Modern Statutory
Interpretation

Modern Statutory Interpretation

Problems, Theories, and
Lawyering Strategies

Second Edition

Linda D. Jellum

David Charles Hricik

CAROLINA ACADEMIC PRESS
Durham, North Carolina

Library of Congress Cataloging-in-Publication Data

Jellum, Linda D.
  Modern statutory interpretation : problems, theories, and lawyering strategies / Linda
D. Jellum, David Charles Hricik. -- 2nd ed.
      p. cm.
  Includes bibliographical references and index.
  ISBN 978-1-59460-675-5 (alk. paper)
  1. Law--United States--Interpretation and construction. 2. Law--Interpretation and
construction. I. Hricik, David Charles. II. Title.

  KF425.J45 2009
  348.73'2--dc22

                              2009021590

Carolina Academic Press
700 Kent Street
Durham, North Carolina 27701
Telephone (919) 489-7486
Fax (919) 493-5668
www.cap-press.com

Printed in the United States of America

Contents

Table of Cases

Table of Authorities

Introduction

A. The Statutorification of U.S. Law

Let's begin with the most basic point: Why should judges be the ones to interpret statutes? Two very fundamental concepts create the need for judges to interpret statutes. One is the application of statutes to actual cases. We will see that the imprecise nature of language, drafting mistakes by legislatures, and the fact that legislatures simply cannot foresee all circumstances that can arise when they enact statutes lead to the need for interpretation. The second is the fundamental judicial principle that it "is emphatically the province and duty of the judicial department to say what the law is." *Marbury v. Madison*, 5 U.S. (1 Cranch) 137, 177 (1803). As a consequence, judges must apply statutes to particular cases, and in doing so, "must of necessity expound and interpret" statutory language. *Id.*

Once we recognize the need for interpretation, then the question of what is the proper methodology arises. A bit of history will help to bring clarity. Statutes have become pervasive only recently (in terms of the law). Until the late Nineteenth century, statutes were enacted comparatively infrequently. In addition, most of those addressed specific, narrow problems not addressed by the common law. At that time, most statutes were private— meaning they applied only to specific individuals—rather than public. Thus, for "more than a century after the American Revolution, ideals about the meaning of the rule of law were developed within an entirely judge- and court-centered system of thought." Ellen Ash Peters, *Common Law Judging in a Statutory World: An Address at the University of Pittsburgh School of Law*, 43 U. Pitt. L. Rev. 995, 995 (1982).

Around the end of the Nineteenth century, however, Congress and state legislatures became more prolific and enacted statutes that applied more generally. Statutes regulating social and economic behavior became common. Legislatures also enacted statutes that were specifically intended to modify, and sometimes even abrogate, existing common law. *See* John M. Walker, *Judicial Tendencies in Statutory Construction: Differing Views on the Role of the Judge*, 58 N.Y.U. Ann. Surv. Am. L. 203, 207–08 (2001). At the onset of this change, most statutes were very short and general. As such, they left room for judicial development almost in the same manner as the common law. The Sherman Act, for example, was enacted in 1890. It constituted the entire federal law on a comprehensive and expansive subject (federal antitrust law); yet, the entire statute fit easily on a single page, leaving much for judicial development.

Although the number of statutes increased, these short, generalized statutes were the norm for many decades. Judges typically applied their usual common law methods of reasoning when interpreting these statutes; they discerned the purpose of the statute and its broader context, likely because statutes were so broad that deferring to the text would have been a hollow proposition. Instead, when determining a statute's contours, courts largely did not treat statutes differently from common law.

Statutory evolution intensified before World War II during the creation of the New Deal, which had as its foundation the enactment of an unprecedented number of statutes. The breadth and suddenness of this change was remarkable. Statutes not only became more common, they became much more detailed and, consequently, longer. "Judicial habits die hard, however." Walker, *supra*, at 208. Despite the changes, judges did not "abandon what was familiar to them—common law methods of judging"—but "adapted their common law reasoning to the modern statutory and administrative state." *Id.* Beginning at this time, some thought that treating statutes like the common law was improper. Suggestions were made as to how to approach statutory interpretation, and that debate still rages today.

Another development that made statutory interpretation increasingly important was the advent of the modern form of administrative government. Particularly after World War II, regulatory agencies proliferated. Each agency adopted its own regulations, which had to be interpreted in much the same manner as statutes. In addition, agencies had to interpret statutes, and their interpretations had to be reviewed by courts. Consequently, the proliferation of agencies and of regulations increased the importance of codified law.

As a consequence of their increasing need to decide cases that implicated statutes, the change in the kind of statutes, and a growing belief that separation of powers and functional principles required statutes to be treated differently from common-law judicial decisions, judges began to develop ways to resolve statutory interpretation issues. Early on, for example, judges developed a set of "canons"* to help determine meaning or resolve apparent ambiguity. Courts also looked beyond the text of the statute to discern meaning. For example, some judges turned to the "legislative history" of the statute—the recorded debates and proceedings that led to the enactment of the statute in question. These judges believed that while the words of the statute were important, so, too, was the intent behind the statute as expressed by legislators during debates and hearings. But not all judges agreed—then or now.

Law continues to become "statutorified" (a term coined by Professor Guido Calabresi), and the trend toward greater length of and detail in statutes continues unabated. The Patriot Act, for example, was enacted in 2001 and has 132 pages. Thus, "starting with the Progressive Era but with increasing rapidity since the New Deal, we have become a nation governed by written laws." GUIDO CALABRESI, A COMMON LAW FOR THE AGE OF STATUTES 5 (Harvard Univ. Press 1982). Likewise, the number of regulatory bodies and the number of regulations they promulgate continues to grow. Hence, statutory interpretation has become increasingly important to our legal society.

You should understand that we are still in the midst of this fundamental change, and several aspects of statutory interpretation are, as a consequence, very much in a state of dynamic and important flux. Even today the appropriate "way" to interpret a statute is far from settled. Yet, the question of whether there ought to be "rules" governing statutory interpretation did not become the subject of extensive inquiry until the mid 1980s. *See* Philip P. Frickey, *From the Big Sleep to the Big Heat: The Revival of Theory in Statutory Interpretation*, 77 MINN. L. REV. 241, 248 (1992). As a result, statutory interpretation only recently became the focus of scholarly treatment as judges, professors, and lawyers dis-

---

* Authors' footnote: "Cannon" and "canon" are used somewhat interchangeably in the legal opinions and scholarship in this area. We have chosen to use "canon."

agreed about the relative importance to be placed on the text, the legislative intent as expressed in the legislative history, and the statutory purpose.

It is an exciting time to study this subject. Unlike many areas of law, critical jurisprudential, conceptual, and philosophical issues are being hotly debated. Beginning in just the last decade, courts began debating the proper method of statutory interpretation "at a level of theory that far transcends the details of the case at hand" and in a way "that implicates the very question of the" interpretive role of the courts in democratic government. *Id.* at 256. As you will see, even the basic question of what the ultimate goal of statutory interpretation is—to find the legislature's intent, the statute's purpose, or to merely apply the written text—is currently in dispute. Much is unsettled and evolving.

To summarize, today there are more statutes, and they are more detailed. The greater detail that Congress and legislatures include in statutes ostensibly narrows, or at least changes, the role of the courts in interpreting statutes. The words of the statute themselves—and the precise meaning of those words—are critically important. "What does the statute mean?" has become the initial and, often, the most important inquiry that lawyers must make every day in all areas of practice.

That question is the subject of this book. Answering the question of "What does the statute mean?" is more complex than it may seem. "Statutory interpretation requires some of the most complex mental processing that ordinary human beings are called upon to perform." Morell E. Mullins, Sr., *Tools, Not Rules: The Heuristic Nature of Statutory Interpretation*, 30 J. Legis. 1, 5 (2003).

B. Why Statutory Interpretation Requires Its Own Skill Set

Although you may not recognize it—in light of the focus on the common law in most of your other courses—most of the work lawyers do today centers on federal and state statutes or regulations. In the course of representing clients, every lawyer interprets and, sometimes, challenges statutes. Statutes and regulations are displacing the common law. Thus, understanding statutes is critical to your future career.

You may think you've already learned how to discern "the law," at least if you've completed a semester or more of law school. After all, you've learned to analyze and brief cases. But learning to interpret statutes requires skills and knowledge different from those needed to interpret cases. To interpret cases, you analyze the findings, reasoning, and holding of a single court concerning a specific problem. The limited, relevant facts are identified in the opinion. The reason for the decision is explained. A limited number of authors are involved.

Statutory interpretation is remarkably different. First, the *process* of judicial decision making is *never* relevant to a case's meaning. In fact, the judicial decision making process is shielded from public scrutiny: For example, drafts of opinions are not available for review. In contrast, the process of legislative decisionmaking, in large measure, takes place in a public forum, and that process can be relevant to a statute's meaning. Second, approaches and interpretive rules have been developed on how to interpret a statute. There are no similar rules or approaches regarding interpretation of the rule of law announced in a common-law decision. Third, statutory interpretation routinely implicates separation-of-powers principles. When a court interprets a prior common-law decision, such issues are not raised. Finally (and partly as a consequence of the foregoing), there are functional and political consequences of the approach that a court takes to statutory interpretation. For example, if courts refuse to look past the statutory text to legislative history, the refusal may create incentives for legislatures to be clearer in their drafting, but it may also mean that statutes are given meaning that they clearly were not intended to have and may also result in increased costs as legislatures must too often undo what courts have done.

In sum, although they share analytical similarities, statutory interpretation is distinct from common law interpretation. It requires a different set of skills to answer the question, "What does the statute mean?" than it does to answer the question, "What does the case mean?"

C. Why Study the Theories of Statutory Interpretation?

Why should you care about statutory interpretation and, in particular, its theories, or approaches? You'll come to appreciate the multiple answers to that question as you move onward, but a word about it here. First, it is of extreme practical importance. Because the meaning of a statute can be definitively decided only by a court, lawyers must know how the courts in the pertinent jurisdiction interpret statutes. Accordingly, when litigating or advising clients about legal issues that implicate statutory interpretation, lawyers must know the theoretical approach of the pertinent jurisdiction to statutory interpretation. If you know the jurisdiction's preferred approach to statutory interpretation, you can determine which sources of meaning will prove most convincing or which interpretation of a statute might later be adopted if you are advising a client in a transaction.

For example, if the jurisdiction in which your case is pending takes a textualist approach (one that focuses on the text of the statute), you know that you must persuade the judge that the statute's plain meaning supports your client's position. If it does, you know to be ready to discount and oppose the other side's reliance on other sources. Yet, if the text itself does not favor your client, but the legislative intent or purpose does, you know you must persuade the judge that there is a reason (typically ambiguity or absurdity) to turn to other sources. In contrast, if the jurisdiction takes an intentionalist or purposivist approach, you should start with the language but speak in terms of intent or purpose respectively. You know to look at all the relevant evidence including the text, legislative history, and more.

Lest you think we're exaggerating about the importance of the adopted approach, consider, for example, that whether your client will have any recovery or any liability can turn directly on which approach to statutory interpretation a court applies. *E.g., Cotto v. Citibank, N.A.*, 247 F. Supp. 2d 44, 47 (D. P.R. 2003) (recognizing that the "split in court opinions on the issue of individual liability [under Title VII] is based on differing approaches to the statutory interpretation of Title VII."). There is "much room within which to advocate an understanding of a statute that best suits" a client's needs. Paul E. McGreal, *Slighting Context: On the Illogic of Ordinary Speech in Statutory Interpretation*, 52

U. Kan. L. Rev. 325, 352 (2004). Part of your success as a lawyer will depend upon your ability to persuade courts on proper interpretation.

Second, there are profound political, constitutional, and jurisprudential issues implicated by statutory interpretation. What does it mean to say that a judge is a "strict constructionist," for example? Does that mean she defers to the legislature or keeps power to herself in the guise of deferring to "plain meaning"? What does it mean when courts ignore legislative history, even where that history clearly shows that the plain meaning of the text was not intended?

Third, perhaps for the first time ever, judges are openly "debating statutory interpretation methodologies at a level of theory that far transcends the details of the case at hand, and that implicates the very question of the [judiciary's] role in a democracy." Philip P. Frickey, *supra*, at 256.

D. How This Book Will Teach These New Skills

This book will teach you the art of statutory interpretation. It will not only help you develop the skills to advise a client how a statute will *likely* be interpreted, but will also give you skills to convince a court that a statute *should* be interpreted in a way that will benefit your client. This book will help you understand the different approaches to statutory interpretation and methods to analyze statutory meaning.

In this second edition, we have remained true to our original goals while improving content. We have replaced cases that were overly complicated, included a number of new problems, reorganized topics, and expanded our coverage of some areas, including preemption, clear statement rules, and the relevance of administrative interpretations. We think the changes further our objectives. In addition, we have continued several things from the first edition. First, this book is organized by process: We will learn the art of interpretation in a logical way. We begin by examining the typical legislative process; we then explore the approaches to, or theories of, interpretation, which permeate every ensuing chapter; hence, theory comes early in this edition. Next, we turn to the relevance of the text of the statute, the starting point for interpretation. While it may be the starting point, text is not the stopping point. Hence, after examining the importance of text, we turn to *when* courts will consider information beyond the text and *what* sources of information they will consider. In this part of the book, we begin with the sources that courts are most likely to consider (the textual canons and component parts of bills, for example) and then proceed to those sources that courts are less likely to consider, at least explicitly (legislative history and statutory purpose, for example). Finally, we consider constitutional implications, administrative interpretations, and other, critical topics.

Second, within each chapter we introduce the concepts with concise statements and explanation. After the introduction, we include one or more cases that illustrate the key concepts of the section. We have selected cases and other materials that are interesting and, whenever possible, modern (sometimes even funny!). The cases almost invariably are close cases and typically include at least one dissenting opinion. Notes and questions follow the cases. The questions are designed to help focus your understanding of the case and the issues it raises to better prepare you for class. The notes point out issues to consider to help you delve more deeply into the topic.

Third, we have edited the cases to clarify the issues and relevant analyses. To make the cases as easy as possible to read, we have heavily edited them, eliminating irrelevant information. While we have remained faithful to the text, we have omitted most extraneous citations and quotation marks without so noting. We have included ellipses to indicate all substantive deletions (excluding deleted citations to legal authority, quotations, and internal brackets).

Fourth, we include problems for you to resolve using the skills you learned not only in the chapter housing the problem, but in previous chapters as well. The problems commonly take place in the hypothetical state of Mercer. Each problem lends itself to at least two arguments, sometimes more. Each problem relies upon and further explores the concepts you are learning in your studies. The problems are a central part of the book and should help you learn lawyering skills.

Our approach is unique. It provides a logical and practical approach to this topic while also probing the theoretical approaches to interpretation. When you are done with your studies, you should have a respect for the breadth of arguments that can be made to convince a court to interpret a statute in a way that favors your client's position and that might be made against your client. In sum, this book is intended to provide you with a thorough understanding of modern statutory interpretation: the conceptual, doctrinal, and jurisprudential origins and the skills to be a successful lawyer in this area. Of course, your journey does not end with this course and this book; it is only your beginning. Yet, we hope that we will have helped you acquire the skills you need to be an effective lawyer at a time when statutes are becoming ever more critical to legal practice.

In writing and rewriting this book, we had the goal of making this important journey interesting and informative. We hope that we have succeeded. Along the way, we have benefitted from the generous assistance of a few individuals. We would like to thank the following for their support and assistance with this second edition: Dean Stephen Johnson, Professor Michael Dimino, the editors at Carolina Academic Press, and, especially, Christopher Featherstun, class of 2009.

The second edition is dedicated to our families, who were supportive beyond belief, and (again) to each other. We survived the process once again!

David Hricik
Linda Jellum

Macon, GA (April 2009)

Modern Statutory Interpretation

Chapter 1

The Legislative Process and Judicial Deference to Internal Legislative Processes

To understand statutory interpretation, you must understand how a bill becomes a law. This chapter provides a brief and simplified overview of the legislative process. It provides a general discussion of the actions that typically lead to the adoption of a statute. Not every bill follows the path discussed here, and Congress and state legislatures often have somewhat different processes. There are entire courses and books devoted solely to the legislative process. We will not be so detailed, but you should understand some basics about the legislative process, which is important to statutory interpretation for at least three reasons.

First, in determining the meaning of a statute, some courts consider statements that were made during the legislative process by committees or individual members of the legislature that enacted the statute. Some believe that the legislature's decision to reject one word in favor of another can be important to statutory interpretation. Likewise, some believe that the statements made during the legislative process can provide context for interpreting the words that were actually chosen. Thus, for example, some courts might give weight to statements concerning the meaning of statutory language that were made by legislators during the legislative process. Such statements are part of the "legislative history" of the statute.*

Second, and more broadly, an understanding of the legislative process will help you appreciate how statutory language differs from statements written by judges. Unlike judicial decisions, the words codified in a statute result from a democratic, political process. The words chosen ostensibly reflect the will of a majority of the people and so ought to be viewed somewhat differently than the words that were used by a court in explicating the common law.

Third, because the precise words in the statute are the result of legislative compromise, statutes are — as a result of the legislative process — not as precise as they could have been if drafted in a "perfect world." We will see, for example, statutes where the language that a legislature adopted — after full deliberation and careful analysis —

---

* Authors' footnote: We will examine the role of legislative history in statutory interpretation much later in this text. This chapter includes a few examples of specific items affecting interpretation, however. Why do we split what could be one topic into two? Because we don't want you to incorrectly give too much weight to legislative history. As will become clear during the book, courts today are giving less weight to legislative history than in the past. You need to understand the legislative process in order to fully apprehend the issues involved in interpretation generally, but spending too much time on legislative history early in your study can lead you astray.

makes absolutely no sense! At other times, the language makes sense, but it is reasonably susceptible to two (or more) equally plausible meanings. In part, ambiguity, lack of clarity, and imprecision arise from the way legislation is drafted. "It has been said that one should never watch laws or sausage being made...." *In re Butler*, 186 B.R. 371, 372 (Bankr. D. Vt. 1995).

Perhaps it is obvious to you, but the precise words that are chosen to be codified can be critical because even slight changes in language can radically alter meaning. It is one thing to say that a judge "must" consider mitigating circumstances in determining punishment to be given to a criminal, but quite another to say that she "may." Legislators are keenly aware of that fact, so it is common for sharp and important disagreements to occur over precisely which words to use.

This chapter describes the legislative process. In a later chapter, we'll take a much deeper look at whether (and if so, when) courts look at statements made during the legislative process in interpreting the resulting statute. For now, only an overview is necessary. After we describe the legislative process, we'll end the chapter by examining a case that identifies the legislative process of a particular bill in some additional detail and also explores the "enrolled bill doctrine."

A. The Legislative Process

Congress, state legislatures, and other deliberative bodies adopt legislation. This chapter focuses on the process that occurs in the U.S. Congress. The House and Senate each has its own separate, though somewhat similar, internal structure. Likewise, each chamber has its own internal procedural rules that govern the progress of bills. For our purposes, the differences between them are unimportant.

Article I, Section 1 of the U.S. Constitution vests legislative power "in a Congress of the United States, which shall consist of a Senate and House of Representatives." A bill must be approved by both houses before it can be presented to the president for approval, after which it becomes codified as a statute. (If the president vetoes a bill, then absent an override by both houses, the bill does not become law.) Most states have similar systems.

The process of enacting a statute truly begins when someone believes there is a need to change the law, either by enacting a new law or by amending an existing one. Constituents, lobbyists, government agencies, or the executive can propose legislation to a legislator, such as a member of Congress. However, only a member of the House or Senate can introduce a bill. A bill must have at least one sponsor who introduces it.

Thus, the first step in the legislative process is introduction of a bill by at least one sponsor. A bill can have many cosponsors. To increase the likelihood that a bill will receive attention, sponsors try to seek cosponsors and often try to have an identical bill, called a "companion bill," introduced in the other chamber.

Once a sponsor introduces a bill, it is given a number for tracking purposes. When a bill is introduced in the House, it is designated "H.R.," followed by a number; in the Senate, it is designated "S.," followed by the number. Numbering starts over with each new Congress. Each session lasts two years, which is the term of a member of the House of Representatives. As a result, a senator's six-year term will last through three sessions. Thus, to identify a particular bill, you must designate not only its number, but also whether it was a House or Senate bill and in which session of Congress it was introduced. So, "H.R. 1081 in the 107th Congress" adequately identifies a specific bill.

Nearly 9,000 bills were introduced in a recent session of Congress. Most bills do not become law; in fact, most do not even get any consideration at all. Of those 9,000 introduced bills, only about 225 became law.

Legislative deliberations take place in two different forums within each chamber: (1) in committee, where only members of the committee discuss, propose amendments to, and vote on whether to approve the bill for consideration by the entire chamber; and, (2) in the "Committee of the Whole," if approved by the committee first, when a full chamber of Congress discusses, proposes amendments to, and votes on the bill.

To become law, a bill is usually first sent to committee. There are numerous committees in the House and Senate, each with jurisdiction over specified subject matters. For example, the House has committees on the judiciary, on defense, and on ways and means. Each committee has the right to hold hearings on bills that fall within the committee's jurisdiction. Thus, any bill introduced in the House that affects the judiciary will be referred to the House Committee on the Judiciary for a hearing and must generally be heard by that committee and be approved by a majority vote of its members. On occasion, bills are referred to a smaller subcommittee for consideration prior to consideration by the full committee.

Some bills must be heard by and approved by more than one committee. For example, a bill may impact the judiciary and also the Department of Defense. In that case, aspects of the bill would fall into the jurisdiction of both committees, and both committees would have to hold hearings on the bill and would need to vote to approve it.

It is important for you to recognize that Congress and state legislatures have chosen to adopt procedures that give the majority party significant control over which bills receive the attention of a committee. Committee chairs, for example, are all members of the majority party. A majority of the committee will be comprised of members of the majority party. "This unequal distribution of power means that the statements of some actors in some situations can provide reliable information about what a procedurally, and hence constitutionally, empowered subset of legislators meant when they constructed a statute's meaning." Cheryl Boudreau et al., *What Statutes Mean: Interpretive Lessons from Positive Theories of Communication and Legislation*, 44 San Diego L. Rev. 957, 968 (2007). As those authors explain:

> [S]ince the late nineteenth century, legislative procedures have given extraordinary powers to a chamber's majority party. This is particularly true in the U.S. House of Representatives. The first act of every legislative session typically entails legislators delegating the legislature's agenda-setting authority and the task of allocating the legislature's scarce resources to the majority party leadership. At the same time, however, legislators do not give away all authority, nor do they grant authority unconditionally. The distribution of power is regulated by an internal system of checks and balances. Legislative procedures provide some actors with a veto over the actions of agenda setters and give others an opportunity and incentive to act as checks. These procedures may be very subtle. In the House, backbenchers may check the actions of their leaders through the committee process and must give their consent and approval to their leaders' actions in plenary meetings.
>
> As a given proposal approaches the floor, the Rules Committee and the Speaker—as well as the Appropriations Committee if any funding is required to implement the proposal—check committee members' ability to propose legislation, for these two central coordinating bodies control access to plenary time.

All of these entities are strongly controlled by the majority party. Therefore, during floor debates, the bill manager for the majority party controls the time devoted to debate and to particular amendments, determining which members speak and for how long. It is not unusual for a number of amendments to be added to a proposal during this stage, unless, of course, the majority party-controlled Rules Committee grants a special rule that limits the number and nature of amendments.

As this discussion makes clear, the congressional process reflects a conversation among members of the majority party. Indeed, in passing legislation, legislators in the majority party communicate with each other and with other members about the meaning of statutes. They also present evidence and arguments about proposed laws, trying to secure support or build opposition.

Id. at 970 (footnotes omitted).

During committee hearings, a bill generally receives the most intense scrutiny and analysis. The hearings are public. Lobbyists, representatives of the government, and other interested parties can testify — generally through written submissions, with only brief oral appearances, if any — about the impact that the bill will have if it is enacted. Each member of the committee is permitted to question (for brief periods, typically five minutes) any witness who appears.

Amendments may be offered to change the language of the bill to avoid negative consequences identified during the hearings or to achieve different goals or to achieve the same goal through different means. The original language in the bill will then be "marked up" and considered by the committee. Ultimately, the committee will have a final version of the bill to vote on: It will approve the bill, defeat the bill, or "table" it for further study and, perhaps, later consideration.

Legislators are aware that the language in a bill will be the subject of litigation and interpretation. They realize, too, that in litigation lawyers will argue for an interpretation that favors their client's position. *See* Paul E. McGreal, *Slighting Context: On the Illogic of Ordinary Speech in Statutory Interpretation*, 52 U. KAN. L. REV. 325, 351–52 (2004). Because they know that the language in the statute will be used strategically, legislators engage in various approaches to drafting to attempt to stem off strategic behavior. For example, statutes that prohibit "A, B, and C" often include a catchall that says "or similar behavior."

Statements made by members of a committee during committee hearings can be important in determining statutory meaning. Statements made by the sponsor of a bill are sometimes given substantial weight by courts, which presume that the sponsor was more knowledgeable about the bill than other legislators. *E.g., In re Duda*, 182 B.R. 662, 668 (Bankr. D. Conn. 1995) (giving "great weight" to a statement by state legislator who had been bill's sponsor). But the Supreme Court has, over time, given conflicting views on how much weight to give to statements made by the sponsor of a bill. *Compare Gen. Dynamics Land Sys., Inc. v. Cline*, 540 U.S. 581 (2004) (discounting the sponsor's statements), *with Fed. Energy Admin. v. Algonquin SNG, Inc.*, 426 U.S. 548, 564 (1976) ("As a statement of one of the legislation's sponsors, this explanation deserves to be accorded substantial weight in interpreting the statute."). Some say that statements by key members of the majority party — such as the majority whip or the majority leader — are much more likely to be accurate and sincere statements of intended meaning because such communications "signal the meaning of the statutes they have written to the remaining members of the chamber." Boudreau, *supra*, at 971.

If the committee approves a bill for consideration by the full chamber, the committee staff generally writes a committee report to accompany the bill. As one court noted, "Committee materials are properly consulted to understand legislative intent, since it is reasonable to infer the legislators considered explanatory materials and shared the understanding expressed in the materials when voting to enact a statute." *Oden v. Bd. of Admin. of the Pub. Employees' Ret. Sys.*, 23 Cal. App. 4th 194, 205 (1994). Committee reports ostensibly "represen[t] the considered and collective understanding of those Congressmen involved in drafting and studying proposed legislation." *Garcia v. United States*, 469 U.S. 70, 76 (1984).

In addition to describing existing law and the problem that the bill addresses, committee reports often include a markup of the bill, showing the language as originally considered by the committee, along with all of the changes to the bill adopted by the committee. Generally, language that the committee has added to the bill is printed in italics, and language that the committee voted to delete from the bill is still shown but struck through by a line. Thus, for example, a markup might look like this:

> (a) As used in this Chapter, the ~~word~~ *phrase* "law school" shall mean only those law schools ~~which~~ *that* have been approved by the American Bar Association *and are in good standing with that organization.*

If a bill is passed out of the committee, the bill can then be heard by the Committee of the Whole on the floor of the House or Senate. Generally, a bill must be approved by every committee to which it was referred for hearing before it can be debated by the Committee of the Whole.

During consideration by the Committee of the Whole, witnesses are not called. Instead, legislators debate the impact of the bill, explaining why they believe the bill should or should not be adopted or why it should be adopted only if amended. During these debates, individual legislators who were not members of a committee that held any hearings on the bill may propose amendments to the bill. Courts do not often give much weight to statements made by individual legislators during debates in the Committee of the Whole. Much later we'll explore why this is true, but a passage from a case involving the role of these statements is important for you to consider here:

> [D]iscerning the subjective motivation of those enacting the statute is, to be honest, almost always an impossible task. The number of possible motivations, to begin with, is not binary, or indeed finite.... [The legislator] may have thought the bill would provide jobs for his district, or may have wanted to make amends with a faction of his party he had alienated on another vote, or he may have been a close friend of the bill's sponsor, or he may have been repaying a favor he owed the Majority Leader, or he may have hoped the Governor would appreciate his vote and make a fundraising appearance for him, or he may have been pressured to vote for a bill he disliked by a wealthy contributor or by a flood of constituent mail, or he may have been seeking favorable publicity, or he may have been reluctant to hurt the feelings of a loyal staff member who worked on the bill, or he may have been settling an old score with a legislator who opposed the bill, or he may have been mad at his wife who opposed the bill, or he may have been intoxicated and utterly unmotivated when the vote was called, or he may have accidentally voted "yes" instead of "no," or, of course, he may have had (and very likely did have) a combination of some of the above and many other motivations.

Edwards v. Aguillard, 482 U.S. 578, 636–37 (1987) (Scalia, J., dissenting). Another court gave a more mundane, but equally legitimate, reason for giving greater weight to the words written in committee reports than to oral statements: "In the course of oral argument on the Senate Floor, the choice of words by a Senator is not always accurate or exact. For this reason, courts have held that statements in debate are not a proper measure of the contents of a statute." *In re Carlson*, 292 F. Supp. 778, 783 (C.D. Cal. 1968).

Although courts disagree on whether much weight should be given to legislative history, courts that do give some weight to it generally give more weight to conference committee reports than to other pieces of legislative history. "When examining the legislative history," some courts "first look to the conference report because, apart from the statute itself, it is the most reliable evidence of congressional intent." *In re Silicon Graphics, Inc. Sec. Litig.*, 183 F.3d 970, 977 (9th Cir. 1999). Courts place greater reliance on conference committee reports because both chambers rely on these reports in approving the bill. *Id.*

Do not lose sight of the fact that statutes are communications from the legislature. Legislation is a form of communication that arrives in a particular form: a bill that has been approved by both chambers and presented to the president for signature. Additionally, to satisfy due process, this bill must provide effective notice of its import. During this process, some say a "compression" must occur: All of the meaning that the legislature may ascribe to words must be compressed into the statutory text. "In other words, statutes are manufactured by a constitutionally authorized legislative body, and are directed toward those who are constitutionally obligated to implement, enforce, or follow the law." Boudreau, *supra*, at 958.

Let's return to our discussion of the process. During debate, the Committee of the Whole will vote to accept or reject each proposed amendment. Once this process is complete, the Committee of the Whole rises and reports the bill to the full chamber (the same individuals in the Committee of the Whole). The full chamber then considers and votes on the bill as amended by the Committee of the Whole.

If one chamber approves the bill, an "engrossed bill" is then sent to the other body where, essentially, the process is repeated. If the other body approves the bill without any changes, then it is sent on to the president. If the other chamber amends the bill in any way, however, the bill cannot become law without further action. Unless the one chamber votes to accept the other's amendments, a conference committee is formed where members of the House and Senate meet to confer about the differences in the House and Senate versions of the bill. This process can result in a conference committee report, which can contain additional statements about the meaning and intent of the bill. The conferees then report back to their respective chambers on the conference committee's resolution of the competing language, and then the chambers vote to approve or reject the proposal.

If both chambers approve the bill, then an "enrolled bill" is created. The Constitution requires that before legislation may become law, the *same bill* signed by the president must have been approved by both chambers. Thus, if both chambers pass a bill, an "enrolled bill" is prepared, printed, and then signed by both the Speaker of the House and the President of the Senate, who attest that the bill has been approved by the House and Senate, respectively. *See generally* Ittai Bar-Siman-Tov, *Legislative Supremacy in the United States?: Rethinking the 'Enrolled Bill' Doctrine*, 97 Geo. L.J. 323 (2009). The enrolled bill is then presented to the president for signature or veto.

If the president signs the bill and it becomes law, it is then assigned a public law number. Statutes passed for a given Congress are numbered sequentially. Thus, the first law approved by the 107th Congress was designated as Public Law 107-1 and so on. Each statute is also paginated in the Statutes at Large in the order it was enacted into law. In addition, all enacted laws are codified and consolidated in the United States Code, where, unlike the Statutes at Large, they are organized by subject. States have similar systems.

A dose of reality is probably in order here. "Congress is no longer [was it ever?] made up of part-time citizen-legislators, extemporaneous orators, who burn the midnight oil as they themselves draft the laws needed to resolve the social and political problems revealed during the day's interchange of spontaneous debate." Stephen Breyer, *On the Uses of Legislative History in Interpreting Statutes*, 65 S. Cal. L. Rev. 845, 858 (1992). The same is true of state legislatures. Today's legislatures are bureaucratic organizations—Congress has more than 20,000 employees—that generate "legislation through a complicated, but organized, process of interaction with other institutions and groups, including executive branch departments, labor unions, business organizations and public interest groups." *Id.* These third parties not only ask their representatives to address problems through legislation, they also "may suggest content and text, not only for statutes, but also for reports or floor statements; they review proposed changes; and they negotiate and compromise with staff, with legislators and with each other." *Id.*

As we will see, some commentators oppose the use of legislative history to interpret statutes because often staff, not legislators, write some of the documents that make up legislative history. You should realize that legislators do not write every word of a statute, and even the language in a committee report may have been prepared by a lobbyist, not a legislator. Legislatures approve only the actual text of a bill. Chart 1.1 summarizes the legislative process.

The importance of legislative process on statutory interpretation will become clear as you proceed through this book. The deliberations that occur in committee, the Committee of the Whole, and the full chamber are often recorded and transcribed. As you will see, there is considerable debate about how much weight, if any, to give to the statements made during this deliberative process. We mentioned a few reasons already. There are others. For example, legislators are obviously aware that a court may later give their statements meaning. Could this lead to strategic behavior, with legislators making statements designed to influence courts? Some courts and commentators believe so. Likewise, even if one legislator clearly understood a statutory term to mean "X," is that any evidence that other legislators, let alone a majority, gave that term the same meaning? Also, does it truly signify much about the *legislature's* understanding of a term if a committee staff member wrote something about the term in a committee report, which many legislators may not have read? We've only scratched the surface here. Keep these issues in mind for later in the text, when we discuss the debate over whether—and if so, how much—weight to give statements made during the legislative process.

Finally, as noted above, legislation is a compressed form of communication: All meaning must be distilled into the statutory text. Interpretation, in contrast, expands the meaning of the statutory language:

> Statutes are compressed policy instructions or procedural guidelines. Legislators who pass them choose their meanings, as well as the words used to convey these meanings. Subsequent recipients of the message are charged with expanding meaning from these words when applying or interpreting them. Recipients have no constitutional authority to add or subtract their own meaning.

Boudreau, *supra*, at 967.

Notes and Questions

(1) *Most Bills Die.* As noted above, it is not uncommon for only one in thirty bills to get enacted into law. One reason for this is time: Those bills deemed unimportant by a

Chart 1-1: **How a Bill Becomes a Law**

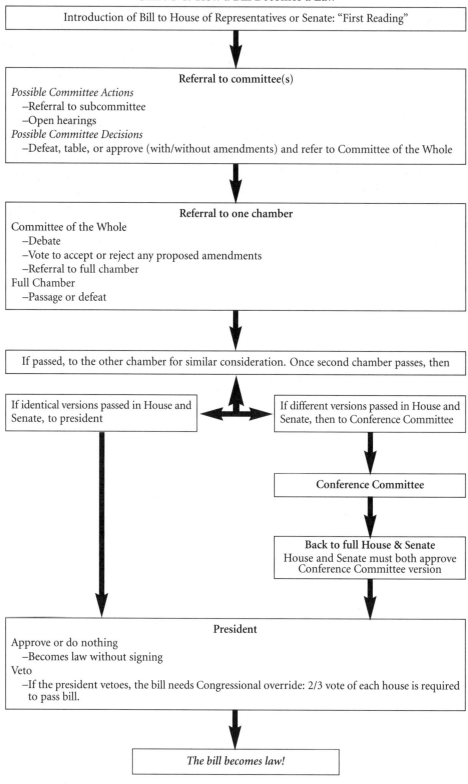

Introduction of Bill to House of Representatives or Senate: "First Reading"

Referral to committee(s)
Possible Committee Actions
    –Referral to subcommittee
    –Open hearings
Possible Committee Decisions
    –Defeat, table, or approve (with/without amendments) and refer to Committee of the Whole

Referral to one chamber
Committee of the Whole
    –Debate
    –Vote to accept or reject any proposed amendments
    –Referral to full chamber
Full Chamber
    –Passage or defeat

If passed, to the other chamber for similar consideration. Once second chamber passes, then

If identical versions passed in House and Senate, to president

If different versions passed in House and Senate, then to Conference Committee

Conference Committee

Back to full House & Senate
House and Senate must both approve Conference Committee version

President
Approve or do nothing
    –Becomes law without signing
Veto
    –If the president vetoes, the bill needs Congressional override: 2/3 vote of each house is required to pass bill.

The bill becomes law!

committee chair, for example, will simply not be considered. The chair's decision not to bring a bill up for committee consideration is the most common form of "veto" possessed by a legislative majority. Even when bills are placed upon a committee calendar for action, opponents have many ways to defeat the bill. For example, opponents may defeat the bill in committee, prevent the bill from being considered by the full chamber of the House or Senate, defeat it in conference, utilize a filibuster in the Senate, or even persuade the president to veto it. A group seeking to prevent legislation from passing has the advantage over those seeking its passage.

(2) *This Balance is the One the Framers Chose.* Alexander Hamilton wrote that "the power of preventing bad laws includes that of preventing good ones; and may be used to the one purpose as well as to the other.... The injury that may possibly be done by defeating a few good laws, will be amply compensated by the advantage of preventing a few bad ones." THE FEDERALIST No. 73 (Alexander Hamilton). Do you agree? Is it relevant to your answer that Senate filibustering—preventing a bill from being voted on by the Committee of the Whole—was responsible for gutting and delaying civil rights bills proposed during the 1950s? A comprehensive act was not enacted until 1964 and only after intense lobbying and compromising. *See* 42 U.S.C. §§ 2000e *et. seq.*

(3) *Party Power.* Our discussion of the legislative process emphasized the power possessed by the majority party and committee chairs, who are chosen by the majority party. Even if a legislative body is controlled by a thin majority (*e.g.*, if the U.S. Senate were comprised of 51 Republicans and 49 Democrats), the majority has substantial control over which bills will be considered by committees because the majority appoints committee chairs. Also, as noted above, many argue that statements by key members of the majority party and the bill sponsor (very likely to be a majority party member as well) should be given more weight than statements by other legislators, particularly minority members. Yet, when a legislature with a thin majority passes a bill only because some members of the minority party vote for it, should not statements from minority members matter? Isn't it more accurate to say that only when no member of the minority party voted for a bill should the minority's views be irrelevant? Or, is majority control irrelevant? That is, if a member of the minority party explains why he is voting for a bill, isn't this statement an accurate statement of meaning? Isn't it the statements of the majority of those who *vote* for the bill, not those who are members of the majority party, that should "count" more?

(4) *Sponsorship is Important.* Choosing a sponsor for a bill is critically important. Why might you want to have a sponsor from the majority party? From the chair of the committee that will have jurisdiction to hold hearings on the bill? Why might you want cosponsors? Would you want cosponsors from the same or a different party?

(5) *The Role of Lobbyists.* A brief word about lobbyists is in order. Lobbyists are generally employed by a company or by an association of companies in a particular industry, such as a steel trade association, to propose and influence legislation. On the one hand, lobbyists perform a positive function in that they educate legislators and regulators on the need for the legislation (or lack of need), the appropriate boundaries for legislative response, and even the potential obstacles for passage. On the other hand, the client for whom the lobbyist is working may have interests that do not comport with the interests of the public-at-large or with other industries. As an example, one of the authors of this casebook has seen lobbyists sitting with state legislators drafting a bill that was designed to protect the public by regulating the lobbyist's client. Lobbyists are paid to further the interest of their constituency, not the public, and not other in-

dustries. Lobbyists have both pernicious and beneficial influences on the legislative process.

Problem 1-1

Assume you are a staff attorney for a minority member of the Senate Energy Committee. Your boss is a sponsor of a bill that you have been charged with drafting. What she thought would be a relatively straightforward bill allowing tax breaks for consumers who purchase hybrid automobiles has become rather involved. There was strong opposition to the bill within the committee (including the chair of the committee). However, the committee reached a compromise.

After the committee had completed its mark-up and issued its final report, a lobbyist contacted you and identified an ambiguity in the bill. What should you do? Should you advise your boss to raise the concern with the committee chair—who would likely send it back to committee—and risk the possibility that it will not pass out of committee? Should you advise her to raise the concern during the debate and offer a floor amendment? Should you advise her to simply be quiet, let the bill pass, and let the courts resolve the ambiguity? If so, should you advise her to talk about what she believes the bill means during the debate so that her comments will be waiting if a court looks to legislative history? Do you advise her to let the bill pass and then attempt to amend it in the next legislative session?

B. The Enrolled Bill Doctrine

As mentioned above, the Speaker of the House and the President of the Senate must attest that the same bill passed both chambers. On occasion, they make a mistake, and the two chambers in fact pass bills that are not identical. Despite the constitutional requirement that both chambers actually approve the same bill, the Supreme Court long ago held that the "enrolled bill doctrine" precludes courts from questioning the validity of the "enrolled bill" or to impeach the attestation by other evidence. *See* Bar-Siman-Tov, Legislative *Supremacy in the United States?: Rethinking the 'Enrolled Bill' Doctrine*, 97 Geo. L.J. 323 (2009). Is this rule sound?

Onesimpleloan v. U.S. Sec'y of Educ.
496 F.3d 197 (2d Cir. 2007)

Jose A. Cabranes, Circuit Judge:

The question presented is whether the "enrolled bill rule" articulated by the Supreme Court in *Marshall Field & Co. v. Clark*, 143 U.S. 649 (1892), requires the dismissal of plaintiffs' claims that the Deficit Reduction Act of 2005 ("DRA"), Pub.L. No. 109-171, 120 Stat. 4 (2006), was enacted in violation of the Bicameralism and Presentment Clause, U.S. Const. art. I, §7, cl. 2.... Agreeing with the recent decision of the United States Court of Appeals for the District of Columbia in *Public Citizen v. United States District Court for the District of Columbia*, 486 F.3d 1342 (D.C.Cir.2007), we conclude that the holding of *Marshall Field* is directly on point and that the Supreme Court has not overruled or narrowed that holding....

BACKGROUND

Plaintiff OneSimpleLoan is a company that markets and finances student loans. Plaintiffs Carina D. Ball and Nathan Bazyk are individual borrowers who consolidated their student loans under the Federal Family Education Loan ("FFEL") Program. Plaintiffs allege that they have suffered injury on account of provisions in the DRA that (1) prohibit a method of refinancing FFEL consolidated loans and (2) impose conditions that inhibit companies from providing lower interest rates and better benefits on FFEL consolidated loans. They brought an action against defendant[], the United States Secretary of Education ... seeking injunctive and declaratory relief. Plaintiffs alleged ... that the DRA was unconstitutional because the bill passed by the House of Representatives was not identical to the bill passed earlier by the Senate and presented later to the President. As evidence of this failure to pass identical texts, plaintiffs pointed to a difference between (1) the "engrossed bill" transmitted from the Senate to the House of Representatives after the Senate vote, and (2) the "enrolled bill" presented to the President after having been signed by the Speaker of the House of Representatives and the President Pro Tempore of the Senate.

A. The Bicameralism and Presentment Clause, the Appropriations Clause, Engrossed Bills, and Enrolled Bills

The Bicameralism and Presentment Clause mandates that "[e]very Bill which shall have passed the House of Representatives and the Senate, shall, before it become a Law, be presented to the President of the United States...." U.S. Const. art. I, §7, cl. 2. A law has been enacted in conformance with this constitutional mandate only if (1) a bill containing its exact text was approved by a majority of the Members of the House of Representatives; (2) the Senate approved precisely the same text; and (3) that text was signed into law by the President. Plaintiffs claim that the DRA never became a law because the House of Representatives and the Senate did not pass "precisely the same text." ...

Congress has established specific procedures governing passage of a bill. Those procedures are currently codified at 1 U.S.C. §106, which provides in relevant part:

> Every bill ... in each House of Congress shall, when such bill ... passes either House, be printed, and such printed copy shall be called the *engrossed bill*.... Said engrossed bill ... shall be signed by the Clerk of the House or the Secretary of the Senate, and shall be sent to the other House, and in that form shall be dealt with by that House and its officers, and, if passed, returned signed by said Clerk or Secretary. When such bill ... shall have passed both Houses, it shall be printed and shall then be called the *enrolled bill*, ... and shall be signed by the presiding officers of both Houses and sent to the President of the United States.

1 U.S.C. §106 (emphasis added). An 'engrossed bill' is thus one that has passed one chamber of Congress, while an 'enrolled bill' has passed both the House and the Senate. In the instant case, plaintiffs allege that a discrepancy between the version of the bill passed by the House and the version of the bill passed by the Senate was introduced by a transcription error made during preparation of the engrossed bill and corrected during preparation of the enrolled bill.

B. Enactment of the DRA

The DRA, signed by the President on February 8, 2006, is an omnibus budget act whose broad-ranging provisions affect not just educational lending, but also, *inter alia,* Medicare and Medicaid laws, Hurricane Katrina relief, the transition to digital television broadcasting, and the filing fees for civil actions in federal district courts....

Most of the facts contained in the complaint are summarized by the District of Columbia Circuit in *Public Citizen*:

> [I]n the Fall of 2005, the House and Senate passed different versions of a budget bill referred to as S.1932. To iron out the differences, the legislation was sent to a conference committee. The committee produced a conference report which failed to pass the Senate. Shortly thereafter the Senate passed an amended version of S.1932 wherein § 5101 specified a 13-month duration of Medicare payments for certain durable medical equipment. However, when the Senate clerk transmitted the engrossed S.1932 to the House, he mistakenly changed § 5101 of the bill to reflect a 36-month duration of payments for durable medical equipment rather than the 13-month duration actually approved by the Senate. The House voted on this engrossed bill, including the erroneous duration figure. Because the legislation originated in the Senate, the House returned it to the Senate for enrollment. The Senate clerk, recognizing the transcription error in the engrossed bill, altered the text of the enrolled bill so that it included a 13-month rather than a 36-month duration. The version of the DRA signed by the presiding officers contains the 13-month figure. Thus, since the 13-month duration term in the enrolled bill passed the Senate but not the House, the President signed legislation that did not actually pass both houses of Congress in precisely the same form.

Id. at 1345. Additionally, plaintiffs in the instant case allege that (1) there existed a "legally improper arrangement among certain representatives of the House, Senate and Executive Branch to have the President sign" legislation that had not been enacted pursuant to the Constitution; (2) the Speaker of the House of Representatives and the President Pro Tempore of the Senate were aware of the discrepancy between the engrossed bill and the enrolled bill when they signed the enrolled bill; and (3) after the President signed the DRA, the Senate passed a concurrent resolution hoping to rectify the constitutional deficiency, but the House of Representatives never passed this resolution.

DISCUSSION

A. Marshall Field

In *Marshall Field*, several importers protesting the assessment of duties under the Tariff Act of October 1, 1890 claimed that "the act was not a law of the United States." 143 U.S. at 665–66. The Supreme Court described the importers' principal contention as follows:

> The contention of the appellants is that [the] enrolled act, in the custody of the Secretary of State, and appearing, upon its face to have become a law in the mode prescribed by the Constitution, is to be deemed an absolute nullity, in all its parts, because—such is the allegation—it is shown by the Congressional record of proceedings, reports of committees of each house, reports of committees of conference, and other papers printed by authority of Congress, and having reference to [the bill in question], that a section of the bill, as it finally passed, was not in the bill authenticated by the signatures of the presiding officers of the respective houses of Congress, and approved by the President.

---

6. The Journal Clause states that "[e]ach House shall keep a Journal of its Proceedings, and from time to time publish the same, excepting such Parts as may in their Judgment require Secrecy; and the Yeas and Nays of the Members of either House on any question shall, at the Desire of one fifth of those Present, be entered on the Journal." U.S. Const. art. I, § 5, cl. 3.

In other words, the importers were arguing that neither house of Congress had passed a version of the bill identical to the enrolled bill. The importers "rest[ed] their contention" on the Journal Clause of the Constitution, U.S. Const. art. I, § 5, cl. 3,[6] which they claimed made congressional journals "the best, if not conclusive evidence upon the issue as to whether a bill was, in fact, passed by the two houses of Congress." *Marshall Field*, 143 U.S. at 670.

The Supreme Court rejected this interpretation of the Journal Clause and stated that nothing in the Constitution "prescribe[s] the mode in which the fact of the original passage of a bill by the House of Representatives and the Senate shall be authenticated, or preclude[s] Congress from adopting any mode to that end which its wisdom suggests." *Id.* at 671. Noting that the Constitution does not "expressly require bills that have passed Congress to be attested by the signatures of the presiding officers of the two houses," the Court observed that "usage, the orderly conduct of legislative proceedings and the rules under which the two bodies have acted since the organization of the government, require that mode of authentication." *Id.* The Court then concluded that "when a bill, thus attested, receives [the President's] approval, and is deposited in the public archives, its authentication as a bill that has passed Congress should be deemed complete and unimpeachable." *Id.* at 672. Recognizing that separation-of-powers concerns were at issue, the Court elaborated that "[t]he respect due to coequal and independent departments requires the judicial department to act upon that assurance, and to accept, as having passed Congress, all bills authenticated in the manner stated." *Id.*

The Supreme Court in *Marshall Field* admitted that the rule thereby established would allow the continued enforcement of legislation that had not been enacted in the manner prescribed by the Constitution. However, it noted that

> [b]etter, far better, that a provision should occasionally find its way into the statute through mistake, or even fraud, than that every act, state and national, should at any and all times be liable to be put in issue and impeached by the journals, loose papers of the legislature, and parole evidence. Such a state of uncertainty in the statute laws of the land would lead to mischiefs absolutely intolerable.

Id.

In concluding its discussion of Congress's alleged failure to pass the precise text of the act in question, the Court set forth "a clear rule" requiring the judicial branch to treat an enrolled bill signed by the presiding officers of the House and Senate as conclusive evidence of the text passed by both houses of Congress. *Public Citizen*, 486 F.3d at 1350. Under *Marshall Field*, "it is not competent" for a plaintiff alleging that a statute is void because Congress did not pass the exact text appearing in an authenticated enrolled bill "to show, from the journals of either house, from the reports of committees, or from other documents printed by authority of Congress," that the bills actually passed by the two houses of Congress differed from the enrolled bill. *Marshall Field*, 143 U.S. at 680.

The rule articulated by the Supreme Court in *Marshall Field* became known as the "enrolled bill rule" and has been described by our Court as "a longstanding rule, invoked by many courts, including the Supreme Court and our own Court." *United States v. Pabon-Cruz*, 391 F.3d 86, 99 (2d Cir. 2004) (holding that the enrolled bill rule does not prevent courts from considering legislative history when determining how to interpret and apply statutory language). As we have observed, the enrolled bill rule "provides that [i]f a legislative document is authenticated in regular form by the appropriate officials, the court[s] treat [ ] that document as properly adopted." *Id.*

The plain language of *Marshall Field* appears to foreclose plaintiffs' constitutional claims in the instant case, which would require our Court to look beyond the authenticated enrolled bill for evidence that the House and Senate did not pass identical texts. Yet plaintiffs present a variety of arguments urging us to decide that *Marshall Field* does not mean what it says.... We conclude that plaintiffs' arguments regarding the inapplicability of the enrolled bill rule are without merit, and we note that it is for the Supreme Court rather than a court of inferior jurisdiction to determine whether the venerable enrolled bill rule requires revision in light of technological and political developments since *Marshall Field* was decided in 1892....

B. The Enrolled Bill Rule Is a "Non-Merits Threshold Ground for Dismissal"

We first consider whether it is necessary for a court to determine if a plaintiff satisfies the "irreducible constitutional minimum of standing" before deciding whether the enrolled bill rule applies. *Lujan*, 504 U.S. at 560. We agree with the District of Columbia Circuit that "[a]t a minimum, the *Marshall Field* rule is ... a non-merits threshold ground for dismissal" that cuts off judicial inquiry into a plaintiff's constitutional claims based on the alleged failure of Congress (whether one house or both) to pass the precise text of a statute. *Public Citizen*, 486 F.3d at 1349; *see Marshall Field*, 143 U.S. at 675 (recognizing that application of the enrolled bill rule will allow unconstitutional laws to survive). Like other rules that are "designed not merely to defeat the asserted claims, but to preclude judicial inquiry," *Tenet v. Doe*, 544 U.S. 1, 6 n.4 (2005), or that "deny[ ] audience to a case on the merits," *Ruhrgas AG v. Marathon Oil Co.*, 526 U.S. 574, 585 (1999), the enrolled bill rule may support dismissal of a claim before a court assesses its authority to hear that claim....

Consequently, a district court need not accept as true the facts alleged in a plaintiff's pleadings when a defendant moves to dismiss pursuant to the enrolled bill rule. Rather, the district court must determine (1) whether the presiding officers of the House and Senate in fact signed the enrolled bill, thereby attesting to its passage, and (2) whether the enrolled bill rule requires dismissal of a particular claim as a matter of law....

In the instant case, there is no dispute as to whether the Speaker of the House of Representatives and the President Pro Tempore of the Senate signed the enrolled bill that would subsequently become the DRA. Thus, we need only review the District Court's legal conclusions regarding application of the enrolled bill rule to the particular claims at issue.

C. The Enrolled Bill Rule Was Not Dicta

Plaintiffs and *amicus* Public Citizen argue that the Supreme Court's holding in *Marshall Field* extended only to congressional journals and that the prohibition against considering all "other documents printed by authority of Congress," *Marshall Field*, 143 U.S. at 680, was merely expansive dicta. *Marshall Field*'s plain language and justification cannot be read to create a rule of dismissal limited to the claims of plaintiffs who rely primarily upon journals to rebut an attested enrolled bill." *Public Citizen*, 486 F.3d at 1351. The Supreme Court articulated an expansive rule in *Marshall Field* because such a rule was necessary to answer the expansive question before the Court, notwithstanding that the appellants' strongest argument lay in their interpretation of the Journal Clause. Moreover, neither the Supreme Court's concern for stability nor its attentiveness to the constitutional doctrine of separation of powers "applies solely to impeachment by journals." *Public Citizen*, 486 F.3d at 1351. Permitting litigants to impeach the text of an enrolled bill by other congressional documents would likewise create "uncertainty in the statute laws," *Marshall Field*, 143 U.S. at 675, and require courts to conduct inquiries that impinge upon the "respect due to coequal and independent departments," *id.* at 672. Finally, the Supreme Court's own subsequent interpretation of *Marshall Field*'s holding requires us to reject plaintiffs' argument that *Marshall Field* did nothing but prevent litigants from challenging the text of an enrolled bill through congressional journals.

Plaintiffs also argue that the scope of the holding of *Marshall Field* was cast into doubt by the Supreme Court's inspection of congressional journals in *United States v. Ballin*, 144 U.S. 1 (1892), a case decided on the same day as *Marshall Field*. This argument, which would render *Marshall Field* meaningless with respect to the one source of evidence plaintiffs concede was at issue, is without merit. In *Ballin,* the Court considered whether another tariff act had been "legally passed." The Court addressed whether a quorum of the House of Representatives had been present "to do Business," U.S. Const. art I, § 5, cl. 1, and whether the bill before the House received a sufficient number of votes. The Court first observed that, as a general matter, "whenever a question arises in a court of law of the existence of a statute…, the judges who are called upon to decide it have a right to resort to any source of information which in its nature is capable of conveying to the judicial mind a clear and satisfactory answer to such question." *Id.* at 3. The Court then noted its decision in *Marshall Field* and stated "[i]t is unnecessary to add anything here to that general discussion." *Id.* at 4. *Ballin* in no way purported to disturb *Marshall Field*'s holding as expressed by the plain language of that case itself.…

Indeed, the Supreme Court's analysis in *Ballin* appears to reinforce its reasoning in *Marshall Field*. In *Ballin*, the Court inspected the House's journal only after "[a]ssuming that by reason of [the Journal Clause] reference may be had to the journal, to see whether the yeas and nays were ordered, and if so, what was the vote disclosed thereby." *Id.* In contrast, the *Marshall Field* Court made plain that the Constitution grants Congress full discretion in deciding how to authenticate the particular text of a bill passed by both houses. Moreover, in *Ballin*, the Court noted that the House of Representatives had itself implemented a rule requiring that certain information regarding voting be recorded in the journal. The Court respected the House's discretion "to determine its rules of proceedings," *id.* at 5, accepting as true the information contained in the journal even though it might be erroneous. In the same way, the Court in *Marshall Field* respected Congress's discretion to prescribe the authentication of an enrolled bill's text, even though that text might not have actually passed both houses.…

E. We May Not Create Exceptions to the Enrolled Bill Rule Based on Technological and Political Developments Since Marshall Field Was Decided

Plaintiffs and *amici* offer two additional reasons why the enrolled bill rule should not apply in the instant case: (1) the engrossed bill, whose production is required by statute, is more reliable than the congressional documents presented as evidence of a constitutional violation in *Marshall Field*; and (2) plaintiffs allege a conspiracy to subvert the Constitution by the presiding officers of Congress and the President. Neither of these arguments is availing.

First, although technological advances in printing and copying since the late nineteenth century may have removed some of the sources of unreliability in congressional documents, the facts alleged by plaintiffs in this case reveal that even engrossed bills printed today are subject to error or mishandling. Indeed, such advances may provide new ways to alter a bill's text during the legislative process. Additionally, while the Supreme Court in *Marshall Field* contemplated that Congress could change its internal bill authentication procedure if it wanted to, Congress has not done so. Nothing in 1 U.S.C. § 106, expressly or otherwise, limits the longstanding authority of the presiding officers of the House and Senate to attest to the passage of an enrolled bill's text.

Second, we do not agree with plaintiffs' argument (supported by several members of the House of Representatives acting as *amici*) that *Marshall Field* creates an exception to the enrolled bill rule in certain cases involving allegations that the presiding officers of Congress and the President of the United States conspired to violate the Constitution by enacting legislation that had not passed both the House and Senate. As it happens, the Supreme Court in *Marshall Field* responded to the contention that under the enrolled bill rule "it becomes possible for the Speaker of the House of Representatives and the President of the Senate to impose upon the people as a law a bill that was never passed by Congress":

> But this possibility is too remote to be seriously considered in the present inquiry. It suggests a deliberate conspiracy to which the presiding officers, the committees on enrolled bills, and the clerks of the two houses must necessarily be parties, all acting with a common purpose to defeat an expression of the popular will in the mode prescribed by the Constitution.

Marshall Field, 143 U.S. at 672–73. Plaintiffs and *amici* seize upon the Court's statement that the possibility of a conspiracy was "too remote to be considered in the present inquiry," arguing that where the likelihood of a conspiracy is greater, the enrolled bill rule does not apply. Yet the Court's next sentence warned that "[j]udicial action based upon ... a suggestion [of conspiracy] is forbidden by the respect due to a co-ordinate branch of the government." *Id.* at 673. In light of the separation-of-powers concerns at the forefront of *Marshall Field*, which are surely undiminished by the passage of time, we do not think it plausible that the judicial branch must, before deciding if the enrolled bill rule applies, conduct threshold inquiries into how likely it was for a particular set of legislative and executive actors to conspire in alleged constitutional violations. Whether the enrolled bill rule has come to serve as an incentive for politicians to avoid the rigors of constitutional law-making is a different question. The answer might provide a policy argument against strict application of the enrolled bill rule, but we are bound to follow Supreme Court precedent as it currently exists.

In the last analysis, even if plaintiffs' arguments support the creation of exceptions to the enrolled bill rule in some circumstances (or militate toward abandoning the rule altogether), we are not at liberty to depart from binding Supreme Court precedent "unless and until [the] Court reinterpret[s]" that precedent. Plaintiffs' constitutional claims are therefore foreclosed by *Marshall Field*, and dismissal by the District Court was appropriate....

Notes and Questions

(1) *Deference Taken Too Far?* Do you believe that the deference embodied in the enrolled bill doctrine is proper, given that the question of whether the same text was approved is a fairly objective, constitutional question? What purpose does the enrolled bill doctrine serve?

(2) *Some States Reject the Enrolled Bill Doctrine.* Some states do permit attacks on an enrolled bill. *See, e.g., Bd. Of Comm'rs of Laramie County v. Wright*, 163 P.2d 190 (Wyo. 1945). Why do you suppose some states disagree with the federal approach established in *Marshall Field?*

(3) *Much Ado About Nothing?* Bicameralism and presentment are, of course, at the core of the constitutional requirements of legislation. If only one chamber passes a bill, it cannot be law. Doesn't this fact suggest that the enrolled bill doctrine should be abolished?

C. Judicial Deference to Internal Legislative Processes

The previous section gave a broad overview of the legislative process. This section explores what happens when the legislature does not follow its own rules. In addition to providing further background on legislative process, it introduces an important principle in statutory interpretation that we will see repeatedly: separation of powers.

As a general matter, judges routinely avoid interjecting themselves into matters that require them to determine the meaning of a legislature's rules or to determine whether the legislature complied with its own rules. Courts uniformly hold that the validity of a statute may not be attacked "by showing that in its enactment some form or proceeding had not been properly followed or adopted by the legislature, the supreme law maker." *Heimbach v. State*, 454 N.Y.S.2d 993, 999 (N.Y. App. Div. 1982) (holding that court would not review validity of a statute even though it was undisputed that a legislator whose vote was necessary for passage was not actually present during the vote). A typical explanation for this hands-off approach follows:

> Our policy of restraint in venturing into the internal operations of the Legislature ... is rooted in longstanding recognition of the wisdom of such restraint as expressed in *Ex parte Wren*, 63 Miss. 512 (1886).... In *Wren*, the appellant who challenged the efficacy of a statute as signed by the Governor, tried to delve into the legislative process, specifically to offer journals to show that amendments had been adopted but dropped from the bill when it was submitted to the Governor. The Court disallowed this saying:

>> The fundamental error of any view which permits an appeal to the journals to see if the constitution has been observed in the passage by both houses of their enactments, is the assumed right of the judicial department to revise and supervise the legislative as to the manner of its performance of its appointed constitutional functions. It is the admitted province of the courts to judge and declare if an act of the legislature violates the constitution, but this duty of the courts begins with the completed act of the legislature. It does not antedate it. *The legislature is one of the three co-ordinate and co-equal departments into which the powers of government are divided by the constitution, possessing all legislative power and not subject to supervision and control during its performance of its constitutional functions, nor to judicial revision afterward of the manner in which it obeyed the constitution its members are sworn to support. From necessity the judicial department must judge of* [sic] *the conformity of legislative acts to the constitution, but what are legislative acts must be determined by what are authenticated as such according to the constitution.*

>> That instrument [the constitution] contains many provisions as to the passage of bills which are admitted to be addressed to legislators exclusively, and for non-observance of which there is confessedly no remedy which courts can apply.... *The sound view ... is to regard all of the provisions of the constitution as mandatory, and those regulating the legislative department as addressed to and mandatory to that body, and with which the courts have nothing to do in the way of revision of how the legislature has performed its duty in the matters confided exclusively to it by the constitution.*

Tuck v. Blackmon, 798 So. 2d 402, 406–07 (Miss. 2001) (quoting *Wren*, 63 Miss. at 533–34).

This reasoning is widely accepted by courts, which generally give broad deference to the legislature by holding that disputes over the meaning or operation of internal legislative rules present "political questions" that are "nonjusticiable." *See, e.g., Baker v. Carr*, 369 U.S. 186, 210 (1962). What, if anything, is different about the holding of the *Des Moines Register* decision, which follows?

Des Moines Register & Tribune Co. v. Dwyer
542 N.W.2d 491 (Iowa 1996)

SNELL, JUSTICE.

[After an Iowa newspaper requested detailed phone records from the Iowa legislature, a legislative committee adopted a policy that denied public access to records that showed any details of a call, such as the number from which the call originated. The newspaper then filed suit, arguing that Iowa's open records act, codified in Iowa Code Chapter 22, required the custodian of the records, Dwyer and Gamble, to release them. The trial court granted summary judgment in favor of Dwyer and Gamble, and the newspaper appealed.]

It is a firmly-established principle that when a challenge to a legislative action involves a "political question," the judiciary may not intervene or attempt to adjudicate the matter. This principle stems primarily from the separation of powers doctrine which requires we leave intact the respective roles and regions of independence of the coordinate branches of government. *Baker v. Carr*, 369 U.S. 186, 210 (1962). *See also* 1 William Blackstone, Commentaries on the Laws of England 164 (13 ed. 1800) ("for it hath not been used aforetime that the justices should in any wise determine the privileges of the … parliament … the determination and knowledge of that privilege belongs to the … parliament and not to the justices"). Whether a matter involves a political question requires a case-by-case inquiry and constitutes a "delicate exercise in constitutional interpretation." *Baker*, 369 U.S. at 210–11….

At issue in this case is … whether a textually demonstrable constitutional commitment to the senate renders nonjusticiable the senate's decision to keep specific detailed phone records confidential. The text of the Iowa Constitution commits to the senate the power to determine its own rules of proceedings. The Iowa Constitution, article III, section 9 states as follows:

> Each house shall sit upon its own adjournments, keep a journal of its proceedings, and publish the same; *determine its rules of proceedings*, punish members for disorderly behavior, and with the consent of two-thirds, expel a member, but not a second time for the same offense; and shall have all other powers necessary for a branch of the general assembly of a free and independent state.

(Emphasis added.)

It is within the power of the judiciary to review the senate's rules for constitutionality and to ensure they do not violate individual fundamental rights. *Marbury v. Madison*, 5 U.S. (1 Cranch) 137 (1803).

It is entirely the prerogative of the legislature, however, to make, interpret, and enforce its own procedural rules, and the judiciary cannot compel the legislature to act in accordance with its own procedural rules so long as constitutional questions are not implicated. Furthermore, the legislature has complete control and discretion whether it shall observe, enforce, waive, suspend, or disregard its own rules of procedure, and violations of such rules are not grounds for the voiding of legislation.

The question here is not one involving a preservation of the independence of the judiciary in construing and interpreting statutes as suggested by the Register and Council but of recognizing and respecting the prerogatives of the Iowa Senate as committed to it by the Iowa Constitution. To view it as a matter of protecting our judicial independence from legislative incursions inappropriately inverts the legal posture of the case. This is because a study of the scope of chapter 22, The Open Records Statute, does not, nay cannot precede our authority and duty to first determine what rights are exclusively given to the legislature by our Constitution. Were it otherwise, we could always preempt a consideration of a constitutional question involving the legislature's exclusive domain where a statute could be interpreted to apply to the legislature itself. We believe that to embrace an imbalance of this magnitude between the judicial and legislative branches would be inconsistent with the principle of respect due to co-equal branches and would undermine the founded independence of all three branches of state government....

The determinative issue in the case at bar is whether the senate's policy on release of detailed phone records constitutes a senate rule of proceeding. The Register and Council argue the constitutional grant of procedural rule-making authority to the senate does not embrace the actions of individual senators but only actions of the senate as a "body," and because actions of individual senators are at issue here, the matter in controversy is justiciable. Dwyer argues for a broader interpretation of "rules of proceedings" and essentially contends procedural rules encompass any actions carried out in accordance with the constitutional functions of the senate. Inasmuch as privileged communication with constituents is an integral part of the senate's lawmaking process, Dwyer argues, the senate's policy regarding confidentiality of phone records constitutes a rule of proceeding and senate adherence to such a rule is beyond judicial intervention.

Whether an action constitutes a senatorial proceeding clearly requires a case-by-case analysis, and we do not believe it would be necessary or even feasible to establish a "bright line" definition of a senatorial rule of proceeding as the Register and Council request....

The Iowa Constitution vests the general assembly with the "'authority to pass rules of law for the government and regulation of people or property.'" *Schneberger v. Board of Social Welfare*, 291 N.W. 859, 861 (1940). Public communication with senators is an integral part of the senate's performance of its constitutionally granted authority to enact laws....

In order to perform the constitutionally-granted power and duty to enact laws, the Iowa Senate has provided a means by which individuals can communicate their thoughts with senators at public expense. Part of the procedure of the senate as a whole is to communicate on matters of legislation with the public. The phone conversations at the heart of the controversy before us constitute actions taken by the senate as it proceeds in the exercise of its power, in the transaction of its business, and in the performance of duties conferred upon it by the constitution. Recognizing that an accounting of the expenses incurred from use of senate telephone lines is appropriate, the senate authorized Dwyer to provide information that showed the total long distance charges for each senate telephone. This information was given to appellants....

The call detail records at issue here were not provided, however, by Dwyer. He believed that distribution of such records would violate senate policy, violate privacy rights and constitutional guarantees of freedom of speech, and would have a chilling effect on our citizens' rights and willingness to contact their elected officials....

The Iowa Senate has determined that a wholesale disclosure of its itemized call detail telephone records would be harmful to the public and to the senate's ability to carry out its responsibilities. Implicit in the senate's decision is a citizen's right to contact a legislator in person, by mail, or by telephone without any fear or suspicion that doing so would subject the citizen to inquiries from the press or anyone else regarding the nature of the conversation. Apart from the inconvenience or possible harassment generated, a citizen subjected to inquiry about contacting a senator, may, on refusing to discuss the content, find negative inferences are drawn from that fact alone.

The weighing of these factors is indigenous to the political process and is distinctly within the province of the senate. As elected representatives involved with the political process, senators are conditioned to decide political questions. A senatorial policy governing these actions therefore clearly constitutes a "rule of proceeding." We therefore affirm the trial court's ruling that release of the phone records by the senate constitutes a nonjusticiable political question. The proper forum for a challenge of the senate's policy on this matter lies not in the courts, but in the political process....

Affirmed.

Harris, Justice. (dissenting).

According to a venerable principle of disputation, the power to frame the question includes also the power to control the answer. Although the majority may have employed the proper analysis it has not reached the correct controlling question and has thus reached the incorrect conclusion. The question should be whether the legislature can suspend a self-imposed statutory obligation without first amending or repealing the statute. The answer should be no. I dissent because I think the trial court should be reversed.

As the majority notes, the political-question doctrine stems primarily from the principle of separation of powers. I enthusiastically agree that those of us who serve in any branch of government should be scrupulous in according respectful deference to the other branches concerning those matters entrusted to them. I also agree with the majority that the test for determining the existence of a political question is that set out in *Baker v. Carr*, 369 U.S. 186, 217 (1962). I further concur that the present case involves the first factor of that test: whether there is a textually demonstrable constitutional commitment of the issue to a coordinate political department. Indeed the majority is on solid ground in observing that responsibility and authority for establishing its own rules of proceedings rests with the General Assembly and not the courts.

This is not what is involved here. We are not dealing with rules of proceedings. Rather we are faced with an interpretation of a statute carefully fashioned years ago by the legislature when it provided for open access to public records. The legislature did not fashion this statute without difficulty. On the one hand it had to consider the interest of the taxpayers' right to information on where their dollars were being spent. On the other hand the legislature had also to consider the interests of citizens seeking comfortable access to their elected legislators. I freely acknowledge it was for the legislature to sort through these competing considerations in the legislative process and strike a balance that would be judged in the forum of public opinion. I would be the last to intrude into that process.

What the legislature should not be allowed to do is the very thing authorized by the majority: to resolve the question by enacting the open-records law, now Iowa Code chapter 22 (1995), in favor of access to the information, expressly making the access binding on itself, and then, on an ad hoc determination—actually judicial in nature—to withhold the statute's application. The majority is misguided in according this authority to the legislature on a ground of separation of powers because to do so abdicates authority that properly belongs exclusively to the courts. Under well established authority, later discussed, it is the province of the legislature to enact the laws, but once enacted it is the exclusive province of the courts to interpret the law.

Once a statute is lawfully enacted, all members of society, even legislators, must comply with its provisions. The General Assembly should be required to abide by Iowa Code chapter 22. A careful analysis of article III section 9 of the Iowa Constitution mandates this conclusion....

The heart of the dispute is the holding that the General Assembly's prerogative to set its own rules of proceedings authorizes it to suspend operation of a statute it has made binding upon itself. For two reasons I think it cannot. First, not by any stretch of imagination, can I believe this policy, concerning as it does the individual legislator's interface with the public, is a rule of proceeding. Secondly, I am convinced we should persist in our view that the legislature cannot excuse itself from the binding effect of its own enactments without first amending or repealing them....

My strongest disagreement with the majority lies with its authorization of the "political question" escape route: a legislative claim of a direct constitutional power used in order to avoid the legal consequences of its own enactments. The "claim" was triggered by a transparent legal ruling. The defendant secretary of the senate, John F. Dwyer, refused to produce call detail records because, he said, "production of such records would violate privacy rights and constitutional guarantees of freedom of speech and would have a detrimental chilling effect on citizens' rights and willingness to petition their elected officials." I am sure Mr. Dwyer is a person of considerable ability but nevertheless is a person who obviously has never taken an oath of judicial office. It cannot be seriously argued that his ruling did not involve interpretation of laws, a function we have vigilantly claimed exclusively for the courts.

> We have often expressed our acknowledgment that under the separation of powers doctrine, it is the prerogative of the legislature to declare what the law shall be, but the prerogative of the courts alone to declare what the law is.

State ex rel. Lankford v. Mundie, 508 N.W.2d 462, 463 (Iowa 1993).

Cases can be found that acknowledge a legislature's right to ignore or contradict existing statutes. This view seems to have originated with commentators, such as Blackstone, who were familiar with a system of parliamentary responsibility, in which the parliament did indeed reign supreme, even to the extent of holding final jurisdiction to consider appeals from the courts. This orientation has led many courts to misconstrue a valid principle: one legislative session cannot bind its successors. But this limitation properly exists only in the sense that it cannot bind future legislatures to renew legislation or to be bound not to repeal it....

Article III section 9 of the Iowa Constitution accords each house of the General Assembly authority to "determine its rules of proceedings." The trial court interpreted this authority to include the subject matter of this suit, an interpretation I believe to be at odds with the Constitution's plain language. This provision was obviously intended to accord each legislative house the power to establish a system for the orderly processing of bills. How individual legislators meet or communicate with the public is a matter of considerable importance, but has absolutely nothing to do with the General Assembly's rules of proceedings. *See Watson v. California Fair Political Practices Comm'n,* 266 Cal.Rptr. 408, 413

(2 Dist.1990) (term "rules of proceedings" confined to manner in which a legislature drafts its rules, appropriates its funds, or chooses officers or employees, and does not concern legislators' relationships with constituents); *Sweeney v. Tucker*, 473 Pa. 493, 375 A.2d 698, 708–09 (1977) ("rules of proceedings" defined as internal operating procedures of the legislature)....

Appellate judges writing, as I am, in dissent are often tempted to exaggerate the importance of the holding with which they disagree. I recognize that the immediate fallout from the majority opinion, though profoundly disappointing to me, will not shake the cosmos. The public, if sufficiently motivated, has political ways of acquiring information on the details of public expenditures. What I do find alarming is our surrender of vital ground in the separation of powers. We acquired this ground at considerable cost. In some future controversy the majority holding will surely haunt us.

Like my respected colleagues I have a profound reluctance to question the actions of either other branch of state government. It is however no compliment to them, especially when they are confronted by members of the public, to accord other branches more deference than is proper. Neither is it an insult to them to preserve to our branch those responsibilities exclusively entrusted to us. I think the judgment of the trial court should be reversed and the case remanded for the further proceedings I have described.

Notes and Questions

(1) *What is this Case About?* The *Des Moines Register* case divided the court. What was the essence of their disagreement? What is a "law" compared to a "rule" if a rule can vitiate a law? Why does that matter? Or does it—was this just a fight about form, not substance?

(2) *Was it a "Rule" or Something Else?* As a matter of plain English, do you believe a rule about whether the public can have access to phone records is a "rule of proceeding?" Why did the majority hold that it was? Why did the dissent argue otherwise?

(3) *Separation of Powers.* In what fundamental way does *Des Moines Register* stretch the principle that courts should respect the interpretation of the legislature's internal rules and at the same time respect that the judiciary's function is to interpret statutes while the legislature's function is to write them?

D. The Single Subject Rule

Some state constitutions impose procedural requirements on legislatures. A common one is the so-called "one subject rule." Single subject rules require that a bill address only "one subject." Virtually all state constitutions require that bills relate to only a "single subject." *Franklin v. State*, 887 So. 2d 1063, 1072 (Fla. 2004) (noting that 43 states had such provisions). *E.g.*, FLA. CONST. art. III, §6 ("Every law shall embrace but one subject and matter properly connected therewith, and the subject shall be briefly expressed in the title."); GA. CONST. art. III, §V, ¶III (no bill shall "refer[] to more than one subject matter or contain[] matter different from what is expressed in the title thereof."); PA. CONST. art. III, §3 ("No bill shall be passed containing more than one subject, which shall be clearly expressed in its title, except a general appropriation bill or a bill codifying or compiling the law or a part thereof.'"). Despite the fact that the single subject rule is constitutionally required, courts tend to be highly deferential in determining whether a bill complies with the single subject rule. Consider the following case.

Lutz v. Foran
427 S.E.2d 248 (Ga. 1993)

FLETCHER, JUSTICE.

This appeal challenges the constitutionality of the affidavit requirement in professional malpractice actions. We hold that O.C.G.A. §9-11-9.1 does not violate the constitutional prohibition against the inclusion of more than one subject matter in a bill or a matter in the body different from the title. Because the law was unsettled on the act's coverage of professionals when the complaint was filed, we reverse and remand to enable the plaintiffs to file an appropriate affidavit.

Reid Lutz owned a shrimp boat that sunk in the Savannah River. The boat was salvageable, and Lutz marked it with buoys. He had raised it within five feet of the surface when a ship piloted by Michael Foran, a licensed harbor pilot, hit and damaged it beyond repair. Lutz and the owner of the salvage equipment sued Foran for negligence in failing to control his vessel and causing the collision of boats. Foran denied that a collision occurred and moved to dismiss for Lutz's failure to attach an expert affidavit in compliance with O.C.G.A. §9-11-9.1. Lutz appeals from the trial court's order dismissing the complaint....

The expert affidavit requirement provides:

> In any action for damages alleging professional malpractice, the plaintiff shall be required to file with the complaint an affidavit of an expert competent to testify, which affidavit shall set forth specifically at least one negligent act or omission claimed to exist and the factual basis for each such claim.

O.C.G.A. §9-11-9.1(a) (1982 & Supp.1992). This court relied on the plain language of the statute to hold in *Housing Auth. v. Greene*, 259 Ga. 435, 437, 383 S.E.2d 867 (1989), that it "applies to 'any action for damages alleging professional malpractice' on the part of an architect or other professional." Subsequently, we held that affidavits are required only in lawsuits filed against a professional in one of the occupations enumerated in O.C.G.A. §14-7-2(2) or subject to licensing and regulation under O.C.G.A. §§14-10-2(2) and 43-1-24. A harbor pilot is a member of a profession listed in §14-7-2. Therefore, Lutz must file an affidavit with his complaint if the allegations involve professional malpractice....

The allegations in the complaint establish that Lutz filed a claim for professional, rather than simple, negligence.... Because conducting an ocean-going ship in the Savannah River calls for the professional skill of a harbor pilot, Lutz must file an expert affidavit with his complaint.

Lutz alleges that the affidavit requirement in O.C.G.A. §9-11-9.1 should be struck down as unconstitutional because it is part of an act that contains more than one subject matter and a subject different from the matter expressed in the title. Specifically, he argues that the Medical Malpractice Reform Act of 1987 cannot apply to professions other than medicine without violating Article III, Section V, Paragraph III of the Georgia Constitution.

---

2. This court has construed the word "title" in the constitution to mean the act's caption. This opinion uses the terms "title" and "caption" interchangeably.

This constitutional provision provides that "[n]o bill shall pass which refers to more than one subject matter or contains matter different from what is expressed in the title thereof." Ga. Const. Art. III, Sec. V, Par. III. The legislature enacted this paragraph to prevent surreptitious legislation such as the "Yazoo Fraud" and omnibus bills that combine several adverse matters to secure their passage. Requiring the act's title to alert the reader to the matters contained in its body is to protect against surprise legislation.

The provision requiring the title to express what is in the act must be given a reasonable interpretation.[2]

> It was never intended that the substance of the entire act should be set forth in the caption. It was not contemplated that every detail stated in the body should be mentioned in the caption. If what follows after the enacting clause is definitely related to what is expressed in the title, has a natural connection, and relates to the main object of legislation, ... there is no infringement of the constitutional [provision].... Any provision in the body which is germane to [the act's] general purpose as embraced in the title [does not violate] the [Constitution].

Id. at 10–11, 193 S.E. 869. The caption must indicate only the general object to be dealt with in the act to protect the people against covert legislation.

Applying a reasonable interpretation of the statute, we hold that the title of the act gives the reader sufficient notice that the affidavit requirement will apply in professional malpractice actions. The caption states that the act is "to provide that in any case in which *professional* malpractice is alleged, an affidavit of an expert competent to testify setting forth the particulars of the claim shall be filed with the complaint." Ga.L. 1987, p. 887 (emphasis supplied). The language in section three of the act tracks the words in the caption. Section three is one of only three substantive provisions of the four-page act and receives its proportionate share of the lines in the caption.[3] Thus, despite the short title of "Medical Malpractice Reform Act of 1987," the caption gives the General Assembly and the public adequate notice that the act contains matter relating to malpractice actions against professionals.

The act's legislative history supports this conclusion. The Governor's Advisory Committee on Tort Reform in its final report in 1986 recommended the affidavit requirement in "medical malpractice and other professional liability cases." A conference committee composed of three leaders of both the house and senate added the affidavit provision to Senate Bill 2. The bill was passed as part of an intensely debated effort to reform the state's

---

3. The entire caption states as follows:

To provide substantive and comprehensive reforms affecting claims for medical malpractice; to provide a short title; to amend Title 9 of the Official Code of Georgia Annotated, relating to civil practice, so as to provide that minors who have attained the age of five years and incompetents shall be subject to limitations of actions provisions regarding medical malpractice; to provide for periods of limitation and repose; to provide exceptions; to provide findings; to provide that certain actions shall not be revived or extinguished; to provide that in any case in which professional malpractice is alleged, an affidavit of an expert competent to testify setting forth the particulars of the claim shall be filed with the complaint; to provide the contents of such affidavit; to provide exceptions; to provide procedures; to provide that no period of limitation is extended by such filing requirements; to amend Chapter 1 of Title 51 of the Official Code of Georgia Annotated, relating to general provisions affecting torts, so as to provide immunity from civil liability to certain health care providers or other entities providing professional services without compensation or the expectation thereof; to provide exceptions; to provide for applicability; to repeal conflicting laws; and for other purposes.

tort laws. Presumably, members of the General Assembly looked beyond the short title and read the caption of the bill to determine its contents before voting.

Although no one has previously challenged the constitutionality of O.C.G.A. § 9-11-9.1, we have previously considered the arguments on which the dissenting opinion relies. We rejected the argument that the affidavit requirement applies solely to medical malpractice actions, despite the reference in the 1989 amendment to medical malpractice, because of the presumption that the General Assembly enacts statutes with full knowledge of the existing condition of the law and that statutes are to be interpreted with reference to prior decisions of the courts. Prior to the passage of the 1989 amendment, the Court of Appeals interpreted the statute to apply to any professional malpractice action.

Moreover, if legislators and citizens lacked notice that the affidavit requirement applied to professions outside the medical field, as the dissent contends, the surprise resulted from this court's interpretation of the statute, not the act itself. In concluding that the statute is unconstitutional, the dissenting opinion ignores the rule of statutory construction that we must construe a statute as valid when possible. The statute would be constitutional, even under the analysis of the dissent, if the affidavit requirement were limited to the medical profession. Yet, the legislature has declined invitations in 1989, 1990, and 1991 to amend the statute to limit the affidavit requirement to the medical profession.

To conclude that the caption gives inadequate notice because the professional affidavit requirement is located between provisions on medical malpractice and health care providers is to place in jeopardy a major portion of the bills that the legislature passes. Our court has never held either the legislature or the bills it passes to such a strict standard of notice. The test is reasonableness, and the title of the challenged act gives reasonable notice to any reader of the act's contents.

Whether an act violates the multiple subject matter rule depends on whether all of the bill's provisions seek to accomplish a single objective. The Constitution looks to "unity of purpose."

> As used in the Constitution, [the term "subject matter"] is to be given a broad and extended meaning so as to allow the legislature authority to include in one Act all matters having a logical or natural connection. To constitute plurality of subject matter, an Act must embrace two or more dissimilar and discordant subjects that by no fair intendment can be considered as having any logical connection with or relation to each other. All that our Constitution requires is that the Act embrace only one general subject.

Crews v. Cook, 139 S.E.2d 490 (1964). This court has upheld several acts against constitutional challenges that they embraced multiple subject matters. See *Wall*, 242 Ga. at 570, 250 S.E.2d 408 (upholding act extending city limits by annexation and changing the method of electing a city's governing body); *Crews*, 220 Ga. at 481, 139 S.E.2d 490 (upholding act dealing with wills and the administration of estates); *Capitol Distrib. Co. v. Redwine*, 206 Ga. 477, 486, 57 S.E.2d 578 (1950) (upholding act increasing excise taxes on both malt beverages and wine).

---

1. While the allegation of invalidity in this case is based on the Georgia Constitution, the "single subject" constitutional provision at issue pertains to a procedural irregularity which, while not in the least trivial or unimportant, is not of the magnitude of an ongoing equal protection or substantive due process violation.

The general purpose of the challenged act is to reform tort liability of both medical providers and other professionals. The act seeks to reduce the number of liability claims against professionals. By establishing a new statute of limitation for suits against medical providers by minors or incompetents, requiring injured persons to support their allegations of professional malpractice with an affidavit by an expert, and granting immunity from civil liability to health care providers who render services without pay. All three provisions are logically related to the general subject of professional liability and do not embrace discordant subjects. Therefore, the act is constitutional under the multiple subject matter provision....

HUNT, PRESIDING JUSTICE, concurring.

One cannot argue with the logic of the dissent. In the abstract, it is entirely correct: the title of the Medical Malpractice Reform Act of 1987 gives no clue that it applies to malpractice other than medical malpractice.[1]

But the reality is that, time and again, over the last five years, we, and the Court of Appeals, have applied the Act to all aspects of professional negligence. See *Cheeley v. Henderson*, 261 Ga. 498, 405 S.E.2d 865 (1991) (lawyers); *Kneip v. Southern Eng'g Co.*, 260 Ga. 409, 395 S.E.2d 809 (1990) (engineers); *Housing Authority v. Greene*, 259 Ga. 435, 383 S.E.2d 867 (1989) (architects); *Precision Planning v. Wall*, 193 Ga.App. 331, 387 S.E.2d 610 (1989) (engineers); *Frazier v. Merritt*, 190 Ga.App. 832, 380 S.E.2d 495 (1989) (lawyers). Surely if the members of the General Assembly were surprised by these holdings or disagreed with them, they would have cured the problem by clarifying the scope of the Act. To now declare the Act unconstitutional, while an interesting academic exercise, serves no practical purpose.

SEARS-COLLINS, JUSTICE, dissenting.

... [T]his Georgia contribution to American constitutional law[2] contains two separate restrictions: a "single subject" requirement and a title requirement. The single subject provision is designed to "inhibit the passage of what is often termed 'omnibus' or 'log-rolling' bills," in which many diverse matters are contained in one bill with the view of combining in their favor the advocates of all and thus securing the passage of several measures no one of which could succeed upon its own merits. The title requirement facilitates the legislative process in two important ways. First, it prevents the surprise that may result when the title of an act does not fully inform legislators of the act's contents. Second, the title requirement alerts the citizens of this state, especially affected groups and parties, to the subjects the legislature is considering.

In this case, the question of impermissible "log-rolling" need not be addressed because I conclude, as the appellants contend, that the title of the Act gave citizens and legislators notice that the body of the Act would contain matter related to medical malpractice actions only and did not fairly apprise citizens and their legislators that Section 3 of the Act ... would apply to professional malpractice actions in general.

---

2. Georgia was the first state to adopt a constitutional title and single-subject requirement.... Our provision had its genesis in the notorious Yazoo Land Fraud, in which an obscure legislative provision not indicated in the title of its statute authorized the sale of over 35,000,000 acres of land which now comprise the states of Alabama and Mississippi to certain land speculation companies for a mere $500,000 dollars, or less than two cents per acre. By an act of February 13, 1796, the Georgia Legislature tried to declare this egregious fraud null and void. The United States Supreme Court held that an innocent purchaser of the land held good title which could not be abrogated by the 1796 act. *Fletcher v. Peck*, 10 U.S. (6 Cr.) 87(1810) (the first case in which the Supreme Court struck down a state law as unconstitutional).

In this regard, § 9-11-9.1 provides, in relevant part, that "[i]n any action for damages alleging professional malpractice, the plaintiff shall be required to file with the complaint an affidavit of an expert competent to testify." Id. at (a). In [another case], this court correctly held that "under its *plain language,* O.C.G.A. § 9-11-9.1 applies to 'any action for damages alleging professional malpractice'... [and] is not restricted to medical-malpractice actions." In [a second case] we subsequently held that the reach of § 9-11-9.1 was limited to the definition of "professional" contained in the O.C.G.A., currently §§ 14-7-2(2), 14-10-2(2), and 43-1-24. Given the plain meaning of the statutory language, our rules of statutory construction prohibited us from relying on the short title and caption of the Act to hold that the statute was limited to medical malpractice actions only....

This issue puts the focus on the language of the short title and the caption of the Act ...

In deciding whether this caption and the short title put citizens and their legislators on notice of the broad impact of § 9-11-9.1, we must bear in mind the purpose of the constitutional provision. "The purpose of this constitutional provision is to protect the people against covert or surprise legislation," *Nelson,* supra, 147 S.E.2d 424, particularly since "[i]t is a common practice to pass bills by their title only...." In short, the title of a bill must be honest. It must provide adequate notice to citizens and their legislators of the subjects contained therein. To this end, we have held that the title must not be "deceiving upon a *casual reading* of only the [caption] of the [a]ct."

In this case, the majority opinion undermines the purpose of the constitutional provision by focusing on the phrase "professional malpractice" in the caption in isolation instead of determining what is communicated to legislators or concerned citizens by the Act's short title and entire caption. Examining the caption, we see, first, that the opening clause states that the Act is "to provide substantive and comprehensive reforms affecting claims for medical malpractice." A legislator or citizen reading this clause, especially given that the short title preceding that opening clause is the "Medical Malpractice Reform Act of 1987," would, with some justification, believe that the remaining clauses of the caption would set forth the substantive and comprehensive medical malpractice reforms mentioned in the opening clause. Moreover, the phrase "professional malpractice" is mentioned only once in the twenty-one lines of the caption, is buried in the middle of the caption, and is bracketed by a provision affecting *medical* malpractice statutes of limitation and repose and another provision reforming the liability of *health care* providers in emergency or charitable settings. The contents of the caption, especially when read alongside the Act's short title, gave inadequate notice that the affidavit requirement would apply to suits against riverboat captains and harbor pilots. Rather, the title probably left most reasonable legislators and concerned citizens with the distinct impression that the affidavit requirement was designed to reform medical malpractice only.

In addition to focusing on the phrase "professional malpractice" in isolation, the majority invokes the legislative history of the affidavit requirement to support its conclusion that the title of the Act gave legislators and citizens adequate notice. This reliance on legislative history, however, is misplaced. First, the constitutional provision in question requires the title of the act to provide adequate notice; it does not say that the legislative history will suffice. Considering the profusion of bills that legislators must review, it is contrary to the spirit of the constitutional provision to rely on legislative history to determine if legislators received adequate notice of what was contained in the body of an act.

Moreover, the legislative history of the affidavit requirement leads to the inescapable conclusion that the legislators were not adequately notified that the affidavit requirement extended beyond the medical profession to other professionals. The Senate included a blanket affidavit requirement in the Senate substitute for the House bill that eventually became the broadly applicable Tort Reform Act of 1987, but the House *rejected* the substitute bill. The caption of the rejected bill, like the caption of the Tort Reform Act of 1987, began with the comprehensive statement: "To provide substantial and comprehensive civil justice reform affecting tort claims litigation." The caption of the rejected bill then proposed that "in any case in which professional malpractice or product liability is alleged, an affidavit of an expert competent in the field setting forth the particulars of the claim shall be filed with the complaint." Since the opening clause of the caption dealt with tort reform in general, any citizen or legislator who read the clause of the caption dealing with "professional malpractice or product liability" would have obtained real notice of the comprehensive nature of the affidavit requirement. Perhaps because of such clear notice, the members of the legislature *rejected* the bill, and the affidavit requirement contained therein was not included in the equally comprehensive Tort Reform Act of 1987.

Instead, it can be surmised that the defeated supporters of the broad affidavit requirement smuggled the requirement, Trojan Horse fashion, and without the words "product liability," into the body and the caption of the more limited Medical Malpractice Reform Act of 1987, which begins its much less ambitious caption with: "To provide substantive and comprehensive reforms affecting claims for medical malpractice." Had the words "product liability" remained in the affidavit requirement and had they accompanied the words "professional malpractice" in the caption of the Medical Malpractice Reform Act, a legislator, upon reading the caption, might have been reminded of the broad affidavit requirement defeated as part of the Tort Reform Act. The words "product liability" were possibly deleted for just that reason. Given the medical malpractice reform orientation of the caption of the Medical Malpractice Reform Act, and given the deletion of the words "product liability" from the rejected provision of the Tort Reform Act, the majority's reliance on the legislative history of the affidavit requirement in the Tort Reform Act to conclude that citizens and legislators received adequate notice from the caption of the Medical Malpractice Reform Act is misplaced.

Moreover, the 1989 amendment to the 1987 Act, which refers to O.C.G.A. § 9-11-9.1 as requiring an affidavit in *medical* malpractice actions, supports the conclusion that many legislators believed that the Act applied to medical malpractice actions only....

However laudable the purpose of reforming other types of malpractice actions, both good government and our state constitution require that the titles of our laws give citizens and their legislators adequate notice of the actual substance of laws to whose passage they give assent.

Since the citizens of Georgia and their legislators were not fairly apprised of O.C.G.A. § 9-11-9.1's true breadth, I conclude that the application by our courts of O.C.G.A. § 9-11-9.1 to other than medical professional malpractice actions, despite being warranted by the plain language of that provision, nevertheless is unconstitutional.... I, therefore, must respectfully dissent to the majority opinion in this case.

Notes and Questions

(1) *Are Some Constitutional Rights More Important than Others?* Arguably, the difference of opinion among the judges in this case turns on the importance they ascribe to the single subject rule. In footnote 1, the concurring opinion goes so far as to rank the single subject rule of lesser importance than other constitutional rights. Doesn't the history of Georgia's constitutional requirement suggest that close judicial scrutiny was intended?

(2) *Who has the Stronger Arguments on the Merits?* Looking at the legislative history, doesn't the dissent have the stronger argument? If so, then isn't the only explanation for the difference of opinion the "scrutiny" that the judges give to the rule, or, to put it another way, the deference that they will give to legislators?

(3) *Purposes of the Single Subject Rule.* Single subject rules serve several purposes, including (a) encouraging a deliberative and accountable government; (b) curbing the practice of hiding the significant part of a bill; (c) reducing the ability of legislators to regulate unpopular subjects in bills that will pass; and (d) providing fair notice to legislators and the public as to a bill's subject. *Pennsylvanians Against Gambling Expansion Fund, Inc. v. Commonwealth*, 877 A.2d 383 (Pa. 2005). "[R]easonable notice is the keystone" requirement. *Id.* at 395. Given these important policies, does judicial deference make sense?

(4) *Deference on a Constitutional Question?* Even where the legislature's action implicates principles imposed by a state constitution, such as the single subject rule, courts "interpret[] procedural limitations liberally and will uphold the constitutionality of a statute against such an attack unless the act clearly and undoubtedly violates the constitutional limitation." *Fust v. Attorney General*, 947 S.W.2d 424, 427 (Mo. 1997). The courts generally resolve "every reasonable doubt in favor of validity." *Franklin v. State*, 887 So. 2d 1063, 1075 (Fla. 2004). Accordingly, courts broadly construe what "a single subject" means. *See Pennsylvanians Against Gambling*, 877 A.2d at 394–97 (holding that "regulation of gaming" was the subject of a bill, so the bill did not violate single subject rule even though, among other things, it authorized issuance of gambling licenses, created numerous funds to distribute tax proceeds from gaming, and established subject matter jurisdiction in the Pennsylvania Supreme Court over disputes over the issuance of gaming licenses). As a consequence, bills that have been found to have violated the single subject rule are scarce. *E.g., Sloan v. Wilkins*, 608 S.E.2d 579 (S.C. 2005) (holding that the single subject rule was violated by the "Life Sciences Act" because it was "teeming with subjects, from life sciences provisions to the establishment of a culinary arts institute.") If a bill does cover more than one "subject," however, then some or all of the provisions that were part of the bill may be unconstitutional. *See id.* (finding those provisions of the statute that were within "one subject" to be enforceable, but not the other provisions). Do you believe that is a correct balance of power? Isn't it the courts' job to apply constitutional requirements? *See Tuck v. Blackmon*, 798 So. 2d 402, 406 (Miss. 2001) ("An interpretation by the Senate of the extent of its power under the Constitution, while not binding on the courts, should be accepted unless manifestly wrong.").

(5) *Subsequent Action.* Several years after the events in the principal case, the Georgia Legislature adopted a bill that identified 24 professions that would be subject to the affidavit requirement. *See Minix v. Dep't of Transp.*, 533 S.E.2d 75 (Ga. 2000). We'll address subsequent legislative actions later, but can you argue that this later action shows the *Lutz* court was wrong in holding that all professions were covered by the bill?

Chapter 2

Sources, Approaches, and Theories of Interpretation

As a leading commentator noted, "legislation is an act of communication to be understood on the simple model of speaker and audience, so that the commanding question in legislative interpretation is what a particular speaker or group 'meant' in some canonical act of utterance." RONALD DWORKIN, LAW'S EMPIRE 348 (1986). Thus, interpretation is a "quest by judges to use the best available theory and information to determine 'what statutes mean.'" Cheryl Boudrea, et al., *What Statutes Mean: Interpretive Lessons from Positive Theories of Communication and Legislation*, 44 SAN DIEGO L. REV. 957, 958 (2007).

This chapter introduces the theory and sources of information that are used to determine what a statute means. First, this chapter discusses the sources judges look to for evidence of meaning, and second, the principal theories, or approaches, to statutory interpretation. Broadly speaking, there are three primary theories of statutory interpretation: textualism, intentionalism, and purposivism. This chapter explains the theories, then explores judicial disagreement about the appropriate theory, or as we call it, the appropriate approach to interpretation. These approaches influence not only how judges think about the text, but what judges do when the text doesn't resolve the issue before them. Approach arguably influences all aspects of statutory interpretation; hence, this challenging subject comes early in your studies. Before we discuss the approaches, you must first understand the sources judges consider when determining a statute's meaning.

A. The Sources for Statutory Interpretation

To answer the question "What does the statute mean?" a judge may look to a variety of different sources for insights as to meaning. These sources of statutory interpretation fall into three general categories: intrinsic (or textual), extrinsic (including legislative history), and policy-based. *See generally*, William N. Eskridge, Jr., & Philip P. Frickey, *The Supreme Court, 1993 Term Foreword: Law As Equilibrium*, 108 HARV. L. REV. 26, 97 (1994). (As we'll see, courts sometimes characterize a particular source differently than we have, but the label is not critical to your understanding of the role the sources play in interpretation.)

1. Intrinsic Sources

First are sources intrinsic to the statutory text being interpreted—principally the words. For all courts, the words are the starting point of interpretation. Thus, more than any other source, words play the most critical role in interpretation. But a statute is larger than simply its words; syntax, punctuation, grammar, and related statutes are also important intrinsic sources. You might think of intrinsic sources as those coming from the legislative pen and passing through the constitutionally required enactment process.

One intrinsic source is the linguistic, or textual, canons. Because words are inherently ambiguous, judges developed canons of statutory construction related to this expression of the legislature. These textual canons help judges draw inferences from the words, grammar, and structure of the statute. Examples of these canons include:

- *Expressio unius*: read the expression of one thing to mean the exclusion of other things.
- *Noscitur a sociis*: interpret a general term to be similar to more specific terms in a series.
- *Ejusdem generis*: interpret a general term to reflect the class of objects reflected in more specific terms accompanying it.
- The Rule Against Surplusage: avoid interpreting a provision in a way that would render other words, sections, or provisions of the act superfluous or unnecessary.
- The Identical Words Presumption: interpret the same or similar words in statutes to mean the same thing.

See id. at 97–108. This list is not exhaustive, but merely representative of some of the commonly used textual canons. For a more detailed list, see Appendix A. Moreover, although these canons are important, they are merely guidelines or presumptions that help judges and lawyers interpret language. We will explore them in more detail later, and we will see that courts sometimes refuse to rely on textual canons if the text is clear. For now, you need simply be aware of their role as a source of statutory meaning.

Another intrinsic source is the components of the bill, such as titles, preambles, and section headings. In some situations, these components play a role in interpretation. In summary, intrinsic sources include those sources that come directly from the legislature during the enactment process.

2. Extrinsic Sources

Second are sources extrinsic to the statutory text, but related to the legislative process. Examples include legislative history, subsequent legislative inaction (*i.e.*, sometimes courts ascribe meaning to inaction when a legislature fails to act in response to a judicial interpretation of a statute), and agency interpretations. These sources of meaning are not in enacted text. Something more must be consulted.

Different courts find different forms of extrinsic evidence relevant to a statute's meaning. Legislative history is perhaps the most controversially used source within this category. Reliance on subsequent legislative inaction is also controversial. In contrast, deferring to administrative interpretations is increasingly common, even mandated, in some situations. We examine the legislative process and the documents that comprise the legislative history in other chapters. We will also explore subsequent legislative inaction and agency action in more detail later. But you should notice that with all these extrinsic sources, a court looks beyond the text itself to discern the statute's meaning. Just when courts are willing to do so will vary, as we will see below.

3. Policy-Based Sources

Third, and finally, are sources that reflect important policy choices. Many of these policy-based sources are derived from the Constitution or from existing common law concepts. For example, the rule of lenity is a canon derived from the Due Process Clause. It directs that criminal statutes be given the narrower of two reasonable interpretations to ensure that citizens have notice of what is, and is not, criminal conduct. Similarly, another canon directs courts to avoid constitutional questions and, by doing so, furthers separation of powers. Two other canons also reflect substantive policies: first, statutes in derogation of the common law should be strictly construed, and second, remedial statutes should be broadly construed. We will study each canon in detail later.

Thus, judges have a variety of sources from which to discern meaning, some within the statute and some outside of it. However, all judges give primacy to the text. The text has always been important, and it has become more important in recent years as courts have grown more reluctant to look at sources beyond the text. Whether, and to what extent, a judge will give weight to the other sources, and the extent to which that judge will permit those other sources to overcome the plain meaning of the text, turns on the clarity of the text and the approach to statutory interpretation that the particular judge follows—a topic we explore in detail next.

For now, see if you can distinguish between the sources. In the following case, note the wide variety of sources that are used and when they can be used (*i.e.,* must ambiguity be found first?).

Beiswenger v. Psychiatric Sec. Review Bd.

84 P.3d 180 (Or. Ct. App. 2004)

LANDAU, P.J.,

Petitioner seeks judicial review of an order of the Psychiatric Security Review Board (PSRB or the board) denying his request for conditional release. We reverse and remand for further proceedings.

I. STATUTORY BACKGROUND

A brief review of the relevant statutes and rules will aid in understanding the facts and arguments in proper context. ORS 161.295 provides:

> "(1) A person is guilty except for insanity if, as a result of mental disease or defect at the time of engaging in criminal conduct, the person lacks substantial capacity either to appreciate the criminality of the conduct or to conform the conduct to the requirements of law.

> "(2) ... [T]he terms 'mental disease or defect' do not include an abnormality manifested only by repeated criminal or otherwise antisocial conduct, nor do they include any abnormality constituting solely a personality disorder." ...

Pursuant to ORS 161.341(4), a person committed to a state mental hospital may petition for discharge from PSRB's jurisdiction or for conditional release:

> "Any person who has been committed to a state hospital ... may apply to the board for an order of discharge or conditional release upon the grounds:

"(a) That the person is no longer affected by mental disease or defect...."

Obviously, a determinative issue often is whether the petitioner is affected by a "mental disease or defect." The statutes do not define the term other than to specify what is not included, that is, "an abnormality manifested only by repeated criminal or otherwise antisocial conduct, nor do they include any abnormality constituting solely a personality disorder." ORS 161.295(2). PSRB [an administrative agency] has promulgated administrative rules that define the terms "mental disease" and "mental defect" as follows:

"(4) 'Mental disease.' Mental disease is defined as any diagnosis of mental disorder which is a significant behavioral or psychological syndrome or pattern that is associated with distress or disability causing symptoms or impairment in at least one important area of an individual's functioning and is defined in the current Diagnostic and Statistical Manual of Mental Disorders (DSM-IV) of the American Psychiatric Association.

"(5) 'Mental defect.' Mental defect is defined as mental retardation, brain damage or other biological dysfunction that is associated with distress or disability causing symptoms or impairment in at least one important area of an individual's functioning and is defined in the current Diagnostic and Statistical Manual of Mental Disorders (DSM-IV) of the American Psychiatric Association."

OAR 859-010-0005(4), (5).

The DSM is a standard reference manual published by the American Psychiatric Association....

II. FACTUAL BACKGROUND

The relevant facts are not disputed. In 1988, petitioner was found guilty except for insanity, ORS 161.295, of kidnapping in the second degree, menacing, and unlawful use of a weapon. Petitioner was diagnosed at that time as suffering from "incipient paranoid schizophrenia" and "chronic residual schizophrenia." The trial court ordered that petitioner be placed under the jurisdiction of PSRB for a maximum period of 16 years....

In January 2002, petitioner applied to the board for conditional release. In March 2002, a psychiatrist prepared a progress note update in which he diagnosed petitioner as suffering from ... paraphilia..., alcohol abuse, cocaine abuse, cannabis abuse, and amphetamine abuse.... In April 2002, the board held a hearing for the purpose of determining whether petitioner should be conditionally released.... At the close of the hearing, petitioner argued that he was entitled to release because he was not currently suffering from a mental disease or defect. According to petitioner, his current drug- and alcohol-related diagnoses and his sexual disorder diagnosis of paraphilia demonstrated that he suffered only from "personality disorders," which by definition are not mental diseases or defects within the meaning of the relevant statutes.

The board found as fact that petitioner was affected by a mental disease or defect, that he continued to present a substantial danger to others, and that he could not adequately be treated or controlled in the community if conditionally released.... The board continued petitioner's commitment to the state hospital.

III. DISPOSITION OF THE MERITS

On judicial review, petitioner argues that PSRB erred in concluding that he suffers from a mental disease or defect within the meaning of ORS 161.295(1). He argues that, because the term is not defined in the statute and otherwise has no settled meaning, it is appropriate to turn to the legislative history of the statute, which he contends clearly demonstrates that conditions such as sexual conduct disorders, alcohol dependence, and drug dependence were intended to be classified as personality disorders, not mental diseases or defects.

The state contends that the statute is clear on its face and that resort to legislative history is unnecessary. It argues that … whether a given condition is a "mental disease or defect" may be determined by reference to PSRB rules and to the edition of the DSM in effect at the time that those rules were adopted. The state further argues that, under PSRB's current rules, the relevant edition is the DSM-IV and, in that edition, each of petitioner's diagnosed conditions is a mental disease or defect.

Petitioner in turn argues that, to the extent that PSRB is relying on its own rules and on the DMS, those rules are clearly at odds with the intended meaning of the statute and that, at the very least, the board cannot define statutory terms by reference to editions of professional publications that did not even exist at the time the statute was enacted.

The meanings of the terms "mental disease or defect" and "personality disorder" pose questions of statutory construction… [W]e attempt to determine the intended meaning of the statute by reference to its text in context and, if necessary, its legislative history and other aids to construction.

A. *Textual analysis*

At the first level of statutory construction, we examine—among other things—the wording of the statute in context and any prior judicial constructions of it. Our objective is to determine whether the legislature unambiguously expressed the intended meaning of the terms in dispute. A statutory term is "ambiguous" if more than one interpretation is not "wholly implausible." If the term is ambiguous, we must resort to legislative history to determine which among the competing interpretations the legislature intended.

In this case, as we have noted, the statutes do not expressly define the term "mental disease or defect." In common parlance, a mental disease is "a disease characterized esp. by mental symptoms: mental disorder: INSANITY." *Webster's Third New Int'l Dictionary* 1411 (unabridged ed. 1993). "Defect" is similarly broadly defined as "want or absence of something necessary for completeness, perfection, or adequacy in form or function: DEFICIENCY, WEAKNESS." *Id.* at 591. Thus, the phrase "mental disease or defect" could refer to virtually any infirmity of a nonphysical nature, including sexual misconduct disorders and alcohol and drug dependence.

ORS 161.295, however, explicitly imposes some limits on the term by describing what is not included, namely, "an abnormality manifested only by repeated criminal or otherwise antisocial conduct, nor do they include any abnormality constituting solely a personality disorder." ORS 161.295(2). The problem is that the statute does not define what constitutes a "personality disorder." The ordinary meaning of the term is a "psychopathological condition or group of conditions in which an individual's entire life pattern is considered deviant or nonadaptive." *Webster's* at 1687. In light of that definition, it is plausible that the legislature intended such deviant or nonadaptive life patterns as sexual misconduct disorders and alcohol and drug dependence to be regarded as "personality disorders" within the meaning of the statute and, as a result, to be excluded from the meaning of "mental disease or defect." …

In short, the statutory references to "mental disease or defect" and "personality disorder" are ambiguous. Resort to legislative history therefore is necessary.…

B. *Legislative history*

ORS 161.295 originated as House Bill (HB) 2075 during the 1983 legislative session. The bill was the product of an interim legislative committee that focused on public concerns with the so-called "insanity defense" in criminal cases....

The original version of the bill did not exclude "personality disorders" from the "mental disease[s] or defect[s]" that would be subject to a defense of guilty except for insanity. At an early hearing on the bill, the Executive Director of PSRB suggested that the bill should address that issue:

> "The legislature should take a position to either include or exclude 'personality' disorders' from the definition [of 'mental disease or defect']. It should be noted that personality disorders include the following diagnoses: antisocial, inadequate, passive-aggressive, sexual conduct disorders, drug dependent, alcohol dependent and paranoid."

Minutes, House Committee on Judiciary, HB 2075, Apr. 27, 1983, Ex D (statement of Felicia Gniewosz).

At the same hearing, the chair of PSRB testified that the board supported the exclusion of "personality disorders" from the definition of "mental disease or defect." She explained to the House Judiciary Committee that "personality disorders" include child molestation, other sex offenses, and persons "suffering from a drug-induced syndrome." Tape Recording, House Committee on Judiciary, HB 2075, Apr. 27, 1983, Tape 270, Side A (statement of Judy Snyder). She added as a further example of a "personality disorder":

> "[P]eople who have an alcohol problem and who maybe stabbed someone while they were in an alcoholic stupor and they're put under our jurisdiction.... The problem the board has is that kind of person can be very dangerous if they drink alcohol but the doctors will testify that's not a mental illness, they don't have a mental illness[.]"

Id. at Tape 269, Side B....

It was at that point that the current wording of the statute was first proposed. Representative Courtney asked Jeffrey Rogers, the chair of the legislative interim task force that had drafted the bill, to propose wording that would accomplish the exclusion of "personality disorders" from the statutory definition of "mental disease or defect." Rogers responded with the wording that is, in substance, the current law. The wording was adopted by the House Judiciary Committee without objection. Tape Recording, House Committee on Judiciary, HB 2075, May 13, 1983, Tape 324, Side A.

The House Judiciary Committee ultimately approved the bill, including the exclusion for "personality disorders." Interestingly, in the staff measure analysis prepared for the benefit of the committee members, the ... bill was summarized ...:

> "The bill as amended further limits the scope of mental diseases or defects for which a person may be found, under present law, 'not responsible.' Existing law excludes abnormalities manifested only by repeated criminal or otherwise antisocial conduct. The bill would exclude, in addition, any abnormality which constitutes solely a personality disorder, which includes such diagnoses as sexual conduct disorders, drug dependent and alcohol dependent."

Staff Measure Analysis, House Committee on Judiciary, HB 2075, 1983.

The bill moved to the floor of the House, where the floor manager, Representative Courtney, explained that it contained a "personality exclusion" that accomplished a narrowing of the definition of "mental disease or defect." Quoting from a letter from PSRB's Executive Director to the House Judiciary Committee, he explained:

> "Right now if a person has what is considered a personality disorder, by that I mean what they call 'anti-social, inadequate, passive-aggressive, sexual conduct disorders, drug dependent, alcohol dependent, or paranoid,' if they fit into that personality disorder category they're able to claim that they have a mental disease or defect. We now no longer, with this piece of legislation, will allow an individual to say that I have a mental disease or defect because I have a personality disorder."

House Floor Debate, HB 2075, June 16, 1983, Reel 19, Track I (Rep Peter Courtney).

After passage by the House, the bill was referred to the Senate Judiciary Committee. At the first hearing on the bill, Representative Courtney introduced it to the committee and explained that it "would remove personality disorders as a category that could be relied on for use of the insanity plea." Tape Recording, Senate Committee on Judiciary, HB 2075, June 29, 1983, Tape 234, Side A (Rep. Peter Courtney). A "personality disorder," he explained, included such conditions as "anti-social, inadequate, passive-aggressive, sexual conduct disorders, drug dependent, alcohol dependent, paranoid, etc." *Id.*…

The Senate Judiciary Committee, concerned that the concept of "personality disorder" was too difficult to define, deleted the exclusion from the bill, and the Senate approved the bill as amended.

The bill then moved to a conference committee. The first topic of discussion was the deletion of the "personality disorder" exclusion.… The committee ultimately agreed to restore the "personality disorder" exclusion. The staff measure analysis of the final version of the bill explained that, as amended, the bill "would exclude … any abnormality which constitutes solely a personality disorder, which includes such diagnoses as sexual conduct disorders, drug dependent and alcohol dependent." Staff Measure Analysis, House Committee, HB 2075, 1983. As amended by the conference committee, the bill was passed by both houses and signed into law.

Several things are worth noting about the legislative history. First, although legislative history frequently is sparse and equivocal, in this case, it is anything but that. From the first hearing before the House Judiciary Committee, to the House floor debates, to the Senate hearings and the conference committee negotiations, the legislative history consistently and pervasively reflects an understanding that the statutory term "personality disorder" includes, among other things, sexual conduct disorders, alcohol dependency, and drug dependency.

Second, the reason for the legislature's concern with defining the term "personality disorder" also comes through rather clearly in the records of the enactment history. The "mental disease[s] or defect[s]" to which the statute refers are important not just for purposes of determining whether an individual who is subject to the jurisdiction of the PSRB may be released; they are also critical to determining whether a defendant may, in the first instance, avoid responsibility for the commission of a criminal act by reason of such a mental condition. Legislators repeatedly expressed concern that criminal defendants not be permitted to avoid criminal responsibility and incarceration merely by asserting that they suffered from some "mental disease or defect," as broadly defined. As Representative Courtney explained at several key junctures during the enactment process, the legislature believed it was necessary to provide an exclusion for "personality disorders" so that criminal defendants could not avail themselves of an insanity defense on the basis of such conditions as sexual conduct disorders, alcohol dependency, and drug dependency. In other words, as Courtney explained, by narrowly defining "mental disease or defect," the legislature intended to make the insanity defense less broadly available to criminal defendants. *See, e.g.,* House Floor Debate, HB 2075, June 16, 1983, Reel 19, Track I ("We now no longer, with this piece of legislation, will allow an individual to say that I have a mental disease or defect because I have a personality disorder.") ...

The objective of resorting to the legislative history is to ascertain what the legislature most likely would have understood as to the purpose and meaning of the wording of its enactments. Whether or not witnesses, in fact, were "mistaken" in indicating to the legislature that the mental health profession currently classified certain conditions as "personality disorders," the fact remains that the legislature clearly enacted the legislation based on that understanding....

C. Relevant maxims of construction

Even assuming ... that the state is correct that the legislative history is equivocal, that would not end our analysis. We would be required to resort to relevant maxims of statutory construction to resolve the persistent ambiguity. One of the maxims ... is that, in the absence of other clear indications of legislative intent, courts should attempt to reconstruct what the legislature would have done had it confronted the issue at hand. The court accomplishes that by selecting the construction that most completely effectuates the general policies reflected by the available indicia of legislative intent.

In this case, that task is not especially difficult. As we have noted, the legislature clearly stated that the general policy motivating its creation of the "personality disorder" exclusion was that the statutory term "mental disease or defect" be narrowly defined to limit the extent to which criminal defendants can avail themselves of the insanity defense. The state's proposed construction would run afoul of that general policy. Specifically, giving the term "mental disease or defect" the broad reading that the state suggests would expand the availability of the insanity defense to cover precisely those individuals whom the legislature explicitly intended to exclude.

We therefore conclude that the legislature intended the reference to "personality disorder" in ORS 161.295(2) to include sexual conduct disorders, alcohol dependency, and drug dependency and that, as a result, those disorders do not constitute a "mental disease or defect" within the meaning of ORS 161.295(1). The only conditions on which the state relies in this case for its assertion that petitioner was affected by a "mental disease or defect" are paraphilia—a sexual conduct disorder—and alcohol and drug dependency. Those conditions are not "mental disease[s] or defect[s]" within the meaning of ORS 161.295. It necessarily follows that PSRB erred in reaching a contrary conclusion....

Reversed and remanded for reconsideration.

Notes and Questions

(1) *Sources of Interpretation.* Can you identify the sources used by the court? Which do you find most persuasive? Did the court find the statute ambiguous before looking beyond the text?

(2) *Purpose v. Intent.* The court looked both for the specific intent of the legislature regarding the words "personality disorder," as well as the statutory purpose. What did the court decide the legislature's intent regarding these words was? What did the court determine that purpose was? Were they the same?

(3) *Does the Result Further the Purpose?* Does it seem strange to you that the court used the purpose for the exception (to prevent individuals with drug, sexual, and alcohol additions from escaping criminal responsibility) to help justify its holding that Beiswenger should no longer be confined to a mental hospital because he only had these types of addictions?

(4) *Affidavits of Meaning from Legislators.* Generally, courts reject as irrelevant affidavits from legislators, even those who voted on the statute in issue. Why do you think judges consider these affidavits irrelevant? Does the fact that one legislator had one intent necessarily indicate the intent of the remaining members of that legislature? What if the affidavit is from the bill's sponsor, the principal author? The governor who signed the bill into law? What if a majority of the legislature that had enacted the bill signed an affidavit as to their collective intent? Should any of these factors matter?

Problem 2-1

You represent Maria Fogg. Ms. Fogg was living with Chris Blanchard in a rent-controlled apartment located at 405 East 54th Street from the summer of 1995 until Blanchard's death this past September. Blanchard and Fogg were involved in an exclusive relationship; however, they never married.

In November of this year, Simon Associates Company, the owner of the apartment building, served Fogg a notice to evict. The notice contended that she was a mere licensee since only Blanchard was the tenant of record; thus, she had no right to occupy the apartment after Blanchard's death. The notice stated that she had one month to vacate the apartment and that, if the apartment were not vacated, Simon Associates would commence eviction proceedings. In the city in which your client lives, there is a rent-control statute that prohibits landlords from evicting spouses and family members of tenants who die.

First, identify the statutory text implicated by this problem. Then, using the materials below, determine how you would argue that your client is entitled to remain in the apartment. What sources of meaning best support your client's position? What arguments might Simon Associates make in response? Which sources of meaning best support its position?

Problem Materials

Mercer Rev. Stat. § 2204.6: Rent and Eviction Regulations

> (a) A certificate shall be issued for the eviction of the tenant and subtenants where the landlord seeks in good faith to recover possession of housing accommodations for which the tenant's lease or other rental agreement has expired or otherwise terminated, and at the time of termination the occupants of the housing accommodation are subtenants or other persons who occupied under a rental agreement with the tenant, and no part of the accommodations is used by the tenant as his dwelling.

> (1) The city rent agency shall not issue an order granting an eviction under subsection (a) of this provision, and any member of the tenant's family including the tenant's spouse shall not be evicted under this section where the tenant has permanently vacated the housing accommodation and such family member has resided with the tenant in the housing accommodation as a primary residence for a period of no less than two years.

The Preamble to the Rent Control Act provides:

> This act is intended to address a serious public emergency created by an acute shortage in dwellings, which resulted in speculative, unwarranted, and abnormal increases in rents. These measures were designed to regulate and control the housing market so as to prevent exactions of unjust, unreasonable and oppressive rents and rental agreements and to forestall profiteering, speculation, and other disruptive practices tending to produce threats to the public health and to prevent uncertainty, hardship, and dislocation. Although initially designed as an emergency measure to alleviate the housing shortage attributable to the end of World War II, a serious public emergency continues to exist in the housing of a considerable number of persons. Consequently, the Legislature has found it necessary to continually reenact the rent-control laws, thereby providing continued protection to tenants.

> To accomplish its goals, the Legislature recognized that not only would rents have to be controlled, but that evictions would have to be regulated and controlled as well. Hence, section 2204.6 of the Rent and Eviction Regulations, which authorizes the issuance of a certificate for the eviction of persons occupying a rent-controlled apartment after the death of the named tenant, provides, in subdivision (a), non-eviction protection to those occupants who are dependent upon the deceased tenant, for example, the surviving spouse or some other member of the deceased's family who has been living with the tenant. The manifest intent of this section is to restrict the landowners' ability to evict a small class of occupants other than the tenant of record who were closely related to the former tenant.

A Committee Report from the legislative history provides:

> Rent stabilization is necessary to protect family members from being uprooted from their homes. Because of the premium landlords can charge, family members must be protected. Thus, the bill provides that when a tenant dies, no eviction notice may issue to any family member or spouse. However, juxtaposed against this intent favoring the protection of tenants and their families, is the over-all objective of a gradual transition from regulation to a normal market of free bargaining between landlord and tenant. One way in which this goal is to be achieved is "vacancy decontrol," which automatically makes rent-control units subject to the less rigorous provisions of rent stabilization upon the termination of the rent-control tenancy.

Mercer Rev. Stat. §788.1: State's Intestacy Law Definitions (A different statute)

> (1) The following words shall have the provided definitions unless the context of the statute provides otherwise. All definitions in this section shall be construed in order to effectuate the over-all goal of orderly succession to real property.

> (a) "Family member" means anyone related to the intestate by blood, consanguinity, or adoption.

Dictionary Definitions from a dictionary published in the same year that the statute was enacted:

> Family: 1. A fundamental social group in society typically consisting of one or two parents and their children; 2. Two or more people who share goals and values, have long-term commitments to one another, and reside usually in the same dwelling place; 3. All the members of a household under one roof; 4. A group of persons sharing common ancestry; 5. Lineage, especially distinguished lineage.

Consanguinity: 1. Relationship by blood or by a common ancestor; 2. A close affinity or connection.

B. An Introduction to the Approaches to Statutory Interpretation

Courts approach their obligation to interpret statutes differently. Academics call these approaches the theories of statutory interpretation. We use the term "approach" because we believe it better explains what judges are doing. But the terms are interchangeable. Fundamentally, the approaches differ in whether, when, and to what extent their adherents will consider sources other than the statutory text when interpreting that text.

The question of which approach to take, we will see, can be outcome determinative in a particular case. "The proper method of interpreting statutes is an enormously important legal issue that has seen enormous theoretical discussion, including some by Supreme Court Justices themselves." Frank B. Cross, *The Significance of Statutory Interpretative Methodologies*, 82 Notre Dame L. Rev. 1971 (2007). These theories matter—greatly.

Broadly speaking, there are three dominant approaches to statutory interpretation: (1) *textualism*, in which the statutory language directs interpretation; (2) *intentionalism*, in which legislative intent guides interpretation; and (3) *purposivism*, in which the statute's purpose elucidates meaning. These approaches are not as distinct as you might at first think. Many judges blend these approaches—for example, relying on the text but giving some weight to intent or purpose. There are few distinct lines. So, perhaps a more accurate way of looking at these approaches is as separate emphases that judges give to the process of interpretation. Thus, regardless of which approach a judge emphasizes or begins with, a typical judge will often examine various sources for evidence to better understand statutory meaning.

Critically, though, textualists, intentionalists, and purposivists all agree that a statute's text is the starting point for interpretation.

> [T]he language of the statute is the most important factor to be considered, for three very fundamental reasons. First, the language of the statute is what the legislature enacted and the governor signed. It is, therefore, the law. Second, the process of interpretation is, in essence, the search for the meaning *of that language* as applied to the facts of the case, including the question of whether it does apply to those facts. Third, all language has limits, in the sense that we are not free to attribute to legislative language a meaning that it simply will not bear in the usage of the English language.

State v. Courchesne, 816 A.2d 562, 579 (Conn. 2003). Thus, all theorists agree that the first step in determining "what the statute means" is to look at the language of the statute. If statutes were always clear, error-free, and never led to absurd or illogical results, any other source might be irrelevant. In other words, if the process were perfect, if the resulting text were always clear, and if the statute always reflected what the legislature had intended, then it would be unnecessary for a court to consider any source other than text in determining statutory meaning.

But language and legislatures are imperfect. And judges, who are imperfect too, are left to deal with those realities. When the language in the statute is unclear or just makes no sense, where should judges turn? And even when the text is clear, should a court look beyond the words to extrinsic sources, such as the legislative history? Can the intent of the legislature matter? If so, can it matter more than the words that the legislature as a whole adopted and codified so that legislative intent overcomes the plain meaning of the statute? What if the sources lead to conflicting, but equally plausible, interpretations? What should direct interpretation: the text alone, legislative intent, legislative purpose, or some combination of these sources with differing weight (how much?) given to each one?

C. Exploring the Three Dominant Approaches to Statutory Interpretation

This section explores each of the three dominate approaches to interpretation, and we will explore them further in subsequent chapters. At this point, it is important for you to recognize that whether a court will give any weight to sources beyond the text, and if so to which ones and to what extent, depends on the approach that the jurisdiction or individual judge takes to statutory interpretation. Most often in the past, the approach was a matter for judicial decision, but in Chapter 16 you will see that some legislatures have tried to direct how courts should approach statutory interpretation.

At the outset, there is no empirical way to show that one of these approaches is "better" than the others, in the sense that one approach more often than the others captures the "true meaning" of a statute. Moreover, the Supreme Court's preferred approach has changed over time, leading to some confusion in the courts below. For example, the importance of legislative history has shifted dramatically in recent years; yet, not long ago, legislative history was routinely consulted by the Justices. At bottom, there is simply no "best" approach to statutory interpretation if "accuracy" is the measure of success. But, as we next show, each approach has its strengths, its weaknesses, its proponents, and its critics.

1. Textualism[*]

The approach that examines the fewest sources is textualism. Textualists look to the text to find "a sort of 'objectified' intent—the intent that a reasonable person would gather from the text of the law, placed alongside the remainder of the *corpus juris*." ANTONIN SCALIA, A MATTER OF INTERPRETATION: FEDERAL COURTS AND THE LAW 17 (1997). Textualists believe that by adopting the "plain meaning" of the text, they most effectively carry out the legislature's objectified intent. They contend that courts should seek to hear the "ring the words [of the statute] would have had to a skilled user of words at the time, thinking about the same problem." Frank H. Easterbrook, *The Role of Original Intent in Statutory Construction*, 11 HARV. J.L. & PUB. POL'Y 59, 61 (1988). Thus, they look at the text at issue, the language of other statutes—but not to legislative history unless, as we

---

* Authors' footnote: Textualism is often labeled as "the plain meaning" approach because it relies almost exclusively on the plain meaning canon of interpretation. For clarity and consistency, we use "textualism" to refer to the approach and "plain meaning" to refer to the canon. But if you see either a legislature or a court referring to its approach as "plain meaning," it likely means "textualism."

will see, they have a very strong reason to doubt the plain meaning of the text. In addition, they do not rely on any unarticulated "purpose" for the statute in discerning the meaning of the text. Textualists justify their reluctance to consider other sources with several reasons, three of which we note here.

First, textualists view themselves as agents, not of the legislature, but of the Constitution. They believe that by holding Congress to its words, they ensure that only language actually enacted will be given the force of law. Further, by focusing so predominantly on text, judges will not legislate, which, textualists believe, is the exclusive province of Congress. In addition, a text-centered approach "accompanied by a reduced reliance on legislative history ... tend[s] to shift the spotlight away from the judge and back to the legislature." John M. Walker, Jr., *Judicial Tendencies in Statutory Construction: Differing Views on the Role of the Judge*, 58 N.Y.U. Ann. Surv. Am. L. 203, 238 (2001). As a result, this refocus may reduce the controversy of interpretations and put the "political heat" back on the legislative branch which, after all, is accountable to the electorate, unlike many judges. *Id.*

Second, and related to the first point, textualists contend that looking beyond the text raises other constitutional concerns. Textualists "would hold Congress to the words it used.... [T]o do otherwise would permit Congress to legislate without completing the required process for enactment of legislation." Carol Chomsky, *Unlocking the Mysteries of Holy Trinity: Spirit, Letter, and History in Statutory Interpretation*, 100 Colum. L. Rev. 901, 951 (2000). Only the text of a statute is approved by both houses and presented to the president for signature; committee reports, for example, are neither approved nor presented. Hence, textualists argue that if Congress were able to dictate meaning through committee reports, floor debates, or other forms of legislative history, legislators would be able to legislate while circumventing the constitutionally required legislative process.

• Third, textualists contend that it is difficult, if not impossible, to discern the intent or purpose of a group, when each member of that group may have had a different reason for supporting the legislation; so, looking for meaning expressed in a form other than the text would be misguided. For that reason, they contend it is wrong to attribute words used by one or more legislators during the legislative process to the entire legislature. Moreover, legislative history is often contradictory. As Judge Harold Leventhal used to say, "[T]he trick is to look over the heads of the crowd and pick out your friends." Scalia, *supra*, at 36.

Textualism takes a variety of forms. Its strictest form has the fewest defenders. In its strictest form, textualism is probably best understood as literalism. Strident literalists believe that it is improper to consider anything beyond the text without first finding that the text is either ambiguous, absurd, or contains a scrivener's error. A true literalist would not take into account, for example, the fact that words have different meanings depending on context. Although at times judges have made statements that sound as if they are literalists, *see Koons Buick Pontiac GMC, Inc. v. Nigh*, 543 U.S. 50, 67 (2004) (Thomas, J., concurring) ("If the text ... [is] clear, resort to anything else [is] unwarranted."); *Union Bank v. Wolas*, 502 U.S. 151, 163 (1991) (Scalia, J., concurring) ("Since there was here no contention of a 'scrivener's error' producing an absurd result, the plain text of the statute should have made this litigation unnecessary and unmaintainable."), in fact there are few modern adherents to this form of textualism.

Instead, and despite their rhetoric, even today's most stridently "textualist" judge is decidedly not a literalist. *See* Miranda McGowan, *Do as I Do, Not as I Say: An Empirical Investigation of Justice Scalia's Ordinary Meaning Method of Statutory Interpretation*, 78

Miss. L. Rev. 129 (2008) (concluding that even in those cases where he believes the text controls, more often than not Justice Scalia decides that the presumption of ordinary meaning has been overcome in the particular case). In contrast to literalists, a moderate or "new" textualist will look more broadly at other sources although always against the primacy of text. As the leading commentator wrote:

> Modern textualists ... are not literalists. In contrast to their early-twentieth-century predecessors in the "plain meaning" school, they do not claim that interpretation can occur "within the four corners" of a statute, or that "the duty of interpretation does not arise" when a text is "plain." Rather, modern textualists acknowledge that language has meaning only in context.... [T]hey believe that statutory language, like all language, conveys meaning only because a linguistic community attaches common understandings to words and phrases, and relies on shared conventions for deciphering those words and phrases in particular contexts. Hence, textualists ask how "a skilled, objectively reasonable user of words" would have understood the statutory text, as applied to the problem before the court.
>
> The "reasonable user" approach gives textualists significant room to account for the nuances of language, a factor that is especially significant in a mature legal system with a rich set of background legal understandings and conventions.... Like any reasonable language user, textualists pay attention to the glosses often put on language (even in ordinary usage), the specialized connotations of established terms of art, and the background conventions that sometimes tell readers how to fill in the gaps inevitably left in statutory directions.

John F. Manning, *Textualism and the Equity of the Statute*, 101 Colum. L. Rev. 1, 108–09 (2001).

Obviously, the foregoing excerpt shows that there are ranges of textualism. The more strictly a judge adheres to textualism, the less frequently that judge will find a reason to go beyond the text, the fewer extratextual sources she will consider, and the less weight she will give to them. As a general principle, though, after looking at the language in context, a textualist may well be finished unless there is reason to consult other sources.

There are criticisms of textualism, and, particularly in its most stringent, literalistic form, textualism has not been universally embraced. Rather, it has been criticized as quite formalistic—if the language was not enacted then it cannot be "law." Yet, "[n]o one claims that legislative history is a statute, or even that, in any strong sense, it is 'law.' Rather, legislative history is helpful in trying to understand the meaning of the words that do make up the statute or the 'law.'" Stephen Breyer, *On the Uses of Legislative History in Interpreting Statutes*, 65 S. Cal. L. Rev. 845, 863 (1992).

Two other criticisms are worth mentioning.

First, many judges believe that courts can most accurately interpret language only by looking at all possible sources of meaning. "Though often applied, [textualism] is often condemned as simplistic because the meaning of words varies with the verbal context and the surrounding circumstances, not to mention the linguistic ability of the users and readers (including judges)." Black's Law Dictionary 1188 (8th ed. 2004). As one commentator wrote, it is "a blunt, frequently crude, and certainly narrowing device, cutting off access to many features of some particular conversational or communicative or interpretive context that would otherwise be available to the interpreter or conversational participant." Frederick Schauer, *Statutory Construction and the Coordinating Function of Plain Meaning*, 1990 Sup. Ct. Rev. 231, 251 (1990).

Second, by limiting the search for meaning to just the text, a judge has more discretion to decide that a statute means what that judge thinks it should mean. In other words, a more narrow approach enables judges to frustrate the intent of the legislature as expressed elsewhere. As proof of the accuracy of this criticism, critics point to the fact that the appellate courts routinely split as to whether a statute is ambiguous. This fact suggests that a judge may find or not find ambiguity, depending on the judge's desired result. Justice Stevens explained that to avoid usurpation, the purpose of the statute must always be considered:

> [T]he "minimalist" judge "who holds that the purpose of the statute may be learned only from its language" has more discretion than the judge "who will seek guidance from every reliable source." A method of statutory interpretation that is deliberately uninformed, and hence unconstrained, may produce a result that is consistent with a court's own view of how things should be, but it may also defeat the very purpose for which a provision was enacted.

Circuit City Stores, Inc. v. Adams, 532 U.S. 105, 133 (2001) (Stevens, J., dissenting). In this regard, some argue that there is no "ordinary" or "plain" meaning and that the act of ascribing plain meaning is itself a subjective act that masks judicial reasoning from public scrutiny. *See* Paul E. McGreal, *Slighting Context: On the Illogic of Ordinary Speech in Statutory Interpretation,* 52 U. KAN. L. REV. 325 (2004).

Thus, despite the appeal of textualism, it has not garnered universal following, although the moderate and more modern form of textualism has increased textualism's popularity. Nonetheless, it is undeniable that the text of the statute has, in recent years, gained dramatically in importance.

2. Intentionalism

Intentionalism is a broader approach than textualism. Intentionalists start with the statutory language but also seek to discern meaning from the author's (authors'?) intent. An intentionalist does not need a reason — like ambiguity or absurdity — to consider sources beyond the text. Intentionalists attempt to discern intent by perusing all available sources, including, principally, legislative history. Not that long ago, courts routinely cited legislative history, going so far as to find "that a crucial committee or a powerful sponsor had authoritatively revealed the specific intent behind general statutory language." John F. Manning, *Legal Realism & The Canons' Revival,* 5 GREEN BAG 2d 283, 287–88 (2002).

There is a profound philosophical difference about the role of language between textualists and intentionalists. Intentionalists believe that in interpreting language it is imperative to be truthful to the intent of the author, and to do so, one must consult extrinsic sources. Proponents of intentionalism argue that it supports the separation of powers expressed in the Constitution. The legislative branch, not the judiciary, has the constitutional power to legislate. In order to avoid "making law," courts should strive to carry out the legislature's intent. Intentionalists view themselves as agents of the legislature that enacted the statute who must avoid imposing their own preferences rather than furthering the choices of the legislature. As stated by Alexander Hamilton:

> It can be of no weight to say, that the courts on the pretense of repugnancy, may substitute their own pleasure to the constitutional intentions of the legislature....
> The courts must declare the sense of the law; and if they should be disposed to

exercise will instead of judgment, the consequence would equally be the substitution of their pleasure to that of the legislative body. The observation, if it proved any thing, would prove that there ought to be no judges distinct from that body.

ALEXANDER HAMILTON, THE FEDERALIST No. 78 (Terence Ball ed., 2003). Examining legislative history helps to achieve the goal of furthering legislative intent.

But there are criticisms. Foremost, many question whether courts are equipped to discern the legislature's "intent." How should a court discern the intent of a group of individuals, all of whom may have had different agendas? Because each individual legislator may have had a unique reason for voting for a bill and even one that conflicted with others who voted for it, the idea that there is one unified legislative intent, particularly one expressed anywhere other than in the enacted words, is arguably a fantasy. *See, e.g.,* Max Radin, *Statutory Interpretation*, 43 HARV. L. REV. 863, 870 (1930) ("The chances that several hundred [individuals] each will have exactly the same determinate situations in mind as possible reductions of a given [statutory issue], are infinitesimally small.") Thus, one criticism is that the intent of a legislative body cannot be ascertained from anything less than the language of the statute approved by that body.

Moreover, critics point out that not every legislator reads every committee report or hears all floor debates, and yet intentionalists use statements made in those legislative documents to discern the entire body's intent. The impact on the legislative process of attributing too much meaning to such statements could be troublesome: If courts attribute meaning to a statement made by one legislator during debate, then other legislators would have to express their disagreement. But they do not regularly do so, and invoking a judicial rule of interpretation that "required" them to do so would create inefficiencies. (Do you see why?) And many committee reports and other documents are drafted by staff members and so, arguably, reflect the intent of the staff members who drafted them, not the legislature. Moreover, because constitutions require legislatures to enact laws, not staff members, reliance on these statements is, arguably, unconstitutional. Even if a report were drafted by a legislator, reliance upon statements in the reports implicates constitutional concerns because constitutions delegate legislative powers to legislatures as a whole, not to committees or individual members. As Justice Scalia, a leading critic of using legislative history, wrote:

> As anyone familiar with modern-day drafting of congressional committee reports is well aware, the [language was] ... inserted, at best by a committee staff member on his or her own initiative, and at worst by a committee staff member at the suggestion of a lawyer-lobbyist; and the purpose of [that language] was not primarily to inform Members of Congress about what the bill meant, ... but rather to influence judicial construction. What a heady feeling it must be for a young staffer, to know that this or her [language became] ... the law of the land....

Blanchard v. Bergeron, 489 U.S. 87, 98–99 (1989).

In addition, critics believe that judges can manipulate legislative history to support their own interpretation. Justice Scalia wrote that in "any major piece of legislation, the legislative history is extensive, and there is something for everyone." ANTONIN SCALIA, A MATTER OF INTERPRETATION: FEDERAL COURTS AND THE LAW, 36 (1997).

Finally, the state and federal constitutions require a specific legislative process: approval by the legislature and presentment to the executive for approval or veto. Legislative history is neither approved by a legislature nor presented to the executive. Thus, intentionalism elicits sharp criticism.

In response to these criticisms, consider, this point made by then-judge Stephen Breyer:

> Conceptually, … one can ascribe an "intent" to Congress in enacting the words of a statute if one means "intent" in its … sense of "purpose" rather than its sense of "motive." One often ascribes "group" purposes to group actions. A law school raises tuition to obtain money for a new library. A basketball team stalls to run out the clock…. Obviously, one of the best ways to find out the purpose of an action taken by a group is to ask some of the group's members about it. But, this does not necessarily mean that the group's purposes and the members' motives or purposes must be identical. The members … may have different, private *motives* for their own actions; but that fact does not necessarily change the proper characterization of the group's purpose.…
>
> In practice, we ascribe purposes to group activities all the time without many practical difficulties.

Breyer, *supra*, at 864–65.

Also in response to these criticisms, many have pointed out that statutes are drafted with the assumption that lawyers will later interpret them strategically to favor the position of a client. "If the legislative process has its own assumptions and word usages, the process itself should be the context within which we seek a statute's meaning." McGreal, *supra*, at 373. Because legislators (and their staff) chose the words on the assumption that they will be manipulated, the words ought to be interpreted in that context, not in some other context, and so legislative history may reveal an intended meaning. *Id.* at 374.

Finally, isn't it disrespectful to assume that legislators included language in a committee report, not because the legislators approved of the language, but because a lobbyist manipulated them? Further, should it be the courts responsibility to police the legislative process? *See* Bernard W. Bell, *Metademocratic Interpretation and Separation of Powers*, 2 N.Y.U. J. LEGIS. & PUB. POL'Y 1, 7–8 (1998). Assuming not, then why should we ignore the committee reports, which are part of this process? Further, even if all of the textualist criticisms of legislative history are justified, should judges ignore *all* legislative history under *all* circumstances?

3. Purposivism

Purposivism, the final dominant approach (there are many others and various permutations of each of these three), is similar to intentionalism. Both approaches advocate searching beyond the text to discern meaning. Purposivism differs, however, in its focus. While intentionalists seek the legislative intent, purposivists focus on the statutory purpose. Thus, they view themselves as agents of the legislature but seek to further statutory purpose, rather than legislative intent.

Purposivism "focuses on the broad goals of a statute, on the problem the legislatures meant to address by passing the statute. Both the text and the legislative history help a court determine those goals." Daniel A. Farber & Brett H. McDonnell, *"Is There a Text in This Class?" The Conflict Between Textualism and Antitrust*, 14 J. CONTEMP. LEGAL ISSUES 619, 666 (2005). To illustrate:

> [C]onsider the hypothetical city ordinance that prohibits operation of a "vehicle" in a public park. In deciding whether a bicycle falls within the meaning of the statute, one might ask why the city adopted the ordinance. If the city did so

to protect the park from air and noise pollution, banning bicycles would not further that purpose. If, however, the city did so to protect pedestrian safety, banning bicycles might make sense. To the extent that legislative history explains the evil at which a statute is aimed, it can aid in this analysis.

McGreal, *supra,* at 375. "If a statute is to make sense, it must be read in the light of some assumed purpose. A statute merely declaring a rule, with no purpose or objective, is nonsense." Karl N. Llewellyn, *Remarks on the Theory of Appellate Decision and the Rules or Canons About How Statutes Are To Be Construed,* 3 VAND. L. REV. 395, 400 (1949). (*See* Appendix A.)

Like intentionalists, but unlike textualists, purposivists do not need a reason — like ambiguity, absurdity, or scrivener's error — to look to extratextual sources to discern meaning. Instead, and like intentionalists, they believe that the interpretive function cannot be completed without considering other sources.

Purposivism has its advocates and its critics. One argument in support of purposivism is that it, even more than intentionalism, allows courts to seek meaning from the broadest number of sources to make a more informed decision. It urges the court to consider *all* of the relevant evidence bearing on the meaning of the language at issue because the underlying premise is that the more such evidence the court considers, the more likely it is that the court will arrive at a proper conclusion regarding that meaning. *State v. Courchesne,* 816 A.2d 562, 575 (Conn. 2003). Moreover, unlike intentionalism, purposivism allows its adherents to interpret statutes in situations never contemplated by the enacting legislature. For example, if we return to our hypothetical city ordinance prohibiting "vehicles" in the park, purposivists could determine whether the ordinance applied to Segways™ (motorized scooters) even though these scooters did not exist when the ordinance had been adopted. In contrast, intentionalists might say that the ordinance could not apply because the city council could not have intended to regulate something not then in existence. Thus, purposivism offers flexibility that intentionalism might not.

Judge Learned Hand was a purposivist; one who acknowledged that searching for purpose was "a hazardous process," but who believed that judges could not "escape it, once we abandon literal interpretation," which he characterized as "a method far more unreliable." *Borella v. Borden Co.,* 145 F.2d 63, 64–65 (2d Cir. 1944), *aff'd,* 325 U.S. 679 (1945). Judge Hand recognized the risk of purposivism:

> On the one hand [a judge] must not enforce whatever he thinks is best; he must leave that to the common will expressed by the government. On the other, he must try as best he can to put into concrete form what that will is, not by slavishly following the words, but by trying honestly to say what was the underlying purpose expressed.

Learned Hand, *How Far is a Judge Free in Rendering a Decision?,* reprinted in John M. Walker, Jr., *Judicial Tendencies in Statutory Construction: Differing Views on the Role of the Judge,* 58 N.Y.U. ANN. SURV. AM. L. 203, 215 (2001). Additionally, purposivists believe that by openly stating their approach, they will reduce "judicial legislation," and they believe that judges should "do [their] best to enforce the policy of a statute even when [they] detest[] its aim." *Id.* at 216. Purposivism, probably more than the other approaches, allows judges to do justice in a particular case because it is more directly focused on the circumstances in the particular case than, for example, textualism.

But, like the other theories, purposivism has its critics. Just as some question whether legislative intent can be gleaned from anything less than the language adopted by the legislature, some question the competency of the courts to ascertain the purpose of a statute:

"legislation is the product of bargaining between various interest groups rather than an underlying common will or purpose among legislators. Thus … statutes will rarely have a single purpose that can guide interpretation." *Courchesne*, 816 A.2d at 610 (Zarella, J. dissenting). Others are concerned that "consultation of extrinsic, non-textual sources of interpretation in every case, regardless of whether the language of the statute is clear … subordinates the statutory text and renders the analysis more vulnerable to subjectivity." *State ex rel. Kalal v. Circuit Court of Dane County*, 681 N.W.2d 110, 125 n.8 (Wis. 2004). In addition, some suggest that purposivism, like textualism and intentionalism, encourages "activist" or "unintended" interpretation. *Courchesne*, 816 A.2d at 609 (Zarella, J., dissenting) ("[P]urpose … is normally of such generality as to be useless as an interpretative tool, unless … it is being used as a cover for the judge to 'do justice' as he sees fit.")

Finally, some view purposivism as a vestige of a time when statutes were broader and more general and so were more in need of and more amenable to such interpretations. *See* Walker, *supra*, at 237. Purposivism, they say, may be a relic of early common law reasoning improperly brought from that realm into the modern realm.

Notes and Questions

(1) *What Do Your Instincts Say?* You've no doubt read a lot about "judges who legislate." What is your view on the proper approach? Should courts ever look beyond the text? If so, why? When? Write down your answer in the margin of this text. See whether your view changes as you progress through the course.

(2) *Plain Meaning?* Humpty Dumpty famously said that words mean whatever he says they should mean. In his view, the power to interpret words is greater than the power to form them. Is he accurate? If so, what, if anything, should rein that power in?

(3) *Justifying the Result?* Some say that judges simply justify the result they want by using one of these approaches or by saying a statute is ambiguous so that they can cherry-pick statements from extrinsic sources that favor the interpretation they want the statute to have. Thus, for example, some say a judge is more likely to find a statute ambiguous if he disagrees with its plain meaning so that he can pick out statements from the legislative history that support his view while ignoring the others. Do you think such a process happens? How can it be prevented? Will requiring judges to find ambiguity, absurdity, or scrivener's error before they can rely on legislative history do the trick? Will requiring judges to rely on the "plain meaning" of the text do so? Is justifying the result more a matter of judicial integrity and intellectual honesty?

D. Judicial Disagreement over the Competing Approaches

The case law reflects disagreement between and even within courts on virtually all the questions about the appropriate approach to statutory interpretation. Cases can be found with judges arguing that legislative intent must be considered along with the text; other cases state that the textual canons must be considered along with the text; and others state that those positions are wrong. *See, e.g., Chisom v. Roemer*, 501 U.S. 380, 404 (1991) (Scalia, J., dissenting) ("I thought we had adopted a regular method for interpreting the meaning of a statute: first, find the ordinary meaning of the language in its textual context; and second, using established canons of construction, ask whether there is any clear indication that some permissible meaning other than the ordinary one applies."); *Wilt v. Brunswick Plaza L.L.C.*, 703 N.Y.S.2d 700, 702 (N.Y. 2000) ("If the words ... have a definite meaning, which involves no absurdity or contradiction, then there is no room for construction and courts have no right to add to or take away from that meaning."); *Cohen v. Comm'r of the Div. of Med. Assistance*, 668 N.E.2d 769, 774 (Mass. 1996) ("Only if the legislative history compelled a different conclusion might we depart from the plain meaning of the statute."); *Tello v. McMahon*, 677 F. Supp. 1436, 1441 (E.D. Cal. 1988) ("analysis begins with application of the plain meaning rule and is followed by examination of the legislative history. If any ambiguity remains after application of these two primary means of statutory construction, the court may apply other textual means of construction...."). These debates are important and can be critical in certain courts on certain issues.

There is a dose of practicality we'll mention here. Most judges want to be right on the substance, rather than rigid in their approach to statutory interpretation. Doing justice— both to the parties in a particular case and more broadly—is going to be more important to many judges than is adhering to rigid doctrine. *See also* Walker, *supra*, at 232. In this regard, an Alaska court wrote what could be an honest assessment of what many judges may, despite their rhetoric, be doing and which probably is good guidance for approaching statutory interpretation in many jurisdictions, if not all:

> Alaska does not adhere to a "plain meaning rule" of statutory interpretation that disregards any consideration of legislative purpose or intent. Instead, we consider a statute's meaning by applying a "sliding scale" such that, the plainer the statutory language, the more convincing the evidence of a contrary legislative purpose or intent must be.

LeFever v. State, 877 P.2d 1298, 1299–1300 (Alaska Ct. App. 1994) (holding evidence of legislative intent outweighed the defendant's plain meaning construction). Alaska's sliding scale approach allows judges to consider extratextual sources regardless of whether the text is clear:

> We have rejected that formulation of the plain meaning rule which mandates that we must disregard all legislative history if the statute's wording is clear and unambiguous on its face. To do so would overly restrict our inquiry, since reference to legislative history may provide an insight which is helpful to making a judgment concerning what a statute means, and since words are necessarily inexact and ambiguity is a relative concept. Even if the statute under consideration here were facially unambiguous, then, the plain meaning rule would not foreclose the possibility that consideration of legislative history would reveal an ambiguity not apparent on the face of the statute.

Mun. of Anchorage v. Sisters of Providence in Wash., Inc., 628 P.2d 22, 27 n.6 (Alaska 1981). Notice, though, that this approach is closer to textualism than it may appear at first blush. The plainer the text, the more convincing the contrary indications of meaning must be.

The New Mexico Supreme Court also recognized the common sense notion that other sources may have weight even when language seems clear on its face:

> [Plain meaning's] beguiling simplicity may mask a host of reasons why a statute, apparently clear and unambiguous on its face, may for one reason or another give rise to legitimate (*i.e.*, nonfrivolous) difference of opinion concerning the statute's meaning.... [T]his rule is deceptive in that it implies that words have

intrinsic meanings. A word is merely a symbol which can be used to refer to different things. Difficult questions of statutory interpretation ought not to be decided by the bland invocation of abstract jurisprudential maxims.... The assertion in a judicial opinion that a statute needs no interpretation because it is "clear and unambiguous" is in reality evidence that the court has already considered and construed the act.

State ex rel. Helman v. Gallegos, 871 P.2d 1352, 1359 (N.M. 1994); *see also Helvering v. Gregory,* 69 F.2d 809, 810 (2d Cir. 1934) ("as the articulation of a statute increases, the room for interpretation must contract"), *aff'd,* 293 U.S. 465 (1935).

Thus, even where a decision-maker appears to follow textualism, a lawyer should consult the legislative history and other sources for persuasive arguments. They may be more compelling than you might think:

> In deciding a question of statutory interpretation in the real, as opposed to the theoretical, world, few judges approach the interpretive task armed with a fixed set of rigid rules. In briefs, the parties make all of the arguments they can think of, whether based on the relevant case law, the "plain text," the legislative history, or the statute's underlying purpose or purposes in effectuating a policy or remediating mischief. I have difficulty imagining that any judge, presented with such arguments, would, for example, simply evaluate the so-called plain meaning of the statute and then stop reading the brief. Even a judge's strongest theoretical inclinations are tempered by the judge's desire to accord a fair hearing to the parties' arguments and to be open to all credible materials that might enhance the judge's understanding of the case.

Walker, *supra,* at 232–33. (The author was, at the time of the article, the Chief Judge of the Second Circuit.)

The importance of text has no doubt grown in recent years. The quote above suggests that the movement in both the courts and the legislatures is toward a more encompassing approach, but plain meaning remains the focal point. *See Train v. Colo. Pub. Interest Research Group, Inc.,* 426 U.S. 1, 10 (1976) ("[W]hen aid to construction of the meaning of words, as used in the statute, is available, there certainly can be no 'rule of law' which forbids its use, however clear the words may appear on 'superficial examination.'") (quoting *United States v. Am. Trucking Ass'ns,* 310 U.S. 534, 543–44 (1940)). Even Justice Scalia finds rigid adherence to strict textualism unworkable: "I play the game like everybody else.... I'm in a system which has accepted rules and legislative history is used.... You read my opinions, I sin with the rest of them." Frank H. Easterbrook, *What Does Legislative History Tell Us?,* 66 Chi.-Kent L. Rev. 441, 442 n.4 (1990) (quoting *Judges and Legislators: Toward Institutional Comity,* 174–75 (R. Katzmann ed. 1988) (Justice Scalia's comments during a panel discussion)).

As we explore these issues further, not just in this chapter but also in the rest of this book, bear in mind that—apart from when the statute is ambiguous, absurd, or contains a scrivener's error (all explored elsewhere)—whether courts should consider extratextual sources, which ones, and what weight they should be given, are fundamental issues about which the law is keenly undeveloped. Therein lies the opportunity and challenge for you.

Now that you understand the various approaches, see if you can identify the position of the majority and dissent in the case below. Read closely because the majority is not as clear as you might think at first. Note too the arguments raised to support their adopted approach. Which, if any, do you find convincing?

State v. Courchesne

816 A.2d 562 (Conn. 2003)

BORDEN, J.

Under our statutory scheme, a defendant becomes eligible for the death penalty if he is convicted of a capital felony for the "murder of two or more persons at the same time or in the course of a single transaction...." General Statutes (Rev. to 1997) § 53a-54b (8). One of the aggravating factors that permits the imposition of the death penalty is that "the defendant committed the offense in an especially heinous, cruel or depraved manner...." General Statutes (Rev. to 1997) § 53a-46a(i)(4).... The present case ... requires us to decide [whether it was necessary for the state, in order to seek the death penalty based on that factor, to prove the defendant had killed "both ... of the victims in an especially cruel manner"]....

We conclude that proof that the defendant committed at least one of the murders in the specified aggravated manner is sufficient. Accordingly, we reverse....

[T]he following facts may be considered as undisputed.... [T]he defendant stabbed Demetris Rodgers to death [over a $410 drug debt]. At the time she was stabbed, she was pregnant with Antonia Rodgers. Although Demetris Rodgers was dead on arrival at the hospital, the physicians at the hospital ... delivered Antonia Rodgers, who lived for forty-two days before dying from ... deprivation of oxygen to the brain....

This claim presents a question of statutory interpretation. The process of statutory interpretation involves a reasoned search for the intention of the legislature. In other words, we seek to determine, in a reasoned manner, the meaning of the statutory language as applied to the facts of this case, including the question of whether the language actually does apply. In seeking to determine that meaning, we look to the words of the statute itself, to the legislative history and circumstances surrounding its enactment, to the legislative policy it was designed to implement, and to its relationship to existing legislation and common law principles governing the same general subject matter....

The defendant contends ... that the plain language of §§ 53a-46a (i)(4) and 53a-54b (8) compels the conclusion that both murders must be committed in the manner proscribed by the aggravating factor in order for the factor to be established. The defendant points to the language of § 53a-46a (i)(4): "[T]he defendant committed *the offense* in an especially heinous, cruel or depraved manner...." (Emphasis added.) He then points to the language of § 53a-54b (8) defining the relevant capital felony as the "*murder of two or more persons* at the same time or in the course of a single transaction...." (Emphasis added.) Thus, the defendant argues, "the essential gravamen of the offense set forth at § 53a-54b (8) that must be 'especially heinous' is the 'murder of two or more persons,' not the murder of one person."

We acknowledge that, if we were to apply the applicable language literally, as a purely linguistic matter the defendant's contention probably carries more weight than that of the state. It would be linguistically appealing to adopt the syllogism embodied in the defendant's contention, namely, that: (1) § 53a-46a (i)(4) requires that "the offense" be committed in the aggravated manner; (2) the likely referent of "the offense" is the capital felony of which the defendant has been convicted; (3) that capital felony at issue in the present case is the "murder of two or more persons," as defined in § 53a-54b (8); and (4) therefore, the murder of *two* persons must be committed in the aggravated manner. Thus, under the defendant's position, there is a direct linguistic line between the language, "the offense," contained in § 53a-46a (i)(4), and the definition of the capital felony as the "murder of two ... persons," contained in § 53a-54b (8)....

The conclusion that would flow from the linguistic analysis suggested by the defendant, however, cannot withstand further scrutiny. Although the language of the statute, viewed literally and in isolation, suggests a conclusion consistent with the interpretation offered by the defendant, when viewed in its context and history leads us to conclude, to the contrary, that when § 53a-46a (i)(4) refers to "the offense," as applied in the circumstances of the present case, it means the murder of either of the "two" persons referred to in § 53a-54b (8), and does not mean both murders.... [Although the majority acknowledges that the text favors the defendant's interpretation, the majority nevertheless concludes that the statute's "context and history" support the state's interpretation. The majority concludes that the "context and history" show the meaning of the statute, *i.e.*, that the existence of the aggravating factor need not be established by showing that both murders were committed in an especially heinous manner.]

We now make explicit that our approach to the process of statutory interpretation ... namely, engaging in a "reasoned search for the intention of the legislature," which we further defined as a reasoned search for "the meaning of the statutory language as applied to the facts of [the] case, including the question of whether the language actually does apply."[21] The rest of the formulation sets forth the range of sources that we will examine in order to determine that meaning. That formulation admonishes the court to consider all relevant sources of meaning of the language at issue—namely, the words of the statute, its legislative history and the circumstances surrounding its enactment, the legislative policy it was designed to implement, and its relationship to existing legislation and to common-law principles governing the same general subject matter. We also now make explicit that we ordinarily will consider all of those sources beyond the language itself,[22] without first having to cross any threshold of ambiguity of the language.

We emphasize, moreover, that the language of the statute is the most important factor to be considered, for three very fundamental reasons. First, the language of the statute is what the legislature enacted and the governor signed. It is, therefore, the law. Second, the process of interpretation is, in essence, the search for the meaning *of that language* as applied to the facts of the case, including the question of whether it does apply to those facts. Third, all language has limits, in the sense that we are not free to attribute to legislative language a meaning that it simply will not bear in the usage of the English language.

Therefore—and we make this explicit as well—we always *begin* the process of interpretation with a searching examination of that language, attempting to determine the range of plausible meanings that it may have in the context in which it appears and, if possible, narrowing that range down to those that appear most plausible. Thus, the statutory

21. We need not enter a semiotic debate with the dissent about whether a group such as a legislature can have an "intent," as opposed to a "purpose," in enacting legislation. Both this court and courts throughout the nation have long employed the language of "legislative intent," both within and outside the confines of the plain meaning rule, without any apparent confusion about what it means. Furthermore, our own legislature has no difficulty with the notion that it can have and express an "intent." *See, e.g.*, General Statutes § 47-210(a) ("[i]t is the *intent* of the General Assembly that this section is remedial and does not create any new cause of action to invalidate any residential common interest community lease, but shall operate as a statutory prescription on procedural matters in actions brought on one or more causes of action existing at the time of the execution of such lease" [emphasis added]).

22. We say "ordinarily" because, of course, in any given case not all of the extratextual sources will be relevant or available. For example, in any given case there may not be any legislative history available, or what is available may not shed any light on the question of interpretation. The same may be said of the other sources noted. In sum, we will examine those extratextual sources to the extent that they are ascertainable.

language is always the starting point of the interpretive inquiry. [But] ... we do not end the process with the language.

The reason for this ... is that the legislative process is purposive, and ... the meaning of legislative language (indeed, of any particular use of our language) is best understood by viewing not only the language at issue, but by its context and by the purpose or purposes behind its use....

Thus, the purpose or purposes of the legislation, and the context of that legislative language ... are directly relevant to its meaning as applied to the facts ... before us....

Indeed, in our view, the concept of the context of statutory language should be broadly understood. That is, the context of statutory language necessarily includes the other language used in the statute or statutory scheme at issue, the language used in other relevant statutes, the general subject matter of the legislation at issue, the history or genealogy of the statute, as well as the other, extratextual sources.... All of these sources, textual as well as contextual, are to be considered, along with the purpose or purposes of the legislation, in determining the meaning of the language of the statute as applied to the facts of the case....

[This approach] requires the court, in *all* cases, to consider *all* of the relevant evidence bearing on the meaning of the language at issue. Thus, [our] underlying premise is that, the more such evidence the court considers, the more likely it is that the court will arrive at a proper conclusion regarding that meaning....

In summary, we now restate the process by which we interpret statutes as follows: The process of statutory interpretation involves a reasoned search for the intention of the legislature. In other words, we seek to determine, in a reasoned manner, the meaning of the statutory language as applied to the facts of [the] case, including the question of whether the language actually does apply. In seeking to determine that meaning, we look to the words of the statute itself, to the legislative history and circumstances surrounding its enactment, to the legislative policy it was designed to implement, and to its relationship to existing legislation and common law principles governing the same general subject matter. Thus, this process requires us to consider all relevant sources of the meaning of the language at issue, without having to cross any threshold or thresholds of ambiguity. Thus, we do not follow the plain meaning rule.

In performing this task, we begin with a searching examination of the language of the statute, because that is the most important factor to be considered. In doing so, we attempt to determine its range of plausible meanings and, if possible, narrow that range to those that appear most plausible. We do not, however, end with the language. We recognize, further, that the purpose or purposes of the legislation, and the context of the language, broadly understood, are directly relevant to the meaning of the language of the statute.

This does not mean, however, that we will not, in a given case, follow what may be regarded as the plain meaning of the language, namely, the meaning that, when the language is considered without reference to any extratextual sources of its meaning, appears to be *the* meaning and that appears to preclude any other likely meaning. In such a case, the more strongly the bare text supports such a meaning, the more persuasive the extratextual sources of meaning will have to be in order to yield a different meaning....

[R]eversed....

ZARELLA, J., with whom SULLIVAN, C.J., joins, dissenting.

The majority's opinion is nothing short of breathtaking. The majority expressly abandons the plain meaning rule and fails to apply the rule of lenity in a death penalty case.

in which the majority states that the text of the statutory provision at issue favors the defendant's interpretation. Moreover, application of the sources of interpretation that the majority employs in reaching its conclusion lead to a flawed assessment of the rationality of the legislature's choices in drafting this state's death penalty statute. I believe, for reasons distinct from those offered by the majority, that the text of the statute at issue suggests that the defendant's interpretation of the statute should be rejected.... Finally, in my view, the majority's abandonment of the plain meaning rule in favor of an alternative and novel method of statutory interpretation represents an incorrect deviation from our traditional mode of statutory interpretation and an impermissible usurpation of the legislative function. Accordingly, I dissent....

In contrast to the majority's determination that the defendant has a strong textual argument, I believe that the text of §53a-46a (i)(4) does not require the state to prove the existence of the aggravating factor as to each individual constituent part, in the present case, each individual murder. I also would conclude, however, that, after interpreting the statute, a reasonable doubt persists about whether the legislature expressly intended that the death penalty be imposed under the circumstances of the present case. Therefore, I would uphold the trial court's application of the rule of lenity and require that the state prove beyond a reasonable doubt that both murders were committed in a cruel manner in order to satisfy its burden of establishing the existence of the aggravating factor enumerated in §53a-46a (i)(4)....

The majority's method of statutory interpretation is radical, its central premise is misguided, and its application is likely to lead to an unpredictable and unconstrained statutory interpretation jurisprudence....

As the majority acknowledges, its approach to statutory interpretation "has not been adopted in the same specific formulation by *any* other court in the nation." ... I think for good reason.

My most fundamental disagreement with the majority's approach to statutory interpretation is its heavy reliance upon unexpressed statutory purposes. Such reliance is particularly inappropriate when a statute's text is plain and unambiguous. Indeed, even proponents of the purposive approach to statutory interpretation that the majority embraces acknowledge that nontextual sources should be resorted to only when a statute is *unclear*. *See, e.g.,* S. Breyer, "On the Uses of Legislative History in Interpreting Statutes," 65 S. Cal. L. Rev. 845, 848 (1992) (legislative history is useful in interpreting *unclear* statutes). Thus, the majority's contention that a statute's unremunerated purpose can trump statutory language that is plain and unambiguous is truly beyond the pale. I am particularly troubled by such an approach because I agree with ... the chief judge of the ... Second Circuit, who recently assessed the lack of usefulness of the purposive method of statutory interpretation: "[A legislative] purpose, whether derived from legislative history, the entirety of the statute, the mischief at which the statute is aimed, or the judge's imagination, is normally of such generality as to be useless as an interpretative tool, unless, of course, it is being used as a cover for the judge to 'do justice' as he sees fit." ...

Moreover, ... even if it were theoretically possible to uncover a statute's purpose with sufficient specificity to guide the interpretative process of the particular issue before the court, public choice theory presents a "substantial" critique of such a method. Such a theory teaches that legislation is the product of bargaining between various interest groups rather than an underlying common will or purpose among legislators. Thus, the theory suggests, as an empirical matter, that statutes will rarely have a single purpose that can guide interpretation....

For the foregoing reasons, I respectfully dissent.

Notes and Questions

(1) *Deference to Legislative Power.* One consideration in evaluating the various approaches is to consider their impact on judicial power. The decision by a court as to which approach to choose is viewed by many as indicating that court's view on the extent to which it should defer to the legislature. In that regard, some believe that textualism is the most deferential to the legislative branch. But, Judge Learned Hand believed that a textualist approach gave judges too much power. Articulate reasons to support the view that textualists are the least deferential, that intentionalists are, and that purposivists are.

(2) *Intellectual Dishonesty.* As with intentionalism, an argument against purposivism is that it lets judges rely on their own ideas about goals and policies to "legislate from the bench." Consider this argument from *Courchesne*:

> The dissent also suggests that judges, by employing a purposive approach to statutory interpretation rather than the plain meaning rule, will substitute our own notions of wise and intelligent policy for the policy of the legislature. We agree that this may happen; any court *may* be intellectually dishonest in performing *any* judicial task, whether it be interpreting a statute or adjudicating a dispute involving only the common law. We suggest, however, that the risk of intellectual dishonesty is just as great, or as minimal, in employing the plain meaning rule as in employing the method of interpretation that we articulate. If a court is determined to be intellectually dishonest and reach the result that it *wants* the statute to mandate, rather than the result that an honest and objective appraisal of its meaning would yield, it will find a way to do so under any articulated rubric of statutory interpretation. Furthermore, by insisting that *all* evidence of meaning be considered and explained before the court arrives at the meaning of a statute, we think that the risk of intellectual dishonesty in performing that task will be minimized. Indeed, resort to and explanation of extratextual sources may provide a certain transparency to the court's analytical and interpretive process that could be lacking under the employment of the plain meaning rule. In sum, we have confidence in the ability of this court to ascertain, explain and apply the purpose or purposes of a statute in an intellectually honest manner.

816 A.2d at 587–88. Doesn't this criticism presume judges are intellectually dishonest and will not abide by their constitutional duties? Isn't this criticism demeaning to the judiciary?

(3) *Better Drafting?* One argument in favor of strict textualism is that it encourages legislators to write clearer statutes. Can you explain why this is true? But if, as many posit, language will inevitably have ambiguity when applied to particular fact patterns, does strict textualism actually guide legislators on how to draft for the difficult or unanticipated cases? If you believe that the textualist approach encourages better drafting, what do you say in response to these arguments:

> [W]e also reject the dissent's suggestion that, by employing the plain meaning rule, we will give the legislature an incentive to write clear statutes and, presumably, therefore, also give it a disincentive to write poorly drafted statutes. We do not regard it as appropriate for the judiciary, by creating incentives or disincentives, to instruct the legislature on how to write statutes, any more than it would be appropriate for the legislature, directly or indirectly, to instruct the judiciary on how to write opinions. We presume that the legislature, within the constraints of time and other resources, does the best it can in attempting to capture in legislative language what it is attempting to accomplish by its legisla-

tion. No legislature, or legislative drafter, has the ability to foresee all of the questions that may arise under the language that it employs. Our task is to do the best we can in interpreting its language, within the context of specific factual situations presented by specific cases and within the limits of that language, so as to make sense of the statute before us and so as to carry out the legislature's purpose or purposes in enacting that statute.

Courchesne, 816 A.2d at 588 n.32.

(4) *Distinguishing Between Intent and Purpose.* In footnote 21, the majority in *Courchesne* discussed the ability of a legislature to express its intent. Did it ignore the distinction between "intent" and "purpose," or is there in fact no real distinction?

(5) *Legislative Reaction.* As a direct response to *Courchesne*, the legislature acted quickly by enacting this statute:

> The meaning of a statute shall, in the first instance, be ascertained from the text of the statute itself and its relationship to other statutes. If, after examining such text and considering such relationship, the meaning of such text is plain and unambiguous and does not yield absurd or unworkable results, extratextual evidence of the meaning of the statute shall not be considered.

CONN. GEN. STAT. ANN. § 1-2z (West 2005). Do you see how this statute changed the approach articulated by the majority? In a subsequent case, the majority explained:

> In *State v. Courchesne*, this court explained that, as part of the judicial task of statutory interpretation, we would not follow the so-called "plain meaning rule," which operates to preclude the court, in certain cases, from considering sources in addition to the statutory text in order to determine its meaning. We are cognizant that, subsequent to our decision in *Courchesne*, [the legislature] has legislatively overruled that part of *Courchesne* in which we stated that we would not require a threshold showing of linguistic ambiguity as a precondition to consideration of sources of the meaning of legislative language in addition to its text.... This case does not present an appropriate occasion to consider [§ 1-2z because] the applicable statutory text is plain and unambiguous....

Paul Dinto Elec. Contractors, Inc. v. City of Waterbury, 835 A.2d 33, 39–40 n.10 (Conn. 2003). By statute then, the legislature specifically prohibited courts from considering any extratextual sources absent textual ambiguity or absurdity. Why might a legislature prefer a narrower judicial approach to statutory interpretation, while courts prefer a broader one? Does the Connecticut statute implicate separation of powers? *See* Linda D. Jellum, *"Which is to Be Master," the Judiciary or the Legislature? When Statutory Directives Violate Separation of Powers*, 56 U.C.L.A. L. REV. 837 (2009) (arguing that when a legislature directs the approach a court is to take for statutory interpretation, the legislature violates separation of powers). We explore this issue in more detail in Chapter 16.

(6) The final irony from the *Courchesne* case is this:

> It is ironic that the legislative debate surrounding [§ 1-2z] specifically indicated that its purpose was to overrule that part of *Courchesne*. If we were to read [§ 1-2z] literally, and assume that it is not ambiguous in any way, we would be barred by it from consulting that very legislative history in order to determine that its purpose was to overrule *Courchesne*.

Carmel Hollow Assoc. Ltd. P'ship v. Town of Bethlehem, 848 A.2d 451, 470 n.1 (Conn. 2004) (Borden J., concurring). Judge Borden authored *Courchesne*.

State *ex rel.* Kalal v. Circuit Court of Dane County
681 N.W.2d 110 (Wis. 2004)

DIANE S. SYKES, J.

In Wisconsin, the district attorney is primarily responsible for the decision whether to charge a person with a crime....

There are exceptions to this rule, however, and this case arises from one of them. Subsection (3) of Wis. Stat. §968.02 provides that "[i]f a district attorney *refuses or is unavailable* to issue a complaint, a circuit judge may permit the filing of a complaint, if the judge finds there is probable cause to believe that the person to be charged has committed an offense." Wis. Stat. §968.02(3)(2001–02) (emphasis added.)

This case involves an effort by a Madison attorney to invoke this procedure against her former employer and his wife for allegedly stealing funds earmarked for her retirement account. The attorney, Michele Tjader, first complained to the Madison Police Department and the Dane County District Attorney about the alleged theft by Ralph and Jackie Kalal. Several months later, after receiving word from the district attorney that she "was free to proceed legally in whatever manner she believed necessary," Tjader filed a motion pursuant to Wis. Stat. §968.02(3) for the issuance of a criminal complaint against the Kalals. A circuit judge authorized the filing of the proposed complaint.

The Kalals moved for reconsideration, arguing that ... the district attorney had [not] "refused" to issue a complaint as required by Wis. Stat. §968.02(3). The circuit judge ... denied [the motion]....

By its terms, Wis. Stat. §968.02(3) requires the circuit judge to make two determinations prior to authorizing the issuance of a complaint: 1) that "the district attorney *refuses* or *is unavailable* to issue a complaint;" and 2) that "there is probable cause to believe that the person to be charged has committed an offense." ...

Probable cause is not at issue here, nor is there a challenge to the judge's exercise of discretion to permit the filing of the complaint. We are confronted only with a question about the meaning of the term "refuses" in the statute....

Wisconsin's statutory interpretation case law has evolved in something of a combination fashion, generating some analytical confusion. The typical statutory interpretation case will declare that the purpose of statutory interpretation is to discern and give effect to the intent of the legislature, but will proceed to recite principles of interpretation that are more readily associated with a determination of statutory meaning rather than legislative intent—most notably, the plain-meaning rule. Although ascertainment of legislative intent is the frequently-stated goal of statutory interpretation, our cases generally adhere to a methodology that relies primarily on intrinsic sources of statutory meaning and confines resort to extratextual sources of legislative intent to cases in which the statutory language is ambiguous.

Accordingly, we now conclude that the general framework for statutory interpretation in Wisconsin requires some clarification. It is, of course, a solemn obligation of the judiciary to faithfully give effect to the laws enacted by the legislature, and to do so requires a determination of statutory meaning. Judicial deference to the policy choices enacted

↱focus on language

into law by the legislature requires that statutory interpretation focus primarily on the language of the statute. We assume that the legislature's intent is expressed in the statutory language. Extrinsic evidence of legislative intent may become relevant to statutory interpretation in some circumstances, but is not the primary focus of inquiry. It is the enacted law, not unenacted intent, that is binding on the public. Therefore, the purpose of statutory interpretation is to determine what the statute means so that it may be given its full, proper, and intended effect.

Thus, we have repeatedly held that statutory interpretation begins with the language of the statute. If the meaning of the statute is plain, we ordinarily stop the inquiry. Statutory language is given its common, plain, and accepted meaning, except that technical or specially-defined words or phrases are given their technical or special definitional meaning....

If this process of analysis yields a plain, clear statutory meaning, then there is no ambiguity, and the statute is applied according to this ascertainment of its meaning. Where statutory language is unambiguous, there is no need to consult extrinsic sources of interpretation, such as legislative history. In construing or interpreting a statute the court is not at liberty to disregard the plain, clear words of the statute.

ambiguity

The test for ambiguity generally keeps the focus on the statutory language: a statute is ambiguous if it is capable of being understood by reasonably well-informed persons in two or more senses. It is not enough that there is a disagreement about the statutory meaning; the test for ambiguity examines the language of the statute to determine whether well-informed persons should have become confused, that is, whether the statutory ... language reasonably gives rise to different meanings.... *Test for ambiguity*

At this point in the interpretive analysis the cases will often recite the following: If a statute is ambiguous, the reviewing court turns to the scope, history, context, and purpose of the statute.... [T]his common formulation is somewhat misleading: scope, context, and purpose are perfectly relevant to a plain-meaning interpretation of an unambiguous statute as long as the scope, context, and purpose are ascertainable from the text and structure of the statute itself, rather than extratextual sources, such as legislative history.

Some statutes contain explicit statements of legislative purpose or scope.... Accordingly, it cannot be correct to suggest, for example, that an examination of a statute's purpose or scope or context is completely off-limits unless there is ambiguity. It is certainly not inconsistent with the plain-meaning rule to consider the intrinsic context in which statutory language is used; a plain-meaning interpretation cannot contravene a textually or contextually manifest statutory purpose.[8] ...

---

8. In her concurrence the chief justice represents that "[t]his opinion correctly concludes that a court resorts to the scope, context, and purpose of the statute without having to declare an ambiguity in the statute." This somewhat overstates our holding. We have noted that a statute's scope, context, and purpose are often apparent from the statutory text itself. A plain meaning, text-based approach to statutory interpretation certainly does not prohibit the interpretation of a statute in light of its textually manifest scope, context, or purpose. We do not by this conclusion endorse the methodology advanced by the chief justice in her concurrence that calls for consultation of extrinsic, non-textual sources of interpretation in every case, regardless of whether the language of the statute is clear. Such an approach subordinates the statutory text and renders the analysis more vulnerable to subjectivity....

Wisconsin courts ordinarily do not consult extratextual sources of statutory interpretation unless the language of the statute is ambiguous. By "extrinsic sources" we mean interpretive resources outside the statutory text—typically items of legislative history.

We have repeatedly emphasized that traditionally, resort to legislative history is not appropriate in the absence of a finding of ambiguity. This rule generally prevents courts from tapping legislative history to show that an unambiguous statute is ambiguous. That is, the rule prevents the use of extratextual sources of interpretation to vary or contradict the plain meaning of a statute, ascertained by application of the foregoing principles of interpretation. Thus, as a general matter, legislative history need not be and is not consulted except to resolve an ambiguity in the statutory language, although legislative history is sometimes consulted to confirm or verify a plain-meaning interpretation....

An interpretive method that focuses on textual, intrinsic sources of statutory meaning and cabins the use of extratextual sources of legislative intent is grounded in more than a mistrust of legislative history or cynicism about the capacity of the legislative or judicial processes to be manipulated. The principles of statutory interpretation that we have restated here are rooted in and fundamental to the rule of law. Ours is a government of laws not men, and it is simply incompatible with democratic government, or indeed, even with fair government, to have the meaning of a law determined by what the lawgiver meant, rather than by what the lawgiver promulgated. It is the law that governs, not the intent of the lawgiver.... Men may intend what they will; but it is only the laws that they enact which bind us....

[W]e conclude that the language ... is clear and unambiguous. More particularly, the term "refuse" (as in "the district attorney refuses") has a common and accepted meaning, ascertainable by reference to the dictionary definition.

To refuse is "[t]o indicate unwillingness to do, accept, give, or allow." The American Heritage Dictionary of the English Language 1519 (3d ed. 1992). As the term is ordinarily understood, a "refusal" involves a decision to reject a certain choice or course of action. This definition is reasonable in the statutory context and consistent with the manifest statutory purpose. Accordingly, the statute's meaning is plain, there is no ambiguity to clarify, and no need to consult extrinsic sources such as legislative history....

[The Kalals "argue, however, that the statutory term 'refuses' must be accorded a strict and literal interpretation, to require a direct and explicit statement of refusal from the district attorney, in order to avoid conflict between the branches in this area of shared power. While we recognize the constitutional tension inherent in this statute, we see no reason to depart from a straightforward, plain-meaning interpretation of the statutory term 'refuses.' We therefore reject the Kalals' argument that only a direct and unequivocal statement from the district attorney—e.g., 'I refuse to issue a complaint'—can satisfy the statute. Such a literal reading would nullify the statute by permitting the district attorney to defeat the statutory procedure by responding to the complainant in equivocal or vague terms. On the other hand, to equate refusal with mere inaction runs contrary to the accepted meaning of the term and could undermine the district attorney's exercise of prosecutorial discretion or interfere with ongoing criminal investigations."]*

The decision of the court of appeals is affirmed.

---

* Authors' footnote: We have moved this portion of the case for clarity; hence, it is in brackets.

SHIRLEY ABRAMSON, Chief Justice (concurring).

I join the mandate, but I return once again to this court's approach(es) to statutory interpretation. It is important, as I have written before, that litigants, lawyers, legislators, courts, and the people of Wisconsin know and understand our approach....

This opinion makes what I consider a significant advance in explaining what the court is actually doing in statutory interpretation. I think, however, it will be difficult to understand and apply parts of this opinion because it works at cross purposes in several respects. For example, the opinion strongly emphasizes textualism but broadens textualism to include many matters the plain meaning folk (including those on this court) have rejected. It recognizes that the purposes of the legislation should be considered in interpretation but refuses to consider the consequences of different interpretations as an aid to interpretation....

The most significant advance is that the court at long last abandons its too-oft quoted but erroneous aphorism that to determine the intent of the legislature "if a statute is ambiguous, the reviewing court turns to the scope, history, context, and purpose of the statute."

This opinion correctly concludes that a court resorts to the scope, context, and purpose of the statute without having to declare an ambiguity in the statute. The majority opinion states: "[S]cope, context, and purpose are perfectly relevant to a plain-meaning interpretation of an unambiguous statute as long as the scope, context, and purpose are ascertainable from the text and structure of the statute itself, rather than extrinsic sources, such as legislative history." The trick in understanding and applying this sentence is to give meaning to the phrase "ascertainable from the text and structure of the statute itself." "Ascertainable," "text," and "structure of the statute itself" have elasticity. From my perspective that is a saving grace.

Our cases have been inconsistent in stating whether an ambiguity must be declared before a court examines the terms of a statute in relation to the scope, history, context, and subject matter of the legislation, the spirit or nature of the act, the evil intended to be remedied, the general object sought to be accomplished, and the consequences. The majority opinion now separates "history" from the other listed sources of legislative intent, without defining history, and discusses only legislative history. Before a court uses legislative history, a court must declare the statute ambiguous, according to the majority opinion.

I part company with the majority opinion when it declares that extrinsic sources (not defined) such as legislative history may be used only when the statutory language is ambiguous or when the legislative history supports (but does not contradict) the plain meaning of the statute. I have criticized this approach to plain meaning, ambiguity, and legislative history before. Language is often ambiguous; the distinction between "plain" and "ambiguous" is in the eye of the beholder; and both words too often are conclusory labels a court pins on a statute, making its decision appear result-oriented.

I have argued that a court may examine history without declaring an ambiguity and that a court "must engage in an analysis of both the evidence that supports a given interpretation as well as the evidence that contradicts a given interpretation." ...

My view is that "proper statutory interpretation requires that a court take a comprehensive view toward determining legislative intent." ...

Without this comprehensive approach, this court risks usurping the legislative role and substituting its judgment for the legislature's intent. It is only through complete analysis and weighing of available materials that we can ascertain the meaning of a statute and effectuate legislative intent. . . .

ANN WALSH BRADLEY, J. (concurring).

I agree with the majority . . . that the district attorney's actions constituted a "refusal" under Wis. Stat. § 968.02(3). . . . Although I commend both the majority and concurrence for their endeavors, I ultimately join neither.

Notes and Questions

(1) *The Different Views.* How did the approaches of the majority and the first concurrence differ? How would the first concurrence have used legislative history differently than the majority? As a lawyer in Wisconsin, what argument must you make to ensure consideration of, and that weight be given to, extratextual sources?

(2) *Which Approach Appeals to You?* When would the majority review the "scope, context, and purpose of a statute"? How did the first concurrence's approach differ? If nothing else, these three opinions should make it clear that there is no uniform approach to interpretation. Hence, as an attorney, you must be ready to use all the statutory sources of construction to make your arguments.

(3) *A Workable Approach?* The first concurrence argued that the majority "strongly emphasizes textualism but broadens textualism to include many matters the plain meaning folk . . . have rejected. It recognizes that the purposes of the legislation should be considered in interpretation but refuses to consider the consequences of different interpretations as an aid to interpretation. . . ." How would the majority respond?

(4) *Later Reexamination.* Not long after *Kalal*, the same majority revisited the proper approach to statutory interpretation. Reiterating the "common" and "misleading formulation" it eschewed in *Kalal*, the majority explained:

> If the statute is unambiguous, we must give effect to the words within the statute according to their common meanings. As a general rule, we do not review extrinsic sources, unless there is ambiguity. If the statutory language is ambiguous, however, *we then may use the scope, history, context, and subject matter of the statute in order to ascertain legislative intent.*

Keup v. Wis. Dept. Health & Family Serv., 675 N.W.2d 755, 763 (Wis. 2004) (emphasis added). How does this approach differ from the majority's approach in *Kalal*? Why do you think the majority ignored the formulation it took great pains to articulate in *Kalal*?

Problem 2-2

Now you are equipped. You have learned the approaches to statutory interpretation and know how to convince a judge that your interpretation of a statute is the accurate one. But, how do you know which approach will persuade a particular judge? One way to prepare is to read the statutory interpretation opinions from that judge and identify whether the judge is a textualist, a purposivist, or an intentionalist. If you can figure out first what sources matter to your judge, then you can explain how those sources lead to the result you want. We give you a chance to practice below.

The following is an excerpt from a law review article written in 1949 by Lon L. Fuller, Professor at Harvard Law School. While the case is fictional, the judicial analysis exemplifies some of the approaches to statutory interpretation still in use today. See if you can identify the theory followed by each of the judges below, then answer the questions following the excerpt.

Problem Materials

The Case of the Speluncean Explorers

In the Supreme Court of Newgarth, 4300*

The defendants, having been indicted for the crime of murder, were convicted and sentenced to be hanged.... They bring a petition of error before this Court....

CHIEF JUSTICE TRUEPENNY.

The four defendants are members of the Speluncean Society, an organization of amateurs interested in the exploration of caves. Early in May of 4299 they, in the company of Roger Whetmore, then also a member of the Society, penetrated into the interior of a limestone cavern of the type found in the Central Plateau of this Commonwealth. While they were in a position remote from the entrance to the cave, a landslide occurred. Heavy boulders fell in such a manner as to block completely the only known opening to the cave. When the men discovered their predicament they settled themselves near the obstructed entrance to wait until a rescue party should remove the detritus that prevented them from leaving their underground prison. On the failure of Whetmore and the defendants to return to their homes, the Secretary of the Society was notified by their families. It appears that the explorers had left indications at the headquarters of the Society concerning the location of the cave they proposed to visit. A rescue party was promptly dispatched to the spot.

The task of rescue proved one of overwhelming difficulty. It was necessary to supplement the forces of the original party by repeated increments of men and machines, which had to be conveyed at great expense to the remote and isolated region in which the cave was located. A huge temporary camp of workmen, engineers, geologists, and other experts was established. The work of removing the obstruction was several times frustrated by fresh landslides. In one of these, ten of the workmen engaged in clearing the entrance were killed. The treasury of the Speluncean Society was soon exhausted in the rescue effort, and the sum of eight hundred thousand frelars, raised partly by popular subscription and partly by legislative grant, was expended before the imprisoned men were rescued. Success was finally achieved on the thirty-second day after the men entered the cave.

Since it was known that the explorers had carried with them only scant provisions, and since it was also known that there was no animal or vegetable matter within the cave on which they might subsist, anxiety was early felt that they might meet death by starvation before access to them could be obtained. On the twentieth day of their imprisonment it was learned for the first time that they had taken with them into the cave a portable wireless machine capable of both sending and receiving messages. A similar machine was promptly installed in the rescue camp and oral communication established with the unfortunate men within the mountain. They asked to be informed how long a time would be required to release them. The engineers in charge of the project answered that at least ten days would be required even if no new landslides occurred. The explorers then asked

* Lon L. Fuller, *The Case of the Speluncean Explorers*, 62 HARV. L. REV. 616 (1949). Copyright Lon L. Fuller, Professor. Used by permission.

if any physicians were present, and were placed in communication with a committee of medical experts. The imprisoned men described their condition and the rations they had taken with them, and asked for a medical opinion whether they would be likely to live without food for ten days longer. The chairman of the committee of physicians told them that there was little possibility of this. The wireless machine within the cave then remained silent for eight hours. When communication was re-established the men asked to speak again with the physicians. The chairman of the physicians' committee was placed before the apparatus, and Whetmore, speaking on behalf of himself and the defendants, asked whether they would be able to survive for ten days longer if they consumed the flesh of one of their number. The physicians' chairman reluctantly answered this question in the affirmative. Whetmore asked whether it would be advisable for them to cast lots to determine which of them should be eaten. None of the physicians present was willing to answer the question. Whetmore then asked if there were among the party a judge or other official of the government who would answer this question. None of those attached to the rescue camp was willing to assume the role of advisor in this matter. He then asked if any minister or priest would answer their question, and none was found who would do so. Thereafter no further messages were received from within the cave, and it was assumed (erroneously, it later appeared) that the electric batteries of the explorers' wireless machine had become exhausted. When the imprisoned men were finally released it was learned that on the twenty-third day after their entrance into the cave Whetmore had been killed and eaten by his companions.

From the testimony of the defendants, which was accepted by the jury, it appears that it was Whetmore who first proposed that they might find the nutriment without which survival was impossible in the flesh of one of their own number. It was also Whetmore who first proposed the use of some method of casting lots, calling the attention of the defendants to a pair of dice he happened to have with him. The defendants were at first reluctant to adopt so desperate a procedure, but after the conversations by wireless related above, they finally agreed on the plan proposed by Whetmore. After much discussion of the mathematical problems involved, agreement was finally reached on a method of determining the issue by the use of the dice.

Before the dice were cast, however, Whetmore declared that he withdrew from the arrangement, as he had decided on reflection to wait for another week before embracing an expedient so frightful and odious. The others charged him with a breach of faith and proceeded to cast the dice. When it came Whetmore's turn, the dice were cast for him by one of the defendants, and he was asked to declare any objections he might have to the fairness of the throw. He stated that he had no such objections. The throw went against him, and he was then put to death and eaten by his companions.

After the rescue of the defendants, and after they had completed a stay in a hospital where they underwent a course of treatment for malnutrition and shock, they were indicted for the murder of Roger Whetmore. At the trial, after the testimony had been concluded, the foreman of the jury (a lawyer by profession) inquired of the court whether the jury might not find a special verdict, leaving it to the court to say whether on the facts as found the defendants were guilty. After some discussion, both the Prosecutor and counsel for the defendants indicated their acceptance of this procedure, and it was adopted by the court. In a lengthy special verdict the jury found the facts as I have related them above, and found further that if on these facts the defendants were guilty of the crime charged against them, then they found the defendants guilty. On the basis of this verdict, the trial judge ruled that the defendants were guilty of murdering Roger Whetmore. The judge then sentenced them to be hanged, the law of our Commonwealth permitting him no discretion with respect to the penalty to be imposed. After the release of the jury, its members joined in a communication to the [President] asking that the sentence be commuted to an imprisonment of six months. The trial judge addressed a similar communication to the [President]. As yet no action with respect to these pleas has been taken, as the [President] is apparently awaiting our disposition of this petition of error....

The language of our statute is well known: "Whoever shall willfully take the life of another shall be punished by death." N. C. S. A. (N. S.) § 12-A. This statute permits of no exception applicable to this case, however our sympathies may incline us to make allowance for the tragic situation in which these men found themselves.

In a case like this the principle of executive clemency seems admirably suited to mitigate the rigors of the law, and I propose to my colleagues that we follow the example of the jury and trial judge by joining in the communications they have addressed to the [President]. There is every reason to believe that these requests for clemency will be heeded, coming as they do from those who have studied the case and had an opportunity become thoroughly acquainted with all its circumstances.... I think we may therefore assume that some form of clemency will be extended to these defendants. If this is done, then justice will be accomplished without impairing either the letter or spirit of our statutes and without offering any encouragement for the disregard of law.

Justice Foster.

I am shocked that the Chief Justice, in an effort to escape the embarrassments of this tragic case, should have adopted, and should have proposed to his colleagues, an expedient at once so sordid and so obvious. I believe something more is on trial in this case than the fate of these unfortunate explorers; that is the law of our Commonwealth. If this Court declares that under our law these men have committed a crime, then our law is itself convicted in the tribunal of common sense, no matter what happens to the individuals involved in this petition of error. For us to assert that the law we uphold and expound compels us to a conclusion we are ashamed of, and from which we can only escape by appealing to a dispensation resting within the personal whim of the Executive, seems to me to amount to an admission that the law of this Commonwealth no longer pretends to incorporate justice.

For myself, I do not believe that our law compels the monstrous conclusion that these men are murderers. I believe, on the contrary, that it declares them to be innocent of any crime....

Now it is, of course, perfectly clear that these men did an act that violates the literal wording of the statute which declares that he who "shall willfully take the life of another" is a murderer. But one of the most ancient bits of legal wisdom is the saying that a man may break the letter of the law without breaking the law itself. Every proposition of positive law, whether contained in a statute or a judicial precedent, is to be interpreted reasonably, in the light of its evident purpose. This is a truth so elementary that it is hardly necessary to expatiate on it....

The statute before us for interpretation has never been applied literally. Centuries ago it was established that a killing in self-defense is excused. There is nothing in the wording of the statute that suggests this exception. Various attempts have been made to reconcile the legal treatment of self-defense with the words of the statute, but in my opinion these are all merely ingenious sophistries. The truth is that the exception in favor of self-defense cannot be reconciled with the *words* of the statute, but only with its *purpose*.

The true reconciliation of the excuse of self-defense with the statute making it a crime to kill another is to be found in the following line of reasoning. One of the principal objects underlying any criminal legislation is that of deterring men from crime. Now it is apparent that if it were declared to be the law that a killing in self-defense is murder such a rule could not operate in a deterrent manner. A man whose life is threatened will repel his aggressor, whatever the law may say. Looking therefore to the broad purposes of criminal legislation, we may safely declare that this statute was not intended to apply to cases of self-defense.

When the rationale of the excuse of self-defense is thus explained, it becomes apparent that precisely the same reasoning is applicable to the case at bar. If in the future any group of men ever find themselves in the tragic predicament of these defendants, we may be sure that their decision whether to live or die will not be controlled by the contents of our criminal code. Accordingly, if we read this statute intelligently it is apparent that it does not apply to this case. The withdrawal of this situation from the effect of the statute is justified by precisely the same considerations that were applied by our predecessors in office centuries ago to the case of self-defense....

I therefore conclude that on any aspect under which this case may be viewed these defendants are innocent of the crime of murdering Roger Whetmore, and that the conviction should be set aside.

JUSTICE TATTING.

In the discharge of my duties as a justice of this Court, I am usually able to dissociate the emotional and intellectual sides of my reactions, and to decide the case before me entirely on the basis of the latter. In passing on this tragic case I find that my usual resources fail me. On the emotional side I find myself torn between sympathy for these men and a feeling of abhorrence and disgust at the monstrous act they committed. I had hoped that I would be able to put these contradictory emotions to one side as irrelevant, and to decide the case on the basis of a convincing and logical demonstration of the result demanded by our law. Unfortunately, this deliverance has not been vouchsafed me.

As I analyze the opinion just rendered by my brother Foster, I find that it is shot through with contradictions and fallacies....

The gist of my brother's argument may be stated in the following terms: No statute, whatever its language, should be applied in a way that contradicts its purpose. One of the purposes of any criminal statute is to deter. The application of the statute making it a crime to kill another to the peculiar facts of this case would contradict this purpose, for it is impossible to believe that the contents of the criminal code could operate in a deterrent manner on men faced with the alternative of life or death. The reasoning by which this exception is read into the statute is, my brother observes, the same as that which is applied in order to provide the excuse of self-defense.

On the face of things this demonstration seems very convincing indeed....

It is true that a statute should be applied in the light of its purpose, and that *one* of the purposes of criminal legislation is recognized to be deterrence. The difficulty is that other purposes are also ascribed to the law of crimes. It has been said that one of its objects is to provide an orderly outlet for the instinctive human demand for retribution. *Commonwealth v. Scape.* It has also been said that its object is the rehabilitation of the wrongdoer. *Commonwealth v. Makeover.* Other theories have been propounded. Assuming that we must interpret a statute in the light of its purpose, what are we to do when it has many purposes or when its purposes are disputed?

A similar difficulty is presented by the fact that although there is authority for my brother's interpretation of the excuse of self-defense, there is other authority which assigns to that excuse a different rationale.... The taught doctrine of our law schools, memorized by generations of law students, runs in the following terms: The statute concerning murder requires a "willful" act. The man who acts to repel an aggressive threat to his own life does not act "willfully," but in response to an impulse deeply ingrained in human nature....

Now the familiar explanation for the excuse of self-defense just expounded obviously cannot be applied by analogy to the facts of this case. These men acted not only "willfully" but with great deliberation and after hours of discussing what they should do. Again we encounter a forked path, with one line of reasoning leading us in one direction and another in a direction that is exactly the opposite....

But what are we to do with one of the landmarks of our jurisprudence, which again my brother passes over in silence? This is *Commonwealth v. Valjean.* Though the case is somewhat obscurely reported, it appears that the defendant was indicted for the larceny of a loaf of bread, and offered as a defense that he was in a condition approaching starvation. The court refused to accept this defense. If hunger cannot justify the theft of wholesome and natural food, how can it justify the killing and eating of a man? Again, if we look at the thing in terms of deterrence, is it likely that a man will starve to death to avoid a jail sentence for the theft of a loaf of bread? My brother's demonstrations would compel us to overrule *Commonwealth v. Valjean,* and many other precedents that have been built on that case....

There is still a further difficulty in my brother Foster's proposal to read an exception into the statute to favor this case, though again a difficulty not even intimated in his opinion. What shall be the scope of this exception? Here the men cast lots and the victim was himself originally a party to the agreement. What would we have to decide if Whetmore had refused from the beginning to participate in the plan? Would a majority be permitted to overrule him? Or, suppose that no plan were adopted at all and the others simply conspired to bring about Whetmore's death, justifying their act by saying that he was in the weakest condition. Or again, that a plan of selection was followed but one based on a different justification than the one adopted here, as if the others were atheists and insisted that Whetmore should die because he was the only one who believed in an afterlife. These illustrations could be multiplied, but enough have been suggested to reveal what a quagmire of hidden difficulties my brother's reasoning contains.

Of course I realize on reflection that I may be concerning myself with a problem that will never arise, since it is unlikely that any group of men will ever again be brought to commit the dread act that was involved here. Yet, on still further reflection, even if we are certain that no similar case will arise again, do not the illustrations I have given show the lack of any coherent and rational principle in the rule my brother proposes? Should not the soundness of a principle be tested by the conclusions it entails, without reference to the accidents of later litigational history? Still, if this is so, why is it that we of this Court so often discuss the question whether we are likely to have later occasion to apply a principle urged for the solution of the case before us? Is this a situation where a line of reasoning not originally proper has become sanctioned by precedent, so that we are permitted to apply it and may even be under an obligation to do so? ...

I have given this case the best thought of which I am capable. I have scarcely slept since it was argued before us. When I feel myself inclined to accept the view of my brother Foster, I am repelled by a feeling that his arguments are intellectually unsound and approach mere rationalization. On the other hand, when I incline toward upholding the conviction, I am struck by the absurdity of directing that these men be put to death when their lives have been saved at the cost of the lives of ten heroic workmen. It is to me a matter of regret that the Prosecutor saw fit to ask for an indictment for murder. If we had a provision in our statutes making it a crime to eat human flesh, that would have been a more appropriate charge. If no other charge suited to the facts of this case could be brought against the defendants, it would have been wiser, I think, not to have indicted them at all. Unfortunately, however, the men have been indicted and tried, and we have therefore been drawn into this unfortunate affair.

Since I have been wholly unable to resolve the doubts that beset me about the law of this case, I am with regret announcing a step that is, I believe, unprecedented in the history of this tribunal. I declare my withdrawal from the decision of this case.

Justice Keen.

I should like to begin by setting to one side two questions which are not before this Court.... [First, the justice suggests that whether the executive should grant clemency is a question for the President, not the court].

The second question that I wish to put to one side is that of deciding whether what these men did was "right" or "wrong," "wicked" or "good." That is also a question that is irrelevant to the discharge of my office as a judge sworn to apply, not my conceptions of morality, but the law of the land....

The sole question before us for decision is whether these defendants did, within the meaning of N. C. S. A. (N. S.) § 12-A, willfully take the life of Roger Whetmore. The exact language of the statute is as follows: "Whoever shall willfully take the life of another shall be punished by death." Now I should suppose that any candid observer, content to extract from these words their natural meaning, would concede at once that these defendants did "willfully take the life" of Roger Whetmore.

Whence arise all the difficulties of the case, then, and the necessity for so many pages of discussion about what ought to be so obvious? The difficulties, in whatever tortured form they may present themselves, all trace back to a single source, and that is a failure to distinguish the legal from the moral aspects of this case. To put it bluntly, my brothers do not like the fact that the written law requires the conviction of these defendants. Neither do I, but unlike my brothers I respect the obligations of an office that requires me to put my personal predilections out of my mind when I come to interpret and apply the law of this Commonwealth.

Now, of course, my brother Foster does not admit that he is actuated by a personal dislike of the written law. Instead he develops a familiar line of argument according to which the court may disregard the express language of a statute when something not contained in the statute itself, called its "purpose," can be employed to justify the result the court considers proper....

[W]e now have a clear-cut principle, which is the supremacy of the legislative branch of our government. From that principle flows the obligation of the judiciary to enforce faithfully the written law, and to interpret that law in accordance with its plain meaning without reference to our personal desires or our individual conceptions of justice....

My brother Foster's penchant for finding holes in statutes reminds one of the story told by an ancient author about the man who ate a pair of shoes. Asked how he liked them, he replied that the part he liked best was the holes. That is the way my brother feels about statutes; the more holes they have in them the better he likes them. In short, he doesn't like statutes.

One could not wish for a better case to illustrate the specious nature of this gap-filling process than the one before us. My brother thinks he knows exactly what was sought when men made murder a crime, and that was something he calls "deterrence." My brother Tatting has already shown how much is passed over in that interpretation. But I think the trouble goes deeper. I doubt very much whether our statute making murder a crime really has a "purpose" in any ordinary sense of the term. Primarily, such a statute reflects a deeply-felt human conviction that murder is wrong and that something should be done to the man who commits it. . . .

If we do not know the purpose of § 12-A, how can we possibly say there is a "gap" in it? How can we know what its draftsmen thought about the question of killing men in order to eat them? . . . [I]t remains abundantly clear that neither I nor my brother Foster knows what the "purpose" of § 12-A is. . . .

Now I know that the line of reasoning I have developed in this opinion will not be acceptable to those who look only to the immediate effects of a decision and ignore the long-run implications of an assumption by the judiciary of a power of dispensation. A hard decision is never a popular decision. Judges have been celebrated in literature for their sly prowess in devising some quibble by which a litigant could be deprived of his rights where the public thought it was wrong for him to assert those rights. But I believe that judicial dispensation does more harm in the long run than hard decisions. Hard cases may even have a certain moral value by bringing home to the people their own responsibilities toward the law that is ultimately their creation, and by reminding them that there is no principle of personal grace that can relieve the mistakes of their representatives. . . .

I conclude that the conviction should be affirmed.

JUSTICE HANDY.

I have listened with amazement to the tortured ratiocinations to which this simple case has given rise. I never cease to wonder at my colleagues' ability to throw an obscuring curtain of legalisms about every issue presented to them for decision. . . . My only disappointment was that someone did not raise the question of the legal nature of the bargain struck in the cave—whether it was unilateral or bilateral, and whether Whetmore could not be considered as having revoked an offer prior to action taken thereunder. . . .

The problem before us is what we, as officers of the government, ought to do with these defendants. . . . When the case is approached in this light, it becomes, I think, one of the easiest to decide that has ever been argued before this Court. . . .

I have never been able to make my brothers see that government is a human affair, and that men are ruled, not by words on paper or by abstract theories, but by other men. They are ruled well when their rulers understand the feelings and conceptions of the masses. They are ruled badly when that understanding is lacking. . . .

Now when these conceptions are applied to the case before us, its decision becomes, as I have said, perfectly easy. . . .

The first of these is that this case has aroused an enormous public interest, both here and abroad. Almost every newspaper and magazine has carried articles about it; columnists have shared with their readers confidential information as to the next governmental move; hundreds of letters-to-the-editor have been printed. One of the great newspaper chains made a poll of public opinion on the question, "What do you think the Supreme Court should do with the Speluncean explorers?" About ninety per cent expressed a belief that the defendants should be pardoned or let off with a kind of token punishment. It is perfectly clear, then, how public feels about the case. . . .

This makes it obvious, not only what we should do, but what we must do if we are to preserve between ourselves and public opinion a reasonable and decent accord. Declaring these men innocent need not involve us in any undignified quibble or trick. No principle of statutory construction is required that is not consistent with the past practices of this Court. Certainly no layman would think that in letting these men off we had stretched the statute any more than our ancestors did when they created the excuse of self-defense. If a more detailed demonstration of the method of reconciling our decision with the statute is required, I should be content to rest on the arguments developed in ... my brother Foster's opinion....

This brings me to the concluding portion of my remarks, which has to do with executive clemency....

I come now to that most crucial fact in this case, a fact known to all of us on this Court, though one that my brothers have seen fit to keep under the cover of their judicial robes. This is the frightening likelihood that if the issue is left to him, the [President] will refuse to pardon these men or commute their sentence. As we all know, our [President] is a man now well advanced in years, of very stiff notions. Public clamor usually operates on him with the reverse of the effect intended. As I have told my brothers, it happens that my wife's niece is an intimate friend of his secretary. I have learned in this indirect, but, I think, wholly reliable way, that he is firmly determined not to commute the sentence if these men are found to have violated the law....

I conclude that the defendants are innocent of the crime charged, and that the conviction and sentence should be set aside....

* * *

The Supreme Court being evenly divided, the conviction and sentence of the Court of General Instances is *affirmed.* It is ordered that the execution of the sentence shall occur at 6 A.M., Friday, April 2, 4300, at which time the Public Executioner is directed to proceed with all convenient dispatch to hang each of the defendants by the neck until he is dead.

Notes and Questions

(1) *You Make the Call.* Assume you are the tie-breaking vote on this case. How would you vote? How would you support that decision using statutory interpretation approaches and sources? Are there any approaches or sources that were not discussed that you believe are relevant?

(2) *Whetmore's Choice.* Had they thought about it, how do you think the defendants would have expected a court to vote at the time they made their pact? Is it relevant that Whetmore was the individual who originally proposed the idea? Would you decide the case any differently had Whetmore not withdrawn his consent? Are principles of contract law at all relevant?

(3) *Multiple Purposes.* What should happen when a statute has more than one purpose? Does finding these men guilty or innocent further more of the purposes? (*See* Chapter 10.)

Chapter 3

Determining the Meaning of the Text: Words

This chapter focuses on the starting point for statutory interpretation: the words. You will learn from this chapter how to use the text to discern meaning as we explore both the plain meaning and the technical meaning canons. You will learn the role that audience plays in determining meaning, and you will discover how important it can be to identify the "right" language for a court to interpret.

A. Determining *Ordinary* Meaning

1. The Plain Meaning Rule

As we've mentioned, the place to start when interpreting a statute is with the words themselves. We begin with the most basic question: How do you know what a word means?

At some levels, there is of course inherent indeterminacy in language and, in particular, at the margins of meaning. "When does a hill become a mountain? On a continuum of shapes, when does a cup become a bowl? … When we ask people to Come here, how close do they have to be before they have reached the state of herehood?" Lawrence Solan, *When Judges Use the Dictionary*, 68 Am. Speech 50, 59 (1993). Words have a range of meaning and at the margins become imprecise.

But even at the core, language is imprecise. "The philosophy of language, and [especially the writings of Ludwig Wittgenstein], has established that sets of words do not possess intrinsic meanings and cannot be given them; to make matters worse, speakers do not even have determinative intents about the meanings of their own words." Frank H. Easterbrook, *Statutes' Domains*, 50 U. Chi. L. Rev. 533, 536 (1983). Some say that, as a result, the "invocation of 'plain meaning' just sweeps under the rug the process by which meaning is divined." *Id.* This chapter explores these and related issues. Recently, one commentator used a simple illustration to underscore that fundamental point:

> Imagine shells washing up on the shore in the shape of the letters "CAT." There we could ask what would be the most likely understanding of those letters, and the answer would be, the household pet. But this method raises a few hard questions. First, how do we know what the culture in question believed to be the most likely meaning? Second, for many words, there will be several possible meanings, and picking the most likely one, although fine for our seashells example, will seem awfully silly in the context of specific statutes. For example, reading "CAT"

73

to refer to the household pet works for the most likely meaning, but if the setting involves a girl named Catherine whose nickname is "Cat," or if it involves "the fur of a domestic cat" or "a cat-o'-nine tails" or "a catfish" or "a catamaran" or "a player or devotee of jazz music"—all acceptable definitions of "cat" in the American Heritage Dictionary—then reading "CAT" to mean the household pet would seem odd, missing something we all learn very early on about language— that the same word can have different meanings. Furthermore, some serious problems are raised, in the statutory setting, by arguing that we should always interpret words according to their most likely meaning as a default rule, forcing the legislature to further specify a term's meaning if it doesn't want the most likely meaning. Is the legislature going to conduct a linguistic analysis of every word in every statute, determine the most likely meaning of each, and then write elaborate subsections and definition sections each time it wants to define a term differently? This seems extraordinarily costly, highly unlikely, and it still wouldn't account for the unforeseen circumstances problem (although in theory this kind of "strict liability" approach could force legislatures, at the margins, to write more carefully).

Abner S. Greene, *The Jurisprudence of Justice Stevens Panel III: The Missing Step of Textualism*, 74 Fordham L. Rev. 1913, 1917 (2006).

The following three cases explore language in the same statute to address the issue of whether words have fixed, ordinary meanings.

Smith v. United States
508 U.S. 223 (1993)

Justice O'Connor delivered the opinion of the Court.

Petitioner ... and his companion went from Tennessee to Florida to buy cocaine.... Upon arriving at [the] motel room, [an] undercover officer presented himself to petitioner as a pawnshop dealer. Petitioner, in turn, presented the officer with a proposition: He had an automatic MAC-10 and silencer with which he might be willing to part.... Rather than asking for money, however, petitioner asked for drugs. He was willing to trade his MAC-10, he said, for two ounces of cocaine. The officer told petitioner ... that he wanted the MAC-10 and would try to get the cocaine. The officer then left, promising to return within an hour....

But petitioner was not content to wait.... When law enforcement authorities tried to stop petitioner, he led them on a high-speed chase. Petitioner eventually was apprehended....

[Petitioner was convicted of] two drug trafficking crimes ... [and] knowingly us[ing] the MAC-10 and its silencer during and in relation to a drug trafficking crime. Under 18 U.S.C. §924(c)(1), a defendant who so uses ... a "machinegun" or [a gun] fitted with a silencer, [may be sentenced to] 30 years....

On appeal, petitioner argue[s] that §924(c)(1)'s penalty for using a firearm during and in relation to a drug trafficking offense covers only situations in which the firearm is used as a weapon. According to petitioner, the provision does not extend to defendants who use a firearm solely as a medium of exchange or for barter....

By its terms, the statute requires the prosecution ... demonstrate that the defendant "use[d] or carrie[d] a firearm." ...

Petitioner argues … that he cannot be said to have "use[d]" a firearm unless he used it as a weapon, since that is how firearms most often are used.…

There is a significant flaw to this argument. It is one thing to say that the ordinary meaning of "uses a firearm" *includes* using a firearm as a weapon, since that is the intended purpose of a firearm and the example of "use" that most immediately comes to mind. But it is quite another to conclude that, as a result, the phrase also *excludes* any other use. Certainly that conclusion does not follow from the phrase "uses … a firearm" itself. As the dictionary definitions and experience make clear, one can use a firearm in a number of ways. That one example of "use" is the first to come to mind when the phrase "uses … a firearm" is uttered does not preclude us from recognizing that there are other "uses" that qualify as well. In this case, it is both reasonable and normal to say that petitioner "used" his MAC-10 in his drug trafficking offense by trading it for cocaine.…

Both a firearm's use as a weapon and its use as an item of barter fall within the plain language of § 924(c)(1), so long as the use occurs during and in relation to a drug trafficking offense; both must constitute "uses" of a firearm for § 924(d)(1) to make any sense at all.… We therefore hold that a criminal who trades his firearm for drugs "uses" it during and in relation to a drug trafficking offense within the meaning of § 924(c)(1).… The judgment of the Court of Appeals, accordingly, is affirmed.…

JUSTICE SCALIA, with whom JUSTICE STEVENS and JUSTICE SOUTER join, dissenting.

Section 924(c)(1) mandates a sentence enhancement for any defendant who "during and in relation to any crime of violence or drug trafficking crime … uses … a firearm." 18 U.S.C. § 924(c)(1). The Court begins its analysis by focusing upon the word "use" in this passage, and explaining that the dictionary definitions of that word are very broad. It is, however, a fundamental principle of statutory construction (and, indeed, of language itself) that the meaning of a word cannot be determined in isolation, but must be drawn from the context in which it is used. That is particularly true of a word as elastic as "use," whose meanings range all the way from "to partake of" (as in "he uses tobacco") to "to be wont or accustomed" (as in "he used to smoke tobacco"). *See* Webster's New International Dictionary 2806 (2d ed. 1950).

In the search for statutory meaning, we give nontechnical words and phrases their ordinary meaning. To use an instrumentality ordinarily means to use it for its intended purpose. When someone asks, "Do you use a cane?," he is not inquiring whether you have your grandfather's silver-handled walking stick on display in the hall; he wants to know whether you *walk* with a cane. Similarly, to speak of "using a firearm" is to speak of using it for its distinctive purpose, *i.e.*, as a weapon. To be sure, "one can use a firearm in a number of ways," including as an article of exchange, just as one can "use" a cane as a hall decoration — but that is not the ordinary meaning of "using" the one or the other. The Court does not appear to grasp the distinction between how a word *can be* used and how it *ordinarily is* used. It would, indeed, be both reasonable and normal to say that petitioner "used" his MAC-10 in his drug trafficking offense by trading it for cocaine. It would also be reasonable and normal to say that he "used" it to scratch his head. When one wishes to describe the action of employing the instrument of a firearm for such unusual purposes, "use" is assuredly a verb one could select. But that says nothing about whether the *ordinary* meaning of the phrase "uses a firearm" embraces such extraordinary employments. It is unquestionably *not* reasonable and normal, I think, to say simply "do not use firearms" when one means to prohibit selling or scratching with them.…

For the foregoing reasons, I respectfully dissent.

Bailey v. United States
516 U.S. 137 (1995)

JUSTICE O'CONNOR delivered the opinion of the Court.

These consolidated petitions each challenge a conviction under 18 U.S.C. § 924(c)(1). In relevant part, that section imposes a 5-year minimum term of imprisonment upon a person who "during and in relation to any crime of violence or drug trafficking crime ... uses or carries a firearm." We are asked to decide whether evidence of the proximity and accessibility of a firearm to drugs or drug proceeds is alone sufficient to support a conviction for "use" of a firearm during and in relation to a drug trafficking offense under 18 U.S.C. § 924(c)(1).

In May 1989, petitioner Roland Bailey was stopped by police officers after they noticed that his car lacked a front license plate and an inspection sticker. When Bailey failed to produce a driver's license, the officers ordered him out of the car. As he stepped out, the officers saw Bailey push something between the seat and the front console. A search of the passenger compartment revealed one round of ammunition and 27 plastic bags containing a total of 30 grams of cocaine. After arresting Bailey, the officers searched the trunk of his car where they found, among a number of items, a large amount of cash and a bag containing a loaded 9-mm. pistol.

Bailey was charged on several counts, including using and carrying a firearm in violation of 18 U.S.C. § 924(c)(1)....

Section 924(c)(1) requires the imposition of specified penalties if the defendant, "during and in relation to any crime of violence or drug trafficking crime..., uses or carries a firearm." ...

In *Smith*, we faced the question whether the barter of a gun for drugs was a "use," and concluded that it was. As the debate in *Smith* illustrated, the word "use" poses some interpretational difficulties because of the different meanings attributable to it....

We agree with the majority below that "use" must connote more than mere possession of a firearm by a person who commits a drug offense....

This conclusion — that a conviction for "use" of a firearm under § 924(c)(1) requires more than a showing of mere possession — requires us to answer a more difficult question. What must the Government show, beyond mere possession, to establish "use" for the purposes of the statute? ...

We start, as we must, with the language of the statute.... If Congress had intended to deprive "use" of its active connotations, it could have simply substituted a more appropriate term — "possession" — to cover the conduct it wished to reach.

The Government nonetheless argues that our observation in *Smith* that "§ 924(c)(1)'s language sweeps broadly," precludes limiting "use" to active employment. But our decision today is not inconsistent with *Smith*. Although there we declined to limit "use" to the meaning "use as a weapon," our interpretation of § 924(c)(1) nonetheless adhered to an active meaning of the term. In *Smith*, it was clear that the defendant had "used" the gun; the question was whether that particular use (bartering) came within the meaning of § 924(c)(1). *Smith* did not address the question we face today of what evidence is required to permit a jury to find that a firearm had been used at all....

Having determined that "use" denotes active employment, we must conclude that the evidence was insufficient to support ... Bailey's ... conviction for "use" under § 924(c)(1).

The police stopped Bailey for a traffic offense and arrested him after finding cocaine in the driver's compartment of his car. The police then found a firearm inside a bag in the locked car trunk. There was no evidence that Bailey actively employed the firearm in any way....

Because the Court of Appeals did not consider liability under the "carry" prong of §924(c)(1) for Bailey..., we remand for consideration of that basis for upholding the conviction[].

Watson v. United States

552 U.S. 74 (2007)

JUSTICE SOUTER delivered the opinion of the Court.

The question is whether a person who trades his drugs for a gun "uses" a firearm "during and in relation to ... [a] drug trafficking crime" within the meaning of 18 U.S.C. §924(c)(1)(A). We hold that he does not.... The statute leaves the term "uses" undefined, though we have spoken to it twice before.

Smith v. *United States*, 508 U.S. 223 (1993) raised the converse of today's question, and held that "a criminal who trades his firearm for drugs 'uses' it during and in relation to a drug trafficking offense within the meaning of §924(c)(1)." We rested primarily on the "ordinary or natural meaning" of the verb in context, and understood its common range as going beyond employment as a weapon: "it is both reasonable and normal to say that petitioner 'used' his MAC-10 in his drug trafficking offense by trading it for cocaine."

Two years later, the issue in *Bailey* v. *United States*, 516 U.S. 137 (1995), was whether possessing a firearm kept near the scene of drug trafficking is "use" under §924(c)(1). We looked again to "ordinary or natural" meaning, and decided that mere possession does not amount to "use": "§924(c)(1) requires evidence sufficient to show an *active employment* of the firearm by the defendant, a use that makes the firearm an operative factor in relation to the predicate offense."

This third case on the reach of §924(c)(1)(A) began to take shape when petitioner, Michael A. Watson, told a Government informant that he wanted to acquire a gun. On the matter of price, the informant quoted no dollar figure but suggested that Watson could pay in narcotics. Next, Watson met with the informant and an undercover law enforcement agent posing as a firearms dealer, to whom he gave 24 doses of oxycodone hydrocholoride (commonly, OxyContin) for a .50 caliber semiautomatic pistol. When law enforcement officers arrested Watson, they found the pistol in his car, and a later search of his house turned up a cache of prescription medicines, guns, and ammunition. Watson said he got the pistol "to protect his other firearms and drugs." ...

The Government's position that Watson "used" the pistol under §924(c)(1)(A) by receiving it for narcotics lacks authority in either precedent or regular English.... With no statutory definition or definitive clue, the meaning of the verb "uses" has to turn on the language as we normally speak it; there is no other source of a reasonable inference about what Congress understood when writing or what its words will bring to the mind of a careful reader. So, in *Smith* we looked for "everyday meaning," revealed in phraseology that strikes the ear as "both reasonable and normal." This appeal to the ordinary leaves the Government without much of a case.

The Government may say that a person "uses" a firearm simply by receiving it in a barter transaction, but no one else would. A boy who trades an apple to get a granola bar is sensibly said to use the apple, but one would never guess which way this commerce actually flowed from hearing that the boy used the granola. So, when Watson handed over the drugs for the pistol, the informant or the agent "used" the pistol to get the drugs, just as *Smith* held, but regular speech would not say that Watson himself used the pistol in the trade. "A seller does not 'use' a buyer's consideration[.]" ...

The Government would trump ordinary English with two arguments. First, it relies on *Smith* for the pertinence of a neighboring provision, 18 U.S.C. § 924(d)(1), which authorizes seizure and forfeiture of firearms "intended to be used in" certain criminal offenses listed in § 924(d)(3). Some of those offenses involve receipt of a firearm,[8] from which the Government infers that "use" under § 924(d) necessarily includes receipt of a gun even in a barter transaction....

We agree with the Government that § 924(d) calls for attention; the reference to intended use in a receipt crime carries some suggestion that receipt can be "use" (more of a hint, say, than speaking of intended "use" in a crime defined as exchange). But the suggestion is a tepid one ... because the utility of § 924(d)(1) is limited by its generality and its passive voice; it tells us a gun can be "used" in a receipt crime, but not whether both parties to a transfer use the gun, or only one, or which one. The nearby subsection (c)(1)(A), however, requires just such a specific identification. It provides that a person who uses a gun in the circumstances described commits a crime, whose perpetrator must be clearly identifiable in advance.

The agnosticism on the part of § 924(d)(1) about who does the using is entirely consistent with common speech's understanding that the first possessor is the one who "uses" the gun in the trade, and there is thus no cause to admonish us to adhere to the paradigm of a statute "as a symmetrical and coherent regulatory scheme, ... in which the operative words have a consistent meaning throughout," or to invoke the "standard principle of statutory construction ... that identical words and phrases within the same statute should normally be given the same meaning." Subsections (d)(1) and (c)(1)(A) as we read them are not at odds over the verb "use"; the point is merely that in the two subsections the common verb speaks to different issues in different voices and at different levels of specificity. The provisions do distinct jobs, but we do not make them guilty of employing the common verb inconsistently.

The second effort to trump regular English is the claim that failing to treat receipt in trade as "use" would create unacceptable asymmetry with *Smith*.... [I]t would be strange to penalize one side of a gun-for-drugs exchange but not the other.... [However,] policy-driven symmetry cannot turn "receipt-in-trade" into "use." Whatever the tension between the prior result and the outcome here, law depends on respect for language and would be served better by statutory amendment (if Congress sees asymmetry) than by racking statutory language to cover a policy it fails to reach....

Given ordinary meaning and the conventions of English, we hold that a person does not "use" a firearm under § 924(c)(1)(A) when he receives it in trade for drugs. The judgment of the Court of Appeals is reversed, and the case is remanded for further proceedings consistent with this opinion.

JUSTICE GINSBURG, concurring in the judgment.

It is better to receive than to give, the Court holds today, at least when the subject is guns. Distinguishing, as the Court does, between trading a gun for drugs and trading

---

8. See, *e.g.,* 18 U.S.C. § 922(j) (prohibiting, *inter alia,* the receipt of a stolen firearm in interstate commerce); § 924(b) (prohibiting, *inter alia,* the receipt of a firearm in interstate commerce with the intent to commit a felony).

drugs for a gun, for purposes of the 18 U.S.C. § 924(c)(1) enhancement, makes scant sense to me. I join the Court's judgment, however, because I am persuaded that the Court took a wrong turn in *Smith* when it held that trading a gun for drugs fits within § 924(c)(1)'s compass as "use" of a firearm "during and in relation to any ... drug trafficking crime." For reasons well stated by JUSTICE SCALIA in his dissenting opinion in *Smith*, I would read the word "use" in § 924(c)(1) to mean use as a weapon, not use in a bartering transaction. Accordingly, I would overrule *Smith*, and thereby render our precedent both coherent and consistent with normal usage.

Notes and Questions

(1) *Does Even "Cane" Have an Ordinary Meaning?* In *Smith*, Justice Scalia contended that there is an objective difference between how a word *can be used* and how it is *ordinarily used,* and he proffered the example of the cane to make the point. "But is Justice Scalia's hypothetical question ["Do you use a cane?"] intelligible outside of some context?" Paul E. McGreal, *Slighting Context: On the Illogic of Ordinary Speech in Statutory Interpretation,* 52 U. KAN. L. REV. 325, 357 (2004). "What if the question comes as I am thinking about how I played stickball as a child? ... And what if I am thinking about beating dust and dirt out of a rug?" *Id.* Does "cane" have meaning independent of context? If it does not, doesn't the judge's subjective choice of context dictate plain meaning? If that is the case, should the judge be required to explain why that context was chosen as the one most appropriate for "plain" meaning? *See id.* at 357–58. Don't we need something more than a judge giving an example and saying "this is how the word is ordinarily used"?

(2) *Plain Meaning as Incompatible with Legislative Drafting.* You hopefully recognized long ago that people write differently than they speak. As you have no doubt concluded, legislators do not write as people ordinarily speak or even as people ordinarily write. In part, writing statutes is different from writing anything else because statutes are drafted with the anticipation that someone will try to avoid obligations contained within them. Does the fact that statutes are not "ordinary speech" (or even "ordinary writing") mean that it is wrong to try to look for ordinary meaning within them? Or, given that statutes are largely intended to govern everyone and not just lawyers, should plain meaning be the appropriate choice?

(3) *Ordinary Meaning as Defeating Legislative Drafting Techniques.* Legislatures recognize that the meaning of their language will be litigated and, accordingly, draft with that purpose in mind. Does application of "plain meaning" defeat their goal of reducing strategic behavior? In *Smith*, the legislature chose the word "use" rather than "fire" or "discharge" perhaps to avoid "clever" circumvention: "If the more specific words were used, the *Smith* defendant could say, 'I didn't fire the gun, I just exchanged it for the drugs....'" McGreal, *supra*, at 367. If the legislature's choice of the word "use" was deliberate, using "plain meaning" may defeat the legislature's goal. *See id.*

(4) *Where Does "Ordinary" Meaning Come From?* Judges often write that they simply determine the plain and ordinary meaning of the words in issue. But where does this meaning come from? Words mean different things to different people; language is imperfect. Thus, any effort to rely on "ordinary" or "plain" meaning presents obvious hurdles. How, for example, is "ordinary" usage determined? One possible "neutral" source: dictionaries. What is the purpose of dictionaries? One commentator summed it up as follows:

> In most cases, dictionary definitions reflect the commonly-shared understanding of the terms, so the court is not distorting the meaning of the statute

by noting the dictionary definition. The court is simply providing additional authority for the plain meaning it would give the words in the absence of a dictionary definition.

Steven J. Johansen, *What Does Ambiguous Mean? Making Sense of Statutory Analysis in Oregon*, 34 Willamette L. Rev. 219, 229 (1998).

(5) *Are Dictionaries the Best Place to Look for Meaning?* But even that question raises a whole series of questions, such as: Which dictionary? Are all dictionaries equally valuable when interpreting text? In answering those questions, consider what your answer means for the interpretive process. Should a judge be required, for example, to explain why she chose a particular dictionary and, if there are different meanings within the "chosen one," to explain why the judge chose that definition? One commentator, noting that often "[t]here are a wide variety of dictionaries from which to choose, and all of them usually provide several entries for each word," then argued that the judge's "selection of a particular dictionary and a particular definition is not obvious and must be defended on some other grounds of suitability." Note, *Looking It Up: Dictionaries and Statutory Interpretation*, 107 Harv. L. Rev. 1437, 1445 (1994). What should influence the choice? The purpose? The intent? The "most likely" or "ordinary" definition? Does the existence of these choices suggest that, even as to plain meaning, something more than text must be considered?

In considering "plain meaning" in this context and more broadly, consider whether the word "grass" in "keep off the grass" means "lawn" or "marijuana." Both might be included in a modern dictionary, but what must you know in order to know which definition was intended? *See* McGreal, *supra*, at 340–41. Or, consider this example: two men meet in a bar, agreeing to leave at 6 o'clock as each has a commitment. A few minutes before six, as the men are discussing their children, one finishes his drink. The other says, "Are you going to have another one?" *See id.* Was the question about drinking or children?

(6) *The Ambiguity of Dictionaries.* If a court looks to a dictionary to define a word and finds more than one definition, does that mean that word is inherently ambiguous? Should a court always use the first definition listed? What if different dictionaries have different definitions? Should one dictionary be more persuasive than another? What about the meaning identified by most dictionaries as first? Should the meaning with the greatest number of dictionaries supporting it prevail? In *MCI Telecomms. Corp. v. Am. Tel. & Tel. Co.*, 512 U.S. 218 (1994), the Court had to interpret the word "modify," as used in 47 U.S.C. §203(b)(2). The parties supported their proposed, but inconsistent, meanings with different dictionaries. The Court explained that different dictionaries carry different weight:

> The dispute between the parties turns on the meaning of the phrase "modify any requirement" in §203(b)(2). Petitioners argue that it gives the [Federal Communications] Commission authority to make even basic and fundamental changes in the scheme created by that section. We disagree.... Virtually every dictionary we are aware of says that "to modify" means to change moderately or in minor fashion. *See, e.g.*, Random House Dictionary of the English Language 1236 (2d ed. 1987) ("to change somewhat the form or qualities of; alter partially; amend"); Webster's Third New International Dictionary 1452 (1981) ("to make minor changes in the form or structure of: alter without transforming"); 9 Oxford English Dictionary 952 (2d ed. 1989) ("[t]o make partial changes in; to change (an object) in respect of some of its qualities; to alter or vary without radical trans-

formation"); Black's Law Dictionary 1004 (6th ed. 1990) ("[t]o alter; to change in incidental or subordinate features; enlarge; extend; amend; limit; reduce").

In support of their position, petitioners cite dictionary definitions contained in, or derived from, a single source, Webster's Third New International Dictionary 1452 (1981) (Webster's Third), which includes among the meanings of "modify," "to make a basic or important change in." ...

[W]hat we have here [is] one dictionary whose suggested meaning contradicts virtually all others....

Most cases of verbal ambiguity in statutes involve ... a selection between accepted alternative meanings shown as such by many dictionaries. [That is not the case here. Instead,] what petitioners demand that we accept as creating an ambiguity here is a rarity even rarer than that: a meaning set forth in a single dictionary ... which not only supplements the meaning contained in all other dictionaries, but contradicts one of the meanings contained in virtually all other dictionaries. Indeed, contradicts one of the alternative meanings contained in the out-of-step dictionary itself—for as we have observed, Webster's Third itself defines "modify" to connote both (specifically) major change and (specifically) minor change. It is hard to see how that can be. When the word "modify" has come to mean both "to change in some respects" and "to change fundamentally" it will in fact mean neither of those things. It will simply mean "to change," and some adverb will have to be called into service to indicate the great or small degree of the change.

If that is what the peculiar Webster's Third definition means to suggest has happened—and what petitioners suggest by appealing to Webster's Third—we simply disagree. "Modify," in our view, connotes moderate change....

Id. at 225–28.

What process permits a judge, where dictionaries contain different meanings, to assume that the legislators all had the identical meaning in mind when enacting the statute? Does the use of a dictionary appear objective, but in fact mask subjective choices that may be driven by more than discernment of "plain meaning"?

(7) *Timing?* Should courts consult dictionaries that were "current" at the time the statute was enacted, at the time the events in the lawsuit occurred, or at the time the court is rendering its decision? Does your answer to this question change depending on the interpretative approach the court has adopted?

(8) *Some Other Examples.* We can't resist including the following cases. In *Durst v. Newby*, 685 F. Supp. 250 (S.D. Ga. 1988), the plaintiff truck driver sued a cow-owning defendant for injuries sustained when the plaintiff's tractor-trailer, filled with gasoline, collided "with a bovine standing completely in the roadway—a pensive all-black heifer oblivious to its fate." *Id.* Arguing that there was no evidence that the cow belonged to him, the defendant moved for summary judgment. The court denied the motion. In so doing, the court discussed the sufficiency of the evidence plaintiff offered to prove that the cow belonged to the defendant:

Both parties have discussed the admissibility of evidence regarding prior wanderings of defendant Newby's cows. The defendant contends this evidence is inadmissible character evidence [under § 404 of the Federal Rules of Evidence].... The plaintiff asserts the admissibility of such evidence as an exception with this scope of Rule 404(b).... The Court notes, however, that evidence regarding a cow's character is probably not rendered inadmissible by Rule 404 because the rule refers to "evidence of a *person's* character." Rather, the wanderlust of cows is simply a relevant fact not relating to the character of a party or witness.

Id. at 252 n.2. *See also United States v. Sproed,* 628 F. Supp. 1234 (D. Or. 1986) (affirming the dismissal of defendant's citation for catching butterflies in Crater Lake National Park in violation of a federal regulation prohibiting possessing "living … wildlife."); *Jett v. Mun. Court,* 223 Cal. Rptr. 111 (Cal. Ct. App. 1986) (finding that Rocky, a "slow-moving, grass-grazing giant tortoise" was not a "fighting animal").

2. The Relevance of Audience

Assuming that ordinary meaning matters, whose understanding of ordinary meaning is relevant? Should a court look to the ordinary meaning the drafters of the statute would have had, the ordinary meaning the legislators voting for the bill would have had, the ordinary meaning the public has a whole would have had, or some other ordinary meaning? The case that follows explores that question.

Patrie v. Area Coop. Educ. Serv.

37 Conn. L. Rptr. 470 (Conn. Super. Ct. 2004)

CORRADINO, J.

[P]laintiff was injured inside the premises of the defendant school when a student jumped on his back [playfully]. For his injuries he received compensation under the Workers' Compensation Act, and he has now brought a civil statutory action pursuant to § 10-236a of the General Statutes for a recovery beyond that provided for in the compensation act.…

Subsection (a) of § 10-236a recites as follows:

Sec. 10-236a. Indemnification of education personnel assaulted in the line of duty. (a) Each board of education shall protect and save harmless any member of such board or any teacher … from financial loss and expense, including payment of expenses reasonably incurred for medical or other service necessary as a result of an assault upon such teacher or other employee.…

The question … is the definition of the word "assault" in § 10-236a. There is no appellate case law that interprets the word and both sides agree that the legislative history is of no direct help so this court must try to interpret the meaning of the word "assault".…

Excusing the redundancy, what does the phrase "plain meaning" actually mean? Or, to approach the problem of the meaning of a statute from another perspective, should we not be concerned with the audience a statute is directed at, whose lives or interests does it try to affect, and is it not a worthwhile goal that our statutory scheme and decisions interpreting it should give the people a clear idea of what statutes mean? A discussion cannot become so abstract that these considerations are forgotten.…

For quite a period of time we have had a statute regarding "words and phrases" now at § 1-1 of the General Statutes which says:

(a) In the construction of the statutes, words and phrases shall be construed according to the commonly approved usage of the language; and technical words and phases, and such as have acquired a peculiar and appropriate meaning in the law, shall be construed and understood accordingly.

"Assault" is hardly a technical word....

Words generally do not acquire a peculiar and different meaning when used in a statute. Thus words in a statute normally must be given their usual, natural, plain, ordinary, and commonly understood meaning in the absence of any indication to the contrary....

Where then do we turn to find the usual, plain, natural or ordinary meaning? ... It is not unusual to find cases which indicate that approved usage of words can be established by the definition of a recognized dictionary....

Random House Dictionary of the English Language:

> assault ... N. 1: A violent attack; onslaught....

American Heritage Dictionary of the English Language:

> N. 1: a violent attack, either physical or verbal....

Webster's Third New International Dictionary

> 1: a violent attack with physical means (as blows or weapons)....

The common meaning of the word as reflected in these dictionary definitions and the ordinary understanding of people using our language is that an assault is an intentionally violent and hostile attack on another person.

The foregoing definitions are remarkably similar and convey the same meaning of the word "assault" in common English usage....

What is the plaintiff's alternative to the common meaning definition of "assault" in § 10-236a? In a very thorough brief the plaintiff first argues, without any support for the proposition advanced, that "the legislature most probably did not intend to use the word 'assault' in its strictest, most limiting definition. 'Assault' technically represents the interest in freedom from apprehension of a harmful or offensive, contact, as distinguished from the contact itself...."

The plaintiff then makes an argument that there is no intent requirement for civil assault in our state.... [Alternatively, plaintiff suggests that assault means criminal assault as defined in the penal code. Criminal assault similarly does not require intent.]

The definition of "assault" the plaintiff advocates forgets the audience the statute was aimed at — school administrators trying to meet budgets and run their schools and teachers concerned with their rights above and beyond workers' compensation. The word "assault" would have a common meaning for them as the word is ordinarily used — they would not be expected to reference civil case law and the entire penal code to find out how § 10-236a applies to them.

Furthermore, although ... the court ... does not base its decision on this observation the effect of legislation on the actions of those affected must be kept in mind. In other words if the strict definition of assault suggested by common usage of that word and ordinary meaning controls § 10-236a the schools would be expected to and the legislature might have thought it would be desirable for school districts to take certain steps to control violence prone students — special classes, identifying problem children, counseling, hallway monitoring, home tutoring etc. School districts could take a variety of steps to limit their exposure under this worthwhile act. If the broad definition of "assault" suggested by the plaintiff is adopted the only way school districts could protect themselves is by having schools become highly regimented places — negligent assault, would that include injury to a teacher by a twelve-year-old rambunctiously running down a hallway and bumping into him or her, how about the teacher walking through a merry game of tag during recess?

For all of the foregoing reasons the court concludes as previously indicated that an "assault" under § 10-236a means an intentionally violent and hostile attack on another person.

Notes and Questions

(1) *Is "Assault" a "Technical Word"?* The court didn't think so. Do you agree? Do lawyers and laypersons share a common definition of "assault?" Is it more or less likely that the legislature intended to use the ordinary meaning of "assault" as opposed to its legal meaning? *Compare Dickens v. Puryear*, 276 S.E.2d 325 (N.C. 1981) (holding that the term "assault" in a statute of limitations was intended in the legal sense).

(2) *Whose Perspective Counts?* According to this court, from whose perspective is ambiguity of a statute resolved? Does this audience make sense given that the statute was written by legislators, who are often lawyers?

(3) *Legislative History.* Note that the court began by lamenting that "the legislative history is of no direct help so this court must try to interpret the meaning of the word assault." Which approach does this court likely follow? Had the legislature provided guidance in a statement from a sponsor or a committee report, would this court have viewed its job as complete? Should it have? Has the court reversed the typical interpretative process?

(4) *Specialty Dictionaries.* There are countless specialty dictionaries: medical, engineering, scientific, and legal. Does the fact that many legislators are lawyers but fewer are doctors or scientists suggest that legal dictionaries should be preferred to ordinary dictionaries? To technical dictionaries? What about a technical term in a medical malpractice statute? Should the statute's context or audience matter more? Should words in a statute concerning the regulation of prescription drugs be interpreted in light of a medical dictionary or an ordinary dictionary? In other words, should it be the context of the statute or the intended audience that matters?

3. Identifying the Language at Issue

Litigators must be able to identify for a court the relevant language in a statute to be interpreted. In the cases below, notice how the two courts focus on different language in the same statute to reach opposite results on virtually identical facts.

Dixon v. Florida

812 So. 2d 595 (Fla. Dist. Ct. App. 2002)

PER CURIAM.

Richard L. Dixon appeals his convictions for forgery of a written instrument and driving without a valid driver's license. He argues that the trial court erred in denying his motion ... by which he sought to exclude, on the authority of section 316.650(9) the admission into evidence of a traffic citation issued to him....

Upon being stopped by a police officer following the commission of several traffic infractions, appellant provided a false name to the officer. That name was placed on the traffic citation, which appellant signed using the false name. When it was learned that appellant gave a false name, he was charged with forgery under section 831.01 and driving without a valid driver's license.... [A]ppellant sought to preclude the admission of the traffic citation into evidence. The trial court denied the motion, finding that the legislature could not have intended the exclusion of a traffic citation when the execution of the citation is the basis of the offense at trial. Appellant thereafter entered a plea of *nolo contendere,* reserving the right to appeal the issue of whether it was error to admit the traffic citation into evidence....

Florida courts have recognized that signing another person's name to a traffic citation constitutes a forgery. Nevertheless, section 316.650(9) provides that a traffic citation "shall not be admissible evidence in any trial." The statute contains no exceptions to this clear and unambiguous prohibition. It is a well-established principle of statutory interpretation that an unambiguous statute is not subject to judicial construction, no matter how wise it may seem to alter the plain language of the statute. Moreover, even where a court is convinced that the legislature really meant and intended something not expressed in the phraseology of the act, it will not deem itself authorized to depart from the plain meaning of the language which is free from ambiguity. Further, although courts may interpret a statute to give effect to discernable legislative intent even though such intent may contradict the strict language of the statute, here we have been presented with no basis to discern a legislative intent contrary to the unambiguous language of section 315.650(9)....

While following the unambiguous mandate of section 315.650(9) will make convictions for forgery of a traffic citation more difficult, the application of the plain and ordinary meaning of the words of the statute do not lead to either an unreasonable or ridiculous result. As the Florida Supreme Court stated in *Jett*:

> We trust that if the legislature did not intend the result mandated by the statute's plain language, the legislature itself will amend the statute at the next opportunity.

Accordingly, in view of the absolute mandatory terms of section 316.650(9), we conclude that the trial court erred in denying appellant's motion....

Maddox v. Florida
862 So. 2d 783 (Fla. Dist. Ct. App. 2003)

DAVIS, JUDGE.

Robert E. Maddox challenges his convictions and sentences for two counts of forgery, two counts of uttering forged instruments, and one count each of giving false information to a law enforcement officer and driving while license suspended or revoked. We affirm Maddox's convictions and sentences without comment but write to address the issue of the admissibility of the forged traffic citations at his trial.

A Polk County Deputy Sheriff stopped Maddox for an improper lane change. Upon being asked for his driver's license and proof of insurance, Maddox advised the deputy that he did not have his license or proof of insurance with him. The deputy then asked for his name and date of birth, in response to which Maddox said his name was Nathaniel Lewis Maddox and his date of birth was November 1, 1980. Based on this information, the deputy issued two citations in the name of Nathaniel Lewis Maddox—one for improper lane change and the other for failure to produce proof of insurance. When Maddox was hesitant to sign the citations, the deputy advised that failure to sign was a criminal offense. Maddox then signed the citations.

During the traffic stop, a second deputy arrived on the scene. The owner of the car ... gave permission for the deputies to search the vehicle. During the search, the second deputy found an identification card that identified Maddox as Robert Edwin Maddox. A license check for Robert Edwin Maddox showed that his driver's license was suspended.... Later, while in custody, Maddox volunteered that Nathaniel Maddox was his brother. Accordingly, Maddox was charged with two counts of forgery for signing the citations issued in the name of Nathaniel and two counts of uttering a forged instrument.

Maddox went to trial on the forgery and uttering counts.... He was found guilty as charged.

On appeal, Maddox argues that, pursuant to section 316.650(9) the trial court erred by admitting these traffic citations into evidence. In making this assertion, Maddox relies on the First District's opinion in *Dixon* ("Because the language of section 316.650(9) unambiguously provides that traffic citations are not admissible in any trial, we must reverse [appellant's forgery conviction]."). We, however, do not agree with the reasoning in *Dixon*....

[W]e do not believe the trial court erred in admitting the citations as evidence of the forgeries. Although section 316.650(9) does provide that traffic citations "shall not be admissible evidence in any trial," that statutory proscription does not apply to the facts of this case. Based on our reading of the statute, we conclude that the purpose of the statute is to protect the person to whom the citation is issued. Here, the citation was issued to a person the deputy believed to be Nathaniel Maddox; the deputy charged Nathaniel Maddox with two civil infractions. When the deputy learned that Maddox was, in fact, not Nathaniel Maddox, but rather Robert Maddox, he withdrew the charges against Nathaniel Maddox and retained the documents as evidence of the criminal offenses of forgery. Maddox misrepresented himself to be Nathaniel and signed the ticket to carry out the misrepresentation. Maddox was not on trial for either of the civil infractions, nor was Nathaniel Maddox. In fact, after the withdrawal of the citations, the charges of improper lane change and failure to show proof of insurance were no longer pending against anyone. Thus, the documents were not "citations" as contemplated by the statute, but rather were documentary evidence of Maddox's criminal conduct. Thus, the statute does not apply.

Accordingly, we affirm the trial court's ruling admitting the citations into evidence against Robert Maddox....

Notes and Questions

(1) *Which Language Mattered?* Which language did the *Dixon* court focus on? The *Maddox* court? Which court's holding was right? Could the legislature really have intended the result in *Dixon*? But if the legislature intended the result in *Maddox*, shouldn't the legislature have used clearer text?

(2) *Ambiguity?* We haven't yet studied ambiguity, but it means that reasonable people could give a statute two equally plausible meanings. When a statute is silent, is it ambiguous? Wasn't the statute here unambiguous and clear? Had the legislature not wanted any exceptions, how else could the legislature have said so? Should we expect legislatures to consider every possibility and specifically exclude those it does not want included?

(3) *Interpretative Approach.* Which approach did the *Dixon* court use? The *Maddox* court?

(4) *Later Action.* The Florida Supreme Court granted review of *Maddox* in mid 2004. *Maddox v. State*, 879 So. 2d 622 (Fla. 2004). How do you think the court ruled (*see* 923 So. 2d 442)?

Problem 3-1

You represent Tim Thompson, who has been charged with unlawfully attempting to sell marijuana in violation of the federal drug trafficking laws. A sentence-enhancing statute requires courts to impose a five year mandatory prison term on any person who, "during and in relation to any crime of violence or a drug trafficking crime, *uses or carries* a firearm." 18 U.S.C. §924(c)(1)(A) (emphasis added).

Tim tells you that as he was driving his truck to the drug sale police arrested him and searched his truck. In a locked glove compartment, the police discovered a handgun. During the plea proceeding, Tim admitted he was bringing the handgun "for protection in relation to" the drug sale but denied he had used it. Review the statutory and common law materials below and determine what arguments you can make on behalf of Tim that "uses or carries a firearm" does not apply to his case.

Problem Materials

18 U.S.C. §924(c)(1)(A) provides:

> [A]ny person who, during and in relation to any crime of violence or drug trafficking ... for which the person may be prosecuted in a court of the United States, uses or carries a firearm ... shall, in addition to the punishment provided for such crime of violence or drug trafficking crime—
>
> (i) be sentenced to a term of imprisonment of not less than 5 years;
>
> (ii) if the firearm is brandished, be sentenced to a term of imprisonment of not less than 7 years; and
>
> (iii) if the firearm is discharged, be sentenced to a term of imprisonment of not less than 10 years.

Dictionary definitions:

> "Use:" verb (used, using, uses) meaning: To put into service or apply for a purpose; employ. To avail oneself of; practice: *use caution.* To conduct oneself toward; treat or handle: "the peace offering of a man who once used you unkindly" (Laurence Sterne). To seek or achieve an end by means of; exploit: *used their highly placed friends to gain access to the president; felt he was being used by seekers of favor.* To take or consume; partake of: *She rarely used alcohol.*
>
> "Carry:" verb (carried, carrying, carries) meaning: To hold or support while moving; bear: *carried the baby in my arms; carrying a heavy backpack.* To take from one place to another; transport: *a train carrying freight; a courier carrying messages....* To serve as a means for the conveyance of; transmit: *pipes that carry waste water; a bridge that carries traffic between the two cities.* To communicate; pass on: *The news was carried by word of mouth to every settlement....*

B. Determining *Technical* Meaning

Generally, "[u]nless otherwise defined in the statute, or understood to have a technical or peculiar meaning in the law, every word or phrase of a statute will be given its plain and ordinary meaning." *Van Reken v. Darden, Neef & Heitsch*, 674 N.W.2d 731, 733 (Mich.

Ct. App. 2003). The word "conviction," for example, has a legal meaning distinct from its ordinary one. It is not always clear whether the legislature intended the technical or ordinary meaning, as the case below illustrates. Notice also how that determination is critical to the outcome of the case.

St. Clair v. Commonwealth

140 S.W.3d 510 (Ky. 2004)

[Per Three Justices]

A ... jury found Appellant, Michael D. St. Clair, guilty of murdering Frances C. Brady. At the subsequent capital sentencing proceeding, the jury found the presence of an aggravating circumstance and fixed Appellant's punishment at death....

[W]hile he was awaiting final sentencing for two (2) Oklahoma state Murder convictions, Appellant escaped from a jail ... accompanied by another inmate, Dennis Gene Reese ("Reese"). The two men fled ... Oklahoma for the suburbs of Dallas, Texas.... When Reese was subsequently arrested several months later in Las Vegas, Nevada, he confessed to his involvement in an ensuing crime spree.

According to Reese, after hiding out in Dallas for a few days, the men: (1) boarded a Greyhound bus bound for the Pacific Northwest but disembarked in Colorado, where Appellant kidnapped a man, Timothy Keeling ("Keeling"), and took his vehicle—again, a pickup truck—and Appellant and Reese began driving back towards Texas; (2) while driving through New Mexico ... Appellant used the stolen handgun to execute Keeling in the desert; (3) the men then drove Keeling's pickup truck to ... Kentucky, where Appellant kidnapped another man, Frances C. Brady ("Brady") and took his vehicle—another pickup truck; (4) the men then set fire to Keeling's pickup truck in order to destroy any incriminating evidence and Appellant used his handgun to execute Brady....

[T]he jury found Appellant guilty of Murder....

Appellant argues ... that he was entitled to a directed verdict of acquittal as to the aggravating circumstance because KRS 532.025(2)(a)(1) required that his "conviction for a capital offense" exist prior to the time of Brady's murder. Appellant argues that, although he had four (4) capital convictions for murders committed in Oklahoma by the time he came to trial in Kentucky, he did not have a "prior record of conviction for a capital offense" at the time he murdered Brady because final judgment and sentence had not yet been entered in two (2) of his Oklahoma murder cases and he had yet to stand trial in the others....

[I]n *Thompson v. Commonwealth, Ky.*, 862 S.W.2d 871 (1993), we reversed the appellant's death sentence because a murder conviction that remained on appeal had been used to prove the KRS 532.025(2)(a)(1) aggravating circumstance:

> ... The language in KRS 532.025(2)(a)(1) refers to an aggravator as being a "prior record of conviction." It has long been held by Kentucky courts that a "conviction, which of course means the final judgment" cannot be relied upon as a conviction if an appeal is being taken because "an appeal in a criminal case suspends the judgment, and this (sic) does not become final until a termination of the appeal." ...

Id. at 877.

The parties' positions on this interpretive question are in clear opposition as to whether KRS 532.025(2)(a)(1) requires that the "prior record of conviction for a capital offense" exist at the time of the present capital offense. Appellant emphasizes the past tense of "was committed" and cites *Thompson* in support of its [sic] claim that the Commonwealth can demonstrate the applicability of the KRS 532.025(2)(a)(1) aggravating circumstance only by proving that, at the time that a defendant committed the present offense of Murder or Capital Kidnapping, the defendant had exhausted all of his or her appeals under a preexisting final judgment of conviction for a capital offense. In contrast, the Commonwealth ... argues that, to satisfy its burden of proof as to the KRS 532.025(2)(a)(1) aggravating circumstance, it need only demonstrate that, at the time a capital sentencing proceeding is conducted, the defendant's criminal record contains a conviction for a capital offense.

Without question, the specific language utilized in an aggravating circumstance is critical to interpreting its scope....

Thus, as is the case in any issue of statutory construction, our responsibility is to ascertain and give effect to the intention of the legislature. In so doing, we are required by KRS 446.080(4) to construe words and phrases according to the common and approved use of language.

> The best way in most cases to ascertain such intent or to determine the meaning of the statute is to look to the language used, but no intention must be read into the statute not justified by the language. The primary rule is to ascertain the intention from the words employed in enacting the statute and not to guess what the Legislature may have intended but did not express. Resort must be had first to the words, which are decisive if they are clear.

[W]e find the verb tense and phraseology ... in KRS 532.025(2)(a)(1) to be unequivocal, i.e., "[t]he offense of murder or kidnapping *was committed by a person with* a prior record of conviction for a capital offense[.]" (emphasis added). We find KRS 532.025(2)(a)(1) susceptible to but one natural and reasonable construction: the aggravating circumstance is implicated only when the defendant has already been convicted of a capital offense prior to the commission of the present capital offense....

A second interpretative question remains, however, as to what level of finality is contemplated by "a prior record of conviction for a capital offense." We recognize that we stated in *Thompson* that "a 'conviction, which of course means the final judgment' cannot be relied upon as a conviction if an appeal is taken because 'an appeal in a criminal case suspends the judgment, and this (sic) does not become final until a termination of the appeal.'" In doing so, however, it appears that we quoted out-of-context the authority upon which we relied ... and overlooked nearly a century of jurisprudence from this Court which recognizes that the word "conviction" has a twofold meaning. One is the determination of the fact of guilt, as by the verdict of a jury. The other ... denotes the final judgment in the prosecution. The definition of "convict" or "conviction" ... has a meaning dual in nature: The word "conviction" has two meanings: its ordinary or popular meaning, which refers to a finding of guilt by plea or verdict, and its legal or technical meaning, which refers to the final judgment entered on plea or verdict of guilty....

Turning to that inquiry, we again find guidance in KRS 446.080(4): "(a)ll words and phrases shall be construed according to the common and approved use of language." As the Court of Appeals has observed, the ordinary or popular meaning of conviction refers to a finding of guilt by plea or verdict. Further, our rules of statutory construction presume that the legislature is aware of the state of the law at the time it enacts a statute.... We therefore find it significant that the General Assembly chose the phrase "prior record of conviction" in KRS 532.025(2)(a)(1) — a phrase that invokes the vernacular notion of a person's "criminal record" — instead of "judgment of conviction," which would have had not only a defined legal meaning but also a body of precedent ... interpreting it to mean a final judgment of conviction. Accordingly, we conclude that, for purposes of KRS 532.025(2)(a)(1), "prior record of conviction for a capital offense" includes a plea of guilty accepted by the trial court or a jury's or judge's verdict of guilty. To the extent that *Thompson* reaches a contrary holding, it is overruled.

In light of our construction of the KRS 532.025(2)(a)(1) ... we find that the ... trial court ... correctly denied Appellant's motion for a directed verdict of acquittal with respect to the KRS 532.025(2)(a)(1) aggravating circumstance. Although the final judgments were not entered in Appellant's first two Oklahoma Murder convictions until ... approximately six (6) weeks after Brady's murder, Appellant acknowledged ... that he had been convicted of those two (2) counts of Murder following a trial.... Because these two (2) murder convictions demonstrated that Brady was murdered by "a person with a prior record of conviction for a capital offense," the trial court correctly denied Appellant's motion for a directed verdict as to the aggravating circumstance....

KELLER, JUSTICE, Concurring in Part and Dissenting in Part.

I would hold that, if Appellant were to be found guilty upon remand for a new trial..., he should receive a sentence of imprisonment of between twenty (20) to fifty (50) years or life. In *Thompson v. Commonwealth*, this Court correctly interpreted KRS 532.025(2)(a)(1)'s "prior record of conviction for a capital offense" to mean a final judgment of conviction for a capital offense. By overruling *Thompson* and adopting a contrary and novel interpretation of the same language, today's opinion ... turns its back on common sense and its own rules of statutory construction. The Opinion of the Court concedes that the term "conviction" is inherently ambiguous and is susceptible to different interpretations, but then fails to apply the "rule of lenity" that requires us to give it the more lenient interpretation when faced with such ambiguity. The opinion correctly observes that KRS 446.080(4) states that "[a]ll words and phrases shall be construed according to the common and approved usage of language[.]" However, the statute continues further, "but technical words and phrases, and such others as may have acquired a peculiar and appropriate meaning in the law shall be construed according to such meaning." And, although the popular meaning of "conviction" may apply where rights of persons other than the "convict" are involved, in situations where legal disabilities, disqualifications, and forfeitures are to follow, the strict legal meaning is to be applied, absent some indication of contrary intent.... Today's Opinion of the Court interprets KRS 532.025(2)(a)(1)'s "prior record of conviction for a capital offense" language in a manner inconsistent with the technical meaning of "conviction" and thereby creates an anomaly of epic proportions where a non-final capital "conviction" would be insufficient to trigger [Persistent Felony Offender] enhancement, but sufficient to render a defendant death-eligible. The death penalty cannot be imposed simply because we or the jury believe the actions or motives of a particular defendant are deserving of capital punishment, and this Court must interpret the scope of KRS 532.025(2)(a)'s aggravating circumstance in the same manner that it interprets any legislative enactment — i.e., by applying the rules of statutory construction. A proper application of those rules demonstrates that the Commonwealth was unable to prove that Brady's murder "was committed by a person with a prior record of conviction for a capital offense." Accordingly, the trial court should have directed a verdict in Appellant's favor and instructed the jury to fix Appellant's punishment at a sentence of imprisonment between twenty (20) years to fifty (50) years or life....

Notes and Questions

(1) *Ordinary or Technical?* Did the majority conclude that the ordinary or technical meaning of the term "conviction" was intended? Did the dissent agree? With whom do you agree?

(2) *How Should Courts Decide Between Technical or Ordinary Meaning?* Should the ordinary meaning apply unless the legislature has expressly adopted a technical meaning in the statute? Or, should courts use the technical meaning if the statute is directed to a technical audience? If the technical meaning should be used, are tariffs on vegetables and fruits directed towards botanists, businessmen, or accountants?

(3) *Statutory Directive.* Both the majority and dissent turned to the statutory directive for guidance. The statutory directive here required the court "to construe words and phrases according to the common and approved use of language," but "technical words and phrases, and such others as may have acquired a peculiar and appropriate meaning in the law shall be construed according to such meaning." Do you find this directive enlightening as to whether the legislature intended the ordinary or technical meaning? What part of the directive did the majority focus on? The dissent? Which focus makes more sense?

Problem 3-2

C.J. Powers, Inc. seeks your advice regarding whether fresh rhubarb should be classified as a fruit or as a vegetable under the U.S. Tariff Act. Rhubarb is typically eaten either as a sweet sauce or in dessert pies. C.J. Powers, Inc. imports rhubarb from Canada and would prefer to pay the lower tariff amount charged for fruit. What do you advise?

Problem Materials

19 U.S.C. §751

Duty shall be paid on vegetables in their natural state at 50 per centum ad valorem....

19 U.S.C. §752.

Duty shall be paid on fruits in their natural state at 35 per centum ad valorem....

Dictionary Definitions:

Fruit: The edible, more or less succulent, product of a perennial or woody plant, consisting of the ripened seeds and adjacent tissues, or of the latter alone. In popular usage there is no exact distinction between a fruit and a vegetable, except where the latter consists of the stem, leaves, or root of the plant. Thus the apple, pear, orange, lemon, peach, plum, grape, banana, persimmon, pineapple, and most berries are generally recognized as fruits; the pea, bean, pumpkin, squash, eggplant, cucumber, etc., are vegetables; while the tomato, melon, and rhubarb are variously regarded.

Vegetable: any plant whose fruit, seeds, roots, tubers, bulbs, stems, leaves, or flower parts are used as food, as the tomato, bean, beet, potato, onion, asparagus, spinach, or cauliflower. Vegetables and fruits are sometimes loosely distinguished by the usual need of cooking the former for the use of man, while the latter may be eaten raw; but the distinction often fails, as in the case of quinces, barberries, and other fruits, and lettuce, celery, and other vegetables. Tomatoes if cooked are vegetables, if eaten raw are fruits.

Rhubarb: A vegetable, in the popular sense, is any part of a herbaceous plant commonly used for culinary purposes, and may consist of the root, as in the beet and turnip; the stem, as in the asparagus, celery, and rhubarb.

Nix v. Hedden
149 U.S. 304 (1893)

JUSTICE GRAY … delivered the opinion of the court.

The single question in this case is whether tomatoes, considered as provisions, are to be classed as "vegetables" or as "fruit," within the meaning of the tariff act of 1883.

The only witnesses called at the trial testified that neither "vegetables" nor "fruit" had any special meaning in trade or commerce different from that given in the dictionaries, and that they had the same meaning in trade to-day that they had in March, 1883.

The passages cited from the dictionaries define the word "fruit" as the seed of plaints, or that part of plaints which contains the seed, and especially the juicy, pulpy products of certain plants, covering and containing the seed. These definitions have no tendency to show that tomatoes are "fruit," as distinguished from "vegetables," in common speech, or within the meaning of the tariff act.

There being no evidence that the words "fruit" and "vegetables" have acquired any special meaning in trade or commerce, they must receive their ordinary meaning. Of that meaning the court is bound to take judicial notice, as it does in regard to all words in our own tongue; and upon such a question dictionaries are admitted, not as evidence, but only as aids to the memory and understanding of the court.

Botanically speaking, tomatoes are the fruit of a vine, just as are cucumbers, squashes, beans, and peas. But in the common language of the people, whether sellers or consumers of provisions, all these are vegetables which are grown in kitchen gardens, and which, whether eaten cooked or raw, are, like potatoes, carrots, parsnips, turnips, beets, cauliflower, cabbage, celery, and lettuce, usually served at dinner in, with, or after the soup, fish, or meats which constitute the principal part of the repast, and not, like fruits generally, as dessert.

The attempt to class tomatoes as fruit is not unlike a recent attempt to class beans as seeds, of which Mr. Justice Bradley, speaking for this court, said: "We do not see why they should be classified as seeds, any more than walnuts should be so classified. Both are seeds, in the language of botany or natural history, but not in commerce nor in common parlance. On the other hand in speaking generally of provisions, beans may well be included under the term 'vegetables.' As an article of food on our tables, whether baked or boiled, or forming the basis of soup, they are used as a vegetable, as well when ripe as when green. This is the principal use to which they are put. Beyond the common knowledge which we have on this subject, very little evidence is necessary, or can be produced."

Judgment affirmed.

Chapter 4

Beyond the Text: Absurdity, Ambiguity, and Scrivener's Error

What, if anything, comes after a court determines the ordinary meaning of the text? That central question occupies the next several chapters. First the good news: no matter which approach to statutory interpretation a court uses, if the plain meaning of the text is ambiguous, absurd, or contains a scrivener's error, the court will go beyond the text. Under every approach, a finding of one of these three things requires the court to look beyond the text for meaning. It opens the door for consideration of other sources of meaning. That issue is the subject of this chapter. We will see that beyond opening the door, however, there is disagreement.

This chapter focuses on the three universally recognized exceptions to the plain meaning rule: ambiguity, absurdity, and scrivener's error.* Suppose that the plain meaning of the statute lends itself to more than one plausible interpretation. What does a court do to resolve this ambiguity? Suppose instead that the plain meaning of the statute is clear, but that meaning simply makes no sense—it is absurd. What, if anything, should a court do? Or, assume the legislature simply made a mistake. Should a court correct the mistake? We will explore these somewhat related questions in this chapter. We will see that, when statutory language is ambiguous, absurd, or contains a scrivener's error, courts are generally willing to look beyond the text to determine meaning. They may disagree on what sources other than the text to consider, but they are almost all willing to go beyond the text under these circumstances.

Theoretical disagreements aside, you should realize what these principles mean to you as a lawyer: If the plain meaning of the text does not favor your client's position, then you need to be prepared to argue that the statute is ambiguous, absurd, contains a scrivener's error, or that under the court's approach, analysis does not stop with clear text. That is the hurdle we examine in this chapter, and also in the chapters that follow. These important philosophical and jurisprudential differences have important, perhaps outcome-determinative, practical lawyering applications.

---

* Authors' footnote: There is one other exception: the constitutional avoidance doctrine. We cover this exception later.

A. Ambiguity

Often, the statute at issue is not clear. Statutory language can be ambiguous. Defining "ambiguity" is somewhat difficult. This issue is far from academic. How a court defines ambiguity will directly impact you and your clients.

Let's start out by what ambiguity is not: "Ambiguous" does not mean "vague" or "broad" or "general." "Vehicles" is a very broad, vague, and general word. Its meaning is not, however, in the abstract, ambiguous.

Instead, ambiguity means that a statute can be read in two ways when applied to particular facts. For example, under one reading of a statute, there is liability, but under another reading, there is no liability. While some language theorists would no doubt contend that all language is ambiguous, the courts do not go so far.

Most courts state that statutes are ambiguous when two or more reasonable people disagree as to its meaning. It sounds right, doesn't it? But, think about that definition for a moment: any time there is a lawsuit over the meaning of a statute, unless the court finds that one party's interpretation was unreasonable, a court using that definition would have to find the statute ambiguous. What would that mean for the importance of text? Similarly, if "two reasonable people disagree" is the test, then won't every statutory interpretation decision where there is a dissent mean that the statute is ambiguous? In this regard, consider the fact that often the cases that the Supreme Court decides arise from circumstances where the appellate judges split not only over the application of the statute but the meaning of the text as well. A finding of ambiguity requires, like every judicial finding, that a majority of the judges believe that the statute is ambiguous. Thus, if only four of nine judges believe a statute is ambiguous, four is not enough to warrant a finding of ambiguity. Similarly, the fact that circuits split on the meaning is not enough for a court to hold that there is ambiguity. Thus, ambiguity is a narrower exception than it may appear.

Although "reasonable people disagree" is often stated as the test, we think that most courts are actually applying a higher standard. Some courts expressly require a higher threshold, saying that simply because two litigants or two judges disagree about what a statute means does not lead to a finding that the statute is ambiguous. They are correct: ambiguity in application means more than just that "two reasonable people's disagree." Instead, it probably means that the language is "equally susceptible to more than a single meaning." *Mayor of Lansing v. Mich. Pub. Serv. Comm'n*, 680 N.W.2d 840, 847 (Mich. 2004). In other words, ambiguous has to mean more than just two *reasonable* interpretations — it has to mean two *equally plausible* interpretations or some similar standard.

The Michigan Supreme Court explained why "that reasonable minds can differ" should not be the test for "ambiguity:"

> Especially in the context of the types of cases and controversies considered by this Court — those in which the parties have been the most determined and persistent, the most persuaded by the merits of their own respective arguments — it is extraordinarily difficult to conclude that reasonable minds cannot differ on the correct outcome. That is not, and has never been, the standard either for resolving cases or for ascertaining the existence of an ambiguity in the law. The law is not ambiguous whenever a dissenting (and presumably reasonable) justice would interpret such law in a manner contrary to a majority. Where a majority finds the law to mean one thing and a dissenter finds it to mean another,

neither may have concluded that the law is "ambiguous," and their disagreement by itself does not transform that which is unambiguous into that which is ambiguous. Rather, a provision of the law is ambiguous only if it irreconcilably conflicts with another provision, or when it is equally susceptible to more than a single meaning. In lieu of the traditional approach to discerning "ambiguity"—one in which only a few provisions are truly ambiguous and in which a diligent application of the rules of interpretation will normally yield a "better," albeit perhaps imperfect, interpretation of the law—the dissent would create a judicial regime in which courts would be quick to declare ambiguity and quick therefore to resolve cases and controversies on the basis of something other than the words of the law.

Id.

Is it possible that a judge's desire to look beyond the text might affect the breadth of that judge's definition of ambiguity? There may also be a contraction of "ambiguity" that is happening by design, and whose importance you should ponder. One reason for some courts' hesitancy to broadly define "ambiguity"—and perhaps a growing trend to narrow the circumstances in which a statute can be found ambiguous—is that a finding of ambiguity opens the door to consideration of extratextual sources, such as the purpose or legislative history, which some courts view dimly. "A finding of ambiguity, of course, enables an appellate judge to bypass traditional approaches to interpretation and either substitute presumptive rules of policy, or else to engage in a largely subjective and perambulatory reading of legislative history." *Id.* at 846.

The following opinion and notes explore the different approaches to ambiguity and the propriety of reliance on extratextual sources. Some judges believe reliance on extratextual sources is required; others believe it is improper. See if you can identify the approach to statutory interpretation used by the majority and dissent. How does their choice affect their willingness to resort to extratextual sources to resolve ambiguity?

Fla. Dep't of Revenue v. Piccadilly Cafeterias, Inc.
128 S.Ct. 2326 (2008)

Justice Thomas delivered the opinion of the Court.

Piccadilly was founded in 1944 and was one of the Nation's most successful cafeteria chains until it began experiencing financial difficulties in the last decade. On October 29, 2003, Piccadilly declared bankruptcy under Chapter 11 of the Bankruptcy Code, § 1101 *et seq.* (2000 ed. and Supp. V), and requested court authorization to sell substantially all its assets.... Piccadilly prepared to sell its assets as a going concern and sought an exemption from any stamp taxes* on the eventual transfer under § 1146(a) of the Code. The Bankruptcy Court conducted an auction in which the winning bidder agreed to purchase Piccadilly's assets for $80 million.

On January 26, 2004, as a precondition to the sale, Piccadilly entered into a global settlement agreement ... [which] dictated the priority of distribution of the sale proceeds among Piccadilly's creditors. On February 13, 2004, the Bankruptcy Court approved the

---

* Authors' footnote: To generate revenue, Florida requires that taxes be paid when parties transfer mortgages, deeds, notes, and other documents indicating indebtedness. These taxes are known as document stamp taxes.

proposed sale.... The court also ruled that the transfer of assets was exempt from stamp taxes under § 1146(a). The sale closed on March 16, 2004.

Piccadilly filed its ... Chapter 11 plan in the Bankruptcy Court on ... on July 31, 2004.... Before the Bankruptcy Court confirmed the plan, Florida filed an objection, seeking a declaration that the $39,200 in stamp taxes it had assessed on certain of Piccadilly's transferred assets fell outside § 1146(a)'s exemption because the transfer had not been "under a plan confirmed" under Chapter 11. On October 21, 2004, the bankruptcy court [denied the objection, and Florida appealed.]

The Court of Appeals for the Eleventh Circuit affirmed.... The Court of Appeals acknowledged that its holding conflicted with the approach taken by the Courts of Appeals for the Third and Fourth Circuits....

We granted certiorari to resolve the conflict among the Courts of Appeals as to whether § 1146(a) applies to preconfirmation transfers.

II

Section 1146(a), entitled "Special tax provisions," provides: "The issuance, transfer, or exchange of a security, or the making or delivery of an instrument of transfer *under a plan confirmed under Section 1146(a) of this title,* may not be taxed under any law imposing a stamp tax or similar tax." (Emphasis added.) Florida asserts that § 1146(a) applies only to postconfirmation sales; Piccadilly contends that it extends to preconfirmation transfers as long as they are made in accordance with a plan that is eventually confirmed....

A

Florida contends that § 1146(a)'s text unambiguously limits stamp-tax exemptions to postconfirmation transfers made under the authority of a confirmed plan. It observes that the word "confirmed" modifies the word "plan" and is a past participle, *i.e.,*"[a] verb form indicating past or completed action or time that is used as a verbal adjective in phrases such as *baked beans* and *finished work*." American Heritage Dictionary 1287 (4th ed.2000). Florida maintains that a past participle indicates past or completed action even when it is placed after the noun it modifies, as in "beans baked in the oven," or "work finished after midnight." Thus, it argues, the phrase "plan confirmed" denotes a "confirmed plan"—meaning one that has been confirmed in the past.

Florida further contends that the word "under" in "under a plan confirmed" should be read to mean "with the authorization of" or "inferior or subordinate" to its referent, here the confirmed plan. Florida points out that, in the other two appearances of "under" in § 1146(a), it clearly means "subject to." Invoking the textual canon that "'identical words used in different parts of the same act are intended to have the same meaning,'" Florida asserts the term must also have its core meaning of "subject to" in the phrase "under a plan confirmed." Florida thus reasons that to be eligible for § 1146(a)'s exemption, a transfer must be subject to a plan that has been confirmed subject to § 1129.... Florida concludes that a transfer made prior to the date of plan confirmation cannot be subject to, or under the authority of, something that did not exist at the time of the transfer—a confirmed plan.

Piccadilly counters that the statutory language does not unambiguously impose a temporal requirement. It contends that "plan confirmed" is not necessarily the equivalent of "confirmed plan," and that had Congress intended the latter, it would have used that language, as it did in a related Code provision. See § 1142(b) (referring to "any instrument required to effect a transfer of property dealt with by a confirmed plan"). Piccadilly also argues that "under" is just as easily read to mean "in accordance with." It observes that the variability of the term "under" is well-documented, noting that the American Heritage Dictionary 1395 (1976) provides 15 definitions, including "[i]n view of," "because of," "by virtue of," as well as "[s]ubject to the restraint ... of." Although "under" appears several times in §1146(a), Piccadilly maintains there is no reason why a term of such common usage and variable meaning must have the same meaning each time it is used, even in the same sentence. As an illustration, it points to §302(a) of the Bankruptcy Code, which states, "The commencement of a joint case under a chapter of this title constitutes an order for relief under such chapter." Piccadilly contends that this provision is best read as: "The commencement of a joint case *subject to the provisions of* a chapter of this title constitutes an order for relief *in* such chapter." Piccadilly thus concludes that the statutory text—standing alone—is susceptible of more than one interpretation.

While both sides present credible interpretations of §1146(a), Florida has the better one. To be sure, Congress could have used more precise language—*i.e.,*"under a plan *that has been* confirmed"—and thus removed all ambiguity. But the two readings of the language that Congress chose are not equally plausible: Of the two, Florida's is clearly the more natural. The interpretation advanced by Piccadilly ...—that there must be "some nexus between the pre-confirmation transfer and the confirmed plan" for §1146(a) to apply—places greater strain on the statutory text than the simpler construction advanced by Florida....

Although we agree with Florida that the more natural reading of §1146(a) is that the exemption applies only to postconfirmation transfers, ultimately we need not decide whether the statute is unambiguous on its face. Even assuming, *arguendo*, that the language of §1146(a) is facially ambiguous, the ambiguity must be resolved in Florida's favor. We reach this conclusion after considering the parties' other arguments, to which we now turn.

B

Piccadilly insists that, whatever the degree of ambiguity on its face, §1146(a) becomes even more ambiguous when read in context with other Bankruptcy Code provisions. Piccadilly asserts that if Congress had intended §1146(a) to apply exclusively to transfers occurring after confirmation, it would have made its intent plain with an express temporal limitation similar to those appearing elsewhere in the Code....

For its part, Florida argues that the statutory context of §1146(a) supports its position that the stamp-tax exemption applies exclusively to postconfirmation transfers. It observes that the subchapter in which §1146(a) appears is entitled, "POSTCONFIRMATION MATTERS." ...

We find it informative that Congress placed §1146(a) in a subchapter entitled, "POSTCONFIRMATION MATTERS." To be sure, a subchapter heading cannot substitute for the operative text of the statute. Nonetheless, statutory titles and section headings "'are tools available for the resolution of a doubt about the meaning of a statute.'" The placement of §1146(a) within a subchapter expressly limited to postconfirmation matters undermines Piccadilly's view that §1146(a) covers preconfirmation transfers.

But even if we were fully to accept Piccadilly's textual and contextual arguments, they would establish at most that the statutory language is ambiguous. They do not—and largely are not intended to—demonstrate that §1146(a)'s purported ambiguity should be resolved in Piccadilly's favor. Florida argues that various nontextual canons of construction require us to resolve any ambiguity in its favor. Piccadilly responds with substantive canons of its own. It is to these dueling canons of construction that we now turn.

C

Florida contends that even if the statutory text is deemed ambiguous, applicable substantive canons compel its interpretation of § 1146(a). Florida ... invokes the substantive canon ... that courts should "'proceed carefully when asked to recognize an exemption from state taxation that Congress has not clearly expressed.'" In light of this directive, Florida contends that § 1146(a)'s language must be construed strictly in favor of the States to prevent unwarranted displacement of their tax laws....

In response, Piccadilly contends that the federalism principle articulated in *Sierra Summit* does not apply where there is a "clear expression of an exemption from state taxation" overriding a State's authority to tax. In Piccadilly's view, that is precisely the case with regard to § 1146(a), which proscribes the imposition of stamp taxes and demonstrates Congress' intent to exempt a category of state taxation....

We agree with Florida that the federalism canon articulated in *Sierra Summit* and elsewhere obliges us to construe § 1146(a)'s exemption narrowly. Piccadilly's effort to evade the canon falls well short of the mark because reading § 1146(a) in the manner Piccadilly proposes would require us to do exactly what the canon counsels against. If we recognized an exemption for preconfirmation transfers, we would in effect be "'recogniz[ing] an exemption from state taxation that *Congress has not clearly expressed*'"—namely, an exemption for preconfirmation transfers. Indeed, Piccadilly proves precisely this point by resting its entire case on the premise that Congress has expressed its stamp-tax exemption in ambiguous language. Therefore, far from being inapposite, the canon is decisive in this case.

The canons on which Piccadilly relies are inapposite....

As for Piccadilly's assertion that reading § 1146(a) to allow preconfirmation transfers to be taxed while exempting others moments later would amount to an "absurd" policy, we reiterate that "'it is not for us to substitute our view of ... policy for the legislation which has been passed by Congress.'" That said, we see no absurdity in reading § 1146(a) as setting forth a simple, bright-line rule instead of the complex, after-the-fact inquiry Piccadilly envisions....

Lastly, to the extent the "practical realities" of Chapter 11 reorganizations are increasingly rendering postconfirmation transfers a thing of the past, it is incumbent upon the Legislature, and not the Judiciary, to determine whether § 1146(a) is in need of revision.

III

The most natural reading of § 1146(a)'s text, the provision's placement within the Code, and applicable substantive canons all lead to the same conclusion: Section 1146(a) affords a stamp-tax exemption only to transfers made pursuant to a Chapter 11 plan that has been confirmed. Because Piccadilly transferred its assets before its Chapter 11 plan was confirmed by the Bankruptcy Court, it may not rely on § 1146(a) to avoid Florida's stamp taxes. Accordingly, we reverse the judgment below and remand the case for further proceedings consistent with this opinion....

JUSTICE BREYER, with whom JUSTICE STEVENS joins, dissenting.

The Bankruptcy Code provides that the "transfer" of an asset "*under a plan confirmed under section 1129 of this title*, may not be taxed under any law imposing a stamp tax or similar tax." In this case, the debtor's reorganization "plan" provides for the "transfer" of assets. But the "plan" itself was not "confirmed under section 1129 of this title" (*i.e.*, the Bankruptcy Judge did not formally approve the plan) until *after* the "transfer" of assets took place.

Hence we must ask whether the time of transfer matters. Do the statutory words "under a plan confirmed under section 1129 of this title" apply only where a transfer takes place "under a plan" that at the time of the transfer *already has been* "confirmed under section 1129 of this title"? Or, do they also apply where a transfer takes place "under a plan" that *subsequently is* "confirmed under section 1129 of this title"? The Court concludes that the statutory phrase applies only where a transfer takes place "under a plan" that at the time of transfer *already has been* "confirmed under section 1129 of this title." In my view, however, the statutory phrase applies "under a plan" that at the time of transfer either *already has been* or *subsequently is* "confirmed." In a word, the majority believes that the time (pre- or post-transfer) at which the bankruptcy judge confirms the reorganization plan matters. I believe that it does not. (And construing the provision to refer to a plan that simply "is" confirmed would require us to read fewer words into the statute than the Court's construction, which reads the provision to refer only to a plan "that has been" confirmed.)

The statutory language itself is perfectly ambiguous on the point. Linguistically speaking, it is no more difficult to apply the words "plan confirmed" to instances in which the "plan" *subsequently is* "confirmed" than to restrict their application to instances in which the "plan" *already has been* "confirmed." But [the majority believes its reading is "clearly the more natural"].

Nor can I find any text-based argument that points clearly in one direction rather than the other. Indeed, the majority, after methodically combing the textualist beaches, finds that a comparison with other somewhat similar phrases in the Bankruptcy Code sheds little light. For example, on the one hand, if Congress thought the time of confirmation mattered, why did it not say so expressly as it has done elsewhere in the Code? On the other hand, if Congress thought the time of confirmation did *not* matter, why did it place this provision in a subchapter entitled "POSTCONFIRMATION MATTERS"?

The canons of interpretation offer little help. And the majority, for the most part, seems to agree. It ultimately rests its interpretive conclusion upon this Court's statement that courts "must proceed carefully when asked to recognize an exemption from state taxation that Congress has not clearly expressed." But when, as here, we interpret a provision the *express point of which* is to exempt some category of state taxation, how can the statement in *Sierra Summit* prove determinative? ... I suspect that the majority's reliance upon *Sierra Summit's* "canon" reflects no more than an effort to find the proverbial "any port" in this interpretive storm.

The absence of a clear answer in text or canons, however, should not lead us to judicial despair. Consistent with Court precedent, we can and should ask a further question: *Why* would Congress have insisted upon temporal limits? What reasonable *purpose* might such limits serve? In fact, the majority's reading of temporal limits in § 1146(a) serves *no reasonable congressional purpose at all.*

The statute's purpose is apparent on its face. It seeks to further Chapter 11's basic objectives: (1) "preserving going concerns" and (2) "maximizing property available to satisfy creditors." ... It furthers these objectives where, *e.g.*, asset transfers are at issue, by turning over to the estate (for the use of creditors or to facilitate reorganization) funds that otherwise would go to pay state stamp taxes on plan-related transferred assets. The requirement that the transfers take place pursuant to a reorganization "plan" that is "confirmed" provides the bankruptcy judge's assurance that the transfer meets with creditor approval and the requirements laid out in § 1129.

How would the majority's temporal limitation further these statutory objectives? It would not do so in any way. From the perspective of these purposes, it makes no difference whether a transfer takes place before or after the plan is confirmed. In both instances the exemption puts in the hands of the creditors or the estate money that would otherwise go to the State in the form of a stamp tax. In both instances the confirmation of the related plan assures the legitimacy (from bankruptcy law's perspective) of the plan that provides for the assets transfer....

[I]f the potential loss of stamp tax revenue threatens delay in implementing any such decision to sell, then creditors (or the remaining reorganized enterprise) could suffer far more serious harm. They could lose the extra revenues that a speedy sale might otherwise produce....

What conceivable reason could Congress have had for silently writing into the statute's language a temporal distinction with such consequences? The majority can find none. It simply says that the result is not "'absurd'".... I agree that the majority's interpretation is not absurd.... But I see no reason to adopt the majority's preferred construction (that only transfers completed after plan confirmation are exempt), where it conflicts with the statute's purpose.

Of course, we should not substitute "'*our view* of ... policy'" for the statute that Congress enacted. But we certainly should consider *Congress'* view of the policy for the statute it created, and that view inheres in the statute's purpose. "Statutory interpretation is not a game of blind man's bluff. Judges are free to consider statutory language in light of a statute's basic purposes." It is the majority's failure to work with this important tool of statutory interpretation that has led it to construe the present statute in a way that, in my view, runs contrary to what Congress would have hoped for and expected.

For these reasons, I respectfully dissent.

Notes and Questions

(1) *Plain Meaning.* Both sides argued that their interpretation of the language was the more plausible interpretation. What were their arguments? According to the majority, why was Florida's plain meaning interpretation "the more natural"?

(2) *The Different Views.* Did the majority and dissent disagree that the language was ambiguous or did they disagree about how to resolve any ambiguity? Assuming the latter, how did each side resolve the ambiguity? Which source or canon was most important to the majority? Which source or canon was most important to the dissent? Which argument did you find most convincing?

(3) *Federalism.* The majority cited *Sierra Summit* for the proposition that courts should not recognize an exemption from state taxation that Congress has not clearly expressed. Was the dissent correct to challenge the majority's reliance upon this canon as reflecting "no more than an effort to find the proverbial 'any port' in this interpretive storm"? Does the dissent convincingly counter this argument?

(4) *Approach.* Which approach did the majority take? The dissent? Do you think that the selected approach was outcome determinative here?

(5) *Absurdity.* Piccadilly argued that Florida's interpretation would be absurd. Why? Did the majority agree? The dissent? We turn to absurdity in the next section, but for now, do you find these arguments convincing?

(6) *What to Consider in Determining Whether a Statute is Ambiguous.* As noted above, there is some disagreement as to whether ambiguity is determined solely on the basis of

the plain meaning or whether other sources can be examined first. *Compare State v. Stenklyft*, 697 N.W.2d 769, 774 (Wis. 2005) ("To this end, absent ambiguity in a statute, we do not resort to extrinsic aids of interpretation and instead apply the plain meaning of the words of a statute in light of its textually manifest scope, context, and purpose."), *with Smith v. Yurkovsky*, 830 A.2d 743, 748 (Conn. 2003) ("In seeking to determine that meaning, we look to the words of the statute itself, to the legislative history and circumstances surrounding its enactment, to the legislative policy it was designed to implement, and to its relationship to existing legislation and common law principles governing the same general subject matter.... Thus, this process requires us to consider all relevant sources of the meaning of the language at issue, without having to cross any threshold or thresholds of ambiguity.") Indeed, courts disagree even on what is "intrinsic" and what is "extratextual."

This issue can be critical, of course. If legislative history may be considered in determining whether a statute is ambiguous, then statements from the legislature are appropriately considered, at least for the purpose of determining ambiguity. On the other hand, if only the plain meaning matters, then the legislative history is irrelevant. What approach would a textualist more likely take? An intentionalist? A purposivist?

Problem 4-1

You are a prosecutor for the Mercer District Attorney's office. The following case has just crossed your desk. Analyze whether you will bring child abandonment changes against Mr. Staton for abandoning any of his nine children. In doing so, determine whether the statute is ambiguous.

Claiming he could no longer care for them, Lee Staton dropped off his nine children at the emergency room in Mercer University Medical Center Wednesday night at 8 p.m. His wife, and the mother of nine kids, died from a brain aneurysm seventeen months ago, just days after delivering the youngest child. The oldest child was fifteen, the youngest was seventeen months. When he dropped the children off, Mr. Stanton said, "I was with her for seventeen years, and then she was gone. What was I going to do with nine kids? We raised them together. I don't think I can do it alone. I can't take care of them."

Staton said he was overwhelmed by his family responsibilities and had to quit his job. He said he couldn't pay the rent or utilities. "I was able to get the kids to a safe place before they were homeless," he said. He handed the nurse the children's birth certificates and said he was there to surrender his kids. "I hope they know I love them," he said. "I hope their future is better without me around them."

In the past, Staton and his wife were cited three years ago for child neglect, according to police records.

Problem Materials

Mercer Rev. Stat. § 157.010:

A BILL FOR AN ACT relating to children; to prohibit prosecution for leaving a child at a hospital; and to provide a duty for the hospital.

Be it enacted by the people of the State of Mercer,

Section 1: Findings & Purpose: The legislature finds that many parents of newborns and infant children are overwhelmed with the responsibilities of parenting children and have limited financial and social means to care for these children. For these reasons, some parents choose to abandon their children in unsafe ways. The purpose of this act is to protect the children of this state by allowing parents to give up their children in safe ways.

Section 2: No person shall be prosecuted for abandonment based solely upon the act of leaving a child in the custody of an employee on duty at a hospital licensed by the State of Mercer. The hospital shall promptly contact appropriate authorities to take custody of the child.

Governor's signing statement:

> I am delighted to sign this bill entitled "Mercer's Safe Haven Law." This Act will protect young children from the danger of unsafe abandonment. It's important to recognize the potential trauma abandonment can cause for children of any age. This bill is designed to encourage parents to act promptly and safely in choosing to give up their children.

Dictionary definition:

"Child": a noun meaning

1. a person between birth and full growth;

2. a son or daughter; an offspring;

3. a baby or infant;

4. a person who has not attained maturity or the age of legal majority;

5. a member of a tribe; descendant.

B. Absurdity (The Golden Rule Exception)

Counter-intuitively, the plain meaning of a statute may be "wrong." The so-called "Golden Rule Exception" to plain meaning recognizes that when the plain meaning leads to an absurd result, then the court must go beyond the plain meaning to see if other sources demonstrate that the absurd—but plain—meaning was not intended. *See City of Winder v. McDougald,* 583 S.E.2d 879, 882 (Ga. 2003) (Benham, J., dissenting). For example, in *Holy Trinity Church v. United States,* 143 U.S. 457, 459 (1892), the Court looked to legislative intent because "of the absurd results which follow from giving such [plain] meaning to the words." The reason to go beyond the words is that it is "unreasonable to believe that the legislator intended" the absurd result. *Id.*

In addition to the fact that language is inherently imperfect, the legislative process may lead to ambiguity or absurdity. For example, a statute "may be deliberately imprecise to accommodate political interests.... [C]areful draftsmanship is all too often absent; perhaps it is impossible in the crush of competing interests and activities that occur in the final moments of legislative enactments. Mistakes are made. In addition, a case that comes before the court ... may present an issue that was not in the minds of ... the legislators." John M. Walker, Jr., *Judicial Tendencies in Statutory Construction: Differing Views on the Role of the Judge,* 58 N.Y.U. Ann. Surv. Am. L. 203, 204 (2001).

Despite its near-universal acceptance, the Golden Rule Exception is not without controversy. If a court disregards the plain meaning of a statute for some other "non-absurd" meaning, isn't the court inappropriately "legislating"? Even if it is appropriate to ignore plain meaning, where should a court turn to discern meaning? Should a court be guided solely by *one* extrinsic source, such as the purpose or legislative history? Should it consider *all* extrinsic sources and give each the same weight? Different weight?

Another issue is the question of what exactly do judges mean when they say that a statute is absurd? There is no universally accepted definition of absurdity. Veronica M. Dougherty, *Absurdity and the Limits of Literalism: Defining the Absurd Result Principle in Statutory Interpretation*, 44 Am. U. L. Rev. 127, 133 (1994). Rather, judges often attempt to define absurdity by simply identifying, without explaining, other cases in which absurdity has been found. *Id.* at 139; *see, e.g., Pub. Citizen v. U.S. Dep't of Justice*, 491 U.S. 440, 470–71 (Kennedy, J., concurring). In the case that follows, identify the definition of absurdity the majority and dissent use. Do you agree with either definition? Should absurdity be relatively easy to establish (*i.e.*, the plain meaning is inconsistent with the statutory purpose) or fairly difficult (*i.e.*, the plain meaning is wholly irrational)? Does your answer to that question depend on your approach to interpretation?

A final question is how absurdity is determined. Does a court determine plain meaning and then determine whether there is absurdity? Assuming so, do the textual canons, legislative history, and purpose help resolve the absurdity? Or, does a court determine meaning by looking at all sources—including plain meaning, the textual canons, the legislative history, and purpose—and only then determine whether there is absurdity? The following case and the notes explore these and other issues: When is a statute absurd? When it is absurd, what sources can provide the "right" meaning?

Robbins v. Chronister

402 F.3d 1047 (10th Cir. 2005), *rev'd*,
435 F.3d 1238 (10th Cir. 2006) (en banc)

Seymour, Circuit Judge.

Plaintiff-appellee Ralph Robbins prevailed in a § 1983 civil rights suit against Larry Chronister, a police officer who violated his Fourth Amendment rights. The court awarded Mr. Robbins nominal damages of one dollar. Applying the Supreme Court's absurdity exception to the plain language rule of statutory construction, the court then held that the provision of the Prison Litigation Reform Act (PLRA) limiting attorney's fee awards in prisoner suits to 150% of the money judgment, 42 U.S.C. § 1997e(d), does not apply to civil rights claims arising before the victim of the constitutional violation was incarcerated. The court awarded Mr. Robbins reasonable attorney's fees under 42 U.S.C. § 1988 without regard to the PLRA's fee cap. We affirm.

In December 1995, Mr. Robbins was sitting in his car at a gas station ... waiting for a gas pump to become available.... Officer Chronister recognized Mr. Robbins ... and knew there were five outstanding traffic warrants for Mr. Robbins's arrest.... Officer Chronister approached ... Mr. Robbins's car with his baton in his hand. Officer Chronister identified himself and ordered Mr. Robbins out of the car. Mr. Robbins engaged the door locks of his car, put the car in reverse, and began to back towards Officer Chronister's truck. Officer Chronister swung his baton into the driver's side window of Mr. Robbins's car, shattering it, and attempted to pull Mr. Robbins from the car. Mr. Robbins managed to maneuver the car away from Officer Chronister's truck, and tried unsuccessfully to accelerate on the icy pavement. He skidded and spun around the parking lot, eventually fish-tailing toward Officer Chronister. As the car approached him, Officer Chronister shot at its hood and windshield. Mr. Robbins ultimately left the parking lot and wrecked the car a few blocks away. He was taken to the University of Kansas Medical Center for treatment of two gunshot wounds to the chest and one to his lower left side.

Mr. Robbins subsequently pled guilty to attempted aggravated assault on a law enforcement officer and was incarcerated at the Federal Correctional Institution in Greenville, Illinois. While he was incarcerated, he filed a *pro se* civil rights complaint under 42 U.S.C. § 1983, alleging that Officer Chronister used excessive force in their encounter in violation of Mr. Robbins's Fourth Amendment rights. The court appointed counsel for him. After conducting a three-day bench trial, the court ruled that Officer Chronister's use of deadly force in firing the shots was reasonable under the Fourth Amendment, but that shattering Mr. Robbins's driver's side window with a baton was not. Because Mr. Robbins was not physically injured as a result of the shattered window, the court awarded him nominal damages of one dollar, a determination he does not appeal.

Mr. Robbins filed a motion for attorney's fees pursuant to 42 U.S.C. § 1988(b), which allows the court to award a reasonable attorney's fee to the prevailing party in a § 1983 action. Officer Chronister opposed the motion, arguing the plain language of § 1997e(d) of the PLRA caps Mr. Robbins's attorney's fees at 150% of his damages, or $1.50, because he was a prisoner when he filed suit.... [T]he court declined to apply the PLRA cap. It held that applying the PLRA in these circumstances would produce an absurd result because Congress could not have intended the statute to apply to meritorious civil rights claims that arose prior to a prisoner's confinement.... [T]he court awarded Mr. Robbins $9,680 in fees and $915.16 in expenses. On appeal, Officer Chronister contends the court should have applied the PLRA and capped Mr. Robbins's attorney's fees at $1.50....

We review issues of statutory construction *de novo,* and begin by examining the plain language of the statute. The plainness or ambiguity of statutory language is determined by reference to the language itself, the specific context in which that language is used, and the broader context of the statute as a whole.

The PLRA provides in relevant part:

> (1) In any action brought by a prisoner who is confined to any jail, prison, or other correctional facility, in which attorney's fees are authorized under section 1988 of this title, such fees shall not be awarded, except to the extent that—

> > (A) the fee was directly and reasonably incurred in proving an actual violation of the plaintiff's rights protected by a statute pursuant to which a fee may be awarded under section 1988 of this title;....

> (2) Whenever a monetary judgment is awarded in an action described in paragraph (1), a portion of the judgment (not to exceed 25 percent) shall be applied to satisfy the amount of attorney's fees awarded against the defendant. If the award of attorney's fees is not greater than 150 percent of the judgment, the excess shall be paid by the defendant.

42 U.S.C. § 1997e(d) (footnotes omitted).... The statute's plain language indicates the 150% fee cap applies if (1) the plaintiff was "a prisoner" at the time he brought the action and (2) he was awarded attorney's fees pursuant to § 1988. It is undisputed that Mr. Robbins was a prisoner when he filed his § 1983 action and that the court entered judgment in his favor by awarding him one dollar in nominal damages and reasonable attorney's fees pursuant to § 1988(b). Under the plain language rule ... therefore, the fee cap contained in § 1997e(d) would apply ... limiting the award to $1.50.

Statute

If the language of a statute is clear in its application, the general rule is that we are bound by it. Nevertheless, where applying the plain language would produce an absurd and unjust result which Congress could not have intended, we need not apply the language in such a fashion. This is because interpretations of a statute which would produce absurd results are to be avoided if alternative interpretations consistent with the legislative purpose are available. This absurdity exception to the plain language rule is consistent with the doctrine that the function of the courts ... is to construe ... statutory language so as to give effect to the intent of Congress.

Although the absurdity doctrine is "exceptional" in character, we have applied it where construing the plain language of a statute would produce an illogical result....

Turning to application of the PLRA in this case, and as we discuss below, it is clear that Congress intended to curb frivolous lawsuits brought by prisoners relating to the conditions and circumstances of their incarceration. Conversely, Congress gave no indication of any intent to impose a fee limitation on *pre-incarceration civil rights claims* brought by plaintiffs who *subsequently* become prisoners and file their action while in prison. The PLRA's legislative history is silent as to civil rights claims arising prior to incarceration, and Congress could have addressed this issue expressly had it so intended.

The PLRA was attached as a rider to an omnibus appropriations act and apparently was not subjected to committee markup or extensive hearings. Cases have noted the paucity of information available in the PLRA's legislative history for divining Congress's intent, but the unmistakable purpose of the legislation was to limit the rapidly increasing number of frivolous prisoner claims arising from alleged prison-related civil rights violations.... As one court has explained:

> Although the legislative history regarding the PLRA is sparse, Congress's general purpose in passing the act is relatively clear. According to Senator Hatch, the PLRA "will help bring relief to a civil justice system overburdened by frivolous prisoner lawsuits.... Our legislation will also help restore balance to *prison conditions litigation* and will ensure that Federal court orders are limited to remedying actual violations of prisoners' rights...." 141 Cong. Rec. S14408-01, *S14418 (daily ed. Sept. 27, 1995) (statement of Sen. Hatch). *See also* 141 Cong. Rec. S7498-01, *S7526 (daily ed. May 25, 1995) (statement of Sen. Kyl) (PLRA "will deter frivolous inmate lawsuits. Statistics compiled by the Administrative Office of the U.S. Courts show that inmate suits are clogging the courts and draining precious judicial resources"); *id.*, at *S7524 (statement of Sen. Dole) ("Frivolous lawsuits filed by prisoners tie up the courts, waste valuable judicial and legal resources, and affect the quality of justice enjoyed by the law-abiding population.").

Zehner v. Trigg, 952 F.Supp. 1318, 1324–25 (S.D.Ind.1997) (emphasis added). The Supreme Court has cautioned against construing a statute literally where the clause in question was added on the Senate floor and the legislative history gave no indication that Congress intended the broad reading the plain language would indicate.

We, of course, do not quibble with Congress's legislative judgment that too many frivolous lawsuits and appeals are filed by prisoners; indeed, our own docket is heavy with prison litigation....

Our society has long recognized the importance of preventing and deterring civil rights violations.... Moreover, because the law recognizes the importance to organized society that those rights be scrupulously observed and every individual's civil rights are equally valuable regardless of ability to hire an attorney to pursue their vindication, Congress intended for attorney's fees to be awarded in civil rights cases regardless of the amount of damages....

Constitutional claims arising *before* the events causing the plaintiff's incarceration are unrelated to prison confinement. Nor does a pre-existing constitutional claim fall into the category of "frivolous prisoner litigation" that Congress was trying to discourage by its passage of the PLRA. As evidenced by the statute's limited legislative history, it was frivolous confinement cases Congress was attempting to deter....

We apply the Supreme Court's absurdity exception to the PLRA's plain language because there is no indication Congress intended to limit an award of attorney's fees to a civil rights plaintiff simply because he crossed the threshold of a prison before filing his lawsuit. Failing to distinguish between pre-incarceration cases and post-incarceration cases would lead to absurd results we are not persuaded Congress intended when it passed the PLRA. This narrow absurdity exception will not undercut Congress's purpose of curbing frivolous prison litigation. The PLRA fee cap will still fully apply to cases "brought by a prisoner who is confined to any jail, prison, or other correctional facility," § 1997e(d)(1), where the claims are based on violations that arise during a prisoner's incarceration. By distinguishing temporally between these cases and those concerning constitutional violations that occurred prior to an individual's period of imprisonment, we give effect to Congress's intent without being overinclusive.

In sum, we hold that it would be absurd to limit Mr. Robbins's attorney's fees merely because he happened to file his pre-existing constitutional claim while he was in prison. We therefore affirm.

HARTZ, CIRCUIT JUDGE, dissenting.

… What I cannot agree with … is the majority's view that it would be absurd to think Congress wished to apply § 1997e(d) to suits alleging preconfinement misconduct.

We have said that an interpretation of a statute is absurd if it leads to results so gross as to shock the general moral or common sense. Applying § 1997e(d) here does not come close to meeting that standard.

It is worth remembering that 42 U.S.C. § 1988, which provides for attorney-fee awards in civil-rights litigation, is a departure from the American Rule, under which the losing party is not required to reimburse the prevailing party's attorney fees. Concerned that the prospect of attorney-fee awards was encouraging the high volume of frivolous prisoner litigation burdening the courts and defendants, Congress reduced the incentive, restricting recovery of attorney fees to no more than 150% of the damages awarded, thereby encouraging only suits likely to recover substantial damages. According to the majority opinion it would be absurd to reduce the incentives for prisoners to file suits alleging preconfinement civil-rights violations. But it seems to me eminently reasonable.

The likely reason why prisoners file so many groundless suits is that they have so much time, time to file suits alleging preconfinement misconduct as well as suits concerning prison conditions. This explains why § 1997e(d) looks to the status of the plaintiff when suit is filed (is the plaintiff a prisoner?) not the nature of the civil-rights claim. Not only is the provision inapplicable to suits filed before incarceration that allege preconfinement misconduct, but it also is inapplicable to suits filed after release that allege unlawful prison conditions. If it makes sense to try to reduce the volume of frivolous prisoner litigation regarding prison conditions by restricting attorney-fee awards, it also makes sense to use the same means to try to reduce the volume of frivolous prisoner litigation alleging preconfinement misconduct.

The majority opinion's reliance on congressional floor debate is unpersuasive. The perils of relying on that source for interpreting statutory language are well-known. But even when relied upon, floor debate has been used only to indicate what Congress meant by certain language. I do not see how floor debate could show that a particular interpretation of statutory language would be absurd; it would, at most, show that the interpretation was not the intended one. The absurdity doctrine, however, requires more than a showing that the statutory language does not mean what Congress intended; it requires a showing that it would have been absurd for Congress to have intended what the statute says....

I would reverse the judgment below and remand with instructions to award an attorney fee of $1.50. I can certainly sympathize with an attorney appointed by the court who is not compensated for the services rendered. But this could occur even under the majority's rule, as when the prisoner loses entirely or the appointment is for a prison-conditions lawsuit. The remedy, however, would be to have the attorney paid with court funds, not to impose an obligation on the defendant contrary to an unambiguous, non-absurd statute.

Notes and Questions

(1) *Is Legislative History Relevant to a Finding of Absurdity?* Was the absurdity apparent solely from the text of the statute? The question of whether a court should look beyond the text as part of determining absurdity is a critical philosophical and practical question. How might textualists address that issue? Would purposivists or intentionalists disagree?

(2) *Absurd or Not?* Does the question of whether the statute was absurd in the case turn on what the judge thought the purpose of the statute was? Look at the statute carefully. Was the purpose to limit lawsuits brought by people in prison or to limit lawsuits brought by people challenging prison conditions? What did the majority think the purpose of this statute was? The dissent? If you believe the dissent's version of the purpose of the statute, then is the plain meaning absurd? Who was right? In answering that question, consider this: whether a person's attorneys' fees are capped turns on whether they are in jail when they bring the suit, not on whether they bring suit because of the conditions of their incarceration. If you conclude that purpose should be considered in determining whether language is absurd, then what does that mean for a textualist?

(3) *Purpose from Legislative History?* The plain meaning of the statute clearly barred recovery of more than $1.50 in attorney's fees in this case. The dissent took the majority to task for defining the purpose of the statute as to deter litigation over prison conditions as opposed to suits by prisoners. Look at the language quoted by the majority for its support. Isn't that language ambiguous, at best, with respect to whether the purpose was only to limit suits about prison conditions?

(4) *Doesn't the Majority Just Disagree with Congress's Language?* Normally, courts say that a statute is not "absurd" simply because the court thinks the statute reflects a poor policy choice. *E.g., Mayor of Lansing v. Mich. Pub. Serv. Comm'n,* 680 N.W.2d 840 (Mich. 2004). Isn't that precisely what the majority did here? In rehearing the case *en banc*, the court adopted the dissent's approach. *Robbins v. Chronister,* 435 F.3d. 1238 (10th Cir. 2006)(en banc).

(5) *Supreme Court's Use of the Absurdity Doctrine.* In recent years, the Supreme Court has relied on the absurdity doctrine at least five times to depart from a plain reading of the text. *Clinton v. City of New York,* 524 U.S. 417, 428–29 (1998) (invoking doctrine to expand meaning of "individuals" to include corporations as those who could seek expe-

dited review under Line Item Veto Act); *United States v. X-Citement Video, Inc.*, 513 U.S. 64, 69 (1994) (holding it would be absurd to apply term "knowingly" only to relevant verbs in criminal statute and not to elements of the crime concerning minor age of participant and sexually explicit nature of material); *Burns v. United States*, 501 U.S. 129, 135–37 (1991) (relying on absurdity to hold that district courts may not depart upward from sentencing range established by Sentencing Guidelines without first notifying parties of court's intent to depart); *Pub. Citizen v. U.S. Dep't of Justice*, 491 U.S. 440, 454–55 (1989) (relying on absurdity, in part, to interpret Federal Advisory Committee Act "federal advisory committee" narrowly); *Green v. Bock Laundry Mach. Co.*, 490 U.S. 504, 509–11 (1989) (some justices reasoned that it would be absurd not to apply FED. R. EVID. 609(a)(1) to civil as well as criminal defendants). As we noted, a finding of absurdity is necessary before a textualist-oriented court will go beyond the text. Do five relatively recent cases from the Supreme Court sound like the doctrine is expansive or narrow?

(6) *Textualism.* Consider the tension between the Golden Rule Exception and textualism. The Golden Rule Exception allows courts to rely on extrinsic sources when the text leads to absurd results. Under that circumstance, courts may ignore the text and peruse extratextual sources for the meaning of the statute. Does the Golden Rule Exception undermine textualism?

(7) *Purposivism.* As part of the process of interpretation, purposivists analyze the text and also ask what evil, or mischief, the statute was designed to remedy, and they seek to give a meaning to the text that furthers that goal. Thus, right from the start and without need to rely on the Golden Rule Exception to do so, purposivists look to extratextual sources along with the text. Similarly, intentionalists look to the legislative history, along with the text, right from the start and without a threshold requirement of ambiguity or absurdity. Does the existence of the Golden Rule Exception suggest that purposivism and intentionalism are "better" than textualism?

(8) *Absurdity Doctrine as Undermining Plain Meaning?* A recent academic debate has centered on whether the absurdity doctrine undermines separation of powers. As one professor summarized the critique, "the exercise of judicial discretion to temper the harsh results that are occasionally mandated by applying general rules to particular circumstances conflicts with the constitutional structure and principles of separation of powers." Glen Staszewski, *Avoiding Absurdity*, 81 IND. L.J. 1001, 1008 (2006). Does it respond to this argument to say that a reasonable legislature could not have intended a harsh result, or does it simply beg the question?

Problem 4-2

In late August 2005, while answering a disturbance call, police officers went to the home of Lillian Sands. Upon entering, they found five people, including Ms. Sands and Anthony Baker, a juvenile. There was a bench warrant for the arrest of Baker for failing to appear at trial on burglary charges. Burglary is a felony. Ms. Sands knew about the burglary charge; Baker had lived at the Sands' residence for some time. Police officers had gone to the Sands' house looking for Baker on several occasions between May and August, and Ms. Sands stated that she did not know Baker's whereabouts. The investigation also revealed that Baker's mother reported him as a runaway and that Ms. Sands is not related to Baker.

Analyze whether Ms. Sands can be prosecuted for harboring a felon under Mercer Rev. Stat. § 30-22-4. Note that juveniles who commit "delinquent acts" are "delinquent offenders." "Felon" is not defined in § 30-22-4, but is defined in another statute. What are

Ms. Sands' strongest argument(s) that applying the statute to the facts of her case would be absurd? What are the State's strongest argument(s) that applying the statute to the facts of her case would not be absurd? Ignore the rule of lenity.

Problem Materials

Mercer Rev. Stat. § 30-22-1: Findings

> Harboring anyone who has committed a crime is not in the state's interest. And harboring will likely be more successful if the felon knows that someone intends to help him or her. The consequences of harboring rest on society, which has strong interest in enforcement of its laws.

Mercer Rev. Stat. § 30-22-4: Harboring a Felon

> Harboring or aiding a felon consists of any person who knowingly conceals any felon or gives such person any other aid, knowing that he or she has committed a felony, with the intent that he or she escape or avoid arrest, trial, conviction, or punishment. In a prosecution under this section it shall not be necessary to aver, nor on the trial to prove, that the principal felon has been either arrested, prosecuted, or tried. Whoever commits harboring or aiding a felon is guilty of a fourth degree felony.

Mercer Rev. Stat. § 32A-2-3. Definitions: As used in a separate act entitled: the Child Delinquency Act:

> A. "Delinquent act" means an act committed by a child that would be designated as a crime under the law if committed by an adult;
>
> B. "Delinquent offender" means a child who has committed a delinquent act;
>
> C. "Felony" means an act committed by an adult that has been designated as a crime under the laws of this state;
>
> D. "Felon" means anyone who has committed a felony;
>
> E. "Child" for purposes of this code section only includes people between the ages of 7 and 17, unless found after hearing to be triable as an adult.

C. Scrivener's Error

Sometimes a legislature errs when it drafts or amends a statute. The ensuing error, called a scrivener's error, creates ambiguity in the statute: Should the statute be interpreted as written or as intended? This exception to the plain meaning rule permits judges "to correct" the error, but the exception is limited.

When statutes contain an obvious clerical or typographical error, judges will correct that scrivener's error. *U.S. Nat'l Bank of Or. v. Indep. Ins. Agents of Am., Inc.*, 508 U.S. 439, 462 (1993) (correcting misplaced punctuation); *United States v. Coatoam*, 245 F.3d 553, 557 (6th Cir. 2001) (correcting an incorrect cross-reference to another section in the statute); *United States v. Scheer*, 729 F.2d 164 (2nd Cir. 1984) (changing the word "request" to "receipt" where language in statute provided that a certificate would be furnished "upon *request* of the ... request"). These statutes each contained a relatively obvious error—one due to inattention or oversight. Yet, the scrivener's error exception to the plain meaning rule is a narrow one. A court should not turn to this exception simply because the court believes that an error might have been made. "It is beyond [a court's] province to rescue Congress from its drafting errors, and to provide for what [it] might think ... is the preferred result." *United States v. Granderson*, 511 U.S. 39, 68 (1964)(Kennedy, J., concurring). Rather, a court should only fix obvious drafting errors. In the case that follows, is there an obvious error?

Koons Buick Pontiac GMC, Inc. v. Nigh

543 U.S. 50 (2004)

Justice GINSBURG delivered the opinion of the Court.

The meaning of a subparagraph in a section of the Truth in Lending Act (TILA or Act), 15 U.S.C. § 1601 et seq., is at issue in this case....

Less-than-meticulous drafting of the 1995 amendment created an ambiguity....

As originally enacted in 1968, the Act provided for statutory damages of twice the finance charge in connection with the transaction, except that recovery could not be less than $100 or greater than $1,000. The original civil-liability provision stated:

"(a) [A]ny creditor who fails in connection with any consumer credit transaction to disclose to any person any information required under this chapter to be disclosed to that person is liable to that person in an amount ... of

"(1) twice the amount of the finance charge in connection with the transaction, except that liability under this paragraph shall not be less than $100 nor greater than $1,000...."

In 1974, Congress amended TILA's civil-liability provision, 15 U.S.C. § 1640(a), to allow for the recovery of actual damages in addition to statutory damages.... Congress reworded the original statutory damages provision to limit it to individual actions, moved the provision from § 1640(a)(1) to § 1640(a)(2)(A), and retained the $100/$1,000 brackets on recovery. In order to account for the restructuring of the statute, Congress changed the phrase "under this paragraph" to "under this subparagraph." The amended statute provided for damages in individual actions as follows:

"(a) [A]ny creditor who fails to comply with any requirement imposed under this chapter ... is liable to such person in an amount equal to the sum of—

"(1) any actual damage sustained by such person as a result of the failure;

"(2)(A) in the case of an individual action twice the amount of any finance charge in connection with the transaction, except that the liability under this subparagraph shall not be less than $100 nor greater than $1,000...."

[I]n 1976 ... [,] Congress inserted a clause into § 1640(a)(2)(A) setting statutory damages for individual actions relating to consumer leases at 25% of the total amount of monthly payments under the lease. Again, Congress retained the $100/$1,000 brackets on statutory damages. The amended § 1640(a)(2)(A) provided for statutory damages equal to

"(2)(A)(i) in the case of an individual action twice the amount of any finance charge in connection with the transaction, or (ii) in the case of an individual action relating to a consumer lease ... 25 per centum of the total amount of monthly payments under the lease, except that the liability under this subparagraph shall not be less than $100 nor greater than $1,000...."

[C]ourts consistently held that the $100/$1,000 limitation remained applicable to all consumer financing transactions, whether lease or loan.

In 1995, Congress amended [the statute again]. The 1995 amendment, which gave rise to the dispute in this case, added a new clause (iii) at the end of § 1640(a)(2)(A), setting a $200 floor and $2,000 ceiling for statutory damages in an individual action relating to a closed-end credit transaction "secured by real property or a dwelling." These closed-end real estate loans, formerly encompassed by clause (i), had earlier been held subject to the $100/$1,000 limitation. Section 1640(a), as amended in 1995, thus provides for statutory damages equal to

> "(2)(A)(i) in the case of an individual action twice the amount of any finance charge in connection with the transaction, (ii) in the case of an individual action relating to a consumer lease … 25 per centum of the total amount of monthly payments under the lease, except that the liability under this subparagraph shall not be less than $100 nor greater than $1,000, or (iii) in the case of an individual action relating to a credit transaction not under an open end credit plan that is secured by real property or a dwelling, not less than $200 or greater than $2,000…."

… On February 4, 2000, respondent Bradley Nigh attempted to purchase a used 1997 Chevrolet Blazer truck from petitioner Koons Buick Pontiac GMC. Nigh traded in his old vehicle and signed a buyer's order and a retail installment sales contract reflecting financing to be provided by Koons Buick. Koons Buick could not find a lender to purchase an assignment of the payments owed under the sales contract and consequently restructured the deal to require a larger down payment. On February 25, after Koons Buick falsely told Nigh that his trade-in vehicle had been sold, Nigh signed a new retail installment sales contract. Once again, however, Koons Buick was unable to find a willing lender. Nigh ultimately signed, under protest, a third retail installment sales contract.

Nigh later discovered one reason why Koons Buick had been unable to find an assignee for the installment payments due under the second contract: That contract contained an improperly documented charge of $965 for a Silencer car alarm Nigh never requested, agreed to accept, or received. Nigh made no payments on the Blazer and returned the truck to Koons Buick.

On October 3, 2000, Nigh filed suit against Koons Buick alleging, among other things, a violation of TILA. Nigh sought uncapped recovery of twice the finance charge, an amount equal to $24,192.80. Koons Buick urged a $1,000 limitation on statutory damages under § 1640(a)(2)(A)(i). The District Court held that damages were not capped at $1,000, and the jury awarded Nigh $24,192.80 (twice the amount of the finance charge).

A divided panel of the Fourth Circuit affirmed.…

Statutory construction is a "holistic endeavor." "A provision that may seem ambiguous in isolation is often clarified by the remainder of the statutory scheme—because the same terminology is used elsewhere in a context that makes its meaning clear, or because only one of the permissible meanings produces a substantive effect that is compatible with the rest of the law." In this case, both the conventional meaning of "subparagraph" and standard interpretive guides point to the same conclusion: The $1,000 cap applies to recoveries under clause (i).

Congress ordinarily adheres to a hierarchical scheme in subdividing statutory sections. This hierarchy is set forth in drafting manuals prepared by the legislative counsel's offices in the House and the Senate. The House manual provides:

> "To the maximum extent practicable, a section should be broken into—

"(A) subsections (starting with (a));

"(B) paragraphs (starting with (1));

"(C) subparagraphs (starting with (A));

"(D) clauses (starting with (i))...."

Congress followed this hierarchical scheme in drafting TILA. The word "subparagraph" is generally used to refer to a subdivision preceded by a capital letter, and the word "clause" is generally used to refer to a subdivision preceded by a lower case Roman numeral. Congress applied this hierarchy in § 1640(a)(2)(B), which covers statutory damages in TILA class actions and states: "[T]he total recovery *under this subparagraph* (3) shall not be more than the lesser of $500,000 or 1 per centum of the net worth of the creditor...." (Emphasis added.) In 1995, Congress plainly meant "to establish a more generous minimum and maximum" for closed-end mortgages. On that point, there is no disagreement. Had Congress simultaneously meant to repeal the longstanding $100/$1,000 limitation on § 1640(a)(2)(A)(i), thereby confining the $100/$1,000 limitation solely to clause (ii), Congress likely would have flagged that substantial change. At the very least, a Congress so minded might have stated in clause (ii): "liability under this clause."

The statutory history resolves any ambiguity whether the $100/$1,000 brackets apply to recoveries under clause (i). Before 1995, clauses (i) and (ii) set statutory damages for the entire realm of TILA-regulated consumer credit transactions. Closed-end mortgages were encompassed by clause (i). As a result of the addition of clause (iii), closed-end mortgages are subject to a higher floor and ceiling. But clause (iii) contains no other measure of damages. The specification of statutory damages in clause (i) of twice the finance charge continues to apply to loans secured by real property as it does to loans secured by personal property. Clause (iii) removes closed-end mortgages from clause (i)'s governance only to the extent that clause (iii) prescribes $200/$2,000 brackets in lieu of $100/$1,000.[9] ...

It would be passing strange to read the statute to cap recovery in connection with a closed-end, real-property-secured loan at an amount substantially lower than the recovery available when a violation occurs in the context of a personal-property-secured loan or an open-end, real-property-secured loan. The text does not dictate this result; the statutory history suggests otherwise; and there is scant indication Congress meant to change the well-established meaning of clause (i).

For the reasons stated, the judgment of the Court of Appeals for the Fourth Circuit is reversed, and the case is remanded for further proceedings consistent with this opinion.

JUSTICE SCALIA, dissenting.

The Court views this case as a dispute about the meaning of "subparagraph" in 15 U.S.C. § 1640(a)(2)(A). I think it involves more than that.... The ultimate question here is not the meaning of "subparagraph," but the scope of the exception which contains that term. When is "liability under this subparagraph" limited by the $100/$1,000 brackets? In

---

9. The dissent's reading, we note, hinges on an assumed alteration in Congress' design, assertedly effected by the bare addition of "(iii)" and the transposition of "or." If Congress had not added "(iii)" when it raised the cap on recovery for closed-end mortgages, the meaning of the amended text would be beyond debate. The limitations provision would read: "except that the liability under this subparagraph shall not be less than $100 nor greater than $1,000, or in the case of an individual action relating to a credit transaction not under an open end credit plan that is secured by real property or a dwelling, not less than $200 or greater than $2,000."

answering that question, I would give dispositive weight to the structure of §1640(a)(2)(A), which indicates that the exception is part of clause (ii) and thus does not apply to clause (i)....

The structure of subparagraph (A) provides the best indication of whether the exception is part of clause (ii). In simplified form, the subparagraph reads: "(i)..., (ii)..., or (iii)...." Clauses (i), (ii), and (iii) are separated by commas, and an "or" appears before clause (iii). It is reasonable to conclude that the exception—which appears between "(ii)" and the comma that precedes "or (iii)"—is part of clause (ii). In fact, the Court admits in passing that the exception appears "*in* clause (ii)." Yet the Court's holding necessarily assumes that the exception somehow stands outside of clause (ii)—someplace where its reference to "subparagraph" can have a different effect than "clause" would. The Court effectively requires the exception to be either part of clauses (i) and (ii) simultaneously, or a part of subparagraph (A) that is not within any of the individual clauses. The legislative drafting manuals cited by the Court, reveal how unnatural such an unanchored subdivision would be.

In its second step, the Court notes that, before 1995, the exception was generally read as applying to both clauses (i) and (ii). But the prior meaning is insufficient to reveal the meaning of the current version.... [T]he placement of the exception "at the end of (A)" used to "indicat[e] that it was meant to refer to the whole of (A)." That inference, however, is no longer available, since Congress eliminated the "or" between clauses (i) and (ii) and added clause (iii). If the "or" were still there, it might just be possible to conceive of clauses (i) and (ii) as a sub-list to which the exception attached as a whole. But one simply does not find a purportedly universal exception at the end of the second item in a three-item list....

In its ... final step, the Court asserts that it would be "anomalous" for liability to be "uncapped by the [$1,000] limit" when real property secures an open-end loan but capped by the $2,000 limit when it secures a closed-end loan, and that it would be "passing strange" for damages to be "substantially lower" under clause (iii) than under clause (i). The lack of a $1,000 limit does not, of course, make liability under clause (i) limitless. In all cases under clause (i), the damages are twice the finance charge, and the 1-year statute of limitations, 15 U.S.C. §1640(e), naturally limits the amount of damages that can be sought.

More importantly, Congress would have expected the amounts financed (and thus the finance charges) under clause (i) to be generally much lower than those under clause (iii). In cases (like this one) where loans are not secured by real property, the amount financed can be no greater than $25,000....

As the Court noted earlier this year: "If Congress enacted into law something different from what it intended, then it should amend the statute to conform it to its intent. It is beyond our province to rescue Congress from its drafting errors, and to provide for what we might think is the preferred result." I would apply the exception only to the clause with which it is associated and affirm the judgment of the Court of Appeals.

Notes and Questions

(1) *Drafting Error?* What was the scrivener's, or drafting, error in this case? How did the majority and dissent "fix" the error, if at all?

(2) *Should Structure Be Dispositive?* The majority essentially ignored the structure of the statute, while the dissent found it dispositive. Should structure be so critical? Does the fact that the statute had been amended four times affect your answer?

(3) *Which Words Were Being Interpreted?* The majority stated that it was interpreting the word "subparagraph:" specifically, did "subparagraph" mean clauses (i) and (ii), or did

it mean just clause (ii)? The dissent suggested that the ultimate question was "the scope of the exception, which contains that term," and looked to the structure, including Congress's use of commas and the word "or," to resolve the issue.

(4) *Who Should Correct Drafting Errors?* The dissent noted: "It is beyond our province to rescue Congress from its drafting errors, and to provide for what we might think is the preferred result." Did the majority simply correct a drafting error to reach a preferred result? Or, did the majority more accurately discern the intent of the legislature by looking beyond the text? If it is clear that Congress intended one result, but drafted the statute poorly, what is the appropriate role of the court: to hold Congress to its words or to interpret the words as Congress intended?

(5) *Statutory Approach.* This case clearly illustrates how the judges' approach to interpretation dictates the outcome. Because the majority was willing to look broadly for Congressional intent, it found that Congress did not intend what the text said. In contrast, Justice Scalia, following textualism, concluded that the text meant what it said despite other evidence to the contrary. Interestingly, Justice Thomas, also text-focused, joined the majority. In doing so, Justice Thomas wrote separately:

> If the text were clear, resort to anything else would be unwarranted.... But I agree with the Court that § 1640(a)(2)(A) is ambiguous ... because on its face it is susceptible of several plausible interpretations.... The statutory history of § 1640(a)(2)(A) resolves this ambiguity.... [Justice Thomas recounts the various versions of the statute and that prior to 1995, the $100–$1,000 bracket applied to both clause (i) and (ii)]. Congress's 1995 amendment did not materially alter the text of § 1640(a)(2)(A)(i) or (ii).... The only substantive change that amendment wrought was the creation of clause (iii), which established a higher $2,000 cap on damages for a very specific set of credit transactions.... By so structuring the amendment, Congress evinced its intent to address only the creation of a different limit for a specific set of transactions.

Did Justice Thomas look to extrinsic or intrinsic sources to resolve the ambiguity created by the drafting error?

Justice Rehnquist joined Justice Kennedy's concurring opinion, which also found the text ambiguous:

> The Court properly chooses not to rest its holding solely on the words of the statute.... That means that examination of other interpretive resources, including predecessor statutes, is necessary for a full and complete understanding of congressional intent. This approach is fully consistent with cases in which, because the statutory provision at issue had only one plausible textual reading, we did not rely on such sources. In the instant case, the Court consults extratextual sources and, in my view, looking to these materials confirms the usual interpretation of the word "subparagraph."

How, if at all, did the two concurrences differ? If they did not, then why do you think the justices wrote separately?

D. Ambiguous or Absurd?

The following case is frequently considered to be an absurdity case. Is that correct: Was absurdity found, was ambiguity found, or did the majority find neither?

Green v. Bock Laundry Mach. Co.
490 U.S. 504 (1989)

Justice Stevens delivered the opinion of the Court.

This case presents the question whether Rule 609(a)(1) of the Federal Rules of Evidence requires a judge to let a civil litigant impeach an adversary's credibility with evidence of the adversary's prior felony convictions....

While in custody at a county prison, petitioner Paul Green obtained work-release employment at a car wash. On his sixth day at work, Green reached inside a large dryer to try to stop it. A heavy rotating drum caught and tore off his right arm. Green brought this product liability action against respondent Bock Laundry Co. (Bock), manufacturer of the machine. At trial Green testified that he had been instructed inadequately concerning the machine's operation and dangerous character. Bock impeached Green's testimony by eliciting admissions that he had been convicted of conspiracy to commit burglary and burglary, both felonies. The jury returned a verdict for Bock. On appeal Green argued that the ... impeaching evidence [should have been excluded]. The Court of Appeals ... affirmed....

[C]riticism of [cases that have admitted impeachment evidence] is longstanding and widespread. Our task in deciding this case, however, is not to fashion the rule we deem desirable but to identify the rule that Congress fashioned. We begin by considering the extent to which the text of Rule 609 answers the question before us. Concluding that the text is ambiguous with respect to civil cases, we then seek guidance from legislative history and from the Rules' overall structure.

Federal Rule of Evidence 609(a) provides:

> General Rule. For the purpose of attacking the credibility of a witness, evidence that the witness has been convicted of a crime shall be admitted if elicited from the witness or established by public record during cross-examination but only if the crime (1) was punishable by death or imprisonment in excess of one year under the law under which the witness was convicted, and the court determines that the probative value of admitting this evidence outweighs its prejudicial effect to the defendant....

By its terms the Rule requires a judge to allow impeachment of any witness with prior convictions for felonies not involving dishonesty "only if" the probativeness of the evidence is greater than its prejudice "to the defendant." It follows that impeaching evidence detrimental to the prosecution in a criminal case "shall be admitted" without any such balancing.

The Rule's plain language commands weighing of prejudice to a defendant in a civil trial as well as in a criminal trial. But that literal reading would compel an odd result in a case like this. Assuming that all impeaching evidence has at least minimal probative value, and given that the evidence of plaintiff Green's convictions had some prejudicial effect on his case—but surely none on defendant Bock's—balancing according to the strict language of Rule 609(a)(1) inevitably leads to the conclusion that the evidence was admissible. In fact, under this construction of the Rule, impeachment detrimental to a civil plaintiff always would have to be admitted.

No matter how plain the text of the Rule may be, we cannot accept an interpretation that would deny a civil plaintiff the same right to impeach an adversary's testimony that it grants to a civil defendant. The Sixth Amendment ... guarantees a criminal defendant certain fair trial rights not enjoyed by the prosecution.... In contrast, civil litigants in federal court share equally the protections of the Fifth Amendment's Due Process Clause. Given liberal federal discovery rules, the inapplicability of the Fifth Amendment's protection against self-incrimination, and the need to prove their case, civil litigants almost always must testify in depositions or at trial. Denomination as a civil defendant or plaintiff, moreover, is often happenstance based on which party filed first or on the nature of the suit. Evidence that a litigant or his witness is a convicted felon tends to shift a jury's focus from the worthiness of the litigant's position to the moral worth of the litigant himself. It is unfathomable why a civil plaintiff—but not a civil defendant should be subjected to this risk. Thus ... as far as civil trials are concerned, Rule 609(a)(1) "can't mean what it says."

Out of this agreement flow divergent courses, each turning on the meaning of "defendant." The word might be interpreted to encompass all witnesses, civil and criminal, parties or not. It might be read to connote any party offering a witness, in which event Rule 609(a)(1)'s balance would apply to civil, as well as criminal, cases. Finally, "defendant" may refer only to the defendant in a criminal case. These choices spawn a corollary question: must a judge allow prior felony impeachment of all civil witnesses as well as all criminal prosecution witnesses, or is Rule 609(a)(1) inapplicable to civil cases, in which event Rule 403 would authorize a judge to balance in such cases? Because the plain text does not resolve these issues, we must examine the history leading to enactment of Rule 609 as law....

[The Court analyzed the legislative history in some detail and concluded that "a defendant" in Rule 609 should be interpreted to mean "a criminal defendant." Thus, it held that the rule does not apply in civil litigation.]

In summary, we hold that Federal Rule of Evidence 609(a)(1) requires a judge to permit impeachment of a civil witness with evidence of prior felony convictions regardless of ensuant unfair prejudice to the witness or the party offering the testimony. Thus no error occurred when the jury in this product liability suit learned through impeaching cross-examination that plaintiff Green was a convicted felon. The judgment of the Court of Appeals is

Affirmed.

JUSTICE SCALIA, concurring in the judgment.

We are confronted here with a statute which, if interpreted literally, produces an absurd, and perhaps unconstitutional, result. Our task is to give some alternative meaning to the word "defendant" in Federal Rule of Evidence 609(a)(1) that avoids this consequence....

I think it entirely appropriate to consult all public materials, including the background of Rule 609(a)(1) and the legislative history of its adoption, to verify that what seems to us an unthinkable disposition (civil defendants but not civil plaintiffs receive the benefit of weighing prejudice) was indeed unheard of, and thus to justify a departure from the ordinary meaning of the word "defendant" in the Rule. For that purpose, however, it would suffice to observe that counsel have not provided, nor have we discovered, a shred of evidence that anyone has ever proposed or assumed such a bizarre disposition....

The meaning of terms on the statute books ought to be determined, not on the basis of which meaning can be shown to have been understood by a larger handful of the Members of Congress; but rather on the basis of which meaning is (1) most in accord with context and ordinary usage, and thus most likely to have been understood by the whole Congress which voted on the words of the statute (not to mention the citizens subject to it), and (2) most compatible with the surrounding body of law into which the provision must be integrated—a compatibility which, by a benign fiction, we assume Congress always has in mind. I would not permit any of the historical and legislative material discussed by the Court, or all of it combined, to lead me to a result different from the one that these factors suggest.

I would analyze this case, in brief, as follows:

(1) The word "defendant" in Rule 609(a)(1) cannot rationally (or perhaps even constitutionally) mean to provide the benefit of prejudice-weighing to civil defendants and not civil plaintiffs. Since petitioner has not produced, and we have not ourselves discovered, even a snippet of support for this absurd result, we may confidently assume that the word was not used (as it normally would be) to refer to all defendants and only all defendants.

(2) The available alternatives are to interpret "defendant" to mean (a) "civil plaintiff, civil defendant, prosecutor, and criminal defendant," (b) "civil plaintiff and defendant and criminal defendant," or (c) "criminal defendant." Quite obviously, the last does least violence to the text. It adds a qualification that the word "defendant" does not contain but, unlike the others, does not give the word a meaning ("plaintiff" or "prosecutor") it simply will not bear. The qualification it adds, moreover, is one that could understandably have been omitted by inadvertence—and sometimes is omitted in normal conversation ("I believe strongly in defendants' rights"). Finally, this last interpretation is consistent with the policy of the law in general and the Rules of Evidence in particular of providing special protection to defendants in criminal cases....

I am frankly not sure that, despite its lengthy discussion of ideological evolution and legislative history, the Court's reasons for both aspects of its decision are much different from mine. I respectfully decline to join that discussion, however, because it is natural for the bar to believe that the juridical importance of such material matches its prominence in our opinions—thus producing a legal culture in which, when counsel arguing before us assert that "Congress has said" something, they now frequently mean, by "Congress," a committee report; and in which it was not beyond the pale for a recent brief to say the following: "Unfortunately, the legislative debates are not helpful. Thus, we turn to the other guidepost in this difficult area, statutory language."

For the reasons stated, I concur....

JUSTICE BLACKMUN with whom JUSTICE BRENNAN and JUSTICE MARSHALL join, dissenting.

Federal Rule of Evidence 609(a) has attracted much attention during its relatively short life. This is due in no small part to its poor and inartful drafting. As noted by the majority, the Rule's use of the word "defendant" creates inescapable ambiguity. The majority concludes that Rule 609(a)(1) cannot mean what it says on its face. I fully agree.

I fail to see, however, why we are required to solve this riddle of statutory interpretation by reading the inadvertent word "defendant" to mean "criminal defendant." I am persuaded that a better interpretation of the Rule would allow the trial court to consider the risk of prejudice faced by any party, not just a criminal defendant. Applying the balancing provisions of Rule 609(a)(1) to all parties would have prevented the admission of unnecessary and inflammatory evidence in this case and would prevent other similar unjust results until Rule 609(a) is repaired, as it must be. The result the Court reaches today, in contrast, endorses "the irrationality and unfairness," of denying the trial court the ability to weigh the risk of prejudice to any party before admitting evidence of a prior felony for purposes of impeachment....

It may be correct, as Justice Scalia notes in his opinion concurring in the judgment, that interpreting "prejudicial effect to the defendant" to include only "prejudicial effect to [a] criminal defendant," and not prejudicial effect to other categories of litigants as well, does the "least violence to the text," if what we mean by "violence" is the interpolation of excess words or the deletion of existing words. But the reading endorsed by Justice Scalia and the majority does violence to the logic of the only rationale Members of Congress offered [in the legislative history] for the Rule they adopted....

As I see it, therefore, our choice is between two interpretations of Rule 609(a)(1), neither of which is completely consistent with the Rule's plain language. The majority's interpretation takes protection away from litigants—*i.e.*, civil defendants—who would have every reason to believe themselves entitled to the judicial balancing offered by the Rule. The alternative interpretation—which I favor—also departs somewhat from the plain language, but does so by extending the protection of judicial supervision to a larger class of litigants—*i.e.*, to all parties. Neither result is compelled by the statutory language or the legislative history, but for me the choice between them is an easy one. I find it proper, as a general matter and under the dictates of Rule 102, to construe the Rule so as to avoid "unnecessary hardship." ...

This case should have been decided on the basis of whether the Bock Laundry Machine Company designed and sold a dangerously defective machine without providing adequate warnings. The fact that Paul Green was a convicted felon, in a work-release program at a county prison, has little, if anything, to do with these issues. We cannot know precisely why the jury refused to compensate him for the sad and excruciating loss of his arm, but there is a very real possibility that it was influenced improperly by his criminal record. I believe that this is not a result Congress conceivably could have intended, and it is not a result this Court should endorse.

As the majority concludes otherwise, my hope is that Rule 609(a)(1) will be corrected without delay, preferably into a form that allows judicial oversight over, at the least, the use of any felony conviction that does not bear directly on a witness' honesty. It is encouraging that some efforts in this direction appear to be underway and that the damage Congress caused by its poor draftsmanship soon may be undone.

I respectfully dissent.

Notes and Questions

(1) *Ambiguity or Absurdity?* This case is frequently cited as illustrating absurdity. Which Justices found it absurd? Why was the ordinary meaning "absurd" to the concurring justice but "ambiguous" and "odd" to the majority and dissenting justice? Given the fact that the majority looked at legislative history without first finding ambiguity or absurdity, do you think the majority used a textualist approach?

(2) *Disagreement over Meaning.* What sources did the majority use to resolve the statute's meaning? The concurrence? The dissent? The concurrence agreed with the conclusion reached by the majority, but disagreed in its rationale. Explain why this disagreement was important.

(3) *The Choices.* The majority interpreted (is "rewrote" the right word?) the statute to allow conviction evidence only if a court determined that the probative value of ad-

mitting the evidence outweighed its prejudicial effect to a *criminal defendant;* the dissent, in contrast, to a *party.* The majority's interpretation makes no sense in a civil case, where there are no criminal defendants. Does the dissent's interpretation make more sense?

(4) *Another Approach.* Judge Frank Easterbrook has suggested another option: "What makes us think that Rule 609 applies to civil cases?" Frank H. Easterbrook, *What Does Legislative History Tell Us?* 66 CHI.-KENT L. REV. 441, 443 (1991). He suggested that the "jarring reference" to "the defendant" in the rule suggests that the rule was only meant to apply in criminal cases. He then pointed to evidence in the legislative history to support his interpretation. *Id.* Thus, even Judge Easterbrook, a strong advocate of textualism, finds a role for legislative history when the plain meaning of a statute is absurd (or ambiguous).

(5) *What if?* Suppose the legislative history in *Bock Laundry* showed that every draft of Rule 609, except for the last one, had contained "criminal" before "defendant" and, further, that every committee report and other reference in the legislative history reflected the appropriateness of weighing prejudice in criminal, but not civil, cases. Would it still make sense to reject legislative history? *See* John M. Walker, Jr., *Judicial Tendencies in Statutory Construction: Differing Views on the Role of the Judge,* 58 N.Y.U. ANN. SURV. AM. L. 203, 232 (2001) (concluding that this constitutes a proper use of legislative history). What would the concurrence have said about it?

(6) *Pending Amendment.* At the time *Bock Laundry* was before the Court, a proposed amendment to Rule 609(a) was pending. After the decision, the amendment was adopted: the relevant portion of Rule 609(a), as amended, now provides:

> a. General Rule. — For purposes of attacking the creditability of a witness,
>
> > (1) evidence that a witness other than an accused has been convicted of a crime shall be admitted, subject to Rule 403 ... and evidence that an accused has been convicted of such a crime shall be admitted if the court determines that the probative value of admitting this evidence outweighs its prejudicial effect to the accused....

FED. R. EVID. 609(a). Should the Court have considered the pending amendment as relevant to its decision? Does this amendment show that the majority, dissent, or Judge Easterbrook was right after all? Or, does it show nothing about who was correct?

Problem 4-3

Your client, Lyndsey Hearst, has been charged with driving under the influence of a controlled substance.

According to the police report, the authorities received a call around midnight Saturday, June 14, about someone riding a horse down Main Street. Passing cars had to avoid the horse and rider. Many almost hit the horse. Responding to the call, an officer found your client on horseback and tried to stop her. She wouldn't stop. She kept riding the horse and, in fact, rammed the police car. After ramming the car with the horse, she tried to run away. She tried to jump off the horse, but caught her foot in a stirrup. The officer then took her into custody and found she had crystal methamphetamine, a small amount of marijuana, pills, and a small pipe. She later tested positive for both methamphetamines and marijuana.

Analyze whether your client would likely be convicted of the charge under the following statute.

Mercer Rev. Stat § 32-5A-191: Driving a motor vehicle while under influence of alcohol, controlled substances, etc.

a. Purpose: To make Mercer safe for all citizens who use its roadways, the general assembly finds that mixing any form of drugs or alcohol and driving any means of transportation is dangerous and will not be tolerated.

(b) A person shall not drive or be in actual physical control of any vehicle while:

(1) There is 0.08 percent or more by weight of alcohol in his or her blood;

(2) Under the influence of alcohol,

(3) Under the influence of a controlled substance to a degree that renders him or her incapable of driving safely.

Chapter 5

Determining the Meaning of the Text: Punctuation and Grammar

Not only does the plain-meaning rule "presuppose[] the ordinary usage of words ... [it] relies on accepted punctuation and syntax...." *Occhino v. Grover*, 640 N.W.2d 357, 359 (Minn. Ct. App. 2002). The plain-meaning rule "relies on conventional rules of grammar." *Advantage Capital Mgmt. v. Northfield*, 664 N.W.2d 421, 425 (Minn. Ct. App. 2003). Thus, in this chapter, we turn to the use of punctuation and grammar to determine meaning. You will see that these intrinsic sources matter much less than you might expect.

As with many areas of the law, there is a general rule that applies in most cases; some specific rules that apply in unique situations; and a few "quirks" that are opposite of what grammar might dictate. We address each below.

A. Punctuation & Grammar: The General Rule

The strict English rule presumed that punctuation was irrelevant for the very practical reason that members of the English parliament did not write the punctuation: clerks did. *See generally* Raymond B. Marcin, *Punctuation and the Interpretation of Statutes,* 9 Conn. L. Rev. 227 (1977). In contrast, legislators in the United States write statutes, including punctuation, so punctuation and grammar matter. Consequently, in the United States, a "legislature is presumed to know the meaning of words and the rules of grammar, and the only way the court is advised of what the legislature intends is by giving the generally accepted construction, not only to the phraseology of an act, but to the manner in which it is punctuated." *State v. Bodden*, 877 So. 2d 680, 685 (Fla. 2004); *see U.S. Nat'l Bank of Or. v. Indep. Ins. Agents of Am., Inc.,* 508 U.S. 439, 455 (1993) (excerpted below) ("Statutory construction is a holistic endeavor and, at a minimum, must account for a statute's full text, language[,] as well as punctuation, structure, and subject matter.")

As a consequence of the presumption that legislators know and use punctuation accurately, "an act should be read as punctuated unless there is some reason to do otherwise." 2A Statutes and Statutory Construction § 47.15 at p. 264 (6th ed. 2000 Norman Singer ed.). But,

> [p]unctuation is a most fallible standard by which to interpret a writing; it may be resorted to, when all other means fail; but the Court will first take the in-

strument by its four corners, in order to ascertain its true meaning; if that is apparent on judicially inspecting the whole, the punctuation will not be suffered to change it.

Ewing v. Burnet, 36 U.S. (11 Pet.) 41 (1837). The following case illustrates the general rule and its corollary: when there is a reason to ignore punctuation, courts will ignore it. Be sure that you discern the general punctuation rule as you read this case. As for the factual background, it is very challenging to understand. Should you wish for this level of factual detail, turn to the notes following the case. We include a detailed summary of the legislative background there.

U.S. Nat'l Bank of Or. v. Indep. Ins. Agents of Am., Inc.
508 U.S. 439 (1993)

JUSTICE SOUTER delivered the opinion of the Court.

Almost 80 years ago, Congress authorized any national bank "doing business in any place the population of which does not exceed five thousand inhabitants ... [to] act as the agent for any fire, life, or other insurance company." [12 U.S.C. § 92; otherwise known as section 92]. The 1952 edition of the Code, however, omitted the insurance provision, with a note indicating that Congress had repealed it in 1918....

Despite the absence of section 92 from the Code, Congress has assumed that it remains in force, on one occasion actually amending it....

Though the appearance of a provision in the current edition of the United States Code is "prima facie" evidence that the provision has the force of law, it is the Statutes at Large that provides the "legal evidence of laws," and despite its omission from the Code section 92 remains on the books if the Statutes at Large so dictates....

[The issue is whether Congress located section 92 in section 5202 or in section 13 of the 1913 Federal Reserve Act.]

[Respondents'] argument that section 92 is no longer in force ... is simply stated: [the Federal Reserve Act enacted section 13 and amended section 5202. Section 5202 was amended again in 1916. This amendment] placed section 92 in ... § 5202.... [Then, in 1918, the legislature again amended section 5202, but in doing so, the legislature omitted section 92. Under traditional rules of statutory construction, material omitted on reenactment is deemed repealed. W]e conclude with petitioners that the 1916 Act placed section 92 not in ... § 5202 but in § 13 of the Federal Reserve Act; since the 1918 Act did not touch § 13, it did not affect, much less repeal, section 92.

A reader following the path of punctuation of the 1916 Act would no doubt arrive at the opposite conclusion, that the statute added section 92 to ... § 5202.... The unavoidable inference from familiar rules of punctuation is that the 1916 Act placed section 92 in ... § 5202.

A statute's plain meaning must be enforced, of course, and the meaning of a statute will typically heed the commands of its punctuation. But a purported plain-meaning analysis based only on punctuation is necessarily incomplete and runs the risk of distorting a statute's true meaning. Along with punctuation, text consists of words living "a communal existence," in Judge Learned Hand's phrase, the meaning of each word informing the others and all in their aggregate tak[ing] their purport from the setting in which they are used. Over and over we have stressed that in expounding a statute, we must not be guided by a single sentence or member of a sentence, but look to the provisions of the whole law, and to its object and policy. No more than isolated words or sentences is punctuation alone a reliable guide for discovery of a statute's meaning. Statutory construction is a holistic endeavor, and, at a minimum, must account for a statute's full text, language as well as punctuation, structure, and subject matter.

Here, though the deployment of quotation marks in the 1916 Act points in one direction, all of the other evidence from the statute points the other way. It points so certainly, in our view, as to allow only the conclusion that the punctuation marks were misplaced and that the 1916 Act [did not include] section 92 [in section 5202]....

Against the overwhelming evidence from the structure, language, and subject matter of the 1916 Act there stands only the evidence from the Act's punctuation, too weak to trump the rest. In these unusual cases, we are convinced that the placement of the quotation marks in the 1916 Act was a simple scrivener's error, a mistake made by someone unfamiliar with the law's object and design. Courts ... should "disregard the punctuation, or repunctuate, if need be, to render the true meaning of the statute." The true meaning of the 1916 Act is clear beyond question, and so we repunctuate.... Because the 1918 Act did not amend the Federal Reserve Act, it did not repeal section 92, despite the Court of Appeals's conclusion to the contrary.[11]

Section 92 remains in force, and the judgment of the Court of Appeals is therefore reversed....

Notes and Questions

(1) *Much Ado about Nothing?* The Court in *U.S. National Bank* made two points: first, punctuation matters, but second, it can't trump the plain meaning of the text. In point of fact, courts regularly state that "punctuation is not decisive" and that it "is a minor, and not a controlling, element in interpretation, and courts will disregard the punctuation of a statute, or re-punctuate it, if need be, to give effect to what otherwise appears to be its purpose and true meaning." *United States v. Ron Pair Enters., Inc.*, 489 U.S. 235, 250 (1989) (O'Connor, J., dissenting). Similarly, it has been called "a most fallible standard by which to interpret a writing." *Ewing's Lessee v. Burnet*, 36 U.S. (11 Pet.) 41, 54 (1837). Are these rules much ado about nothing?

(2) *Interpretative Approach.* The Court, in its footnote, stated that it found the statute unambiguous and, thus, did not need to look at the legislative history. The court of appeals had found the statute ambiguous, noting that the relevant section of the 1918 Act (the one which amended section 5202 and omitted section 92) originated as a floor amendment and was adopted without debate. The court of appeals presumed that the author of the amendment would have had section 5202 in front of him when he proposed the amendment; thus, "absent concrete evidence to the contrary, we must assume that the 65th Congress understood section 92 to be part of section 5202, and that its exclusion from the amended section 5202 signaled its repeal." *Indep. Ins. Agents of Am., Inc. v. Clarke*, 955 F.2d 731, 736 (D.C. Cir. 1992). Do you find this information compelling? Which approach to statutory interpretation was used by the court of appeals? By the majority? Are the approaches the same? If so, why did these courts reach opposite results?

---

11. Because we conclude that the meaning of the 1916 Act is plain, and because respondents do not argue that the law's plain meaning is demonstrably at odds with the intentions of its drafters, we need not consider the 1916 Act's legislative history....

(3) *Say What You Mean and Mean What You Say.* Are these rules about grammar consistent with the idea that courts generally require legislatures to clearly articulate their intent and refuse to "correct" perceived errors? If not, why the change?

(4) *Is This Presumption Accurate?* In the United States, rules of statutory construction presume that legislators know and correctly use grammar. Does it make sense to give a lot of weight to punctuation? In answering that question, you might want to consider that many "rules" of punctuation and grammar are optional or subject to disagreement, including, for example, the rule of the serial comma, which we'll discuss in a moment.

(5) *Legislative Detail.* The series of legislative enactments that lead to this case is complicated. In case you want more detail, we provide the following summary. A 1916 federal statute permitted national banks in small communities to sell insurance. Not surprisingly, insurance agents did not like the statute, called section 92, and sued. The parties had admitted throughout the lower court proceedings that section 92 had been in effect during the litigation. On its own motion, however, the Court of Appeals held that the section 92 had been repealed by a 1918 amendment.

Below, we have excerpted the relevant language from the four statutes. Because the location of quotation marks was essential in the case, we depart from ordinary block quotations and include quotation marks *only if they appeared in the original bills or statute.*

In 1863, Congress enacted the National Bank Act. Section 5202, which placed limits on indebtedness, originally provided:

> No association shall at any time be indebted, or in any way liable, to an amount exceeding the amount of its capital stock at such time actually paid in and remaining undiminished by losses or otherwise, except on account of demands of the nature following:

> First. Notes of circulation.

> Second. Moneys deposited with or collected by the association.

> Third. Bills of exchange or drafts drawn against money actually on deposit to the credit of the association, or due thereto.

> Fourth. Liabilities to the stockholders of the association for dividends and reserved profits.

Section 5202 contained no quotation marks.

In 1913, Congress created Federal Reserve Banks and enacted the Federal Reserve Act. It amended section 5202 by adding a fifth exception (known as section 13) to the limitations on indebtedness. The first five paragraphs of the 1913 amendment set forth the powers of the new Federal Reserve Banks. Then came the following statement (without quotation marks):

> Section fifty-two hundred and two of the Revised Statutes of the United States is hereby amended so as to read as follows: No national banking association shall at any time be indebted, or in any way liable, to an amount exceeding the amount of its capital stock at such time actually paid in and remaining undiminished by losses or otherwise, except on account of demands of the nature following: …

> Fifth. Liabilities incurred under the provisions of the Federal Reserve Act.

In 1916, Congress amended several provisions of the 1913 Act. Unlike the 1913 Act, the 1916 Act included quotation marks. The 1916 amendment added what came to be known as Section 92. The 1916 Act provided (without quotation marks):

That section thirteen be, and is hereby, amended to read as follows: ...

Following this introduction were several paragraphs, *in quotation marks*, that tracked the first five paragraphs of section 13 of the 1913 Act and that generally expanded the powers of Federal Reserve Banks. After the quotation marks closed, the following language appeared:

Section fifty-two hundred and two of the Revised Statutes of the United States is hereby amended so as to read as follows (quotation marks in original): "No national banking association shall at any time be indebted, or in any way liable, to an amount exceeding the amount of its capital stock at such time actually paid in and remaining undiminished by losses or otherwise, except on account of demands of the nature following:

"First. Notes of circulation.

"Second. Moneys deposited with or collected by the association.

"Third. Bills of exchange or drafts drawn against money actually on deposit to the credit of the association, or due thereto.

"Fourth. Liabilities to the stockholders of the association for dividends and reserve profits.

"Fifth. Liabilities incurred under the provisions of the Federal reserve Act.

[The following language was codified at 12 U.S.C. §92; hence its name "section 92."] "The discount and rediscount and the purchase and sale by any Federal reserve bank of any bills receivable and of domestic and foreign bills of exchange, and of acceptances authorized by this Act, shall be subject to such restrictions, limitations, and regulations as may be imposed by the Federal Reserve Board.

"That in addition to the powers now vested by law in national banking associations organized under the laws of the United States any such association located and doing business in any place the population of which does not exceed five thousand inhabitants, as shown by the last preceding decennial census, may, under such rules and regulations as may be prescribed by the Comptroller of the Currency, act as the agent for any fire, life, or other insurance company authorized by the authorities of the State in which said bank is located to do business in said State....

"Any member bank may accept drafts or bills of exchange drawn upon it having not more than three months' sight to run, exclusive of days of grace, drawn under regulations to be prescribed by the Federal Reserve Board by banks or bankers in foreign counties or dependencies or insular possessions of the United States for the purpose of furnishing dollar exchange as required by the usages of trade in the respective countries, dependencies, or insular possessions. Such drafts or bills may be acquired by Federal reserve banks in such amounts and subject to such regulations, restrictions, and limitations as may be prescribed by the Federal Reserve Board...."

Finally, in 1918, section 5202 was again amended; a sixth exception was added:

Section fifty-two hundred and two of the Revised Statutes of the United States is hereby amended so as to read as follows: "Sec. 5202. No national banking association shall at any time be indebted, or in any way liable, to an amount exceeding the amount of its capital stock at such time actually paid in and remaining undiminished by losses or otherwise, except on account of demands of the nature following: …

> "Sixth. Liabilities incurred under the provisions of the War Finance Corporation Act." …

Each paragraph began with a quotation mark but did not end with a quotation mark, until the added section 6. Section 92 was not included in the 1918 amendment of section 5202.

B. Punctuation: Specific Rules

1. Commas

The next two subsections focus on the impact of the placement of commas and a canon of construction known as the last antecedent rule. Commas, perhaps more than any other punctuation, may create critical issues of interpretation. At least three rules concerning commas are often important in statutory interpretation. First, the serial comma rule directs that in a series of three items, if each is set off by a comma, then each item should be viewed as independent of the others. The case below addresses the "proper" role of a comma in a series. We will return to the other two rules after this case.

Peterson v. Midwest Sec. Ins. Co.
636 N.W.2d 727 (Wis. 2001)

DIANE S. SYKES, J.

[The plaintiff, Peterson, was injured when the tree stand from which he was bow hunting collapsed, and he fell to the ground. At the time of his injury, Peterson was hunting with permission on land owned by Vernon and Culleen Peterson (no relation). The tree stand, however, had been built and was owned by the Petersons' nephew, Shaw. Peterson sued Shaw's insurance company, which, by motion for summary judgment, raised the defense afforded by Wisconsin's "Recreational Immunity Statute." The courts below held for the insurance company. The plaintiff appealed to the Wisconsin Supreme Court.]

The recreational immunity statute immunizes property owners against liability "for any injury to a person engaged in a recreational activity on the owner's property." If the statute applies, a property owner owes no duty of inspection, warning or safety to "any person who enters the owner's property to engage in a recreational activity," and is otherwise immune from liability for injuries to any person engaged in recreational activity on the owner's property....

Whether Shaw is entitled to immunity depends upon whether he qualifies as a property owner under the statute. "Owner" and "property" are defined terms. An "owner" is "a person ... that owns, leases or occupies property." Wis. Stat. §895.52(l)(d)l. "Property" is "real property and buildings, structures and improvements thereon, and the waters of the state."

The parties agree that Shaw owned the tree stand from which Peterson fell. Their dispute centers on whether the tree stand by itself is "property" under the statute. The circuit court and the court of appeals concluded that the tree stand was a "structure" and therefore "property" within the meaning of Wis. Stat. §895.52(l)(f). We agree.

The term "structure" is not defined in Wis. Stat. § 895.52, and is therefore given its common and ordinary meaning. A "structure" is "something constructed," or "something made up of a number of parts that are held or put together in a particular way." *American Heritage Dictionary of the English Language,* 1782 (3d ed.1992). "Structure" is also defined as "[a]ny construction, or any production or piece of work artificially built up or composed of parts joined together in some definite manner." *Black's Law Dictionary,* 1424 (6th ed.1991).

Shaw's tree stand was made of wood and cinched in against the tree with a chain, and had a metal ladder. In other words, it was constructed, built, or put together in a particular way, and was made up of parts joined together. The tree stand was therefore a "structure" as that term is commonly and ordinarily understood. Shaw was therefore an owner of "property" within the meaning of the recreational immunity statute.

Peterson reads the definition of "property" differently. He argues that the phrase "buildings, structures and improvements" merely modifies "real property," so that a person who owns a building, structure or improvement but does not also own the underlying real property does not own "property" within the meaning of the statute. He interprets the statute to create two categories of "property": 1) real property, along with any buildings, structures, or improvements thereon; and 2) the waters of the state. He bases this interpretation on the lack of punctuation between the phrases "real property" and "buildings, structures and improvements" in the definition.

We decline to give the absence of a comma such interpretive significance. Peterson's punctuation-based interpretation operates to impose a requirement that does not appear on the face of the statute: that the owner of a building, structure or improvement implicated in a recreational injury must also own the underlying real property in order to own "property" as that term is defined in the statute. But the statute does not say '[p]roperty' means real property and buildings, structures and improvements thereon *that are owned by the real property owner,*' and we cannot rewrite it in the exercise of interpreting it. According to the unambiguous language of the statute, a person who owns a "building, structure or improvement" on real property owns "property" under the statute, regardless of whether he also owns the underlying real estate. Where the language of a statute is clear and unambiguous, we do not look beyond it to ascertain its meaning....

This interpretation is also consistent with the expression of legislative purpose ... :

> **Legislative intent.** The legislature intends by this act to limit the liability of property owners toward others who use their property for recreational activities under circumstances in which the owner does not derive more than a minimal pecuniary benefit. While it is not possible to specify in a statute every activity which might constitute a recreational activity, this act provides examples of the kinds of activities that are meant to be included, and the legislature intends that, where substantially similar circumstances or activities exist, this legislation should be liberally construed in favor of property owners to protect them from liability....

1983 Wis. Act 418, § 1.

Thus, while it has often been said that the intent of sec. 895.52, Stats., is to encourage landowners to open up their land for recreational activity, it is abundantly clear from the language of the statute and the statement of legislative intent that the purpose of the statute is broader, and recreational immunity is not in fact limited only to *landowners....*

Peterson's interpretation operates to exclude from the definition of "property" any building, structure or improvement owned by someone other than the real property owner, or, conversely, to include only those buildings, structures or improvements that are owned by the real property owner. This sort of restrictive interpretation is inconsistent with the language of the statute and the legislative directive that it be liberally construed in favor of immunity for property owners.[7]

Accordingly, we conclude that a person who owns a "building, structure or improvement" on real property owns "property" as that term is defined in Wis. Stat. § 895.52(1)(f), even if he does not own the underlying real property.... Shaw is entitled to recreational immunity under Wis. Stat. § 895.52(2).... [W]e affirm....

ANNE WALSH BRADLEY, J. (dissenting).

The recreational immunity statute defines "property" as: "real property and buildings, structures and improvements thereon, and the waters of the state, as defined under § 281.01(18)."

The essence of the majority opinion rests on its conclusion that this definition of property unambiguously [includes any buildings, structures, and improvements]. Yet, the majority is able to reach this conclusion only by dismissing or ignoring rules of grammar and glossing over the ambiguity inherent in this definition. I conclude that the statute's definition of property is ambiguous and that the majority's bright-line ... interpretation conflicts with the legislative intent to provide immunity for outdoor activity....

The majority declares, "[w]e decline to give the absence of a comma such interpretive significance."

I question whether the legislature's choice of punctuation in a statute may be dismissed so easily. Case law abounds with disputes that revolve around the placement of a comma in a statute or other writing.

The sentence we are interpreting in subsection (f) defines property as "real property and buildings, structures and improvements thereon, and the waters of the state." (Emphasis [underlined commas] added.) There are two commas in the above quoted definition. Why is that important to note? The foundation of the majority opinion rests on dismissing the placement of the first comma and completely ignoring the second comma. If the majority acknowledges the placement of these commas, it cannot reach its conclusion that the statute unambiguously creates immunity for owners of three distinctly defined categories of property.

Admittedly, the rules of grammar are only tools to assist in interpretation and should not be mechanistically applied at the expense of a natural reading of the text and its purpose. [But in this case] without explanation, the majority attempts to divorce its interpretation from the accepted use of grammar. Such an attempt calls into question the validity of the majority's approach....

---

7. The dissent argues that our reading of the statute violates the rules of grammar and punctuation. We do not disagree that courts sometimes look to grammatical rules when interpreting legal texts. But interpreting a legal text is not like diagramming a sentence or correcting an English paper. The rules of grammar and punctuation should not be applied at the expense of a natural, reasonable reading of the statutory language (taking into account the context in which it appears and the purpose of the statute), or when the result is an expansion or contraction of the statute contrary to its terms. Here, strict adherence to the "rule of the serial comma" as advocated by the dissent operates to add a substantive requirement to the statute that it other-wise does not contain.

The First Comma

The majority's interpretation violates the rule of the serial comma: in a series of three or more, a comma shall appear after the first term or category listed. *See The Gregg Reference Manual* 15 (9th ed.2001). The majority contends that the first distinct category listed is "real property." Thus, a comma should appear after this first category—but none appears. Instead, the first comma appears after the word "buildings." Such a placement is inconsistent with the majority's interpretation. The majority cannot reconcile its interpretation with the legislature's placement of this comma. Unable to explain it, the majority dismisses the placement of the comma as insignificant.

The Second Comma

A review of the surrounding text of the statute demonstrates that the drafter of the statute adheres to the rule: in a series of three or more, no comma is used preceding the final conjunction. Let me illustrate.

In the text of the recreational immunity statute, the definition of "recreational activity" immediately follows the sentence that we are interpreting in this case. The definition contains a serial listing. "Recreational activity" is defined as an activity undertaken "for the purpose of exercise, relaxation or pleasure." Consistent with the rule, no comma is used preceding the final conjunction, "or." ...

The majority's interpretation of three distinct categories of property, however, is inconsistent with the rule. The drafter placed a comma before the conjunction, "and." Such a placement suggests that the drafter did not intend to create three categories.

The opinion of the majority fails to discuss or even acknowledge the placement of the second comma. Instead, it ignores it. The majority offers no explanation why the surrounding text of the statute adheres to the rule while the majority's interpretation is inconsistent with the rule.

The Use of the Term "thereon"

The majority concludes that "buildings, structures and improvements thereon," is one of three clearly distinct categories. In arriving at this conclusion, it ignores the dictionary meaning of "thereon." The term means "on that" or "concerning that subject." Webster's New Universal Unabridged Dictionary 1894 (2d ed.1983) (emphasis added).

The definition of property set forth in subsection (f) states: "real property and buildings, structures and improvements thereon, and the waters of the state." If the drafter had intended "buildings, structures and improvements thereon," to be a distinct category, the statute should read "buildings, structures and improvements on real property." Instead, the drafter used the term "thereon," which signals that the buildings, structures and improvements are to be on that specific real property referred to in the first part of the definition. The plain meaning of the term "thereon" conflicts with the majority's conclusion that the drafter clearly intended to create three distinctly defined categories of property....

We cannot ignore punctuation when interpreting a statute. The above discussion demonstrates, at the very least, that the definition of "property" is ambiguous. The majority is simply incorrect in its conclusion that the statute clearly and unambiguously creates immunity for owners of three distinctly defined categories of property.

I conclude that there are several constructions of the language in subsection (f). First, as Peterson advances, the definition could be interpreted to identify two categories of property: (1) real property along with the buildings, structures, and improvements on that real property, and (2) the waters of the state. Second, as a variation on Peterson's approach, the definition could be interpreted to include three categories, but a different three than those identified by Midwest and the majority: (1) real property, (2) buildings, structures and improvements on that real property, and (3) the waters of the state. Third, as Midwest argues, the definition could be interpreted to identify the following three categories: (1) real property, (2) any buildings, structures, and improvements on any real property, and (3) the waters of the state. Fourth, the definition could be interpreted to identify three categories of property, but again a different three than those identified by Midwest and the majority: (1) real property and buildings, (2) structures and improvements thereon, and (3) the waters of the state. Rather than addressing the ambiguity, the majority summarily concludes that the "clear" language is consistent with legislative intent....

The purpose of the statute focuses on recreational activity. Because recreational activity is defined as outdoor activity under the statute, it makes little sense for the majority to define all buildings and structures as "property." The majority's definition of property that includes any buildings and structures, regardless of where they stand, can hardly be said to comport with the idea that recreational activity takes place outdoors. How does one enter a building or structure in order to engage in an outdoor activity? ...

In this case, the fact that Peterson was hunting upon a "structure" that happened to be nothing more than a non-enclosed platform attached to a tree obscures the breadth of the majority's ... rule. The result may appear to comport with the legislative intent in this case, but what of others down the road?

I disagree with the majority's basic premise that the statute unambiguously creates immunity for owners of [buildings, structures, and improvements]. Additionally, I conclude that the majority's broad definition cannot be what the legislature intended. Accordingly, I respectfully dissent.

Notes and Questions

(1) *What Language is at Issue?* It is critical in this case to know exactly how the majority and dissent read the statutory language. As defined in the statute, property is "real property and buildings, structures and improvements thereon, and the waters of the state." The dissent suggested that the statute as punctuated was ambiguous. One possibility was that the statute recognized real property together with any buildings, structures, and improvements on *that* real property. Another possibility, one the majority adopted, was that the statute identified: (1) real property and (2) buildings, structures, and improvements on *any* real property. Which result is more consistent with the punctuation, specifically the rule of the serial comma?

(2) *Serial Comma.* What is a serial comma? According to the dissent, the legislature regularly omitted the serial comma when drafting; hence, it likely intended to omit the comma in this section of the statute. How, if at all, did the majority respond to this argument?

(3) *Resolving Ambiguity.* Did the dissent rely more heavily on grammar rules concerning punctuation, while the majority gave more weight to legislative purpose? Is the dissent correct that the majority "ignores" punctuation? Or, did it instead simply follow the Court's admonition in *U.S. National Bank* to ignore punctuation when doing so is necessary to effect the true meaning of the statute? Is the dissent too much of a grammarian, putting true meaning to the side? Does the dissent rely too heavily on grammar or just enough? Does purpose resolve any ambiguity?

(4) *Addition or Omission of a Statutory Element.* In footnote 7, the majority chastised the dissent for strictly adhering to the "rule of the serial comma" to add a substantive element to the statute that the statute otherwise did not contain. Is it fairer to say that the majority, by ignoring this comma rule, omitted a substantive element contained in the statute?

(5) *Who was Right?* It is not common for one person to own land while someone else owns the buildings or structures on that land. Thus, it is entirely likely that the legislature intended this statute to apply exactly as it was punctuated to real property and structures on that property, which are owned by the same person. However, given its broad purpose, isn't it likely that had the legislature thought about the possibility that someone other than the landowner would own a building or structure on the land, the legislature would have wanted the statute to apply to those buildings and structures regardless of whether the underlying property owner also owned them? But should it be the court's responsibility to redraft poorly drafted statutes? In a different vein, do some of the approaches perhaps allow courts more freedom to do justice in a particular case?

(6) *Thereon.* According to the dissent, what was the role of the word "thereon" in the statute? Did the majority explain how "thereon" fit within its interpretation of the statute?

(7) *Another Example.* Suppose you have these two statutes:

> Sec. 116 "Whenever through error a person is named in a patent application as the inventor, or through error an inventor is not named in patent application, and such error arose without any deceptive intention on his part, the Commissioner may correct such error."

> Sec. 256 "Whenever through error a person is named in an issued patent as the inventor, or through error an inventor is not named in an issued patent and such error arose without any deceptive intention on his part, the Commissioner may correct such error."

Under section 256, if a person is named as an inventor, can the error be corrected if it was done with deceptive intent? Under section 116? *See Stark v. Advanced Magnetics, Inc.,* 119 F.3d 1551 (Fed. Cir. 1997) (relying on the presence of the extra comma in section 116 to hold that deceptive intent would prevent correction under section 116 but not 256 where the person is named as an inventor).

2. The Rule of Last Antecedent

We need to return to our second and third comma rules to understand the rule of last antecedent. The second rule is that when a modifier is set off from a series of antecedents by a comma, the modifier should be interpreted to apply to all of the antecedents. Thus, "people may drive cars, motorcycles, and bikes, but only on Thursday" means that driving cars, motorcycles, or bikes is allowed only on Thursday. The phrase "but only on Thursday" is the modifier; "cars, motorcycles, and bikes" are all antecedents. But the sentence, "people may drive cars, motorcycles, and bikes but only on Thursday" does not mean the same thing. It means that bikes, and bikes alone, may be driven only on Thursdays; cars and motorcycles may be driven at any time. Be sure you identify the difference, punctuation-wise, of the last two sentences. This is the third rule: When a modifier is not set off from an antecedent by a comma, then the modifier should be interpreted to apply to only that antecedent. This third rule is known as the "rule of last antecedent."

In the cases below, the courts apply the last antecedent rule to a statute requiring people to forfeit their vehicles when the vehicles are used to transport drugs. Notice that the statute, specifically the punctuation, was amended before the second case was decided.

In re Forfeiture of 1982 Ford Bronco

673 P.2d 1310 (N.M. 1983)

PAYNE, CHIEF JUSTICE.

This appeal challenges the trial court's order forfeiting a 1982 Ford Bronco to the Clovis Police Department, pursuant to NMSA 1978, Section 30-31-34(D).

On December 12, 1982, Wayne Thatcher and Glen Corbin went to Scott Stevens' house, where they were informed that they could get some marijuana. Stevens told them that it would cost two hundred dollars apiece. After he received four hundred dollars, Stevens drove to Tahoka, Texas to make the purchase....

On December 13, 1982, the Clovis Police were tipped off regarding Stevens' activities. At 1:30 a.m., December 14, 1983, two officers stopped the 1982 Ford Bronco driven by him. A search warrant was executed and a shopping bag, which contained 11.4 ounces of marijuana, was found in the Bronco.

Stevens was arrested and charged with possession of over eight ounces of marijuana with the intent to distribute in violation of the Controlled Substances Act. In addition, the police department requested judgment forfeiting the Ford Bronco to the Department.

Although the criminal charges were dismissed..., the trial court ordered the forfeiture. It held that the vehicle was used to transport marijuana for the purpose of sale. We affirm....

Stevens ... challenges the trial court's finding that the "sole purpose of transportation of the marijuana was to complete the sale." Stevens alleges that this is an erroneous legal conclusion. His argument is that he, Corbin, and Thatcher were all partners. Title passed to all three upon delivery of the goods to him as an agent in Tahoka, Texas, as it does in a commercial transaction. The sale was completed before transporting the marijuana. Accordingly, Stevens cites *State v. Barela*, 93 N.M. 700, 604 P.2d 838 (Ct.App.1979), cert. denied, 94 N.M. 674, 615 P.2d 991 (1980) and argues his vehicle is not subject to forfeiture.

In *Barela*, the undercover police agent purchased marijuana from Barela in his kitchen. Then Barela gave the undercover agent a ride from his house, transporting the marijuana. The court of appeals held that Barela's vehicle was not subject to forfeiture because the sale was completed before the drug was transported.

Stevens' argument lacks merit. Although *Barela* held that transportation of the marijuana must be for the purpose of sale, we find this interpretation to be contrary to the meaning of NMSA 1978, Subsection 30-31-34(D) (Repl.Pamp.1980). The statute reads in relevant part:

The following are subject to forfeiture: ...

D. all conveyances, including aircraft, vehicles or vessels, which are used, or intended for use, to transport, or in any manner to facilitate the transportation for the purpose of sale of [drugs]....

According to our interpretation of Subsection 30-31-34(D), a vehicle is subject to forfeiture if used to transport an illegal substance. The transportation need not be for the purpose of sale. Section 30-31-34 must be read according to its "grammatical sense." Of primary importance is the rule that a restrictive clause only applies to the words or phrase immediately preceding it, and not to others more remote. A comma must not be placed between the restrictive clause and that which it restricts. *[S]ee generally* J. Hodges & M. Whitten, *Harbrace College Handbook*, § 12d at 120 (7th ed. 1972), which states that restrictive clauses follow and limit the words they modify and are not set off by commas.

Applying these rules, the restrictive clause at issue in Section 30-31-34 is "for the purpose of sale." It is not separated by a comma from "or in any manner to facilitate transportation", which is the immediately preceding phrase. The clause restricts this phrase. But it does not restrict "to transport", which is set off by a comma and is more remote. The only way in which the restrictive clause could apply to the phrase "to transport" is if commas were to enclose the clause "for the purpose of sale." If so, then the restriction would apply to several antecedents which are themselves separated by a comma....

For the reasons stated, we affirm the trial court in forfeiting the vehicle.

State v. One 1990 Chevrolet Pickup
857 P.2d 44 (N.M. Ct. App. 1993)

CHAVEZ, JUDGE,

[This case] raises the issue of whether NMSA 1978, Section 30-31-34(D) (Repl.Pamp.1989), provides for forfeiture of vehicles and other property when the owner of the property is in possession of a small amount of controlled substances designated solely for personal use. We hold that, in order for property to be forfeited under Section 30-31-34, possession of a controlled substance must be for the purpose of sale....

On July 20, 1991, Thomas Ortega (Ortega) was arrested in Luna County for driving while intoxicated. An inventory search of Ortega's possessions was conducted pursuant to his arrest. The officers conducting the search discovered a folded $100 bill in Ortega's wallet. When the officers unfolded the bill, a very small amount of cocaine was found. The City of Deming (City) instituted forfeiture proceedings against Ortega's truck on August 2, 1991. The parties stipulated that the cocaine found was for Ortega's personal use. The trial court denied Ortega's motion to dismiss and ordered that the truck be forfeited. Ortega appealed the trial court's order....

The current version of Section 30-31-34(D) subjects the following property to forfeiture: "... all conveyances, including aircraft, vehicles or vessels, which are used or intended for use to transport or in any manner to facilitate the transportation for the purpose of sale of property described in Subsection A or B of this section...." The parties ... argue a range of positions about how the phrase "for the purpose of sale" should be interpreted as a modifying or limiting phrase....

[The] earlier version of the statute ... read as follows: "... all conveyances, including aircraft, vehicles or vessels, which are used, or intended for use, to transport, or in any manner to facilitate the transportation for the purpose of sale of property described in Subsections A or B."

The 1981 amendment to Section 30-31-34(D) removed three commas: one between the words "used" and "or," one between the words "use" and "to," and one between the words "transport" and "or." The City ... argue[s] that the legislative amendment resulting in the removal of the commas does not matter ... and that the phrase "for the purpose of sale" modifies only the phrase directly before it; i.e., "in any manner to facilitate the transportation." Interpreting the statute in this manner would result in forfeiture of property any time an individual "transports" a controlled substance in a vehicle, regardless of the amount or whether the drugs were for personal use, as long as the government entity shows that a controlled substance was being transported. The *Stevens* Court made such a determination, and in doing so, the Court relied heavily on the placement of the commas in the earlier version of the statute. The *Stevens* Court also relied heavily on the "last antecedent rule." Specifically, the Court stated that a statute must be read to make "grammatical sense," that a comma must not be placed between the restrictive clause and that which it restricts, and that a restrictive clause only applies to the words or the phrase immediately preceding it. Applying these rules, the *Stevens* Court determined that "for the purpose of sale" only modified the phrase "in any manner to facilitate the transportation." Finally, the Supreme Court stated that the only manner in which the restrictive clause could apply to the phrase "to transport" would be to enclose the clause "for the purpose of sale" by commas.

In the present appeal[], the trial court ... determined that because the Supreme Court relied heavily on commas that no longer exist, *Stevens* cannot be relied upon for the proposition that a vehicle merely transporting controlled substances, whether or not the substances are intended for sale, may be forfeited. In contrast, the trial court in [another] case determined that *Stevens* is still applicable, and that since the legislature has not followed the Supreme Court's directive about how it should draft a modifying phrase, the trial court was required to interpret the current statute in the same manner as *Stevens*.

The cardinal rule of statutory construction is to determine legislative intent. Legislative intent is first sought by reference to the plain meaning found in the language used by the legislature. However, both this court and the New Mexico Supreme Court have rejected formalistic and mechanistic interpretation of statutory language. The "last antecedent rule" utilized in *Stevens* and other cases is a valid method of statutory interpretation, however, the doctrine is merely a tool of statutory interpretation and is not an end to itself. Instead, the last antecedent rule is merely an aid to interpretation, and is not inflexible and uniformly binding. Where the context requires that a qualifying word or phrase apply to several preceding phrases, the qualifying word or phrase will not be restricted to its immediate antecedent.

Applying a less technical version of the "last antecedent rule" to Section 30-31-34(D), we hold that the phrase "for the purpose of sale" modifies the following three clauses that are connected by the word "or": (1) conveyances which are used to transport controlled substances; (2) conveyances which are intended for use to transport controlled substances; or (3) conveyances which are used in any manner to facilitate the transportation of controlled substances. Thus, reading the section in its entirety, forfeiture is allowed only in those instances where an individual possesses a controlled substance for the purpose of selling it....

The order of the Luna County District Court granting forfeiture is reversed.

Notes and Questions

(1) *Identify the Specific Grammatical Change(s).* What specific grammatical changes did the legislature make to the statute that lead this court to a reach a result different from *Stevens*? How did the City interpret this change? The car owner? How is the last antecedent rule implicated?

(2) *Ignoring Rules of Grammar?* What did the court mean when it wrote: "Where the context requires that a qualifying word or phrase apply to several preceding phrases, the qualifying word or phrase will not be restricted to its immediate antecedent"?

(3) *Other Statements of the Rule.* Courts typically say that under the last antecedent rule, "qualifying words, phrases, or clauses will ordinarily be construed as referring to the words, phrases and clauses *immediately preceding,* not to more remote words, phrases, or clauses[ ] [u]nless the context or evident meaning of the statute requires a different construction." *Demchuk v. State Dep't of Health Servs.,* 6 Cal. Rptr. 2d 635, 636 (Cal. Ct. App. 1991). Similarly, others say that a modifier's reference "is to the closest noun 'absent a clear intention to the contrary.'" *Fed. Election Comm'n. v. Arlen Specter '96,* 150 F. Supp. 2d 797, 805 (E.D. Pa. 2001). Do these statements of the rule provide more guidance?

(4) *Judicial and Academic Criticism and Qualification.* The United States Supreme Court has essentially taken the position that it will apply the rule of last antecedent when it makes sense to do so and will ignore the rule when it does not. *Compare Barnhart v. Thomas,* 540 U.S. 20, 26 (2003) (applying rule of the last antecedent and saying, "While this rule is not an absolute and can assuredly be overcome by other indicia of meaning, we have said that construing a statute in accord with the rule is 'quite sensible as a matter of grammar.'") *with Nobelman v. Am. Savings Bank,* 508 U.S. 324, 330 (1993) (declining to apply rule of last antecedent and instead adopting an interpretation which "is the more reasonable one"). A commentator, who has investigated the origins of the rule, wrote:

> By the late 1880s, Jabez Sutherland, who wrote Sutherland on Statutory Construction, had grappled with enough legal ambiguity after investigating complicated and litigated statutes that he invented a grammar/punctuation rule in hopes of resolving future statutory problems:
>
>> Referential and qualifying phrases, where no contrary intention appears, refer solely to the last antecedent. The last antecedent is the last word, phrase, or clause that can be made an antecedent without impairing the meaning of the sentence. This proviso usually is construed to apply to the provision or clause immediately preceding it. The rule is another aid to discovery of intent or meaning and is not inflexible and uniformly binding. Where the sense of the entire act requires that a qualifying word or phrase apply to several preceding or even succeeding sections, the word or phrase will not be restricted to its immediate antecedent.
>>
>> Evidence that a qualifying phrase is supposed to apply to all antecedents instead of only to the immediately preceding one may be found in the fact that it is separated from the antecedents by a comma.

Terri LeClercq, *Doctrine of the Last Antecedent: The Mystifying Morass of Ambiguous Modifiers,* 2 J. Legal Writing Inst. 81, 86–87 (1996) (footnote omitted; emphasis added) (quoting 1891 version of Sutherland on Statutory Construction).

Professor LeClercq went further in her criticism: "the Doctrine of the Last Antecedent is problematic: it contradicts other linguistic principles; it contradicts the historical use of the comma; and the doctrine, itself poorly drafted, does not provide a concrete conclusion to the problem of ambiguous modifiers." *Id.* at 89. "Thus, rather than becoming 'one more aid' in interpretation as Sutherland hoped, the Doctrine of the Last Antecedent has, in its hundred-plus year history, created as much confusion and disagreement as the ambiguous modifier its drafter set out to clarify." *Id.* Finally, she wrote:

> Unfortunately for those who need to depend on it, the Doctrine of the Last Antecedent itself calls for interpretation because Sutherland begins with what seems the fall-back rule of statutory interpretation and concludes with his specific point. He begins with a qualifier, that interpreters should use the Doctrine of the Last Antecedent "where no contrary intention appears." Appears where? Within the

phrase or within the document as a whole? In the notes of a committee that wrote the original rule? If the language offers no "contrary intention," then the meaning is already "plain." If the contrary intent shows up within the sentence itself, then there is no need for the rule. And legislative intent or the drafter's intent is usually in question to begin with, so that search rarely clarifies the sentence in question. But Sutherland's fifth sentence "where the sense of the entire act requires …" implies that the reader has already investigated the phrase within the context of the entire act. Thus the Sutherland rule is a jumble. He probably meant to emphasize intent, and the sense of the act as a whole, over the announced doctrine.

Id. at 92–93. *See Kasischke v. State,* 991 So.2d 803 (Fla. 2008) (collecting these and other criticisms of the rule).

Problem 5-1

You are a prosecutor in *People v. McDonald.* On February 5, McDonald and her two children spent the day at a friend's house. During the day, McDonald drank several glasses of wine. That evening, McDonald left her friend's house with her two young sons.

At approximately 10:00 p.m., a police officer discovered McDonald's car in a park seven miles from her friend's house. McDonald was asleep in the driver's seat and her two children were asleep in their car seats. When the officer found them, the temperature was below freezing, the car's engine was running, the car doors were unlocked, and the driver's window was open about six inches.

After several attempts, the officer woke McDonald. After attempting to start her already running car, McDonald eventually opened her window fully and spoke to the officer. When she did, the officer smelled the odor of alcohol and observed that McDonald's eyes were dilated, watery, and unfocused.

McDonald told the officer that she had been drinking and that she had driven from her friend's house to the park. The most obvious route from her friend's house to the park would have required her to drive on several busy streets. She also told the officer that upon reaching the park, she decided not to drive any further because she knew she was too intoxicated to drive on the freeway.

The officer administered a portable breath test and drove McDonald to the hospital. Based on his observations, training, and experience, the officer believed that McDonald was extremely intoxicated. The children were treated and released unharmed.

The State has charged McDonald with two counts of second degree criminal mistreatment (for driving with the children while intoxicated) under Mercer statute 9A.42.030(1)(a), one count for each child, and with driving under the influence. McDonald is willing to plead guilty to the DUI charge, but disputes the criminal mistreatment charges. Analyze whether the phrase (in the statute below) "by withholding any of the basic necessities of life" applies to both (a) and (b) or whether it applies only to (b).

Problem Materials

Mercer Rev. Stat. §9A.42.005 provides:

> The legislature finds that there is a significant need to protect children and dependent persons, including frail elder and vulnerable adults, from abuse and

neglect by their parents, by persons entrusted with their physical custody, or by persons employed to provide them with the basic necessities of life. The legislature further finds that such abuse and neglect often takes the forms of either withholding from them the basic necessities of life, including food, water, shelter, clothing, and health care, or abandoning them, or both. Therefore, it is the intent of the legislature that criminal penalties be imposed on those guilty of such abuse or neglect.

Mercer Rev. Stat. § 9A.42.030(1) provides:

A parent of a child ... is guilty of criminal mistreatment in the second degree if he or she recklessly, as defined in Mercer Code § 9A.08.010(1)(c), either (a) creates an imminent and substantial risk of death or great bodily harm, or (b) causes substantial bodily harm by withholding any of the basic necessities of life.

Mercer Rev. Stat. § 9A.08.010(1)(c) provides:

A person is reckless or acts recklessly when he knows of and disregards a substantial risk that a wrongful act may occur and his disregard of such substantial risk is a gross deviation from conduct that a reasonable man would exercise in the same situation.

C. Grammar: Specific Rules

1. Conjunctive or Disjunctive: "And" versus "Or"

In statutory interpretation, "and" usually means and, while "or" usually means or, but not always. As one court explained,

According to Black's Law Dictionary 79 (5th ed. 1979), the word "and" is used as

"[a] conjunction connecting words or phrases expressing the idea that the latter is to be added to or taken along with the first....

"It expresses a general relation or connection, a participation or accompaniment in sequence, having no inherent meaning standing alone but deriving force from what comes before and after. In its conjunctive sense the word is used to conjoin words, clauses, or sentences, expressing the relation of addition or connection, and signifying that something is to follow in addition to that which proceeds and its use implies that the connected elements must be grammatically co-ordinate, as where the elements preceding and succeeding the use of the words refer to the same subject matter."

... It is ordinarily presumed that the word "and" should be interpreted according to its plain and ordinary meaning and that it is not interchangeable with the word "or." C. Sands, 1A *Sutherland Statutory Construction* § 21.14 (4th ed. 1972 and Cum.Supp. 1984).... [C]ircumstances may require courts to construe the word "and" to mean "or" whenever such a conversion is mandated by the context of the words used; the principle is applicable to legislative enactments where it is necessary to effectuate the obvious intention of the legislature.

Comptroller of the Treasury v. Fairchild Indus., Inc., 493 A.2d 341 (Md. 1985) (holding that "and" in a tax statute meant "or").

Thus, "and" is generally thought of as conjunctive (joining or connecting), while "or" is more commonly thought to be disjunctive (separating or contrasting). But sometimes, in both statutory interpretation and life, "and" means "or." For example, if someone asks if you want pepperoni or sausage pizza, you may say "pepperoni and sausage is fine," which may mean that they are good together or that one or the other is fine. The following case shows that courts may replace "and" with "or" when "it is necessary to effectuate the obvious intention of the legislature." Interestingly, both sides acknowledged that "and" could not mean and in this case. Why?

United States v. Pabon-Cruz

391 F.3d 86 (2d. Cir. 2004)

José A. Cabranes, Circuit Judge.

Jorge L. Pabon-Cruz, who had just turned 18 at the time of the conduct at issue, was charged with and convicted of both advertising and distributing child pornography over the Internet. Pabon-Cruz is a first-time offender. He had been living with his mentally disabled mother and studying computer science as a scholarship student at the University of Puerto Rico, and the District Court found that he had not been involved in the creation of any child pornography. Count One of the indictment charged Pabon-Cruz with violating 18 U.S.C. §2251(c)(1)(A), which applies to any person who "knowingly makes, prints, or publishes, or causes to be made, printed, or published, any notice or advertisement seeking or offering ... to receive, exchange, buy, produce, display, distribute, or reproduce, any visual depiction, if the production of such visual depiction involves the use of a minor engaging in sexually explicit conduct and such visual depiction is of such conduct." At the time of Pabon-Cruz's conduct, that advertising offense was understood to carry a ten-year mandatory minimum prison sentence. *Id.* §2251(d).[3]

Count Two of the indictment charged Pabon-Cruz with violating 18 U.S.C. §2252A(a)(2)(B), which applies to any person who "knowingly receives or distributes ... any material that contains child pornography...." That offense, unlike the advertising offense, carried no mandatory minimum sentence when Pabon-Cruz engaged in the conduct at issue.[4] ... The jury convicted defendant on both counts of the indictment....

In advance of sentencing, defendant asked the District Court to declare the ten-year minimum penalty then mandated by 18 U.S.C. §2251(d) unconstitutional in light of the Eighth Amendment's prohibition on cruel and unusual punishment....

DISCUSSION

In the course of preparing this opinion, we discovered that the version of 18 U.S.C. §2251(d), the penalty provision governing the advertising charge, set forth in the printed copy of the Conference Report at the time of voting by both houses of Congress provided

---

3. At the time of Pabon-Cruz's conduct, 18 U.S.C. §2251(d) provided, in relevant part, that "[a]ny individual who violates, or attempts or conspires to violate, this section shall be fined under this title or imprisoned not less than 10 years nor more than 20 years, and both." The provision has been changed to read "[a]ny individual who violates, or attempts or conspires to violate, this section shall be fined under this title and imprisoned not less than 15 years nor more than 30 years," and 18 U.S.C. §2251(d) has been reclassified as 18 U.S.C. §2251(e). See PROTECT Act, §103, 117 Stat. at 653.

4. The PROTECT Act subsequently established a five-year mandatory minimum for receiving or distributing child pornography. See PROTECT Act §103(b)(1)(E), 117 Stat. at 653 (codified at 18 U.S.C. §2252A(b)(1)).

that "[a]ny individual who violates ... this section, shall be fined under this title or imprisoned not less than 10 years nor more than 20 years, *or both*...." 142 Cong. Rec. H11, 652 (Sept. 28, 1996); 142 Cong. Rec. S11,842 (Sept. 30, 1996) (emphasis added). This language differs from that included in the bill signed by the President and printed in the Statutes at Large, which provides that "[a]ny individual who violates ... this section, shall be fined under this title or imprisoned not less than 10 years nor more than 20 years, *and both*...." Pub.L. No. 104-208, § 121(4), 110 Stat. 3009-30 (1996) (emphasis added). Because ... this case turns on the penalty provision, and the language and interpretation of this provision was addressed neither by the parties nor by the District Court, we requested ... supplemental briefing on ... how the provision should be construed, and whether it allows a violator to be sentenced to a fine in lieu of imprisonment. We ... now turn to a consideration of the language of the penalty provision.

The parties agree that the text of the bill signed by the President does not match the text of the Conference Report. Defendant argues that the "and both" language makes no sense; that the appropriate reading of the statute is thus "or both"; and that the District Court consequently has the discretion to sentence anyone convicted under the statute to a fine, a term of imprisonment of at least ten years, or both. The Government contends that the "and both" language controls and that, despite its ungrammatical phrasing, it should be read to require a minimum ten-year term of imprisonment....

Accordingly, before evaluating the constitutionality of the sentence imposed by the District Court, we must determine exactly what the statutory penalty provision in effect at the time of sentencing provided. We note that a subsequent Congress revised this statute, and opted unmistakably for a mandatory prison sentence, by providing in the PROTECT Act in 2003 that "[a]ny individual who violates, or attempts or conspires to violate, this section shall be fined under this title and imprisoned not less than 15 years...." 18 U.S.C. § 2251(e); H.R. Conf. Rep. 108-66, at 4 (2003), U.S. Code Cong. & Admin. News 683. Thus any decision we make with respect to the penalty provision will apply to an extremely small universe of cases.

We begin with the observation that the "and both" language in the Statutes at Large makes no sense. As a grammatical matter, one cannot choose between "A, or B, and both." Rather, it seems obvious that Congress intended the provision to mean either "A, *or* B, *or* both," or "A *and* B." Both parties are in agreement on this point. The Government acknowledges that the "and both" language is "simply illogical" and "essentially [a] scrivener's error[]." We thus ... find the statutory language ambiguous, and recognize the need to consult the legislative history as an aid to its interpretation.

Turning to the legislative history, we observe that one of the possible constructions of the statutory language—"A, or B, or both"—was prevalent in the drafting history of the text, while the other possible construction—"A and B"—was never part of the text. The penalty provision was originally part of the Child Pornography Prevention Act of 1996, which itself was inserted into H.R. 3610, an omnibus appropriations act for fiscal year 1997, at the House-Senate Conference on that bill. The Conference Report on H.R. 3610, which contained the presumptively final, non-amendable version of the language agreed to by the House of Representatives and the Senate, stated that violators "shall be fined under this title or imprisoned not less than 10 years nor more than 20 years, or both...." H.R. Conf. Rep. No. 104-863, at 32 (1996). The Conference Report on H.R. 3610, containing the "or both" language, was also inserted into the Congressional Record. *See* 142 Cong. Rec. H11,644, 11,652 (Sept. 28, 1996). Confusingly, the Senate Judiciary Committee Report on the Child Pornography Prevention Act employs the "and both" language when it sets forth the terms of the bill, S.Rep. No. 104-

358, at 4 (1996), and the "or both" language in its analysis of the bill's provisions. *Id.* at 23. Because only the analysis section of the Senate Report was inserted into the Congressional Record during the Senate debate on H.R. 3610, the Congressional Record report of that debate contains only the "or both" language. *See* 142 Cong. Rec. S11,838, 11,842 (Sept. 30, 1996)....

There is no question that the text of the bill signed by the President provides that violators "shall be fined ... or imprisoned not less than 10 years...., and both," and that this is the law we are considering. It is equally clear that the "and both" language makes no sense in this sentence. We are thus required to determine how the language of the statute should be interpreted and applied. The legislative history of § 2251(d) discussed above suggests that the "and both" language passed into law was, as the Government suggests, a scrivener's error. The same sources suggest that throughout much of the debate on the provision, the materials on which Congress could have been expected to rely for authoritative understandings of the bill's language specified that the bill provided that violators should be "fined under this title *or* imprisoned not less than 10 years nor more than 20 years, *or* both." By contrast, no version of the text of which we are aware ever provided that violators should be "be fined under this title *and* imprisoned not less than 10 years nor more than 20 years." In light of those sources, and the fact that the "or both" language is both grammatically unambiguous and logical as a matter of English usage, the "or both" language seems to us the most appropriate construction of the provision.

The Government contends that we should instead construe § 2251(d) as if it provided that violators "shall be fined under this title *and* imprisoned not less than 10 years nor more than 20 years." In support of this argument, the Government does not point to anything in the legislative history suggesting that language to that effect was ever put before or considered by Congress. Rather, the Government contends that whatever language Congress intended to adopt, that language should be construed as mandating a minimum of ten years' imprisonment on the basis of (i) the overall structure of § 2251(d); (ii) various statements made by individual legislators in support of and in opposition to the provision; and (iii) the alleged absurdity of any contrary interpretation. We disagree.

First, the Government contends that the structure of the statute was devised to set forth a regime of mandatory minimums, based on a defendant's prior convictions. The clauses of Section 2251(d) following the clause in question here, which apply only to recidivists, specify longer mandatory minimums and, more importantly, specify that such defendants "shall be fined under this title *and* imprisoned...." Pub.L. No. 104-208, § 121(4) (emphasis added).[16] Contrary to the Government's arguments, however, we do not find the other clauses in the paragraph to be irrefutable proof of Congress' intent to ensure mandatory minimum sentences for all offenders without exception; the discrepancy could as easily suggest Congress' intent to allow a more lenient sentence for first-time offenders.

---

16. The complete passage reads:
>   (d) Any individual who violates, or attempts or conspires to violate, this section shall be fined under this title or imprisoned not less than 10 years nor more than 20 years, and both, but if such person has one prior conviction under this chapter or chapter 109A, or under the laws of any State relating to the sexual exploitation of children, such person shall be fined under this title and imprisoned for not less than 15 years nor more than 30 years, but if such person has 2 or more prior convictions under this chapter or chapter 109A, or under the laws of any State relating to the sexual exploitation of children, such person shall be fined under this title and imprisoned not less than 30 years nor more than life.

Pub.L. No. 104-208, § 121(4).

The Government next argues, based on the legislative history of the provision, that the "plain import" was to mandate a ten-year minimum sentence. As evidence of this theory, the Government presents statements made in the report of the Senate Judiciary Committee describing the penalty provision, noting that "[t]he purpose of Senator Grassley's amendment [the amendment which resulted in the provision at issue here] is to toughen Federal penalties for the sexual exploitation of children." S.Rep. No. 104-358, at 22 (1996). However, it is immediately after describing this purpose that the report notes that "an individual who violates section 2251 would be fined *or* imprisoned for not less than 10 years nor more than 20 years, or both." *Id.* at 23 (emphasis added). Furthermore, no matter how we read the first-time offender provision of § 2251(d), the Child Pornography Prevention Act indisputably "toughen[ed] Federal penalties for the sexual exploitation of children." The previous version of the statute provided a ten-year *maximum* for first-time offenders, and a fifteen-year maximum for recidivists. *See* 18 U.S.C. § 2251(d) (1994). H.R. 3610 increased the maximum penalty for first-time offenders by ten years, changed the fifteen-year maximum for recidivists to a fifteen-year minimum, and added a new 30 years-to-life category for third-time offenders.

The Government also points to the statements in the Senate Report of three Senators opposed to the mandatory minimum provisions as evidence of the Congressional intent to mandate minimum sentences for all offenders. As we have noted before, however, it is well established that speeches by opponents of legislation are entitled to relatively little weight in determining the meaning of the Act in question. We do not find the statements of the Senators opposed to mandatory minimum provisions to constitute persuasive evidence against the clear meaning of the provision.

Next, the Government notes that Senator Grassley, the sponsor of the amendment including the penalty provisions, stated on the floor of the Senate: "In the Judiciary Committee, I offered an amendment which would create a three-strikes-and-you're-out penalty structure for the production of child pornography. First time offenders will receive a 10-year minimum sentence.... My amendment passed the committee after much debate." 142 Cong. Rec. S11, 285 (1996). While we acknowledge that these remarks by Senator Grassley contribute meaningfully at least to the understanding of his views, these remarks do not furnish sufficient evidence that Congress as a whole intended to mandate minimum terms of imprisonment and cannot suffice to overcome the more substantial indications that Congress intended to permit a choice. See *Chrysler Corp. v. Brown*, 441 U.S. 281, 311 (1979) ("The remarks of a single legislator, even the sponsor, are not controlling in analyzing legislative history.").[19]

Finally, the Government contends that the penalty provision in question should be understood as mandating at least ten years' imprisonment because any other result would be nonsensical. We disagree....

The Government argues that it simply makes no sense to permit a fine-only sentence, but to mandate that if any imprisonment is imposed, it must be at least ten years. This argument ignores the fact that the statute, passed in 1996, would operate against

---

19. In any event, even if the statements by individual members of Congress that the Government has drawn from the legislative history were weighty enough to counterbalance the evidence that the grammatically clear "or both" language was the version of the statute intended by Congress, we would hesitate to adopt the Government's position that an ambiguous penalty provision should be construed on that basis against a criminal defendant [based on the rule of lenity].

the backdrop of the Sentencing Guidelines. Depending on the particular circumstances of the crime and the offender, the Guidelines will almost always call for a sentence of at least several years' imprisonment for the offenses covered by § 2251(d), in which case § 2251(d) will mandate that the sentence be at least ten years. Only if there exist reasonable grounds for a very substantial downward departure will a federal judge have authority to consider imposing only a fine on an offense punishable under§ 2251(d). In other words, the Government contends that it is patently absurd to read the statute, in line with significant textual support in the legislative history, to permit a court to sentence an offender to no prison time if his case is extraordinary enough to justify a substantial downward departure. In place of such a construction the Government suggests we read the provision, without any textual support, and largely on the basis of isolated comments by individual members of Congress, to mandate that all offenders be sentenced to ten years' imprisonment no matter what the facts may be in the individual case. We cannot agree that there is any absurdity in prescribing a mandatory sentence for violations regarded as serious enough to warrant imprisonment while allowing a sentence without confinement where sufficient mitigating circumstances are found to justify withholding imprisonment altogether. Without doubt Congress could rationally have prescribed mandatory imprisonment for all violations. We recognize that Congress has indeed since amended the Act to provide unambiguously for such a result. But we cannot accept that it would have been absurd for Congress to *avoid* such a result....

Accordingly, we hold that the "and both" language contained in the enrolled version of the statute makes no sense as a matter of grammar, usage, or law; that the "or both" language in the Conference Report does make some sense; that the stronger evidence of Congress' intent points to an understanding that the "or both" text is what Congress contemplated; [and] that there is no textual support for the government's interpretation.... We therefore conclude that the District Court had the discretion to sentence defendant to either a fine or a term of imprisonment of not less than ten years or both....

Accordingly, the finding of guilt is affirmed, the sentence is vacated, and the cause is remanded for further proceedings consistent with this opinion.

Notes and Questions

(1) *Bad Lawyering.* Who first raised this interpretation issue? Why do you think defendant's counsel missed this critical argument?

(2) *Government's Arguments.* The state makes three arguments to support its interpretation that a court must impose both a fine and a ten year sentence. What are those arguments? Which, if any, do you find most persuasive?

(3) *Scrivener's Error.* The court rejected the ordinary meaning of the text, concluding that the statute contained a scrivener's error. And both sides agreed that the text could not mean what it said. Where does this court turn to discern meaning given that the text does not provide the answer? Do you find the analysis persuasive? How would a textualist likely have resolved this case given that intrinsic sources were of little value?

(4) *Should "And" Mean Only And?* As the text has gained currency, courts have increasingly refused to interpret "and" and "or" in anything other than in their denotative way. For example, the Florida courts will change the meanings of "and" and "or" only when the literal reading results in an unreasonable or ridiculous interpretation. *Corfan Banco Asuncion Paraguay v. Ocean Bank*, 715 So. 2d 967, 970 (Fla. Dist. Ct.

App. 1998). Florida courts assume that the conjunction's literal meaning was intended, and, if not, it is for the legislature to address by amendment, not for the court to address through interpretation. Given that we are talking about the use of "and" and "or" in a statute that may run for dozens or hundreds of pages, does Florida expect too much of its legislators?

Problem 5-2

You represent Loree Powers. Her husband, Mercer State Trooper Mark Powers died on September 27. On the date of his death, Powers was a trooper on active duty with the Mercer State Patrol and was a member of the Mercer State Patrol Retirement System (MSPRS). Powers is survived by his wife and seven children. Powers and Loree had four children, who all lived with them at the time of Powers' death. Powers' other three children were from his previous marriage to Patti Holloway, with whom they resided. All seven children were under the age of 19 when Powers died.

Loree seeks benefits on behalf of herself as Powers' surviving spouse and on behalf of the couple's four children who live with her. Loree wants to know whether §81-2026(3) excludes Holloway's children from sharing in Powers' annuity.

Allocation of benefits from MSPRS is governed by the Mercer State Patrol Retirement Act, Mercer Rev. Stat. §81-2026(3), which provides:

> Upon the death of an officer before retirement, benefits shall be provided as follows: (a) To the surviving spouse, regardless of the length of time the spouse and officer had been married, and dependent child or children of the officer under the age of nineteen years in such spouse's care, the benefit shall be one hundred percent of the amount of such officer's annuity until such time as the youngest dependent child attains the age of nineteen years after which time the benefit shall be reduced to seventy-five percent of the officer's annuity for the remainder of his or her life or until he or she remarries; (b) if there is no spouse living at the date of the officer's death, his or her child or children, if any, shall continue to receive seventy-five percent of the amount of such officer's annuity until such time as the youngest child attains the age of nineteen years; (c) if there is more than one child of the officer under the age of nineteen years at the date of the officer's death, the benefit shall be divided equally among such children and, as they attain the age of nineteen years, only the child or children under the age of nineteen years shall participate therein; and (d) if there is no child or children of the officer under the age of nineteen years living at the date of the officer's death, the surviving spouse, regardless of the length of time the spouse and officer had been married, shall receive seventy-five percent of the amount of such officer's annuity for the remainder of his or her life or until he or she remarries.

According to the legislative history, the MSPRS was established in 1947 to "provide certain retirement and other benefits" for officers of the Mercer State Patrol. 1947 Mercer Laws, ch. 211, §2, p. 687. The officer death benefit found in §81-2026 was initially added in 1953 to provide benefits for an officer's widow and/or children upon the officer's death after retirement. 1953 Mercer Laws, ch. 333, §2, p. 1093. In 1957, the preretirement benefit was added. 1957 Mercer Laws, ch. 276, §1, p. 1004. In 1969, the statute was amended to provide that a greater percentage of the annuity be paid out when the trooper left behind both a widow and children. 1969 Mercer Laws, ch. 511, §8, p. 2095.

Analyze whether Loree is entitled to recover 100% of the benefits given that some surviving children resided with her and some with the former spouse.

2. Singular and Plural, Masculine, Feminine, and Neuter Words

While courts generally presume that the ordinary rules of grammar apply, in two instances ordinary rules do not. First, singular words in a statute can include the plural. "In determining the meaning of any Act of Congress, unless the context indicates otherwise—words importing the singular include and apply to several persons, parties, or things; words importing the plural include the singular...." 1 U.S.C. § 1 (2000). Some states have similar provisions. *See, e.g.,* N.J. Stat. Ann. § 1:1-2 (West 2005); Ariz. Rev. Stat. § 1-214(B) (2005).

For example, *Homebuilders Ass'n v. City of Scottsdale*, 925 P.2d 1359 (Ariz. Ct. App. 1996), was a suit to have a referendum rejected for having an insufficient number of signatures. At issue was whether the term "councilmen" was plural or singular:

> [R]ules of statutory construction are unnecessary when the meaning of a statute can be discerned from the plain meaning of its language. However, ... we reject the argument that the meaning of "councilmen" as either singular or plural is clear and unambiguous. Not only have the parties in these consolidated appeals presented considerable argument in two courts disputing the interpretation of this term, but two superior court judges have ruled differently on the meaning of this word in this context. Under these circumstances, we find an ambiguity sufficient for us to resort to general principles of statutory construction....
>
> We also concur with the general principle that the legislature is presumed to mean what it says. However, we also presume that the legislature meant what it said when it enacted its own general rules of statutory construction. We further presume the legislature was aware of those statutory rules of construction when it enacted [the statute being interpreted]....
>
> In this case, those rules also include the statutory directive that words in the plural be interpreted to include the singular. A.R.S. § 1-214(B).
>
> This general principle of statutory interpretation has been widely adopted in most statutory schemes. The historical purpose of construing plural and singular nouns and verbs interchangeably is to avoid requiring the legislature to use such expressions as "person or persons," "he, she, or they," and "himself or themselves." Under this principle, the plural has often been held to apply to the singular in a statute, absent evidence of contrary legislative intent. [The court holds that the term councilmen includes both the plural and singular in this instance.]

Id. at 1365–66.

Second, under federal and many state statutes, the masculine pronoun can also include the feminine (and neuter) and *vice versa. See* 1 U.S.C.A. § 2 (West 2005); *see, e.g.,* 1 Pa. Cons. Stat. § 1902; O.R.S. 174.110(2) ("Words used in the masculine gender may include the feminine and the neuter.") Oregon's policy is to write statutes in gender neutral language. Or. Rev. Stat. § 174.129 (2005). As with all the principles of statutory construction, a judge will ignore these rules if they lead to absurd results. *See* MINN. STAT. ANN. §645.08 (West 2005); 1 PA. CONS. STAT. §1922 (2005).

Notes and Questions

(1) *An Example of the Singular Not Meaning the Plural.* In *Van Horn v. William Blanchard Co.*, 438 A.2d 552 (N.J. 1981), the court analyzed New Jersey's Comparative Negligence Act, which provided:

> Contributory negligence shall not bar recovery in an action by any person or his legal representative to recover damages for negligence resulting in death or injury to person or property, if such negligence was not greater than the negligence of the person against whom recovery is sought, but any damages sustained shall be diminished by the percentage sustained of negligence attributable to the person recovering. (N.J.S.A. 2A:15-5.1).

The specific language at issue was "the person." The majority rejected the plaintiff's argument that the word "person" could include the plural "persons":

> The Legislature's use of the singular "the person" rather than the plural form strongly suggests that a plaintiff's negligence should be compared to the negligence of only one person at a time. Plaintiff would have us reject that sensible construction by resort to N.J.S.A. 1:1-2, which provides that "(w)herever, in describing or referring to any person ... any word imparting the singular number ... is used, the same shall be understood to include and to apply to several persons or parties as well...." The argument is that in its use of the phrase "the person against whom recovery is sought" the Legislature intended to refer to the tortfeasor concept in its collective and adjectival sense....
>
> Whatever persuasive appeal is inherent in that approach is overcome when section 1 of the Act is read in conjunction with section 3. The latter section reads:
>
> > The party so recovering, may recover the full amount of the molded verdict from any party against whom such recovering party is not barred from recovery. Any party who is so compelled to pay more than such party's percentage share may seek contribution from the other joint tortfeasors.
>
> This statute obviously addresses a multi-defendant situation, as in the case before us. Equally obvious is that it contemplates a fact pattern in which the plaintiff is entitled to recover from at least one defendant, while at the same time there are other negligent defendants from whom he is not entitled to recover — the antithesis of aggregating all the defendants' negligence. No other meaning can reasonably be ascribed to the descriptive phrase "any party against whom such recovering party is not barred from recovery." And if there are defendants from whom plaintiff is entitled to recover and others from whom recovery is barred, then it is clear that aggregation of defendants' percentages of fault is not contemplated; for if it were, and if a plaintiff were entitled to recover against any negligent defendant, he would be entitled to recover against all under the minority's theory.
>
> But that is not what section 3 of the statute says. It distinguishes between or among defendants: those from whom recovery is allowed and those against whom recovery is barred. The most obvious point of distinction between the two classes of defendants is the quantum of their respective negligence vis-a-vis the plain-

tiff's negligence. So if plaintiff is thirty-five percent negligent, defendant A is forty-five percent at fault and defendant B's negligence amounts to twenty percent, in keeping with section 3 of the Act plaintiff would be permitted to recover from defendant A but not from defendant B.... N.J.S.A. 2A:15-5.3 convincingly disposes of the argument that defendants' negligence should be aggregated for purposes of determining whether plaintiff is entitled to recover.

Id. at 554–55. The dissent vigorously disagreed:

In reasoning that the emphasized words in these passages dictate the individual approach, the majority has succumbed to a common judicial temptation in the interpretation of statutes. In effect, the Court has already interpreted the statute to require the singular significance of the term "person" and then declares that the "plain language" admits of only one interpretation—the one it has selected.

The essential judicial task, of course, is to ascertain the statutory meaning intended by the Legislature. Where the plain meaning of a statute is revealed by its language, given its ordinary significance and understanding, that meaning, and no other, must be ascribed to the enactment. What constitutes "plain" language, however, is not always obvious. The meaning of language that is seemingly clear and unequivocal may become doubtful and elusive when considered in a wider context. In my estimation, the statutory language at issue does not simply or plainly reveal the intentions of the Legislature.... [I]n ascertaining the legislative intent underlying the Comparative Negligence Act, the inquiry must go beyond the terms of the statute itself.

While the facial or literal terms in question permit the construction chosen by the Court, neither the intrinsic nor contextual meaning of the words of the statute requires this interpretation. The Legislature has provided its own guidelines for the interpretation of statutes, which in this case counsel a different construction from that imposed by the majority. N.J.S.A. 1:1-2 defines certain words and phrases for interpretive purposes and specifically states that unless expressly excepted or repugnant to the subject of the enactment, all defined words and phrases used in New Jersey legislation carry the meaning indicated in N.J.S.A. 1:1-2. That statute explicitly provides that "any word importing the singular number ... shall be understood to include and apply to several persons or parties as well as to one person or party." Thus, the word "person" as used in the Act does not necessarily or plainly denote "one person." ...

The majority's reliance on N.J.S.A. 2A:15-5.3 to extract a contextual meaning from the words "the person" or "any person" as denoting the singular usage does not advance its "plain language" thesis. That provision has to do with the allocation of the recovery of a successful plaintiff. It simply states that such a plaintiff may recover the entire or full amount of the verdict from any defendant "against whom (the plaintiff) is not barred from recovery." This class of defendants, of course, encompasses all, and means any of the defendants who are liable to the plaintiff under N.J.S.A. 2A:15-5.1.

The majority points out that N.J.S.A. 2A:15-5.3 contemplates a multi-defendant situation and recognizes by implication that in a given case some defendants will not be subject to a plaintiff's recovery. The majority reasons that because some defendants may not be subject to a plaintiff's recovery under N.J.S.A. 2A:15-5.3, the Legislature must have intended the individual approach, since the aggregate approach would render all "negligent" defendants liable....

> It is difficult to follow [the majority's reasoning]. Wherever else it leads, it clearly demonstrates that the legislative intent to use the individual or the aggregate approach cannot be fairly resolved solely from the language of the enactment.

Id. at 557–58 (Handler, J., dissenting).

Which approach to interpretation did the majority follow? The dissent? Did the majority ignore the plain meaning to obtain a result it considered more consistent with the legislative intent? The New Jersey Legislature amended this statute in direct response to the holding in this case. The new statute adopted the dissent's interpretation. Does that amendment indicate anything about which interpretation was correct?

(2) *An Example of the Masculine Including the Feminine.* In *Commonwealth. v. Henninger*, 1981 WL 423 (Pa. Ct. Com. Pl. 1981), the court applied the gender neutral rule to the question of whether a female could be charged with statutory rape:

> Defendant argues that the statute does not admit of the capability of a female to commit the crime of statutory rape in Pennsylvania. The prohibition against intercourse with persons under the age of consent is codified at 18 Pa. C. S.A. § 3122. "A person who is 18 years of age or older commits statutory rape, a felony of the second degree, when he engages in sexual intercourse with another person not his spouse who is less than 14 years of age."
>
> First, defendant maintains that the gender-based language in Section 3122 evidences an intent on the part of the legislators to protect only women. Defendant's historical argument is certainly well-founded but, given the more recent pronouncement of the legislators regarding sexual equality in enacting the Equal Rights Amendment, Const. Art. 1 Section 28, we believe the statute must now be read in light of that amendment. Additionally, the Statutory Construction Act, 1 Pa.C.S.A. § 1902, undermines any argument defendant may propose with regard to the masculine pronouns employed in Section 3122. Section 1902 states: ..."Words used in the masculine gender shall include the feminine and neuter."
>
> We conclude ... that females can be charged with ... statutory rape....

(3) *An Example of the Feminine Meaning only the Feminine.* Occasionally, courts refuse to interpret a gender-specific term in a gender-neutral way. An Oregon court faced this statute:

> In case an unmarried man and an unmarried woman have cohabited in this state as husband and wife for over one year prior to the date of an accidental injury received by such man, and children are living as a result of that relation, the woman and the children are entitled to compensation under [another statute] the same as if the man and woman had been legally married.

Or. Rev. Stat. § 656.226. The court refused to interpret "woman" to include "man" despite a statute that directed that "[w]ords used in the masculine gender may include the feminine and the neuter." Or. Rev. Stat. § 174.110(2). The court reasoned:

> Petitioner asks us to interpret the word "woman" to include man. That would not be an interpretation of a word used in the masculine gender.... We cannot apply a "policy" to contradict the obvious meaning of the words employed by the legislature. The word "woman" is clear and merits no interpretation. We cannot employ judicial interpretation to thwart the plain meaning of the statutory language.

In Re Compensation of Williams, 635 P.2d 384, 386 (Or. Ct. App. 1981), *aff'd*, 653 P.2d 970 (Or. 1982). Why did the majority refuse to apply the canon to the word "woman?"

Problem 5-3

Assume the following news story appeared in your jurisdiction. Analyze the judge's decision.

Indecent Exposure Law Applies to Men Only; Drops Charge Against Woman

A judge dismissed an indecent exposure charge against a woman who allegedly disrobed in front of a 14-year-old boy, saying the law applies only to men. The law refers to a person who "exposes his person."

"Usually when a section proscribes conduct, it's 'his or her.' This one is not," the judge said. "It's gender specific."

The county prosecutor argued that the lack of a feminine reference in the penal code was a typo and that solely applying the law to men would violate the state Constitution. But the judge was not convinced and dismissed the case.

The facts are simple. The defendant allegedly gave the boy, her neighbor, a full-frontal view as he played basketball in the yard next door. The defendant had complained to the boy that he was making too much noise as he played. When he didn't stop playing, she went out onto her sundeck. The boy looked up at her, she looked down at him, and she disrobed. The boy ran inside and told his parents. When the defendant threatened to do it every time he played basketball, his parents called the police. The family has since moved out of the neighborhood.

Earlier in the day, the judge told the prosecutor he thought the defendant's disrobing was "very silly and illegal conduct" but not serious enough to require her to register as a sex offender for the rest of her life.

Chapter 6

The Textual Canons

This chapter surveys the canons that lay somewhere between the text and purely extrinsic sources, such as legislative history. These canons are often called the linguistic, or syntactic, canons. We have chosen to call them "textual" canons of construction to emphasize that the focus of these canons is on the legislature's enacted "expression." We will see that other canons—the rule of lenity, for example—reflect substantive policies. In contrast, the textual canons "do not, on their face at least, reflect any policy preference, but simply purport to be helpful ways of divining the nature and limits of what the drafters of the legislation were trying to achieve." David L. Shapiro, *Continuity and Change in Statutory Interpretation*, 67 N.Y.U. L. Rev. 921, 927 (1992). This chapter covers the more common textual canons.

Because many textual canons go by Latin names, the direction they offer appears clouded in legal mystery. Some academics have widely criticized the textual canons for their ostensible inconsistency. These academics argue that for every canon there is an equal and opposite canon. We think that the criticism is overstated, but as you study the canons, keep that criticism in mind.

A. When Should the Textual Canons Affect Plain Meaning?

Before discussing the textual canons, we must first ask: At what point in the interpretative process are they appropriate to consider? Perhaps by now you will not be surprised to learn that there is no agreement on the answer to that question. Instead, when a judge will use the textual canons turns on the judge's approach to interpretation. Pertinent here, you need to recognize that there is disagreement over the role of the textual canons. Do they apply in determining plain meaning, or, instead, should they be used only if a judge first concludes that the text is ambiguous, absurd, or contains a scrivener's error? Let's explore this question further.

You will see that the textual canons often state what might seem to be the obvious. For example, one canon (*ejusdem generis*) advises that general words following a series should be limited in type to the specific words preceding them. Thus, a statute that applies to "cars, SUVs, motorcycles, and *other vehicles*," seemingly would not apply to bicycles. They are not motorized, and ordinarily people do not call bikes "vehicles." But why and how does "other vehicles" become limited by the language that precedes it?

As we've said, words are inherently ambiguous. At a minimum, the textual context surrounding the words at issue (meaning the remainder of the statute) will play a role in their interpretation. After all, "other vehicles" is completely unclear without "cars, SUVs, [and] motorcycles" preceding it. A very strict textualist might stop there. But should a judge look further?

What if the statute at issue regulated maximum speeds on roads? The ordinary meaning of "vehicle" would not seem to cover bikes, but the purpose of the statute (ostensibly to limit speeds to protect people and property) might suggest that "other vehicles" was meant to be broad and inclusive; hence, the interpretation of the phrase should not be limited by the fact that cars, SUVs, and motorcycles have engines. This example suggests that sometimes the words preceding a general catchall narrow the catchall phrase. But why does "other vehicles" become limited by the words that precede it? Does the purpose of the statute, the text, or both suggest the limitation?

And how does "other vehicles" become so limited? Suppose, instead, that the statute imposed a tax on "cars, SUVs, motorcycles, and other vehicles." Should the tax apply to bikes? It should if "other vehicles" is limited to things that can be used for transportation, but it should not if "other vehicles" applies only to things with engines.

The point here is fundamental. Textualists believe that the text, in its context, gives the most likely meaning of the words. But consider whether a judge can determine what "other vehicles" means without considering something more than the surrounding words? Our simple example illustrates one key issue that the cases in this book often wrestle with: Should anything but the words in the text be considered in determining the "plain," or "ordinary," meaning of a statute?

If consideration of something more is sometimes necessary, then the question becomes: What should courts properly consider besides the words themselves? Does the purpose of the statute matter? Does legislative intent, as reflected in the legislative history, matter? Should those things matter only under some circumstances, such as when the statute is ambiguous? If so, then does a judge determine ambiguity only by looking at the ordinary meaning of the words, or does a judge look beyond the text itself in determining whether an ambiguity exists?

Who do you think would be more amenable to using the textual canons: textualists, intentionalists, or purposivists? Textualists use the canons as a way to avoid finding ambiguity altogether or to resolve such a finding promptly. By applying the textual canons so readily, textualists ensure that consideration of extrinsic sources will be foreclosed in all but the rarest occasions. Simply put, "if one doubts the judicial capacity to find ... legislative intent or purpose, it may seem important, if not essential, to emphasize and develop effective rules of thumb to resolve the doubts that inevitably arise out of statutory language." John F. Manning, *Legal Realism & The Canons' Revival*, 5 GREEN BAG 283, 285 (2002). To a textualist, turning to the textual canons first is also one way to further the legislative process: If the courts apply the canons in a predictable way and if legislators know how the canons will be applied, then it is more likely that legislators will draft text that can be interpreted to reflect the intended meaning. The textual canons, thus, become an efficient means to ensure accurate communication of meaning from legislatures to courts. *See id.* In other words, using the textual canons furthers predictability.

In contrast, if "one believes that legislative history (or some other type of evidence [*e.g.*, purpose]) can reliably reveal specific intent or at least the ultimate goal behind words and phrases ... then using [textual canons] to resolve ambiguity might appear technical, formal, and perhaps insensitive to the true will of the democratically elected legislature." *Id.* Hence, intentionalists and purposivists also rely on these canons because they simply reflect the reality of American speaking and writing, but these theorists do not value these canons to the degree that textualists do.

B. The Rule of Lenity: An Introduction

Before beginning our discussion of the textual canons, we first mention the rule of lenity: a canon based, not on text, but on constitutional concerns. Due Process requires that criminal statutes give fair warning of the scope of criminal law. Consequently, a person can only be punished for engaging in conduct that a reasonable person would know was illegal. We will explore this canon more fully in another chapter because it is generally applied only when the statute at issue is both penal in nature *and* ambiguous (however identified).

We mention the rule of lenity here, however, because several cases in this chapter refer to the rule of lenity. In fact, many judges expansively state that, pursuant to the rule of lenity, they must interpret criminal statutes narrowly. *E.g., Commonwealth v. O'Keefe*, 723 N.E.2d 1000 (Mass. Ct. App. 2000). Actually, judges generally do not turn to the rule of lenity unless the ambiguity persists even after the court has examined many other sources of meaning. With that background in mind, let's turn to the textual canons.

C. The Common Textual Canons

1. *In Pari Materia*

We start with a textual canon that directs judges on what textual context to consider when interpreting statutes: *in pari materia*. The words *"in pari materia"* mean "part of the same material." Simply put, this canon reflects the common sense notion that statutory language should not be looked at in isolation; rather, the entire textual context is relevant. The canon has two distinct aspects.

context matters

The first aspect directs that the words of a single section of a statute must be construed in light of the entire statute and not in isolation. This aspect is merely common sense. "Statutory construction ... is a holistic endeavor. A provision that may seem ambiguous in isolation is often clarified by the remainder of the statutory scheme...." *United Sav. Ass'n of Tex. v. Timbers of Inwood Forest Assocs., Ltd.*, 484 U.S. 365, 371 (1988). Simply put, words must be construed in light of the act as a whole. This aspect of *in pari materia* is relatively non-controversial.

The second aspect of *in pari materia* directs that the same word in "related" statutes, statutes on the same subject matter, be given the same meaning. This aspect leads to more disagreement and controversy for what does "related" (or of the same subject) mean? We will explore this question below in *Commonwealth v. Smith*.

Taken together, *in pari materia* presumes internal consistency within a single statute, as well as coherence among different statutes on the same subject. Likewise, it presumes that courts can readily discern when two statutes are "related" enough so that the same word used in each statute should be given the same meaning. Both presumptions may be unrealistic, as the following cases show.

a. The Whole Act Rule

Rhyne v. K-Mart Corp.

594 S.E.2d 1 (N.C. 2004)

BRADY, Justice.

On or about 28 April 1998, K-Mart employees confronted plaintiffs as the couple was walking near a K-Mart retail store.... Roberts, one of the employees, inquired of plaintiffs as to whether they had been rummaging through K-Mart's dumpsters. Mr. Rhyne responded that plaintiffs had not touched the dumpsters and were walking for exercise purposes only.

The following day, plaintiffs were again walking in the store's parking lot when they were approached by Roberts and Hoyle. This time, Roberts grabbed Mr. Rhyne, placed him in a choke-hold, and forced him to the ground. As Mrs. Rhyne attempted to assist her husband, who was at that time struggling to break free from Roberts, Hoyle pushed Mrs. Rhyne to the ground....

As a result of the incident, plaintiffs sought and received medical attention for various physical and psychological ailments. Mr. Rhyne sustained a total of $5,376.12 in medical bills and lost wages, while Mrs. Rhyne sustained a total of $13,582.40 in medical bills.

[P]laintiffs filed a civil action against K-Mart, Roberts, and Hoyle....

Regarding K-Mart, the jury returned a verdict finding that the corporation, through its agent Roberts, falsely imprisoned or unlawfully detained plaintiffs, inflicted intentional emotional distress on plaintiffs, ... and negligently injured both plaintiffs. The jury awarded compensatory damages to Mr. Rhyne in the amount of $8,255.00.... The jury awarded compensatory damages to Mrs. Rhyne in the amount of $10,730.00. [Further,] the jury found that each plaintiff was entitled to an award of punitive damages in the amount of $11.5 million.... The statute at issue in the present appeal, N.C.G.S. §1D-25, instructs trial courts to reduce awards of punitive damages to an amount that is three times the compensatory damages award or $250,000.00, whichever amount is greater. Pursuant to that statute, the trial court reduced the amount awarded each plaintiff to $250,000.00....

Plaintiffs and K-Mart appealed.... [The appellate court affirmed].

K-Mart argues that the Court of Appeals misinterpreted section 1D-25(b). Subsection (b) provides as follows:

> Punitive damages awarded against a defendant shall not exceed three times the amount of compensatory damages or two hundred fifty thousand dollars ($250,000), whichever is greater. If a trier of fact returns a verdict for punitive damages in excess of the maximum amount specified under this subsection, the trial court shall reduce the award and enter judgment for punitive damages in the maximum amount.

The Court of Appeals concluded that section 1D-25(b) applied per plaintiff, such that each plaintiff should receive the greater of three times his individual compensatory damages award or $250,000.00. Because the trebling of each plaintiff's compensatory damages award resulted in an amount less than $250,000.00, the Court of Appeals determined that each plaintiff in the instant case should receive $250,000.00, requiring K-Mart to pay a total of $500,000.00 in punitive damages.

K-Mart argues that the punitive damages limitation should apply per defendant, such that it should be required to pay a total of $250,000.00 in punitive damages. According to K-Mart, a per-defendant application is dictated by the plain meaning of the statute as it directs a trial court to reduce "[p]unitive damages awarded against *a defendant.*" We do not agree with K-Mart's argument.

The meaning of N.C.G.S. § 1D-25(b) is easily resolved through applying the well-established rules of statutory construction. A statute that is clear and unambiguous must be construed using its plain meaning. But where a statute is ambiguous, judicial construction must be used to ascertain the legislative will.

K-Mart supports its argument that the punitive damages limitation applies per defendant by isolating one particular portion of section 1D-25(b) — that "[p]unitive damages awarded against *a defendant* shall not exceed" the amount specified therein. However, this Court does not read segments of a statute in isolation. Rather, we construe statutes *in pari materia*, giving effect, if possible, to every provision.

The use of other singular terms in section 1D-25(b) suggests that the statute applies to reduce each plaintiff's individual punitive damages award. The second sentence of section 1D-25 refers to that which is to be reduced as "*a verdict*" and "*the* award." We acknowledge that when a jury returns multiple verdicts, it will, more than likely, submit one verdict sheet to the trial court. Furthermore, in our everyday parlance, we may refer to the verdict sheet as a verdict or declare that the jury has returned its verdict or a verdict. However, as the verdict sheet reflects in th[is] case ..., the jury may actually return two separate punitive damages awards, as there are two distinct verdicts based upon causes of action for individual plaintiffs.

Here, the jury returned one verdict against K-Mart for Mr. Rhyne in the amount of $11.2 million and a separate verdict for Mrs. Rhyne in the same amount. Mr. and Mrs. Rhyne joined in one civil action to bring their claims, and K-Mart was, in essence, a separate defendant with respect to each plaintiff's action. Thus, reading N.C.G.S. 1D-25 in its entirety, as we must, the statute directs the trial court to reduce both the award for Mr. Rhyne and the award for Mrs. Rhyne and to enter judgment against K-Mart in the amount of $250,000.00 for each plaintiff.

This construction of section 1D-25(b) is further supported by the operation of other statutes within Chapter 1D. Most significantly, section 1D-15(a) directs the trier of fact to consider an exclusive list of aggravating factors when determining whether to award punitive damages. In the absence of some legislative directive, it is assumed that the trier of fact should, as it did at common law, consider these factors as to each plaintiff's cause of action and not as to each defendant. It follows that, like section 1D-15(a), section 1D-25(b) applies to the individual jury verdict of each plaintiff.

For the reasons stated above, we hold that N.C.G.S. § 1D-25 ... applies to limit the recovery of each plaintiff. We therefore affirm....

Notes and Questions

(1) *Did the Majority First Find that the Statute Was Ambiguous?* Remember that some textualists require such a finding before they will look past the text. Assuming there was ambiguity, did *in pari materia* resolve it?

(2) *Singular Includes the Plural.* We saw earlier that the singular includes the plural and *vice versa.* (*See* Chapter 5.) Would this latter canon have aided the court's interpretation? Why do you suppose the court failed to discuss this canon and instead relied on *in pari materia*?

(3) *No Mention of Intent or Purpose.* Why do you think the court never addressed legislative intent or purpose? Is there any clear purpose you can discern? If it is to ensure that conduct is punished only once, what should be the proper result? If it is to limit punitive damages, what result?

(4) *Absurd Result?* In an omitted section of the opinion, the majority concluded that any other interpretation would lead to absurd results because it would encourage a proliferation of multiple punitive damages lawsuits. In other words, civil litigants would bring separate suits rather than combine them like the Rhymes did. Do you find that argument convincing? Does it presume a legislative intent about avoiding lawsuits that may not be reflected in the language of the statute?

b. The Same Word in Related Statutes Should Have the Same Meaning

The foregoing case illustrates the first aspect of *in pari materia*: how the same words in different provisions in a single statute or act should be interpreted. The case below illustrates its more controversial and difficult-to-apply form: how the same word in related statutes should be interpreted. Before you read the case, a warning: the subject matter—incest and child abuse—is difficult. We have chosen to include the case despite this difficulty because it develops the second aspect of *in pari materia* very clearly.

Here is some background information to help make this case clearer for you. In 1974, the Massachusetts legislature amended the rape statute (contained in the chapter entitled "Crimes Against the Person") by substituting the terms "sexual intercourse" and "unnatural sexual intercourse" for "ravishes and carnally knows." In *Commonwealth v. Gallant*, 369 N.E.2d 707 (Mass. 1977), the court interpreted those terms: *Sexual intercourse* was defined as "the penetration of the female sex organ by the male sex organ, with or without emission," while *unnatural sexual intercourse* was defined as "oral and anal intercourse, including fellatio, cunnilingus, and other intrusions of a part of a person's body or other object into the genital or anal opening of another person's body." *Id.* at 712.

But the incest statute, which criminalized only *sexual intercourse* not *unnatural sexual intercourse* between consanguineous relatives, was not amended at that time. Moreover, section 3, another section within the same code where the incest statute was codified ("Crimes Against Chastity, Morality, Decency and Good Order"), was amended in 1998 to substitute the terms "sexual intercourse or unnatural sexual intercourse" for the term "unlawful sexual intercourse." As you read the case, be sure you understand why both the majority and dissent refuse to apply the rape definition to the incest statute yet disagree as to what the proper definition is.

Commonwealth v. Smith
728 N.E.2d 272 (Mass. 2000)

Lynch., J.

A Plymouth County grand jury indicted the defendant on two charges of incest pursuant to G.L. c. 272, §17 (incest statute), based on conduct he allegedly engaged in with his daughter.[1] The defendant moved in the Superior Court ... to dismiss the indictments,

---

1. The defendant was also indicted for indecent assault and battery on a child under the age of fourteen years, G.L. c. 265, §13B, and assault and battery, G.L. c. 265, §13A, for acts allegedly perpetrated against his daughter. Neither of these indictments is before us on appeal. The defendant was

arguing that, because there was no evidence of penile-vaginal penetration, the grand jury lacked sufficient evidence that he had engaged in "sexual intercourse" with his daughter, as required by the incest statute.[2] The judge allowed this motion to dismiss, and the Appeals Court affirmed.... We granted the Commonwealth's application for further appellate review. We now affirm....

1. *Facts and prior proceedings.* The charges against the defendant arose from allegations made by his daughter.... The daughter testified ... that the defendant had fondled her in an inappropriate manner after she was eleven years old and that, after she reached the age of sixteen years, he put his hands down her pants and digitally penetrated her vagina and also had her perform oral sex on him....

In allowing the defendant's motion to dismiss the incest indictments, the judge concluded that the alleged acts of digital penetration and oral intercourse did not satisfy the requirement in G.L. c. 272, § 17, of "sexual intercourse" between consanguineous relations. In the absence of a definition of "sexual intercourse" in the incest statute, the judge relied on this court's construction of this term, and of the related term "unnatural sexual intercourse," in the context of the rape statutes. In *Commonwealth v. Gallant,* ... this court concluded that, "[b]y sexual intercourse, the Legislature undoubtedly intended the traditional common law notion of rape, the penetration of the female sex organ by the male sex organ, with or without emission," whereas "unnatural sexual intercourse," by contrast, refers to "oral and anal intercourse, including fellatio, cunnilingus, and other intrusions of a part of a person's body or other object into the genital or anal opening of another person's body." Because the incest statute explicitly criminalizes "sexual intercourse" but not "unnatural sexual intercourse" between consanguineous relations, the judge concluded that the defendant's alleged conduct with his daughter did not warrant a finding of probable cause that the defendant had committed the statutory crime of incest and, therefore, dismissed the indictments....

2. *Discussion....* The Legislature has not explicitly defined the term "sexual intercourse" in G.L. c. 272, § 17, and in prior cases brought under the statute we have not been required to determine whether this term extends to forms of sexual conduct other than penile-vaginal penetration. We conclude that, but for the Legislature's post-1974 amendments of statutes in G.L. c. 272 that contain the term "sexual intercourse" and its addition of the term "unnatural sexual intercourse" to G.L. c. 272, § 3, the term "sexual intercourse" in the incest statute, G.L. c. 272, § 17, could properly be construed to encompass the acts here alleged to have been engaged in by the defendant with his daughter. However, in light of that legislative activity, we are compelled to limit the meaning of "sexual intercourse" in G.L. c. 272, § 17, to penile-vaginal penetration ... and to conclude that the incest indictments against the defendant were properly dismissed....

In our view, it is too facile to rely directly ... on the rape statutes for the meaning of "sexual intercourse" in the incest statute. When interpreting undefined terms in a statute, it is certainly permissible to draw on the meaning that has settled on the same language in other legislation. However, such an interpretive approach is more properly utilized when the legislation that the court consults for guidance is *in pari materia* with the statute

---

not indicted for rape or statutory rape. The alleged acts of intercourse occurred after the victim had reached the age of sixteen years, thus precluding statutory rape charges. *See* G.L. c. 265, § 23. Moreover, at oral argument, the Commonwealth explained that no indictment was sought for rape, G.L. c. 265, § 22, because there was insufficient evidence of the daughter's lack of consent to the alleged acts of intercourse.

2. General Laws c. 272, § 17, provides, in pertinent part: "Persons within the degrees of consanguinity within which marriages are prohibited or declared by law to be incestuous and void, who intermarry or have sexual intercourse, shall be punished...."

being construed, that is, when the two statutes relate to the same class of persons or things or share a common purpose. When the two statutes are not so related, this approach is, at best, an uncertain means of discerning the intended meaning of statutory language and should be employed cautiously. The rape statutes appear in a chapter entitled "Crimes Against the Person," whereas the incest statute appears in a chapter entitled "Crimes Against Chastity, Morality, Decency and Good Order." G.L. c. 272. Rape is a violent invasion of personal integrity and dignity committed in a sexual manner, an essential element of which is the absence of the victim's consent. In the case of rape of a child under the age of sixteen years committed without the use of force or threat, such lack of consent is, nevertheless, conclusively presumed by law. By contrast, the crime of incest is committed where persons within a specified "degree[] of consanguinity" engage in sexual intercourse; the consensual or nonconsensual character of the conduct is immaterial. Moreover, in *Commonwealth v. Gallant*, where "sexual intercourse" in [the rape statutes] was held to refer to penile-vaginal penetration, this court noted that the Legislature's 1974 amendment of the rape statutes to encompass also "unnatural sexual intercourse" reflected a nation-wide reform effort that explicitly sought to "broaden the scope of the crime" to include forms of sexual intrusion that had escaped prosecution as rape under a narrower definition of intercourse. Our construction of these terms in *Gallant* was thus influenced by the history of legislative activity specifically aimed at redefining and modernizing the crime of rape. All of this warrants the conclusion that the rape statutes are not *in pari materia* with the incest statute and that the meaning attributed to "sexual intercourse" in the context of rape would be inconclusive as to its meaning in the context of incest, absent an indication that the Legislature intended this same meaning to apply to statutes defining and proscribing "crimes against chastity, morality, decency and good order."

In the absence of such an indication, a better interpretive approach would have implemented the following two canons of statutory interpretation: first, a statute must be interpreted according to the intent of the Legislature ascertained from all its words construed by the ordinary and approved usage of the language, considered in connection with the cause of its enactment, the mischief or imperfection to be remedied and the main object to be accomplished, to the end that the purpose of its framers may be effectuated, and second, the statutory language itself is the principal source of insight into the legislative purpose. Limiting "sexual intercourse" in G.L. c. 272, §17, to penile-vaginal penetration would be appropriate if the sole purpose of the incest prohibition were the prevention of genetic or biological abnormalities in the offspring of incestuous unions. However, the plain language of the incest statute indicates that its drafters sought to advance purposes different from, and more compelling than, eugenics. For the statute does not define the crime of incest exclusively in terms of sexual intercourse between consanguineous relations, but also criminalizes the intermarriage of persons so related. Moreover, the "[p]ersons within the degrees of consanguinity" to whom the statute's prohibitions of intermarriage and sexual intercourse apply are not limited to blood relations, but include also certain affinal kin as well as stepparents. The Legislature's purpose in criminalizing incestuous conduct must thus extend beyond the prevention of genetic defects, as this goal would clearly not be advanced by criminalizing marriage itself, without more, between blood relations, and still less by prohibiting coitus between affinal kin who do not share a common bloodline. Indeed, the scope of the incest statute, as it relates to both conduct and persons, strongly suggests that its framers valued and sought to promote the sanctity and integrity of familial relationships, as well as to protect children within the family from sexual impositions by their elders. Accordingly, were there no other relevant legislative pronouncement, we would conclude that the term "sexual intercourse" in the in- cest statute, interpreted so as to realize all of the statute's purposes, is not properly lim- ited to heterosexual coitus—a restrictive definition consistent only with a debatable eugenics rationale—but instead should be construed according to the term's ordinary and approved usage, which includes "intercourse involving genital contact between indi- viduals other than penetration of the vagina by the penis." Webster's New Collegiate Dic- tionary 1055 (1980 ed.)....

That having been said, however, statutory amendments to G.L. c. 272, the same chap- ter of the General Laws as the incest statute, that contain the term "sexual intercourse" compel us to construe this term in G.L. c. 272, § 17, more narrowly than would other- wise be the case. The term "sexual intercourse" also appears in [five other sections of] G.L. c. 272. Since its 1974 amendment of the rape statutes, which substituted the terms "sexual intercourse" and "unnatural sexual intercourse" ... and our decision construing these terms in *Commonwealth v. Gallant, supra,* the Legislature has amended [three of these sections in] G.L. c. 272, but has not expanded the scope of the proscribed offenses to include "unnatural sexual intercourse." Moreover, the Legislature recently rewrote G.L. c. 272, § 3 (an act criminalizing the overpowering of another by means of an intoxicat- ing substance for sexual purposes), substituting the terms "sexual intercourse or unnat- ural sexual intercourse" for the term "unlawful sexual intercourse." This same legislation rewrote [a final section of] G.L. c. 272, which criminalizes "induc[ing] any person under 18 years of age of chaste life to have unlawful sexual intercourse," to revise the penalty provisions, but did not similarly expand the scope of this offense to include "unnatural sexual intercourse."

Assuming, as we must, that the Legislature, in enacting these various amendments, was aware of this court's prior construction of the terms "sexual intercourse" and "unnatural sex- ual intercourse," we must infer from this legislative activity that it intends these terms to be similarly defined where they appear in G.L. c. 272. Because statutes which relate to a com- mon subject matter "should be construed together so as to constitute an harmonious whole," we interpret G.L. c. 272, § 17, in conjunction with other statutes in G.L. c. 272 that con- tain the term "sexual intercourse" (in particular G.L. c. 272, § 3, that also contains the term "unnatural sexual intercourse"), and conclude, regrettably, that the term "sexual inter- course" in the incest statute excludes such forms of sexual conduct as are encompassed by the term "unnatural sexual intercourse." As the conduct allegedly engaged in by the defen- dant with his daughter falls within the scope of the latter term, as we have construed it, the judge did not err in allowing the defendant's motion to dismiss the incest indictments.[10]

We acknowledge ... that the ... conduct is shocking and abhorrent in nature.... While the result in this case undoubtedly offends both common sense and fundamental decency, it is an outcome that is compelled by the Legislature's choice of language in G.L. c. 272, coupled with the limits on this court's powers that flow from [the State Constitution]. Accordingly, if the statutory crime of incest is to encompass the conduct here alleged, it is incumbent on the Legislature to use the terms it has adopted to convey this purpose.

We affirm the order ... allowing the motion to dismiss....

IRELAND, J. (dissenting).

I write separately because I believe the court, while correctly acknowledging that the purpose of the incest statute is to "promote the sanctity and integrity of familial rela-

---

10. This conclusion comports with the maxim that criminal statutes are to be strictly construed and that any reasonable doubt as to a statute's meaning must be resolved in a defendant's favor.

tionships, as well as to protect children within the family from sexual impositions," fails to interpret the statute to further those purposes. The court's overly narrow definition of "sexual intercourse" does not accord with a commonsense understanding of the term and leaves the children of the Commonwealth inadequately protected from sexual exploitation by relatives. I therefore respectfully dissent.

To begin, I agree that the court is not bound by its previous construction of the term "sexual intercourse," as used in the rape statutes, when construing the term as used in the incest statute. I also agree that it is appropriate for the court to look to other statutes for interpretive guidance when those statutes are *in pari materia*. I disagree though, that the Legislature, by [amending] G.L. c. 272, § 3, intended to import the Court's construction of "sexual intercourse" in the context of the rape statutes, into all sections of c. 272.

First, the title of the act and its provisions indicates that the legislative purpose was to address the issue of drug facilitated rape and kidnapping.[1] The statutes affected by the legislation seem to be no more *in pari materia* with the incest statutes than the other rape statutes. Although the court implies that the statutes amended [in 1998], and the incest statute relate "to a common subject matter," the court does not identify one, and seems to rest that conclusion on the mere fact that the statutes appear in the same chapter.

Furthermore, and more fundamentally, the court's interpretation fails to further all of the purposes served by the statute. The Legislature may choose to employ a term differently in two different statutes. In each statute, the term should be construed to effectuate the purposes of that particular statute. The court acknowledges that the plain language of the incest statute indicates that it was intended to "advance purposes different from, *and more compelling* than, eugenics," including the promotion of the family unit and the protection of children (emphasis added). The court also acknowledges that an interpretation of sexual intercourse limited only to "heterosexual coitus" is "a restrictive definition consistent only with a debatable eugenics rationale." The court proceeds, however, to interpret the statute in such a way to cover only "heterosexual coitus." This result is in direct contravention to the fundamental principle of statutory interpretation, that is, the court should construe a statute in order to effectuate its purpose or purposes, and disregards dictionary definitions of the term on which we have traditionally relied to help us determine the ordinary and common usage of a word.

Under the court's interpretation, a mother who had vaginal intercourse with her son would be committing incest, whereas a father who had anal intercourse with his son or his daughter would not be committing incest. As the Pennsylvania courts have noted, such a result would be arbitrary, and we should not interpret the statute to lead to such an absurd result.[3]

In sum, I dissent because the court's interpretation does not serve all of the purposes of the incest statute and thus is not consistent with the legislative intent, leads to an unfair and absurd result, fails adequately to protect the children of our Commonwealth from sexual abuse within their families, and, as the court itself acknowledges, "offends both common sense and fundamental decency." I would urge the Legislature to act as quickly as possible to correct the situation created by the court's decision today.

---

1. [The 1998 Act] is entitled "An Act relative to the prevention of drug induced rape and kidnapping," and in addition to substituting "sexual intercourse or unnatural sexual intercourse" for "unlawful sexual intercourse" in G.L. c. 272, § 3....

3. It is true that penal statutes are to be strictly construed. The purpose behind the rule of strict construction, however, is to put defendants properly on notice of what types of behavior are criminalized. Here, the defendant should have understood that his alleged actions constituted the crime of incest.

Notes and Questions

(1) *Incest*. Do you believe that the conduct here was "incestuous"? Why wasn't the ordinary meaning enough to reverse?

(2) *Plain Meaning*. Be sure you understand the majority's conclusion. According to the majority, did the plain meaning of "sexual intercourse" include the defendant's conduct or not? What was the purpose, or what were the purposes, of the incest statute? If the purpose of the incest statute was more than eugenics, then why did the court construe "sexual intercourse" to exclude the defendant's conduct? Why did it hold that the defendant's conduct was not "sexual intercourse" when it was within the ordinary meaning?

(3) *In Pari Materia or Not?* Did the two statutes (the incest statute and the drug-facilitated-rape statute) relate to the same subject? Did the majority think so? Did the dissent agree with the majority's conclusion on *in pari materia*? If the statutes did not relate to the same subject, then should *in pari materia* apply? If it should not apply, what is the proper result?

(4) *Ambiguity Before Application or Not?* As we mentioned above, some courts hold that *in pari materia* may not be relied upon without first finding ambiguity. *See City of Columbiana v. J & J Car Wash, Inc.*, 2005 WL 678750, at *6 (Ohio Ct. App. 2005) ("we cannot use the doctrine of *in pari materia* at this point since this rule of construction is to be used only after some doubt or ambiguity exists.") In considering whether that is the approach most likely to result in proper interpretation, consider *Village of Chatham v. County of Sangamon*, 814 N.E.2d 216 (Ill. Ct. App. 2004). There, the majority held that "when a statute is not ambiguous, the rule of *in pari materia* is not applicable," while the dissent rejected this "isolated" view. The dissent wrote:

> The doctrine of *in pari materia* is a long-established, fundamental statutory construction principle. Under this doctrine of construction, two legislative acts that address the same subject are considered with reference to one another, so that they may be given harmonious effect. The United States Supreme Court, in *United States ex rel. Chott v. Ewing*, 237 U.S. 197, 200 (1915), was faced with two provisions, which, when "[l]ooked at isolatedly," had "absolute conflict between" them. The Court rejected the isolated approach and stated as follows: "[E]ven if the method of isolated consideration were not otherwise plainly a mistaken one, it follows that it cannot be adopted since it affords no possible solution of the controversy." *Ewing*, 237 U.S. at 200. The Court then held: "[S]uch solution must therefore be sought ... by turning primarily to the context of the section and secondarily to provisions *in pari materia* as affording an efficient means for discovering the legislative intent in enacting the statute thereby vivifying and enforcing the remedial purposes which it was adopted to accomplish." *Ewing*, 237 U.S. at 200.

Id. at 230 (Myerscough, J., dissenting). Should the canon be applied regardless of whether there is ambiguity? Does it matter whether it is the same statute or a different, but related one, where the same word appears?

(5) *Subsequent Legislative Action*. Perhaps not surprisingly, Massachusetts amended the incest statute in 2002. The statute now reads:

> Persons within degrees of consanguinity within which marriages are prohibited or declared by law to be incestuous and void, who intermarry or have sexual intercourse with each other, or who engage in sexual activities with each other, including but not limited to, oral or anal intercourse, fellatio, cunnilin-

gus, or other penetration of a part of a person's body, or insertion of an object into the genital or anal opening of another person's body, or the manual manipulation of the genitalia of another person's body, shall be punished by imprisonment in the state prison for not more than 20 years or in the house of correction for not more than 2 1/2 years.

Mass. Gen. Laws Ann. ch. 272, § 17 (West 2005). Does this fact show that the dissent was right or that the majority was right to make the legislature write a clearer statute?

Problem 6-1

You represent T.J. DiGiacomo, who was fourteen years old when he engaged in inappropriate sexual activity with Marie Williams, an eight-year-old neighborhood girl. The girl "had a crush" on T.J. and was close to his family. Taking advantage of Marie's vulnerability, her feelings for him, and the disparity in their ages, T.J. kissed and hugged Marie and rubbed the genital area of his clothed body against the genital area of her clothed body in order to gratify his own sexual desires. Marie initially submitted to his sexual advances, but then asked him to stop. T.J. never threatened Marie or used force during the incident, and he stopped immediately when she asked him to stop. Marie told her mother shortly after the incident took place. T.J. admitted kissing, hugging, and "rubbing bodies" with Marie, but denies that he attempted to have intercourse with her.

The state has filed a delinquency petition against T.J., alleging that he engaged in lewd and lascivious conduct with a child under the age of sixteen. Draft a motion to dismiss the petition, arguing that as a juvenile, T.J. could not have violated § 2602. As you develop your argument, pay particular attention to the penalty provisions of the criminal statutes included below. Does the severity of the penalty structure makes sense if T.J. is guilty? Ignore the rule of lenity.

Problem Materials

Mercer Juvenile Proceedings Code § 632(a)

(3) a juvenile who is alleged to have committed a delinquent act may be subject to delinquency proceedings....

(a) "delinquent act" means "an act designated as a crime under the laws of this state."

Mercer Criminal Code § 2602: Lewd or Lascivious Conduct with Child

A person who shall willfully commit any lewd or lascivious act upon or with the body, or any part or member thereof, of a child under the age of sixteen years, with the intent of arousing, appealing to, or gratifying the lust, passions or sexual desires of such person or of such child, shall be guilty of a felony and imprisoned not less than one year nor more than five years.

Mercer Juvenile Code § 3202. Carnal Knowledge by Person under Sixteen

If a juvenile under the age of sixteen years unlawfully and carnally knows a juvenile person under the age of sixteen years with her consent, both juveniles shall be guilty of a misdemeanor and may be committed to the juvenile detention school.

2. The Rule against Surplusage

We turn now from discussing a canon that defines the scope for interpretation to the canons that apply to the words and phrases actually used. We start with the rule against surplusage. Simply put, every word matters. It is "a cardinal principle of statutory construction" that "a statute ought, upon the whole, to be so construed that, if it can be prevented, no clause, sentence, or word shall be superfluous, void, or insignificant." *Duncan v. Walker*, 533 U.S. 167, 174 (2001). Consequently, a statute should not be interpreted in a way that renders a word superfluous. This canon is particularly true as to "pivotal" words of a statute. *Id.* Thus, any construction of a statute that does not give meaning to every word implicates the rule against surplusage.

This canon is based on the assumption that the legislature put every word in the statute for a reason. There are two distinct aspects. First, every word must be given meaning. A statute cannot be interpreted in a way that some words or provisions are rendered superfluous by the interpretation. Second, different words in the same statute, particularly those in a list, cannot mean precisely the same thing. If they did, one word would be redundant. So, if a statute imposes liability only if a defendant has acted with "malice and intent," both "malice" and "intent" must be proved, and "malice" and "intent" must mean something different from one another.

As with all textual canons, however, the rule against surplusage is not absolute; there are exceptions. One commonly recognized exception is that courts may reject words as surplusage if the words are completely meaningless or inconsistent with the legislature's intention as plainly expressed in the statute. *E.g.*, *Guitierrez v. Ada*, 528 U.S. 250 (2000) (refusing to apply the rule against surplusage when other canons of construction and common sense suggested the opposite result). Additionally, when words are clearly "inadvertently inserted" or where they are "repugnant to the rest of the statute," the rule does not apply. *Chickasaw Nation v. United States*, 534 U.S. 84, 94 (2001). Finally, words can be ignored if they are "patently" surplusage. *Thornburgh v. Am. College of Obstetricians & Gynecologists*, 476 U.S. 747, 769 (1986). You might question whether the exceptions swallow the rule.

The following case raises the issue of whether, and if so how, the rule against surplusage should be applied.

Feld v. Robert & Charles Beauty Salon
459 N.W.2d 279 (Mich. 1990)

Riley, Chief Justice.

[T]he plaintiff, Sylvia Feld, was injured in a work-related accident. Three days later, she filed an application for workers' compensation benefits, alleging a twisted neck and a sprain to the upper back, neck, and right hand. She later amended the petition to include a torn ligament in her left knee.

Pursuant to [section 385] the defendants, Robert & Charles Beauty Salon and its insurance carrier, requested that the plaintiff undergo a medical examination to be conducted by a physician of their choice. The plaintiff refused ... unless she was accompanied by her attorney ... [T]he hearing referee granted a motion for the defendants to suspend the payment of benefits until the plaintiff submitted herself for the medical examination. The referee held that "[p]laintiffs attorney (sic) has no right under the statute to be present at such examination." ...

[T]he Court of Appeals reversed ... and held that the plaintiff did have the right to have her attorney present at the medical examination requested by the defendants.... The defendants ... appeal[ed]....

The limited issue in this case centers on the statutory construction of [section 385], which provides in relevant part:

> After the employee has given notice of injury and from time to time thereafter during the continuance of his or her disability, if so requested by the employer or the carrier, he or she shall submit himself or herself to an examination by a physician or surgeon authorized to practice medicine under the laws of the state, furnished and paid for by the employer or the carrier ... *The employee shall have the right to have a physician provided and paid for by himself or herself present at the examination.* If he or she refuses to submit himself or herself for the examination, or in any way obstructs the same, his or her right to compensation shall be suspended and his or her compensation during the period of suspension may be forfeited.... (Emphasis added.)

Section 385 grants an employer or its carrier the authority to have a physician of its choice conduct a medical examination of an employee. The statute is clear and unambiguous in that it permits the employee "the right to have a physician provided and paid for by himself or herself present at the examination." It is equally clear that § 385 does not provide the employee with the right to have counsel present at the examination....

Our analysis is buttressed by the fundamental rule of construction that every word of a statute should be given meaning and no word should be treated as surplusage or rendered nugatory if at all possible....

The plaintiff advances the argument that an employee has the right to have counsel present during a § 385 medical examination because the statute does not expressly preclude attorneys.[14] This rationale ignores the obvious fact that the Legislature has *expressly prescribed* that an employee has the right to have a personal physician present. To extend the right of an employee to include the presence of an attorney merely because the statute does not *expressly prohibit* counsel would neutralize the effect of the entire § 385 sentence in question and render it nothing more than surplusage. This is a conclusion that may only be reached when we are presented with a strong countervailing legislative implication, and that is not the case here....

We find that ... the fundamental rule of construction that every word in a statute should be given meaning and no word should be treated as surplusage if at all possible, [is] applicable to the question before us today. Therefore, we determine that the legislative intent of § 385 is to limit the right of an employee to the presence of a personal physician during an examination requested by an employer. Thus, we conclude that § 385 does not grant an employee the right to have counsel present during a physical examination requested by the employer....

Accordingly, we reverse....

BOYLE, JUSTICE (concurring).

It would be naive not to recognize the inherently adversarial nature of a physical examination requested by an employer or its carrier under [§ 385].... Where the Legislature

---

14. If we were to accept this argument, the next question would have to be, "Then why did the Legislature include within § 385 the sentence '[t]he employee shall have the right to have a physician provided and paid for by himself or herself present at the examination?'"

has declined to provide the right to an attorney at a § 385 physical examination, such a right may not be created by judicial action, no matter how well justified....

Cavanaugh, Justice (dissenting).

I reject the majority's conclusion that its interpretation of the statute is compelled by the rule[] of construction [that] ..."no word should be treated as surplusage...." The absence of any reference to the presence of nonphysicians at the examination is ambiguous. The Legislature may have either assumed an employee already had the right to the presence of nonphysicians, or even neglected, failed, or refused to decide whether or not an employee could bring along a nonphysician observer.

[handwritten margin note: "]ambiguous"]

Nothing in § 385 denies an employee the right to the presence of a person other than a personal physician at the examination, be that person the employee's spouse, an interpreter, a friend of the employee, the employee's attorney or that attorney's representative, or a nurse. More generally, the section does not deny an employee the right to insist that the examination be subject to reasonable conditions; it only prohibits the employee from "refus[ing] to submit" to or "in any way obstruct[ing]" the examination....

The Legislature has conditioned the continued receipt of benefits upon the worker's cooperation with the defendant's doctor's physical examination. The examination clearly forces a surrender of the worker's privacy. The statute's specific allowance of the worker's own physician at the examination must arise only rarely. How many injured workers, living on the very compensation threatened to be forfeited, can afford to pay a physician to attend? If the worker is fortunate to have hospitalization insurance, would such attendance by a personal physician be reimbursable as a necessary expense? I hardly think so! It is for this reason, as well, that I find it unfortunate that the majority today reaches out to find a statutory prohibition against an injured worker's ability to be accompanied by a person the worker chooses during this personal and intrusive, albeit required, experience.

I am unwilling to attribute to the Legislature an intent to authorize the severe sanction of forfeiture of an employee's right to compensation benefits whenever that employee insists, under § 385, upon the presence of ... a person other than a personal physician ... at an examination.

Notes and Questions

(1) *Was there Surplusage?* Was the majority correct to contend that the canon was implicated here? Would it render the words in the sentence that allow for doctors to attend the examination superfluous if anyone else, including attorneys, could attend? Did the dissent contest this issue?

(2) *Silence as Ambiguity?* The legislature had authorized the presence of one category of professionals. By doing so, was it excluding others? The dissent contended that § 385 was ambiguous because it was silent on whether others could be present. Was it? In contrast, the majority went so far as to say it was "clear" that no one else could attend. Was it? Remember that, for some judges, reliance on any textual canon is inappropriate unless the text is ambiguous; hence, this issue could be critical.

(3) *Test the Majority's Construction.* Under the majority's construction, could the employee have a physician present at the medical examination who was paid for by the attorney or the employee's parents? Does that suggest to you that the majority's interpretation is wrong or that there is ambiguity?

(4) *The Purpose of the Sentence.* In a footnote, the majority implied that the purpose for the sentence allowing physicians to attend was unclear. Based solely on the text, is the purpose to ensure that a physician can be present along with anyone else or to ensure that no one but a physician can be present? If the purpose of the statute is the latter, which words are surplusage? The former? Does this difference suggest that more than the words should be considered in determining plain meaning? Does it suggest that, at least sometimes, whether language is ambiguous turns on an understanding of the purpose of or the intent behind the language?

(5) *Does the Rule Make Sense?* Judge Posner questioned whether the rule is realistic: "No one would suggest that judicial opinions or academic articles contain no surplusage; are these documents less carefully prepared than statutes? There is no evidence for this improbable proposition; what evidence we have, much of it from the statutes themselves, is to the contrary.... [A] statute that is the product of compromise may contain redundant language as a by-product of the strains of the negotiating process." Richard A. Posner, *Statutory Interpretation—In the Classroom and the Courtroom,* 50 U. Chi. L. Rev. 800, 812 (1983). If you believe that statutes are more likely to have surplusage than articles, what does that observation mean for the canon?

(6) *Write a Clear Statute.* The legislature could have identified everyone it wished to include or exclude as one way of making the statute clear. But there is probably a simpler way. We think the legislature could have included one word, and only one, and removed all doubt. What word was missing in this statute as drafted?

3. *Noscitur a Sociis*

Under *noscitur a sociis,* the meaning of words that are placed together in a statute should be determined in light of the words with which they are associated. *Noscitur a sociis* literally means "it is known from its associates." The canon simply dictates that "the coupling of words together shows that they are to be understood in the same sense. And where the meaning of any particular word is doubtful or obscure ... the intention of the party who has made use of it may frequently be ascertained and carried unto effect by looking at the adjoining words." *Neal v. Clark,* 95 U.S. 704, 709–10 (1877). As Justice Scalia put it more recently: "If you tell me, 'I took the boat out on the bay,' I understand 'bay' to mean one thing; if you tell me, 'I put the saddle on the bay,' I understand it to mean something else." Antonin Scalia, A Matter of Interpretation 26 (Princeton University Press 1997). The canon thus expresses the common sense notion that although a phrase or a word may mean one thing in isolation, it may mean something substantially different when read in context.

Despite its apparent simplicity, the canon can be challenging to apply. Among other things, the rule against surplusage and *noscitur a sociis* can be in tension. Legislatures often use long lists of words. When legislatures do so, they risk repetition. When words in a list are interpreted under *noscitur a sociis,* it may be hard to give each word a separate, independent meaning so as to avoid the rule against surplusage. This tension between the rule against surplusage and *noscitur a sociis* is just one example of how these canons can conflict.

Another issue is whether the canon applies to unambiguous text. Perhaps more than any other canon, it makes sense to apply *noscitur a sociis* regardless of ambiguity because context provides meaning. Some courts take that approach. For example, the Sixth Circuit recently stated that the canon was to be used as part of the textual analysis. *Limited, Inc. v. Comm'r*, 286 F.3d 324, 332 (6th Cir. 2002) ("As a further aide in determining the meaning of an undefined term, the maxim … directs us to look to accompanying words to deduce the undefined word's meaning. Where this textual analysis fails to produce a conclusive result, or where it leads to ambiguous or unreasonable results, a court may look to legislative history to interpret a statute.") In contrast, several courts hold that the canon cannot be used if the text is unambiguous. *E.g., Stryker Corp. v. Dir., Div. of Taxation*, 773 A.2d 674, 684 (N.J. 2001) (holding that the canon had no application where the text was unambiguous).

In the following case, pay attention to how the various judges approach the interpretive process. Do they look for the plain meaning first and turn to the canon only after the plain meaning is ambiguous, or do they use the canon to determine which plain meaning was intended?

Also, consider whether it is appropriate to apply *noscitur a sociis* to the list of words in the case; it's one thing to say that words influence each other (*i.e.*, in the list "boiling, hot, warm, and cold" the list of words might suggest various temperatures) and entirely another to say what that influence should be (*i.e.*, that these words are all synonyms for the same temperature). What trait or similarity do the words share, and how should that trait influence the meaning of the other words? Notice also how each opinion offers a slightly different interpretation.

People v. Vasquez
631 N.W.2d 711 (Mich. 2001)

MARKMAN, J.

While investigating a complaint about a loud party, a police officer found defendant urinating on the front lawn of a private residence…. The officer suspected that defendant was an intoxicated minor. When the officer asked defendant his name and age, defendant said that his name was "John Wesley Chippeway" and that he was sixteen years old. In fact, defendant's name was Mark John Vasquez, Jr., and he was seventeen years old….

The prosecutor charged defendant with "resisting and obstructing" a police officer. The trial court quashed the "resisting and obstructing" charge….

The "resisting and obstructing" statute [MCL 750.479] states in relevant part:

> Any person who shall knowingly and willfully … obstruct, resist, oppose, assault, beat or wound … any person or persons authorized by law to maintain and preserve the peace, in their lawful acts, attempts and efforts to maintain, preserve and keep the peace shall be guilty of a misdemeanor….

The … issue is whether defendant "obstructed," within the meaning of the "resisting and obstructing" statute, the police officer when he lied to him. The meaning of statutory language, plain or not, depends on context. Contextual understanding of statutes is generally grounded in the doctrine of *noscitur a sociis*: It is known from its associates. This doctrine stands for the principle that a word or phrase is given meaning by its context or setting. In seeking meaning, words and clauses will not be divorced from those which precede and those which follow. It is a familiar principle of statutory construction that words grouped in a list should be given related meaning.

In the present case, the statute uses the word "obstruct" as part of a list containing five other words, namely, "resist, oppose, assault, beat [and] wound." The meaning of the word "obstruct" should be determined in this particular context, and be given a meaning logically related to the five surrounding words of the statute. "Resist" is defined as "to withstand, strive against, or oppose." *Random House Webster's College Dictionary* (1991) at 1146. "Resistance" is additionally defined as the opposition offered by one thing, force, etc. "Oppose" is defined as to act against or furnish resistance to; combat. "Assault" is defined as a sudden violent attack; onslaught. "Beat" is defined as to strike forcefully and repeatedly; ... to hit repeatedly as to cause painful injury. "Wound" is defined as to inflict a wound upon; injure; hurt. Each of these words, when read together, clearly implies an element of threatened or actual *physical* interference.

The accompanying term "obstruct" is susceptible to several potential meanings. "Obstruct" is defined as: 1. to block or close up with an obstacle. 2. to hinder, interrupt, or delay the passage, progress, course, etc. of. 3. to block from sight; be in the way of (a view, passage, etc.). Accordingly, we understand the dissent's definition of "obstruct," which defines it as including both physical and nonphysical conduct. Although we understand that "obstruct" can be defined in such a manner, *when read in context*, we believe that the more reasonable interpretation is one that communicates an actual, or a threat of, physical interference.

The words "assault, beat, or wound" necessarily contain an element of violence; whereas, the words "obstruct, resist [or] oppose" may, but do not necessarily, contain an element of violence. For example, one cannot "assault, beat, or wound" an officer without being violent; however, one can "obstruct, resist, [or] oppose" an officer without necessarily being violent. What this leads us to believe is that when the Legislature used these six words together, it intended to proscribe both violent and nonviolent physical interference; physical interference being the only element common to all six words. Therefore, by grouping these six words together as a part of a single type of prohibited conduct, the Legislature has demonstrated a purpose of proscribing conduct amounting to actual or threatened physical interference.[2] In this case, defendant's conduct did not constitute threatened or actual physical interference. Defendant instead lied to the officer about his name and age. While certainly not laudatory, defendant's conduct did not physically interfere with or threaten to physically interfere with the officer. Moreover, the principal "purpose of [the 'resisting and obstructing' statute] is to protect officers from physical harm." The statute attempts to punish an assault upon an officer while in the discharge of his duty by a penalty more severe than that imposed for other assaults, *i.e.*, assaults on private citizens. In our judgment, defendant's conduct, *i.e.*, the giving of a false name

---

2. The dissent asserts that "the fact that the word 'obstruct' later appears with the words 'assault, beat, or wound' should not be given any special significance," because "[a]t the beginning of the statute, regarding the service of process, the words 'obstruct, resist, or oppose' are specifically set apart from the words 'assault, beat, or wound.'" We respectfully disagree. Rather, that the Legislature initially separated the six terms into two groups in the statute does suggest that the two groups of words have a distinct meaning. This distinction is that the words "obstruct, resist, [and] oppose," refer to nonviolent physical interference; while, the words "assault, beat, [and] wound" refer to violent physical interference. However, the fact that the Legislature then combined the two sets of words, in the portion of the statute that we are interpreting here, suggests that it is referring to both violent and nonviolent physical interference, with physical interference being the only element common to both sets of words.

Further, in our judgment, the Legislature used six verbs in the "resisting and obstructing" statute, not to prohibit six discrete forms of conduct, but rather to prohibit one general category of conduct in as thorough a manner as possible, by ensuring that there were no obvious gaps that could be exploited in the statute. Therefore, we must interpret each of the six words by looking at them together in order to determine the general category of conduct that the Legislature intended to prohibit.

and age to an officer, does not fit within the range of conduct that M.C.L. §750.479 was meant to prohibit.

It is clear that the principal purpose of this statute is to protect police officers from harm. However, from its language, we do not believe that this is the *only* purpose. Because one may threaten to or actually physically interfere with a police officer without threatening to or actually hurting a police officer, we believe that one may physically "obstruct" an officer without necessarily posing a threat to the officer's safety. For example, one may "obstruct" an officer by placing an object in the way of the officer with the intent of making it less accessible to the officer. This may pose no real threat to the officer's safety, but it may nevertheless "obstruct" because of the physical barrier interposed to the officer's performance of his duties. Therefore, both physical interference that poses a threat to the safety of police officers ("assault, beat, or wound") *and* physical interference that does not necessarily, but nevertheless may, pose a threat to the safety of police officers ("obstruct, resist, [or] oppose") are proscribed.

If the Legislature had intended to proscribe any manner of interference with a police officer, as the dissent asserts, why did the Legislature not clearly express this intent? If the Legislature intended to proscribe nonphysical forms of "obstruction," it could have used such terms as "lies," "falsifies," "refuses to cooperate," "interferes with" or "objects to." It did not. Instead, the Legislature chose six words that, when read together, evidence an intent to proscribe only threatened or actual physical interference.

Indeed, the fact that the Legislature used six separate terms to describe the types of conduct that it sought to proscribe, makes it even more probable that, had the Legislature truly intended to proscribe "lying" to a police officer, it would have expressly included such a term in its litany. That is, to the extent that the Legislature sought to proscribe the types of conduct that the dissent attributes to the statute, what more obvious starting point could there have been than to prohibit "lying?" Why, in light of its laundry list of proscribed activities, its literal thesaurus of forms of misconduct, would the Legislature have been so cryptic in setting forth such an obvious form of wrongdoing as "lying"? After all, "lying" is something more than an obscure verb describing an abstruse form of misconduct; rather, it describes a form of misconduct that, by itself, has been made the subject of numerous significant criminal statutes....

Under the plain meaning of M.C.L. §750.479, conduct that rises to the level of threatened or actual *physical* interference is proscribed. Michigan's resisting and "obstructing" statute does not proscribe *any* manner of interference with a police officer, and it also does not proscribe *only* conduct that poses a threat to the safety of police officers; rather, it proscribes threatened, either expressly or impliedly, physical interference and actual physical interference with a police officer. Defendant's conduct did not constitute threatened or actual physical interference. Therefore, defendant did not "obstruct" the police officer, within the meaning of M.C.L. §750.479, when he lied to him. Accordingly, we would reverse the decision of the Court of Appeals and reinstate the trial court's order dismissing the charges against defendant.

MARILYN J. KELLY, [concurring].

The prosecution and our dissenting colleagues argue that the term "obstruct" should be construed broadly. They view it as encompassing any physical or oral act that causes delay or presents an obstacle to an officer's efforts to gather information. While such an expansive meaning may be consistent with a literal reading of the word, it does not comport with the legislative intent underlying §479. This Court often consults dictionary definitions to ascertain the generally accepted meaning of a term that is not expressly defined by statute. Random House Webster's College Dictionary (1984) defines "obstruct" as: 1. to block or close up with an obstacle or obstacles, as a road. 2. to interrupt, hinder or oppose the passage, progress, course, etc., of. 3. to block from sight.

However, as with the word "obstruct," dictionaries often contain multiple definitions and define a term using multiple terms that, themselves, have multiple definitions. Thus, exclusive reliance on dictionary definitions can blur, as much as clarify, the meaning of a word. Dictionaries are therefore properly regarded as mere interpretive aids for the court.

Keeping the lay definition in mind, along with the purpose of the statute, we next examine the statutory context in which the word "obstruct" appears. Our consideration of context involves an examination of the family of words or phrases associated with the word "obstruct" in § 479. This analytical concept is known in law by the Latin phrase *noscitur a sociis*("It is known from its associates"). It stands for the proposition that, when we seek the meaning of words and clauses, we do not divorce them from those that precede and those that follow. Words grouped in a list should be given related meaning....

Here, the statute uses the word "obstruct" in a six-term list that contains "resist," "oppose," "assault," "beat" and "wound." ...

The six words, presented as they are in the statute, create a continuum. The first, "obstruct," is the mildest manner of violating the statute; and the final, "wound," the most severe. The dissent opines that the first three words preclude a finding that § 479 was intended to address only actual or threatened harm to police officers. This is so, surmises the dissent, because the word "assault" would be rendered nugatory if the "obstruct," "resist" and "oppose" were narrowed to the physical realm.

We cannot agree. Where broadly defined words are grouped with terms of specificity, the general words are interpreted as belonging to the same class as the narrowest in the list. Here, none will deny the terms "assault," "beat," and "wound" necessarily involve a physical component of actual or threatened harm.... Indeed, the only common thread that reasonably can be woven through the entire list is the element of actual or threatened physical interference or action. Such an interpretation provides the most effective way of addressing the mischief the statute was designed to remedy. On this basis, we find that the Legislature drafted the list of six verbs to describe a fluid string of behavior that constitutes a violation of the statute. And, it follows, the words and the concepts covered are interrelated.

"Obstruct," "resist," "oppose," and "assault" address actions or words that threaten physical harm to an officer or impose a physical barrier to the officer's performance of official duties. The final two, "beat" and "wound," proscribe actual physical harm to an officer. When viewed together, in proper context, the words depict the range of conduct. The behavior runs from verbal utterances and physical acts that threaten to physically interfere with an officer to the erection of physical barriers, physical interference, and the perpetration of physical harm....

Thus, Vasquez' conduct was not of the kind that the statute was designed to prevent....

CORRIGAN, C.J. (dissenting).

I respectfully dissent.... I reject [the majority's] unnecessarily narrow reading of the word "obstruct." In effect, the lead opinion inserts a new element—actual or threatened physical interference—into the resisting and obstructing statute. In my view, defendant's alleged conduct—lying to the officer about his name and age—clearly falls within a common understanding of the word "obstruct." ...

Resolution of this case turns on our interpretation of the word "obstruct" as it refers to police attempts to keep the peace. Consistent with the principles of statutory interpretation…, we must examine the common and approved usage of the word.… *Random House Webster's College Dictionary* (1991) defines "obstruct" as: "1. to block or close up with an obstacle.… 2. to hinder, interrupt, or delay the passage, progress, course, etc. of. 3. to block from sight; be in the way of (a view, passage, etc.)." Although this definition of "obstruct" clearly encompasses physical interference, it is not limited to physical interference. Certainly, it is possible to hinder, interrupt, or delay an officer's attempts to keep the peace without resorting to actual or threatened physical interference, as the lead opinion would require.…

Applying the statute to these facts, defendant's alleged conduct falls within the plain meaning of the word "obstruct." A state trooper tried to gather information to investigate his suspicion that defendant was an intoxicated minor. When asked to provide his name and age, defendant had two lawful choices: he could have answered truthfully or exercised his constitutional right not to answer at all. Instead, defendant chose to lie. By doing so, he impeded the officer's investigation by creating a nonphysical obstacle to the officer's attempt to gather accurate information.[3]

The lead opinion, relying on the doctrine of *noscitur a sociis*, concludes that the word "obstruct" refers only to physical obstruction despite the fact that the common understanding of the word clearly encompasses both physical and nonphysical obstruction. The *noscitur a sociis* doctrine stands for the simple proposition that the words of a statute should be understood in context. While I have no objection to interpreting the word "obstruct" in the context of its placement in the statute, I disagree with the lead opinion's conclusion that the Legislature's placement of the word "obstruct" in a list of words also including "resist, oppose, assault, beat or wound," indicates an intent to limit the common meaning of the word to include only physical obstruction. The lead opinion's conclusion that physical interference is the only element common to all six words overlooks the fact that the simple notion of interference also connects all six words. While all six words are verbs that could be used to describe acts of physical interference, only two of them, "beat" and "wound," definitely require a physical act; the other four may also be used to describe nonphysical acts. Thus, read in context, it is at least equally likely that the Legislature meant to criminalize all types of interference, both physical and nonphysical.

More fundamentally, the unique structure of the statute at issue demonstrates that the Legislature did not intend that its grouping of the six words together give special meaning to any of the words. At the beginning of the statute, regarding service of process, the words "obstruct, resist, or oppose" are specifically set apart from the words "assault, beat, or wound." Later, however, when the statute refers to keeping the peace, all six words are listed together. Notably, in the second instance the list is preceded by the word "so," which refers readers directly back to the statute's earlier use of the same words. Because the meaning of each word contained in the list of six is established by reference to the first part of the statute, where "obstruct, resist, or oppose" are set apart from "assault, beat, or wound," the fact that the word "obstruct" later appears with the words "assault, beat or wound" should not be given any special significance.

To the extent that the meaning of the word "obstruct" can be determined from context, the only relevant comparable words are "resist" and "oppose." Because resistance and

---

3. While the facts of this case indicate a *de minimis* violation of the statute, I caution my colleagues that hard facts make bad law. It is certainly conceivable that under different factual circumstances, lying to a police officer during an investigation could have grave consequences.

opposition can be oral or nonphysical just as easily as they can be physical, proper application of the doctrine of *noscitur a sociis* does not support the conclusion that the Legislature intended the word "obstruct" to have a limited meaning. If anything, the Legislature's decision to initially separate the words "obstruct, resist, or oppose" from the words "assault, beat, or wound" suggests an intention to avoid an interpretation that would *require* a physical component.

The lead opinion's conclusion that the crime of resisting and obstructing requires actual or threatened physical interference has no basis in the text of the statute.... For these reasons, I respectfully dissent.

Notes and Questions

(1) *What is the Unifier?* The majority relied on *noscitur a sociis* to reason that the pertinent words should be construed in light of each other and be interpreted to include physical obstruction. The concurrence contended that the list represented a continuum beginning with the least harmful and ending with "the most severe." Does this difference matter? The dissent first looked to the plain meaning of "obstruct" to interpret the statute. While the dissent "ha[d] no objection to interpreting the word 'obstruct' in the context of its placement in the statute," he suggested that interference, rather than physical obstruction, was the unifying element. Who was right? If the dissent's argument makes sense, does it respond to the majority's point that the legislature did not intend to include mere "lies" because the legislature did not include the word "lies" or similar words in the statute? How does the dissent respond to this argument, if at all?

(2) *The Rule Against Surplusage.* The rule against surplusage directs that each of these words must have a different meaning from the others. Didn't the majority, by relying on *noscitur a sociis*, treat them as synonyms for each other rather than as words with independent meaning? Does "oppose," for example, now mean the same thing as "obstruct"? Doesn't the majority's interpretation violate the rule against surplusage? Can you explain what each word now means in a way that makes each have a separate meaning?

(3) *Dictionary Definition.* Is the majority's statement that "physical interference" is the only commonality to all six words accurate? The dictionary definition cited in the majority opinion of "obstruct" includes "to interrupt, hinder, or oppose the passage, progress, course, etc., of." Why doesn't this definition show that any hindrance or opposition— with or without physical interference—is enough? Did the majority, in concluding that "obstruct" included "physical interference" "*when read in context*" err? Isn't a person who lies to a police officer obstructing the officer?

(4) *Not Enough Words?* The majority wrote that the legislature should have used "lies" or "refuses to cooperate" and similar phrases if it had wanted to preclude simply giving false statements. Is this argument persuasive? While the legislature could simply have included the word "lies" in the statute, should the legislature have to identify every possible way a defendant could interfere with a police investigation? Or, is it preferable for the legislature to make clear the "evil" it is legislating against and give the court broad interpretative authority? The legislature put in six words—how many more are needed? Yet, does the majority's point—that "lying" is such an obvious word that it should have been included, so the omission means something—have any merit? Can you write a statute to cover what the dissent believed was covered? (See Problem 6-2 below).

(5) *What Influence?* The majority relied on the purpose of the statute to conclude that "obstruct" meant only "actual or threatened physical interference." The dissent saw the

purpose much differently and believed the separation of the words "oppose," "resist," and "obstruct" from "assault, beat, or wound" suggested that the legislature intended to "avoid an interpretation that would *require* a physical component." What is the purpose of the statute? Can you tell? Should the purpose influence how the word "obstruct" is construed?

(6) *Should Noscitur a Sociis Apply to Lists of Independent Words?* We introduced the case with this question. It was also argued in a later case, *G.C. Timmis & Co. v. Guardian Alarm Co.*, 662 N.W.2d 710 (Mich. 2003), where the dissent wrote:

> I offer the following as an example to illustrate the majority's abuse and mis-application of this canon of statutory construction. Suppose that a hypothetical statute were to preclude ownership of the following animals without a license:
>
> Duck, Goose, Bittern, Swan, Heron
>
> Presume that the word "bittern" had no commonly understood meaning that could be discerned by resort to a dictionary. In order to determine the meaning of the word, the doctrine of *noscitur a sociis* could be utilized to reasonably come to the conclusion that a bittern is a type of waterfowl. That is, where the meaning of the word is not apparent, the meaning could be ascertained by reference to the meaning of words associated with it.
>
> Now suppose that the hypothetical example were altered slightly, and the statute listed these animals:
>
> Duck, Goose, Pig, Swan, Heron
>
> Unlike bittern, the word "pig" does have a fixed, commonly understood meaning, and it is *not* "waterfowl."[5] However, under the majority's analysis, the doctrine of *noscitur a sociis* could properly be used to come to the conclusion that a pig is a waterfowl (despite the clear, unambiguous meaning of pig), because all the surrounding terms were waterfowls.

Id. at 723 (Young, J., dissenting). The majority responded:

> [W]e believe that the dissent's "pig" hypothetical example makes our point. Concerning this hypothetical example, *noscitur a sociis* can not only be "accurately" applied, but must necessarily be applied. Contrary to the dissent's assertion, the term "pig" does not have a single, invariable meaning. Rather, it has several separate and distinct meanings, including: (1) a swine; (2) a person who is gluttonous, greedy, or slovenly; or (3) an oblong mass of metal that has been run into a mold of sand while still molten. *Random House Webster's College Dictionary* (2d ed.).... That the first of these definitions would suggest itself to a "native speaker of English as the common, most likely meaning of the term," is surely a correct, but an irrelevant, observation on the part of the dissent. We do not accord words "default" definitions on the basis of their order of appearance in the dictionary. Rather, because the term "pig" has several different meanings, we initially apply *noscitur a sociis* (whether or not in an explicit fashion) to accord it one of these meanings—that which is contextually related to the language that surrounds "pig." Such a meaning, we assume, is that which is most likely intended by the lawmaker.

---

5. We agree with the majority that "pig" does have many meanings beyond swine. However, none of the alternatives cited in the majority opinion, such as an "oblong mass of metal," would suggest themselves to a native speaker of English as the common, most likely meaning of the term as used in our hypothetical statute.

In the dissent's hypothetical example, after examining the immediately surrounding terms, all of which have in common that they relate to animals, we
accord "pig" its only meaning possessed in common with these other terms, *i.e.,*
"a swine." Moreover, our analysis would not necessarily stop there. Instead, depending on the matter in controversy, *noscitur a sociis* might have to be further
applied to determine an even narrower common characteristic between "a swine"
and the other listed terms, for example, that each of these terms can be characterized as an animal that is a mammal.

Id. at 718 n.12 (majority opinion). Who was right? Does "pig" have only one common *ordinary* meaning, as the dissent suggested? Or, does the fact that there are multiple dictionary
meanings suggest that "pig" has more than one common ordinary meaning, as the majority argued? Assuming that the dissent was correct—that a word may have many dictionary meanings, while it has only one *ordinary* meaning—was *noscitur a sociis* even
necessary? Or, was the majority correct that English readers and speakers would intuitively apply *noscitur a sociis* when reading the list above and assume that the animal
meaning of "pig" was intended, rather than, for example, the derogatory terms for an
overweight individual or police officer? In other words, don't readers intuitively apply
noscitur a sociis all the time so that a finding of ambiguity should not be necessary for
this canon to apply?

Problem 6-2

Assume that you are a member of the legislature in Michigan. Additionally, you were
part of the legislature that enacted MCL § 750.479, which was discussed in the *Vasquez*
case above. You are angry at the result in *Vasquez* and want to draft legislation to overrule the case. Draft an amendment to the statute that would cover not only the *Vasquez*
facts, but the following factual situations as well:

(1) Suppose a man witnesses a robbery on the street. Suspecting that the man saw
the crime, an officer approaches and queries, "Which way did he go?" The man,
a friend of the robber, does not respond for a full minute. Then, he says, "He went
that way," and points in the direction the robber fled.

(2) Suppose a defendant weighs 500 pounds. When a police officer working alone
tries to arrest the defendant, she sits down and waits for the officer to carry her.

(3) Suppose a defendant screams obscenities at an arresting officer.

How would you draft differently if you did not want to include subparagraphs 2 and 3
above? Can you think of other situations that you would want to cover, but are not already addressed with your language?

4. *Ejusdem Generis*

Ejusdem generis is a species of *noscitur a sociis. See New Castle County, DE v. Nat'l
Union Fire Ins. Co.,* 243 F.3d 744 (3rd Cir. 2001). *Ejusdem generis* literally means "of the
same kind, class, or nature." When general words in a statute precede or follow the designation of specific things (as in a list, such as "cars, boats, and other vehicles"), the general words should be construed to include only objects similar in nature to the specific words.
The specific words indicate the class of items to which the statute applies (cars and boats),
while the general words extend the statute to everything else in the identified class in-

cluding things that might not have existed when the statute was enacted. "Whereas *ejusdem generis* tells us how to find items outside the list expressed in the statute, *noscitur a sociis* tells us how the list gives meaning to the items within it." *Stebbins v. Wells*, 2001 WL 1255079, at *3 fn.3 (R.I. Sup. Ct. 2001).

As with *noscitur a sociis*, the courts disagree on whether *ejusdem generis* should be applied to unambiguous text. Some courts hold that application of the canon is part of the determination of plain meaning. *E.g.*, *Silverstreak, Inc. v. Wash. State Dep't of Labor & Indus.*, 104 P.3d 699, 704 (Wash. Ct. App. 2005). Other courts hold that it is improper to apply the canon absent a finding of ambiguity. *E.g.*, *State v. Malik*, 839 A.2d 67, 74 (N.J. Super. Ct. App. Div. 2003). As noted above, the willingness to apply the canons absent ambiguity may reflect whether the court is more generally willing to move beyond the text to other sources.

Like all the textual canons, *ejusdem generis* is not an iron-clad rule but rather an aid to interpretation. When the list of things is not sufficiently similar, *ejusdem generis* should not apply. *See, e.g., Jones v. State*, 149 S.W. 56 (Ark. 1912) (refusing to apply *ejusdem generis* to this list: "incompetency, corruption, gross immorality, criminal conduct amounting to a felony, malfeasance, or nonfeasance in office" because the listed items were not sufficiently similar). As with *noscitur a sociis*, *ejusdem generis* raises the issue of what trait the words share. The specific issue *ejusdem generis* raises is whether, and if so how, that trait should constrain the meaning of generalized catchalls.

It is common for legislatures to use these catchalls. A legislature could write statutes that do not include catchalls, but doing so would invite "clever evasions" by lawyers, who would simply avoid the literal list and do something slightly different. Frank H. Easterbrook, *Statutes' Domains*, 50 U. Chi. L. Rev. 533, 537 (1983). "Zipper clauses" that say "this statute covers X, Y, and Z but nothing else" are therefore, deliberately avoided by legislatures to prevent these clever evasions. *Id.* But clearly the list of specific items must somehow limit the catchall. Precisely how, however, is sometimes difficult to determine.

Ali v. Fed. Bureau Of Prisons
552 U.S. 214 (2008)

Justice Thomas delivered the opinion of the Court.

... Petitioner Abdus-Shahid M.S. Ali was a federal prisoner.... Before being transferred [to another federal prison], he left two duffle bags containing his personal property in the [prison to be transferred to the new prison].... Upon inspecting his property, he noticed that several items were missing.... Many of the purportedly missing items were of religious and nostalgic significance, including two copies of the Qur'an, a prayer rug, and religious magazines. Petitioner estimated that the items were worth $177.

... Petitioner ... filed a complaint alleging ... violations of the Federal Tort Claims Act (FTCA). The BOP maintained that petitioner's claim was barred by the exception in § 2680(c) for property claims against law enforcement officers. The District Court agreed and dismissed petitioner's FTCA claim.... [T]he Eleventh Circuit affirmed[.]

In the FTCA, Congress waived the United States' sovereign immunity for claims arising out of torts committed by federal employees. As relevant here, the FTCA authorizes "claims against the United States, for money damages ... for injury or loss of property ... caused by the negligent or wrongful act or omission of any employee of the Government while acting within the scope of his office or employment." The FTCA exempts from this waiver certain categories of claims. Relevant here is the exception in subsection (c), which provides that § 1346(b) shall not apply to "[a]ny claim arising in respect of the assessment or collection of any tax or customs duty, or the detention of any goods, merchandise, or other property by any officer of customs or excise or any other law enforcement officer." § 2680(c).

This case turns on whether the BOP officers who allegedly lost petitioner's property qualify as "other law enforcement officer[s]" within the meaning of § 2680(c). Petitioner argues that they do not because "any other law enforcement officer" includes only law enforcement officers acting in a customs or excise capacity. Noting that Congress referenced customs and excise activities in both the language at issue and the preceding clause in § 2680(c), petitioner argues that the entire subsection is focused on preserving the United States' sovereign immunity only as to officers enforcing those laws.

Petitioner's argument is inconsistent with the statute's language. The phrase "*any* other law enforcement officer" suggests a broad meaning. We have previously noted that "[r]ead naturally, the word 'any' has an expansive meaning, that is, 'one or some indiscriminately of whatever kind.'" ... Congress' use of "any" to modify "other law enforcement officer" is most naturally read to mean law enforcement officers of whatever kind.[4] The word "any" is repeated four times in the relevant portion of § 2680(c), and two of those instances appear in the particular phrase at issue: "*any* officer of customs or excise or *any* other law enforcement officer." Congress inserted the word "any" immediately before "other law enforcement officer," leaving no doubt that it modifies that phrase. To be sure, the text's references to "tax or customs duty" and "officer[s] of customs or excise" indicate that Congress intended to preserve immunity for claims arising from an officer's enforcement of tax and customs laws. The text also indicates, however, that Congress intended to preserve immunity for claims arising from the detention of property, and there is no indication that Congress intended immunity for those claims to turn on the type of law being enforced.

Petitioner would require Congress to clarify its intent to cover all law enforcement officers by adding phrases such as "performing any official law enforcement function," or "without limitation." But Congress could not have chosen a more all-encompassing phrase than "any other law enforcement officer" to express that intent. We have no reason to demand that Congress write less economically and more repetitiously....

Against this textual and structural evidence that "any other law enforcement officer" does in fact mean any other law enforcement officer, petitioner invokes numerous canons of statutory construction. He relies primarily on *ejusdem generis*, or the principle that "when a general term follows a specific one, the general term should be understood as a reference to subjects akin to the one with specific enumeration." In petitioner's view, "any officer of customs or excise or any other law enforcement officer" should be read as a three-item list, and the final, catchall phrase "any other law enforcement officer" should be limited to officers of the same nature as the preceding specific phrases....

... We disagree. The structure of the phrase "any officer of customs or excise or any other law enforcement officer" does not lend itself to application of the canon. The phrase is disjunctive, with one specific and one general category, not ... a list of specific items separated by commas and followed by a general or collective term. The absence of a list of specific items undercuts the inference embodied in *ejusdem generis* that Congress remained focused on the common attribute when it used the catchall phrase.

---

4. Of course, other circumstances may counteract the effect of expansive modifiers....

Moreover, it is not apparent what common attribute connects the specific items in § 2680(c). Were we to use the canon to limit the meaning of "any other law enforcement officer," we would be required to determine the relevant limiting characteristic of "officer of customs or excise." ... Petitioner suggests that the common attribute is that both types of officers are charged with enforcing the customs and excise laws. But we see no reason why that should be the relevant characteristic as opposed to, for example, that officers of that type are commonly involved in the activities enumerated in the statute: the assessment and collection of taxes and customs duties and the detention of property.

Petitioner's appeals to other interpretive principles are also unconvincing. Petitioner contends that his reading is supported by the canon *noscitur a sociis*, according to which "a word is known by the company it keeps." But the cases petitioner cites in support of applying *noscitur a sociis* involved statutes with stronger contextual cues. Here, although customs and excise are mentioned twice in § 2680(c), nothing in the overall statutory context suggests that customs and excise officers were the exclusive focus of the provision. The emphasis in subsection (c) on customs and excise is not inconsistent with the conclusion that "any other law enforcement officer" sweeps as broadly as its language suggests.

Similarly, the rule against superfluities lends petitioner sparse support. The construction we adopt today does not necessarily render "any officer of customs or excise" superfluous; Congress may have simply intended to remove any doubt that officers of customs or excise were included in "law enforcement officers." Moreover, petitioner's construction threatens to render "any other law enforcement officer" superfluous because it is not clear when, if ever, "other law enforcement officer[s]" act in a customs or excise capacity. In any event, we do not woodenly apply limiting principles every time Congress includes a specific example along with a general phrase....

In the end, we are unpersuaded by petitioner's attempt to create ambiguity where the statute's text and structure suggest none. Had Congress intended to limit § 2680(c)'s reach as petitioner contends, it easily could have written "any other law enforcement officer *acting in a customs or excise capacity*." Instead, it used the unmodified, all-encompassing phrase "any other law enforcement officer." ... Section 2680(c) forecloses lawsuits against the United States for the unlawful detention of property by "any," not just "some," law enforcement officers....

JUSTICE KENNEDY, with whom JUSTICE STEVENS, JUSTICE SOUTER, and JUSTICE BREYER join, dissenting.

Statutory interpretation, from beginning to end, requires respect for the text. The respect is not enhanced, however, by decisions that foreclose consideration of the text within the whole context of the statute as a guide to determining a legislature's intent. To prevent textual analysis from becoming so rarefied that it departs from how a legislator most likely understood the words when he or she voted for the law, courts use certain interpretative rules to consider text within the statutory design. These canons do not demand wooden reliance and are not by themselves dispositive, but they do function as helpful guides in construing ambiguous statutory provisions. Two of these accepted rules are *ejusdem generis* and *noscitur a sociis*, which together instruct that words in a series should be interpreted in relation to one another....

As the Court states, at issue here is the extent of the exception for suits arising from the detention of goods in defined circumstances. The relevant provision excepts from the general waiver "claim[s] arising in respect of the assessment or collection of any tax or customs duty, or the detention of any goods, merchandise, or other property by any officer of customs or excise or any other law enforcement officer."

Both on first reading and upon further, close consideration, the plain words of the statute indicate that the exception is concerned only with customs and taxes. The provision begins with a clause dealing exclusively with customs and tax duties. And the provision as a whole contains four express references to customs and tax, making revenue duties and customs and excise officers its most salient features.

This is not to suggest that the Court's reading is wholly impermissible or without some grammatical support. After all, detention of goods is not stated until the outset of the second clause and at the end of the same clause the words "any other law enforcement officer" appear; so it can be argued that the first and second clauses of the provision are so separate that all detentions by all law enforcement officers in whatever capacity they might act are covered. Still, this ought not be the preferred reading; for between the beginning of the second clause and its closing reference to "any other law enforcement officer" appears another reference to "officer[s] of customs or excise," this time in the context of property detention. This is quite sufficient, in my view, to continue the limited scope of the exception. At the very least, the Court errs by adopting a rule which simply bars all consideration of the canons of *ejusdem generis* and *noscitur a sociis*. And when those canons are consulted, together with other common principles of interpretation, the case for limiting the exception to customs and tax more than overcomes the position maintained by the Government and adopted by the Court.

The *ejusdem generis* canon provides that, where a seemingly broad clause constitutes a residual phrase, it must be controlled by, and defined with reference to, the "enumerated categories ... which are recited just before it," so that the clause encompasses only objects similar in nature. The words "any other law enforcement officer" immediately follow the statute's reference to "officer(s) of customs or excise," as well as the first clause's reference to the assessment of tax and customs duties.

The Court counters that § 2680(c) "is disjunctive, with one specific and one general category," rendering *ejusdem generis* inapplicable. The canon's applicability, however, is not limited to those statutes that include a laundry list of items. In addition, *ejusdem generis* is often invoked in conjunction with the interpretative canon *noscitur a sociis*, which provides that words are to be "known by their companions." The general rule is that the "meaning of a word, and, consequently, the intention of the legislature," should be "ascertained by reference to the context, and by considering whether the word in question and the surrounding words are, in fact, *ejusdem generis*, and referable to the same subject-matter."

A proper reading of § 2680(c) thus attributes to the last phrase ("any other law enforcement officer") the discrete characteristic shared by the preceding phrases ("officer[s] of customs or excise" and "assessment or collection of any tax or customs duty"). Had Congress intended otherwise, in all likelihood it would have drafted the section to apply to "any law enforcement officer, including officers of customs and excise," rather than tacking "any other law enforcement officer" on the end of the enumerated categories as it did here....

The Court reaches its contrary conclusion by concentrating on the word "any" before the phrase "other law enforcement officer." It takes this single last phrase to extend the statute so that it covers all detentions of property by any law enforcement officer in whatever capacity he or she acts. There are fundamental problems with this approach, in addition to the ones already mentioned.

First, the Court's analysis cannot be squared with the longstanding recognition that a single word must not be read in isolation but instead defined by reference to its statutory context. This is true even of facially broad modifiers. The word "any" can mean "different things depending upon the setting," and must be limited in its application "to those objects to which the legislature intended to apply them." ...

Second, the Court's construction of the phrase "any other law enforcement officer" runs contrary to "our duty to give effect, if possible, to every clause and word of a statute." The Court's reading renders "officer[s] of customs or excise" mere surplusage, as there would have been no need for Congress to have specified that officers of customs and officers of excise were immune if they indeed were subsumed within the allegedly all-encompassing "any" officer clause.

Third, though the final reference to "any other law enforcement officer" does result in some ambiguity, the legislative history, by virtue of its exclusive reference to customs and excise, confirms that Congress did not shift its attention from the context of revenue enforcement when it used these words at the end of the statute.

Indeed, the Court's construction reads the exception to defeat the central purpose of the statute, an interpretative danger the Court has warned against in explicit terms. It is difficult to conceive that the FTCA, which was enacted by Congress to make the tort liability of the United States "the same as that of a private person under like circumstance[s]," would allow any officer under any circumstance to detain property without being accountable under the Act to those injured by his or her tortious conduct. If Congress wanted to say that all law enforcement officers may detain property without liability in tort, including when they perform general law enforcement tasks, it would have done so in more express terms; one would expect at least a reference to law enforcement officers outside the customs or excise context either in the text of the statute or in the legislative history. In the absence of that reference, the Court ought not presume that the liberties of the person who owns the property would be so lightly dismissed and disregarded....

For these reasons, in my view, the judgment of the Court of Appeals ought to be reversed.

JUSTICE BREYER, with whom JUSTICE STEVENS joins, dissenting.

... As with many questions of statutory interpretation, the issue here is not the *meaning* of the words. The dictionary meaning of each word is well known. Rather, the issue is the statute's *scope*. What boundaries did Congress intend to set? To what circumstances did Congress intend the phrase, as used in *this* statutory provision, to apply? ...

The word "any" is of no help because all speakers (including writers and legislators) who use general words such as "all," "any," "never," and "none" normally rely upon context to indicate the limits of time and place within which they intend those words to do their linguistic work. And with the possible exception of the assertion of a universal truth, say by a mathematician, scientist, philosopher, or theologian, such limits almost always exist. When I call out to my wife, "There isn't any butter," I do not mean, "There isn't any butter in town." The context makes clear to her that I am talking about the contents of our refrigerator. That is to say, it is context, not a dictionary, that sets the boundaries of time, place, and circumstance within which words such as "any" will apply.

Context, of course, includes the words immediately surrounding the phrase in question. And canons such as *ejusdem generis* and *noscitur a sociis* offer help in evaluating the significance of those surrounding words. Yet that help is limited. That is because other contextual features can show that Congress intended a phrase to apply more broadly than the immediately surrounding words by themselves suggest....

In this case, not only the immediately surrounding words but also every other contextual feature supports Justice Kennedy's conclusion. The textual context includes the location of the phrase within a provision that otherwise exclusively concerns customs and revenue duties. And the nontextual context includes several features that, taken together, indicate that Congress intended a narrow tort-liability exception related to customs and excise.

First, drafting history shows that the relevant portion of the bill that became the Federal Tort Claims Act concerned only customs and excise. Initially, the relevant provision of the bill exempted only claims "arising in respect of the assessment or collection of any tax or customs duty." In 1931, a Special Assistant to the Attorney General, Alexander Holtzoff, wrote additional draft language, namely, "or the detention of any goods or merchandise by any officer of customs or excise or *any other law enforcement officer*" (emphasis added). Holtzoff, in a report to a congressional agency, said that the expanded language sought "to include immunity from liability in respect of loss in connection with the detention of goods or merchandise by any officer of customs or excise." Holtzoff explained that the language was suggested by a similar British bill that mentioned only customs and excise officials. And Members of Congress repeatedly referred to the exception as encompassing claims involving customs and excise functions.

Second, insofar as Congress sought, through the Act's exceptions, to preclude tort suits against the Government where "adequate remedies were already available," a limited exception makes sense; a broad exception does not. Other statutes already provided recovery for plaintiffs harmed by federal officers enforcing customs and tax laws but not for plaintiffs harmed by all other federal officers enforcing most other laws.

Third, the practical difference between a limited and a broad interpretation is considerable, magnifying the importance of the congressional silence to which Justice Kennedy points. A limited interpretation of the phrase "any other law enforcement officer" would likely encompass only those law enforcement officers working, say, at borders and helping to enforce customs and excise laws. The majority instead interprets this provision to include the tens of thousands of officers performing unrelated tasks. The Justice Department estimates that there are more than 100,000 law enforcement officers, not including members of the armed services. And although the law's history contains much that indicates the provision's scope is limited to customs and excise, it contains *nothing at all* suggesting an intent to apply the provision more broadly, indeed, to multiply the number of officers to whom it applies by what is likely one or more orders of magnitude. It is thus not the Latin canons, *ejusdem generis* and *noscitur a sociis*, that shed light on the application of the statutory phrase but Justice Scalia's more pertinent and easily remembered English-language observation that Congress "does not ... hide elephants in mouseholes." *Whitman* v. *American Trucking Assns., Inc.*, 531 U.S. 457, 468 (2001)....

Notes and Questions

(1) *Any.* Is the word "any" ambiguous according to the majority? What about to Justice Kennedy? Justice Breyer? Wasn't Justice Breyer correct that the true issue was what is the statute's scope because the term "any" is so broad? Aren't the textual canons appropriate precisely when a broad term is used in a catchall? Why then did the majority refuse to apply any of the canons identified by the petitioner? Which other textual canons were identified? Did you find any of these canons compelled a particular result?

(2) *Ejusdem Generis and Noscitur a sociis.* Do either of these the canons apply? The majority thought not because there was no list of items, just a specific item and a catch-all. In contrast, both dissents thought the canons were relevant. Why this difference?

(3) *Elephants and Mouseholes.* In *Whitman*, identified above, Justice Scalia said, "Congress … does not alter the fundamental details of a regulatory scheme in vague terms or ancillary provisions—it does not, one might say, hide elephants in mouseholes." What did Justice Scalia mean? Why do you think Justice Breyer quoted this memorable phrase in *Ali*? At bottom, this cases illustrates the impact a judge's approach has on interpretation. The majority refused to look beyond what it viewed as clear text. Both dissents looked more broadly, but to different sources. Justice Kennedy focused on the textual canons and legislative history, while Justice Breyer focused on the drafting history and the dog does not bark canon.

(4) *Narrowing the Meaning. Ejusdem generis* is typically used to narrow broad catchalls or statutes that include examples, such as "including but not limited to." For example, in *McKinney v. Robbins*, 892 S.W.2d 502 (Ark. 1995), the plaintiff sued the defendant for intentionally killing the plaintiff's dog, which had attacked the defendant's cat. The defendant relied upon ARK. CODE ANN. § 20-19-102 (Repl. 1991), which provided in part:

> (a)(1) "Domesticated animals" includes, but is not limited to, sheep, goats, cattle, swine, and poultry. . . .

> (b)(2) Any person knowing that any dog has killed or is about to catch, injure, or kill any domesticated animal shall have the right to kill the dog, without in any way being liable to the owner of the dog in any courts of this state.

The question for the court was whether a cat was a "domesticated animal" protected by this statute. If so, the defendant could not be liable. Most of us would likely concede that cats are "domesticated animals." However, relying on both *ejusdem generis* and *noscitur a sociis*, the court rejected defendant's argument: "[T]he definition of 'domesticated animals' which is limited by its terms to examples of livestock to include pets would expand the effect of the Act far beyond what, we believe, was intended by the General Assembly." Applying *ejusdem generis*, the court held that the broad term "domesticated animal" was narrowed by the specific examples. The court used the narrower, specific examples to confine the broader term and to limit "including but not limited to." Narrowing language should be the real function of *ejusdem generis.* Do you see why broadening the general term could implicate the rule against surplusage?

(5) *Broadening the Meaning.* Should the canon only be applied to narrow the meaning of a broad term? Consider *People v. Fields*, 105 Cal. App. 3d 341 (1980). There, the court construed a statute titled "destroying or concealing documentary evidence" and penalizing the destroying of any "book, paper, record, instrument in writing, or other matter or thing" to apply to marijuana. It refused to apply *ejusdem generis* or *noscitur a sociis* to narrow the broad term. Instead, the court held that "*other matter or thing*" was not ambiguous and included "an unending variety of physical objects." Did the *Fields* court err by failing to apply the rule against surplusage when the court's interpretation rendered "book, paper, record, instrument in writing" superfluous because, under the court's interpretation, the statute covered everything?

(6) *Consider the Purpose of these Catchalls.* Then-judge Stephen Breyer noted that legislatures do not attempt to put forth "complete lists" but instead use general catchalls out of the fear that "they would not be able to imagine, in advance, every possible kind of [conduct] that should be included. Such a reason is a common cause of generality, or lack of precision, in statutes." Stephen Breyer, *On the Uses of Legislative History in Inter-*

preting Statutes, 65 S. CAL. L. REV. 845, 854 (1992). Should that fact have some impact on whether, and if so how, *ejusdem generis* is applied? If so, what?

(7) *Ejusdem Generis v. Noscitur a Sociis: What is the Difference?* Judges often argue about which canon is appropriate. *See, e.g., People v. Jacques*, 572 N.W.2d 195 (Mich. 1998) (where the dissent noted that *ejusdem generis* was inapplicable because the term "structure" was used in the statute without the word "other" preceding it, while the majority disagreed that the word "other" was needed because "structure" was a general word).

How do you decide when to use *ejusdem generis* and *noscitur a sociis*? These are similar, related canons. While the courts are not always consistent in their use of these canons, we believe that the two canons serve different purposes when lists are involved. When there is a list of items with a general collective (or catchall) often preceded by phrases such as "other," *ejusdem generis*, not *noscitur a sociis*, is the proper canon. Or, another way to think of it is that "[t]he *ejusdem generis* rule is generally applied to general and specific words clearly associated in the same sentence in a pattern such as '[specific], [specific], or [general]' or '[general], including [specific] and [specific].'" *State v. Van Woerden*, 967 P.2d 14, 18 (Wash. Ct. App. 1998). *Noscitur a sociis* is better used to identify the meaning of items within the list (obstruct, resist, oppose), but not within the catch-all. As we quoted earlier: "Whereas *ejusdem generis* tells us how to find items outside the list expressed in the statute, *noscitur a sociis* tells us how the list gives meaning to the items within it." *Stebbins v. Wells*, 2001 WL 1255079, at *3 fn.3 (R.I. Sup. Ct. 2001). For example, if a statute states that it applies to "cars, trucks, motorcycles, and other vehicles," *ejusdem generis* would limit "other vehicles," to motorized vehicles or vehicles that travel on public highways. *Noscitur a sociis* would be inappropriate to use to interpret the catch-all. Yet, if any of the listed words—cars, trucks, or motorcycles—were in dispute, then *noscitur a sociis* would be appropriate. This distinction preserves the purposes of these two different canons.

5. *Expressio* (or *Inclusio*) *Unius Est Exclusio Alterius*

Expressio or *inclusio unius est exclusio alterius* literally means the inclusion of one thing excludes the other. By including a list of specific items and not using a catchall, the legislature meant to exclude items not listed. It is a rule of negative implication: by including some things, the legislature intentionally left out others. As one court explained:

> The maxim is a product of logic and common sense, properly applied only when it makes sense as a matter of legislative purpose.... [T]he ... principle describes what we usually mean by a particular manner of expression, but does not prescribe how we must interpret a phrase once written. Understood as a descriptive generalization about language rather than a prescriptive rule of construction, the maxim usefully describes a common syntactical implication. 'My children are Jonathan, Rebecca and Seth' means 'none of my children are Samuel.' Sometimes there is no negative pregnant: 'get milk, bread, peanut butter and eggs at the grocery' probably does not mean 'do not get ice cream.'

Silvers v. Sony Pictures Entm't, Inc., 402 F.3d 881, 899 (9th Cir. 2005). In law, for example, Federal Rule of Civil Procedure 9(b) requires allegations of "fraud or mistake" be pleaded with particularity. Applying this canon, courts have held that no other allegations need be pleaded that way. *E.g., Swierkiewicz v. Sorema N.A.*, 453 U.S. 506 (2002); *Leatherman v. Tarrant County Narcotics Intelligence & Coordination Unit*, 507 U.S. 163 (1993).

This canon, like so many others, presumes that the legislature acted in a particular way. Specifically, it presumes that the legislature actually considered all possible options and selected only those it wanted. *Nat'l Petroleum Refiners Ass'n v. FTC*, 482 F.2d 672, 676 (D.C. Cir. 1973). In some circumstances, of course, considering all options is impossible. For these and other reasons, a few judges have suggested that this canon is unreliable and should not be followed. *Id.* Despite isolated criticism, it is used regularly by the courts.

Chevron U.S.A., Inc. v. Echazabal
536 U.S. 73 (2002)

JUSTICE SOUTER delivered the opinion of the Court.

A regulation of the Equal Employment Opportunity Commission authorizes refusal to hire an individual because his performance on the job would endanger his own health, owing to a disability. The question in this case is whether the Americans with Disabilities Act of 1990, 104 Stat. 328, 42 U.S.C. § 12101et seq. (1994 ed. and Supp. V), permits the regulation. We hold that it does.

I.

Beginning in 1972, respondent Mario Echazabal ... [twice] applied for a job directly with Chevron, which offered to hire him if he could pass the company's physical examination. Each time, the exam showed liver abnormality or damage, the cause eventually being identified as Hepatitis C, which Chevron's doctors said would be aggravated by continued exposure to toxins at Chevron's refinery. In each instance, the company withdrew the offer....

Echazabal filed suit ... claiming, among other things, that Chevron violated the Americans with Disabilities Act (ADA or Act) in refusing to hire him.... Chevron defended under a regulation of the Equal Employment Opportunity Commission (EEOC) permitting the defense that a worker's disability on the job would pose a "direct threat" to his health....

On appeal, the Ninth Circuit ... held that [the EEOC's regulation recognizing a threat-to-self defense exceeded the scope of permissible rulemaking under the ADA]. The court rested its position on the text of the ADA itself in explicitly recognizing an employer's right to adopt an employment qualification barring anyone whose disability would place others in the workplace at risk, while saying nothing about threats to the disabled employee himself. The majority opinion reasoned that "by specifying only threats to 'other individuals in the workplace,' the statute makes it clear that threats to other persons — including the disabled individual himself — are not included within the scope of the [direct threat] defense,"....

We granted certiorari and now reverse.

II.

Section 102 of the ADA prohibits "discriminate(ion) against a qualified individual with a disability because of the disability ... in regard to" a number of actions by an employer, including "hiring." 42 U.S.C. § 12112(a). The statutory definition of "discriminate(ion)" covers a number of things an employer might do to block a disabled person from advancing in the workplace, such as "using qualification standards ... that screen out or tend to screen out an individual with a disability." § 12112(b)(6). By that same definition, as well as by separate provision, § 12113(a), the Act creates an affirmative defense for action under a qualification standard "shown to be job-related for the position in question and ... consistent with business necessity." Such a standard may include "a requirement that an individual shall not pose a direct threat to the health or safety of other individuals in the workplace," § 12113(b), if the individual cannot perform the job safely with reasonable accommodation, § 12113(a). By regulation, the EEOC carries the defense one step further, in allowing an employer to screen out a potential worker with a disability not only for risks that he would pose to others in the workplace but for risks on the job to his own health or safety as well: "The term 'qualification standard' may include a requirement that an individual shall not pose a direct threat to the health or safety of the individual or others in the workplace." 29 CFR § 1630.15(b)(2) (2001).

Chevron relies on the regulation here, since it says a job in the refinery would pose a "direct threat" to Echazabal's health. In seeking deference to the agency, it argues that nothing in the statute unambiguously precludes such a defense.... Echazabal, on the contrary, argues that as a matter of law the statute precludes the regulation....

A.

As for the textual bar to any agency action as a matter of law, Echazabal says that Chevron loses on the threshold question whether the statute leaves a gap for the EEOC to fill.... The argument follows the reliance of the Ninth Circuit majority on the interpretive canon, *expressio unius est exclusio alterius,* "expressing one item of [an] associated group or series excludes another left unmentioned." The rule is fine when it applies, but this case joins some others in showing when it does not.

The first strike against the expression-exclusion rule here is right in the text that Echazabal quotes. Congress included the harm-to-others provision as an example of legitimate qualifications that are "job-related and consistent with business necessity." These are spacious defensive categories, which seem to give an agency (or in the absence of agency action, a court) a good deal of discretion in setting the limits of permissible qualification standards. That discretion is confirmed, if not magnified, by the provision that "qualification standards" falling within the limits of job relation and business necessity "may include" a veto on those who would directly threaten others in the workplace. Far from supporting Echazabal's position, the expansive phrasing of "may include" points directly away from the sort of exclusive specification he claims.

Just as statutory language suggesting exclusiveness is missing, so is that essential extrastatutory ingredient of an expression-exclusion demonstration, the series of terms from which an omission bespeaks a negative implication. The canon depends on identifying a series of two or more terms or things that should be understood to go hand in hand, which is abridged in circumstances supporting a sensible inference that the term left out must have been meant to be excluded. E. Crawford, Construction of Statutes 337 (1940) (*expressio unius* "'properly applies only when in the natural association of ideas in the mind of the reader that which is expressed is so set over by way of strong contrast to that which is omitted that the contrast enforces the affirmative inference.'")

Strike two in this case is the failure to identify any such established series, including both threats to others and threats to self, from which Congress appears to have made a deliberate choice to omit the latter item as a signal of the affirmative defense's scope. The closest Echazabal comes is the EEOC's rule interpreting the Rehabilitation Act of 1973, a precursor of the ADA. That statute ... says nothing about threats to self that particular employment might pose. The EEOC nonetheless extended the exception to cover threat-to-self employment, and Echazabal argues that Congress's adoption only of the threat-to-others exception in the ADA must have been a deliberate omission of the Rehabilitation Act regulation's tandem term of threat-to-self, with intent to exclude it.

But two reasons stand in the way of treating the omission as an unequivocal implication of congressional intent. The first is that the EEOC was not the only agency interpreting the Rehabilitation Act.... While the EEOC did amplify upon the text of the Rehabilitation Act exclusion by recognizing threats to self along with threats to others, three other agencies adopting regulations under the Rehabilitation Act did not. It would be a stretch, then, to say that there was a standard usage, with its source in agency practice or elsewhere, that connected threats to others so closely to threats to self that leaving out one was like ignoring a twin....

Instead of making the ADA different from the Rehabilitation Act on the point at issue, Congress used identical language, knowing full well what the EEOC had made of that language under the earlier statute. Did Congress mean to imply that the agency had been wrong in reading the earlier language to allow it to recognize threats to self, or did Congress just assume that the agency was free to do under the ADA what it had already done under the earlier Act's identical language? There is no way to tell. Omitting the EEOC's reference to self-harm while using the very language that the EEOC had read as consistent with recognizing self-harm is equivocal at best. No negative inference is possible.

There is even a third strike against applying the expression-exclusion rule here. It is simply that there is no apparent stopping point to the argument that by specifying a threat-to-others defense Congress intended a negative implication about those whose safety could be considered. When Congress specified threats to others in the workplace, for example, could it possibly have meant that an employer could not defend a refusal to hire when a worker's disability would threaten others outside the workplace? If Typhoid Mary had come under the ADA, would a meat packer have been defenseless if Mary had sued after being turned away? Expressio unius just fails to work here.

[Since Congress has not spoken exhaustively on threats to a worker's own health, and the EEOC's interpretation was reasonable,] we reverse the judgment of the Court of Appeals and remand the case for proceedings consistent with this opinion.

Notes and Questions

(1) *Three Reasons.* What are the three reasons why *expressio unius est exclusio alterius* was inappropriate in this case? Which do you find most compelling, or are none persuasive?

(2) *Introduction to* Chevron. This case involves an agency, the EEOC, interpreting a statutory grant of authority from Congress. We explore the role that agencies play in statutory interpretation in more detail later. For now though, you should be aware that when a court reviews an agency's interpretation of a statute, the court will determine first whether Congress has directly spoken to the issue, and if not, will next determine whether the agency's interpretation of the statutory language was reasonable. *Chevron U.S.A., Inc. v. Natural Res. Def. Council, Inc.*, 467 U.S. 837 (1984). This two-step analysis is called the *Chevron* two-step. In the case above, we have included the Court's analysis of the first step only: whether Congress spoke directly to the issue. Because the Court found that Congress had not so spoken, the Court then turned to the second step and found the EEOC's interpretation reasonable.

(3) *The* Feld *Case.* In the *Feld* case, *supra* (about having an attorney present at a medical exam), the court did not mention *expressio unius est exclusio alterius*. Would that canon have provided support for the majority's interpretation? The other interpretations?

Problem 6-3

You have been asked for advice regarding whether your client should obtain a license under Mercer Rev. Stat. § 41.0.

Your client maintains an electrically operated mechanical pony, which is fixed on a base. A single child sits on the saddle. After fifty cents is inserted, the pony vibrates up and down with either a bucking or undulating motion. The pony vibrates for about two minutes. This mechanical pony is located in the front of your client's store, to which the public is invited. Children and shoppers are amused by its use. Your client retains the money from the pony. If at all possible, your client would prefer not to seek the very expensive license.

Determine (1) whether the term "common show" is ambiguous and why, (2) which, if any, of the textual canons that you have learned would likely be applied and why, and (3) what interpretation a court would most likely adopt.

Problem Materials

Mercer Rev. Stat. § 41.0 provides:[*]

> It shall be unlawful for any person to act as a common show operator without a license therefor.

Mercer Rev. Stat. § 40.0 provides:

> Definitions — a. Whenever used in this article, the term "common show" means: a carousel, Ferris wheel, a gravity steeplechase ride, a flume ride, a rock climbing wall, a fun house, a scenic railway, a roller coaster, a merry-go-round, an arcade, and all other rides or places of like character.

Subdivision (1) was added by Local Law No. 45 of 1908, and amended by Local Law 78 of 1975.

6. The Presumption that Identical Words in the Same Statute Have the Identical Meaning

One long-standing canon is "that identical words used in different parts of the same act are intended to have the same meaning." *United States v. Cleveland Indians Baseball Co.*, 532 U.S. 200, 213 (2001). However, "the presumption is not rigid and readily yields whenever there is such variation in the connection in which the words are used as reasonably to warrant the conclusion that they were employed in different parts of the act with different intent." *Atlantic Cleaners & Dyers, Inc. v. United States*, 286 U.S. 427, 433 (1932). "Where the subject-matter to which the words refer is not the same in the several places where they are used, or the conditions are different, or the scope of the legislative power exercised in one case is broader than that exercised in another, the meaning well may vary to meet the purposes of the law, to be arrived at by consideration of the language in which those purposes are expressed, and of the circumstances under which the language was employed." *Id.*

Thus, the use of identical words in different places in a statute or act creates a presumption that each should be given the same meaning, but other facts may overcome the presumption and, as a consequence, allow a court to ascribe different meanings to the

---

[*] It is common for attorneys to have to interpret archaic statutes, like the one above.

same word. *E.g.*, *Guiterrez v. Ada*, 528 U.S. 250 (2000) (holding that presumption did not apply where statute was later amended and terminology had changed between time of later amendment and original enactment). Consider the following cases—the first decided by the Illinois Court of Appeals and the second from the Illinois Supreme Court reversing the lower court opinion—which illustrate the challenges that this presumption creates.

To understand the cases that follow, you must first understand the difference between a survival action and a wrongful death action. A wrongful death action is a suit brought by those dependent upon the decedent for the losses they suffered as a result of their loved one's death. Any recovery belongs to the relatives in their own right. In contrast, a survival action arises when the victim sues and then dies, for whatever reason. In early common law, the suit died with the victim, and so survival actions were created to allow the lawsuit to continue; the administrator of the victim's estate is substituted for the victim. Thus, damages are for the injuries the victim sustained prior to death and go to the victim's estate. While any recovery may ultimately flow to the beneficiaries, the beneficiaries' loss is not what is being remedied in a survival action.

Jensen v. Elgin, Joliet & Eastern Ry. Co.
175 N.E.2d 564 (Ill. Ct. App. 1961)

BURKE, Presiding Justice.

This is an appeal from a judgment awarding the plaintiff, Nancy Jensen, Administratrix of the Estate of Ole Jensen, deceased, $10,000 for damages under the survival provision of the Federal Employers' Liability Act (45 U.S.C.A. §59). The decedent, a switching foreman, sustained a back injury when he attempted to throw a puzzle switch which was in an unsafe and inoperative condition by reason of the fact that it had not been properly oiled and maintained. The ... defendant's liability was previously ascertained. An earlier judgment for $50,000 was reversed and the cause remanded for a new determination of the amount of damages. Ole Jensen died from other causes pending the former appeal, his administratrix was substituted and the complaint amended, limiting the recovery sought to damages which her decedent might or could have recovered in his lifetime for the injuries he sustained from the date of his injuries to the date of his death, for the benefit of Ole Jensen's three adult children. As Ole Jensen's three marriages terminated in divorce decrees prior to the instant litigation, the former wives are not concerned with these proceedings. Recovery is sought for the benefit of the three children, two of whom are married and living with their families. None is dependent on the father....

The principal question presented is whether the right of action of an injured employee under the Federal Employers' Liability Act which survives his death from other causes may be prosecuted for the benefit of his adult nondependent children. The FELA, enacted in 1908, created a right of action in the injured employee and a right of action for wrongful death in his personal representative 'for the benefit of the surviving widow or husband and children of such employee; and, if none, then of such employee's parents' and, if none, then of the next of kin dependent upon such employee,'[§1]; but made no provision for survival of the injured employee's right of action in the event of his later death from his injuries or from other causes.... [The statute was amended in 1910 to include] Section 9, [which reads] as follows:

> Any right of action given by this chapter to a person suffering injury shall survive to his or her personal representative, for the benefit of the surviving widow or husband and children of such employee, and, if none, then of such em-

ployee's parents; and, if none, then of the next of kin dependent upon such employee, but in such cases there shall be only one recovery for the same injury.

It will be noted that the statutory designation in section 9 of the beneficiaries of the survival action is identical with the designation in section 1 of the beneficiaries of the wrongful death action. By the recognized rule of statutory interpretation, identical language in different sections of the same statute must receive the same construction. The persons for whose benefit the survival action may be prosecuted are the same persons as those for whose benefit a wrongful death action may be brought....

[The appellate court believed that the term "children" in § 1 had been interpreted to mean "dependent minor children" by the Supreme Court.] Plaintiff maintains that pecuniary loss to children or dependency of children is not a prerequisite to the vesting of a survival action under Sec. 9 of the FELA. She says that this section remedied the oversight in Sec. 1 and that damages under Sec. 9 are not measured by pecuniary loss to the specific beneficiaries but by those damage elements which accrued to the decedent during his lifetime. She insists that pecuniary loss to the next of kin is not necessary where the action is based on the surviving right of action of a deceased employee....

We are of the opinion that the same construction given by the courts to the meaning of Sec. 1 must be given to the phrase 'children of such employee' in Sec. 9. No different legislative purpose can be discerned as the language is identical. No sound reason can be suggested why adult children should be permitted to share in the recovery for their parent's pain and suffering but not in the proceeds of a wrongful death action. *The McGinnis case* holds that a wrongful death action may not be prosecuted for the benefit of an adult, married daughter not 'in any way dependent upon the decedent.' One cannot find any congressional purpose to include nondependent sons and daughters as beneficiaries of a survival action when their father dies of other causes and exclude them when his death is the result of the defendant's negligence. Plaintiff, citing Black's Law Dictionary, says that the term 'child' as used in the law when speaking of a decedent means a son or daughter of a parent irrespective of age. It is obvious that if 'children' under Sec. 1, the wrongful death section, means children during their minority, it means the same under Sec. 9, irrespective of any dictionary definition. Neither the 26-year old married son living with his family in Florida, nor the 33-year old daughter living in Bellwood, sustained any loss as a result of their father's accident. Nancy, the administratrix, 23 years old, neither alleged nor proved any dependency on her father and the offer of proof was that her father had not supported her since she was 18. Since under the *McGinnis* case no judgment on their behalf could have been recovered if their father died as a result of defendant's negligence, they are not in a position to ask for a judgment in their favor when their father died of other causes.

For these reasons the judgment is reversed....

Jensen v. Elgin, Joliet & Eastern Ry. Co.
182 N.E.2d 211 (Ill. 1962)

HOUSE, Justice.

The first question presented by this appeal is whether a cause of action which an injured employee has under section 1 of the Federal Employers' Liability Act will under provisions of section 9 of the act survive his death for the benefit of his adult nondependent children. Section 9 provides that 'Any right of action given by this chapter to a person suffering injury shall survive to his or her personal representative, for the benefit of the widow or husband and children of such employee.' The Appellate Court, First District, construed 'children' as used in section 9 to mean 'minor dependent children' and reversed a judgment of the circuit court of Cook County awarding to the personal representative of Ole Jensen, deceased, for the benefit of his three adult nondependent children, $10,000 for damages sustained by Jensen during his lifetime.

Section 1 of the act … provides that in case of the wrongful death of such employee a cause of action accrues 'to his or her personal representative, for the benefit of the surviving widow or husband and children of such employee.' The Appellate Court, after reviewing a number of decisions interpreting the wrongful death provisions of section 1, concluded that the word 'children' as used in that section had been construed to mean 'minor dependent children.' Since the phraseology defining the beneficiaries in section 1 is identical with that defining the beneficiaries for whose benefit an action survives under section 9 the Appellate Court held that the word 'children' as used in section 9 must also be construed to mean 'minor dependent children.' In this we believe the court erred. An examination of the cases construing the provisions of section 1 leads us to the conclusion that the word 'children' has not been given other than its ordinary meaning and that the inability of any of the beneficiaries designated in section 1 to recover is simply the result of the measure of damages and basis of liability under that section. [In other words, a wrongful death action is brought to recover for the injury to those relatives actually dependent on the decedent.]

In *Michigan Central Railroad Co. v. Vreeland*, the Supreme Court in considering the wrongful death provisions stated: 'This cause of action is independent of any cause of action which the decedent had, and includes no damages which he might have recovered for his injury if he had survived. It is one beyond that which the decedent had,—one proceeding upon altogether different principles. It is a liability for the loss and damage sustained by relatives dependent upon the decedent. It is therefore a liability for the pecuniary damages resulting to them, and for that only.'

In *Craft*, the court pointed out that the basis of liability under the wrongful death provisions of section 1 is the wrong to the beneficiaries in causing their pecuniary loss. If a child has suffered no pecuniary loss then he has not been damaged and there is no basis of liability.

The basis of liability for an action which survives under section 9 is, on the other hand, the wrong to the injured employee and the measure of damages is his personal loss and suffering before he died. Thus, the basis of liability and measure of damages that may operate to prevent some children from recovering under the wrongful death provisions of section 1 are not present in an action which survives under section 9. We are of the opinion that the word 'children' has its ordinary dictionary meaning in both sections 1 and 9. The Appellate Court by construing the word 'children' to mean 'minor dependent children' unnecessarily placed a restriction on beneficiaries clearly designated in section 9, a restriction which exists under section 1 only because of the inherent nature of a wrongful death action.

The judgment … is reversed.… *child = ordinary dictionary meaning*

Notes and Questions

(1) *Why Reverse?* How did the lower court interpret the word "children"? How did the Illinois Supreme Court interpret "children"? Was the identical words presumption relevant according to the Illinois Supreme Court? Assuming not, why then did the court reverse?

(2) *Who was Right?* As we explained above, wrongful death and survival actions serve different purposes. Does that fact or the difference in the recoveries explain the different results in the cases? Which court got it right?

(3) *Is Monotony a Good Thing?* In English composition, variety of word usage is commended. In statutes, however, a change in word signifies a change in meaning. Does this suggest that monotony in statutory drafting is a good thing?

7. Provisos

Provisos are clauses limiting another clause in a substantive provision. They typically begin with the words "provided, that...." The following statute contains two provisos, which we have italicized:

Ala. Code § 32-7-23. Uninsured motorist coverage; "uninsured motorist" defined; limitation on recovery.

(a) No automobile liability or motor vehicle liability policy insuring against loss resulting from liability imposed by law for bodily injury or death suffered by any person arising out of the ownership, maintenance or use of a motor vehicle shall be delivered or issued for delivery in this state with respect to any motor vehicle registered or principally garaged in this state unless coverage is provided therein or supplemental thereto, in limits for bodily injury or death set forth in subsection (c) of Section 32-7-6, under provisions approved by the Commissioner of Insurance for the protection of persons insured thereunder who are legally entitled to recover damages from owners or operators of uninsured motor vehicles because of bodily injury, sickness or disease, including death, resulting therefrom; *provided, that* the named insured shall have the right to reject such coverage; and *provided further,* that unless the named insured requests such coverage in writing, such coverage need not be provided in or supplemental to a renewal policy where the named insured had rejected the coverage in connection with the policy previously issued to him by the same insurer.

Provisos limit the effect of a statutory provision or create an exception to a general rule. "It is a well-recognized rule of statutory construction that exceptions or provisos should be narrowly and strictly construed." *Samara Dev. Corp. v. Marlow*, 556 So. 2d 1097, 1100 (Fla. 1990). The reason for strict construction, of course, is that otherwise the exception would swallow the rule: "[A] proviso states an exception to the general policy which a law embodies, and should be strictly construed and interpreted so as not to destroy the remedial processes intended to be accomplished by the enactment." *Local Union No. 38 v. Pelella,* 350 F.3d 73, 85 (2d Cir. 2003). Even so, some courts only strictly construe provisos if the plain meaning is ambiguous. *E.g., State v. Simms,* 977 P.2d 647, 650 (Wash. Ct. App. 1999).

Lexington Educ. Ass'n v. Lexington
448 N.E.2d 1271 (Mass. Ct. App. 1983)

GREANEY, JUSTICE.

The question in this case is whether, by reason of the definition of the word "employee" in G.L. c. 32B, § 2(d), a municipality is foreclosed from requiring of its employees more than twenty hours of service per week as a qualification for coverage under the municipality's group insurance plan. The town of Lexington takes the position that the statute sets a twenty hour minimum requirement for coverage, above which municipalities are free to set their own standards. Lexington's policy is to provide coverage for employees who work at least twenty-five hours per week. The Lexington Education Association (Association) asserts that a municipality may not set a standard different from the twenty hour test enunciated in the statute. The Association brought an action in the Superior Court for a declaration of rights.... [T]he Superior Court ... granted partial summary judgment to the Association....

General Laws c. 32B, §3 provides that upon acceptance of c. 32B by a governmental unit, that unit must purchase certain group insurance "covering employees." An "employee" is defined ... in G.L. c. 32B, §2(d), as "any person in the service of a governmental unit ... who receives compensation for such service ... ; provided, the duties of such person require no less than twenty hours, regularly, in the service of the governmental unit during the regular work week of permanent or temporary employment." We think this can be taken only as including, within the term "employee," all who work for the governmental entity and are paid for their efforts except those who do not meet the qualifications expressed in the provisos which immediately follow the broad general definition. In other words, we interpret the quoted language of the statute as conferring employee status on all compensated persons engaged in the service of Lexington whose duties require no less than twenty hours per week of regular service to the town. This includes those who work between twenty and twenty-five hours per week—persons currently excluded from coverage by Lexington's self-imposed and super-statutory twenty-five hour minimum requirement. We reject the notion that statutory authority for the imposition of such a standard may be found in the last sentence of §2(d) which provides that "[a] determination by the appropriate public authority that a person is eligible for participation in the plan of insurance shall be final." This clause does no more than authorize the town to make binding final determinations of whether individual employees qualify under the statutory standard. It does not empower the town to adopt a more restrictive standard.

Our interpretation of the proviso as a device to excise a discrete group from the broad general definition of "employee," and no more, is supported by long-standing rules of statutory interpretation. It is a cardinal rule of interpretation that where a provision, general in its language and objects, is followed by a proviso, ... the proviso is to be strictly construed, as taking no case out of the provision that does not fairly fall within the terms of the proviso, the latter being understood as carving out of the provision only specified exception, within the words as well as within the reason of the former. "Where there is doubt ... as to the extent of the restriction imposed by a proviso on the scope of another provision's operation, the proviso is strictly construed. The reason for this is that the legislative purpose set forth in the main or dominant body of an enactment is assumed to express the legislative policy, and only those subjects expressly exempted by the proviso should be freed from the operation of the statute." 2A Sands, Sutherland Statutory Construction §47.08, at 82 (4th ed. 1973). What the proviso does here is to exclude from the statute's coverage all those who work [more than 20 hours per week]. §2(d) proviso was not intended to confer discretion on the town to set higher standards of qualification for insurance coverage than those expressed in the statute....

Judgment affirmed.

Notes and Questions

(1) *The Proviso at Issue.* What is the municipality's argument that the proviso didn't apply? The court stated that where the meaning of the statute was "in doubt," provisos are strictly construed. Is "in doubt" something less than ambiguous?

(2) *Proviso or Not?* The characterization of a clause as a proviso is important because it means the exception will be narrowly construed. In that regard, consider *Gay & Lesbian Law Students Association v. Board of Trustees*, 673 A.2d 484 (Conn. 1996). In that case, the Gay and Lesbian Law Students Association of the University of Connecticut School of Law sought to enjoin the Judge Advocate General Corps (commonly referred to as "JAG Corps") from recruiting at the law school because the military discriminated against homosexuals. A Connecticut gay rights law prohibited discrimination in employment based on sexual orientation. A separate statute, 10a-149a, provided:

> Notwithstanding any other provision of law to the contrary, each ... university ... shall ... provide the same ... on-campus recruiting opportunities to ... the armed forces ... as are offered to nonmilitary recruiters or commercial concerns.

The majority held that 10a-149 was a proviso—an exception to the gay rights law. As a result, the majority applied the rule that "provisos and exceptions to statutes are to be strictly construed with doubts resolved in favor of the general rule rather than the exception and that those who claim the benefit of an exception under a statute have the burden of proving that they come within the limited class for whose benefit it was established." *Id.* The court held (1) that the exception following "notwithstanding" was to be narrowly construed as an exception to the general rule that employers not discriminate on the basis of sexual orientation, (2) that the military's violation of the Gay Rights Law required the school to deny access to the JAG recruiters, and (3) that the exception in 10a-149a did not apply. *Id.*

The dissent disagreed with the majority's characterization of 10a-149 as a proviso:

> I find it necessary to challenge the majority's characterization of that clause as a "proviso" or an "exception" to the Gay Rights Law. The majority utilizes that characterization in order to place upon the defendants "'the burden of proving that they come within the limited class for whose benefit [the law] was established'" and to claim that the "notwithstanding" clause in this case should be "strictly construed with doubts resolved in favor of the general rule...." As the majority asserts, the Reserve Officers' Training Corps provision in the Gay Rights Law is an "exception" in that it is a provision that restricts its general applicability. The "notwithstanding" clause, however, does not represent a specific exception to the Gay Rights Law but rather a legislative pronouncement within § 10a-149a that any conflict between § 10a-149a and any other law will be resolved in favor of § 10a-149a. The "notwithstanding" clause is more analogous to a general saving statute that saves rights and remedies except where a subsequent repealing act indicates that it was not the legislative intention that particular rights and remedies should be saved. This is a situation where one statute provides for the resolution of conflicts between it and other statutes, not a situation where there is a specific exemption within a statute to that statute's general applicability. Moreover, in the only other case in which this court has interpreted a "notwithstanding" clause in a statute, not only did we not "strictly construe" that clause as the majority does in this case, but we interpreted it broadly. Therefore, I believe that the majority's application of the presumptions and burdens associated with exceptions and provisos is simply wrong.

Id. at 509 n.9 (Palmer, A.J., dissenting). Who was right? Why was the characterization so important to the outcome?

D. The Textual Canons in Harmony

We have now canvassed the common textual canons. Some have argued that for each canon, there often is an equal and opposite canon of construction. Professor Karl Llewellyn made that observation many years ago. Karl N. Llewellyn, *Remarks on the Theory of Appellate Decision and the Rules of Cannon about How Statutes are to be Construed*, 3 VAND. L. REV. 395, 401 (1949), reproduced in Appendix A. Professor Llewellyn's chart has become famous in academic circles for the argument that there really are no rules of statutory construction. Additionally, Judge Posner has observed that the canons are not used by legislators in drafting statutes, nor used consistently by judges when interpreting them. *See* Richard Posner, *Statutory Interpretation—In the Classroom and in the Courtroom*, 50 U. CHI. L. REV. 800 (1983).

However, Professor Llewellyn did not believe that the canons were pointless, and Judge Posner relies on the canons in his judicial opinions. Common sense plays an important role in applying these canons. It is important that you understand that the point these authors make is more subtle than the point a deconstructionist would make, namely that none of this really matters. Professor Llewellyn and Judge Posner would instead suggest that the canons are merely sources that lawyers and judges use to argue about or find statutory meaning. Thus, lawyers who rely on one canon to justify their position must be able to explain why the other, opposing canon does not apply or is less compelling given the circumstances of the case.

The case below (known as the Spotted Owl Case) shows the interaction of many of these canons. This case involves a challenge to an agency regulation. As noted above, courts review an agency's interpretation of a statute in two steps. First, the court determines whether Congress directly spoke to the issue. *Chevron U.S.A., Inc. v. Natural Resources Def. Council, Inc.*, 467 U.S. 837 (1984). If so, then the inquiry is over, for the agency has no power to interpret the statute differently than Congress. *Id*. If not, then the court will determine whether the agency's interpretation of the statute was reasonable. Agencies may only adopt regulations within the authority provided to them by Congress. In the case below, the agency enacted a regulation that interpreted the word "harm" in the Endangered Species Act. The issue presented is whether the agency interpreted the word too broadly.

The opinions in *Sweet Home* use many of the canons we have discussed (and some that we will be discussing later) including the following: *in pari materia*; the plain meaning rule and its corollaries regarding ordinary and technical meaning; *noscitur a sociis*; *ejusdem generis*; *expressio unius est exclusio alterius*; the rule against surplusage; the Golden Rule; and the identical words presumption. See if you can find where each canon was used in the majority opinion or dissent. Notice how the different canons compel a different result. When different canons point in different directions, how should the court decide a case? The side with the most canons wins? The side with the most compelling canons wins? The side with the most compelling argument wins, canons notwithstanding? There is simply no answer to this question at this time.

Babbitt v. Sweet Home Chapter Commun.
515 U.S. 687 (1995)

JUSTICE STEVENS delivered the opinion of the Court.

The Endangered Species Act of 1973 (ESA or Act) ... makes it unlawful for any person to "take" any endangered or threatened species. The Secretary [of the Interior] has promulgated a regulation that defines the statute's prohibition on takings to include "significant habitat modification or degradation where it actually kills or injures wildlife." This case presents the question whether the Secretary exceeded his authority under the Act by promulgating that regulation.

Section 9(a)(1) of the Act provides the following protection for endangered species:

> [I]t is unlawful for any person subject to the jurisdiction of the United States to ... take any such species within the United States or the territorial sea of the United States." ...

> The term 'take' means to harass, harm, pursue, hunt, shoot, wound, kill, trap, capture, or collect, or to attempt to engage in any such conduct. 16 U.S.C. § 1532(19).

The Act does not further define the terms it uses to define "take." The Interior Department [an agency] regulations that implement the statute, however, define the statutory term "harm":

> *Harm* in the definition of 'take' in the Act means an act which actually kills or injures wildlife. Such act may include significant habitat modification or degradation where it actually kills or injures wildlife by significantly impairing essential behavioral patterns, including breeding, feeding, or sheltering. 50 CFR § 17.3 (1994).

... Respondents in this action are small landowners, logging companies, and families dependent on the forest products industries in the Pacific Northwest and in the Southeast, and organizations that represent their interests. They brought this ... action ... to challenge the ... Secretary's regulation defining "harm," particularly the inclusion of habitat modification and degradation in the definition.... Their complaint alleged that application of the "harm" regulation to the red-cockaded woodpecker, an endangered species, and the northern spotted owl, a threatened species, had injured them economically.... [The court of appeals agreed basing its reasoning on a canon of statutory construction called *noscitur a sociis*, which holds that a word is known by the company it keeps.]

Our consideration of the text and structure of the Act, its legislative history, and the significance of the 1982 amendment persuades us that the Court of Appeals' judgment should be reversed....

The text of the Act provides three reasons for concluding that the Secretary's interpretation is reasonable. First, an ordinary understanding of the word "harm" supports it. The dictionary definition of the verb form of "harm" is "to cause hurt or damage to: injure." Webster's Third New International Dictionary 1034 (1966). In the context of the ESA, that definition naturally encompasses habitat modification that results in actual injury or death to members of an endangered or threatened species.

Respondents argue that the Secretary should have limited the purview of "harm" to direct applications of force against protected species, but the dictionary definition does not include the word "directly" or suggest in any way that only direct or willful action that leads to injury constitutes "harm." Moreover, unless the statutory term "harm" encompasses indirect as well as direct injuries, the word has no meaning that does not duplicate the meaning of other words that §3 uses to define "take." A reluctance to treat statutory terms as surplusage supports the reasonableness of the Secretary's interpretation.[11]

Second, the broad purpose of the ESA supports the Secretary's decision to extend protection against activities that cause the precise harms Congress enacted the statute to avoid.... Third, the fact that Congress in 1982 authorized the Secretary to issue permits for takings that §9(a)(1)(B) would otherwise prohibit, "if such taking is incidental to, and not the purpose of, the carrying out of an otherwise lawful activity," 16 U.S.C. §1539(a)(1)(B), strongly suggests that Congress understood §9(a)(1)(B) to prohibit indirect as well as deliberate takings....

The Court of Appeals made three errors in asserting that "harm" must refer to a direct application of force because the words around it do. First, the court's premise was flawed. Several of the words that accompany "harm" in the §3 definition of "take," especially "harass," "pursue," "wound," and "kill," refer to actions or effects that do not require direct applications of force. Second, to the extent the court read a requirement of intent or purpose into the words used to define "take," it ignored §11's express provision that a "knowin[g]" action is enough to violate the Act." ... Third, the court employed *noscitur a sociis* to give "harm" essentially the same function as other words in the definition, thereby denying it independent meaning. The cannon, to the contrary, counsels that a word "gathers meaning from the words around it." The statutory context of "harm" suggests that Congress meant that term to serve a particular function in the ESA, consistent with, but distinct from, the functions of the other verbs used to define "take." The Secretary's interpretation of "harm" to include indirectly injuring endangered animals through habitat modification permissibly interprets "harm" to have "a character of its own not to be submerged by its association." ...

The judgment of the Court of Appeals is reversed....

JUSTICE SCALIA, with whom THE CHIEF JUSTICE and JUSTICE THOMAS join, dissenting.

The Endangered Species Act of 1973 provides that "it is unlawful for any person subject to the jurisdiction of the United States to take ... any [protected] species within the United States." §1538(a)(1)(B). The term "take" is defined as "to harass, harm, pursue, hunt, shoot, wound, kill, trap, capture, or collect, or to attempt to engage in any such conduct." §1532(19). The challenged regulation defines "harm" thus:

> *Harm* in the definition of 'take' in the Act means an act which actually kills or injures wildlife. Such act may include significant habitat modification or degradation where it actually kills or injures wildlife by significantly impairing essential behavioral patterns, including breeding, feeding or sheltering. 50 CFR §17.3 (1994)....

The ... most important unlawful feature of the regulation is that it encompasses injury inflicted, not only upon individual animals, but upon populations of the protected

---

11. In contrast, if the statutory term "harm" encompasses such indirect means of killing and injuring wildlife as habitat modification, the other terms listed in §3 — "harass," "pursue," "hunt," "shoot," "wound," "kill," "trap," "capture," and "collect" — generally retain independent meanings. Most of those terms refer to deliberate actions more frequently than does "harm," and they therefore do not duplicate the sense of indirect causation that "harm" adds to the statute. In addition, most of the other words in the definition describe either actions from which habitat modification does not usually result (*e.g.*, "pursue," "harass") or effects to which activities that modify habitat do not usually lead (*e.g.*, "trap," "collect"). To the extent the Secretary's definition of "harm" may have applications that overlap with other words in the definition, that overlap reflects the broad purpose of the Act.

species. "Injury" in the regulation includes "significantly impairing essential behavioral patterns, including *breeding*," 50 CFR § 17.3 (1994) (emphasis added). Impairment of breeding does not "injure" living creatures; it prevents them from propagating, thus "injuring" *a population* of animals which would otherwise have maintained or increased its numbers. What the face of the regulation shows, the Secretary's official pronouncements confirm. The Final Redefinition of "Harm" accompanying publication of the regulation said that "harm" is not limited to "direct physical injury to an individual member of the wildlife species," and refers to "injury *to a population*," (emphasis added)....

The term "harm" in § 1532(19) has no legal force of its own. An indictment or civil complaint that charged the defendant with "harming" an animal protected under the Act would be dismissed as defective, for the only *operative* term in the statute is to "take." ... The verb "harm" has a *range* of meaning: "to cause injury" at its broadest, "to do hurt or damage" in a narrower and more direct sense. See, *e.g.*, 1 N. Webster, An American Dictionary of the English Language (1828).... In fact the more directed sense of "harm" is a somewhat more common and preferred usage; "*harm* has in it a little of the idea of specially focused hurt or injury, as if a personal injury has been anticipated and intended." To define "harm" as an act or omission that, however remotely, "actually kills or injures" a population of wildlife through habitat modification is to choose a meaning that makes nonsense of the word that "harm" defines—requiring us to accept that a farmer who tills his field and causes erosion that makes silt run into a nearby river which depletes oxygen and thereby "impairs [the] breeding" of protected fish has "taken" or "attempted to take" the fish. It should take the strongest evidence to make us believe that Congress has defined a term in a manner repugnant to its ordinary and traditional sense.

Here the evidence shows the opposite. "Harm" is merely one of 10 prohibitory words in § 1532(19), and the other 9 fit the ordinary meaning of "take" perfectly. To "harass, pursue, hunt, shoot, wound, kill, trap, capture, or collect" are all affirmative acts (the provision itself describes them as "conduct," see § 1532(19)) which are directed immediately and intentionally against a particular animal—not acts or omissions that indirectly and accidentally cause injury to a population of animals. The Court points out that several of the words ("harass," "pursue," "wound," and "kill") "refer to actions or effects that do not require direct *applications of force*." (emphasis added). That is true enough, but force is not the point. Even "taking" activities in the narrowest sense, activities traditionally engaged in by hunters and trappers, do not all consist of direct applications of force; pursuit and harassment are part of the business of "taking" the prey even before it has been touched. What the nine other words in § 1532(19) have in common-and share with the narrower meaning of "harm" described above, but not with the Secretary's ruthless dilation of the word—is the sense of affirmative conduct intentionally directed against a particular animal or animals.

I am not the first to notice this fact, or to draw the conclusion that it compels. In 1981 the Solicitor of the Fish and Wildlife Service delivered a legal opinion on § 1532(19) that is in complete agreement with my reading:

> The Act's definition of 'take' contains a list of actions that illustrate the intended scope of the term.... With the possible exception of 'harm,' these terms all represent forms of conduct that are directed against and likely to injure or kill *individual* wildlife. Under the principle of statutory construction, *ejusdem generis*, ... the term 'harm' should be interpreted to include only those actions that are directed against, and likely to injure or kill, individual wildlife.

I would call it *noscitur a sociis*, but the principle is much the same: The fact that "several items in a list share an attribute counsels in favor of interpreting the other items as possessing that attribute as well." The Court contends that the cannon cannot be applied to deprive a word of all its "independent meaning." That proposition is questionable to begin with, especially as applied to long lawyers' listings such as this. If it were true, we ought to give the word "trap" in the definition its rare meaning of "to clothe" (whence "trappings") — since otherwise it adds nothing to the word "capture." In any event, the Court's contention that "harm" in the narrow sense adds nothing to the other words underestimates the ingenuity of our own species in a way that Congress did not. To feed an animal poison, to spray it with mace, to chop down the very tree in which it is nesting, or even to destroy its entire habitat in order to take it (as by draining a pond to get at a turtle), might neither wound nor kill, but would directly and intentionally harm. . . .

The Endangered Species Act is a carefully considered piece of legislation that forbids all persons to hunt or harm endangered animals, but places upon the public at large, rather than upon fortuitously accountable individual landowners, the cost of preserving the habitat of endangered species. There is neither textual support for, nor even evidence of congressional consideration of, the radically different disposition contained in the regulation that the Court sustains. For these reasons, I respectfully dissent.

Notes and Questions

(1) Chevron's *Two-Step*. Note that the majority opinion addresses the second step of *Chevron* only, whether the agency's interpretation was reasonable. To get to this step, the majority must have first found that Congress did not "speak" directly to this issue, but rather left it to the agency to resolve. Had Congress directly spoken to the issue, the agency would have no authority to interpret the language differently from Congress.

(2) *Harm or Take?* What is the statutory language at issue in the statute, "harm" or "take"? Or, are both words at issue? Which term did the agency interpret in its regulation?

(3) *Noscitur a Sociis*. The lower court rested its holding that the agency regulation was an unreasonable interpretation of the statute on this textual canon. Why did the majority disagree? Was it because the lower court's unifying factor depleted the word "take" of any independent meaning or was it because *noscitur a sociis* was simply inapplicable? According to the dissent, what was the unifer?

(4) *Ejusdem Generis v. Noscitur a Sociis*. Legal counsel for the Fish and Wildlife Service, an agency, stated that *ejusdem generis* was the appropriate canon to use. Justice Scalia disagreed and used *noscitur a sociis*. Explain why Justice Scalia was correct. What if the language being interpreted was "or to attempt to engage in any such conduct," which occurs at the end of the listed items: Which canon would be appropriate in that case? Why?

Chapter 7

The Role of Components

The paperwork that contains a proposed statute is called a "bill" or, after it's been enacted, an "act." This chapter explains the various components of a bill and their relevance to statutory interpretation. Even if a bill is enacted into law, not all of the language in a bill is codified as "law." Instead, most bills contain language that will not become part of the statute (*i.e.*, will not be codified). Most of what this book focuses on is called the "purview" of a bill: the words in the bill that follow the "enacting clause," become law, and provide the substance of the statute. *See Atkins v. Deere & Co.*, 685 N.E.2d 342, 346 (Ill. 1997). In this chapter, though, we'll see two things that may, at first, not make much sense: Some of the language that is not officially enacted into law can affect interpretation, while some of the language that *is* enacted into law, meaning it is within the purview of the statute, is not normally relevant to interpretation. Moreover, even when it is relevant, it is given little weight.

To help you understand why this is so, this chapter reprints excerpts from a very short bill that was introduced in the 108th Congress: S. 620, otherwise known as the College Fire Prevention Act. The complete bill is reproduced in full in Appendix B. Below are the first three paragraphs of that act. Normally, the title of the components is not printed in the bill, but we've added titles in brackets, using italicized, bolded letters.

A BILL

[Long Title]: To amend title VII of the Higher Education Act of 1965 to provide for fire sprinkler systems, or other fire suppression or prevention technologies, in public and private college and university housing and dormitories, including fraternity and sorority housing and dormitories.

[Enacting Clause]: Be it enacted by the Senate and House of Representatives of the United States of America in Congress assembled....

SEC. 771. SHORT TITLE.

[Short Title]: This part may be cited as the 'College Fire Prevention Act'.

A good place to start our discussion is with the enacting clause. Enacting clauses are required. 1 U.S.C. § 101 (2005). The enacting clause must precede those sections of the statute intended to have the force of law. 1 U.S.C. § 103 (2005). Only language that follows the enacting clause is, technically, enacted by the legislature and presented to the executive for signature. The enacting clause itself does not become law; only the language following it. *See State v. Phillips*, 560 S.E.2d 852, 856 (N.C. Ct. App. 2002) ("While the enacting clause is required for the act to become law, it does not itself become law, nor is that required to be the case.")

A formalistic approach to statutory interpretation would suggest that nothing before the enacting clause should be considered for statutory interpretation, while everything after it should be considered. After all, language that precedes the enacting clause is not "enacted" nor intended to have the force of law. That's not the approach courts take, however, as we will see below.

A. Long and Short Titles

1. The Differences between Long and Short Titles

Long Title. Immediately following the words "A BILL" is the long title. It typically begins with the words "to" or "relating to" and then expresses the general purpose of the bill. Obviously, the title identifies the subject of the act. But titles can do more than that. Look again at the long title for the College Fire Prevention Act. Notice how it identifies where the bill's substantive provisions will be codified. Thus, in addition to giving a general description of the act, long titles can also identify statutes that will be affected by the bill's enactment, including whether it will be a new statute, or if not, which existing statutes it will amend or repeal. Some long titles can be quite long. *See, e.g., Franklin v. State*, 887 So. 2d 1063, 1084 (Fla. 2004) (quoting a two-page-long title from a bill).

Short Title. Sometimes, and particularly if the title is unusually long, a short title is included following the enacting clause. A short title typically states: "This act may be cited as the _____ Act of _____." The College Fire Prevention Act has a short title.* Notice that the short title, but not the long title, comes after the enacting clause.

Note also that bills typically have section titles. We discuss these later.

2. The Role of Long and Short Titles

While one could argue that a judge should never consider the long title when interpreting a statute because it precedes the enacting clause and was not enacted into law, most judges reject this formalistic approach. Conversely, one could argue that the short title should always be considered because it comes after the enacting clause. In point of fact, however, judges treat long and short titles similarly. Most judges refuse to rely on either the short or long title unless necessary to resolve ambiguous statutory language:

> [T]itles can do no more than indicate the provisions in a most general manner.... For interpretative purposes, they are of use only when they shed light on some ambiguous word or phrase. They are but tools available for the resolution of a doubt. But they cannot undo or limit that which the text makes plain.

Bhd. of R.R. Trainmen v. Baltimore & Ohio R.R., Co., 331 U.S. 519, 528–29 (1947). Thus, the "title cannot control the plain words of the statute," 2A STATUTES AND STATUTORY CONSTRUCTION, § 47:03, 215 (6th ed. 2000, Norman Singer ed.), but they may be considered "if the phraseology of the act is ambiguous or is susceptible of more than one in-

---

* Authors' footnote: While long and short titles such as the ones above are generally descriptive, the drafter may use the long title or short title (or both) for persuasive effect, for example, "The U.S. Patriot Act" or "No Child Left Behind Act."

terpretation...." *Parker v. State*, 406 So. 2d 1089, 1092 (Fla. 1982); *see, e.g., Skeen v. Monsanto Co.*, 569 F. Supp. 232, 233 (S.D. Tex. 1983) (holding that the fact that the short title mentioned only architects and engineers did not require narrow construction of a statute that clearly covered other professions). For example, if the long title of a bill stated that the bill was intended to overrule a prior judicial decision, but the substantive language of the bill did not actually do so, the case would remain good law.

Although these principles appear straightforward, in application they are not. The following cases explore the relevance of short and long titles to statutory interpretation. Pay attention to whether the court is analyzing the long or short title in each of them. The first case is a significant statutory interpretation case.

Church of the Holy Trinity v. United States
143 U.S. 457 (1892)

JUSTICE BREWER delivered the opinion of the Court.

Plaintiff ... is a [church]. E. Walpole Warren was, prior to September, 1887, an alien residing in England. In that month the plaintiff ... made a contract with him, by which he was to remove to the city of New York and enter into its service as rector.... It is claimed by the United States that this contract ... was forbidden ... and an action was commenced to recover the penalty prescribed by that act. The Circuit Court held that the contract was within the prohibition of the statute, and rendered judgment accordingly and the single question presented for our determination is whether it erred in that conclusion.

The first section describes the act forbidden, and is in these words:

> Be it enacted by the senate and house of representatives of the United States of America, in congress assembled, that ... it shall be unlawful for any person, company, partnership, or corporation, in any manner whatsoever, to prepay the transportation, or in any way assist or encourage the importation or migration, of any alien or aliens, any foreigner or foreigners, into the United States ... to perform labor or service of any kind....

It must be conceded that the act of the corporation is within the letter of this section, for the relation of rector to his church is one of service, and implies labor on the one side with compensation on the other.... While there is great force to this reasoning, we cannot think Congress intended to denounce with penalties a transaction like that in the present case. It is a familiar rule that a thing may be within the letter of the statute and yet not within the statute, because not within its spirit nor within the intention of its makers....

Among other things which may be considered in determining the intent of the legislature is the title of the act. We do not mean that it may be used to add to or take from the body of the statute, but it may help to interpret its meaning. In the case of *U. S. v. Fisher*, Chief Justice Marshall said: "... Neither party contends that the title of an act can control plain words in the body of the statute; and neither denies that, taken with other parts, it may assist in removing ambiguities. Where the intent is plain, nothing is left to construction. Where the mind labors to discover the design of the legislature, it seizes everything from which aid can be derived; and in such case the title claims a degree of notice, and will have its due share of consideration." And in the case of *U.S. v. Palmer* the same judge applied the doctrine in this way: "... The words 'any person or persons' are broad enough to comprehend every human being. But general words must not only be limited to cases within the jurisdiction of the state, but also to those objects to which the legislature intended to apply them. Did the legislature intend to apply these words to the subjects of a foreign power, who in a foreign ship may commit murder or robbery on the high seas? The title of an act cannot control its words, but may furnish some aid in showing what was in the mind of the legislature. The title of this act is, 'An act for the punishment of certain crimes against the United States.' It would seem that offenses against the United States, not offenses against the human race, were the crimes which the legislature intended by this law to punish."

It will be seen that words as general as those used in the first section of this act were by that decision limited, and the intent of Congress with respect to the act was gathered partially, at least, from its title. Now, the title of this act is, "An act to prohibit the importation and migration of foreigners and aliens under contract or agreement to perform labor in the United States, its Territories, and the District of Columbia." Obviously the thought expressed in this reaches only to the work of the manual laborer, as distinguished from that of the professional man. No one reading such a title would suppose that Congress had in its mind any purpose of staying the coming into this country of ministers of the gospel, or, indeed, of any class whose toil is that of the brain. The common understanding of the terms labor and laborers does not include preaching and preachers; and it is to be assumed that words and phrases are used in their ordinary meaning. So whatever of light is thrown upon the statute by the language of the title indicates an exclusion from its penal provisions of all contracts for the employment of ministers, rectors, and pastors....

We find, therefore, that the title of the act ... [shows] the intent of Congress was simply to stay the influx of this cheap unskilled labor....

The judgment will be reversed, and the case remanded....

Notes and Questions

(1) *Did Title Trump Plain Meaning?* Did the Court look at the long, short, or section title of the bill? According to the cases cited by the Court, the title of an act cannot control the plain language of the statute. The Court earlier admitted that "the [church's] act ... is within the letter of this" law. Did the Court correctly apply its own canon, or did it latch onto the title as a way to avoid the statute's plain meaning?

(2) *Plain Meaning of "Laborers."* Justice Brewer concluded that the title — ostensibly the words "to perform labor" — demonstrated that the statute covered only manual laborers as distinguished from professional laborers. Can you argue he was incorrect?

(3) *Subsequent Legislative Action.* Unmentioned by the Court is the fact that after the district court had construed the statute to apply to Pastor Warren, Congress amended the statute to exempt ministers and other professionals. Act of March 3, 1891, § 12.26 Stat. 1084, 1086. While the amendment would not have applied to this case, does it support the Court's decision? Consider the fact that in *United States v. Laws*, 163 U.S. 258, 265 (1896), the Court exempted a chemist from the same statute at issue in *Holy Trinity* and referred to the 1891 amendment as support for its decision, even though the amendment did not apply to the chemist's case, either.

(4) *The Golden Rule Exception to Plain Meaning.* The most cited sentence from *Holy Trinity* is: "It is a familiar rule that a thing may be within the letter of the statute and yet not within the statute, because not within its spirit nor within the intention of its makers...." Do you understand what the court is saying? Turn to the discussion of purpose in Chapter 10 and see if you notice any similarity.

Compare the approach of the following case to the *Holy Trinity* case. Are the cases consistent?

Caminetti v. United States
242 U.S. 470 (1917)

JUSTICE DAY delivered the opinion of the Court:

These three cases were argued together, and may be disposed of in a single opinion. In each of the cases there was a conviction and sentence for violation of the so-called White Slave Traffic Act.... The judgments were affirmed ... and writs of certiorari bring the cases here.

[T]he petitioner[s were convicted] ... for ... causing to be transported ... certain wom[en] [across state lines] for the purpose of debauchery, and for an immoral purpose, to wit, that the aforesaid wom[e]n should be and become [their] mistress[es] and concubine[s].... [T]he United States Circuit Court of Appeals ... affirmed....

It is contended that the act of Congress is intended to reach only "commercialized vice," or the traffic in women for gain, and that the conduct for which the several petitioners were indicted and convicted, however reprehensible in morals, is not within the purview of the statute when properly construed in the light of its history and the purposes intended to be accomplished by its enactment. In none of the cases was it charged ... that the transportation was for gain or for ... furnishing women for prostitution for hire, and it is insisted that, such being the case, the acts charged and proved, upon which conviction was had, do not come within the statute.

It is elementary that the meaning of a statute must, in the first instance, be sought in the language in which the act is framed, and if that is plain, and if the law is within the constitutional authority of the law-making body which passed it, the sole function of the courts is to enforce it according to its terms.

Where the language is plain and admits of no more than one meaning the duty of interpretation does not arise and the rules which are to aid doubtful meanings need no discussion. There is no ambiguity in the terms of this act. It is specifically made an offense to knowingly transport or cause to be transported, etc., in interstate commerce, any woman or girl for the purpose of prostitution or debauchery, or for "any other immoral purpose"....

Statutory words are uniformly presumed, unless the contrary appears, to be used in their ordinary and usual sense, and with the meaning commonly attributed to them. To cause a woman or girl to be transported for the purposes of debauchery, and for an immoral purpose, to wit, becoming a concubine or mistress, ... and other immoral practices, for which [the petitioners were] convicted, would seem by the very statement of the facts to embrace transportation for purposes denounced by the act, and therefore fairly within its meaning.

While such immoral purpose would be more culpable in morals and attributed to baser motives if accompanied with the expectation of pecuniary gain, such considerations do not prevent the lesser offense against morals of furnishing transportation in order that a woman may be debauched, or become a mistress or a concubine, from being the execution of purposes within the meaning of this law. To say the contrary would shock the common understanding of what constitutes an immoral purpose when those terms are applied, as here, to sexual relations....

But it is contended that though the words are so plain that they cannot be misapprehended when given their usual and ordinary interpretation, and although the sections in which they appear do not in terms limit the offense defined and punished to acts of "commercialized vice," or the furnishing or procuring of transportation of women for debauchery, prostitution, or immoral practices for hire, such limited purpose is to be attributed to Congress and engrafted upon the act in view of the language of §8 [the short title] and the report which accompanied the law upon its introduction into and subsequent passage by the House of Representatives.

In this connection, it may be observed that while the title of an act cannot overcome the meaning of plain and unambiguous words used in its body, the title of this act embraces the regulation of interstate commerce "by prohibiting the transportation therein for immoral purposes of women and girls, and for other purposes." It is true that §8 of the act provides that it shall be known and referred to as the "White slave traffic Act...." Still, the name given to an act by way of designation or description, ... cannot change the plain import of its words. If the words are plain, they give meaning to the act, and it is neither the duty nor the privilege of the courts to enter speculative fields in search of a different meaning....

The judgment in each of the cases is affirmed.

JUSTICE MCKENNA, dissenting:

Undoubtedly in the investigation of the meaning of a statute we resort first to its words, and when clear they are decisive. The principle has attractive and seemingly disposing simplicity, but that it is not easy of application or, at least, encounters other principles, many cases demonstrate....

The transportation which is made unlawful is of a woman or girl "to become a prostitute or to give herself up to debauchery, or to engage in any other immoral practice." Our present concern is with the words "any other immoral practice," which, it is asserted, have a special office. The words are clear enough as general descriptions; they fail in particular designation; they are class words, not specifications. Are they controlled by those which precede them? If not, they are broader in generalization and include those that precede them, making them unnecessary and confusing. To what conclusion would this lead us? 'Immoral' is a very comprehensive word. It means a dereliction of morals. In such sense it covers every form of vice, every form of conduct that is contrary to good order. It will hardly be contended that in this sweeping sense it is used in the statute. But if not used in such sense, to what is it limited and by what limited? If it be admitted that it is limited at all, that ends the imperative effect assigned to it in the opinion of the court. But not insisting quite on that, we ask again, By what is it limited? By its context, necessarily, and the purpose of the statute.

For the context I must refer to the statute; of the purpose of the statute Congress itself has given us illumination. It devotes a section to the declaration that the "Act shall be known and referred to as the 'White-Slave Traffic Act.'" ... It is a peremptory rule of construction that all parts of a statute must be taken into account in ascertaining its meaning, and it cannot be said that §8 has no object. Even if it gives only a title to the act it has especial weight. But it gives more than a title; it makes distinctive the purpose of the statute. The designation "White-slave traffic" has the sufficiency of an axiom. If apprehended, there is no uncertainty as to the conduct it describes. It is commercialized vice, immoralities having a mercenary purpose, and this is confirmed by other circumstances....

This being the purpose, the words of the statute should be construed to execute it, and they may be so construed even if their literal meaning be otherwise....

In *Holy Trinity Church v. United States*, Mr. Justice Brewer, declared that "it is a familiar rule that a thing may be within the letter of the statute and yet not within the statute, because not within its spirit, nor within the intention of its makers." ...

There is much in the present case to tempt to a violation of the rule. Any measure that protects the purity of women from assault or enticement to degradation finds an instant advocate in our best emotions; but the judicial function cannot yield to emotion — it must, with poise of mind, consider and decide. It should not shut its eyes to the facts of the world and assume not to know what everybody else knows. And everybody knows that there is a difference between the occasional immoralities of men and women and that systematized and mercenary immorality epitomized in the statute's graphic phrase "White-slave traffic." And it was such immorality that was in the legislative mind, and not the other. The other is occasional, not habitual — inconspicuous — does not offensively obtrude upon public notice. Interstate commerce is not its instrument as it is of the other, nor is prostitution its object or its end. It may, indeed, in instances, find a convenience in crossing state lines, but this is its accident, not its aid....

For these reasons I dissent....

Notes and Questions

(1) *Are Caminetti and Holy Trinity Consistent?* The majority in *Caminetti* refused to consider the title because it found the statute to be "unambiguous and neither absurd [n]or wholly impracticable." Is this approach consistent with this statement from *Holy Trinity*: "We do not mean that [the title] may be used to add or take from the body of the statute, but it may help to interpret its meaning"?

(2) *Did Title Placement Matter?* The *Holy Trinity* Court arguably used the long title to override unambiguous statutory text. The majority in *Caminetti* refused to use the short title to circumvent the unambiguous language of that statute. The majority in *Caminetti* did refer to the long title and found it consistent with the text. The *Caminetti* dissent ignored the long title and looked just to the short title to interpret ambiguous text. According to the dissent, the short title provided the statute's purpose. Are these focuses inconsistent? Assuming they are inconsistent, why do you think these various judges don't use a unified focus?

(3) *Statutory Approach.* Which approach to statutory interpretation do you believe the majority adopted? The dissent?

(4) *Subsequent Legislative Action.* In 1986, Congress amended the statute at issue in *Caminetti* to prohibit individuals from "knowingly transport[ing] an individual in interstate or foreign commerce ... with intent that such individual engage in prostitution, or in any sexual activity *for which any person can be charged with a criminal offense....*" 18 U.S.C. §2412 (emphasis added). Does this amendment suggest that *Caminetti* was wrongly decided? Or, does the fact that Congress took almost seventy years to change the statute suggest that the majority was correct?

(5) *A Failed Effort to Use the Short Title to Limit the Statute.* In *Skeen v. Monsanto Co.,* 569 F. Supp. 232 (S.D. Tex. 1983), a statute of repose provided that any claim against an engineer for "performing or furnishing the design, planning, or inspection of construction" of certain improvements to real estate had to be brought within ten years of the completion of the improvement. The defendant had *designed* an improvement but had not been involved in the actual construction. The plaintiff's claim arose more than ten years after construction had been completed, so the defendant moved for summary judgment based on this statute of repose. The plaintiff opposed, pointing out that the short title was "Architects, engineers and persons *performing or furnishing* construction or repairs of improvements to real property." Can you articulate the plaintiff's argument and also explain why the defendant won?

(6) *Popular Names.* Some statutes either are born with or come to be given popular names. The "Controlling Assault of Non-Solicited Pornography and Marketing Act" was, no doubt, given that name because the first letter of each word (its acronym) spelled "CAN-SPAM." The "Patriot Act" and other statutes also were intentionally given titles based on acronyms. Other statutes, such as the Sherman Act (the major antitrust statute) only acquired their names after enactment. For an interesting discussion of popular names, see Mary Whisner, *What's in a Statute Name?*, 97 Law Libr. J. 169 (2005) (recounting the morphing of the "Act of July 2, 1890" into the "Sherman Act" and the advent of Congress including popular names in legislation). What role, if any, should a popular name play in interpretation?

B. Preambles, Purpose Clauses, and Legislative Findings

1. The Role of Preambles

The Supreme Court recently summarized the historical use of preambles:

> [T]he key 18th-century English case on the effect of preambles, *Copeman v. Gallant*, 1 P. Wms. 314, 24 Eng. Rep. 404 (1716), stated that "the preamble could not be used to restrict the effect of the words of the purview." J. Sutherland, Statutes and Statutory Construction, 47.04 (N. Singer ed. 5th ed.1992). This rule was modified in England in an 1826 case to give more importance to the preamble, but in America "the settled principle of law is that the preamble cannot control the enacting part of the statute in cases where the enacting part is expressed in clear, unambiguous terms."

Dist. of Columbia v. Heller, 128 S.Ct. 2783, 2789 n.3 (2008) (reasoning that the preamble to the Second Amendment identifies the purpose of that amendment and thus helps resolve any ambiguity in the operative provision). Even though preambles are not controlling, legislatures continue to use them to determine the reasons for adopting a statute. Simply put, "preambles" identify the policy that led the legislature to enact the law.

There are different types of preambles. True preambles typically identify the purpose for the bill and precede the enacting clause. Bills may also include "findings clauses," which state facts or motivations for the statute. In addition, bills may include "purpose clauses" identifying the mischief, or problem, the legislature sought to correct by enacting the statute. Typically, purpose clauses are contained in the body of the statute, whereas preambles precede the enacting clause. Some bills include all three clauses. Truthfully, there is little substantive difference between these three categories, and courts often treat them as interchangeable. *But see PRB Enterps., Inc. v. S. Brunswick Planning Bd.*, 518 A.2d 1099, 1101 (N.J. 1987) (holding that a purpose clause, which followed the enacting clause, was not simply a statement of purpose, like the preamble, but was intended to be substantive). In this text, we address these technically distinct provisions—preambles, purpose clauses, and findings—collectively as "preambles."

In sum, preambles are relevant to interpretation because they often state considerations that led the legislature to enact the statute. If you want to know why a statute exists, the bill's preamble may be the place to look.

The College Fire Prevention Act included this preamble:

SEC. 772. FINDINGS.

Congress makes the following findings:

(1) On Wednesday, January 19, 2000, a fire occurred at a Seton Hall University dormitory. Three male freshmen, all 18 years of age, died. Fifty-four students, 2 South Orange firefighters, and 2 South Orange police officers were injured. The dormitory was a 6-story, 350-room structure built in 1952, that housed approximately 600 students. It was equipped with smoke alarms but no fire sprinkler system.

(2) On Mother's Day 1996 in Chapel Hill, North Carolina, a fire in the Phi Gamma Delta Fraternity House killed 5 college juniors and injured 3. The 3-story plus basement fraternity house was 70 years old. The National Fire Protection Association identified several factors that contributed to the tragic fire, including the lack of fire sprinkler protection....

(5) New dormitories are generally required to have advanced safety systems such as fire sprinklers. But such requirements are rarely imposed retroactively on existing buildings.

(6) In 1998, 93 percent of the campus building fires reported to fire departments occurred in buildings where there were smoke alarms present. However, only 34 percent had fire sprinklers present.

Courts generally treat preambles in the same manner as they treat long and short titles. Preambles may not be used to "enlarge or confer powers, nor control the words of the act...." *Yazoo & M. V. R. Co. v. Thomas*, 132 U.S. 174, 188 (1889). For example, in *Kavolchyck v. Goldman*, 154 B.R. 793 (Bankr. S.D. Fla. 1993), the Florida legislature passed a bill containing a preamble that stated that the legislature disagreed with a prior judicial interpretation of a Florida statute. Nonetheless, the court examined the substantive text of the statute and found that the legislature had not changed the wording of the statute that had been previously interpreted. The court held that "the Florida Legislature could not overrule established case law concerning a statute merely by passing a preamble without any corresponding change in the wording of the statute." *Id.* at 800. Thus, "legislative policy is law only to extent that enactments incorporate such policy." *Hanson v. Gass*, 267 N.W. 403, 407 (Neb. 1936) (internal quotations omitted).

Preambles do not control and do not expand or narrow the plain meaning of a statute, in part, because the "function of the preamble is to supply reasons and explanations and not to confer power or determine rights." 1A STATUTES AND STATUTORY CONSTRUCTION § 20:3, 123 (6th ed. 2002 Norman Singer ed.). However, as with long and short titles, the preamble can be considered if the statutory language itself is "doubtful or ambiguous." *Id.* Thus, if "'the operative sections [of a statute] are clear and unambiguous,' the preamble of the statute is 'neither essential nor controlling in the construction of the Act.'" *Jurgensen v. Fairfax County*, 745 F.2d 868, 885 (4th Cir. 1983). *See also Price Dev. Co. v. Orem City*, 995 P.2d 1237, 1246 (Utah 2000) (preambles "may be used to clarify ambiguities, but they do not create rights that are not found within the statute, nor do they limit those actually given by the legislation.").

As a final point, some courts may give weight to a preamble only if the preamble follows the enacting clause. However, the modern trend is to give little weight to preambles, regardless of whether they come before or after the enacting clause. 2A STATUTES AND STATUTORY CONSTRUCTION § 47.05, 226 (6th ed. 2000 Norman Singer ed.).

✱ give little weight to preambles ✱

2. Judicial Treatment of Preambles

As with long and short titles, judicial application of the ostensibly straightforward principles concerning preambles is sometimes interesting. The cases below explore the relevance of preambles.

Commonwealth v. Besch

674 A.2d 655 (Pa. 1996)

CAPPY, JUSTICE.

This case presents the Court with the question of whether the prosecution of a wholly illegitimate drug conspiracy which exhibits no legitimate purpose nor encompasses any elements of a legitimate business activity is within the scope of the Pennsylvania Corrupt Organizations Statute (hereinafter referred to as "Pa.C.O.A.")....

Appellant was charged with ... violating Pa.C.O.A. and one count of conspiring to violate Pa.C.O.A. [and other criminal counts]. After a jury trial Appellant was convicted on all counts.... This Court granted ... [the] appeal.

During the course of the trial, the Commonwealth presented a significant number of witnesses, many of whom were members of the drug trafficking network which operated from Appellant's home. This testimony revealed a clearly defined operation wherein Appellant, and his primary conspirator, Douglas Woodward, had by specific agreement developed a business of distributing marijuana and cocaine....

Business went on smoothly for Appellant and Woodward until the arrest of a regular customer, Charlie Miller in 1989....

Miller ... later ... entered into an agreement with the prosecutor for a reduced penalty ... in exchange for his testimony against Appellant....

Based on all the testimony ... the Commonwealth argues that a drug enterprise existed which included Appellant, ... Woodward, [and others]. The enterprise functioned with Appellant's home as the central location for buying, packaging for resale and then selling of cocaine and marijuana.... The entire enterprise existed for the purpose of buying and selling illegal drugs....

Specifically at issue in this case are [appellant's convictions for] the two Pa.C.O.A. violations of 18 Pa.C.S. §911(b)(3) and (b)(4):

> (3) It shall be unlawful for any person employed by or associated with any enterprise to conduct or participate, directly or indirectly, in the conduct of such enterprise's affairs through a pattern of racketeering activity.
>
> (4) It shall be unlawful for any person to conspire to violate any of the provisions of paragraph (1), (2) or (3) of this subsection.

Taking all of the evidence in the light most favorable to the Commonwealth, it is clear that an "enterprise" existed and flourished in Appellant's home centering around the business of buying and selling controlled substances for profit. It is clear that Appellant was a member of the "enterprise" and agreed to participate in all of the activities of that enterprise along with his fellow associates. It was also clearly established that the Appellant along with various members of the "enterprise" engaged in a "pattern of racketeering" activities, as that term is defined within Pa.C.O.A. at §911(h)(4), such as individual acts of possession and/or sales of controlled substances, burglary and receiving stolen property. Thus, the only question to be addressed is whether this "enterprise" comes within the scope of the Pa.C.O.A.

In arguing that this particular "enterprise" violates Pa.C.O.A., the Commonwealth focuses upon the definition within the statute of the word "enterprise."

> "Enterprise" means any individual, partnership, corporation, association or other legal entity, and any union or group of individuals associated in fact although not a legal entity, engaged in commerce.

18 Pa.C.S. §911(h)(3).

The Commonwealth asserts that since the definition given does not restrict itself to "legitimate enterprises" then the statute can clearly extend to a prosecution for wholly illegitimate "enterprises." In other words, what is not prohibited must be permitted. However, by focusing on the definition of the word "enterprise" without reference to the entire piece of legislation, the Commonwealth distorts the intent of the General Assembly ... and violates the primary principles of statutory construction. The very first, and the primary rule of statutory construction states:

> [1 Pa.C.S.] § 1921. Legislative intent controls
>
> (a) The object of all interpretation and construction of statutes is to ascertain and effectuate the intention of the General Assembly. Every statute shall be construed, if possible, to give effect to all its provisions....
>
> (c) When the words of the statute are not explicit, the intention of the General Assembly may be ascertained by considering, among other matters:
>
> > (1) The occasion and necessity for the statute.
> >
> > (2) The circumstances under which it was enacted.
> >
> > (3) The mischief to be remedied.
> >
> > (4) The object to be attained.
> >
> > (5) The former law, if any, including other statutes upon the same or similar subjects....

The intention of the General Assembly is clearly and specifically spelled out at great length in the Pa.C.O.A. statute.

> §911. Corrupt organizations
>
> (a) Findings of fact.—The General Assembly finds that:
>
> > (1) organized crime is a highly sophisticated, diversified, and widespread phenomenon which annually drains billions of dollars from the national economy by various patterns of unlawful conduct including the illegal use of force, fraud, and corruption;
> >
> > (2) organized crime exists on a large scale within the Commonwealth of Pennsylvania, engaging in the same patterns of unlawful conduct which characterizes its activities nationally.
> >
> > (3) the vast amounts of money and power accumulated by organized crime are increasingly used to infiltrate and corrupt legitimate businesses operating within the Commonwealth, together with all of the techniques of violence, intimidation, and other forms of unlawful conduct through which such money and power are derived;....

There is no escaping the clear intent of this statute. The General Assembly went to great pains to set forth the parameters of this piece of legislation. Pa.C.O.A. is directed at preventing the infiltration of legitimate business by organized crime in order to promote and protect legitimate economic development within Pennsylvania. Although the Commonwealth acknowledges this to be the precise intent of the General Assembly in enacting Pa.C.O.A., they choose to ignore same. However, once the intent of the General Assembly has been ascertained that intent cannot be ignored, rather, it must be given effect. 1 Pa.C.S. § 1921(a).

Without reference to the intent of this legislation the specific subsections that Appellant has been convicted under are difficult to comprehend. Following the Commonwealth's argument, what Pa.C.O.A. thus prohibits is any group of criminals from forming an association and engaging in any of the enumerated criminal acts at § 911(h)(1)(i) of the statute, without any connection between the association of criminals, the type of crimes they engage in, and any legitimate Commonwealth business. We find it incomprehensible that the General Assembly would go to such great lengths to explicate that Pa.C.O.A. is designed to deter criminal enterprises from infiltrating legitimate business, yet not require that there be a link between the criminal enterprise, the crimes committed, and an infiltration of, or attempt to infiltrate, a legitimate business enterprise within the Commonwealth of Pennsylvania. Pa.C.O.A. only makes sense when the words of the statute are given their fair meaning in the context of the general purpose and intent of the statute....

In construing the intent of this statute we need not look beyond its actual words. The express intent was to prevent infiltration of legitimate businesses by organized crime.... The statute at issue was enacted to punish persons engaged in organized crime, not "organized" criminals....

Allowing Pa.C.O.A. to be used as a tool in furthering this policy position rather than restricting the reach of the statute to its intended targets violates the intended goal of the General Assembly in drafting Pa.C.O.A. A review of the facts in the instant case illustrates how far from the intended purpose of Pa.C.O.A. the Commonwealth has drifted.

In the case at bar the police began investigating Appellant and his "enterprise" in 1987. The investigation continued until Appellant's arrest in 1989. Nothing came to light during the entire investigation which would indicate an intention on the part of any individual within this particular "enterprise" to use their revenue from the drug sales to infiltrate any business within Pennsylvania. In fact all of Appellant's co-conspirators within the "enterprise" testified that they were drug users and each made their transactions within the ongoing distribution ring in order to get sufficient drugs to satisfy their own personal use. Thus, taking all of the evidence in the light most favorable to the Commonwealth, it has proven beyond a reasonable doubt that an organization existed for the purpose of buying and selling illegal drugs and that the Appellant was a member of the organization and that he engaged in a pattern of activity which included acts that are enumerated offenses under Pa.C.O.A. However, there is not one piece of evidence that connects this drug enterprise even remotely to a legitimate business, or any attempt to infiltrate a legitimate business....

Accordingly, Appellant's convictions under Pa.C.O.A. at 18 Pa.C.S. § 911(b)(3) and (b)(4) are reversed....

Nix, Chief Justice, dissenting.

I believe that the Pennsylvania Corrupt Organizations Act (hereinafter "the Act"), encompasses illegitimate as well as legitimate business enterprises. Accordingly, I respectfully dissent.

both Illegitimate & legitimate businesses

The Act defines a business enterprise as "any ... group of individuals associated in fact although not a legal entity...." 18 Pa.C.S. §911(h)(3). The plain language of this statute would include both legitimate and illegitimate business enterprises....

The majority's sole rationale for disregarding the plain language of the Act as well as the overwhelming weight of federal case law interpreting an identical provision in the federal statute is a single sentence in the preamble to the Act. Finding number (3) in the preamble to the Act states that "vast amounts of money and power accumulated by organized crime are increasingly used to infiltrate and corrupt legitimate businesses operating within the Commonwealth...." 18 Pa.C.S. §911(a)(3). The majority holds that this language evidences the intent of the General Assembly to limit the reach of the Act to legitimate business enterprises. I disagree....

I believe that the conduct of our General Assembly is more revealing of their intent than a preamble.... In fact, the course suggested by the majority is so contrary to the generally accepted interpretation of [the federal] Racketeer Influenced and Corrupt Organizations statute[], that I believe the General Assembly would have clearly and strenuously indicated its departure from the norm. Its failure to do so strongly suggests agreement with the generally accepted interpretation....

Notes and Questions

(1) *Was the Statute Ambiguous?* Did the court first have to find ambiguity before looking to the preamble? Did the fact that the findings were or were not codified affect the weight they were given? Should it?

(2) *Statutory Directives.* What section of 1 Pa. C.S. §1921 allowed the majority to look to the findings for meaning? Is the dissent fair to characterize the "majority's sole rationale for disregarding the plain language of the Act" as being "a single sentence in the preamble to the Act"? Do other facts support the majority's interpretation? Do you agree with the dissent's statement that "the conduct of [the] General Assembly is more revealing of their intent than a preamble ..."?

(3) *Does the Short Title Help?* The short title was "Pennsylvania Corrupt Organizations Act." Does the short title unequivocally aid either side?

(4) *Plain Meaning or Absurd Result?* Would you have felt confident arguing that because your client had absolutely no legitimate purpose in buying and selling drugs his conviction should be reversed? The rule of lenity, which we will study later, gives this counter-intuitive argument weight.

(5) *Statutes Patterned after Another Jurisdiction.* The dissent found it relevant that federal courts had interpreted the federal counterpart to the Pennsylvania statute to apply to illegitimate businesses, and the Pennsylvania legislature had patterned its statute after the federal RICO statute. The federal RICO statute had a preamble and definition which were substantially similar. Should the fact that so many other courts had interpreted "enterprise" more broadly under the federal statute have influenced the majority? In fact, courts treat statutes patterned after other jurisdictions with distinct rules, which we'll study in more detail in a later chapter. Take a look at 1 Pa. C.S. §1921(c)(5), quoted in the majority's opinion. Why doesn't the majority mention this other interpretative aid? If the plain language of the statute and federal interpretations of an identical statute each supports a broad interpretation of the word "enterprise," why wasn't the majority convinced?

(6) *The Legislative Response.* Two months after *Besch* was decided ... the legislature amended the Act to change the definition of "'enterprise' to include legitimate as well

as illegitimate enterprises." *Commonwealth v. Baldwin*, 789 A.2d 728, 730 n.3 (Pa. 2001). Does this mean that the majority erred in determining the legislature's intent? If you think so — if the statute was intended to reach even wholly illegitimate businesses — then why did the legislature use the language "legitimate businesses" in the findings?

Problem 7-1

You represent Lindsey Sabel, age 13, who sold marijuana while in middle school. Her case was referred to an intake worker, who subsequently referred the case to the district attorney with a recommendation that the district attorney file a delinquency petition and enter into a consent decree. The district attorney filed a delinquency petition but did not pursue a consent decree.

Dissatisfied with the district attorney's failure to request a consent decree, you filed a motion to dismiss the petition. You requested that the court refer the case back to the intake worker for deferred prosecution. Over the state's objection, the juvenile court judge granted the motion, dismissed the petition, and referred the matter for deferred prosecution. A deferred prosecution agreement was then signed and sent to the district attorney.

After receiving the deferred prosecution agreement, the district attorney filed a second delinquency petition containing the same charge and factual allegations as set forth in the first petition. You again filed a motion to dismiss, arguing that no new information existed to justify the re-filing of an already dismissed petition.

A "delinquency petition" is the juvenile version of an adult conviction. If convicted, the juvenile will be sent to the juvenile version of jail, generally detention. In contrast, a "consent decree" ends the proceedings and places the juvenile under supervision in the juvenile's own home. For this problem, assume that a "deferred prosecution" does the same thing as a "consent decree."

Based on the materials below, analyze whether the district attorney has the authority under Mercer Rev. Stat. §938.21 to terminate the resulting deferred prosecution agreement by filing a second delinquency petition that contains the same charge and factual allegations as the first petition. Simply put, the issue is whether a deferred prosecution can be given to the juvenile (Lindsey Sabel) without the district attorney's consent.

Problem Materials

The long title of a statute codified as §938.21 is "An Act Relating to the Deferred Prosecution of Juveniles and the District Attorney's Consent to any Such Agreement." There is no short title. The preamble includes this statement: "The legislature finds that the juvenile system works most successfully when all parties agree to a case's resolution. Thus, this act authorizes and promotes the prompt resolution of juvenile cases with the advice and consent of the district attorney, intake worker, and juvenile." Mercer Rev. Stat. §938.21 provides:

(1) *Deferred prosecution agreement.* After investigating the facts leading to the juvenile's arrest, the intake worker may request that a petition be filed, may enter into a deferred prosecution agreement with the juvenile, may recommend a petition be filed and a consent decree sought, or close the case. If the intake worker enters into a deferred prosecution agreement, notification shall be sent to the district attorney.

(2) *Deferred prosecution order.* If the judge determines that the best interests of the juvenile and the public are served, he or she may order the petition dismissed and refer the matter to the intake worker for deferred prosecution.

(3) *Prosecutorial consent to deferred prosecution.* A deferred prosecution agreement arising out of an alleged delinquent act is terminated if the district attorney files a new delinquency petition within 20 days after receipt of notice of the deferred prosecution agreement from the intake worker.

In resolving this problem, consider these questions: Regarding § 938.21 (2), is it clear that the case goes away once the judge dismisses the delinquency petition? Once the judge refers the matter to the intake worker for a deferred prosecution pursuant to subsection (2), what can the prosecutor do under subsection (3)? Once the district attorney files a new delinquency petition under subsection (3) (which is what happened in the problem), is that the end of the case? What can the judge do under subsection (2)? How should the statute be interpreted? Try to figure out each side's arguments about how the three sections should fit together.

C. The Purview: The Substantive Provisions

Following the long title, enacting clause, short title, and preamble are the substantive sections of the bill. Each section, including the short title, must be separately numbered and should contain only a single proposition of enactment. *See* 1 U.S.C. § 104 (2005). Typically, well-drafted legislation follows a specific organization: definitions, general provisions, administrative provisions, and penalty or remedy sections.

Statutes are generally divided into sections, with short "headings," or "section titles," preceding each substantive provision. Look at the College Fire Prevention Act in Appendix B for examples. The headings generally break up the bill and provide short descriptions for the substantive content of each section of the bill.

Section titles and headings come after the enacting clause but generally do not affect the meaning of the substantive statutory text. "For interpretative purposes, they are of use only when they shed light on some ambiguous word or phrase. They are but tools available for the resolution of a doubt. But they cannot undo or limit that which the text makes plain." *Bhd. of R.R. Trainmen v. Baltimore & Ohio R.R., Co.*, 331 U.S. 519, 529 (1947). In some states, this point has been made clear by statute:

> Unless otherwise provided in this Code, the descriptive headings or catch-lines immediately preceding or within the text of the individual Code sections of this Code … do not constitute part of the law and shall in no manner limit or expand the construction of any Code section….

GA. CODE ANN. § 1-1-7 (2004). Further, while section headings may be helpful in construing a statute's meaning, "'it may not be used as a means of creating an ambiguity when the body of the act itself is clear.'" *Bautista v. Star Cruises*, 396 F.3d 1289, 1298 n.12 (11th Cir. 2005) (quoting 2A STATUTES AND STATUTORY CONSTRUCTION § 47:07 (6th ed. 2000 Norman Singer ed.)).

Why do you suppose that these short headings generally do not control and cannot limit, expand, or render ambiguous, substantive statutory text? *See Bhd. of R.R. Trainmen*, 331 U.S. at 528 (explaining that where "the text is complicated and prolific, headings and titles can do no more than indicate the provisions in a most general manner; to attempt to refer to each specific provision would often be ungainly as well as useless").

We now turn to the substantive sections.

1. Definitions

Words in a statute should generally be given their common, ordinary, and accepted meaning. But many words have several common, ordinary, or accepted meanings. Consult a dictionary if you think otherwise. Consequently, to help courts be clear about which common, ordinary, or accepted meaning was intended, legislatures sometimes expressly define certain words in the statute, either within a definitions section or simply in the subsection where the defined word occurs. Definition sections are not required, so not all bills have them. The College Fire Prevention Act, for example, does not have such a section. Furthermore, in some statutes words may have different meanings in one subsection than in the statute generally. If a word is defined to mean something particular "in this section," then it will be given that definition only.

If the legislature has defined particular words, then this definition trumps all other definitions. However, it is not possible or even desirable to define every word used in a statute. Hence, legislatures generally define only those terms that (1) need specific, specialized definitions; (2) have a meaning different from the ordinary dictionary definition (*e.g.*, the word "complaint" in a statute concerning civil procedure); or (3) have been created to refer to a complex concept in a simple way (*e.g.*, "cause of action").

The inclusion of a definition section in a statute can reduce uncertainty and the need for involved judicial interpretation. But what should a court do when the statute does not define the word, but other, related statutes do define that term?

People v. Leal
94 P.3d 1071 (Cal. 2004)

MORENO, J.

Defendant Juan Diego Leal was convicted ... of [violating Penal Code section 288, subdivision (b)(1), which makes it a felony to commit a lewd act upon a child under the age of 14 years "by use of force, violence, duress, menace, or fear of immediate and unlawful bodily injury...."]

Defendant was the boyfriend of [the victim's] aunt....

On numerous occasions, defendant assaulted [the victim] in her mother's bedroom....

Defendant told [the victim] not to tell anyone about these incidents, warning her that if she did she would not be able to see him anymore. [The victim] was concerned that this would mean that she also would not be able to see her aunt ... anymore. Defendant did not hurt her, but [the victim] felt disgusted.

[A friend] urged [the victim] to "tell somebody," but [she] refused because she was afraid she would be taken away from her parents, as had happened to friends of hers who had been molested, and it scared her to think about that....

The court instructed the jury ... that "[t]he term duress means a direct or implied threat of force, violence, danger, hardship or retribution sufficient to coerce a reasonable person of ordinary susceptibilities to 1) perform an act which otherwise would not have been performed or, 2) acquiesce in an act to which one otherwise would not have submitted...."

Defendant appealed his conviction and argued ... that the trial court erred by defining "duress" to include "a direct or implied threat of 'hardship.'" The Court of Appeal affirmed....

Penal Code section 288, subdivision (b)(1), makes it a felony for any person to commit a lewd act upon a child under the age of 14 years "by use of force, violence, duress, menace, or fear of immediate and unlawful bodily injury." ...

[The word "duress" is not defined in the statute at issue. The court thus examines the definition of "duress" contained in other sex crimes statutes.]

Before 1990, the crime of rape differed from [other] sexual crimes ... in that it could not be committed by means of duress....

The Legislature [amended the rape statute] in 1990 ... adding the term[] "duress" ... to expand the definition of rape to include acts accomplished "by means of force, violence, duress, menace, or fear of immediate and unlawful bodily injury on the person or another." The Legislature further amended [the rape statute] to include definitions of the term[] "duress" ... : "As used in this section, 'duress' means a direct or implied threat of force, violence, danger, hardship, or retribution sufficient to coerce a reasonable person of ordinary susceptibilities to perform an act which otherwise would not have been performed, or acquiesce in an act to which one otherwise would not have submitted...."

In 1993, the Legislature rewrote the spousal rape law to define "spousal rape" in terms similar to the definition of "rape".... Subdivision (c) of the new spousal rape statute defines the term "duress." The Assembly Bill that proposed this legislation, as introduced, adopted verbatim the definition of "duress" in the rape statute which included the term "hardship".... The bill was amended in the Senate, however, to remove the term "hardship" from both the spousal rape statute and the rape statute. As enacted, therefore, the bill amended the definition of "duress" in the rape statute to delete the term "hardship" and adopted this same definition of "duress" in the rewritten spousal rape statute....

[The defendant argued that when the legislature amended the statute to define "duress" for rape and spousal rape, it intended its new definition to apply to other sexual offenses that use the term "duress." Defendant observed: "The legislative history does not suggest any rationale for why the Legislature would want its 1993 amendment of the definition of 'duress' to apply only to rape so that it would have one meaning when the rape statutes use the phrase 'force, violence, duress, menace, or fear of immediate and unlawful bodily injury' but another, much more expansive meaning when the identical phrase is used in the statutes defining lewd acts on a child and other sexual offenses."]

Our task in interpreting a statute "is to ascertain and effectuate legislative intent." In order to do so, "[w]e turn first to the words of the statute themselves, recognizing that they generally provide the most reliable indicator of legislative intent. When the language of a statute is clear and unambiguous and thus not reasonably susceptible of more than one meaning, there is no need for construction, and courts should not indulge in it."

The statutory language of the provision defining "duress" in each of the rape statutes is clear and unambiguous. The definition of "duress" in both the rape and spousal rape statutes begins with the phrase, "As used in this section, 'duress' means...." This clear language belies any legislative intent to apply the definitions of "duress" in the rape and spousal rape statutes to any other sexual offenses....

[T]he Legislature was not required to set forth its reasons for providing a different definition of "duress" for rape and spousal rape than has been used in other sexual offenses; it is clear that it did so. "When statutory language is ... clear and unambiguous there is no need for construction, and courts should not indulge in it. The plain meaning of words in a statute may be disregarded only when that meaning is repugnant to the general purview of the act, or for some other compelling reason...." As we said in an analogous situation: "It is our task to construe, not to amend, the statute. 'In the construction of a statute ... the office of the judge is simply to ascertain and declare what is in terms or in substance contained therein, not to insert what has been omitted or omit what has been inserted.'... We may not, under the guise of construction, rewrite the law or give the words an effect different from the plain and direct import of the terms used."

The Legislature clearly confined the definition of "duress" in the rape and spousal rape statutes to apply in those sections. Had the Legislature intended for this definition to apply as well to other sexual offenses, it could easily have said so....

The Legislature might well have wished to apply a somewhat broader definition of "duress" in cases involving sexual abuse of a child under the age of 14 years. The Legislature may have wished to protect children against lewd acts committed by threats of hardship despite its determination that similar threats of hardship should not provide the basis for the crime of rape or spousal rape against an adult....

For the reasons set forth above, we ... affirm....

Dissenting Opinion by Kennard, J.

Unlike the majority, I would hold that the term "duress" in Penal Code section 288, subdivision (b)(1) does not include a threat to inflict "hardship." ...

Section 288, subdivision (b)(1), makes it a felony to commit a lewd act upon a child under the age of 14 years "by use of force, violence, duress, menace, or fear of immediate and unlawful bodily injury...." The quoted phrase also appears in the definitions of three other sexual offenses: forcible sodomy in violation of section 286, subdivision (c)(2), forcible oral copulation in violation of section 288a, subdivision (c)(2), and forcible acts of sexual penetration in violation of section 289, subdivision (a)(1). None of these statutes defines the term "duress."

Twenty years ago, the Court of Appeal in *People v. Pitmon* turned to a dictionary to define the term "duress" in section 288. Choosing from alternative definitions, *Pitmon* held that "duress" means "a direct or implied threat of force, violence, danger, hardship, or retribution sufficient to coerce a reasonable person of ordinary susceptibilities to (1) perform an act which otherwise would not have been performed or (2) to acquiesce in an act to which one otherwise would not have submitted."

When in 1990 the Legislature set out to define "duress" in the rape statute (§ 261), it codified the *Pitmon* definition. That legislation expressly limited its definition of "duress" to section 261.

Three years later, in 1993, the Legislature reversed course. It amended the meaning of "duress" in the rape statute, to delete the reference to "hardship." The statutory definition of duress now reads: "As used in this section, 'duress' means a direct or implied threat of force, violence, danger, or retribution sufficient to coerce a reasonable person of ordinary susceptibilities to perform an act which otherwise would not have been performed, or acquiesce in an act to which one otherwise would not have submitted...." The 1993 Legislature also enacted a spousal rape statute with the just-quoted definition of duress, a definition that does not include the threat of hardship.

Thus, the statutory landscape today shows two statutes [the rape and spousal rape statutes] that exclude "hardship" from the definition of duress, four statutes (§§ 286, 288, 288a, and 289) that contain no definition of duress, and no statute that includes "hardship" in a definition of duress.

In light of this background, ... [the] courts should adopt the definition of duress in [the rape and spousal rape statutes], the only statutes to define that term....

Each of these statutes applies the same consequences to convictions ... [t]herefore, the term "duress" as used in all of these statutes should be given the same meaning, regardless of whether the offense is committed against an adult or a minor....

I can discern no reason why "duress" should be defined differently for sodomy, oral copulation, or sexual penetration than for rape or spousal rape. The majority asserts that the Legislature is not required to set forth a reason for defining duress differently for rape and spousal rape than for other sexual crimes. But if neither the majority nor the Legislature can articulate a reason to distinguish rape from other sex crimes, the more likely explanation is that the Legislature never intended such a distinction....

I would therefore reverse....

Notes and Questions

(1) *Who was Right?* The majority relied on a prior judicial construction of "duress," while the dissent pointed to definitions in other statutes. Whose argument do you find more compelling? Should a court presume that the legislature was aware of common law definitions when it enacted a statute?

(2) *Encouraging the Legislature to be Explicit.* In an earlier case, an appellate court held that the fact that the legislature removed "hardship" from the definition of "duress" for rape and spousal rape reflected legislative intent to remove hardship as a permissible basis for finding duress in any sex crime. *People v. Valentine*, 93 Cal. App. 4th 1241, 1248 (2001). But *Leal* rejected this argument and invited amendment. Does *Leal* require the legislature to be explicit about what it wants?

(3) *In Pari Materia.* As we saw, identical terms in the same statute or statutes on the same subject should generally be given the same meaning. (*See* Chapter 6). Are you persuaded by the dissent's *in pari materia* argument? Would the following general presumption make sense: Whenever a legislature defines a word in a statute, that definition applies in every statute where the word is used unless the legislature specifically indicates otherwise? Would it be easy to research the definitions of terms if they were sprinkled throughout all legislation? Is a legislature likely to know all the defined terms on the books when it enacts later legislation? If the legislature followed that presumption, would the legislation process be streamlined?

(4) *Global Definitions.* The federal and state legislatures have general global definition sections. For example, a federal statute provides:

> In determining the meaning of any Act of Congress, or of any ruling, regulation, or interpretation of the various administrative bureaus and agencies of the United States, the word "marriage" means only a legal union between one man and one woman as husband and wife, and the word "spouse" refers only to a person of the opposite sex who is a husband or a wife.

1 U.S.C. § 7 (2004). Congress made clear that this definition applies to "any act of Congress." *Id.*; *see, e.g.,* 1 U.S.C. §§ 1–8 (2004); Ga. Code Ann. § 1-3-3 (2004) (defining words such as "accident," "following," and "person"). These statutes generally provide that the defined words have the meanings specified unless the context in which the word is used clearly requires that a different meaning was intended. Ga. Code Ann. § 1-3-2 (2004). Can you think of a time when the context might suggest a different meaning than the one the statute provides? What if you had to determine whether a close corporation qualified as a "person" under a state consumer protection statute? Assume that a general definition statute defines "person" as follows: "Person includes a corporation." *See, e.g.,* Ga. Code Ann. § 1-3-3(14) (2004). Would the legislative purpose behind the consumer protection act—to protect the unsophisticated consumer—suggest that this definition should not apply?

(5) *"Including, but not Limited to."* Legislatures also define words in other ways; for example, a word may be defined simply by indicating what it includes. When a definition states what it "includes," it "is more susceptible to extension of meaning by construction than where the definition declares what the term 'means.'" *In re Greg H*, 542 S.E.2d 919, 923 n.6 (W.Va. 2000) (citing 2A Statutes and Statutory Construction § 47:07, 231 (6th ed. 2000 Norman Singer ed.)). Do you see why?

2. Responsibility, Administrative, and Enforcement Provisions

The remaining substantive sections typically follow the definitions section. Below are the substantive sections of the College Fire Prevention Act, in which we identify the types of substantive sections. These sections are provisions of general applicability that identify the rights, privileges, duties, or responsibilities the bill creates. Under the College Fire Prevention Act, eligible colleges may seek federal grants to purchase fire prevention technology, so long as state or local officials provide at least one-half of the amounts sought. If the statute is drafted well, provisions with general applicability precede provisions with specific applicability; general rules precede exceptions. The College Fire Prevention Act states:

————————

[Rights Sections]
SEC. 773. AUTHORIZATION OF APPROPRIATIONS.

There are authorized to be appropriated to carry out this part $80,000,000 for each of the fiscal years 2004 through 2008.

SEC. 774. GRANTS AUTHORIZED.

(a) PROGRAM AUTHORITY—The Secretary, in consultation with the United States Fire Administration, is authorized to award grants to States, private or public colleges or universities, fraternities, and sororities to assist them in providing fire sprinkler systems, or other fire suppression or prevention technologies, for their student housing and dormitories.

(b) MATCHING FUNDS REQUIREMENT—The Secretary may not award a grant under this section unless the entity receiving the grant provides, from State, local, or private sources, matching funds in an amount equal to not less than one-half of the cost of the activities for which assistance is sought.

[Administrative Sections]
SEC. 775. PROGRAM REQUIREMENTS.

(a) APPLICATION—Each entity desiring a grant under this part shall submit to the Secretary an application at such time and in such manner as the Secretary may require.

(b) PRIORITY—In awarding grants under this part, the Secretary shall give priority to applicants that demonstrate in the application submitted under subsection (a) the inability to fund the sprinkler system, or other fire suppression or prevention technology, from sources other than funds provided under this part.

(c) LIMITATION ON ADMINISTRATIVE EXPENSES—An entity that receives a grant under this part shall not use more than 4 percent of the grant funds for administrative expenses.

SEC. 776. DATA AND REPORT.

The Comptroller General shall—

> (1) gather data on the number of college and university housing facilities and dormitories that have and do not have fire sprinkler systems and other fire suppression or prevention technologies; and

> (2) report such data to Congress.

[Enforcement Section]
SEC. 777. ADMISSIBILITY.

Notwithstanding any other provision of law, any application for assistance under this part, any negative determination on the part of the Secretary with respect to such application, or any statement of reasons for the determination, shall not be admissible as evidence in any proceeding of any court, agency, board, or other entity.

Following the rights sections are those sections identifying how the law should be implemented (*i.e.*, the administrative sections). These provisions identify, and perhaps even create, the government agency responsible for administering and enforcing the new law. They also delineate how that agency should do so. For example, the legislature may create a new agency and authorize it to impose and collect fines. In the College Fire Prevention Act, the bill directed an existing agency to issue grants and to collect and report data.

The final substantive provisions are the sanction or remedy provisions. "When Congress creates a cause of action, the provisions describing the new substantive rights and liabilities typically precede the provisions describing enforcement procedures...." *Bank One v. Midwest Bank & Trust Co.*, 516 U.S. 264, 277 (1996) (Stevens, J., concurring). These provisions can include civil and criminal penalties, civil remedies, or various combinations.

In the College Fire Prevention Act, the enforcement provisions relate to the admission of evidence in unrelated proceedings.

Problem 7-2

Your clients, Christina and Jeff Durham, are the parents of Luke, a student at Northeast Elementary School. Luke was injured in a fight with another student, which took place on the school bus. The Cook County School District videotapes the bus rides.

The District allowed the Durhams and the parents of the other child to view the videotape on the date of the incident. But when the Durhams asked the District to produce either the full or a redacted copy of surveillance videotape under Mercer's Public Disclosure Act (PDA), the District refused. The District claimed that because the tape was maintained for disciplinary purposes, the tape was exempt from the disclosure. The District also contended that because of the videotape's format, it could not be edited and that requiring it to provide the tape in a different format would be tantamount to ordering it to create a new record, which the PDA did not require.

Using the statutes below, evaluate whether the District is correct that the PDA does not require disclosure.

Problem Materials

Title 42. Public Officers and Agencies

Chapter 42.17. Disclosure — Public Records

Mercer Rev. Stat. § 42.17.010 (11). Declaration of policy

> That, mindful of the right of individuals to privacy and of the desirability of the efficient administration of government, full access to information concerning the conduct of government on every level must be assured as a fundamental and necessary precondition to the sound governance of a free society.

Mercer Rev. Stat. § 42.17.020. Definitions

> (1) "Agency" includes all state agencies and all local agencies. "State agency" includes every state office, department, division, bureau, board, commission, or other state agency. "Local agency" includes every county, city, town, municipal corporation, quasi-municipal corporation, or special purpose district, or any office, department, division, bureau, board, commission, or agency thereof, or other local public agency.
>
> (2) "Public record" includes any writing containing information relating to the conduct of government or the performance of any governmental or proprietary function prepared, owned, used, or retained by any state or local agency regardless of physical form or characteristics.
>
> (3) "Writing" means handwriting, typewriting, printing, photostating, photographing, and every other means of recording any form of communication or representation, including, but not limited to, letters, words, pictures, sounds, or symbols, or combination thereof, and all papers, maps, magnetic or paper tapes, photographic films and prints, motion picture, film and video recordings, magnetic or punched cards, discs, drums, diskettes, sound recordings, and other documents including existing data compilations from which information may be obtained or translated.

Mercer Rev. Stat. § 42.17.251. Construction

The people of this state do not yield their sovereignty to the agencies that serve them. The people, in delegating authority, do not give their public servants the right to decide what is good for the people to know and what is not good for them to know. The people insist on remaining informed so that they may maintain control over the instruments that they have created. The public records subdivision of this chapter shall be liberally construed and its exemptions narrowly construed to promote this public policy.

Mercer Rev. Stat. § 42.17.255. Invasion of Privacy

A person's "right to privacy," "right of privacy," "privacy," or "personal privacy," as these terms are used in this chapter, is invaded or violated only if disclosure of information about the person: (1) would be highly offensive to a reasonable person and (2) is not of legitimate concern to the public.

Mercer Rev. Stat. § 42.17.260. Documents to Be Made Public

(1) Each agency, in accordance with published rules, shall make available for public inspection and copying all public records, unless the record falls within the specific exemptions of Mercer § 42.17.310, which exempts or prohibits disclosure of specific information or records. To the extent required to prevent an unreasonable invasion of personal privacy interests protected by Mercer § 42.17.310 and § 42.17.255, an agency shall delete identifying details when it makes available or publishes any record; however, in each case, the justification for the deletion shall be explained fully in writing.

Mercer Rev. Stat. § 42.17.310. Certain Personal and Other Records Exempt

(1) The following are exempt from public inspection and copying:

(a) Personal information in any files maintained for students in public schools, patients or clients of public institutions or public health agencies, or welfare recipients.

(b) Personal information in files maintained for employees, appointees, or elected officials of any public agency provided that disclosure would violate their right to privacy.

Chapter 8

Legislative History

As you've seen, the text of a statute is always the starting point for statutory interpretation, but it may not be the ending point. As you know well by now, judges disagree on whether a judge should look to extratextual sources (such as legislative history) as a source of interpretation. The English Rule stated that "for the purpose of ascertaining the intention of the legislature, no extrinsic fact, prior to the passage of the bill, which is not itself a rule of law or an act of legislation, can be inquired into or in any way taken into view." William N. Eskridge, Jr., *Legislative History Values*, 66 Chi.-Kent L. Rev. 365, 365 (1990). Yet, American courts rejected this narrow view. Prior to Justice Scalia's appointment to the Supreme Court in 1986 and the advent of "New Textualism," legislative history was routinely considered as part of the statutory interpretation process. Today, a growing number of judges refuse to look to legislative history or at least hesitate to rely on it. Justice Scalia is often credited, or blamed, with this movement away from legislative history.*

But the movement is not universal. Many courts — and even some legislatures — consider legislative history to be pertinent to interpretation even when the statutory language is clear. An intentionalist will rely on legislative history even when text is clear, and a purposivist will do so to the extent it illuminates statutory purpose. Although courts generally give legislative history less weight today than in prior years, legislative history remains an important source of meaning for many judges. Thus, to be an effective lawyer, you should *always* read the legislative history because it may provide your client with powerful arguments that are unavailable solely from the text.

The legislative process takes time. (You may want to review the discussion of legislative process in Chapter 1.) During the process, legislators may make statements or author reports about bills in various forums. For example, comments may be made during committee hearings, during debate in the "committee of the whole," and during final passage. Legislators might even insert statements into the legislative record that were not contemporaneously considered or even heard by the legislature. *See, e.g., City of Harrisburg v. Franklin*, 806 F. Supp. 1181 (M.D. Pa. 1992) (finding a Representative's written remarks — which (1) were made after the bill was passed, (2) were "given to the clerk of the House for inclusions in the ["Extensions of Remarks" section of the Congressional Record, and (3) were] *never actually spoken on the floor of the legislature*" — not indicative of legislative intent). Unlike the statutory text, statements made in committee reports, made during debates, and made in other ways during the legislative process are not approved by the legislative branch, nor presented to the executive for approval. In fact, as we saw in Chapter 7 (on Components), not even all of the text of a bill goes through these processes.

---

* Authors' footnote: Not all members of the Supreme Court reject it. In *Wisconsin Public Intervenor v. Mortier*, 501 U.S. 597, 610 n.4 (1991), several of the Justices explicitly rejected Justice Scalia's disdain for legislative history.

A. Legislative History: A Continuum of Uses

We'll delve into more details below, but let's start with the big picture. There is a continuum of circumstances in which legislative history might be used. At one end of the continuum, some judges, Justice Scalia being one such judge, believe that legislative history should never be consulted, under almost any circumstances. This is the most restrictive end of the continuum. At the other end of this continuum (the most *unrestricted* end), judges believe that legislative history should always be used as a source, whether the text is ambiguous or not.

In truth, few judges are exclusively at either end of this continuum. Rather, judges are willing to use legislative history for a variety of reasons. Some judges are willing to use legislative history to determine the meaning of ambiguous text. Some judges are willing to use legislative history to confirm the meaning of clear text. And, occasionally, judges are willing to use legislative history to defeat the plain meaning of text. In your view, should any or all of these uses be permitted or required? Regardless of your answer, you should know that judges have used legislative history for each of these purposes.

Hence, legislative history may play a strong role in interpretation. Keep in mind, however, that few judges today rely exclusively on legislative history because text is primary. As we have seen, the text is the focus for all of the approaches. But many judges and commentators believe that the meaning of text cannot be understood without also analyzing the context from which the words were chosen. Text should be read in light of the legislative history because the text comes from—and so only has meaning when viewed in—that context: "statutes first gain meaning within the context that gave them life: the give and take of the legislative process," as a result, "we must read [them] within the context of the legislative process, which is reflected in the statute's legislative history." Paul E. McGreal, *Slighting Context: On the Illogic of Ordinary Speech in Statutory Interpretation*, 52 U. Kan. L. Rev. 325, 328 (2004).

The fundamental question this chapter addresses is at what point, if any, along this continuum, does the use of legislative history become unsupportable? The cases below shed light on the issues that underlie that fundamental question: What is the appropriate role of legislative history? We will return to this question at the end of the chapter.

The two cases below address this issue in the following context. When the plain meaning of the text conflicts with the legislative history, how should a judge resolve the conflict? Compare the approaches adopted in each case.

In re Sinclair
870 F.2d 1340 (7th Cir. 1989)

Easterbrook, Circuit Judge.

This case presents a conflict between a statute and its legislative history. The Sinclairs, who have a family farm, filed a bankruptcy petition in April 1985 under Chapter 11 of the Bankruptcy Act of 1978. In October 1986 Congress added Chapter 12, providing benefits for farmers, and the Sinclairs asked the bankruptcy court to convert their case from Chapter 11 to Chapter 12. The bankruptcy judge declined, and the district court affirmed. Each relied on § 302(c)(1) of the Bankruptcy Judges, United States Trustees, and Family Farmer Bankruptcy Act of 1986, Pub.L. 99-554, 100 Stat. 3088:

The amendments made by subtitle B of title II shall not apply with respect to cases commenced under title 11 of the United States Code before the effective date of this Act.

The Sinclairs rely on the report of the Conference Committee, which inserted § 302(c)(1) into the bill:

It is not intended that there be routine conversion of Chapter 11 and 13 cases, pending at the time of enactment, to Chapter 12. Instead, it is expected that courts will exercise their sound discretion in each case, in allowing conversions only where it is equitable to do so.

Chief among the factors the court should consider is whether there is a substantial likelihood of successful reorganization under Chapter 12.

Courts should also carefully scrutinize the actions already taken in pending cases in deciding whether, in their equitable discretion, to allow conversion. For example, the court may consider whether the petition was recently filed in another chapter with no further action taken. Such a case may warrant conversion to the new chapter. On the other hand, there may be cases where a reorganization plan has already been filed or confirmed. In cases where the parties have substantially relied on current law, availability (sic) to convert to the new chapter should be limited.

H.R.Conf.Rep. 99-958, 99th Cong., 2d Sess. 48–49 (1986), U.S.Code Cong. & Admin.News 1986, pp. 5227, 5249–5250. The statute says conversion is impossible; the report says that conversion is possible and describes the circumstances under which it should occur.

Which prevails in the event of conflict, the statute or its legislative history? The statute was enacted, the report just the staff's explanation. Congress votes on the text of the bill, and the President signed that text. Committee reports help courts understand the law, but this report contradicts rather than explains the text. So the statute must prevail....

Yet the advice from the Supreme Court about how to deal with our situation seems scarcely more harmonious than the advice from the legislature. The reports teem with statements such as: "When we find the terms of a statute unambiguous, judicial inquiry is complete", *Rubin v. United States*, 449 U.S. 424, 430 (1981). Less frequently, yet with equal conviction, the Court writes: "When aid to the construction of the meaning of words, as used in the statute, is available, there certainly can be no 'rule of law' which forbids its use, however clear the words may appear on 'superficial examination.'" *United States v. American Trucking Associations, Inc.*, 310 U.S. 534, 543–44, 60 (1940) (footnotes omitted). Some cases boldly stake out a middle ground, saying, for example: "only the most extraordinary showing of contrary intentions from (the legislative history) would justify a limitation on the 'plain meaning' of the statutory language." *Garcia v. United States*, 469 U.S. 70, 75 (1984). This implies that once in a blue moon the legislative history trumps the statute (as opposed to affording a basis for its interpretation) but does not help locate such strange astronomical phenomena. These lines of cases have coexisted for a century, and many cases contain statements associated with two or even all three of them, not recognizing the tension.

What's a court to do? The answer lies in distinguishing among uses of legislative history. An unadorned "plain meaning" approach to interpretation supposes that words have meanings divorced from their contexts—linguistic, structural, functional, social, historical. Language is a process of communication that works only when authors and readers share a set of rules and meanings. What "clearly" means one thing to a reader unacquainted with the circumstances of the utterance—including social conventions prevailing at the time of drafting—may mean something else to a reader with a different background. Legislation speaks across the decades, during which legal institutions and linguistic conventions change. To decode words one must frequently reconstruct the legal and political culture of the drafters. Legislative history may be invaluable in revealing the setting of the enactment and the assumptions its authors entertained about how their words would be understood. It may show, too, that words with a denotation "clear" to an outsider are terms of art, with an equally "clear" but different meaning to an insider. It may show too that the words leave gaps, for short phrases cannot address all human experience; understood in context, the words may leave to the executive and judicial branches the task of adding flesh to bones. These we take to be the points of cases such as *American Trucking* holding that judges may learn from the legislative history even when the text is "clear". Clarity depends on context, which legislative history may illuminate. The process is objective; the search is not for the contents of the authors' heads but for the rules of language they used.

Quite different is the claim that legislative intent is the basis of interpretation, that the text of the law is simply evidence of the real rule. In such a regimen legislative history is not a way to understand the text but is a more authentic, because more proximate, expression of legislators' will. One may say in reply that legislative history is a poor guide to legislators' intent because it is written by the staff rather than by members of Congress, because it is often losers' history ("If you can't get your proposal into the bill, at least write the legislative history to make it look as if you'd prevailed"), because it becomes a crutch ("There's no need for us to vote on the amendment if we can write a little legislative history"), because it complicates the task of execution and obedience (neither judges nor those whose conduct is supposed to be influenced by the law can know what to do without delving into legislative recesses, a costly and uncertain process). Often there is so much legislative history that a court can manipulate the meaning of a law by choosing which snippets to emphasize and by putting hypothetical questions—questions to be answered by inferences from speeches rather than by reference to the text, so that great discretion devolves on the (judicial) questioner. Sponsors of opinion polls know that a small change in the text of a question can lead to large differences in the answer. Legislative history offers willful judges an opportunity to pose questions and devise answers, with predictable divergence in results. These and related concerns have lead to skepticism about using legislative history to find legislative intent. These cautionary notes are well taken, but even if none were salient there would still be a hurdle to the sort of argument pressed in our case.

Statutes are law, not evidence of law. References to "intent" in judicial opinions do not imply that legislators' motives and beliefs, as opposed to their public acts, establish the norms to which all others must conform. "Original meaning" rather than "intent" frequently captures the interpretive task more precisely, reminding us that it is the work of the political branches (the "meaning") rather than of the courts that matters, and that their work acquires its meaning when enacted ("originally"). Revisionist history may be revelatory; revisionist judging is simply unfaithful to the enterprise. Justice Holmes made the point when denouncing a claim that judges should give weight to the intent of a document's authors:

> (A statute) does not disclose one meaning conclusively according to the laws of language. Thereupon we ask, not what this man meant, but what those words would mean in the mouth of a normal speaker of English, using them in the circumstances in which they were used.... But the normal speaker of English is merely a special variety, a literary form, so to speak, of our old friend the pru-

dent man. He is external to the particular writer, and a reference to him as the criterion is simply another instance of the externality of the law.... We do not inquire what the legislature meant; we ask only what the statute means.

Oliver Wendell Holmes, *The Theory of Legal Interpretation*, 12 Harv.L.Rev. 417, 417–19 (1899), reprinted in *Collected Legal Papers* 204, 207 (1920). Or as Judge Friendly put things in a variation on Holmes's theme, a court must search for "what Congress meant by what it said, rather than for what it meant simpliciter." Henry J. Friendly, Mr. Justice Frankfurter and the Reading of Statutes, in Benchmarks 218–19 (1967).

An opinion poll revealing the wishes of Congress would not translate to legal rules. Desires become rules only after clearing procedural hurdles, designed to encourage deliberation and expose proposals (and arguments) to public view and recorded vote. Resort to "intent" as a device to short-circuit these has no more force than the opinion poll—less, because the legislative history is written by the staff of a single committee and not subject to a vote or veto. The Constitution establishes a complex of procedures, including presidential approval (or support by two-thirds of each house). It would demean the constitutionally prescribed method of legislating to suppose that its elaborate apparatus for deliberation on, amending, and approving a text is just a way to create some evidence about the law, while the real source of legal rules is the mental processes of legislators. We know ... that the express disapproval of one house of Congress cannot change the law, largely because it removes the President from the process; it would therefore be surprising if "intents" subject to neither vote nor veto could be sources of law.

If Congress enacts a parens patriae statute "intending" thereby to allow states to represent indirect purchasers of overpriced goods, that belief about the effects of the enactment does not become law. If Congress were to reduce the rate of taxation on capital gains, "intending" that this stimulate economic growth and so yield more in tax revenue, the meaning of the law would be only that rates go down, not that revenue go up—a judge could not later rearrange rates to achieve the "intent" with respect to federal coffers. On the other hand, doubt about the meaning of a term found in the statute could well be resolved by harmonizing that provision with the structure of the rest of the law, understood in light of a contemporaneous explanation. In this sense legislative intent is a vital source of meaning even though it does not trump the text.

Concern about the source of law—is the statute law, or is it just evidence of the law?—lies behind statements such as: "[T]he language being plain, and not leading to absurd or wholly impracticable consequences, it is the sole evidence of the ultimate legislative intent." *Caminetti*, 242 U.S. at 490 [1917]. To treat the text as conclusive evidence of law is to treat it as law—which under the constitutional structure it is. Legislative history then may help a court discover but may not change the original meaning. The "plain meaning" rule of *Caminetti* rests not on a silly belief that texts have timeless meanings divorced from their many contexts, not on the assumption that what is plain to one reader must be clear to any other (and identical to the plan of the writer), but on the constitutional allocation of powers. The political branches adopt texts through prescribed procedures; what ensues is the law. Legislative history may show the meaning of the texts—may show, indeed, that a text "plain" at first reading has a strikingly different meaning but may not be used to show an "intent" at variance with the meaning of the text. *Caminetti* and *American Trucking* can comfortably coexist when so understood. This approach also supplies the underpinning for the belief that legislative history is only admissible to solve doubt and not to create it, which punctuates the U.S. Reports. Legislative history helps us learn what Congress meant by what it said, but it is not a source of legal rules competing with those found in the U.S.Code.

Ours is now an easy case. Section 302(c)(1) of the statute has an ascertainable meaning, a meaning not absurd or inconsistent with the structure of the remaining provisions. It says that Chapter 11 cases pending on the date the law went into force may not be converted to Chapter 12. No legislative history suggests any other meaning. The committee report suggests, at best, a different intent. Perhaps a reader could infer that the committee planned to allow conversion but mistakenly voted for a different text. So two members of the committee have said since, calling § 302(c)(1) an oversight. Not only the committee's remarks on conversion but also the omission of § 302(c)(1) from the section-by-section description of the bill suggest that whoever wrote the report (a staffer, not a Member of Congress) wanted § 302(c)(1) deleted and may have thought that had been accomplished. Still another possibility is that the Conference Committee meant to distinguish Chapter 11 from Chapter 13: to ban conversions from Chapter 11 (covered by § 302(c)(1)) but allow them from Chapter 13. On this reading the gaffe is the failure to delete the reference to Chapter 11 from the report, which could still stand as a treatment of conversions from Chapter 13.

Congress has done nothing to change § 302(c)(1), implying that the statement in the committee report may have been the error. It is easy to imagine opposing forces arriving at the conference armed with their own texts and legislative histories, and in the scramble at the end of session one version slipping into the bill and the other into the report. Whichever was the blunder, we know which one was enacted. What came out of conference, what was voted for by House and Senate, what was signed by the President, says that pending Chapter 11 cases may not be converted. Accordingly, pending Chapter 11 cases may not be converted....

Affirmed.

In re Idalski

123 B.R. 222 (Bankr. E.D. Mich. 1991)

Arthur J. Spector, Bankruptcy Judge.

[In this case, a debtor voluntarily paid money into an employee retirement system [ERISA*]. The money was paid back to her after she filed for bankruptcy and left her employment. The trustee sought the money as part of the bankruptcy estate to distribute among the creditors.] The issue before the Court is whether Mrs. Idalski's interest in the retirement plan is excluded from the estate by operation of § 541(c)(2). This section states: "A restriction on the transfer of a beneficial interest of the debtor in a trust that is enforceable under applicable nonbankruptcy law is enforceable in a case under this title."** 11 U.S.C. § 541(c)(2).... [The issue before the court is whether ERISA is a "nonbankruptcy law" such that the money paid into the retirement account and repaid to the debtor would be exempt from the bankruptcy estate.]

For the reasons which follow ... we hold that ... ERISA constitutes "applicable nonbankruptcy law" for purposes of § 541(c)(2)....

It is well-settled that ... an anti-alienation clause contained in an ERISA-qualified pension plan precludes creditors of a plan beneficiary from levying on the beneficiary's in-

---

* Authors' footnote: The Employee Retirement Income Security Act of 1974, 29 U.S.C. § 1001 et seq. Interests in these plans cannot be assigned or alienated, meaning that creditors generally cannot reach them.

** Authors' footnote: In other words, if creditors cannot reach the individual's money outside of the bankruptcy context, they cannot do so within the bankruptcy context.

terest in the plan. Since ERISA is "nonbankruptcy law," and it is clearly "applicable" to the issue in dispute, it would seem that Mrs. Idalski's interest in the plan would accordingly be excluded from the estate in its entirety under §541(c)(2). Nevertheless, a good number of cases have concluded that, in using the term "applicable nonbankruptcy law," Congress did not mean ERISA. In so holding, these cases have primarily relied on the statute's legislative history. Before launching into an exhaustive analysis of non-statutory material, however, we believe a court must always consider whether reference to such sources is appropriate under the circumstances.

There is support for the proposition that, if a literal construction of an unambiguous statute does not produce an absurd or futile result, then it is inappropriate for a court to examine extrastatutory materials in an effort to determine the "legislative intent" of the statute.

Needs to be ambiguous for leg. history

The Supreme Court has explicitly endorsed the plain·meaning rule. In [one case], the Court stated that "[l]egislative history is irrelevant to the interpretation of an unambiguous statute." Other decisions of the Supreme Court attest to the omnipresence of the plain meaning rule.

However, the Supreme Court also explicitly rejected the plain meaning rule on numerous occasions. *See, e.g., United States v. American Trucking Associations*, 310 U.S. 534, 543–44 (1940). Adding to the confusion, at least two other Supreme Court opinions appear to be self-contradictory with regard to this rule of construction.

In *United States v. Rutherford*, 442 U.S. 544 (1979), the Court stated that "[i]f a legislative purpose is expressed in 'plain and unambiguous language, ... the ... duty of the courts is to give it effect according to its terms." In refusing to create an implicit exception to the statute in question, however, the Court in *Rutherford* cited the statute's legislative history to support its conclusion. *See also United States v. Ron Pair Enterprises*, 489 U.S. 235 (1989) (where the Court again gave a ringing endorsement of the plain meaning rule but proceeded to review the legislative history of a statute whose meaning was "plain" to determine if it was one of those "rare cases [in which] the literal application of a statute will produce a result demonstrably at odds with the intention of its drafters.") A number of other decisions rendered by the Supreme Court vividly reflect the court's indecisiveness as to the validity of the plain meaning rule. *See California v. American Stores Co.*, 495 U.S. 271 (1990) ("Although we do not believe the statutory language is ambiguous, we nonetheless consider the legislative history...."); *John Doe Agency v. John Doe Corp.*, 493 U.S. 146 (1989) ("If, despite what we regard as the plain meaning of the statutory language, it were necessary or advisable to examine the legislative history we would reach the same conclusion."); *Bourjaily v. United States*, 483 U.S. 171, 178–79 (1987) (where the Court stated that "[i]t would be extraordinary to require legislative history to *confirm* the plain meaning of (Federal Rule of Evidence) 104," then proceeded to review the rule's legislative history); *United Airlines v. McMann*, 434 U.S. 192, 199 (1977) ("The dissent relies heavily upon the legislative history, which by traditional canons of interpretation is irrelevant to an unambiguous statute. However, in view of the [dissent's] recourse to the legislative history[,] we turn to that aspect to demonstrate the absence of any indication of congressional intent....").

Under the principle of *stare decisis*, we are of course obligated to adhere to decisions rendered by the Supreme Court. This principle has been described as a means of promoting certainty, stability, and predictability of the law. Unfortunately, the ambivalence which the Supreme Court has demonstrated on the question of the plain meaning rule leads us to conclude that "certainty" will not be served by adhering to any of the Court's conflicting pronouncements.[6] Similarly, we are unable to discern any direction on this issue from our own circuit court; the Sixth Circuit cases…, which support the plain meaning rule, are contradicted by a good number of cases from that court which explicitly or implicitly reject the plain meaning rule. Since there is no clear precedent in this regard, we are in effect writing on a clean slate, and we will analyze the problem accordingly.

As a starting point, we note that virtually all courts agree that the legislative history of a statute is potentially useful in determining what Congress "meant" the statute to say; few courts, after all, have suggested that it is pointless to consult the legislative history even if the meaning of a statute is unclear. That being the case, the question becomes, why should the court ever refuse to consider evidence that may substantiate a statutory construction which a party claims most accurately reflects the legislative intent?

The presumed response by advocates of the plain meaning rule is that, given the inherent limitations of the legislative history,[7] it can never persuade the court that an unambiguous statute means other than what it appears to mean. We believe, however, that there are two problems with this response. First, we tend to agree with those who have questioned whether a statute can ever be fairly characterized as "unambiguous." The fundamental flaw of the plain meaning rule is its reliance on the notion that words can have a fixed, unambiguous meaning independent of the context in which they are used.[8] We are accordingly reluctant to pledge our unquestioning faith to the so-called "literal" meaning of a statute.

Second, and more importantly, we do not accept the premise that legislative histories are of so little value that they could (or should) *never* persuade the court that Congress did not intend a statute to be interpreted literally. To the contrary, we believe that there are a number of examples where a court has appropriately declined to apply the "plain meaning" of a statute, based at least in part on the court's analysis of the statute's legislative history. *See, e.g., Church of the Holy Trinity v. United States,* 143 U.S. 457 (1892) (statute which prohibited the importation of foreigners to perform "labor or service of any kind" was directed toward manual laborers and thus did not apply to a contract between a church in the United States and a pastor residing in England). In [this case], a literal application of the statute in question would have created results that Congress never intended. *Cf. Guiseppi v. Walling,* 144 F.2d 608, 624 (2d Cir.1944) (Learned Hand, J., concurring) ("There is no surer way to misread any document than to read it literally.…").

Another argument which can be made in support of the plain meaning rule is that it limits the ability of judges to make value judgments that should properly be made by the legislature. Moreover, by relying on the statute's "plain meaning," legislators are encouraged to "spell out the nature of their intentions much more clearly on the face of the statutes they pass," and the court's task is simplified. Compliance on the part of those persons "whose conduct is supposed to be influenced by the law" may also be facilitated if they are not expected or required to "delv[e] into legislative recesses" in order to determine a statute's meaning. *In re Sinclair,* 870 F.2d 1340, 1343 (7th Cir.1989).

---

6. Other courts have also struggled with the Supreme Court's schizophrenic attitude vis-a-vis the plain meaning rule. *See, e.g., In re Sinclair,* 870 F.2d 1340, 1341–42 (7th Cir.1989). Contrary to the court in *Sinclair,* however, we do not believe that the various positions taken by the Supreme Court can be satisfactorily reconciled.

7. Legislative histories have been criticized as unauthoritative, and it has been suggested that they are unreliable, easily manipulated and subject to abuse.

8. Indeed, the very fact that ambiguity appears to be in the eye of the beholder, *see e.g., United States v. Ron Pair Enterprises,* 489 U.S. 235 (1989) (5–4 split as to whether the statute in question was unambiguous), suggests that it is something of an illusory concept.

The problem with the first argument is that it assumes that judges who are inclined to manipulate the law to suit their own biases will be constrained to a significant extent by the plain meaning rule. We think that assumption is overly optimistic, given the remarkable skill that some courts have demonstrated in detecting "ambiguities" in a statute where most would have thought none existed.[10]

In short, we do not think the plain meaning rule effectively curbs the propensity or ability of judges to circumvent the legislative will. *→ plain meaning can't help w/ leg. will.*

As for the remaining arguments cited above, we believe that any positive effect that strict adherence to the plain meaning rule would have on either the manner in which statutes are drafted or the extent to which they are obeyed is speculative, at best.[11] More to the point, we think that neither these (theoretical) benefits nor the "simplicity" of adhering to a statute's literal meaning would ordinarily justify incurring the risk that seemingly unambiguous statutory provisions will be applied in a manner that Congress did not intend.

Nevertheless, we do agree that there are situations where the risk of misconstruing an unambiguous statute is so minimal that the benefits gained by invoking the plain meaning rule justify its use. Accordingly, we believe that the rule should be applied where the statutory construction urged by a party is so inherently improbable that it defies common sense.

If, for example, a statute says "the requirements set forth herein do not apply to A," and a party contends that Congress meant to say that the requirements *do* apply to A, the party is, in essence, asking the court to find that Congress, through its statute, said the exact opposite of what it meant. As a means of expediting the judicial process, we believe it is appropriate for the court to exclude non-statutory evidence which is claimed to support such an "interpretation."

In such a situation, application of the plain meaning rule is justified because we are confident that no amount of legislative history could persuade the court that the legislature "meant" other than what the statute appears to be "saying." Alternatively, we believe it is appropriate to take the position that the court simply will not construe a statute in such a nonsensical manner, even if such a construction would in fact accurately reflect the intent of the legislature. We concur with the view stated long ago that, in interpreting statutes, the plain meaning rule should operate in a manner analogous to the parol evidence rule applicable to private contracts, and that the intent of the legislature, as established by review of extra-statutory materials, should accordingly be "relevant to the solution of the case only if consistent with the 'meaning' which may *reasonably* be attached to the words used" in the statute.

If, on the other hand, a party concedes that the hypothetical statute excludes A from its coverage, but contends that Congress did not intend to include some subset of A within

---

10. We also note that some judges are able to uncover the "clear" meaning of a statute that appears more hazy to less talented jurists. In *Ron Pair, supra*, for example, the Supreme Court's conclusion that § 506(b) of the Bankruptcy Code permitted oversecured involuntary lienholders to recover post-petition interest on their claims was based in large part on the "plain language of the statute." The statute's meaning was apparently less "plain" to the four dissenting justices, the Sixth Circuit and the bankruptcy court, each of which concluded to the contrary in that case, as well as the First Circuit, which reached the same conclusion as the Sixth Circuit in [another case].

11. With respect to the drafting of statutes, we find merit in the argument that it would in any event be unreasonable to expect the legislature to enact statutes which are devoid of ambiguity. Anyone who has had experience in the drafting of instruments, whether statutes or contracts, knows the impossibility of creating phrases which are free from doubt.

the scope of the exclusion, we do not believe that the court should ignore evidence which the party claims supports her case. Because the party's premise, that Congress inadvertently used an overly broad term, is at least plausible, the court cannot dismiss the possibility that the party will be able to support her argument with persuasive evidence.[14]

Applying this rationale to the case before us, we do not believe that the plain meaning "rule" should be invoked here. We cannot say with confidence that no amount of evidence, by way of legislative history or other extra-statutory materials, could convince us that Congress did not mean to include ERISA when it referred to "applicable nonbankruptcy law" in § 541(c)(2). We will accordingly consider the legislative history which the trustee claims supports his position....

[The court reviews the House Report and the Senate Report and concludes that Congress intended the term "applicable nonbankruptcy law" to include *state* law spendthrift trusts.] [W]e think it takes a certain leap of faith to infer from that fact that Congress also meant to *exclude* federal spendthrift trust law. The court should refrain from construing a statute in a manner which does not comport with its apparent meaning unless there is strong evidence to support such a construction. We find nothing in the legislative history which *clearly* indicates that the reference to applicable nonbankruptcy law contained in § 541(c)(2) does not include restrictions which are enforceable under applicable federal law.... For the reasons stated above, we hold that Mrs. Idalski's interest in the retirement plan was excluded from property of the estate under § 541(c)(2). An order denying the trustee's request for turnover will enter.

Notes and Questions

(1) *How Does the* Sinclair *Approach Differ from the* Idalski *Approach?* How are the judges in each of the opinions above willing to use legislative history (refer to the continuum discussion above)? Which use do you think leads to the more accurate interpretation? In *Sinclair*, the text was unambiguous, but the legislative history contradicted the plain meaning. In *Idalski*, the text was unambiguous, and the legislative history was ambiguous at best. Could this difference alone explain the different approaches? If you answered the last question positively, consider whether the *Idalski* court would have been willing to reject the plain meaning if the legislative history had been more compelling.

(2) *Coherence in the Supreme Court's Use of Legislative History.* Do you agree with *Sinclair* that the Supreme Court's approach to legislative history is reconcilable or with *Idalski* that the Court's approach is irreconcilable? If you agree with *Idalski*, do you think the Court should articulate a unified approach that would be used in every statutory interpretation case? What are the benefits of one, clear approach? The costs?

(3) *Enactment and Presentment.* For constitutional reasons, critics say it is wrong to rely on legislative history because only statutory text is approved by the legislature, presented to the executive branch, and enacted into law. Article I of the U.S. Constitution requires these actions for a bill to become law. (Recall from Chapter 7 that not all of the language in a bill is enacted into law.) Certainly, committee reports and statements made during debates are not enacted or presented. Thus, it is true that legislative history is not "law." *See Koons Buick Pontiac GMC, Inc. v. Nigh*, 543 U.S. 50, 73 (2004) (Scalia, J., dissenting)

---

14. Other examples where we believe that the plain meaning rule should not be invoked would include situations where a party contends that the statute was (or was not) meant to exclude only A, that A has a technical meaning that differs from its lay definition, and so on.

("I also disagree with the Court's reliance on things that the sponsors and floor managers of the 1995 amendment failed to say. I have often criticized the Court's use of legislative history because it lends itself to a kind of ventriloquism. The Congressional Record or committee reports are used to make words appear to come from Congress's mouth which were spoken or written by others (individual Members of Congress, congressional aides, or even enterprising lobbyists.)") Is reliance on legislative history to determine meaning of the enacted text unconstitutional?

(4) *Textualism.* Textualists may avoid the use of legislative history unless the text is ambiguous or absurd *and* other sources of interpretation (*e.g.,* the textual canons) have failed to provide a plain meaning. Does that approach make sense? Does it make sense to give more weight to statutory canons of interpretation that the legislators may be wholly unaware of (like *expressio unius*) and that may actually conflict with the way lawyers are trained to write (like the rule against surplusage), rather than statements contained in a conference committee report? In thinking about that question, consider this excerpt as well:

> The dissent also makes the point[] that legislative history should be considered only if "the other tools of interpretation fail to produce a single, reasonable meaning, and that, in any event, it is an unreliable method of ascertaining legislative intent.... Thus, the dissent regards the use of legislative history as unreliable evidence of legislative intent, and as insidious in the sense that it permits the court to interpret a statute to reach a meaning that the court *wants* it to have, based on the court's own policy preference, rather than that of the legislature. As a result, in the dissent's ... formulation of the plain meaning rule, consideration of legislative history is relegated to the ... penultimate, step.
>
> In response, we note first that it is difficult to understand why the dissent would consider the use of legislative history at all in its formulation, given that it regards such use as both unreliable and insidious. More importantly, it appears to us that, under the dissent's formulation, only the most difficult cases of statutory interpretation would reach the [legislative history step]. Thus, the dissent reserves what it regards as an unreliable and insidious source of statutory meaning to act as the tiebreaker in the most difficult cases of interpretation. This strikes us as a curiously important role for what the dissent regards so negatively as a source of the meaning of legislative language.
>
> On the merits of the use of legislative history, we simply disagree with the dissent's characterizations of it. The general experience of this court demonstrates to us that legislative history, when reviewed and employed in a responsible, discriminating and intellectually honest manner, can constitute reliable evidence of legislative intent....

State v. Courchesne, 816 A.2d 562, 588–89 (Conn. 2003). Does rejecting legislative history except in extreme cases make sense?

(5) *Unambiguous Text with Unambiguous, But Contrary, Legislative History.* At the start, we asked whether legislative history should be used to overcome clear and unambiguous text. A specific example might help resolve this issue. A federal criminal statute made possession of "counterfeit coin" a crime. A defendant possessed counterfeit Krugerrand (a coin of South Africa). On its face, a counterfeit Krugerrand is a "counterfeit coin," and so conviction seemed inevitable. However, the legislative history showed two things: first, that this statute had been in effect for 150 years and had always prohibited only counterfeiting of coins "in resemblance of" any U.S. coins; second, that when the statute

had been amended, it had been part of a large reorganization of criminal statutes, and no substantive changes were intended. Now what? *United States v. Falvey*, 676 F.2d 871 (1st Cir. 1982) (affirming dismissal of indictment). Does giving the text its "intended" meaning do justice in the individual case, but create poor drafting incentives?

(6) *The Legislative History "Hierarchy."* Are some forms of legislative history more reliable than others? If so, why might that be true? We noted in Chapter 1 that when legislative history is considered, conference committee reports are often given greater weight than other statements. Why is some legislative history more relevant than others? Consider this passage:

> Resort to legislative history is only justified where the face of the Act is inescapably ambiguous, and then I think we should not go beyond Committee reports, which presumably are well considered and carefully prepared.... But to select casual statements from floor debates, not always distinguished for candor or accuracy, as a basis for making up our minds what law Congress intended to enact is to substitute ourselves for the Congress in one of its important functions. The Rules of the House and Senate, with the sanction of the Constitution, require three readings of an Act in each House before final enactment. That is intended, I take it, to make sure that each House knows what it is passing and passes what it wants, and that what is enacted was formally reduced to writing. It is the business of Congress to sum up its own debates in its legislation. Moreover, it is only the words of the bill that have presidential approval, where that approval is given. It is not to be supposed that, in signing a bill the President endorses the whole Congressional Record. For us to undertake to reconstruct an enactment from legislative history is merely to involve the Court in political controversies which are quite proper in the enactment of a bill but should have no place in its interpretation.

Schwegmann Bros. v. Calvert Distillers Corp., 341 U.S. 384, 395–96 (1951) (Jackson, J., concurring); *see United States v. Salim*, 287 F. Supp. 2d 250, 340 (S.D.N.Y. 2003) ("[T]he conference report is the most persuasive evidence of congressional intent, next to the statute itself."); *compare Overseas Educ. Ass'n, Inc., v. Fed. Labor Relations Auth.*, 876 F.2d 960, 967 n.41 (D.C. Cir. 1989) ("[C]ommittee reports ... have traditionally been considered to be the most reliable of historical aids to statutory interpretation[].... [And] explanations by sponsors of legislation during floor discussion are entitled to weight when they cast light on the construction properly to be placed upon statutory language.") (internal citations omitted), *with In re Virtual Network Serv. Corp.*, 98 B.R. 343, 349 (Bankr. N.D. Ill. 1989) ("The floor statements of individual legislators are larded with remarks which reflect a political ("sales talk") rather than a legislative purpose."); *United States v. Pabon-Cruz*, 391 F.3d 86, 101 (2d Cir. 2004) ("[I]t is well established that speeches by opponents of legislation are entitled to relatively little weight in determining the meaning of the Act in question.") Does this last statement make sense? If a legislator makes a statement explaining why she is voting against a bill, why isn't that pertinent to its meaning?

Finally, consider Justice Scalia's concern that committee reports are written "at best by a committee staff member on his or her own initiative and, at worst, by a committee staff member at the suggestion of a lawyer-lobbyist; and the purpose of [any language] was not primarily to inform ... Congress what the bill meant ... but rather to influence judicial construction." *Blanchard v. Bergeron*, 489 U.S. 87, 98–99 (1989) (Scalia, J., concurring). He concluded: "What a heady feeling it must be for a young staffer, to know that" his language has become "the law of the land...." *Id.* Do you believe that, if true, this fact warrants ignoring legislative history? Does it affect your answer to learn that many judicial opinions are drafted by law clerks rather than judges?

Problem 8-1

You are an assistant district attorney and have been assigned to prosecute David Mueller. Mr. Mueller was charged with operating a motor vehicle while intoxicated. The trial court granted his motion to suppress the intoxilyzer breath test. The trial court granted the motion. The state timely appealed. However, the elected District Attorney for the County, Kathleen Holmes, did not sign the notice of appeal. Rather, the first assistant to the DA signed for her. The State's notice of appeal read in relevant part:

> The State of Mercer now gives written notice of appeal to the Court of Appeals sitting in Tompkins County, Mercer. I certify to this court that this appeal is not taken for the purpose of delay and that the evidence suppressed in this cause is of substantial importance.
>
> *Kathleen D. Holmes, by Lisa Maddox* September 4, 2005

The DA was out of town on September 4. The First Assistant was fully authorized to execute the functions of the District Attorney in the DA's absence. Analyze whether the DA herself must have actually signed the notice of appeal.

Problem Materials

Mercer Government Code § 311

> (a) In construing a statute, whether or not the statute is considered ambiguous on its face, a court may consider among other matters the:
>
> (1) object sought to be obtained,
>
> (2) circumstances under which the statute was enacted,
>
> (3) legislative history,
>
> (4) the context surrounding the statute's enactment, and
>
> (5) the title, section headings, and preamble.

Mercer Crim. Proc. Code § 44.01

> (a) The state is entitled to appeal an order of a court in a criminal case if the order: ...
>
> (5) grants a motion to suppress evidence ... if the prosecuting attorney certifies in writing to the trial court that the appeal is not taken for the purpose of delay and that the evidence ... is of substantial importance to the case.
>
> > (i) "Prosecuting attorney" means the county attorney or district attorney, and an assistant prosecuting attorney serving on behalf of the prosecuting attorney in his absence.

Legislative History

During the House floor debate of May 29th, 1987, Representative Hury, the sponsor of H.B. 1035 stated in support, "I feel that the bill is so tightly drawn that it does what it is intended to do, and that is, to give the State a limited right to appeal in situations where it has not previously had that right." Representative Danburg, a member of the House Criminal Jurisprudence Committee, related the objectives of the prosecutors who had testified for passage of the bill during committee hearings: "They made it quite clear that they did not wish to be able to appeal every adverse ruling and not every guilty verdict in every single case they lost, for whatever reason. They really only wanted to be able to appeal the abusive ones...."

Representative Danburg then inquired of Representative Hury: "Is it your intention that this bill should only be applied to situations where there really is abuse and not to just every case the State loses, but should be very narrowly applied to abusive situations?" to which Hury responded, "That is what I believe will happen."

Testimony before the Senate Criminal Justice Committee on April 21, 1987, demonstrates a similar concern about the potential for prosecutorial abuse of the appellate privilege. When asked by Senator Lyons what controls are to be found in the bill, Rusty Hardin of the Harris County District Attorney's Office pointed to section (d) as a check against "individual assistants making the decision to appeal. The D.A. would be controlling resources; the D.A. would be controlling the decision as to what issues are important enough to appeal."

Senators Lyons and Glasgow pressed other witnesses about prosecutors using the appellate mechanism to threaten misdemeanor offenders into guilty pleas. Knox Fitzpatrick, from the Augusta District Attorney's office, assured Senator Lyons that he could lay his fears to rest: "In the bill, there is a safeguard, in that it would be the district attorney who would have to certify these appeals, the prosecuting attorney in this case would mean the county attorney or district attorney and does not include every assistant prosecuting attorney. This would be a safeguard I think so there wouldn't be these frivolous appeals"

Senator Lyons persisted, "What kind of safeguards do you have there about a real fire-breathing young misdemeanor prosecutor if he got upset at a ruling in a misdemeanor case by a judge?" To which Mr. Fitzpatrick responded, "Under this section, it would have to be the county attorney or the district attorney, who would have to certify the appeal."

Despite the thorny problems inherent in discerning whether to consider; when to consider; and, if so, how much weight to give legislative history; few suggest that it should never be consulted. However, as you saw in the last two cases, there is a significant and broad difference of opinion on when it should be consulted and, if so, how much weight it should be given. Consequently, as a practicing attorney, you will need to understand both why this disagreement exists, as well as the different views of the propriety of relying upon legislative history. The first two cases raised these issues; the next two sections explore them further.

B. The Indeterminacy of Legislative History

While reliance on legislative history is longstanding, controversy over this reliance is equally as old. *Church of the Holy Trinity v. United States*, 143 U.S. 457 (1892), is credited with beginning the foray into the legislative record. In that case, Justice Brewer relied on a Senate committee report that indicated that the bill — which prohibited anyone from bringing an alien into the country "to perform labor" — had been intended to apply only to those engaged in "manual labor," but that it had been too late in the legislative session to amend the bill to include more accurate language.

However, did Justice Brewer err in allowing that one report to overcome the clear statutory language? Consider this exchange, which took place during floor debate:

> Mr. Morgan: [If an alien] happens to be a lawyer, an artist, a painter, an engraver, a sculptor, a great author, or what not, and he comes under employment to write for a newspaper, or to write books, or to paint pictures ... he comes under the general provisions of the bill....

> Mr. Blair: If that class of people are [sic] liable to become the subject-matter of such importation, then the bill applies to them. Perhaps the bill ought to be further amended.

> Mr. Morgan: ... I shall propose when we get to it to put an amendment in there. I want to associate with the lecturers and singers and actors, painters, sculptors..., or any person having special skill in any business, art, trade or profession....

16 Cong. Rec. 1633 (Feb. 13, 1885). Does this excerpt support Justice Brewer's interpretation, or does it show that the Senate intended that the statute apply to skilled labor? Is it evidence that Justice Brewer imperfectly analyzed the text? Or is the excerpt evidence that Justice Brewer relied on excerpts that supported his interpretation and ignored those that did not? Arguably, this example shows only that, at best, the legislative history was ambiguous and that Justice Brewer's discussion of it was incomplete.

Consequently, some contend that the "error" in *Holy Trinity* demonstrates that courts are not competent to analyze legislative materials and so should not use them to vary the meaning of the text or otherwise discern meaning. *Compare* Adrian Vermeule, *Legislative History and the Limits of Judicial Competence: The Untold Story of* Holy Trinity Church, 50 Stan. L. Rev. 1833 (1998) (arguing that judges are not competent to make this determination), *with* Carol Chomsky, *Unlocking the Mysteries of* Holy Trinity: *Spirit, Letter, and History in Statutory Interpretation*, 100 Colum. L. Rev. 901 (2000) (arguing that they are). Indeed, the Supreme Court recently characterized legislative history as "murky, ambiguous, and contradictory." *Exxon Mobil Corp. v. Allapattah Serv., Inc.*, 545 U.S. 546, 568 (2005).

In contrast, some argue that the meaning of the text cannot be discerned without considering the legislative process: Legislators assume that lawyers will argue about the meaning of text and so "try to leave as little meaning to context as possible, at times creating word usages that have no parallel in ordinary conversation. This pattern of anticipating and responding to strategic behavior shapes the final text." Paul E. McGreal, *Slighting Context: On the Illogic of Ordinary Speech in Statutory Interpretation*, 52 U. Kan. L. Rev. 325, 373 (2004). "If the legislative process has its own assumptions and word usages, the process itself should be the context within which we seek a statute's meaning." *Id.* Because legislators and their staff study how language can be manipulated, that knowledge shapes the meaning of the text chosen.

No doubt, reliance on legislative history is imperfect. Even so, some argue that textualism in its strictest form gives judges too much power to interpret text. We will consider that issue more fully below. For now, consider this excerpt from Professor Carol Chomsky.

---

* Copyright Carol Chomsky, Professor. Used by permission.

Unlocking the Mysteries of *Holy Trinity*:
Spirit, Letter, and History in Statutory Interpretation

100 Colum. L. Rev. 901 (2000)*
Carol Chomsky

... So just what was the intent of the Senate and the House when they enacted the Alien Contract Labor Act? Or, to ask a more relevant question, was it the intent of Congress to cast the net broadly, to exclude from American shores any person who arrived with a prearranged contract for labor or service of any kind? Determining the intent of a body such as Congress is problematic, of course. But the message of an overwhelming number of comments from committee reports, sponsors, and floor supporters was that the aim of the bill—and therefore, one may infer, the aim of those who voted for it—was to stop the wholesale importation of cheap labor to undermine American workers.

Did Congress choose language that would limit its remedy to that problem? Assuredly not. Why did neither the Senate nor the House amend the bill to narrow its scope, since the breadth of the proposed language was brought to the attention of Congress? The legislative history suggests that there was, at least at some stages in the consideration of the bill, insufficient time to make the necessary changes. It also suggests, repeatedly, that neither the drafters nor the supporters thought the bill was well-drafted to accomplish its purposes. The bill was repeatedly referred to as "crude," and at least one Senator suggested that lawyers would laugh to see what had been written. The bill was amended repeatedly to ensure exceptions for a small number of categories of immigrants—personal or domestic servants, personal friends or members of an individual's family, artists—but the only broad amendment offered-to change "labor or service" to "manual labor or manual service"—would not in any event have matched the language of the bill to the purposes expressed. Indeed, it was clear when the breadth was discussed that supporters were satisfied with language that reached all kinds of workers—if they were being imported in the fashion described. Perhaps one reason for the failure to amend is the difficulty of drafting language that would do what Congress intended, that would draw a workable line between the problematic—workers brought in, often in large numbers, to damage the position of American labor—and the acceptable—voluntary immigrants coming to America, with or without promise of employment, to better their own lives and incidentally to contribute to the society they were joining....

If legislative intent as reflected in legislative history should be considered in construing the statutory words ... then the circumstances leading to passage of the Alien Contract Labor Act provide ample support for limiting, as Brewer did, the extremely broad language of the Act....

Holy Trinity Church took the rather modest step of referring with approval to two committee reports, and using them along with "the title of the act, the evil which was intended to be remedied, [and] the circumstances surrounding the appeal to Congress, ... all [of which] concur in affirming that the intent of Congress was simply to stay the influx of this cheap unskilled labor." The opinion made no effort to establish any particular authority for the statements of legislators or committees beyond the cumulative effect they had when considered with other evidence often used for statutory interpretation, and went no further than [a] prior opinion ... in counting legislative history as relevant to determining legislative intent.

Perhaps the reason *Holy Trinity Church* is so often cited as creating a revolution in statutory interpretation is not the principles upon which it drew, but the fact that the Court used them in this particular case to ignore the literal language of a statute....

[margin note: × Court ignored literal language of the statute]

What should a court do when faced with the question raised in *Holy Trinity Church*? Should the operative and seemingly broad language of a statute be controlling, irrespective of the content of the legislative history? "New textualists" like Scalia ... would hold Congress to the words it used, whatever the content of the legislative history, because of the judiciary's institutional incompetence to determine the true intent of Congress. Even if persuaded of the "true" Congressional intent, and of the possibility of determining legislative meaning in this fashion, they might still enforce the words that Congress actually used because to do otherwise would permit Congress to legislate without completing the required process for enactment of legislation. Reading the words of the statute differently than they were written, they argue, would promote just the kind of sloppy drafting that was evident—and described by the drafters themselves—in the Alien Contract Labor Act.

But the textualist approach prevents a court from attempting to fulfill what it can determine of legislative intent expressed elsewhere than in the statutory language. Although it may be technically impossible to determine the specific legislative intent as to a specific issue ... it is possible to understand the general purposes being served by a statute, which helps to ensure a more complete and historically accurate understanding of the law.

Ignoring legislative history also prevents the interpreter from understanding the con- text in which the legislator used the words written into the statutory text. In construing

[margin note: × context]

the words of the Alien Contract Labor Act as clearly proscribing the importation of any kind of laborer, Justice Scalia ignores not only the legislators' statements of statutory purpose and intent, but also the history of labor and immigration that, even without the legislative history of the Act, helps inform our understanding of the way in which the legislators used "labor" and "service" in the statute. While one cannot avoid being affected by modern contexts and perceptions when attempting to understand legislative history, the same is true when attempting to understand the bare statutory words themselves. The legislative history at least may alert the interpreter to the possible complexities of the language used in the statute. Even if the proper aim of statutory interpretation is to seek "objective meaning" rather than "subjective intent," knowing the legislative and other history surrounding enactment inevitably affects conclusions about what those words— even words as seemingly clear as "labor or service of any kind"—"objectively" mean.

Finally, reading statutory words as written, without recourse to legislative history, amplifies the inevitable vagaries of the legislative process. The history of the Alien Contract Labor Act demonstrates that, even in simpler times, Congress proved incapable of being clear and thorough in its statutory drafting, though it recognized and acknowledged the crudity of its language. A textualist approach will not likely result in better statutes that accurately reflect legislative intent, but instead in unintended consequences resulting from the realities of legislative work....

No doubt the debate will continue about whether legislative history ought to be used in construing statutes.... Lawyers and judges who cite to legislative history may, like Brewer, do a less than thorough job of exploring that history, sometimes from unfamiliarity with the whole, sometimes from an excess of zeal in advocacy. This is no more reason to condemn wholesale any attempt to use legislative history, however, than to condemn efforts to use case law precedent or to explore relevant political, social, or economic history, though both are subject to the same missteps and abuses....

Notes and Questions

(1) *Can Legislators be Imputed with a Common Intent?* Critics of legislative history argue that it is improper to attribute a single intent to a group of legislators because each likely had different reasons to vote for a bill and probably different understandings of what the bill meant. These critics argue that it is fiction to suggest that there is one unified legislative intent expressed anywhere other than in the enacted statutory text. *See, e.g.*, Max Radin, *Statutory Interpretation*, 43 HARV. L. REV. 863, 870 (1930) ("The chances that several hundred [individuals] each will have exactly the same determinate situations in mind as possible reductions of a given [statutory issue], are infinitesimally small.") Did the legislative history in *Holy Trinity* show that every member of both legislative bodies intended that the act only apply to manual laborers?

No doubt, it is true that a court cannot be certain that statements made during the legislative process reflect the will of the legislative majority, at least in the abstract. Should it make a difference if the legislative history showed that every legislator had, on the record, agreed that an ambiguous term had a specific meaning?

(2) *Can Reliance on Legislative History Encourage Strategic Behavior by Legislators?* Suppose a legislator knows that any effort to amend a bill means the bill will fail, and the legislator does not want the bill to fail. As a strategic thinker, she might make a statement during the floor debate suggesting that the text in the bill means what she wants it to mean or otherwise include in the legislative history statements that support her view. Later, when a court looks for legislative intent, the court might rely on her statement as indicative of the meaning, even though the legislature as a whole did not intend that meaning and would have rejected it. Does a rule prohibiting consideration of legislative history for this reason presume improper behavior by legislators? In a recent case, the Supreme Court noted this possibility:

> As we have repeatedly held, the authoritative statement is the statutory text, not the legislative history or any other extrinsic material. Extrinsic materials have a role in statutory interpretation only to the extent they shed a reliable light on the enacting Legislature's understanding of otherwise ambiguous terms. Not all extrinsic materials are reliable sources of insight into legislative understandings, however, and legislative history in particular is vulnerable to ... criticism[].... [J]udicial reliance on legislative materials like committee reports, which are not themselves subject to the requirements of Article I, may give unrepresentative committee members — or, worse yet, unelected staffers and lobbyists — both the power and the incentive to attempt strategic manipulations of legislative history to secure results they were unable to achieve through the statutory text. We need not comment here on whether these problems are sufficiently prevalent to render legislative history inherently unreliable in all circumstances, a point on which Members of this Court have disagreed.

Exxon Mobil Corp. v. Allapattah Serv., Inc., 545 U.S. 546, 568 (2005).

(3) *Does Reliance on Legislative History Allow Judicial Activism?* Judicial intrepretation of a statute is sometimes pejoratively called "judicial activism." Isn't "judicial activism" more appropriately viewed as a label to apply to decisions with which one disagrees? Some say that relying on legislative history expands judicial discretion and facilitates "decisions that are based upon the courts' policy preferences, rather than neutral principles of law." ANTONIN SCALIA, A MATTER OF INTERPRETATION 35 (Princeton University Press 1997); *accord State v. Courchesne*, 816 A.2d 562, 588 (Zarella, J., dissenting). Justice Scalia some-

what sarcastically wrote that "your best shot at figuring out what the legislature meant is to ask yourself what a wise and intelligent person should have meant; and that will surely bring you to the conclusion that the law means what you think it ought to mean...." SCALIA, *supra*, at 18; *see also Exxon Mobil Corp.*, 545 U.S. at 568 ("Judicial investigation of legislative history has a tendency to become ... an exercise in looking over a crowd and picking out your friends.") Do you agree? Consider this response to that argument:

> If a court is determined to be intellectually dishonest and result-oriented in its decision-making, it does not need any particular stated rubric of interpretation—whether purposive, plain meaning, or some other method—to be so. Furthermore, we have confidence in this court's ability to employ legislative history in a responsible, discriminating and intellectually honest manner, so as to determine the legislature's purpose or purposes, and not our own. We think that our history in doing so bears this out, and we are confident that we can continue to do so.

Courchesne, 816 A.2d at 589 (Zarella, J., dissenting). Does ignoring legislative history reduce the likelihood of judicial impropriety? Is reliance on legislative history a doorway to judicial activism, or do those making this argument presume—without empirical evidence—improper behavior by the judiciary?

(4) *Does Abjuring Reliance on Legislative History Result in Better Statutes or Higher Transaction Costs?* On the one hand, critics of the use of legislative history argue that refusing to look at it will result in better-drafted statutes. Legislatures will know that they must say what they mean in the text. On the other hand, does it make sense to reject legislative history where it would show that the plain meaning *clearly* was not what was intended? Won't rigidly rejecting legislative history just result in increased costs, requiring legislatures to amend statutes when courts could easily determine what the statute means by searching broadly for meaning?

(5) *Textualism and Judicial Power.* Legislatures operate efficiently because they delegate to committees: Specific members draft, analyze, amend, recommend, oppose, and explain bills to the other members of the legislature. Thus, only a few members may be fully versed on a particular bill. Legislatures would be paralyzed if every member had to be fully versed on every nuance of every bill. There will seldom, if ever, be a statement from a legislative majority that a certain meaning was intended. (Recall that even preambles, finding clauses, and purpose clauses cannot control the plain meaning of the statute.) Does that mean that legislative history will never be pertinent? If you agree with this statement, consider whether ignoring legislative history gives judges greater freedom to ignore the clear intent of the legislature or prevents judges from giving language a meaning that only a few legislators intended. Can a rule that limits the use of legislative history do either, depending on the judge's goal? Does allowing a judge to interpret ambiguous language contrary to a clear expression of legislative intent contained within the legislative history give the judge more or less power?

Fundamentally, it may be that those who refuse to consider legislative history at all wield greater judicial power to determine meaning. *See Exxon Mobil Corp.*, 545 U.S. at 572 (Stevens, J. and Breyer, J., dissenting) ("I believe that we as judges are more, rather than less, constrained when we make ourselves accountable to *all* reliable evidence of legislative intent.") (emphasis in original). This possibility may explain why some state legislatures have—by statute—required courts to consider legislative history when interpreting statutes.

C. When Legislative History Conflicts

Amid all of these important issues are pressing, but more mundane, questions. How do you, as an attorney, handle conflicting legislative materials? How do you, as an attorney, use legislative history to contradict what appears to be clear statutory language? The case below will help you answer these questions. As you read *Weber*, consider how the majority and dissent used different parts of the legislative history to buttress their interpretations. Note also that their approaches were very different.

United Steelworkers v. Weber
443 U.S. 193 (1979)

JUSTICE BRENNAN delivered the opinion of the Court.

[Kaiser opened its Gramercy, Louisiana plant in 1958. Because the Gramercy facility had no apprenticeship or in-plant craft training program, Kaiser hired as craft workers only persons with prior craft experience. Despite Kaiser's efforts to locate and hire trained black craftsmen, few were available in the Gramercy area, and as a consequence, Kaiser's craft positions were manned almost exclusively by whites. In February 1974, under pressure from the Office of Federal Contract Compliance to increase minority representation in craft positions, and hoping to deter minorities from filing employment discrimination suits, Kaiser made an agreement with the United Steelworkers of America (a labor union), which created a new on-the-job craft training program at several Kaiser facilities including the Gramercy plant. The 1974 collective bargaining agreement required that no less than one minority applicant be admitted to the training program for every non-minority applicant until the percentage of blacks in craft positions equaled the percentage of blacks in the local work force. Eligibility for the craft training programs was to be determined on the basis of plant seniority, with black and white applicants to be selected on the basis of their relative seniority within their racial group.

Brian Weber, a white employee, was hired at Kaiser's Gramercy plant in 1968. In April 1974, Kaiser posted nine positions in three on-the-job training programs for skilled craft jobs. Weber applied for all three programs, but was not selected. Instead, five black and four white applicants were chosen in accordance with the quota in the 1974 collective-bargaining agreement. Two of the successful black applicants had less seniority than Weber. Weber sued, alleging that use of the 50% minority admission quota to fill vacancies in Kaiser's craft training programs violated Title VII, which prohibits racial discrimination in employment.]

---

2. Section 703(a), 78 Stat. 255, as amended, 86 Stat. 109, 42 U.S.C. § 2000e-2(a), provides: (a) ... It shall be an unlawful employment practice for an employer — "(1) to fail or refuse to hire or to discharge any individual, or otherwise to discriminate against any individual with respect to his compensation, terms, conditions, or privileges of employment, because of such individual's race, color, religion, sex, or national origin; or "(2) to limit, segregate, or classify his employees or applicants for employment in any way which would deprive or tend to deprive any individual of employment opportunities or otherwise adversely affect his status as an employee, because of such individual's race, color, religion, sex, or national origin."

3. Section 703(d), 78 Stat. 256, 42 U.S.C. § 2000e-2(d), provides: "It shall be an unlawful employment practice for any employer, labor organization, or joint labor-management committee controlling apprenticeship or other training or retraining, including on-the-job training programs to discriminate against any individual because of his race, color, religion, sex, or national origin in admission to, or employment in, any program established to provide apprenticeship or other training."

The complaint alleged that the ... affirmative action program had resulted in junior black employees' receiving training in preference to senior white employees, thus discriminating against respondent [Weber] and other similarly situated white employees in violation of §§ 703(a)[2] and (d)[3] of Title VII. [The district court and the Court of Appeals agreed, enjoining further use of race as a criterion in admitting applicants to the craft training programs.]

The only question ... is the ... issue of whether Title VII *forbids* private employers and unions from voluntarily agreeing upon bona fide affirmative action plans that accord racial preferences...

Respondent argues that Congress intended in Title VII to prohibit all race-conscious affirmative action plans. Respondent's argument rests upon a literal interpretation of §§ 703(a) and (d) of the Act. Those sections make it unlawful to "discriminate ... because of ... race" in hiring and in the selection of apprentices for training programs. Since ... Title VII forbids discrimination against whites as well as blacks, and since the Kaiser-USWA affirmative action plan operates to discriminate against white employees solely because they are white, it follows that the Kaiser-USWA plan violates Title VII.

Respondent's argument is not without force. But it overlooks the significance of the fact that the Kaiser-USWA plan is an affirmative action plan voluntarily adopted by private parties to eliminate traditional patterns of racial segregation. In this context respondent's reliance upon a literal construction of §§ 703(a) and (d) ... is misplaced. It is a "familiar rule that a thing may be within the letter of the statute and yet not within the statute, because not within its spirit nor within the intention of its makers." *Holy Trinity Church v. U.S.*, 143 U.S. 457, 459 (1892). The prohibition against racial discrimination in §§ 703(a) and (d) of Title VII must therefore be read against the background of the legislative history of Title VII and the historical context from which the Act arose. Examination of those sources makes clear that an interpretation of the sections that forbade all race-conscious affirmative action would "bring about an end completely at variance with the purpose of the statute" and must be rejected.

Congress' primary concern in enacting the prohibition against racial discrimination in Title VII of the Civil Rights Act of 1964 was with "the plight of the Negro in our economy." 110 Cong.Rec. 6548 (1964) (remarks of Sen. Humphrey)....

> The rate of Negro unemployment has gone up consistently as compared with white unemployment for the past 15 years. This is a social malaise and a social situation which we should not tolerate. That is one of the principal reasons why the bill should pass.

Congress feared that the goals of the Civil Rights Act—the integration of blacks into the mainstream of American society—could not be achieved unless this trend were reversed. And Congress recognized that that would not be possible unless blacks were able to secure jobs "which have a future." As Senator Humphrey explained to the Senate: ...

> Without a job, one cannot afford public convenience and accommodations. Income from employment may be necessary to further a man's education, or that of his children. If his children have no hope of getting a good job, what will motivate them to take advantage of educational opportunities? ...

Accordingly, it was clear to Congress that "[t]he crux of the problem [was] to open employment opportunities for Negroes in occupations which have been traditionally closed to them," 10 Cong.Rec. 6548 (1964) (remarks of Sen. Humphrey), and it was to this problem that Title VII's prohibition against racial discrimination in employment was primarily addressed.

It plainly appears from the House Report accompanying the Civil Rights Act that Congress did not intend wholly to prohibit private and voluntary affirmative action efforts as one method of solving this problem. The Report provides:

> No bill can or should lay claim to eliminating all of the causes and consequences of racial and other types of discrimination against minorities. There is reason to believe, however, that national leadership provided by the enactment of Federal legislation dealing with the most troublesome problems *will create an atmosphere conducive to voluntary or local resolution of other forms of discrimination.* H.R.Rep. No. 914, 88th Cong., 1st Sess., pt. 1, p. 18 (1963). (Emphasis supplied.)

Given this legislative history, we cannot agree with respondent that Congress intended to prohibit the private sector from taking effective steps to accomplish the goal that Congress designed Title VII to achieve.... It would be ironic indeed if a law triggered by a Nation's concern over centuries of racial injustice and intended to improve the lot of those who had "been excluded from the American dream for so long," 110 Cong.Rec. 6552 (1964) (remarks of Sen. Humphrey), constituted the first legislative prohibition of all voluntary, private, race-conscious efforts to abolish traditional patterns of racial segregation and hierarchy.

Our conclusion is further reinforced by examination of the language and legislative history of § 703(j) of Title VII.[5] Opponents of Title VII raised two related arguments against the bill. First, they argued that the Act would be interpreted to *require* employers with racially imbalanced work forces to grant preferential treatment to racial minorities in order to integrate. Second, they argued that employers with racially imbalanced work forces would grant preferential treatment to racial minorities, even if not required to do so by the Act. Had Congress meant to prohibit all race-conscious affirmative action ... it easily could have answered both objections by providing that Title VII would not require or *permit* racially preferential integration efforts. But Congress did not choose such a course. Rather, Congress added § 703(j) which addresses only the first objection. The section provides that nothing contained in Title VII "shall be interpreted to *require* any employer ... to grant preferential treatment ... to any group because of the race ... of such ... group on account of" a *de facto* racial imbalance in the employer's work force. The section does *not* state that "nothing in Title VII shall be interpreted to *permit*" voluntary affirmative efforts to correct racial imbalances. The natural inference is that Congress chose not to forbid all voluntary race-conscious affirmative action.

The reasons for this choice are evident from the legislative record. Title VII could not have been enacted into law without substantial support from legislators in both Houses who traditionally resisted federal regulation of private business. Those legislators demanded as a price for their support that "management prerogatives, and union free-

---

5. Section 703(j) of Title VII, 78 Stat. 257, 42 U.S.C. § 2000e-2(j), provides: "Nothing contained in this title shall be interpreted to require any employer ... to grant preferential treatment to any individual or to any group because of the race, color, religion, sex, or national origin of such individual or group on account of an imbalance which may exist with respect to the total number or percentage of persons of any race, color, religion, sex, or national origin employed by any employer ... or employed in, any apprenticeship or other training program, in comparison with the total number or percentage of persons of such race, color, religion, sex, or national origin in any community, State, section, or other area, or in the available work force in any community, State, section, or other area." ...

doms ... be left undisturbed to the greatest extent possible." H.R.Rep. No. 914, 88th Cong., 1st Sess., pt. 2, p. 29 (1963). Section 703(j) was proposed by Senator Dirksen to allay any fears that the Act might be interpreted in such a way as to upset this compromise. The section was designed to prevent § 703 of Title VII from being interpreted in such a way as to lead to undue "Federal Government interference with private businesses because of some Federal employee's ideas about racial balance or racial imbalance." 110 Cong.Rec. 14314 (1964) (remarks of Sen. Miller). *See also id.*, at 9881 (remarks of Sen. Allott); *id.*, at 10520 (remarks of Sen. Carlson); *id.*, at 11471 (remarks of Sen. Javits); *id.*, at 12817 (remarks of Sen. Dirksen). Clearly, a prohibition against all voluntary, race-conscious, affirmative action efforts would disserve these ends. Such a prohibition would augment the powers of the Federal Government and diminish traditional management prerogatives while at the same time impeding attainment of the ultimate statutory goals. In view of this legislative history and in view of Congress' desire to avoid undue federal regulation of private businesses, use of the word "require" rather than the phrase "require or permit" in § 703(j) fortifies the conclusion that Congress did not intend to limit traditional business freedom to such a degree as to prohibit all voluntary, race-conscious affirmative action.

We therefore hold that Title VII's prohibition in §§ 703(a) and (d) against racial discrimination does not condemn all private, voluntary, race-conscious affirmative action plans....

Accordingly, the judgment of the Court of Appeals for the Fifth Circuit is

Reversed.

Justice Rehnquist, with whom The Chief Justice [Justice Burger] joins, dissenting.

Quite simply, Kaiser's racially discriminatory admission quota is flatly prohibited by the plain language of Title VII. This normally dispositive fact, however, gives the Court only momentary pause. An "interpretation" of the statute upholding Weber's claim would, according to the Court, bring about an end completely at variance with the purpose of the statute. To support this conclusion, the Court calls upon the "spirit" of the Act, which it divines from passages in Title VII's legislative history indicating that enactment of the statute was prompted by Congress' desire "'to open employment opportunities for Negroes in occupations which [had] been traditionally closed to them.'" But the legislative history invoked by the Court to avoid the plain language of §§ 703(a) and (d) simply misses the point. To be sure, the reality of employment discrimination against Negroes provided the primary impetus for passage of Title VII. But this fact by no means supports the proposition that Congress intended to leave employers free to discriminate against white persons. In most cases, legislative history ... is more vague than the statute we are called upon to interpret. Here, however, the legislative history of Title VII is as clear as the language of §§ 703(a) and (d), and it irrefutably demonstrates that Congress meant precisely what it said in §§ 703(a) and (d)—that *no* racial discrimination in employment is permissible under Title VII, not even preferential treatment of minorities to correct racial imbalance....

Introduced on the floor of the House of Representatives on June 20, 1963, the bill—H.R. 7152—that ultimately became the Civil Rights Act of 1964 contained no compulsory provisions directed at private discrimination in employment. The bill was promptly referred to the Committee on the Judiciary, where it was amended to include Title VII. With two exceptions, the bill reported by the House Judiciary Committee contained §§ 703(a) and (d) as they were ultimately enacted....

After noting that "[t]he purpose of [Title VII] is to eliminate ... discrimination in employment based on race, color, religion, or national origin," the Judiciary Committee's

Report simply paraphrased the provisions of Title VII without elaboration. In a separate Minority Report, however, opponents of the measure on the Committee advanced a line of attack which was reiterated throughout the debates in both the House and Senate and which ultimately led to passage of §703(j). Noting that the word "discrimination" was nowhere defined in H.R.7152, the Minority Report charged that the absence from Title VII of any reference to "racial imbalance" was a "public relations" ruse and that "the administration intends to rely upon its own construction of 'discrimination' as including the lack of racial balance...." To demonstrate how the bill would operate in practice, the Minority Report posited a number of hypothetical employment situations, concluding in each example that the employer "*may be forced to hire according to race*, to 'racially balance' those who work for him *in every job classification* or be in violation of Federal law."

When H.R. 7152 reached the House floor, the opening speech in support of its passage was delivered by Representative Celler, Chairman of the House Judiciary Committee and the Congressman responsible for introducing the legislation. A portion of that speech responded to criticism "seriously misrepresent[ing] what the bill would do and grossly distort[ing] its effects":

> [T]he charge has been made that the Equal Employment Opportunity Commission to be established by title VII of the bill would have the power to prevent a business from employing and promoting the people it wished, and that a 'Federal inspector' could then order the hiring and promotion only of employees of certain races or religious groups. This description of the bill is entirely wrong....
>
> Even [a] court could not order that any preference be given to any particular race, religion or other group, but would be limited to ordering an end of discrimination. The statement that a Federal inspector could order the employment and promotion only of members of a specific racial or religious group is therefore patently erroneous....
>
> The Bill would do no more than prevent ... employers from discriminating against *or in favor* of workers because of their race, religion, or national origin.
>
> It is likewise not true that the Equal Employment Opportunity Commission would have power to rectify existing 'racial or religious imbalance' in employment by requiring the hiring of certain people without regard to their qualifications simply because they are of a given race or religion. Only actual discrimination could be stopped. (Emphasis added).

Representative Celler's construction of Title VII was repeated by several other supporters during the House debate.

Thus, the battle lines were drawn early in the legislative struggle over Title VII, with opponents of the measure charging that agencies of the Federal Government such as the Equal Employment Opportunity Commission (EEOC), by interpreting the word "discrimination" to mean the existence of "racial imbalance," would "require" employers to grant preferential treatment to minorities, and supporters responding that the EEOC would be granted no such power and that, indeed, Title VII prohibits discrimination "in favor of workers because of their race." Supporters of H.R. 7152 in the House ultimately prevailed by a vote of 290 to 130, and the measure was sent to the Senate to begin what became the longest debate in that body's history.

The Senate debate was broken into three phases: the debate on sending the bill to Committee, the general debate on the bill prior to invocation of cloture, and the debate following cloture.

When debate on the motion to refer the bill to Committee opened, opponents of Title VII in the Senate immediately echoed the fears expressed by their counterparts in the House....

[For example], Senator Robertson [said]:

> It is contemplated by this title that the percentage of colored and white population in a community shall be in similar percentages in every business establishment that employs over 25 persons. Thus, if there were 10,000 colored persons in a city and 15,000 whites, an employer with 25 employees would, in order to overcome racial imbalance, be required to have 10 colored personnel and 15 white. And if by chance that employer had 20 colored employees, he would have to fire 10 of them in order to rectify the situation. Of course, this works the other way around where whites would be fired.

Senator Humphrey interrupted Senator Robertson's discussion, responding: "The bill does not require that at all. If it did, I would vote against it.... There is no percentage quota."

Senator Humphrey, perhaps the primary moving force behind H.R. 7152 in the Senate, was the first to state the proponents' understanding of Title VII. Responding to a political advertisement charging that federal agencies were at liberty to interpret the word "discrimination" in Title VII to require racial balance, Senator Humphrey stated: "[T]he meaning of racial or religious discrimination is perfectly clear.... [I]t means a distinction in treatment given to different individuals because of their different race, religion, or national origin." Stressing that Title VII "does not limit the employer's freedom to hire, fire, promote or demote for any reasons—or no reasons—so long as his action is not based on race," Senator Humphrey further stated that "nothing in the bill would permit any official or court to require any employer or labor union to give preferential treatment to any minority group." ...

In the opening speech of the formal Senate debate on the bill, Senator Humphrey addressed the main concern of Title VII's opponents, advising that not only does Title VII not require use of racial quotas, *it does not permit* their use. "The truth," stated the floor leader of the bill, "is that this title forbids discriminating against anyone on account of race. This is the simple and complete truth about title VII." Senator Humphrey continued:

> Contrary to the allegations of some opponents of this title, there is nothing in it that will give any power to the Commission or to any court to require hiring, firing, or promotion of employees in order to meet a racial 'quota' or to achieve a certain racial balance.
>
> That bugaboo has been brought up a dozen times; but it is nonexistent. In fact, *the very opposite is true. Title VII prohibits discrimination.* In effect, it says that race, religion and national origin are not to be used as the basis for hiring and firing....

Senator Kuchel delivered the second major speech in support of H.R. 7152. In addressing the concerns of the opposition, he observed that "[n]othing could be further from the truth" than the charge that "Federal inspectors" would be empowered under Title VII to dictate racial balance and preferential advancement of minorities. Senator Kuchel emphasized that seniority rights would in no way be affected by Title VII: "Employers and labor organizations could not discriminate *in favor of or against* a person because of his race, his religion, or his national origin. In such matters ... The bill now before us ... is color-blind."

A few days later the Senate's attention focused exclusively on Title VII.... Senators Clark and Case took pains to refute the opposition's charge that Title VII would result in preferential treatment of minorities. Their words were clear and unequivocal:

> There is no requirement in title VII that an employer maintain a racial balance in his work force. On the contrary, any deliberate attempt to maintain a racial balance, whatever such a balance may be, would involve a violation of title VII because maintaining such a balance would require an employer to hire or to refuse to hire on the basis of race. It must be emphasized that discrimination is prohibited as to any individual.

Of particular relevance to the instant litigation were their observations regarding seniority rights. As if directing their comments at Brian Weber, the Senators said:

> Title VII would have no effect on established seniority rights. Its effect is prospective and not retrospective. Thus, for example, if a business has been discriminating in the past and as a result has an all-white working force, when the title comes into effect the employer's obligation would be simply to fill future vacancies on a nondiscriminatory basis. He would not be obliged—*or indeed permitted*—to fire whites in order to hire Negroes, *or to prefer Negroes for future vacancies, or, once Negroes are hired, to give them special seniority rights at the expense of the white workers hired earlier.*

Thus, with virtual clairvoyance the Senate's leading supporters of Title VII anticipated precisely the circumstances of this case and advised their colleagues that the type of minority preference employed by Kaiser would violate Title VII's ban on racial discrimination. To further accentuate the point, Senator Clark introduced another memorandum dealing with common criticisms of the bill, including the charge that racial quotas would be imposed under Title VII. The answer was simple and to the point: "Quotas are themselves discriminatory."

Despite these clear statements from the bill's leading and most knowledgeable proponents, the fears of the opponents were not put to rest. Senator Robertson reiterated the view that "discrimination" could be interpreted by a federal "bureaucrat" to require hiring quotas. Senators Smathers and Sparkman, while conceding that Title VII does not in so many words require the use of hiring quotas, repeated the opposition's view that employers would be coerced to grant preferential hiring treatment to minorities by agencies of the Federal Government. Senator Williams was quick to respond:

> Those opposed to H.R. 7152 should realize that to hire a Negro solely because he is a Negro is racial discrimination, just as much as a 'white only' employment policy. Both forms of discrimination are prohibited by title VII of this bill. The language of that title simply states that race is not a qualification for employment.... Some people charge that H.R. 7152 favors the Negro, at the expense of the white majority. But how can the language of equality favor one race or one religion over another? Equality can have only one meaning, and that meaning is self-evident to reasonable men. Those who say that equality means favoritism do violence to common sense....

On May 25, Senator Humphrey again took the floor to defend the bill.... Turning once again to the issue of preferential treatment, Senator Humphrey remained faithful to the view that he had repeatedly expressed:

> The title does not provide that any preferential treatment in employment shall be given to Negroes or to any other persons or groups. It does not provide that

any quota systems may be established to maintain racial balance in employment. In fact, *the title would prohibit preferential treatment for any particular group*, and any person, whether or not a member of any minority group would be permitted to file a complaint of discriminatory employment practices."

While the debate in the Senate raged, a bipartisan coalition under the leadership of Senators Dirksen, Mansfield, Humphrey, and Kuchel was working with House leaders ... and on a number of amendments to H.R. 7152.... The substitute bill, which ultimately became law, left unchanged the basic prohibitory language of §§ 703(a) and (d).... It added ... § 703(j), [which] was specifically directed at the opposition's concerns regarding racial balancing and preferential treatment of minorities, providing in pertinent part: "Nothing contained in [Title VII] shall be interpreted to require any employer ... to grant preferential treatment to any individual or to any group because of the race ... of such individual or group on account of" a racial imbalance in the employer's work force.

The Court draws from the language of § 703(j) primary support for its conclusion that Title VII's blanket prohibition on racial discrimination in employment does not prohibit preferential treatment of blacks to correct racial imbalance....

Contrary to the Court's analysis, the language of § 703(j) is precisely tailored to the objection voiced time and again by Title VII's opponents. Not once during the 83 days of debate in the Senate did a speaker, proponent or opponent, suggest that the bill would allow employers *voluntarily* to prefer racial minorities over white persons. In light of Title VII's flat prohibition on discrimination "against any individual ... because of such individual's race," ... such a contention would have been, in any event, too preposterous to warrant response. Indeed, speakers on both sides of the issue ... recognized that Title VII would tolerate no *voluntary* racial preference, whether in favor of blacks or whites. The complaint consistently voiced by the opponents was that Title VII, particularly the word "discrimination," would be *interpreted* by federal agencies such as the EEOC to *require* the correction of racial imbalance through the granting of preferential treatment to minorities. Verbal assurances that Title VII would not require—indeed, would not permit—preferential treatment of blacks having failed, supporters of H.R. 7152 responded by proposing an amendment carefully worded to meet, and put to rest, the opposition's charge. Indeed, unlike §§ 703(a) and (d), which are by their terms directed at entities— ... the language of § 703(j) is specifically directed at entities—federal agencies and courts—charged with the responsibility of interpreting Title VII's provisions....

Section 703(j) apparently calmed the fears of most of the opponents; after its introduction, complaints concerning racial balance and preferential treatment died down considerably....

Reading the language of Title VII, as the Court purports to do, "against the background of [its] legislative history ... and the historical context from which the Act arose," one is led inescapably to the conclusion that Congress fully understood what it was saying and meant precisely what it said. Opponents of the civil rights bill did not argue that employers would be permitted under Title VII voluntarily to grant preferential treatment to minorities to correct racial imbalance. The plain language of the statute too clearly prohibited such racial discrimination to admit of any doubt. They argued, tirelessly, that Title VII would be interpreted by federal agencies and their agents to require unwilling employers to racially balance their work forces by granting preferential treatment to minorities. Supporters of H.R. 7152 responded, equally tirelessly, that the Act would not be so interpreted because not only does it not require preferential treatment of minorities, it also does not *permit* preferential treatment of any race for any reason. It cannot be doubted that the proponents of Title VII understood the meaning of their words, for seldom has similar legislation been debated with greater consciousness of the need for 'legislative history,' or with greater care in the making thereof, to guide the courts in interpreting and applying the law.

To put an end to the dispute, supporters of the civil rights bill drafted and introduced § 703(j). Specifically addressed to the opposition's charge, § 703(j) simply enjoins federal agencies and courts from interpreting Title VII to require an employer to prefer certain racial groups to correct imbalances in his work force. The section says nothing about voluntary preferential treatment of minorities because such racial discrimination is plainly proscribed by §§ 703(a) and (d). Indeed, had Congress intended to except voluntary, race-conscious preferential treatment from the blanket prohibition of racial discrimination in §§ 703(a) and (d), it surely could have drafted language better suited to the task than § 703(j). It knew how....

Our task in this case, like any other case involving the construction of a statute, is to give effect to the intent of Congress. To divine that intent, we traditionally look first to the words of the statute and, if they are unclear, then to the statute's legislative history. Finding the desired result hopelessly foreclosed by these conventional sources, the Court turns to a third source — the "spirit" of the Act. But close examination of what the Court proffers as the spirit of the Act reveals it as the spirit animating the present majority, not the 88th Congress. For if the spirit of the Act eludes the cold words of the statute itself, it rings out with unmistakable clarity in the words of the elected representatives who made the Act law. It is *equality*....

In passing Title VII, Congress outlawed *all* racial discrimination, recognizing that no discrimination based on race is benign, that no action disadvantaging a person because of his color is affirmative. With today's holding, the Court introduces into Title VII a tolerance for the very evil that the law was intended to eradicate, without offering even a clue as to what the limits on that tolerance may be.... By going not merely *beyond*, but directly *against* Title VII's language and legislative history, the Court has sown the wind. Later courts will face the impossible task of reaping the whirlwind.

Notes and Questions

(1) *Which Approach?* Which approach to interpretation did the majority use? The dissent? How did they use legislative history differently to further the goals of their approaches? Which canons did the majority use? Do you find these canons compel or merely suggest a particular interpretation?

(2) *The Plain Meaning Rule.* Do you think that when the statute was adopted the ordinary meaning of the word "discriminate" included affirmatively helping minorities to counterbalance the effects of past discrimination? Justice Brennan thought not, while Justice Rehnquist might disagree when that "discrimination" negatively affected non-minorities. Who do you believe was right? Should the meaning of words at the time of enactment be more important than the meaning of words at the time of interpretation? How would adherents of the different approaches answer this question?

(3) *Did the Majority Reach a Desired Result, Further Statutory Purpose, Both, or Neither?* In dissent, Justice Burger wrote: "It is often observed that hard cases make bad law. I suspect there is some truth to that adage, for the 'hard' cases always tempt judges to exceed the limits of their authority, as the court does today by totally rewriting a crucial part of

Title VII to reach a 'desirable' result." *Weber*, 443 U.S. at 218 (Burger, J., dissenting). Justice Burger continued:

> Oddly, the Court seizes upon the very clarity of the Statute almost as a justification for evading the unavoidable impact of its language. The Court blandly tells us that Congress could not really have meant what it said, for a literal construction would defeat the "purpose" of the statute—at least the Congressional "purpose" as five Justices divine it today.

Id. at 216. Should a court ignore statutory language that is clear if it is equally clear that the legislative history shows that legislature did not intend the result mandated by the clear language? Would the different approaches have different answers to that question?

(4) *Evaluate* Weber. Assume that you had represented Weber in his case against Kaiser. What do you think would have been your strongest argument? Which approach to statutory interpretation would allow you to make that argument? Now assume instead that you represented Kaiser. How would you have responded to the arguments made by Weber's attorney, including those regarding the legislative history?

(5) *Evidence of Legislative Intent.* Would an affidavit from a legislator that a particular meaning was intended be relevant? Generally no:

> [v]iews of individuals involved with the legislative process as to intent [are of] no assistance ... for two reasons: (1) it is the intent of the legislative body that is sought, not the intent of the individual members who may have diverse reasons for or against a proposition and (2) it is "universally held" that "evidence of a ... draftsman of a statute is not a competent aid to a court in construing a statute."

Am. Meat Inst. v. Barnett, 64 F. Supp. 2d 906, 916 (D. S.D. 1999) (quoting *S.D.E.A. v. Barnett*, 582 N.W.2d 386, 400 (D. S.D. 1998) (Zinter, J., concurring in part and dissenting in part)).

(6) *Intentionalism v. Purposivism.* As we've seen, legislative intent and statutory purpose are not the same. When seeking to determine legislative intent, judges consider what the legislature intended the answer to be to the particular question under consideration. One way that judges determine intent is by analyzing the legislative history for statements made by legislators that may shed light on the meaning of the text at issue. In contrast, when determining statutory purpose, judges consider the general goal (*i.e.*, purpose) of the statute and give an interpretation to the text that best effectuates that goal. The legislature may or may not have discussed the particular question during the legislative process. With respect to *Weber*, what do you think the legislative intent behind Title VII was? The purpose?

(7) *Imaginative Reconstructionism.* Dean Roscoe Pound suggested that judges should follow the intent of the enacting legislature; however, he admitted that the intent is often difficult to discern. He suggested that when there is clear evidence of the specific intent of the enacting legislature, courts should follow that intent. But because evidence of specific intent is often lacking, courts must usually "imaginatively reconstruct" the legislative intent. To do this, the judge should examine the available historical evidence against a sense of morality and justice to determine what the enacting legislature likely would have intended. Note that, under this approach, the text of the statute is often the best evidence of what the legislature would have intended. Roscoe Pound, *Spurious Interpretation*, 7 COLUM. L. REV. 379, 381 (1907). Does this approach appeal to you?

(8) *The Dog Didn't Bark Canon.* "Silence in the legislative history about a particular provision ordinarily is not a good guide to statutory interpretation and certainly is not more persuasive than the words of a statute." *Am. Online, Inc. v. United States*, 64 Fed. Cl. 571,

578 (2005). However, silence can sometimes be illuminating. Suppose, for example, a statute on its face makes a radical and controversial change in the law—one that you would expect would have been discussed and debated. Yet, the record is silent. Under those circumstances, wouldn't silence speak volumes?

(9) *Returning to the Continuum.* We suggested earlier that there is a continuum of circumstances in which legislative history can be used. On the most *unrestrictive* end, judges should always use legislative history as a source, whether the text is ambiguous or not. On the most *restrictive* end of the continuum, judges should never consult legislative history. Having read this chapter, when do you think it is appropriate to use legislative history? In other words, where do you fall on the continuum?

Problem 8-2

You represent Newhouse, Inc. (the lessee). In March 1997, Newhouse agreed to lease two trucks from Bacon Trucks & Equipment, Inc. (the lessor). On September 20, 1999, Newhouse terminated the lease. On February 13, 2002, Bacon filed a breach of contract suit (under state law) and also asserted claims under the Federal Truth-in-Leasing Regulations, 49 U.S.C. § 14704(a)(2), against Newhouse. Bacon asserts that Newhouse violated the provisions of the act relating to payment of money and provision of documents. The issue is whether the suit is timely.

Newhouse asserts that the statute in question contains a scrivener's error in that Congress intended 49 U.S.C. § 14704(a)(2) to have been enacted as 49 U.S.C. § 14704(b). A two-year statute of limitations in 49 U.S.C. § 14705(c) applies to 49 U.S.C. § 14704(b) generally. Under this two-year statute of limitations, Bacon's claims are time-barred.

Bacon contends that the applicable statute of limitations period is four years because in the absence of a specified limitations period within a statute—49 U.S.C. § 14704(a)(2) has none—pursuant to 28 U.S.C. § 1658(a) the statute of limitations is four years

Bacon's attorney has called you to offer a settlement. In advising your client on whether to accept the offer, use the materials below to assess the likelihood that a court would find that the two-year statute of limitations applies.

Assume that prior to the passage of the ICC Termination Act, the statute of limitations for a claim seeking damages against a common carrier under the Interstate Commerce Act was two years.

Additionally, assume that the ICC Termination Act contains parallel provisions governing rail carriers and that the two-year statute of limitations has been held to apply to them. *Engelhard Corp. v. Springfield Terminal Ry. Co.*, 193 F. Supp. 2d 385, 390 (D. Mass. 2002).

Problem Materials

26 U.S.C. § 1658:

> (a) Except as otherwise provided by law, a civil action arising under an Act of Congress enacted after the date of the enactment of this section may not be commenced later than 4 years after the cause of action accrues.

49 U.S.C.A. § 14704

> (a) In general.—...

(2) Damages for violations.—A carrier or broker providing transportation or service ... is liable for damages sustained by a person as a result of an act or omission of that carrier or broker in violation of this [statute].

(b) Liability and damages for exceeding tariff rate.—A carrier providing transportation or service subject to jurisdiction under [this Act] is liable to a person for amounts charged that exceed the applicable rate for transportation or service contained in a tariff in effect under section 13702.

49 U.S.C.A. § 14705:

(c) Damages.—A person must file a complaint ... to recover damages under section 14704(b) within 2 years after the claim accrues.

Legislative History

In 1995, Congress passed the Interstate Commerce Commission Termination Act (ICC Termination Act), Pub. L. No. 104-88, 109 Stat. 803 (1995), which furthered the deregulation of the rail and motor carrier industries and abolished the Interstate Commerce Commission. H.R. Rep. No. 311, 104th Cong., 1st Sess. 82–83 (1995), reprinted in 1995 U.S.C.C.A.N. 793–94.

During debate on the proposed bill, Congressman Nadler commented on the haste in which the bill was presented.

I need to express my dismay with the process and the haste with which this bill was brought before us. As a member of the Committee on Transportation and Infrastructure, we received a 280-page bill on Thursday night and were asked to review, evaluate, and vote on amendments in 4 days; 4 days to determine how we were going to restructure a body of law that had taken 100 years to develop.

141 Cong. Rec. H. 12248, 12259 (Nov. 14, 1995) (statement of Cong. Nadler).

The current § 14704(a)(2) was originally drafted as § 14704(b)(2). Thus, both the House of Representatives and Senate bills *as originally drafted* authorized a two-year statute of limitations for private actions, which was (and remains) in § 14705(c). H.R. 2539, 104th Cong. (1995); S. 1396, 104th Cong. (1995). Originally, the statute of limitations provision contained in § 14705(c) of the original House of Representatives and Senate versions of the bill specifically referred to § 14704(b)(2). H.R. 2539 ("A person must file a complaint ... to recover damages under section 14704(b)(2) of this title within 2 years after the claim accrues.") (version dated October 27, 1995); S. 1396 ("A person must file a complaint ... to recover damages under section 14704(b)(2) of this title within 2 years after the claim accrues.") (version dated November 6, 1995).

The House of Representatives amended its version of § 14704 after debate on the floor. The record of the debate in the House of Representatives indicates that the amendment to § 14704, in which § 14704(b)(2) became the current § 14704(a)(2), was included along with a larger group of changes to other sections of the statute. This amendment became known as the Whitfield Amendment and mainly dealt with railroad mergers and railroad employees. 141 Cong. Rec. H. 12248, 12253–12307 (Nov. 14, 1995). The Congressional Record is silent regarding the relocation of § 14704(b)(2) to § 14704(a)(2). The amendment to § 14704 did not actually alter the text; it merely moved one sentence to a new location.

The House failed to simultaneously amend § 14705(c) to reflect the change to § 14704(b). Thus, after the Whitfield Amendment to the bill was adopted by the House of Representatives—and thus § 14704(b)(2) was relocated to § 14704(a)(2)—the statute of limitations provision in § 14705(c) continued to refer to the non-existent § 14704(b)(2). H.R.

2359 (version dated November 15, 1995). The statute of limitations provision of § 14705(c) continued to contain a reference to the non-existent § 14704(b)(2) in later versions of the House of Representatives bill as well. H.R. 2359 (version dated November 30, 1995; version dated December 5, 1995). In the final version of the bill signed by the President, the reference in § 14705(c) to the non-existent § 14704(b)(2) was eliminated such that § 14705(c) as enacted refers to § 14704(b) not § 14704(b)(2).

Before the Bill was sent to the President, the House and Senate versions had to be reconciled — for differences not related to this section, — so the Bill went to Conference Committee. The Conference Committee recommended adoption of the House version and issued a report. H.R. Conf. Rep. No. 104-422, at 221–222 (1995), reprinted in 1995 U.S.C.C.A.N. 850, 906–907. The relevant parts of that report are excerpted below:

Conference Report No. 104-422
December 18, 1995

The committee of conference on the disagreeing votes of the two Houses on the amendment of the Senate to the bill (H.R. 2539), to abolish the Interstate Commerce Commission, to amend subtitle IV of title 49, United States Code, to reform economic regulation of transportation, and for other purposes, having met, after full and free conference, have agreed to recommend and do recommend to their respective Houses as follows:

SECTION 1. SHORT TITLE; TABLE OF CONTENTS.

(a) Short Title. — This Act may be cited as the "ICC Termination Act of 1995"....

LIMITATIONS ON ACTIONS

House bill

Sec. 14705. Limitation on actions by and against carriers. This section preserves the current relevant statutes of limitations for bringing court suits by or against carriers and makes the time limits uniform for all types of traffic.

Senate Amendment

The Senate amendment contains an identical provision.

Conference Committee Conclusion:

The Conference adopts the provision.

Chapter 9

The Relevance of Post-Interpretave Legislative Silence

As we have seen, courts frequently interpret statutes. Perhaps surprisingly, silence is the most common legislative reaction to judicial interpretation of a statute. This chapter addresses what meaning, if any, courts should ascribe to legislative silence after a court has interpreted a statute. For example, if lawyers in a subsequent case argue that the initial judicial interpretation was wrong, is there any reason for the judge in a subsequent case to infer from the legislature's silence in the interim that the court's initial interpretation was right?

On the one hand, subsequent legislative silence arguably shows "acquiescence" by the legislative branch to an interpretation previously given the statute by a court. "When a court says to a legislature: 'You (or your predecessor) meant X,' it almost invites the legislature to answer: 'We did not.'" Guido Calabresi, A Common Law for the Age of Statutes 31–32 (1982). The assumption that legislative silence means acquiescence encourages those interested (legislators, lobbyists, and others) in a particular issue to follow judicial interpretations and to seek legislative correction of unintended or incorrect interpretations. If legislators know that their inaction will be construed to constitute acquiescence, they'll move—at least in theory—to legislatively overturn incorrect interpretations. Also, if in fact the court is "wrong" in its interpretation, the presumption will encourage prompt legislative correction.

On the other hand, silence can mean many things: the legislature may be content with the interpretation; the legislature may be busy with more pressing legislation; the legislature may be aware of the interpretation, believe it to be wrong, but be unable to reach a consensus on what the "correction" should be; or, and perhaps most likely, the legislature may be unaware of the interpretation. *See id.* The legislature may be unaware of the interpretation even if the court, when it interpreted the statute, specifically invited the legislature to reaffirm or reject its interpretation. Further, "getting a statute enacted is much easier than getting it revised." *Id.* at 6. Recognizing the practicalities, one justice observed:

> [T]he idea cannot always be accepted that Congress, by remaining silent and taking no affirmative action in repudiation, gives approval to judicial misconstruction of its enactments. It is perhaps too late now to deny that, legislatively speaking as in ordinary life, silence in some instances may give consent. But it would be going even farther beyond reason and common experience to maintain, as there are signs we may be by way of doing, that in legislation any more than in other affairs silence or nonaction always is acquiescence equivalent to action.

There are vast differences between legislating by doing nothing and legislating by positive enactment, both in the processes by which the will of Congress is derived and stated and in the clarity and certainty of the expression of its will. And there are many reasons, other than to indicate approval of what the courts have done, why Congress may fail to take affirmative action to repudiate their misconstruction of its duly adopted laws. Among them may be the sheer pressure of other and more important business. At times political considerations may work to forbid taking corrective action. And in such cases, as well as others, there may be a strong and proper tendency to trust to [sic] the courts to correct their own errors, as they ought to do when experience has confirmed or demonstrated the errors' existence....

More often than not the only safe assumption to make from Congress' inaction is simply that Congress does not intend to act at all. At best the contrary view can be only an inference, altogether lacking in the normal evidences of legislative intent and often subject to varying views of that intent. *In short, although recognizing that by silence Congress at times may be taken to acquiesce and thus approve, we should be very sure that, under all the circumstances of a given situation, it has done so before we so rule and thus at once relieve ourselves from and shift to it the burden of correcting what we have done wrongly....* Just as dubious legislative history is at times much overridden, so also is silence or inaction often mistaken for legislation.

Cleveland v. United States, 329 U.S. 14, 22–24 (1946) (Rutledge, J., concurring) (emphasis added). For all these reasons, many contend that too much is read into legislative silence and that courts find acquiescence too quickly. *See, e.g., Butterbaugh v. U.S. Dep't of Justice*, 336 F.3d 1332, 1342 (Fed. Cir. 2003) ("[C]ongressional inaction is perhaps the weakest of all tools for ascertaining legislative intent, and courts are loath to presume congressional endorsement unless the issue plainly has been the subject of congressional attention."). Yet, lawyers must understand how and when to rely on or refute reliance on silence.

A. Legislative Inaction Following Judicial Interpretation

There's a lot more to silence than may be obvious. The meaning, if any, that judges ascribe to legislative silence implicates both the principle of separation of powers and the doctrine of *stare decisis*.

First, giving meaning to legislative silence implicates separation of powers. In statutory interpretation cases, should a court be more reluctant to overrule a prior interpretation of a statute, as opposed to the common law? Some judges believe that the legislature's silence indicates its adoption of the prior decision; thus, if a court overrules the initial decision, then the court is, in essence, rejecting a legislative act. However, critics of this argument say that ascribing meaning to silence ignores the fact that silence "lacks all the supporting evidences of legislation enacted pursuant to prescribed procedures, including reduction of bills to writing, committee reports, debates, and reduction to final written form, as well as voting records and executive approval." *Cleveland*, 329 U.S. at 22 n.5. Isn't this observation accurate? How can judges be sure why a legislature has not acted? Is it harder to determine the basis for inaction than to determine the basis for action? If so, why should courts be more reluctant to overrule a prior interpretation after silence?

Second, giving meaning to legislative silence implicates *stare decisis*, which requires that prior judicial decisions be followed and not be overruled, absent compelling reasons. This doctrine fosters predictability, furthers the goal of treating like-cases in the same way, and reduces litigation and other social costs. On occasion, of course, courts recognize that a prior decision was incorrect and overrule it. While generally courts should overrule prior decisions that are clearly wrong, it makes a difference when the prior decision interpreted a *statute* and Congress remained silent despite knowing of the erroneous interpretation. Generally, courts apply a "super strong" *stare decisis* rule to statutory interpretation cases: Absent compelling evidence that the initial interpretation was wrong, courts are very reluctant to overrule it. The following law review excerpt from Professor Lawrence Marshall explores the basis for heightened scrutiny in this area and recommends an absolute bar to restore legislative supremacy.

"Let Congress Do It": The Case for an Absolute Rule of Statutory Stare Decisis

88 Mich. L. Rev. 177 (1989)*
Lawrence C. Marshall

The sporadic way that various members of the Supreme Court and the legal community treat the principle of stare decisis is increasingly striking.... In some respects, these problems are inevitable in a system that attempts delicately to balance the stability of the law with the obvious need occasionally to overrule some pernicious precedents.... [For this reason,] the Supreme Court has repeatedly demonstrated its willingness to overrule decisions construing the Constitution....

When the precedent in question involves an issue of statutory interpretation, as opposed to constitutional interpretation, however, the Court has traditionally articulated and followed a different approach. The flip side of the Court's readiness to overrule constitutional precedents has been its general reticence to overrule precedents construing statutes.... *Flood v. Kuhn* is [a] notable example of the Court's hesitance to overrule statutory precedents. The Court's asserted justification for not extending antitrust principles to professional baseball, and therefore treating baseball differently from football, basketball, and other professional leagues, was the existence of two precedents—one from the 1920s and one from 1950s—that Congress had never reversed through legislation. In recent times, the Court frequently has relied on a heightened rule of statutory stare decisis to explain why it declined to overrule a statutory precedent.... Although there are also a great many cases where the Court appears to ignore this doctrine, the rule continues to be invoked frequently, and appears to exert substantial weight with some members of the Court....

The conventional explanation for the heightened role of stare decisis in statutory cases is that congressional failure to enact legislation reversing a judicial decision indicates Congress' approval of the Court's interpretation of an earlier statute. As the Court recently expressed it, "When a court says to a legislature: 'You (or your predecessor) meant X,' it almost invites the legislature to answer: 'We did not.'" This argument has often appeared in Supreme Court decisions and dissents, although for just about "every case where the Court rhapsodizes about deliberative inaction, there is a counter-case subjecting such inferences to scathing critique."... [I]t is worth noting that some of the Court's apparently conflicting rulings on the subject of acquiescence can be harmonized by taking into account the Court's assessment of the probability that members of Congress were actually

---

* Copyright Lawrence C. Marshall, Professor. Used by permission. *Reprinted from* Michigan Law Review, December 1989, Vo. 88, No.2.

aware of the decision in question. The great majority of cases invoking a strong rule of statutory stare decisis have either pointed to actual evidence that members of Congress were aware of the earlier decision, or have presumed that the matter decided was so newsworthy that it is inconceivable that Congress was unaware of it.

The notion of silent acquiescence has long been condemned as based on unrealistic and irrelevant assumptions about the legislative process[: including] ignorance, inertia, interpretational ambiguity, and irrelevance....

One obvious problem with interpreting Congress' inaction as evidence of congressional acquiescence is that members of Congress are often unaware of Supreme Court decisions, particularly on relatively obscure issues...."In fact, most Supreme Court decisions never come to the attention of Congress." This may not have been a major problem many years ago, when the Court began to talk about silent acquiescence. "Life was simpler then." The number of statutes being interpreted was small as compared with the post-New Deal age. Today, however, it seems quite unrealistic to assume that a substantial number of congressional actors are routinely made aware of most court decisions on statutory matters. This being the case, how can a court possibly find acquiescence in Congress' silence? ...

The Court's response to the possibility that Congress' silence was a result of ignorance rather than considered acquiescence has been to attribute more significance to inaction when there is some evidence, or at least strong reason to believe, that a large number of members of Congress were made aware of the decision. This methodology has serious flaws, however. To begin with, it assumes that just because a speech is made or a bill is proposed, a great many members of Congress are aware of the issue. There is no evidence that this is true, and strong reason to believe it is not. In the absence of an actual vote by an entire body, it seems unrealistic to assume that members of Congress are made more knowledgeable about a decision simply because some committee holds hearing or some members make speeches about it.

Moreover, the Court's incremental approach can lead to perverse results. If there has been complete congressional silence on an issue, the Court is likely to attribute only minimal significance to Congress' inaction, at least as long as it is not convinced that members of Congress must have known about the decision. It is possible, however, that Congress' complete silence might actually indicate unanimous agreement with the decision—a factor that would be expected to command substantial respect from a Court looking for evidence of acquiescence. On the other hand, if a large group of senators sponsor an amendment to overrule a decision, and that amendment is never passed, the Court is likely to attribute great significance to Congress' inaction. Unanimous agreement with a decision may thus command less respect from the Court than a sharply divided Congress' failure to overrule a precedent. This paradox can create a strong disincentive for legislators to do what legislators should do when they want to express their intent— attempt to pass laws....

The possibility of ignorance is not the only, or necessarily the most severe, problem of interpreting congressional inaction. Varied explanations of legislative inaction apply even to a Congress full of legislators who are acutely aware of, and strongly disagree with, a court decision construing an act of Congress. For example, as Hart and Sacks suggest, a legislator who believes that a decision should be overruled might decline to support legislation overruling the decision because of a "[b]elief that other measures have a stronger claim on the limited time and energy of the [legislative] body." [Or] "[b]elief that the bill is sound in principle but politically inexpedient to be connected with"; "[u]nwillingness to have the bill's sponsors get credits for its enactment"; "[b]elief that the bill is sound in principle but defective in material particulars"; or "[t]entative approval, but belief that action should be withheld until the problem can be attacked on a broader front"....

In sum, besides the possibility of "unawareness," "[c]ongressional inaction frequently betokens ... preoccupation[] or paralysis." That a bill was never introduced, died in committee, or was defeated in a vote therefore fails to identify the intent of Congress. The point here is not that inaction is wholly non-probative of legislative intent; as a matter of logic it is relevant. But this logical relevance does not demonstrate that the probability of congressional agreement is sufficient to support any form of a presumption of congressional acquiescence.

... But even if one ignores concerns of ignorance and inertia, or dismisses them as part of the political process, it remains difficult to construe Congress' inaction as acquiescence. For how is the Court to define what Congress intended to acquiesce to? Did Congress agree with the Court's decision? Or did it simply agree that the Courts should be accorded considerable flexibility in interpreting the statute? ...

Much as Congress has delegated the job of formulating rules of procedures to the courts, it might plausibly be unwilling to interfere with judicial constructions of specific jurisdictional statutes. The mere fact of congressional inaction does not give the court any guidance as to which of these significantly divergent messages Congress has sent.

Ultimately, the most significant problem facing the silent acquiescence argument is its inconsistency with the Court's own theory of statutory interpretation, that "[i]t is the intent of the Congress that enacted" the statute in question "that controls." [T]he Court has adhered to a basically originalist* model of statutory construction—attempting to understand what the legislature that enacted the statute intended to accomplish by the words it chose.

No one has ever explained how a court attempting to understand the intent of a Congress that passed a statute in 1866 or 1870 can find any guidance in the views of a Congress sitting in the 1970s. Indeed, the irony of the matter is that the Court appears willing to find significance in Congress' silence, while generally declining to rely on far more explicit post-enactment legislative history—even of the Congress that passed the statute being interpreted! ... It is downright silly for a court that takes this stand with respect to rather contemporaneous and explicit post-enactment history to afford extraordinary significance to far removed and ambiguous inaction.

Indeed, it is more than silly; it is contrary to fundamental constitutional principles. A law can be enacted only by being passed in both houses of the Congress and being presented to the President for possible veto. Each of these three institutions—the House, the Senate, and the President—therefore has the constitutional authority to prevent the other two from enacting their will into law. Attributing significance to congressional silence subverts this scheme considerably ...

[T]here is another explanation for the doctrine[: separation of powers]....

One of the central premises of the Constitution's division of powers, and the American system of government, is that the primary federal lawmaking authority belongs to Congress. If separation of powers means anything, it means that the task of creating law falls upon the legislature, and that courts must obey and enforce the constitutionally legitimate enactments of the legislative branch. It is the legislative branch which, to some degree or another, is answerable to the people, "the only legitimate fountain of power."

---

* Authors' footnote: Originalist theories focus on the enacting legislative body.

It is this doctrine of legislative supremacy that fuels the conventional approach to statutory interpretation—in which courts seek to implement the value choices and decisions arrived at by the representative branch. In a perfect world there would be no tension between this judicial function and the notion of legislative supremacy. For in a perfect world, the legislature would be able to contemplate and provide for all contingencies in advance, settle all disputes about the effect of the statute, and overcome all ambiguity in transmitting its decisions to the judiciary and the public. If a legislature were able to accomplish all of these goals, the judicial function in statutory interpretation would be relatively passive. The court would discover what the legislature said about the case before it, and would apply its discovery to the case at hand.

Alas, our world is far from perfect. Language is frequently ambiguous, and it is often impossible to discover any legislative intent about an issue which a court needs to decide. In many instances, the generality of the statutory language seems to be a purposeful invitation to the courts to develop a body of law, reflecting Congress' inability or unwillingness to make certain hard political choices. When faced with statutes whose language and context admit of differing interpretations, a court must necessarily become creative. The conventional view is that at this point the court must try to determine what approach to the question before it fits best with the vision that the enacting legislature (or some relevant portion of it) appeared to share...."[I]nterpretation is inescapably a kind of legislation." ...

By what right does the judiciary exercise the power to make political choices in the course of statutory interpretation? ...

The answer to the legitimacy challenge is, ultimately, a pragmatic one. In the course of adjudicating cases it is often essential for courts to decide how an act of Congress applies. There is no option of deferring consideration of the question—a decision has to be reached for the sake of the parties and for the sake of establishing a reasonable level of certainty so interested observers may plan their conduct.... The judiciary's practice of making difficult value choices in the course of interpreting statutes does not find its justification in the intrinsic value of judicial involvement in that process. It is, rather, an inevitable and perhaps unfortunate byproduct of the need to adjudicate actual cases. As Justice Hugo Black asserted: "The Court undertakes the task of interpretation ... not because the Court has any special ability to fathom the intent of Congress, but rather because interpretation is unavoidable in the decision of the case before it."

That *some* level of judicial lawmaking is inevitable does not provide an excuse for *totally* ignoring the countermajoritarian difficulty with statutory interpretation, however. To the extent that the lawmaking role of the judiciary can be reduced or eliminated without impairing the courts' adjudicative function, there is no excuse for not proceeding in that direction. Corresponding to the two major factors that cause the problem with statutory interpretation—judicial creativity and congressional passivity—there are two complementary approaches to reducing the concern over the judiciary's lawmaking function.

First, one could focus on the judicial role, and try to reduce the creativity that judges exercise in interpreting statutes. It is important to recognize, though, that it will never be possible to eliminate the necessity for judicial policy choices in the course of interpreting statutes....

The second way of approaching the problem is to examine Congress' role in the enterprise of statutory interpretation.... [M]uch of the countermajoritarian difficulty with modern statutory interpretation is attributed to the perception that Congress' oversight of the courts' statutory decisions is not as energetic as it might be. [I]it seems reasonable to conclude that if the level of congressional involvement can be increased (thus making the courts' decisions look much more like conditional decisions) then at least some of the countermajoritarian difficulty will be reduced. Hence, one way to deal with the problem of judicial lawmaking is to adopt measures that will make congressional oversight a more realistically legitimizing element in statutory interpretation.... [I]nvoking a heightened rule, or better yet an absolute rule, of statutory stare decisis is a step in this direction....

The tension between the lawmaking aspects of statutory interpretation and principles of democratic self-governance forms the core of the separation-of-powers-based approach to a heightened or absolute rule of statutory stare decisis. Justice Black, perhaps the Court's strongest advocate of a strong rule of statutory stare decisis, sketched out one way in which uneasiness with judicial creativity relates to stare decisis:

> When the law has been settled by an earlier case[,] then any subsequent "reinterpretation" of the statute is gratuitous and neither more nor less than an amendment: it is no different from a judicial alteration of language that Congress itself placed in the statute.

Altering the important provisions of a statute is a legislative function. And the Constitution states simply and unequivocally: "All legislative Powers herein granted shall be vested in a Congress of the United States...."

... Once the statute has been interpreted, any change in direction can be left for Congress. Taken alone, Justice Black's position appears to be a bit shallow. He is, of course, correct that an absolute rule of statutory stare decisis is bound to limit the number of cases in which judges make policy choices.... But limiting the numerical incidence of judicial lawmaking episodes in that narrow sense is not obviously consistent with the goal of limiting the lawmaking role of the courts in statutory interpretation. Indeed, one might persuasively argue that the lawmaking character of statutory interpretation is intensified by a strong rule of stare decisis for the rule gives statute-like permanence to judge-made law. To those concerned with lawmaking by the judiciary, therefore, it makes little sense to talk quantitatively, without considering the effects that a heightened or absolute rule of statutory stare decisis is likely to have on the relationship between Congress and the courts.

Analyzing those effects suggests that aside from decreasing the *incidence* of judicial lawmaking, adopting a heightened or absolute rule of statutory stare decisis could reduce the *significance* of judicial lawmaking. If the relationship between Congress and the courts could be changed so as to make the specter of congressional oversight of statutory precedents more of a reality, the legitimacy of judicial involvement in initially interpreting statutes would become far less difficult to justify. If a more active colloquy between the branches could be stimulated, the potential for congressional override then could be realistically treated as a meaningful legitimizing factor in the interpretive process. The courts' interpretations then could be treated more like conditional rules, and there would be less need to be concerned with the unaccountable nature of the courts.

How, though, could a heightened or absolute rule of statutory stare decisis stimulate increased congressional involvement in monitoring statutory interpretation? It would do so by articulating a clear and unyielding division of responsibility....

Seen in this light, judicial overruling of statutory precedents is not only unnecessary to the adjudicative process, but it serves to lessen the level of congressional involvement in overseeing and overruling the courts' statutory decisions. If Congress and interested parties believe that statutory decisions can be overruled either by Congress *or* by the courts, the pressure on Congress to become involved is reduced.

Because the Court has never consistently applied a heightened or absolute rule of statutory stare decisis, there is no empirical data available to prove or disprove the hypothesis that such a rule would trigger increased congressional oversight of statutory interpretation. Nonetheless, there are a number of models that may help predict the consequences of such a rule. Imagine two legal systems that are identical except in one respect. One deals with statutory precedents as it does other kinds of precedents: it is willing to overrule them. The other system, by contrast, steadfastly refuses to reconsider any statutory precedents. In which system can Congress be expected to pay more attention to a judicial decision interpreting a statute?

There should be a marginally higher level of congressional oversight in the system in which courts apply a heightened or absolute rule of statutory stare decisis. For in that system the legislators, lobbyists, and public all know that any changes in the interpretation of statutes can come only through legislative action — not through a judicial reversal of the announced interpretation. Thus, legislators will not have the luxury of putting off action in anticipation of a judicial decision, or perhaps more importantly, placating their constituents or those who exert pressure upon them by convincing them that there remains the prospect for judicial self-correction. By the same token, groups and individuals interested in changing the rule will focus all of their attention on the legislature, rather than diluting their energy by continuing their attempts to effectuate change in the courts through litigation as well....

In addition to reducing the pressure on Congress to confront thorny political issues, the possibility of judicial reversal deters congressional action in another respect. There is a limited number of issues with which any Congress can deal. In choosing among potential subjects for attention, reasonable legislators should be expected to take into account the possibility that the problem will solve itself, or that someone else may solve it. All other things being equal, therefore, the utility-maximizing decision under these circumstances is to press for the legislation on the subject over which the legislature has exclusive control, while hoping that the other problem (reversing judicial interpretation) will be solved by the courts. If the possibility of judicial overruling is eliminated, legislative consideration of court decisions will be put on a par with other items on the legislative agenda.

This prediction is consistent with basic principles of organizational design theory. Diffusion of responsibility and authority has been shown to pose significant barriers to responsive action within an organization.... One of the essential principles of delegation is to avoid "overlaps" and "splits" of responsibility that tend to reduce any one individual's sense that she must be the one to act....

The effect that anticipated court involvement can have on congressional willingness to deal with issues has been noted in the area of constitutional decisionmaking. Writing in 1893, James Thayer argued that the specter of judicial review tends to dissipate Congress' feeling of obligation to deal with constitutional issues. There are countless examples of an act being passed and signed based on the expectation that the courts would strike down the resulting statute if it contained any constitutional defect. This "abdication of Congress' role as a constitutional guardian and ... abnegation of its duty of responsible lawmaking" is hard to remedy in the constitutional setting, for few would argue that the judiciary should abandon its essential role of constitutional adjudicator. But the problem is not as intractable in the area of statutory reinterpretation — the kingdom would not collapse if only Congress could reverse the Supreme Court's constructions of statutes. In any event, the factors described above, and the phenomenon that occurs in the constitutional area, confirm Dean Levi's assertion that "if the Court is to have freedom to reinterpret legislation, the result will be to relieve the legislature from pressure." ...

The flaw, then, in the current system of shared authority to overrule statutory precedents is that no one body is given the ultimate job of reviewing interpretations of statutes and deciding whether they represent currently acceptable renditions of the statute's goals, or for that matter, whether the statute is worth keeping around at all. This diffusion of authority lessens the probability of statutory development.... As anyone who has ever let a ball pass down the middle of the tennis court untouched while playing doubles knows, two heads are not always better than one....

Notes and Questions

(1) *Four Problems.* According to Professor Marshall, there are four problems with equating congressional inaction with acquiescence. What are they? He suggests that the Court is more willing to find legislative acquiescence when there is evidence that Congress knew of the judicial interpretation or when the issue is of national importance and so Congress should have known of it. If he is correct, what should members of Congress do when they wish to alter the Court's interpretation of a statute but do not have enough votes within Congress to amend that statute? What if they have enough votes but believe that other matters should take priority, so they choose to do nothing? What do your answers tell you about the Court's basis for implying legislative acquiescence?

(2) *Originalist Theories.* Why does the Court's willingness to view legislative silence as acquiescence conflict with the Court's originalist theory of statutory interpretation? If the goal of interpretation is to determine the intent of the *enacting* legislature, should the acquiescence of a later legislature ever matter? Dynamic theories of interpretation posit that laws must change with society's changing needs. Does legislative acquiescence conflict with dynamic theories?

(3) *An Absolute Bar.* Professor Marshall suggests that a heightened *stare decisis* standard for statutory interpretation cases is not strict enough; rather, an absolute bar is necessary: "Once an absolute rule of stare decisis is rejected, however, there is no objective test for gauging adherence to the rule of precedent." Why? Do you agree? Why does he suggest there should be a different standard for constitutional cases than statutory interpretation cases?

(4) *Stare Decisis and the Constitution.* Professor William Eskridge has attacked the argument that the Constitution limits the degree to which judges can make, as opposed to interpret, law. In doing so, he points out that there is no *stare decisis* bar in the Constitution. Thus, he rejects the separation of powers justification for a "superstrong presumption of statutory stare decisis." William Eskridge, *Overruling Statutory Precedents*, 76 Geo. L.J. 1361, 1398 (1988). In response, Professor Marshall counters, "To the extent that the Constitution speaks to [*stare decisis*], it speaks not to the narrow principle of statutory *stare decisis*, but to the broader principle of discouraging judicial lawmaking." Hence, a specific clause encouraging *stare decisis* is unnecessary. With whom do you agree and why?

The next two cases explore legislative acquiescence and the role of *stare decisis* and separation of powers. In many respects, the first case presents an extreme example of legislative silence. There was no question that Congress knew how the Court had previously interpreted the statute, and there was strong evidence that Congress believed that the prior interpretation was wrong. Moreover, the topic was of popular import, and the legal issue involved was substantive (antitrust law and interstate commerce), rather than procedural.

Flood v. Kuhn
407 U.S. 258 (1972)

JUSTICE BLACKMUN delivered the opinion of the Court.

[Petitioner Flood was a professional baseball player who was traded from one team to another without being consulted. He complained to the Commissioner of Baseball, demanding that he be made a free agent and be given the power to strike his own bargain with any team. When that request was denied, he filed suit claiming a violation of the federal antitrust laws.* The trial court entered judgment for the defendants and the appellate court affirmed. The Supreme Court's majority opinion first identified two cases, *Federal Baseball Club* decided in 1922 and *Toolson* decided in 1953, in which it had held that the federal antitrust laws did not apply to baseball because baseball did not affect interstate commerce. The Court then continued by quoting *Toolson*:]

> Congress has had the ruling under consideration but has not seen fit to bring such business under these laws by legislation having prospective effect. The business has thus been left for thirty years to develop, on the understanding that it was not subject to existing antitrust legislation. The present cases ask us to overrule the prior decision and, with retrospective effect, hold the legislation applicable. We think that if there are evils in this field which now warrant application to it of the antitrust laws it should be by legislation. Without re-examination of the underlying issues, the judgments below are affirmed on the authority of *Federal Baseball Club* so far as that decision determines that Congress had no intention of including the business of baseball within the scope of the federal antitrust laws.

This quotation [from *Toolson*] reveals four reasons for the Court's affirmance [of *Federal Baseball Club*] ... : (a) Congressional awareness for three decades of the Court's ruling in *Federal Baseball*, coupled with congressional inaction. (b) The fact that baseball was left alone to develop for that period upon the understanding that the reserve system was not subject to existing federal antitrust laws. (c) A reluctance to overrule *Federal Baseball* with consequent retroactive effect. (d) A professed desire that any needed remedy be provided by legislation rather than by court decree. The emphasis in *Toolson* was on the determination, attributed even to *Federal Baseball*, that Congress had no intention to include baseball within the reach of the federal antitrust laws.... [After discussing *Federal Baseball* and *Toolson*, the majority then identified other cases in which the court found that the antitrust laws *did* apply to other professional sports, and in which it invited Congress to legislatively overrule *Federal Baseball Club* and *Toolson*.]

Legislative proposals have been numerous and persistent. Since *Toolson* more than 50 bills have been introduced in Congress relative to the applicability or nonapplicability of the antitrust laws to baseball. A few of these passed one house or the other. Those that did would have expanded, not restricted, the reserve system's exemption to other professional league sports....

In view of all this, it seems appropriate now to say that:

---

* Authors' footnote: Antitrust laws are intended to promote competition by prohibiting business practices that restrain competition. Flood argued that baseball's system of preventing free agency constituted a restraint on competition. The issue in *Flood* was whether baseball is an interstate trade or commerce under the antitrust laws.

1. Professional baseball is a business and it is engaged in interstate commerce.

2. With its reserve system enjoying exemption from the federal antitrust laws, baseball is, in a very distinct sense, an exception and an anomaly....

3. Even though others might regard this as 'unrealistic, inconsistent, or illogical,' the aberration is an established one.... It is an aberration that has been with us now for half a century, one heretofore deemed fully entitled to the benefit of *stare decisis*, and one that has survived the Court's expanding concept of interstate commerce. It rests on a recognition and an acceptance of baseball's unique characteristics and needs....

6. The Court has emphasized that since 1922 baseball, with full and continuing congressional awareness, has been allowed to develop and to expand unhindered by federal legislative action. Remedial legislation has been introduced repeatedly in Congress but none has ever been enacted. The Court, accordingly, has concluded that Congress as yet has had no intention to subject baseball's reserve system to the reach of the antitrust statutes. This, obviously, has been deemed to be something other than mere congressional silence and passivity.

7. The Court has expressed concern about the confusion and the retroactivity problems that inevitably would result with a judicial overturning of *Federal Baseball*. It has voiced a preference that if any change is to be made, it come by legislative action that, by its nature, is only prospective in operation....

This emphasis and this concern are still with us. We continue to be loath, 50 years after *Federal Baseball* and almost two decades after *Toolson*, to overturn those cases judicially when Congress, by its positive inaction, has allowed those decisions to stand for so long and, far beyond mere inference and implication, has clearly evinced a desire not to disapprove them legislatively.

Accordingly, we adhere once again to *Federal Baseball* and *Toolson*.... If we were to act otherwise, we would be withdrawing from the conclusion as to congressional intent made in *Toolson*.... Under these circumstances, there is merit in consistency even though some might claim that beneath that consistency is a layer of inconsistency....

And what the Court said in *Federal Baseball* in 1922 and what it said in *Toolson* in 1953, we say again here in 1972: the remedy, if any is indicated, is for congressional, and not judicial, action....

[A]ffirmed.

JUSTICE MARSHALL, with whom JUSTICE BRENNAN concurs, dissenting.

... Has Congress acquiesced in our decisions in *Federal Baseball Club* and *Toolson*? I think not. Had the Court been consistent and treated all sports in the same way baseball was treated, Congress might have become concerned enough to take action. But, the Court was inconsistent, and baseball was isolated and distinguished from all other sports. In *Toolson* the Court refused to act because Congress had been silent. But the Court may have read too much into this legislative inaction....

We do not lightly overrule our prior constructions of federal statutes, but when our errors deny substantial federal rights, like the right to compete freely and effectively to the best of one's ability as guaranteed by the antitrust laws, we must admit our error and correct it. We have done so before and we should do so again here.

To the extent that there is concern over any reliance interests that club owners may assert, they can be satisfied by making our decision prospective only. Baseball should be covered by the antitrust laws beginning with this case and henceforth, unless Congress decides otherwise.

Accordingly, I would overrule *Federal Baseball Club* and *Toolson* and reverse....

Notes and Questions

(1) *Stare Decisis.* The Justices all agreed that *Toolson* and *Federal Baseball Club* had been wrongly decided: If they were to decide the issue for the first time, they would hold that baseball was an activity in interstate commerce. Had *Toolson* and *Federal Baseball Club* been common law cases rather than statutory interpretation cases, the Court would likely have overruled them. Instead, the Court affirmed them. The majority and dissent agreed that prior decisions interpreting statutes should be overruled less readily than those interpreting the common law. Why should a court be more willing to let a clearly erroneous interpretation of a statute stand? What benefits are there in letting a clearly erroneous interpretation stand? *See generally,* Amy Coney Barrett, *Statutory Stare Decisis in the Courts of Appeals,* 73 GEO. WASH. L. REV. 317 (2005).

(2) *The Threshold for Overruling Prior Statutory Interpretations.* The Justices disagreed on whether the Court should have overruled *Toolson* and *Federal Baseball.* When would the majority set aside a prior statutory interpretation? The dissent suggested that the Court could make any decision prospective only. Does that suggestion eliminate the basis for the majority's reluctance? Yet, is the dissent's standard for overruling prior statutory interpretations too low?

(3) *Did Congress Acquiesce?* Some argue that it is inappropriate to give any weight to legislative silence because legislative intent can be discerned only through enactment and presentment. The argument continues: Because a court can never be sure why a legislature has failed to act, silence is inherently ambiguous. And, thus, relying on silence to mean that the legislature agreed with the interpretation is choosing one of two reasonable interpretations. But, the extreme facts in *Flood* suggest that sometimes acquiescence is a compelling conclusion and, perhaps, the only conclusion. In some ways, *Flood* is an easy case for concluding that Congress acquiesced because (1) the statute—the antitrust law—was an important federal statute; (2) the interpretation of the statute implicated the concept of interstate commerce, which is important not just in the antitrust context, but to Congressional power generally; (3) the case involved a high-profile professional sport; (4) the Court had repeatedly pointed out the aberrational nature of its prior interpretation and had suggested that Congress should take action if it disagreed, but Congress had not done so; and (5) Congress clearly was aware of the issue because it had debated many bills on the subject and had passed a few of them out of at least one house.

In contrast to *Flood*, the following case presents much weaker facts for finding legislative acquiesce; yet, the majority reached the same result. When you read this case, ask yourself if it is fair to assume, as the majority did, that the legislature was aware of the prior interpretation. Additionally, ask whether the subject matter at issue—substance or procedure—should be relevant. Are the cases that the majority relies upon so clear that the legislature should have considered amending the statute? Also, ponder the dissent's point: were the cases relied on by the majority even relevant?

This case involved a "failure-of-suit" statute. Such statutes essentially toll statutes of limitation for a brief period of time. The issue in the case was whether the failure-of-suit statute tolled a time limitation included in an insurance policy when the time limitation in the policy was required to be included by law.

Bocchino v. Nationwide Mut. Fire Ins. Co.
716 A.2d 883 (Conn. 1998)

BORDEN, ASSOCIATE JUSTICE.

[Defendant issued a fire insurance policy to plaintiff. As required by Connecticut General Statutes 38a-3081(a) and 38a-307, the policy required that any suit on the policy be brought within one year of any covered loss. A fire occurred, and plaintiff sued within one year. However, because of a computer error the district court dismissed his suit. He refiled the suit within one year of the dismissal, but more than one year after the fire.]

In this action to recover proceeds pursuant to a homeowner's insurance policy, the plaintiff appeals from the judgment of the trial court in favor of the defendant. The trial court determined that the action had not been brought within one year of the date of the loss, as required by the policy, and that the accidental failure of suit statute, General Statutes § 52-592,[2] did not operate to save the plaintiff's action....

The plaintiff claims that the trial court improperly concluded that § 52-592(a) did not save this action, because ... the defendant's insurance policy provision requiring that an action be brought within one year of the date of the loss was mandated by the standard fire insurance policy form delineated in §§ 38a-308(a) and 38a-307, and was, therefore, a "time limited by law" within the meaning of the savings provision of § 52-592(a). Recognizing that prevailing case law has interpreted § 52-592(a) as not applying to such provisions, however, the plaintiff urges us to overrule that case law. We decline to do so.

This case is controlled by our prior decisions in *Chichester v. New Hampshire Fire Ins. Co.*, 74 Conn. 510 (1902) [*Chichester II*], and *Vincent v. Mutual Reserve Fund Life Assn.*, 74 Conn. 684 (1902). In short, *Chichester [II]* and *Vincent* held that the accidental failure of suit statute applies only to actions barred by an otherwise applicable *statute of limitations*, and not to an applicable *contractual* limitation period, irrespective of whether that period was required by a statutory form for an insurance policy. Moreover, *Monteiro v. American Home Assurance Co.*, 177 Conn. 281 (1979), reaffirmed that holding, and, on several occasions since that decision, this court and the Appellate Court have further reaffirmed the limited application of the statute....

In *Chichester[II]*, the plaintiff previously had brought an action on a fire insurance policy within the one year provision of the policy, but that action was nonsuited after the plaintiff had introduced all of his evidence, and his appeal was dismissed [*Chichester I*]. The plaintiff immediately ... commenced another action [*Chichester II*], and was met with the defense of the one year provision of the policy. The plaintiff replied by relying on the accidental failure of suit statute....

This court affirmed the judgment of the trial court [dismissing the case], holding that "[t]he provision in the policy sued upon requiring an action to be brought 'within twelve months next after the fire' does not operate as *a statute of limitations;* it is a part of the contract; the rights of the parties flow from the contract, and must be governed by the rules of law applicable to contracts. Such a provision in a contract of insurance is valid and binding upon the parties." (Emphasis added.)

---

2. General Statutes § 52-592 provides in relevant part: "(a) If any action, commenced within the time limited by law, has failed one or more times to be tried on its merits ... because the action has been dismissed for want of jurisdiction, ... the plaintiff ... may commence a new action, ... for the same cause at any time within one year after the determination of the original action...."

This court then ... specifically rejected, the claimed applicability of the accidental failure of suit statute, and the argument that it applied because the fire insurance policy, which contained the one year suit provision, was a standard policy mandated by our then insurance statutes. "The plaintiff's claim that [the accidental failure of suit statute] authorizes the bringing of this suit within one year after his nonsuit in the former action, is without foundation. *That [statute] is an amendment to the statute of limitations and does not affect this contract.*" (Emphasis added.) "The plaintiff also insists that [the statute] establishing a standard policy of insurance, in some way changes the agreement of the parties to such a policy into *a statute of limitations.* The Act clearly has no effect upon the contracts made in accordance with the form therein provided." (Emphasis added.) Subsequently, this court followed the rule of *Chichester*[*II*] in *Vincent* (allegations that prior dismissed action on life insurance policy had been brought within one year policy provision "are immaterial").

Our decisions in *Chichester* [*II*] and *Vincent* cannot plausibly be read any way other than as holding that § 52-592(a) does not apply to save a second action on an insurance policy brought beyond the applicable contractual limitation period but within one year of a timely, but unsuccessful, prior action on the same loss. Moreover, the decision in *Chichester* [*II*] unequivocally concludes that the fact that the policy's limitation period was mandated by a statutory standard fire insurance form is irrelevant. These precedents dictate the conclusion that the accidental failure of suit statute simply does not apply to the plaintiff's action in the present case. That statute applies to actions that would be time barred by an otherwise applicable statute of limitations, not to actions that are time barred by a contractual policy provision, irrespective of the fact that the policy provision was required by a statutory policy form.

Furthermore, this reading of *Chichester* [*II*] was reaffirmed in 1979 when this court decided *Monteiro*.... Although the accidental failure of suit statute was not involved in that case, this court cited *Chichester* [*II*] for the following propositions: (1) "Since a provision in a fire insurance policy requiring suit to be brought within one year of the loss is a valid contractual obligation, a failure to comply therewith is a defense to an action on the policy unless the provision has been waived or unless there is a valid excuse for nonperformance; *and such a condition requiring suit to be brought within one year does not operate as a statute of limitations*"; (emphasis added); and (2) "This condition is a part of the contract so that it controls the rights of the parties under the contract and, hence, such rights must be governed by the rules of law applicable to contracts." This court then went on to reject the plaintiff's claim, under contract law, that he was excused from compliance with the one year suit provision by his attorney's disability....

Recognizing that *Chichester* [*II*] is indistinguishable from the present case, the plaintiff urges us to overrule it. This we decline to do. We generally have adhered to the notion that "[i]n assessing the force of stare decisis ... we should be especially cautious about overturning a case that concerns statutory construction....

When we construe a statute, we act not as plenary lawgivers but as surrogates for another policy maker, the legislature. In our role as surrogates, our only responsibility is to determine what the legislature, within constitutional limits, intended to do. Sometimes, when we have made such a determination, the legislature instructs us that we have misconstrued its intentions. We are bound by the instructions so provided. More often, however, the legislature takes no further action to clarify its intentions. Time and again, we have characterized the failure of the legislature to take corrective action as manifesting the legislature's acquiescence in our construction of a statute.

In light of our role as surrogates for the legislature, proper respect for the separation of powers has led us to exercise prudence with respect to the overruling of cases that involve the construction of a statute. Once an appropriate interval to permit legislative reconsideration has passed without corrective legislative action, the inference of legislative acquiescence places a significant jurisprudential limitation on our own authority to reconsider the merits of our earlier decision. If ... stare decisis is to continue to serve the cause of stability and certainty in the law—a condition indispensable to any well-ordered system of jurisprudence—a court should not overrule its earlier decisions unless the most cogent reasons and inescapable logic require it. This is especially true when the precedent involved concerns the interpretation or construction of a statute.... A change in the personnel of the court never furnishes reason to reopen a question of statutory interpretation....

The present case does not present "the most cogent reasons" to overrule our prior interpretations of the accidental failure of suit statute, nor does "inescapable logic" require such a result. There is nothing bizarre or irrational about those interpretations. Moreover, there is no showing that those interpretations were of recent origin and had disregarded persuasive legislative history regarding the statute's purpose....

The most that can be said for the plaintiff's position, therefore, is that in 1902, when *Chichester* [*II*] was decided, this court plausibly *could* have interpreted the accidental failure of suit statute as saving an action brought beyond the policy's limitation period when a prior action commenced within that period had been nonsuited, and when the provision containing the limitation period was mandated by statute. That is insufficient justification to sweep away the at least equally plausible interpretation that this court *did* adopt ... and has reaffirmed repeatedly since, and which the legislature presumably has approved.

The judgment is affirmed.

BERDON, ASSOCIATE JUSTICE, with whom JUSTICE McDONALD, joins, dissenting.

... I focus on the language of § 52-592(a) to determine whether the plaintiff's case falls within the letter of the savings statute. Section 52-592(a) provides that, if a plaintiff's "action, commenced within the time limited by law, has failed one or more times to be tried on its merits ... the plaintiff ... may commence a new action ... for the same cause at any time within one year after the determination of the original action...." Clearly, the plaintiff's original action failed to be tried on its merits. Moreover, there is no dispute that the plaintiff filed an identical action within one year of the dismissal of his first action. Consequently, the only real issue for this court to address in this appeal is whether the one year limitation of suit provision in the plaintiff's fire insurance policy is "time limited by law" under § 52-592(a).

I conclude that, although the one year period by which the plaintiff was required to institute his action was a provision in the insurance contract, it was still a limitation period required by law. General Statutes § 38a-307 provides in relevant part that the standard form of fire insurance policy shall include the contractual provision that any action be "commenced within twelve months next after inception of the loss" and General Statutes § 38a-308 (a) mandates that all policies of fire insurance "made, issued or delivered by any insurer or any agent or representative thereof, on any property in this state ... [conform] ... to all provisions, stipulations, agreements and conditions" set forth in the standard policy of § 38a-307....

After reviewing *Chichester II* and *Monteiro,* I conclude that both cases are inapposite to the present case because, unlike the plaintiff in this case, the plaintiffs in *Chichester II* and *Monteiro* failed to meet the prerequisites of § 52-592(a) for commencing a new action on the same cause. To understand *Chichester II*, we must review (*Chichester I*). In *Chichester I*, the plaintiff had brought an action within one year of his date of loss, which was nonsuited after he had introduced all of his evidence at trial on that action. The trial court granted the defendant's motion for nonsuit because the plaintiff failed to make out a prima facie case as a result of his failure to prove "immediate notice" to the defendant after the fire, which, in addition to a contractual limitation period of one year for instituting an action, was a condition of the policy of insurance and an essential element of his case. The plaintiff then attempted in *Chichester II* to bring a second action against the defendant pursuant to … § 52-592[a] …, which this court held was barred as not falling within the provisions of the savings statute. In other words, the plaintiff's original action in *Chichester I*, unlike the plaintiff's original action in the present case, was tried on its merits and did not fall within the letter of § 52-592(a).

The plaintiff in *Monteiro*, unlike the plaintiff in this case, commenced his action against the defendant more than one year after he had suffered his loss, thus failing to comply with his insurance policy's one year limitation of suit provision. Consequently, the *Monteiro* court did not even address whether § 52-592(a) extended the one year limitation period in the plaintiff's policy. Instead, the court determined whether the plaintiff was excused from performance of the contractual condition by virtue of his attorney's tragic illness. The principal issue in the present case, therefore, whether § 52-592(a) extends a contractual limitation period when that limitation period is required by law, has never been squarely decided by this court.

Even if the majority were correct that *Chichester II* holds what the majority claims it does, which it does not, I would overrule it.[11] "The value of adhering to precedent is not an end in and of itself … if the precedent reflects substantive injustice. Consistency must also serve a justice related end. B. Cardozo, The Nature of the Judicial Process (1921) p. 150 (favoring rejection of precedent when it has been found to be inconsistent with the sense of justice or with the social welfare).…"[F]ar from being immune from considerations of justice, [the rule of stare decisis] must always be tested against the ends of justice more generally.… If law is to have a current relevance, courts must have and exert the capacity to change a rule of law when reason so requires.… Those doctrines only will eventually stand which bear the strictest examination and the test of experience."

Reason requires this court to overrule *Chichester II* because that court's construction of the interplay between § 38a-308 and § 52-592(a) contravenes our long-standing liberal interpretation of the accidental failure of suit statute, and its long-standing policy of providing "errant parties with an opportunity for cases to be resolved on their merits rather than dismissed for some technical flaw." …

Furthermore, *Chichester II* should be overruled because adherence to it will lead to unjust results for all insured parties who, like the plaintiff (1) put their insurers on notice of claims, (2) file timely proof of loss for the claims, (3) file actions against the insurer within one year of the date of loss, and (4) suffer nonsuits through no fault of their

---

11. "[P]rinciples of law which serve one generation well may, by reason of changing conditions, disserve a later one.… Experience can and often does demonstrate that a rule, once believed sound, needs modification to serve justice better." In overruling prior case law interpreting a nineteenth century statute, we previously had occasion to quote Justice Oliver Wendell Holmes: "'It is revolting to have no better reason for a rule of law than that so it was laid down in the time of Henry IV. It is still more revolting if the grounds upon which it was laid down have vanished long since, and the rule simply persists from blind imitation of the past.' O. Holmes, 'The Path of the Law,' 10 Harv. L.Rev. 457, 469 (1897)."

own. Simply put, it is manifestly unjust to forbid such persons from prosecuting new actions if the prosecution of the original action fulfilled the essential purpose of the policy's limitation of suit provision. The essential purpose of the fire insurance policy's limitation of suit provision is to "prevent delay in the determination of all questions of loss, and in part to enable the company to know in season whether a claim will be prosecuted." By invoking judicial aid less than one year after his date of loss, the plaintiff in the present case gave timely notice to the defendant that a claim would be prosecuted. Moreover, the defendant knew that the plaintiff's original action was dismissed merely because of a computer generated error. Under such circumstances, it defies justice for the majority to refuse to reverse *Chichester II.*

I would hold, therefore, that the remedial provisions of § 52-592(a) apply to toll the running of the parties' statutorily required contractual limitation period, and that the plaintiff's second action is not barred in this case.

Notes and Questions

(1) *Is the Presumption Realistic?* Is it fair to assume that the legislature was aware of the prior interpretations? Is the subject matter of the same apparent notoriety as professional baseball? Are the holdings of the prior cases here as clear as they were in *Flood*? Should that matter in determining acquiescence? Why? When legislative silence is interpreted as acquiescence, courts rely on the assumption that legislatures are aware of all prior judicial interpretations. Is this assumption realistic? Does it have to be? What functional benefits arise from that assumption?

More broadly, this book explores many similar presumptions. For example, legislators supposedly know of prior interpretations of words in related statutes and of prior interpretations of the statute at issue. Legislatures are deemed to know how the courts of the state from which they adopt a statute interpreted that statute. Are these presumptions realistic? Even if not, do they serve functional purposes? Assuming so, what are those purposes?

(2) *Procedural v. Substantive Statutes.* Does it matter that the statute in *Flood* was substantive, but this one was procedural? Can you make an argument that where the statute addresses a matter of civil procedure, it is improper to find acquiescence as readily as when the statute addresses a matter of substantive policy?

(3) *Requiring the Most Cogent Reasons.* The dissent believed that prior judicial interpretations should be overruled, if erroneous, without regard to whether a common law or a statute was in issue. Do you agree? In contrast, the majority reasoned that the principle of separation of powers required greater deference to prior decisions of statutory interpretation. The majority believed statutory interpretation decisions should be affirmed unless the case presented "the most cogent reasons," such as a bizarre or irrational result. Is that standard too high? Or, is it too low? How would *Flood* come out under this standard?

(4) *An Invitation to Act.* Should it make a difference whether the court has invited the legislature to act, such as occurred after *Federal Baseball Club* and *Toolson*? Or, in light of the difficulty of knowing the reasons for the legislature's failure to act, should legislative inaction ever be relevant to statutory interpretation?

(5) *Rejecting Acquiescence.* In *Stratmeyer v. Stratmeyer*, 567 N.W.2d 220 (S.D. 1997), the court held that a special statute of limitations for cases of child sexual assault applied retroactively. To reach this holding, the majority overruled what was then a two-year-old

case that had held that the statute was not retroactive; in doing so, the court completely ignored the unsuccessful subsequent legislative attempts to overrule the earlier case. The dissent chastised:

> Since [our earlier opinion], the legislature has had two opportunities to amend [the statute] to abrogate our holding and give the statute retroactive application. Twice it has declined to do so. If the legislature had in fact intended the statute to have retroactive effect it would have been a simple matter to supersede our holding by amending [the statute] to expressly so provide. The legislature's reluctance to take issue with our holding is persuasive evidence it did not intend the statute to apply retroactively.

Id. at 225 (Miller, C.J., dissenting). Didn't the dissent attach too much importance to the two failed attempts, while the majority correctly ignored them as irrelevant? Yet, given the prior precedent and the importance of *stare decisis*—especially when statutes are interpreted—did the majority overrule its prior decision too easily?

B. Legislative Inaction Following Executive Interpretation

In the last section, we examined the relevance of Congress's silence in response to judicial interpretations of statutes. This section analyzes a related but distinct issue: What if an agency interprets a statute and Congress tries but fails to act to reject the agency's interpretation? Should that type of legislative inaction also be deemed to be legislative acquiescence? Or, should a court simply ignore Congress's response? The next case explores this question in light of the Internal Revenue's interpretation of sections of the tax code granting tax exempt status to charitable institutions.

Bob Jones Univ. v. United States
461 U.S. 574 (1983)

CHIEF JUSTICE BURGER delivered the opinion of the Court.

We granted certiorari to decide whether petitioner[], nonprofit private school[] that prescribe[s] and enforce[s] racially discriminatory admissions standards on the basis of religious doctrine, qualif[ies]as tax-exempt organization[] under §501(c)(3) of the Internal Revenue Code of 1954.

Until 1970, the Internal Revenue Service granted tax-exempt status to private schools, without regard to their racial admissions policies, ... and granted charitable deductions for contributions to such schools....

On January 12, 1970, a three-judge District Court for the District of Columbia issued a preliminary injunction prohibiting the IRS from according tax-exempt status to private schools in Mississippi that discriminated as to admissions on the basis of race. Thereafter, in July 1970, the IRS concluded that it could "no longer legally justify allowing tax-exempt status [under §501(c)(3)] to private schools which practice racial discrimination." At the same time, the IRS announced that it could not "treat gifts to such schools as charitable deductions for income tax purposes [under §170]...."

Bob Jones University is a nonprofit corporation located in Greenville, South Carolina. It[is] ... dedicated to the teaching and propagation of its fundamentalist Christian religious beliefs. It is both a religious and educational institution. Its teachers are required to be devout Christians, and all courses at the University are taught according to the Bible....

The sponsors of the University genuinely believe that the Bible forbids interracial dating and marriage. To effectuate these views, Negroes were completely excluded until 1971. From 1971 to May 1975, the University accepted no applications from unmarried Negroes, but did accept applications from Negroes married within their race....

Since May 29, 1975, the University has permitted unmarried Negroes to enroll; but a disciplinary rule prohibits interracial dating and marriage.... The University continues to deny admission to applicants engaged in an interracial marriage or known to advocate interracial marriage or dating.

Until 1970, the IRS extended tax-exempt status to Bob Jones University under § 501(c)(3).... On January 19, 1976, the IRS officially revoked the University's tax-exempt status, effective as of December 1, 1970.... [T]he University instituted the present action....

In Revenue Ruling 71-447, the IRS formalized the policy first announced in 1970, that § 170 and § 501(c)(3) embrace the common law "charity" concept. Under that view, to qualify for a tax exemption pursuant to § 501(c)(3), an institution must show, first, that it falls within one of the eight categories expressly set forth in that section, and second, that its activity is not contrary to settled public policy.

Section 501(c)(3) provides that "[c]orporations ... organized and operated exclusively for religious, charitable ... or educational purposes" are entitled to tax exemption. Petitioners argue that the plain language of the statute guarantees them tax-exempt status. They emphasize the absence of any language in the statute expressly requiring all exempt organizations to be "charitable" in the common law sense, and they contend that the disjunctive "or" separating the categories in § 501(c)(3) precludes such a reading. Instead, they argue that if an institution falls within one or more of the specified categories it is automatically entitled to exemption, without regard to whether it also qualifies as "charitable."....

It is a well-established canon of statutory construction that a court should go beyond the literal language of a statute if reliance on that language would defeat the plain purpose of the statute.... Section 501(c)(3) therefore must be analyzed and construed within the framework of the Internal Revenue Code and against the background of the Congressional purposes. [The Court concludes that "underlying all relevant parts of the Code, is the intent that entitlement to tax exemption depends on meeting certain common law standards of charity—namely, that an institution seeking tax-exempt status must serve a public purpose and not be contrary to established public policy...."]

There can thus be no question that the interpretation of § 170 and § 501(c)(3) announced by the IRS in 1970 was correct. That it may be seen as belated does not undermine its soundness. It would be wholly incompatible with the concepts underlying tax exemption to grant the benefit of tax-exempt status to racially discriminatory educational entities, which "exer[t] a pervasive influence on the entire educational process." Whatever may be the rationale for such private schools' policies, and however sincere the rationale may be, racial discrimination in education is contrary to public policy. Racially discriminatory educational institutions cannot be viewed as conferring a public benefit within the "charitable" concept ... or within the Congressional intent underlying § 170 and § 501(c)(3)....

The actions of Congress since 1970 leave no doubt that the IRS reached the correct conclusion in exercising its authority. It is, of course, not unknown for independent agencies or the Executive Branch to misconstrue the intent of a statute; Congress can and often does correct such misconceptions, if the courts have not done so. Yet for a dozen years Congress has been made aware—acutely aware—of the IRS rulings of 1970 and 1971. [F]ew issues have been the subject of more vigorous and widespread debate and discussion in and out of Congress than those related to racial segregation in education. Sincere adherents advocating contrary views have ventilated the subject for well over three decades. Failure of Congress to modify the IRS rulings of 1970 and 1971, of which Congress was, by its own studies and by public discourse, constantly reminded; and Congress' awareness of the denial of tax-exempt status for racially discriminatory schools when enacting other and related legislation make out an unusually strong case of legislative acquiescence in and ratification by implication of the 1970 and 1971 rulings.

Ordinarily, and quite appropriately, courts are slow to attribute significance to the failure of Congress to act on particular legislation. We have observed that "unsuccessful attempts at legislation are not the best of guides to legislative intent." Here, however, we do not have an ordinary claim of legislative acquiescence. Only one month after the IRS announced its position in 1970, Congress held its first hearings on this precise issue. Exhaustive hearings have been held on the issue at various times since then. These include hearings in February 1982, after we granted review in this case.

Non-action by Congress is not often a useful guide, but the non-action here is significant. During the past 12 years there have been no fewer than 13 bills introduced to overturn the IRS interpretation of § 501(c)(3). Not one of these bills has emerged from any committee, although Congress has enacted numerous other amendments to § 501 during this same period, including an amendment to § 501(c)(3) itself. It is hardly conceivable that Congress—and in this setting, any Member of Congress—was not abundantly aware of what was going on. In view of its prolonged and acute awareness of so important an issue, Congress' failure to act on the bills proposed on this subject provides added support for concluding that Congress acquiesced in the IRS rulings of 1970 and 1971.

The evidence of Congressional approval of the policy embodied in Revenue Ruling 71-447 goes well beyond the failure of Congress to act on legislative proposals. Congress affirmatively manifested its acquiescence in the IRS policy when it enacted the present § 501(i) of the Code, Act of October 20, 1976, Pub.L. 94-568, 90 Stat. 2697 (1976). That provision denies tax-exempt status to social clubs whose charters or policy statements provide for "discrimination against any person on the basis of race, color, or religion." Both the House and Senate committee reports on that bill articulated the national policy against granting tax exemptions to racially discriminatory private clubs.

Even more significant is the fact that both reports focus on this Court's affirmance of *Green v. Connally*, [330 F.Supp. 1150, 1160 (D.D.C.)], as having established that "discrimination on account of race is inconsistent with an *educational institution's* tax exempt status." These references in Congressional committee reports on an enactment denying tax exemptions to racially discriminatory private social clubs cannot be read other than as indicating approval of the standards applied to racially discriminatory private schools by the IRS subsequent to 1970, and specifically of Revenue Ruling 71-447.[27] ...

---

27. Reliance is placed on scattered statements in floor debate by Congressmen critical of the IRS' adoption of Revenue Ruling 71-447. Those views did not prevail. That several Congressmen, expressing their individual views, argued that the IRS had no authority to take the action in question, is hardly a balance for the overwhelming evidence of Congressional awareness of and acquiescence in

The judgments of the Court of Appeals are, accordingly,

Affirmed.

JUSTICE POWELL, concurring in part and concurring in the judgment.

… Federal taxes are not imposed on organizations "operated exclusively for religious, charitable, scientific, testing for public safety, literary, or educational purposes…." 26 U.S.C. § 501(c)(3). The Code also permits a tax deduction for contributions made to these organizations. § 170(c). It is clear that petitioner[], [an] organization[] incorporated for educational purposes, fall[s] within the language of the statute. It also is clear that the language itself does not mandate refusal of tax-exempt status to any private school that maintains a racially discriminatory admissions policy. Accordingly, there is force in Justice Rehnquist's argument that §§ 170(c) and 501(c)(3) should be construed as setting forth the only criteria Congress has established for qualification as a tax-exempt organization. Indeed, were we writing prior to the history detailed in the Court's opinion, this could well be the construction I would adopt. But there has been a decade of acceptance that is persuasive in the circumstances of this case, and I conclude that there are now sufficient reasons for accepting the IRS's construction of the Code as proscribing tax exemptions for schools that discriminate on the basis of race as a matter of policy.

I cannot say that this construction of the Code, adopted by the IRS in 1970 and upheld by the Court of Appeals below, is without logical support. The statutory terms are not self-defining, and it is plausible that in some instances an organization seeking a tax exemption might act in a manner so clearly contrary to the purposes of our laws that it could not be deemed to serve the enumerated statutory purposes. And, as the Court notes, if any national policy is sufficiently fundamental to constitute such an overriding limitation on the availability of tax-exempt status under § 501(c)(3), it is the policy against racial discrimination in education. Finally, and of critical importance for me, the subsequent actions of Congress present "an unusually strong case of legislative acquiescence in and ratification by implication of the [IRS'] 1970 and 1971 rulings" with respect to racially discriminatory schools. In particular, Congress' enactment of § 501(i) in 1976 is strong evidence of agreement with these particular IRS rulings.[2] …

---

the IRS rulings of 1970 and 1971. Petitioners also argue that the Ashbrook and Dornan Amendments to the Treasury, Postal Service, and General Government Appropriations Act of 1980; Pub.L. 96-74; §§ 103, 614, 615; 93 Stat. 559, 562, 576–577 (1979), reflect Congressional opposition to the IRS policy formalized in Revenue Ruling 71-447. Those amendments, however, are directly concerned only with limiting more aggressive enforcement procedures proposed by the IRS in 1978 and 1979 and preventing the adoption of more stringent substantive standards. The Ashbrook Amendment, § 103 of the Act, applies only to procedures, guidelines or measures adopted after August 22, 1978, and thus in no way affects the status of Revenue Ruling 71-447. In fact, both Congressman Dornan and Congressman Ashbrook explicitly stated that their amendments would have no effect on prior IRS policy, including Revenue Ruling 71-447, see 125 Cong.Rec. H5982 (daily ed. July 16, 1979) (Cong. Dornan: "[M]y amendment will not affect existing IRS rules which IRS has used to revoke tax exemptions of white segregated academies under Revenue Ruling 71-447…."); 125 Cong.Rec. H5882 (daily ed. July 13, 1979) (Cong. Ashbrook: "My amendment very clearly indicates on its face that all the regulations in existence as of August 22, 1978, would not be touched."). These amendments therefore do not indicate Congressional rejection of Revenue Ruling 71-447 and the standards contained therein.

2. The District Court for the District of Columbia in *Green v. Connally*, 330 F.Supp. 1150 (three-judge court), *aff'd sub nom. Coit v. Green*, 404 U.S. 997, 92 S.Ct. 564, 30 L.Ed.2d 550 (1971) (*per curiam*), held that racially discriminatory private schools were not entitled to tax-exempt status. The same District Court, however, later ruled that racially segregated social clubs could receive tax exemptions under § 501(c)(7) of the Code. *See McGlotten v. Connally*, 338 F.Supp. 448 (D.D.C.1972) (three-judge court). Faced with these two important three-judge court rulings, Congress expressly overturned the relevant portion of *McGlotten* by enacting § 501(i), thus conforming the policy with respect to social

JUSTICE REHNQUIST, dissenting.

The Court points out that there is a strong national policy in this country against racial discrimination. To the extent that the Court states that Congress in furtherance of this policy could deny tax-exempt status to educational institutions that promote racial discrimination, I readily agree. But, unlike the Court, I am convinced that Congress simply has failed to take this action and, as this Court has said over and over again, regardless of our view on the propriety of Congress' failure to legislate we are not constitutionally empowered to act for them.

In approaching this statutory construction question the Court quite adeptly avoids the statute it is construing. This I am sure is no accident, for there is nothing in the language of § 501(c)(3) that supports the result obtained by the Court. Section 501(c)(3) provides tax-exempt status for:

> "Corporations, and any community chest, fund, or foundation, organized and operated exclusively for religious, charitable, scientific, testing for public safety, literary, or educational purposes, or to foster national or international amateur sports competition (but only if no part of its activities involve the provision of athletic facilities or equipment), or for the prevention of cruelty to children or animals, no part of the net earnings of which inures to the benefit of any private shareholder or individual, no substantial part of the activities of which is carrying on propaganda, or otherwise attempting, to influence legislation (except as otherwise provided in subsection (h)), and which does not participate in, or intervene in (including the publishing or distributing of statements), any political campaign on behalf of any candidate for public office." 26 U.S.C. § 501(c)(3).

With undeniable clarity, Congress has explicitly defined the requirements for § 501(c)(3) status. An entity must be (1) a corporation, or community chest, fund, or foundation, (2) organized for one of the eight enumerated purposes, (3) operated on a nonprofit basis, and (4) free from involvement in lobbying activities and political campaigns. Nowhere is there to be found some additional, undefined public policy requirement....

Perhaps recognizing the lack of support in the statute itself ... for the 1970 IRS change in interpretation, the Court finds that "[t]he actions of Congress since 1970 leave no doubt that the IRS reached the correct conclusion in exercising its authority," concluding that there is "an unusually strong case of legislative acquiescence in and ratification by implication of the 1970 and 1971 rulings." The Court relies first on several bills introduced to overturn the IRS interpretation of § 501(c)(3). But we have said before, and it is equally applicable here, that this type of congressional inaction is of virtually no weight in determining legislative intent. These bills and related hearings indicate little more than that a vigorous debate has existed in Congress concerning the new IRS position.

The Court next asserts that "Congress affirmatively manifested its acquiescence in the IRS policy when it enacted the present § 501(i) of the Code," a provision that "denies tax exempt status to social clubs whose charters or policy statements provide for" racial discrimination. Quite to the contrary, it seems to me that in § 501(i) Congress showed that when it wants to add a requirement prohibiting racial discrimination to one of the tax-benefit provisions, it is fully aware of how to do it.

---

clubs to the prevailing policy with respect to private schools. This affirmative step is a persuasive indication that Congress has not just silently acquiesced in the result of *Green*.

The Court intimates that the Ashbrook and Dornan Amendments also reflect an intent by Congress to acquiesce in the new IRS position. The amendments were passed to limit certain enforcement procedures proposed by the IRS in 1978 and 1979 for determining whether a school operated in a racially nondiscriminatory fashion. The Court points out that in proposing his amendment, Congressman Ashbrook stated: "'My amendment very clearly indicates on its face that all the regulations in existence as of August 22, 1978, would not be touched.'" The Court fails to note that Congressman Ashbrook also said:

> "The IRS has no authority to create public policy.... So long as the Congress has not acted to set forth a national policy respecting denial of tax exemptions to private schools, it is improper for the IRS or any other branch of the Federal Government to seek denial of tax-exempt status.... There exists but a single responsibility which is proper for the Internal Revenue Service: To serve as tax collector."

In the same debate, Congressman Grassley asserted: "Nobody argues that racial discrimination should receive preferred tax status in the United States. However, the IRS should not be making these decisions on the agency's own discretion. Congress should make these decisions." The same debates are filled with other similar statements. While on the whole these debates do not show conclusively that Congress believed the IRS had exceeded its authority with the 1970 change in position, they likewise are far less than a showing of acquiescence in and ratification of the new position.

This Court continuously has been hesitant to find ratification through inaction. This is especially true where such a finding "would result in a construction of the statute which not only is at odds with the language of the section in question and the pattern of the statute taken as a whole, but also is extremely far reaching in terms of the virtually untrammeled and unreviewable power it would vest in a regulatory agency." Few cases would call for more caution in finding ratification by acquiescence than the present one. The new IRS interpretation is not only far less than a long standing administrative policy, it is at odds with a position maintained by the IRS, and unquestioned by Congress, for several decades prior to 1970. The interpretation is unsupported by the statutory language, it is unsupported by legislative history, the interpretation has lead to considerable controversy in and out of Congress, and the interpretation gives to the IRS a broad power which until now Congress had kept for itself. Where in addition to these circumstances Congress has shown time and time again that it is ready to enact positive legislation to change the tax code when it desires, this Court has no business finding that Congress has adopted the new IRS position by failing to enact legislation to reverse it.

I have no disagreement with the Court's finding that there is a strong national policy in this country opposed to racial discrimination. I agree with the Court that Congress has the power to further this policy by denying § 501(c)(3) status to organizations that practice racial discrimination. But as of yet Congress has failed to do so. Whatever the reasons for the failure, this Court should not legislate for Congress....

For this reason, I would reverse the Court of Appeals.

Notes and Questions

(1) *Plain Meaning.* Was the statute clear or ambiguous according to the majority and concurrence? According to the dissent? Assuming the majority found the statute ambiguous, how did the majority resolve that ambiguity?

(2) *Executive Interpretation.* Did any justice question whether legislative acquiescence would be appropriate when the executive rather than the judiciary had interpreted the statute? Should there be any difference in how those scenarios are treated?

(3) *Legislative Acquiescence.* According to the majority, how did Congress demonstrate acquiescence to the IRS's interpretation? Was the evidence of acquiescence more or less convincing than the evidence of legislative acquiescence in *Flood v. Kuhn*? Why didn't the dissent find this evidence to be convincing?

(4) *Legislative Silence Doesn't Mean Acquiescence or Does it?* You've now read three cases on legislative acquiescence. In each case, the court stated that legislative silence generally is not considered acquiescence. For example, in this last case, the majority said, "Non-action by Congress is not often a useful guide...." Yet, in each case, the court found acquiescence. Why do you think courts may be so willing to find acquiescence? Professor Marshall suggested that the courts are more likely to find acquiescence when there is evidence that the legislature had been aware of the statutory interpretation. Marshall, *supra*, at 185. Does that observation explain the results in each of the above cases?

Problem 9-1

Return to the case of the Speluncean Explorers excerpted in Chapter 2. You may recall that, because the court was evenly divided, the lower court opinion was left in place. Assume the following new facts:* Ten years have passed since the case was decided. The governor refused to issue a pardon, and all of the defendants were hanged. Amidst public outcry over the result, the legislature attempted — on five separate occasions — to amend the statute by providing an exception for cases of necessity and by defining "willfully" more narrowly. A group of legislators adamantly opposed any change to the statute. During one of the legislative debates, a few such legislators commented that any such changes would eviscerate the purpose of the statute: namely to prevent anyone from valuing his own life above another's. These same legislators offered a floor amendment that would have eliminated the common law exception for self-defense. Other legislators, who also opposed the bill, suggested a different amendment, one that would leave it to the trial judge to use discretion in sentencing defendants. Rather than risk either of these amendments passing, proponents of the bill withdrew it from consideration. This same dance occurred each time the amendment was offered. Eventually, proponents simply gave up trying to amend the statute. Thus, the murder statute remains the same today as when the case was decided: "Whoever shall willfully take the life of another shall be punished by death." N.C.S.A. §12-A.

A fifth explorer has suddenly been found, living in another country as though the events of May 4299 never occurred. He was extradited, tried for murder under the statute above, and found guilty during a jury trial. The Appellate Court affirmed. Public outrage is no less than it was ten years ago.

The case is now pending before the Newgarth Supreme Court. Assume that you are a law clerk to Justice Seizmore, who was recently appointed to the Newgarth Supreme Court. Justice Seizmore replaced Justice Tatting, who withdrew from the earlier opinion (leading to the divided court).

Justice Seizmore has asked you to draft an opinion helping her to resolve the case. In your draft, analyze whether the subsequent legislative activity should have any bearing

---

* Authors' footnote: This problem is loosely derived from Peter Suber, The Case of the Speluncean Explorers, 35–36 (1998).

on the court's decision. Would it affect your analysis if no amendments had been considered? What if fifty amendments had been considered and rejected?

C. What, Exactly, Is "Silence"?

That question lies not too far below the question of whether legislative silence constitutes acquiescence. In *Johnson v. Transportation Agency*, 480 U.S. 616, 629 n.7 (1987), the Court found acquiescence in part because "not one legislator even proposed a bill" to overrule *Weber*:

> As Justice Blackmun said in his concurrence in *Weber*, "[I]f the Court has misperceived the political will, it has the assurance that because the question is statutory Congress may set a different course if it so chooses." Congress has not amended the statute to reject our construction, nor have any such amendments even been proposed, and we therefore may assume that our interpretation was correct. Justice Scalia's dissent faults the fact that we take note of the absence of congressional efforts to amend the statute to nullify *Weber*. It suggests that congressional inaction cannot be regarded as acquiescence under all circumstances, but then draws from that unexceptional point the conclusion that any reliance on congressional failure to act is necessarily a "canard." The fact that inaction may not always provide crystalline revelation, however, should not obscure the fact that it may be probative to varying degrees. *Weber*, for instance, was a widely publicized decision that addressed a prominent issue of public debate. Legislative inattention thus is not a plausible explanation for congressional inaction. Furthermore, Congress not only passed no contrary legislation in the wake of *Weber*, but not one legislator even proposed a bill to do so. The barriers of the legislative process therefore also seem a poor explanation for failure to act. By contrast, when Congress has been displeased with our interpretation of Title VII, it has not hesitated to amend the statute to tell us so. For instance, when Congress passed the Pregnancy Discrimination Act of 1978, "it unambiguously expressed its disapproval of both the holding and the reasoning of the Court in [a prior decision]." Surely, it is appropriate to find some probative value in such radically different congressional reactions to this Court's interpretations of the same statute.

Id.

Was the Court correct that in some circumstances inaction can indicate consent? Suppose, for example, that the House voted on a bill to reverse *Flood* and the vote failed. Would one failure be enough? What if both houses voted down similar bills? What if Congress passed such a bill, but the president vetoed it? What if bills were introduced in one or both houses, but never acted upon? Should a court find it significant if not even one legislator proposes a bill in response to a major holding? How about two legislators? Three? When does failed legislative response of any degree become significant? On the one hand, given the difficulty of the political process, should subsequent legislative inaction ever be relevant? On the other hand, doesn't the fact that Congress has on occasion amended statutes in response to interpretations show that subsequent legislative inaction should always be relevant? Why or why not?

The next case probes the question of acquiescence and silence further. The simple issue in *Brown & Williamson* was whether the Food and Drug Administration ("FDA") had authority to regulate tobacco. The majority relied on the fact that Congress had enacted a number of statutes in related areas to argue that Congress did not intend for the FDA to regulate tobacco, but rather wished to regulate tobacco itself.

The history behind the case is interesting. *See generally*, WILLIAM N. ESKRIDGE, JR., ET AL., CASES AND MATERIALS ON LEGISLATION STATUTES AND THE CREATION OF PUBLIC POLICY 798–99 (3rd ed. 2001). Beginning in the 1980s, if not earlier, FDA research showed that smoking constituted a serious health risk. The FDA had authority to regulate "food," "drugs," and "devices." But, also for many years, the FDA had not attempted to regulate tobacco, most likely because it knew that the tobacco companies had, and still have, an extremely powerful lobby. Further, neither President Ronald Reagan, nor President George H. W. Bush would have supported an FDA effort to regulate tobacco. Thus, the FDA's position for many years had been that tobacco was not a "drug" and cigarettes were not "devices;" hence, the agency concluded that neither was within its regulatory authority.

Then the political climate changed. In 1992, President Bill Clinton was elected. President Clinton opposed smoking. He appointed Dr. David A. Kessler, M.D., to head the FDA and indicated a willingness to support Kessler by vetoing tobacco-friendly legislation. In this changed political context, the FDA, in 1996, changed its policy and promulgated regulations covering tobacco, declaring them to be "drugs" and, thus, within its jurisdiction. Tobacco companies quickly challenged the authority of the FDA to regulate their products. In the case we excerpt below, the Supreme Court held that the agency lacked authority to regulate relying on acquiescence principles.

While you may not have yet studied the deference courts normally give to an administrative agency's interpretation of a statute, you should be aware that courts typically will not invalidate an agency interpretation unless either (1) Congress did not implicitly or explicitly delegate decision-making authority to the agency or (2) the agency has unreasonably interpreted the statute. As you read this opinion, focus on the use of acquiescence. What entity did Congress acquiescence to, the judiciary or the FDA?

Food & Drug Admin. v. Brown & Williamson Tobacco Corp.
529 U.S. 120 (2000)

JUSTICE O'CONNOR delivered the opinion of the Court.

In 1996, the Food and Drug Administration (FDA), after having expressly disavowed any such authority since its inception, asserted jurisdiction to regulate tobacco products. The FDA concluded that nicotine is a "drug" within the meaning of the Food, Drug, and Cosmetic Act (FDCA or Act) and that cigarettes and smokeless tobacco are "combination products" that deliver nicotine to the body. Pursuant to this authority, it promulgated regulations intended to reduce tobacco consumption among children and adolescents....

The FDCA grants the FDA ... the authority to regulate ..."drugs" and "devices." The Act defines "drug" to include "articles (other than food) intended to affect the structure or any function of the body." It defines "device," ... as "an instrument, apparatus, implement, machine, contrivance, ... which is ... intended to affect the structure or any function of the body." § 321(h). The Act also grants the FDA the authority to regulate so-called "combination products," which "constitute a combination of a drug, device, or biological product." § 353(g)(1)....

On August 28, 1996, the FDA ... determined that nicotine is a "drug" and that cigarettes and smokeless tobacco are "drug delivery devices," and therefore it had jurisdiction under the FDCA to regulate tobacco products....

Based on [its] findings, the FDA promulgated regulations concerning tobacco products' promotion, labeling, and accessibility to children and adolescents....

Respondents, a group of tobacco manufacturers, retailers, and advertisers, filed suit ... challenging the regulations. They [argued] that the FDA lacked jurisdiction to regulate tobacco....

[In reviewing an agency's regulation we] must first ask "whether Congress has directly spoken to the precise question at issue." ...

In determining whether Congress has specifically addressed the question at issue, a reviewing court should not confine itself to examining a particular statutory provision in isolation. The meaning—or ambiguity—of certain words or phrases may only become evident when placed in context. It is a fundamental cannon of statutory construction that the words of a statute must be read in their context and with a view to their place in the overall statutory scheme. A court must therefore interpret the statute as a symmetrical and coherent regulatory scheme, and fit, if possible, all parts into an harmonious whole. Similarly, the meaning of one statute may be affected by other Acts, particularly where Congress has spoken subsequently and more specifically to the topic at hand....

In determining whether Congress has spoken directly to the FDA's authority to regulate tobacco, we must ... consider in greater detail the tobacco-specific legislation that Congress has enacted over the past 35 years. At the time a statute is enacted, it may have a range of plausible meanings. Over time, however, subsequent acts can shape or focus those meanings. The classic judicial task of reconciling many laws enacted over time, and getting them to make sense in combination, necessarily assumes that the implications of a statute may be altered by the implications of a later statute. This is particularly so where the scope of the earlier statute is broad but the subsequent statutes more specifically address the topic at hand....

Congress has enacted six separate pieces of legislation since 1965 addressing the problem of tobacco use and human health....

In adopting each statute, Congress has acted against the backdrop of the FDA's consistent and repeated statements that it lacked authority under the FDCA to regulate tobacco absent claims of therapeutic benefit by the manufacturer....

[For example,] in June 1964, the [Federal Trade Commission (FTC)] promulgated a final rule requiring cigarette manufacturers "to disclose ... that cigarette smoking is dangerous to health and may cause death from cancer and other diseases." ...

In response to ... the FTC's proposed rule, Congress convened hearings to consider legislation addressing "the tobacco problem." During those deliberations, FDA representatives testified before Congress that the agency lacked jurisdiction under the FDCA to regulate tobacco products....

The FDA's disavowal of jurisdiction was consistent with the position that it had taken since the agency's inception....

Moreover..., Congress considered and rejected several proposals to give the FDA the authority to regulate tobacco. In April 1963, Representative Udall introduced a bill "[t]o amend the Federal Food, Drug, and Cosmetic Act so as to make that Act applicable to smoking products." Two months later, Senator Moss introduced an identical bill in the Senate. In discussing his proposal on the Senate floor, Senator Moss explained that "this amendment simply places smoking products under FDA jurisdiction, along with foods, drugs, and cosmetics." In December 1963, Representative Rhodes introduced another bill that would have amended the FDCA "by striking out 'food, drug, device, or cosmetic,' each place where it appears therein and inserting in lieu thereof 'food, drug, device, cosmetic, or smoking product.'" And in January 1965, five months before passage of the FCLAA, Representative Udall again introduced a bill to amend the FDCA "to make that Act applicable to smoking products." None of these proposals became law.

Congress ultimately decided in 1965 to subject tobacco products to the less extensive regulatory scheme of the FCLAA [Federal Cigarette Labeling and Advertising Act], which created a "comprehensive Federal program to deal with cigarette labeling and advertising with respect to any relationship between smoking and health." The FCLAA rejected any regulation of advertising, but it required the warning, "Caution: Cigarette Smoking May Be Hazardous to Your Health," to appear on all cigarette packages....

Further, the FCLAA evidences Congress' intent to preclude any administrative agency from exercising significant policymaking authority on the subject of smoking and health. In addition to prohibiting any additional requirements for cigarette labeling, the FCLAA provided that "[n]o statement relating to smoking and health shall be required in the advertising of any cigarettes the packages of which are labeled in conformity with the provisions of this Act." Thus, in reaction to the FTC's attempt to regulate cigarette labeling and advertising, Congress enacted a statute reserving exclusive control over both subjects to itself.

Subsequent tobacco-specific legislation followed a similar pattern. By the FCLAA's own terms, the prohibition on any additional cigarette labeling or advertising regulations relating to smoking and health was to expire July 1, 1969. In anticipation of the provision's expiration, both the [Federal Communication Commission] and the FTC proposed rules governing the advertisement of cigarettes. After debating the proper role for administrative agencies in the regulation of tobacco, Congress amended the FCLAA by banning cigarette advertisements "on any medium of electronic communication subject to the jurisdiction of the Federal Communications Commission" and strengthening the warning required to appear on cigarette packages. Importantly, Congress extended indefinitely the prohibition on any other regulation of cigarette labeling with respect to smoking and health.... Moreover, it expressly forbade the FTC from taking any action on its pending rule until July 1, 1971, and it required the FTC, if it decided to proceed with its rule thereafter, to notify Congress at least six months in advance of the rule's becoming effective. As the chairman of the House committee in which the bill originated stated, "the Congress—the body elected by the people—must make the policy determinations involved in this legislation—and not some agency made up of appointed officials." ...

Meanwhile, the FDA continued to maintain that it lacked jurisdiction under the FDCA to regulate tobacco products as customarily marketed....

Against [the FDA's repeated assertions that it lacked jurisdiction to regulate tobacco products], Congress enacted three additional tobacco-specific statutes over the next four years that incrementally expanded its regulatory scheme for tobacco products. In 1983, Congress adopted the Alcohol and Drug Abuse Amendments, which require the Secretary of HHS to report to Congress every three years on the "addictive property of tobacco" and to include recommendations for action that the Secretary may deem appropriate. A year later, Congress enacted the Comprehensive Smoking Education Act, which amended the FCLAA by again modifying the prescribed warning. Notably, during debate on the Senate floor, Senator Hawkins argued that the FCLAA was necessary in part because "[u]nder the Food, Drug and Cosmetic Act, the Congress exempted tobacco products." And in 1986, Congress enacted the Comprehensive Smokeless Tobacco Health Education Act of 1986 (CSTHEA), which essentially extended the regulatory provisions of the FCLAA to smokeless tobacco products.… Thus, as with cigarettes, Congress reserved for itself an aspect of smokeless tobacco regulation that is particularly important to the FDCA's regulatory scheme.…

Between 1987 and 1989, Congress considered three more bills that would have amended the FDCA to grant the FDA jurisdiction to regulate tobacco products. As before, Congress rejected the proposals.…

Taken together, these actions by Congress over the past 35 years preclude an interpretation of the FDCA that grants the FDA jurisdiction to regulate tobacco products. We do not rely on Congress' failure to act—its consideration and rejection of bills that would have given the FDA this authority—in reaching this conclusion. Indeed, this is not a case of simple inaction by Congress that purportedly represents its acquiescence in an agency's position. To the contrary, Congress has enacted several statutes addressing the particular subject of tobacco and health, creating a distinct regulatory scheme for cigarettes and smokeless tobacco. In doing so, Congress has been aware of tobacco's health hazards and its pharmacological effects. It has also enacted this legislation against the background of the FDA repeatedly and consistently asserting that it lacks jurisdiction under the FDCA to regulate tobacco products as customarily marketed. Further, Congress has persistently acted to preclude a meaningful role for any administrative agency in making policy on the subject of tobacco and health. Moreover, the substance of Congress' regulatory scheme is, in an important respect, incompatible with FDA jurisdiction. Although the supervision of product labeling to protect consumer health is a substantial component of the FDA's regulation of drugs and devices, the FCLAA and the CSTHEA explicitly prohibit any federal agency from imposing any health-related labeling requirements on cigarettes or smokeless tobacco products.

Under these circumstances, it is clear that Congress' tobacco-specific legislation has effectively ratified the FDA's previous position that it lacks jurisdiction to regulate tobacco.… Congress has affirmatively acted to address the issue of tobacco and health, relying on the representations of the FDA that it had no authority to regulate tobacco. It has created a distinct scheme to regulate the sale of tobacco products, focused on labeling and advertising, and premised on the belief that the FDA lacks such jurisdiction under the FDCA. As a result, Congress' tobacco-specific statutes preclude the FDA from regulating tobacco products.…

This is hardly an ordinary case. Contrary to its representations to Congress since 1914, the FDA has now asserted jurisdiction to regulate an industry constituting a significant portion of the American economy. In fact, the FDA contends that, were it to determine that tobacco products provide no "reasonable assurance of safety," it would have the authority to ban cigarettes and smokeless tobacco entirely. Owing to its unique place in American history and society, tobacco has its own unique political history. Congress, for better or for worse, has created a distinct regulatory scheme for tobacco products, squarely rejected proposals to give the FDA jurisdiction over tobacco, and repeatedly acted to preclude any agency from exercising significant policymaking authority in the area.…

It is therefore clear, based on the FDCA's overall regulatory scheme and the subsequent tobacco legislation, that Congress has directly spoken to the question at issue and precluded the FDA from regulating tobacco products.…

[A]ffirmed.…

Justice Breyer, with whom Justice Stevens, Justice Souter, and Justice Ginsburg, join, dissenting.

The Food and Drug Administration (FDA) has the authority to regulate "articles (other than food) intended to affect the structure or any function of the body.…" (FDCA), 21

U.S.C. § 321(g)(1)(C). Unlike the majority, I believe that tobacco products fit within this statutory language.

In its own interpretation, the majority nowhere denies the following two salient points. First, tobacco products (including cigarettes) fall within the scope of this statutory definition, read literally. Cigarettes achieve their mood-stabilizing effects through the interaction of the chemical nicotine and the cells of the central nervous system. Both cigarette manufacturers and smokers alike know of, and desire, that chemically induced result. Hence, cigarettes are "intended to affect" the body's "structure" and "function," in the literal sense of these words.

Second, the statute's basic purpose—the protection of public health—supports the inclusion of cigarettes within its scope.... Indeed, tobacco products kill more people in this country every year than ... AIDS..., car accidents, alcohol, homicides, illegal drugs, suicides, and fires, combined.

Despite the FDCA's literal language and general purpose (both of which support the FDA's finding that cigarettes come within its statutory authority), the majority nonetheless reads the statute as excluding tobacco products ... [because] Congress has enacted other statutes, which, when viewed in light of the FDA's long history of denying tobacco-related jurisdiction and considered together with Congress' failure explicitly to grant the agency tobacco-specific authority, demonstrate that Congress did not intend for the FDA to exercise jurisdiction over tobacco.

In my view, [this] proposition[] is [not] valid....

In the majority's view, laws enacted since 1965 require us to deny jurisdiction, whatever the FDCA might mean in their absence. But why? Do those laws contain language barring FDA jurisdiction? The majority must concede that they do not. Do they contain provisions that are inconsistent with the FDA's exercise of jurisdiction? With one exception, the majority points to no such provision. Do they somehow repeal the principles of law that otherwise would lead to the conclusion that the FDA has jurisdiction in this area? The companies themselves deny making any such claim. Perhaps the later laws "shape" and "focus" what the 1938 Congress meant a generation earlier. But this Court has warned against using the views of a later Congress to construe a statute enacted many years before. And, while the majority suggests that the subsequent history "control[s] our construction" of the FDCA, this Court expressly has held that such subsequent views are not "controlling." [S]ee also Sullivan v. Finkelstein, 496 U.S. 617 (1990) (Scalia, J., concurring) ("Arguments based on subsequent legislative history ... should not be taken seriously, not even in a footnote").

Regardless, the later statutes do not support the majority's conclusion.... [T]he subsequent legislative history is critically ambivalent....

Consider, for example, Congress' failure to provide the FDA with express authority to regulate tobacco—a circumstance that the majority finds significant.... [T]he defeat of various different proposed jurisdictional changes proves nothing. This history shows only that Congress could not muster the votes necessary either to grant or to deny the FDA the relevant authority. It neither favors nor disfavors the majority's position.

The majority also mentions the speed with which Congress acted to take jurisdiction away from other agencies once they tried to assert it. But such a congressional response again proves nothing. On the one hand, the speedy reply might suggest that Congress somehow resented agency assertions of jurisdiction in an area it desired to reserve for itself—a consideration that supports the majority. On the other hand, Congress' quick reaction with respect to other agencies' regulatory efforts contrasts dramatically with its failure to enact any responsive law (at any speed) after the FDA asserted jurisdiction over tobacco more than three years ago. And that contrast supports the opposite conclusion....

[Moreover, w]hen Congress enacted the FCLAA, it focused upon the regulatory efforts of the Federal Trade Commission (FTC), not the FDA. And the Public Health Cigarette Smoking Act of 1969 expressly amended the FCLAA to provide that "[n]othing in this Act shall be construed to affirm or deny the [FTC's] holding that it has the authority to issue trade regulation rules" for tobacco. Why would one read the FCLAA's pre-emption clause—a provision that Congress intended to limit even in respect to the agency directly at issue—so broadly that it would bar a different agency from engaging in any other cigarette regulation at all? The answer is that the Court need not, and should not, do so....

When the FCLAA's narrow pre-emption provision is set aside, the majority's conclusion that Congress clearly intended for its tobacco-related statutes to be the exclusive "response" to "the problem of tobacco and health," is based on legislative silence....

The upshot is that the Court today holds that a regulatory statute aimed at unsafe drugs and devices does not authorize regulation of a drug (nicotine) and a device (a cigarette) that the Court itself finds unsafe. Far more than most, this particular drug and device risks the life-threatening harms that administrative regulation seeks to rectify. The majority's conclusion is counterintuitive. And, for the reasons set forth, I believe that the law does not require it....

Notes and Questions

(1) *Is this a Case of Legislative Inaction?* The dissent claimed the majority relied on legislative acquiescence, but the majority specifically stated it was not doing so. Who was right?

(2) *Plain Text.* Is the dissent's point that the plain text matters more than the agency's interpretation? How does the majority address that argument? Isn't the dissent correct: the FDA's position that it had no jurisdiction to act was irrelevant? If Congress intended for the FDA to have authority, then the FDA had authority. If the language of the statute is clear, isn't that the end of the interpretation process? Why wasn't the clarity of the language the end of the question here?

In this regard, consider that Justice Breyer, dissenting in *Brown & Williamson*, quoted this passage from a concurring opinion by Justice Scalia from an earlier case:

> The legislative history of a statute is the history of its consideration and enactment. "Subsequent legislative history"—which presumably means the *post-enactment* history of a statute's consideration and enactment—is a contradiction in terms. The phrase is used to smuggle into judicial consideration legislators' expressions *not* of what a bill currently under consideration means (which, the theory goes, reflects what their colleagues understood they were voting for), but of what a law *previously enacted* means....
>
> It is assuredly *not* the rule that the legislators or committee members in question must have considered, or at least voted upon, the particular statute in question— or even that they have been members of the particular Congress that enacted it....
>
> In my opinion, the views of a legislator concerning a statute already enacted are entitled to no more weight than the views of a judge concerning a statute

not yet passed. In some situations, of course, the expression of a legislator relating to a previously enacted statute may bear upon the meaning of a provision in a bill under consideration—which provision, if passed, may in turn affect judicial interpretation of the previously enacted statute, since statutes *in pari materia* should be interpreted harmoniously. Such an expression would be useful, if at all, not because it was subsequent legislative history of the earlier statute, but because it was plain old legislative history of the later one.

> Arguments based on subsequent legislative history, like arguments based on antecedent futurity, should not be taken seriously, not even in a footnote.

Sullivan v. Finkelstein, 496 U.S. 617, 631 (1990) (Scalia, J., concurring). Should Justice Scalia's decision to sign the majority's opinion in *Brown & Williamson* "be taken seriously"? Can you reconcile his position in *Brown & Williamson* with his position in *Sullivan*?

(3) *Do the Courts Treat Subsequent Legislative Action and Inaction Consistently? Clearly?* Consider this: "the irony of the matter is that the Court appears willing to find significance in Congress' silence, while generally declining to rely on far more explicit post-enactment legislative history—even of the Congress that passed the statute being interpreted!" Marshall, *supra*, at 193. Can you explain why Professor Marshall finds the legislative acquiescence doctrine so ironic?

(4) *What Do You Do?* As an advocate, how should you use subsequent legislative activity? What makes some subsequent legislative inaction more compelling than others? Isn't *stare decisis* a more compelling reason than subsequent legislative acquiescence for maintaining the status quo?

Problem 9-2

The essay below summarizes many of the statutory interpretation canons you have already studied. And, it is particularly relevant to this chapter on legislative acquiescence. See if you can identify each of the canons in the opinions below, including the plain meaning canon, the rule against surplusage, *in pari materia*, *stare decisis*, legislative acquiescence, absurdity, ambiguity, and the role of purpose, which we will study in the next chapter.

The Food Stays in the Kitchen:
Everything I Needed to Know about Statutory Interpretation
I Learned by the Time I was Nine[*]
12 THE GREEN BAG 3rd 357 (2009)
Hillel Y. Levin

On March 23, 1986, the following proclamation, henceforth known as Ordinance 7.3, was made by the Supreme Lawmaker, Mother:

> I am tired of finding popcorn kernels, pretzel crumbs, and pieces of cereal all over the family room. From now on, no food may be eaten outside the kitchen.

Thereupon, litigation arose.

FATHER, C.J., issued the following ruling on March 30, 1986: Defendant Anne, age 14, was seen carrying a glass of water into the family room. She was charged with violating

---

[*] Copyright Hillel Y. Levin, Professor. Used by permission.

Ordinance 7.3 ("the Rule"). We hold that drinking water outside of the kitchen does not violate the Rule.

The Rule prohibits "food" from being eaten outside of the kitchen. This prohibition does not extend to water, which is a beverage rather than food. Our interpretation is confirmed by Webster's Dictionary, which defines food to mean, in relevant part, a "material consisting essentially of protein, carbohydrate, and fat used in the body of an organism to sustain growth, repair, and vital processes and to furnish energy" and "nutriment in solid form." Plainly, water, which contains no protein, carbohydrate, or fat, and which is not in solid form, is not a food.

Customary usage further substantiates our distinction between "food" and water. Ordinance 6.2, authored by the very same Supreme Lawmaker, declares: "[a]fter you get home from school, have some food and something to drink, and then do your homework." This demonstrates that the Supreme Lawmaker speaks of food and drink separately and is fully capable of identifying one or both as appropriate. After all, if "food," as used in the Family Code, included beverages, then the word "drink" in Ordinance 6.2 would be redundant and mere surplusage. Thus, had the Supreme Lawmaker wished to prohibit beverages from being taken out of the kitchen, she could easily have done so by declaring that "no food or drink is permitted outside the kitchen."

Our understanding of the word "food" to exclude water is further buttressed by the evident purpose of the Rule. The Supreme Lawmaker enacted the Rule as a response to the mess produced by solid foods. Water, even when spilled, does not produce a similar kind of mess.

Some may argue that the cup from which the Defendant was drinking water may, if left in the family room, itself be a mess. But we are not persuaded. The language of the Rule speaks to the Supreme Lawmaker's concern with small particles of food rather than to a more generalized concern with the containers in which food is held. A cup or other container bears a greater resemblance to other bric-a-brac, such as toys and backpacks, to which the Rule does not speak, than it does to the food spoken of in the Rule. Although we need not divine the Supreme Lawmaker's reasons for such a distinction, there are at least two plausible explanations. First, it could be that small particles of food left around the house are more problematic than the stray cup or bowl because they find their way into hard-to-reach places and may lead to rodent infestation. Second, it is possible that the Supreme Lawmaker was unconcerned with containers being left in the family room because citizens of this jurisdiction have been meticulous about removing such containers.

BABYSITTER SUE, J., issued the following ruling on April 12, 1986: Defendant Beatrice, age 12, is charged with violating Ordinance 7.3 by drinking a beverage, to wit: orange juice, in the family room. The Defendant relies on our ruling of March 30, 1986, which "h[e]ld that drinking water outside of the kitchen does not violate the [Ordinance]," and urges us to conclude that all beverages are permitted in the family room under Ordinance 7.3. While we believe this is a difficult case, we agree. As we have previously explained, the term "food" does not extend to beverages.

Our hesitation stems not from the literal meaning of the Ordinance, which strongly supports the Defendant's claim, but rather from an understanding of its purpose. As we have previously stated, and as evidenced by the language of the Ordinance itself, the Ordinance was enacted as a result of the Supreme Lawmaker's concern with mess. Unlike the case with water, if the Defendant were to spill orange juice on the couch or rug in the family room, the mess would be problematic—perhaps even more so than the mess produced by crumbs of food. It is thus difficult to infer why the Supreme Lawmaker would choose to prohibit solid foods outside of the kitchen but to permit orange juice.

Nevertheless, we are bound the plain language of the Ordinance and by precedent. We are confident that if the Supreme Lawmaker disagrees with the outcome in this case, she can change or clarify the law accordingly.

GRANDMA, SENIOR J., issued the following ruling on May 3, 1986: Defendant Charlie, age 10, is charged with violating Ordinance 7.3 by eating popcorn in the family room. The Defendant contends, and we agree, that the Ordinance does not apply in this case. Ordinance 7.3 was enacted to prevent messes outside of the kitchen. This purpose is demonstrated by the language of the Ordinance itself, which refers to food being left "all over the family room" as the immediate cause of its adoption.

Such messes are produced only when one transfers food from a container to his or her mouth outside of the kitchen. During that process—what the Ordinance refers to as "eat[ing]"—crumbs and other food particles often fall out of the eater's hand and onto the floor or sofa.

As the record shows, the Defendant placed all of the popcorn into his mouth prior to leaving the kitchen. He merely masticated and swallowed while in the family room. At no time was there any danger that a mess would be produced.

We are certain that there was no intent to prohibit merely the chewing or swallowing of food outside of the kitchen. After all, the Supreme Lawmaker has expressly permitted the chewing of gum in the family room. It would be senseless and absurd to treat gum differently from popcorn that has been ingested prior to leaving the kitchen.

If textual support is necessary to support this obvious and commonsensical interpretation, abundant support is available. First, the Ordinance prohibits food from being "eaten" outside of the kitchen. The term "eat" is defined to mean "to take in through the mouth as food: ingest, chew, and swallow in turn." The Defendant, having only chewed and swallowed, did not "eat." Further, the Ordinance prohibits the "eat[ing]" rather than the "bringing" of food outside of the kitchen; and indeed, food is often brought out of the kitchen and through the family room, as when school lunches are delivered to the front door for carpool pickup. There is no reason to treat food enclosed in a brown bag any differently from food enclosed within the Defendant's mouth.

Finally, if any doubt remains as to the meaning of this Ordinance as it pertains to the chewing and swallowing of food, we cannot punish the Defendant for acting reasonably and in good faith reliance upon the text of the Ordinance and our past pronouncements as to its meaning and intent.

UNCLE RICK, J., issued the following ruling on May 20, 1986: Defendant Charlie, age 10, is charged with violating Ordinance 7.3 ("the Rule") by bringing a double thick mint chocolate chip milkshake into the family room. Were I writing on a clean slate, I would surely conclude that the Defendant has violated the Rule. A double thick milkshake is "food" because it contains protein, carbohydrate, and/or fat. Further, the purpose of the Rule—to prevent messes—would be undermined by permitting a double thick milkshake to be brought into the family room. Indeed, it makes little sense to treat a milkshake differently from a pretzel or a scoop of ice cream.

However, I am not writing on a clean slate. Our precedents have now established that all beverages are permitted outside of the kitchen under the Rule. The Defendant relied on those precedents in good faith. Further, the Supreme Lawmaker has had ample opportunity to clarify or change the law to prohibit any or all beverages from being brought out of the kitchen, and she has elected not to exercise that authority. I can only conclude that she is satisfied with the status quo.

GRANDMA, SENIOR J., issued the following ruling on July 2, 1986: Defendant Anne, age 14, is charged with violating Ordinance 7.3 by eating apple slices in the family room. As we have repeatedly held, the Ordinance pertains only to messy foods. Moreover, the Ordinance explicitly refers to "popcorn kernels, pretzel crumbs, and pieces of cereal." Sliced apples, not being messy (and certainly being no worse than orange juice and milkshakes, which have been permitted by our prior decisions), and being wholly dissimilar from the crumbly foods listed in the Ordinance, do not come within the meaning of the Ordinance.

We also find it significant that the consumption of healthy foods such as sliced apples is a behavior that this jurisdiction supports and encourages. It would be odd to read the Ordinance in a way that would discourage such healthy behaviors by limiting them to the kitchen.

AUNT SARAH, J., issued the following ruling on August 12, 1986: Defendant Beatrice, age 13, is charged with violating Ordinance 7.3 by eating pretzels, popcorn, cereal, and birthday cake in the family room. Under ordinary circumstances, the Defendant would clearly be subject to the Ordinance. However, the circumstances giving rise to the Defendant's action in this case are far from ordinary.

The Defendant celebrated her thirteenth birthday on August 10, 1986. For the celebration, she invited four of her closest friends to sleep over. During the evening, and as part of the festivities, the celebrants watched a movie in the family room. Chief Justice Father provided those present with drinks and snacks, including the aforesaid pretzels, popcorn, and cereal, for consumption during the movie-watching. Father admonished the Defendant to clean up after the movie, and there is no evidence in the record suggesting that the Defendant failed to do so.

We frankly concede that the Defendant's actions were violative of the plain meaning of the Ordinance. However, given the special and unique nature of the occasion, the fact that Father, a representative of the Supreme Lawmaker—as well as of this Court—implicitly approved of the Defendant's actions, and the apparent efforts of the Defendant in upholding the spirit of the Ordinance by cleaning up after her friends, we believe that the best course of action is to release the Defendant.

In light of the growing confusion in the interpretation of this ambiguous Ordinance, we urge the Supreme Lawmaker to exercise her authority to clarify and/or change the law if and as she deems it appropriate.

FATHER, C.J., issued the following ruling on September 17, 1986: Defendant Derek, age 9, was charged with violating Ordinance 7.3 ("the Rule") by eating pretzels, potato chips, popcorn, a bagel with cream cheese, cottage cheese, and a chocolate bar in the family room. The Defendant argues that our precedents have clearly established a pattern permitting food to be eaten in the family room so long as the eater cleans up any mess. He further maintains that it would be unjust for this Court to punish him after having permitted past actions such as drinking water, orange juice, and a milkshake, as well as swallowing popcorn, eating apple slices, and eating pretzels, popcorn, and cereal on a special occasion. The Defendant avers that there is no rational distinction between his sister's eating foods in the family room during a movie on a special occasion and his eating foods in the family room during a weekly television show.

We agree. The citizens of this jurisdiction look to the rulings of this Court, as well as to general practice, to understand their rights and obligations as citizens. In the many months since the Rule was originally announced, the cumulative rulings of this Court on the subject would signify to any citizen that, whatever the technical language of the Rule, the real Rule is that they must clean up after eating any food outside of the kitchen. To draw and enforce any other line now would be arbitrary and, as such, unjust.

On November 4, 1986, the following proclamation, henceforth known as The New Ordinance 7.3, was made by the Supreme Lawmaker, Mother:

> Over the past few months, I have found empty cups, orange juice stains, milk-shake spills, slimy spots of unknown origin, all manner of crumbs, melted chocolate, and icing from cake in the family room. I thought I was clear the first time! And you've all had a chance to show me that you could use your common sense and clean up after yourselves. So now let me be clearer: No food, gum, or drink of any kind, on any occasion or in any form, is permitted in the family room. Ever. Seriously. I mean it.

Chapter 10

Finding and Using Purpose

In Chapter 8, you learned about the role legislative history plays in statutory interpretation. In this chapter, we move to statutory purpose: What is it? Where do you find it? And what role has it played and should it play in interpretation?

As we have explained, purposivists and intentionalists agree with textualists that the text is the primary focus. But intentionalists and purposivists contend that statutes must be interpreted by relying upon other sources, not just the text. Where purposivism and intentionalism part ways is in their focus: Intentionalists search for the *intent* of the legislature, while purposivists search for the *purpose* of the statute. To purposivists, the "purpose or purposes of the legislation, and the context of the language, broadly understood, are directly relevant to the meaning of the language of the statute." *State v. Courchesne*, 816 A.2d 562, 587 (Conn. 2003). As Justice Learned Hand explained:

> Of course it is true that the words used, even in their literal sense, are the primary, and ordinarily the most reliable, source of interpreting the meaning of any writing: be it a statute, a contract, or anything else. But it is one of the surest indexes of a mature and developed jurisprudence not to make a fortress out of the dictionary; but to remember that statutes always have some purpose or object to accomplish, whose sympathetic and imaginative discovery is the surest guide to their meaning.

Cabell v. Markham, 148 F.2d 737, 739 (2d Cir. 1945).

A. The Evolving Role of Purpose

The importance courts have given to statutory purpose has changed over the years. Understanding how courts used purpose in the past helps explain and give context to its current use. Thus, we start with the past.

The search for purpose has long been a part of statutory interpretation in the United States. Judges considered a statute's purpose when interpreting its text at least as early as the 1600s, as the case below shows. *See also State v. Courchesne*, 816 A.2d 562, 586 (Conn. 2003) (recounting the historical role of purpose in interpretation). This tradition carried over from England where, from the earliest of times, courts considered purpose to be relevant to interpretation.

Heydon's Case

76 Eng. Rep. 637 (Eng. 1584)

And it was resolved by them, that for the sure and true (*a*) interpretation of all statutes in general (be they penal (B) or beneficial, restrictive or enlarging of the common law,) four things are to be discerned and considered:—

(*b*) 1st. What was the common law before the making of the Act.

(*c*) 2nd. What was the mischief and defect for which the common law did not provide.

3rd. What remedy the Parliament hath resolved and appointed to cure the disease of the commonwealth.

And, 4th. The true reason of the remedy; and then the office of all the Judges is always to make such (*d*) construction as shall suppress the mischief, and advance the remedy, and to suppress subtle inventions and evasions for continuance of the mischief, and *pro private commodo*, and to add force and life to the cure and remedy, according to the true intent of the makers of the Act, *pro bono publico*....

Heydon's Case illustrates the process for interpreting a statute in light of its purpose: first, identify the law as it existed prior to enactment of the statute; second, identify the "mischief" the legislature had sought to remedy by enacting the statute; and third, interpret the statute in a way that best "suppresses that mischief" and "advance[s] the remedy." This process is known as the Mischief Rule.

A more recent case expressly addressing the role of purpose provides:

> There is ... no more persuasive evidence of the purpose of a statute than the words by which the legislature under took to give expression to its wishes. Often these words are sufficient in and of themselves to determine the purpose of the legislation. In such cases we have followed their plain meaning. When that meaning has led to absurd or futile results, however, this Court has looked beyond the words to the purpose of the Act. Frequently, however, even when the plain meaning did not produce absurd results but merely an unreasonable one plainly at variance with the policy of the legislation as a whole this Court has followed that purpose, rather than the literal words. When aid to construction of the meaning of words as used in the statute, is available, there certainly can be no rule of law which forbids its use, however clear the words may appear on superficial examination.

United States v. Am. Trucking Ass'ns Inc., 310 U.S. 534, 543–44 (1940).

Thus, purposivism is an old approach to statutory interpretation. It gained importance in the federal courts in the 1940s following *American Trucking* and was popular with the Supreme Court throughout the 50s and 60s. In the 1970s, however, some members of the Court and the federal judiciary began to reject purposivism's broader approach in favor of intentionalism's more narrow focus. More recently, members of the Court have been divided on the appropriate role of purpose as textualism has gained support. As noted elsewhere, Justice Scalia commonly rejects reliance on extratextual sources. In contrast, Justices Stevens and Breyer disagree. As Justice Stevens said:

> [T]he "minimalist" judge who holds that the purpose of the statute may be learned only from its language has more discretion than the judge who will seek guidance from every reliable source. A method of statutory interpretation that is deliberately uninformed, and hence unconstrained, may produce a result that is

consistent with a court's own view of how things should be, but it may also defeat the very purpose for which a provision was enacted.

Circuit City Stores, Inc. v. Adams, 532 U.S. 105, 133 (2001) (Stevens, J., dissenting). In a similar vein, Justice Breyer wrote that a "court often needs to know the purpose a particular statutory word or phrase serves within the broader context of a statutory scheme in order to decide properly whether a particular circumstance falls within the scope of that word or phrase." Stephen Breyer, *On the Uses of Legislative History in Interpreting Statutes*, 65 S. Cal. L. Rev. 845, 853 (1992).

Although judges are divided on the appropriate role of purpose today, many judges agree "that legislation is inherently purposive and that, therefore, it is not only appropriate, but necessary to consider the purpose or purposes of legislation in order to determine its meaning." *Courchesne*, 816 A.2d at 587. Finally, consider this older passage from *Caminetti* (*see* Chapter 7), where the dissent cautioned:

> There is danger in extending a statute beyond its purpose, even if justified by a strict adherence to its words. The purpose is studied, all effects measured, not left at random—one evil practice prevented, opportunity given to another. The present case warns against ascribing such improvidence to the statute under review.... It certainly will not be denied that legal authority justifies the rejection of a construction which leads to mischievous consequences, if the statute be susceptible of another construction.

Caminetti v. United States, 242 U.S. 470, 502 (1917) (McKenna, J., dissenting).

Notes and Questions

(1) *Purposivism's Hardiness.* Using purpose to determine meaning has long been a part of statutory interpretation in the United States. Does it surprise you that purposivism is one of the oldest approaches to statutory interpretation? Why do you think some judges have rejected it in favor of textualism or intentionalism? Is it, perhaps, easier for a judge to discern the plain meaning or read legislative history than discern unarticulated purpose?

(2) *The Diminishing Role of Purpose.* Despite its longevity and as a reflection of the rise of textualism, today some courts state that purpose should be considered only if the text is ambiguous or absurd. *E.g.*, *Intermountain Slurry Seal v. Labor Comm'n*, 48 P.3d 252, 254 (Utah 2002). Does this approach appeal to you? Do you believe that the meaning of statutory language can be understood without purpose? *See* Felix Frankfurter, *Some Reflections on the Reading of Statutes*, 47 Colum. L. Rev. 527, 538–39 (1947) ("Legislation has an aim; it seeks to obviate some mischief, to supply an inadequacy, to effect a change of policy, to formulate a plan of government. That aim, that policy is not drawn, like nitrogen, out of air; it is evinced in the language of the statute as read in light of other external manifestations of purpose."); Lon Fuller, *Positivism and Fidelity to Law—A Reply to Professor Hart*, 71 Harv. L. Rev. 630, 664 (1958) (arguing that it is not "possible to interpret a word in a statute without knowing the aim of the statute").

B. Finding Purpose

As we have seen, the text is the focus for all of the approaches, including purposivism. But which comes first: the meaning of the text or the purpose of the statute? Put another way, should the language of text be determined without first discerning the purpose of that text? A purposivist would say that the text should be read in light of the purpose, and so purpose must be discerned first. *See* Michael Rosensaft, *The Role of Purposivism in the Delegation of Rulemaking Power to the Courts*, 29 Vt. L. Rev. 611, 622–23 (2005). While a textualist might disagree and might look to purpose only if the text is ambiguous or vague, many judges recognize that language has meaning only in context and that part of context is purpose. However, purposivists clearly go further than textualists in emphasizing purpose and do not believe that meaning can be discerned without understanding purpose.

But where is purpose found? And can there be more than one purpose? There are obvious places to look for purpose. For example, the language at issue may reveal a purpose. The statute may also have a purpose clause. (We examined preambles, findings, and purpose clauses in Chapter 7.) Even when it is not part of the enacted text, a purpose clause can "give the courts some guidance in applying the statute." *Id.* at 624. Similarly, the legislative history may document the legislature's reason for enacting the statute. Social context may illustrate purpose as well. For example, consider the Patriot Act and the events of September 11, 2001. Or, consider the Bailout Bill and the recession of 2008.

But statutes can have more than one purpose, and, sometimes, those purposes conflict. Suppose, for example, that a statute has as its broader purpose ensuring that children of low-income families receive qualified daycare opportunities. Assume further that the statute also includes a provision that requires that decision-making be done publicly. Should the text of that decision-making provision be interpreted in light of the whole statute's purpose or just the provision's purpose? *See, e.g., Office Planning Group, Inc. v. Baraga-Houghton-Keweenaw Child Dev. Bd.*, 697 N.W.2d 871 (Mich. 2005) (in which the majority and dissent disagreed on which purpose should guide interpretation of the statute).

Similarly, if a statute has dueling purposes, which purpose should control? For example, one purpose of the Sherman Act is to promote consumer welfare. Another purpose is to shift wealth from large companies to small businesses. *See* Rosensaft, *supra*, at 619. These two purposes could conflict. In that case, which should control?

Finally, consider two other points. First, not that long ago, "in addition to being fewer in number, [statutes] were typically drafted with a greater degree of generality and thus were more amenable to being interpreted in light of a general purpose." John M. Walker, Jr., *Judicial Tendencies in Statutory Construction: Differing Views on the Role of the Judge*, 58 N.Y.U. Ann. Surv. Am. L. 203, 237 (2001). Second, "the work of the … judiciary is more likely to be seen in political terms today" than just a few years ago. *Id.* Has the appropriate role for purpose changed?

In the case below, see if you can identify where the majority and dissent find the statute's purpose(s) and what the purpose(s) is.

Ky. Off-Track Betting, Inc. v. McBurney
993 S.W.2d 946 (Ky. 1999)

Wintersheimer, Justice.

… Late in 1994 and early in 1995, Corbin resident McBurney, sole owner of Waitsboro Fiberglass Boat Manufacturing Company, made substantial unsuccessful bets on horse races at KOTB's Corbin facility, writing a series of checks. McBurney lost many bets and by March 1995, was indebted to KOTB for $389,781.74. McBurney wrote KOTB various personal checks drawn on his bank as evidence of his promise to pay, but because he did not have sufficient funds in the bank to honor the checks, KOTB agreed not to cash them.

On March 16, 1995, KOTB manager Gene McClain asked McBurney about honoring the checks. McBurney told him that the bank account was insufficient to pay for the checks. McClain then asked McBurney to execute a promissory note in the principal amount of $389,781.74 in exchange for the checks, which McBurney did. McBurney paid twelve installments totaling $84,000 through June of 1995, but discontinued payments thereafter. KOTB brought a civil action to collect the outstanding balance on the note.

KOTB emphasizes the legality of the transactions pursuant to the 1992 legislation specifically authorizing off-track betting facilities on simulcast horse racing....

On the other hand, McBurney contends that KRS 372.010 is clearly the law and makes the transaction void and unenforceable. KRS 372.010 provides as follows:

> Every contract, conveyance, transfer or assurance for the consideration, in whole or in part, of money, property or other thing won, lost or bet in any game, sport, pastime or wager, or for the consideration of money, property or other thing lent or advanced for the purpose of gaming, or lent or advanced at the time of any betting, gaming, or wagering to a person then actually engaged in betting, gaming, or wagering, is void.

The trial judge granted KOTB summary judgment but the Court of Appeals reversed, holding that even though the bet is a legal bet, a debt coming within the provisions of KRS 372.010 is void and unenforceable. We accepted discretionary review....

KOTB asks for review of the law in this area from the perspective of our current societal public policy. It points out that in the past decade an amendment to Section 226 of the Kentucky Constitution permits first, a state lottery, and then charitable gaming, with 1992 statutory additions and amendments to KRS 230 not only encouraging betting on horse racing at simulcast facilities pursuant to KRS 230.380, but also permits wagering not limited to cash, telephone accounts and credit cards, pursuant to KRS 230.379.

KRS 230.215 is intended to encourage the horse breeding industry through the allowance of parimutuel wagering subject to regulation by the Kentucky Racing Commission. KRS 230.380 authorizes parimutuel betting at certain simulcast facilities, called off-track betting facilities. The plain language of these statutes indicates that they do not impact the activities prohibited by KRS 372.010. The real issue presented here is whether one may collect money loaned or advanced to a person to bet while that person is actually engaged in betting.

The 1992 General Assembly simply intended to acknowledge the various technological advances of modern times, such as satellites and television when it legalized off-track betting for the benefit of businesses engaged in accepting bets on horse races by licensed facilities. It is now no longer necessary to physically go to a race track to place a bet. The promotion of the horse racing industry and the establishment of simulcast facilities is clearly independent of the issue of advancing money for the purposes of gambling.

The loaning of money or advancing of credit to a person by a betting facility which is itself a party to the gambling transaction is the type of unacceptable social conduct that the General Assembly intended to prevent when it adopted KRS 372.010, and which we must presume the General Assembly chose not to repeal when it legalized off-track betting. Betting is legal, the lending of money by a betting facility in order to bet is not....

The decision of the Court of Appeals is affirmed and this matter is remanded to the circuit court for a judgment consistent with this opinion.

JOHNSTONE, JUSTICE, dissenting.

I respectfully dissent from the majority opinion. The purpose of KRS 372.010 is to prevent illegal gambling by rendering void and unenforceable the gambling contract itself and certain related agreements. In *McDevitt v. Thomas*, 130 Ky. 805, 114 S.W. 273 (1908), this Court held that "[t]he purpose of [KRS 372.010] is to discourage betting or wagering by declaring all contracts relative thereto void, and by this means lessen what is generally regarded as a social evil." [*McDevitt* cited no authority for this statement]. Although KRS 372.010 remains on the books, the "social evil" discouraged in the first decade of this century is viewed in a different context in the last decade of this century. For example, in the past decade, amendments to the Kentucky Constitution have permitted a state lottery and charitable gaming. Statutory additions and amendments in 1992 legalized parimutuel wagering on horse racing at simulcast facilities per KRS 230.380. Further, use of credit cards for betting via telephone lines and credit card cash advances via automated teller machines have been authorized. The social evil that KRS 372.010 was designed to curb was gambling, an illegal activity at the time of the statute's enactment, not money lent for a legal activity. It is preposterous that while it is legal to place a parimutuel wager on a horse race at an authorized facility, and it is legal to loan money, it is illegal to loan money to someone to place a legal wager on a horse race in this Commonwealth.

Further, in today's society a check presented is equivalent with cash. By accepting a personal check as payment for goods and services, KOTB did not make a loan to McBurney. KOTB accepted McBurney's personal check as a payment in good faith, believing that the checks would be honored when presented to the financial institution. Only after McBurney approached KOTB to inform it that the checks would not be honored due to insufficient funds, did McBurney intimate that he would enter into a promissory agreement to pay more than $350,000 to cover the bad checks. It is likely that McBurney entered into this agreement to avoid prosecution for writing the bad checks.

There is no evidence in the record that KOTB made any agreement to loan or advance money, or even advance credit "at the time of any betting, gaming, or wagering" to McBurney who was then engaging in betting. The majority opinion presumes, although not supported by the record, that the parties agreed to loan contemporaneously, with McBurney placing his ill-fated, but legal bets.

For the foregoing reasons, I respectfully dissent.

Notes and Questions

(1) *Which Statute's Purpose Mattered?* According to the majority, which statute's purpose was relevant? What about the dissent? Can the purposes of the two statutes be reconciled? Generally, which should control when the purposes of two statutes conflict? The statute being interpreted? The later-enacted statute? The first enacted? Which statute's purpose do you think should control?

(2) *Finding Purpose.* Where did the majority and dissent find the relevant statute's purpose? How do you identify a statute's purpose when there is no legislative history and no preamble? Is identifying purpose possible and, if so, appropriate? Is discerning purpose an objective inquiry? Is it any less objective than determining "plain meaning"?

(3) *Finding Purpose More Generally.* Should judges determine purpose solely from intrinsic sources? *Compare Wood v. Univ. of Utah Med. Ctr.,* 67 P.3d 436, 445 (Utah 2002) ("Legislators may decide that a statute should be passed for myriad, often even different, reasons, but where the legislative purpose is expressly stated and agreed to as part of the legislation, we do not look to the views expressed by one or more legislators in floor debates, committee minutes, or elsewhere, in determining the intent of the statute. Because the legislature expressly set forth its intent and purpose ... in enacting the instant legislation, we do not look at its legislative history."), *with Bown v. Gwinnett County Sch. Dist.,* 112 F.3d 1464, 1469 (11th Cir. 1997) ("To ascertain a statute's purpose, it is, of course, necessary to examine the language of the statute on its face. It is also appropriate to consider the legislative history of the statute and the specific sequence of events leading up to the adoption of the statute.")

Problem 10-1

You represent Nicolas Manueles, a Mexican national, who entered the United States illegally by walking across the border in January 2004. He then traveled to Phoenix, Arizona, and purchased a false resident alien card and a false social security card for $60.00. Resident alien cards are issued by the Department of Homeland Security's Citizen and Immigration Services. They contain the holder's name, photograph, date of birth, alien registration number, and an expiration date. Alien registrations numbers are used by non-citizens as proof of legal entry into the United States and also demonstrate that the holder is lawfully eligible for employment. Like social security numbers, they are assigned to a single person and are not reassigned to anyone else.

After purchasing the cards, Manueles journeyed from Phoenix to Norfolk, Virginia, where he used them to get a job. As it turns out, the alien registration number contained on the resident alien card that Manueles purchased belonged to a Tanzanian national who was then a naturalized citizen of the United States. Likewise, the social security number that he purchased had already been assigned to a different, unidentified individual. While Manueles was aware that the cards were not authentic when he purchased them and that it was illegal to present them as being otherwise, he did not know that the numbers associated with the cards had already been assigned to other people. He became aware of that fact on or after August 9, when agents from the Immigration and Customs Enforcement Division of DHS took him into custody after learning that he was an illegal immigrant.

A search incident to arrest uncovered the false resident alien card described above. After being apprised of his Fifth Amendment *Miranda* rights, Manueles elected to waive them and admitted to the facts recited above. The state concedes that there are no victims of the alleged offense and that his motive was solely to gain employment.

Using the problem materials below, analyze how the word "knowingly" in 18 U.S.C. § 1028A(a)(1) can be argued to modify only "transfers, possesses or uses," and how it arguably modifies "a means of identification of another person." Given your client's position, what should you contend the purpose of the statute to be and how should a court find that purpose? How would the state respond? Ignore the rule of lenity.

Problem Materials

The "Aggravated Identity Theft Penalty Enhancement Act" was enacted by Congress on July 15, 2003. The Act created 18 U.S.C. § 1028A. The long title of the bill is "An Act

To amend title 18, United States Code, to establish penalties for aggravated identity theft, and for other purposes."

18 U.S.C. § 1028A: Aggravated Identity Theft

(a) Offenses—

> (1) **In General**: Whoever ... knowingly transfers, possesses, or uses, without lawful authority, a means of identification of another person shall, in addition to the punishment provided for such felony, be sentenced to a term of imprisonment of 2 years.

> (2) **Terrorism Offense**: Whoever ... knowingly transfers, possesses, or uses, without lawful authority, a means of identification of another person or a false identification document shall, in addition to the punishment provided for such felony, be sentenced to a term of imprisonment of 5 years.

Legislative History Excerpts from the House Committee Report

PURPOSE AND SUMMARY

The "Identity Theft Penalty Enhancement Act," addresses the growing problem of identity theft. Currently under 18 U.S.C. § 1028 many identity thieves receive short terms of imprisonment or probation; after their release, many of these thieves will go on to use false identities to commit much more serious crimes. [This bill] provides enhanced penalties for persons who steal identities to commit terrorist acts, immigration violations, firearms offenses, and other serious crimes. The bill also amends current law to impose a higher maximum penalty for identity theft used to facilitate acts of terrorism.

BACKGROUND AND NEED FOR THE LEGISLATION

The terms "identity theft" and "identity fraud" refer to all types of crimes in which someone wrongfully obtains and uses another person's personal data in some way that involves fraud or deception, typically for economic or other gain, including immigration benefits. The Federal Trade Commission ("FTC") received 161,819 victim complaints of someone using another's information in 2002. Of these, 22% involved more than one type of identity crime.

For 2002, the FTC breakdown of types of identity theft shows that 42% of complaints involved credit card fraud, 22% involved the activation of a utility in the victim's name, 17% involved bank accounts opened in the victim's name, 9% involved employment fraud, 8% involved government documents or benefits fraud, 6% involved consumer loans or mortgages obtained in the victim's name, and 16% involved medical, bankruptcy, securities and other miscellaneous fraud.

In 2003, the FTC randomly sampled households. A total of 4.6% of survey participants indicated that they had discovered they were victims of some type of identity theft in the past year. This result suggests that almost 10 million Americans were the victims of some form of identity theft within the last year, which means despite all the attention to this type of crime since September 11, 2001, the incidence of this crime is increasing....

Since September 11, 2001, Federal and State officials have taken notice of this crime because of the potential threat to security, but the cost to the consumer and corporations is equally alarming. The FTC estimates the loss to businesses and financial institutions from identity theft to be $47.6 billion. The costs to individual consumers are estimated to be approximately $5.0 billion.

As this crime increases, we must try to find new ways to combat it. Websites developed by the FTC and consumer groups encourage consumers to protect themselves by shredding mail and keeping a close watch over their credit reports; yet, the FTC's statistics suggest that identity thieves are obtaining individuals' personal information for misuse not only through "dumpster diving," but also through accessing information that was originally collected for an authorized purpose. The information is accessed either by employees of the company or of a third party that is authorized to access the accounts in the normal course of business, or by outside individuals who hack into computers or steal paperwork likely to contain personal information....

Under current law, many perpetrators of identity theft receive little or no prison time. That has become a tacit encouragement to those arrested to continue to pursue such crimes. [This bill addresses the lack of prison time as well.]

H.R. Rep. No. 528, 108th Cong., 2nd Sess. 2004, 2004 U.S.C.C.A.N. 779, 2004 WL 1260964 (Leg.Hist.).

C. Using Purpose in Interpretation

Discerning purpose may present unforeseen obstacles. The critical issue, of course, is how you—as a lawyer—can use purpose once it is found. In the next set of cases, you will see the many ways that advocates use purpose on behalf of their clients. We begin with the least controversial, using purpose to resolve ambiguity or absurdity, and move to more controversial uses of purpose, such as using purpose to defeat the plain meaning of the text. In Chapter 8, we talked about the continuum of uses of legislative history: Some judges refuse to use legislative history to interpret statutes in any case, while others use it in all cases. And, of course, there were uses between these extremes. The same continuum applies to the use of purposes. Some judges refuse to use purpose to interpret statutes in any case, while others use it in all cases. And, of course, there are uses between these extremes, which we turn to now. As you read these cases, try to discern how the courts identify the purpose of the relevant statute. See also if you think that any of these uses of purpose is inappropriate.

1. Using Purpose to Resolve Ambiguity or Absurdity

We addressed in Chapter 4 the use of purpose when a statute is absurd or ambiguous. That chapter showed that most judges are willing to look beyond the text when its plain meaning is absurd, ambiguous, or contains a scrivener's error. We further pointed out that some judges use the statute's purpose—as evidenced by the legislative history, a preamble, or context of the statute's enactment—to resolve ambiguity or eliminate absurdity or fix errors.

In the case below, the court described two kinds of absurdity, only one of which the court believed permitted judicial foray into legislative history to find purpose. As you read the case, see if you find the distinction meaningful.

Heppner v. Alyeska Pipeline Serv. Co.

665 F.2d 868 (9th Cir. 1981)

WALLACE, CIRCUIT JUDGE:

In this consolidated appeal, Heppner and Jordan challenge the dismissal by the district court of their causes of action.... On August 10, 1976, Heppner's husband was working in a gravel pit that served as a material site for the pipeline and was within the pipeline right-of-way. He was crushed between a rock and a piece of heavy equipment, suffering injuries resulting in his death. On July 28, 1976, Jordan was a passenger in an automobile that was involved in an accident in which Jordan suffered personal injuries, and as a result of which his wife suffered a loss of consortium. Jordan alleges that the operation of the vehicle and his being a passenger in it were the result of and in connection with activities along or in the vicinity of the pipeline right-of-way.

The only issue on appeal is whether the language of the strict liability provision of the Act covers Heppner's and Jordan's causes of action. The Act provides in part as follows:

> Except when the holder of the pipeline right-of-way granted pursuant to this chapter can prove that damages in connection with or resulting from activities along or in the vicinity of the proposed trans-Alaskan pipeline right-of-way were caused by an act of war or negligence of the United States, other government entity, or the damaged party, such holder shall be strictly liable to all damaged parties, public or private, without regard to fault for such damages, and without regard to ownership of any affected lands, structures, fish, wildlife, or biotic or other natural resources relied upon by Alaska Natives, Native organizations, or others for subsistence or economic purposes.

43 U.S.C. § 1653(a)(1).

The question is, therefore, whether ordinary personal injury and wrongful death claims, unconnected with any environmental injury, are embraced by the language "damages in connection with or resulting from activities along or in the vicinity of the proposed trans-Alaskan pipeline right-of-way...."

We first look to the face of the particular part of the statute in question. Although the language of section 1653 is facially clear and unambiguous, the plain meaning rule ... requires us to approach the statute, not with mechanical literalism, but with the purpose of implementing Congressional intent. Sometimes the literal application of the statute occasions an unexpected or, in the traditional language, an "absurd" result. The Supreme Court has, at times, considered absurd results of statutory language to be a reason for looking beyond the face of the subject to the legislative history. *United States v. American Trucking Ass'n*; 310 U.S. 534, 543; *Church of Holy Trinity v. United States*, 143 U.S. 457, 459 (1892). On the other hand, the Court has sometimes determined that absurd or curious results do not require examination of legislative history. *TVA v. Hill*, 437 U.S. at 172–173, 184 n.29.

It appears to us, on the basis of these cases, that the literal application of statutes may cause two different types of absurd results. In order to implement congressional intent, we must distinguish between them. The first type occurs when a congressional decision produces an unexpected absurd result. It arises out of a failure to trace through the effects of the legislation in cases in which the statute was intended by Congress to apply. If there was a congressional mistake in the Endangered Species Act, the statute in question in *TVA v. Hill*, it was a mistake of this sort. Such mistakes, because they are substantive matters of policy, are for the Congress, not the courts, to correct. In this sense, and short of constitutional error, Congress has a right to be wrong.

The second type of absurdity results from a drafting error. It occurs, for example, when Congress uses more sweeping language than it would if it were attending carefully to fact situations, outside the scope of its purpose, to which the language might be erroneously understood to apply. This second type of mistake is one that a court may correct by interpretation—if the court is in a position to infer the actual intent of Congress.

The first type of absurdity, then, arises within what Congress actually intended, and must normally be let stand. The second type of absurdity results from a misapprehension of the intent of Congress and is usually subject to judicial cure. The first, as in *TVA v. Hill*, does not normally require an investigation of legislative history. The second type, for which the present case is a candidate, often will require an investigation, in order to substantiate the hypothesis that the absurd result is outside the intent of Congress.

We can often distinguish between the two kinds of absurdities by reference to the contexts in which the statutes occur. Frequently, reference to a statute's context will give us some idea of the legislative intent behind the statute. For example, the statute in question in *TVA v. Hill* was part of the Endangered Species Act. Reference to the act as a whole, the context for the statute at issue, indicated that the statute was passed as part of Congress's effort to protect endangered species. The completion of the Teleco Dam, literally proscribed by the statute, genuinely threatened an endangered species. Although application of the literal language of the statute may have lead to an "absurd" result, that result was harmonious with Congressional intent as reflected by the statute's context. In such an instance, we should let stand the literal facial meaning of the statute even though some may conclude that Congress has acted in an "absurd" way—Congress has a right to do so.

In the present case, the statute at issue is the Trans-Alaska Pipeline Authorization Act. Reading that act as a whole, it seems clear that Congress intended to facilitate the development and delivery of oil and gas and, at the same time, to protect the environment. Nothing in the statute's context indicates that Congress meant to expand federal protections for the victims of common personal injury torts.

Furthermore, even when we focus only upon section 1653, we cannot read it without having doubts as to just how wide a net is cast by its strict liability provision. Common sense strongly suggests that the statute does not establish strict liability for every sort of injury that might occur within the pipeline right-of-way. If, as seems logical, a slander shouted or an injury from a fight occurring within the right-of-way are not within the statute, then the reader of the statute is faced with a problem of interpretation. The phrase upon which Heppner and Jordan rely, "damages in connection with or resulting from activities along or in the vicinity of the … right-of-way," is so broad that common sense tells us that line drawing is necessary; but the phrase itself is of no help in telling us where to draw the line. However, the remainder of the section at least raises an inference that the thrust of the strict liability feature was directed to environmental concerns. Immediately after the strict liability language, Congress stated that damages would be paid "without regard to ownership of any affected lands, structures, fish, wildlife, or biotic or other natural resources.…"

When we leave the section itself and review it in context with the other parts of the statute, it becomes clear that environmental damages were at least a special concern of Congress. This suggests the possibility that automobile and construction accidents might not be covered. Thus, though the language of the particular part of the section is clear and unambiguous, … we should consult the legislative history to see if these accidents lie outside the area of strict liability intended by Congress.

We need not detail the legislative history as it supplies overwhelming evidence that the intent of Congress in the strict liability provision of section 1653 was to deal with the environmental risks of the pipeline. Even accepting this, however, Jordan and Heppner argue that they must prevail unless the legislative history explicitly contradicts the interpretation of the statute imposing strict liability for personal injuries. They argue that the literal terms of the statute may be overridden by legislative history only if the literal terms lead to an absurd result and the legislative history explicitly contradicts the literal words.

This argument again represents an overly mechanical approach to statutory interpretation. When the statutory language together with the legislative history makes one interpretation overwhelmingly more plausible than a second interpretation, there is no necessity that the legislative history explicitly rule out the second interpretation.... [I]f evidence drawn from the face of the statute militates strongly for one interpretation, but not quite so strongly that the legislative history may safely be ignored, the legislative history should be considered, but considered cautiously. Under these circumstances a second interpretation should be accepted on the basis of the legislative history only if the evidence is very strong, which will usually require explicit language.

This is not the situation in the present case. Evidence drawn from the face of the statute raises serious questions whether we should read the strict liability language literally and should give it its broadest possible sweep. An explicit denial in the legislative history of the distant possibilities included within that sweep is not required. Instead we need only see if the purpose of the Act, as revealed by the legislative history, confirms that the language should not be read too broadly.

We are not required to turn our backs on the overwhelming evidence of the legislative history that the strict liability provision of the Act was intended to deal with environmental accidents rather than ordinary torts. We conclude, therefore, that the district judge was correct in dismissing the actions of Jordan and Heppner.

Affirmed.

Notes and Questions

(1) *Absurd or Ambiguous.* The court found the text to be clear but absurd. Is it absurd to believe that Congress may have wanted to impose strict liability for all injuries caused by the pipeline, regardless of whether the environment was injured or not? Wouldn't it be more accurate to say that the text of the statute was ambiguous as to whether all injuries were covered or just environmental injuries? Assuming the text was ambiguous, would it then be appropriate to peruse legislative history for purpose?

(2) *Sources.* In addition to legislative history, where did the court look for evidence of purpose?

(3) *Two Types of Absurdity.* According to the Ninth Circuit, absurdity can be distinguished by whether it was unexpected due to a legislature's failure to "trace through the effects of the legislation" or whether it was unexpected due to a legislative drafting error. In the first case, the legislature actually intended the absurdity, while in the second, the legislature did not. According to the Ninth Circuit, courts can legitimately correct only absurdity caused by drafting errors. Does this distinction follow from the scrivener's error exception we studied in Chapter 4? Why? Do you find this absurdity distinction enlightening? Regardless of whether this distinction is helpful, it has not been universally adopted. If a judge is willing to look beyond the text for purpose, then the judge will likely do so regardless of the type of absurdity found.

(4) *Intended Absurdity.* In essence, the court reasoned that sometimes absurdity is intended. Do you think absurdity is ever intended? Isn't absurdity of both types due to the

legislature's failure to do its job completely? But if absurdity can be intended, how can judges determine whether absurdity was intended or inadvertent? Will the statute's context always provide the answer to this question?

(5) *Textualism.* A textualist will examine the legislative history only if the plain meaning is absurd, ambiguous, or contains a scrivener's error. What informs that conclusion? In other words, aren't absurdity, ambiguity, and scrivener's error simply subjective opinions? Should a court be required to justify a finding of either by reference to objective facts?

2. Using Purpose to Confirm the Plain Meaning

Using purpose to help resolve ambiguity, absurdity, and scrivener's error is relatively non-contentious. More controversial is using purpose to confirm a statute's plain meaning. Remember that some judges generally will not look beyond the text when the statute is unambiguous, while other judges are more willing. In the somewhat older case below, the majority and dissent both found the statute unambiguous, yet both reviewed the same legislative history despite the clarity of the text. The majority used the legislative history to identify the purpose of the exception in the statute, while the dissent looked to the legislative history to determine the specific intent of the legislature as to the text in question. Notice that their different focuses — intent versus purpose — lead to different outcomes.

Church of Scientology v. U.S. Dep't of Justice
612 F.2d 417 (9th Cir. 1979)

BARNES, SENIOR CIRCUIT JUDGE:

Church of Scientology of California ("CSC") appeals the district court's upholding of the Drug Enforcement Administration's ("DEA") decision not to disclose certain documents sought by CSC under the Freedom of Information Act ("FOIA"). The main issue on appeal is the scope of the term "confidential source" as used in the 7(D) exemption of the FOIA, 5 U.S.C. § 552(b)(7)(D).[2] ...

[T]he district court judge ... found that the government was justified in withholding the ... documents pursuant to the 7(D) exemption. In reaching his decision, the judge concluded that the term "confidential source" in the 7(D) exemption included foreign, state and local law enforcement agencies....

CSC now appeals.... [W]e ... affirm....

From the language of the statute on its face, the 7(D) exemption excludes from mandatory disclosure investigatory records compiled for law enforcement purposes in two different situations: first, where the production would "disclose the identity of a confidential source" and, second, "in the case of a record compiled by a criminal law enforcement au-

---

2. The 7(D) exemption of the FOIA, 5 U.S.C. § 552(b)(7)(D), exempts from disclosure:
   (7) investigatory records compiled for law enforcement purposes, but only to the extent that the production of such records would ...
       (D) disclose the identity of a confidential source and, in the case of a record compiled by a criminal law enforcement authority in the course of a criminal investigation, ... confidential information furnished only by the confidential source....

thority in the course of a criminal investigation, ... if the production would disclose 'confidential information furnished only by the confidential source.'" 5 U.S.C. § 552(b)(7)(D). If we were only to look at the language of the 7(D) exemption and give the words utilized therein their plain and ordinary meaning,[10] we would be forced to conclude that the term "confidential source" refers simply to the origin of information, without distinction among the types of originators. Following that reading of the exemption, we would hold that "confidential source" includes foreign, state and local law enforcement agencies in its scope....

However, the sufficiency of a court's reliance solely upon the "plain meaning" of the language of a statute in interpreting its terms has come into question. Recent pronouncements by the Supreme Court ... have been somewhat inconsistent on this point. On the one hand, the Court in *Train v. Colorado Pub. Interest Research Group*, 426 U.S. 1 (1976), held ... that there was no "rule of law" which forbids the use of extrinsic aids in construing the meaning of statutory language however clear the words may appear on "superficial examination"....

On the other hand, the Supreme Court recently articulated the opposite position and seemingly reaffirmed the former "plain meaning rule". In *Tennessee Valley Authority v. Hill*, 437 U.S. 153, 184 n. 29 (1978), it was stated that: "When confronted with a statute which is plain and unambiguous on its face, we ordinarily do not look to legislative history as a guide to its meaning." ...

The plain meaning rule can be viewed as consisting of two propositions. Initially, the rule stands for the notion that if the language of a statute is clear and there is no ambiguity, then there is no need to "interpret" the language by resorting to the legislative history or other extrinsic aids. Secondly, and more importantly, the rule stands for the proposition that in the vast majority of its legislation Congress does mean what it says and thus the statutory language is normally the best evidence of congressional intent. [W]here the language of an enactment is clear and construction according to its terms does not lead to absurd or impracticable consequences, the words employed are to be taken as the final expression of the meaning intended. It is the former component of the plain meaning rule which has been called into question by cases such as *Train*..., not the latter proposition....

In the present case, we have concluded that the statutory language is clear and unambiguous if we give the words of the 7(D) exemption their ordinary meaning.... [W]e now turn to the legislative history of the 7(D) exemption and examine the congressional intent. Pursuant to our adherence to the applicable portion of the plain meaning rule, we believe that the plainer the language, the more convincing contrary legislative history must be. Also, we note that the proper function of legislative history is to solve, not create, an ambiguity. In construing a statute, the Court has ruled that legislative materials, if without probative value, or contradictory, or ambiguous, should not be permitted to control the customary meaning of words.

Prior to the 1974 amendments to the FOIA, 5 U.S.C. § 552(b)(7) exempted from disclosure "investigatory files compiled for law enforcement purposes except to the extent available by law to a party other than an agency...." On May 30, 1974, Senator Phillip Hart offered [an amendment] which proposed to change the 7th exemption to read as follows:

> Investigatory records compiled for law enforcement purposes, but only to the extent that the production of such records would ... (C) disclose the identity of an informer....

---

10. Words used in a statute are to be given their ordinary meaning in the absence of persuasive reasons to the contrary.

[The house passed the amended bill. The Senate adopted an amended version of the amended House bill.] On June 6, 1974, the legislation was sent to a joint House and Senate conference committee which [substituted the words] "confidential source" ... for the word "informer" in the exemption. The conference [committee] later added language also protecting confidential information compiled from a confidential source by a criminal law enforcement authority in the course of a criminal investigation....

In the midst of the conference deliberations, President Ford wrote to ... one of the co-sponsors of the legislation, expressing his concern as to ... the proposed amendments.... On October 17, 1974, President Ford returned the bill to the House without his approval noting ... the problem of the abridgement of confidentiality as to law enforcement records. In November 1974, after debate in both the House and the Senate, the veto was overridden....

After a careful reading of the legislative materials, we [find] that the issue of the scope of the term "confidential source" is not "precisely addressed in the legislative history". Admittedly, when Senator Hart initially proposed his amendment to the 7th exemption, he spoke only in terms of "informers" and "concerned citizens". However, even at that time, Senator Hart ... stated that ... [he] did not intend his amendment to inhibit in any way a federal law enforcement agency's ability to conduct its lawful investigation....

From those statements, Senator Hart does not appear to limit the word "source" to only human sources but rather gives an expansive reading of the 7(D) exemption.[13]

In the Joint Explanatory Statement of the Committee of Conference ("Conference Report"), the following reason for the substitution of the term "confidential source" for the word "informer" is given:

> The substitution of the term "confidential source" ... is to make clear that the identity of a person other than a paid informer may be protected if the person provided information under an express assurance of confidentiality or in circumstances from which such an assurance could be reasonably inferred. Under this category, in every case when the investigatory records sought were compiled for law enforcement purposes—either civil or criminal in nature—the agency can withhold the names, addresses, and other information that would reveal the identity of a confidential source who furnished the information. However, where the records are compiled by a criminal law enforcement authority, all of the information furnished only by a confidential source may be withheld if the information was compiled in the course of a criminal investigation....

Likewise, Senator Byrd in his arguments in favor of overriding the presidential veto makes similar remarks:

> ... Another matter that disturbed me was the use of the word "informer", since that could be construed to mean that only the identity of a paid "informer" was to be protected and not the identity of an unpaid confidential source. I was deeply concerned that without such protection, law enforcement agencies would be faced with a "drying-up" of their sources of information and their criminal investigative work would be seriously impaired.
>
> The bill in the form now presented to the Senate has been significantly changed by the conference on these critical issues. The language ... has been changed

---

13. Courts look to the statements by the initiators or sponsors of proposed legislation when the meaning of words used in a statute is in doubt.

from protecting from disclosure the identity of an "informer" to protecting the identity of a "confidential source" to assure that the identity of a person other than a paid informer may be protected. The language has also been broadened substantially to protect from disclosure all of the information furnished by a confidential source to a criminal law enforcement agency if the information was compiled in the course of a criminal investigation. Thus, not only is the identity of a confidential source protected but also protected from disclosure is all the information furnished by that source to a law enforcement agency in the course of a criminal investigation.

In both statements, it is clear that the congressional intent was to broaden the scope of the proposed exemption to include sources of confidential information other than informers. The use of the word "person" in those contexts appears to be similar to the use of any collective noun. The word "person" in legal terminology is perceived as a general word which normally includes in its scope a variety of entities other than human beings. *See e. g.* 1 U.S.C. § 1. Had the Conference Report affirmatively stated that the term "confidential source" was limited to or applies only to persons, we would agree with appellant's position herein.

Likewise, a single comment was made by Senator Kennedy in the course of the debates that "we also provided that there be no requirement to reveal not only the identity of a confidential source, but also any information obtained from him in a criminal investigation." However, the use of a singular masculine pronoun is often made where the sex, if any, of its antecedent reference is unknown or where it refers to a collective noun which consists of entities of more than one sex. Given that the comment was made in the course of the debates on the Senate floor, where grammatical formalities are not always observed, we do not consider that one particular comment to be indicative....

[W]e are hesitant to rely solely upon "grammatical nuances" in the legislative materials to resolve the important issue involved herein....

By giving the term "confidential source" its plain meaning, we will effectuate the stated congressional purpose behind the 7(D) exemption. Congress did not plan to prevent law enforcement agencies from gathering information from sources who would be reluctant to provide such information if their identities or their confidential information were made public. By refusing to accept the plain meaning of the word "source" and excluding foreign, state and local law enforcement agencies from the 7(D) exemption, an impairment to federal law enforcement groups will result which would be contrary to the congressional intent. Foreign, state and local law enforcement agencies are under no obligation to provide information to federal agencies in most instances. There is substantial evidence in the record below that some of those groups would refuse to cooperate with federal agencies if they could not be assured of confidentiality in instances where they thought it was necessary. While CSC argues that Congress intended to limit the scope of the 7(D) exemption to human sources, there is no evidence in the legislative history that the congressional concern was focused on the possibility of physical harm to individuals. Rather, the paramount concern was the loss of sources of confidential information.

A "plain meaning" interpretation of the 7(D) exemption would not be in conflict with the remainder of the FOIA. While the FOIA "is in favor of disclosure, it should be apparent that the subsection (b) exemptions are also a part of the FOIA and in their case Congress decided that there were types of information that the Executive Branch must have the option to keep confidential. While one may employ the general purpose of the act as justification to narrowly construe the exemptions where there is an absence of congressional intent on a particular area covered by one of the exemptions, one must remember that the congressional intent in enacting the exemption was to preserve, not destroy, confidentiality in certain necessary situations. Consequently to say, as appellant does here, that one's interpretation of the exemption is consistent with the general purpose of the FOIA is to ignore the congressional intent which caused and required the enactment of the exemptions in the first place.

The purpose of the FOIA is to serve disclosure of federal agency activity, not as a means for private parties to find out what facts or opinions foreign, state or local law enforcement agencies have collected or made on them. By including foreign, state and local law enforcement agencies in the 7(D) exemption, we would not be preventing any proper disclosure of federal agency action. If we adopt the approach suggested by appellant we would eliminate sources of information which the federal agencies may need without gaining any greater disclosure of the type of information which the FOIA seeks to reveal. . . .

In this case, law enforcement agencies fall within the plain meaning of the statutes. Furthermore, their inclusion within 7(D) furthers the statutory purpose of preventing the "drying up" of sources of confidential information. The legislative history does not evidence an intent specifically to exclude law enforcement agencies. In these circumstances, we should give effect to the plain meaning of the statute even if Congress did not contemplate this particular application. . . .

Affirmed.

WALLACE, CIRCUIT JUDGE, dissenting:

I am in sympathy with the result reached by the majority. The statute is clear enough on its face. It makes eminent sense and I quite frankly wish that it were the law. . . .

If I were looking only to the plain language of the statute, I would agree with the conclusion of my brethren that "source" refers simply to the origin of information, without distinction among types of originators. However, the Supreme Court directed that legislative history should not be ignored when it aids in the resolution of a question of statutory construction. . . .

To be sure, reliance on legislative history in divining the intent of Congress is, as has often been observed, a step to be taken cautiously. . . . I, like my brethren, feel that we should heed the Court's instruction that legislative materials, if without probative value, or contradictory, or ambiguous, should not be permitted to control the customary meaning of words. . . .

I conclude that at the time of the passage of the statute, the legislative history shows that Congress intended the term "source" to mean "person."

As originally proposed by Senator Hart, subsection (b)(7)(D) exempted "(i)nvestigatory records compiled for law enforcement purposes, but only to the extent that the production of such records would . . . disclose the identity of an informer. . . ."

In response to President Ford's concerns, the Conference Committee substituted "confidential source" for "informer."[1] Its joint explanatory report, which represents the con-

---

1. The President wrote that he was:
   concerned with any provision which would reduce our ability to effectively deal with crime. This amendment could have that effect if the sources of information or the information itself are disclosed. These sources and the information by which they may be identified must be protected in order not to severely hamper our efforts to combat crime.

sidered and collective understanding of those (legislators) involved in drafting and studying proposed legislation said:

> The substitution of the term "confidential source" in section 552(b)(7)(D) is to make clear that the identity of a person other than a paid informer may be protected if the person provided information under an express assurance of confidentiality or in circumstances from which such an assurance could be reasonably inferred. Under this category, in every case where the investigatory records sought were compiled for law enforcement purposes either civil or criminal in nature the agency can withhold the names, addresses, and other information that would reveal the identity of a confidential source who furnished the information.

My brethren disregard the clear language of this explanatory report by contending that the Conference Committee used "person" as a collective noun and that the expansive nature of their message precludes any restrictive reading of "confidential source." Not only is it unlikely that the Committee was using the law dictionary definition of person, as my brethren contend, but even if they were, that definition of the term would not include foreign, state, and local law enforcement agencies. *See, e.g.,* 1 U.S.C. § 1. The Committee's use of "person" in explaining the change from "informer" plainly reveals that their intent to protect only human sources had not changed. Moreover, the majority's reliance on the expansive intent of the Committee report is misplaced. General intent should not be used to controvert specific language; indeed, the Committee itself chose to express its intent by the term "person."

While floor debates are accorded less weight than committee reports, the floor discussion in the Senate with respect to this passage supports this view of "source." Statements made both before passage of the amendment in the Senate and following the Conference Committee Report and Presidential veto indicate that Senators Hart and Kennedy, both members of the Conference Committee, and Senator Byrd assumed the exemption referred to persons or individuals. The government argues and the majority agrees that Congress intended to protect law enforcement efforts. I do find throughout the legislative debates broad statements by Senators Hart and Kennedy to the effect that law enforcement would in no way be hampered by the amendment of subsection (b)(7). We should not, however, allow broad statements of assurance made in floor debate to control the clear language of the Committee report, language supported by statements of both senators indicating that they understood that "source" referred to persons or individuals. I think it is clear that "source" was not meant to include foreign, state, and local law enforcement agencies. . . .

This conclusion is consistent with the purposes of the Act in general. The Supreme Court has emphasized that the "'basic policy'" of the Act "is in favor of disclosure." While this consideration is not determinative in this case, it is worth pointing out that a restrictive reading limits the meaning of "source" to persons and thus favors disclosure over secrecy. . . .

I would reverse.

Notes and Questions

(1) *Ambiguity.* Do you agree with the majority and dissent that the plain language is clear: "confidential source" includes other law enforcement agencies, not just individuals? Do you find it surprising that the dissent found the language unambiguous, then found that the plain meaning was not intended? Did the dissent find the plain meaning to be absurd or ambiguous? If not, why did the dissent ignore the plain meaning? In contrast, did the majority find the legislative history to be dispositive or ambiguous?

(2) *Which Purpose Mattered?* What specific statutory purpose did the majority consider: the purpose of the FOIA as a whole or the exception within the Act? Which purpose was relevant to the dissent? Why the difference, and who was right? In other words, when interpreting statutory language, should we look to the purpose of the statute as a whole, the exceptions to that statute, or both?

(3) *The Plain Meaning Rule.* Isn't the majority's articulation of the plain meaning rule somewhat unusual? This opinion was written in 1979. Justice Scalia ascended to the Supreme Court in 1986. Prior to that time, textualism was not consistently favored by the Justices, as the tension between the approaches in *Train* and *Tennessee Valley Authority* make clear. Today, textualism has enjoyed a re-emergence; thus, a judge today would likely be more reluctant to disregard clear text.

(4) *Another Approach.* The majority wrote: "Pursuant to our adherence to the applicable portion of the plain meaning rule, we believe that the plainer the language, the more convincing contrary legislative history must be." This approach is similar to the sliding scale approach used in Alaska.

> Alaska does not adhere to a "plain meaning rule" of statutory interpretation that disregards any consideration of legislative purpose or intent. Instead, we consider a statute's meaning by applying a "sliding scale" such that, the plainer the statutory language, the more convincing the evidence of a contrary legislative purpose or intent must be.

LeFever v. State, 877 P.2d 1298, 1299–1300 (Alaska Ct. App. 1994).

(5) *Intent v. Purpose.* The majority used the legislative history to identify the purpose of the exception in the statute, while the dissent looked to the legislative history to determine the specific intent of the legislature as to the text in question. Be sure that you see that the focus, intent versus purpose, selected by the majority and dissent lead to different outcomes. This case should also make clear the difference between an intentionalist and purposivist approach.

(6) *Using the Textual Canons to Interpret the Legislative History.* The majority used the plain meaning canon (actually its technical counterpart) to interpret "person," as used in the conference committee report, to include non-human entities. Additionally, the majority failed to afford "he," as used during the debates, its ordinary meaning. Instead, the majority applied the following canons: (1) grammar shouldn't control meaning and (2) the masculine can include the feminine and the neuter. Should textual canons be used to understand the meaning of the words used during the legislative process (*i.e.*, in committee reports and debates)? If so, does it matter whether those comments were made orally or in writing? Consider whether you choose your words more carefully when speaking or writing.

3. Using Purpose to Defeat the Plain Meaning

We turn next to the use of purpose to defeat the plain meaning of the statute; this use is the most controversial use of purpose. While only purposivist judges are willing to expressly *admit* to using purpose in this way, we believe that even non-purposivist judges may sometimes use purpose to defeat clear text.

The following case may be one of the most cited statutory interpretation cases of all time. It is cited frequently in cases in which the plain meaning of the text appears to defeat the intent or purpose of the legislature. In fact, Professor Frickey wrote, "*Holy Trinity Church* is the case you always cite when the statutory text is hopelessly against you."

Philip P. Frickey, *From the Big Sleep to the Big Heat: The Revival of Theory in Statutory Interpretation*, 77 MINN. L. REV. 241, 247 (1992). As you read this case, see if you agree with Professor Frickey's comment.

For some of you, this case will be familiar. We included it in Chapter 7 (although we edited it differently), when we addressed the role the title plays in statutory interpretation. For others of you, this case may be new. For your convenience, we repeat the relevant facts.

Church of The Holy Trinity v. United States
143 U.S. 457 (1892)

JUSTICE BREWER delivered the opinion of the Court.

Plaintiff ... is a [church]. E. Walpole Warren was, prior to September, 1887, an alien residing in England. In that month the plaintiff ... made a contract with him, by which he was to remove to the city of New York, and enter into its service as rector.... It is claimed by the United States that this contract ... was forbidden; ... and an action was commenced to recover the penalty prescribed by that act. The Circuit Court held that the contract was within the prohibition of the statute, and rendered judgment accordingly, and the single question presented for our determination is whether it erred in that conclusion.

The first section describes the act forbidden, and is in these words:

> Be it enacted by the Senate and House of Representatives of the United States of America, in Congress assembled, That ... it shall be unlawful for any person, company, partnership, or corporation, in any manner whatsoever, to prepay the transportation, or in any way assist or encourage the importation or migration, of any alien or aliens, any foreigner or foreigners, into the United States ... to perform labor or service of any kind....

It must be conceded that the act of the corporation is within the letter of this section, for the relation of rector to his church is one of service, and implies labor on the one side with compensation on the other. Not only are the general words 'labor' and 'service' both used, but also, as it were to guard against any narrow interpretation and emphasize a breadth of meaning, to them is added 'of any kind;' and, further, as noticed by the Circuit Judge in his opinion, the fifth section, which makes specific exceptions, among them professional actors, artists, lecturers, singers, and domestic servants, strengthens the idea that every other kind of labor and service was intended to be reached by the first section. While there is great force to this reasoning, we cannot think Congress intended to denounce with penalties a transaction like that in the present case. It is a familiar rule, that a thing may be within the letter of the statute and yet not within the statute, because not within its spirit, nor within the intention of its makers. This has been often asserted, and the reports are full of cases illustrating its application. This is not the substitution of the will of the judge for that of the legislator, for frequently words of general meaning are used in a statute, words broad enough to include an act in question, and yet a consideration of the whole legislation, or of the circumstances surrounding its enactment, or of the absurd results which follow from giving such broad meaning to the words, makes it unreasonable to believe that the legislator intended to include the particular act....

[A] guide to the meaning of a statute is found in the evil which it is designed to remedy; and for this the court properly looks at contemporaneous events, the situation as it existed, and as it was pressed upon the attention of the legislative body. The situation which called for this statute was briefly but fully stated by Mr. Justice Brown when, as District Judge, he decided the case of *U. S. v. Craig*, 28 Fed. Rep. 795, 798: "The motives and history of the act are matters of common knowledge. It had become the practice for large capitalists in this country to contract with their agents abroad for the shipment of great numbers of an ignorant and servile class of foreign laborers, under contracts by which the employer agreed, upon the one hand, to prepay their passage, while, upon the other hand, the laborers agreed to work after their arrival for a certain time at a low rate of wages. The effect of this was to break down the labor market, and to reduce other laborers engaged in like occupations to the level of the assisted immigrant. The evil finally became so flagrant that an appeal was made to Congress for relief by the passage of the act in question, the design of which was to raise the standard of foreign immigrants, and to discountenance the migration of those who had not sufficient means in their own hands, or those of their friends, to pay their passage."

It appears, also, from the petitions, and in the testimony presented before the committees of Congress, that it was this cheap, unskilled labor which was making the trouble, and the influx of which Congress sought to prevent. It was never suggested that we had in this country a surplus of brain toilers, and, least of all, that the market for the services of Christian ministers was depressed by foreign competition. Those were matters to which the attention of Congress, or of the people, was not directed. So far, then, as the evil which was sought to be remedied interprets the statute, it also guides to an exclusion of this contract from the penalties of the act.

A singular circumstance, throwing light upon the intent of Congress, is found in this extract from the report of the Senate Committee on Education and Labor, recommending the passage of the bill: "The general facts and considerations which induce the committee to recommend the passage of this bill are set forth in the Report of the Committee of the House. The committee report the bill back without amendment, although there are certain features thereof which might well be changed or modified, in the hope that the bill may not fail of passage during the present session. Especially would the committee have otherwise recommended amendments, substituting for the expression, 'labor and service,' whenever it occurs in the body of the bill, the words 'manual labor' or 'manual service,' as sufficiently broad to accomplish the purposes of the bill, and that such amendments would remove objections which a sharp and perhaps unfriendly criticism may urge to the proposed legislation. The committee, however, believing that the bill in its present form will be construed as including only those whose labor or service is manual in character, and being very desirous that the bill become a law before the adjournment, have reported the bill without change." And, referring back to the report of the Committee of the House, there appears this language: "It seeks to restrain and prohibit the immigration or importation of laborers who would have never seen our shores but for the inducements and allurements of men whose only object is to obtain labor at the lowest possible rate, regardless of the social and material well-being of our own citizens, and regardless of the evil consequences which result to American laborers from such immigration. This class of immigrants care nothing about our institutions, and in many instances never even heard of them; they are men whose passage is paid by the importers; they come here under contract to labor for a certain number of years; they are ignorant of our social condition, and, that they may remain so, they are isolated and prevented from coming into contact with Americans; they are generally from the lowest social stratum, and live upon the coarsest food, and in hovels of a character before unknown to American workmen. They, as a rule, do not become citizens, and are certainly not a desirable acquisition to the body politic. The inevitable tendency of their presence among us is to degrade American labor, and to reduce it to the level of the imported pauper labor."

We find, therefore, that ... the evil which was intended to be remedied, the circumstances surrounding the appeal to Congress, the reports of the committee of each house, all concur in affirming that the intent of Congress was simply to stay the influx of this cheap, unskilled labor.

But, beyond all these matters, no purpose of action against religion can be imputed to any legislation, state or national, because this is a religious people....

If we pass beyond these matters to a view of American life, as expressed by its laws, its business, its customs, and its society, we find every where a clear recognition of the same truth. Among other matters note the following: The form of oath universally prevailing, concluding with an appeal to the Almighty; the custom of opening sessions of all deliberative bodies and most conventions with prayer; the prefatory words of all wills, "In the name of God, amen;" the laws respecting the observance of the Sabbath, with the general cessation of all secular business, and the closing of courts, legislatures, and other similar public assemblies on that day; the churches and church organizations which abound in every city, town, and hamlet; the multitude of charitable organizations existing every where under Christian auspices; the gigantic missionary associations, with general support, and aiming to establish Christian missions in every quarter of the globe. These, and many other matters which might be noticed, add a volume of unofficial declarations to the mass of organic utterances that this is a Christian nation. In the face of all these, shall it be believed that a Congress of the United States intended to make it a misdemeanor for a church of this country to contract for the services of a Christian minister residing in another nation?

Suppose, in the Congress that passed this act, some member had offered a bill which in terms declared that, if any Roman Catholic church in this country should contract with Cardinal Manning to come to this country, and enter into its service as pastor and priest; or any Episcopal church should enter into a like contract with Canon Farrar; or any Baptist church should make similar arrangements with Rev. Mr. Spurgeon, or any Jewish synagogue with some eminent Rabbi, such contract should be adjudged unlawful and void, and the church making it be subject to prosecution and punishment, can it be believed that it would have received a minute of approving thought or a single vote? Yet it is contended that such was in effect the meaning of this statute. The construction invoked cannot be accepted as correct. It is a case where there was presented a definite evil, in view of which the legislature used general terms with the purpose of reaching all phases of that evil, and thereafter, unexpectedly, it is developed that the general language thus employed is broad enough to reach cases and acts which the whole history and life of the country affirm could not have been intentionally legislated against. It is the duty of the courts, under those circumstances, to say that, however broad the language of the statute may be, the act, although within the letter, is not within the intention of the legislature, and therefore cannot be within the statute.

The judgment will be reversed, and the case remanded....

Notes and Questions

(1) *Was the Meaning Plain?* Did Justice Brewer perhaps concede too quickly that the plain meaning of the word "labor" was at odds with the statute's purpose? In other words, isn't it at least arguable that "labor" is ambiguous, meaning either those who (1) perform manual labor for a living or (2) perform all types of labor? *See* William N. Eskridge, Jr., *et al*, Cases and Materials on Legislation Statutes and the Creation of Public Policy 679–80 (3rd ed. 2001). Why do you think Justice Brewer readily conceded that the plain meaning conflicted with purpose? Assuming the meaning was clear, was the purpose of the statute clear enough to overcome the plain meaning?

(2) *Sources for Finding Purpose.* What sources did the Court use to determine the purpose of this statute? Does the fact that legislative history was used necessarily imply that Justice Brewer was an intentionalist? Or, does the use of multiple sources simply show the variety of information that can be used to discern purpose?

(3) *A Nation of Religious People.* Regardless of whether Justice Brewer was right on this point, was it necessary for the decision? Relevant? Congress didn't pass a statute prohibiting religious individuals from entering the country. Isn't it true that Warren's profession was not directly relevant to resolving the issue, at least as the statute was written? For example, would the result have been different if Warren had been a professor or engineer? What about a factory worker?

(4) *Poor Drafting.* If Justice Brewer was correct that Congress had intended to stem the influx of cheap labor into the United States, is the result sustainable? If Congress meant to prevent only cheap laborers from coming into the country, shouldn't Congress have simply said so? Who should "fix" poorly drafted laws: a court or legislature?

(5) *Subsequent Legislative Action.* After the Southern District of New York held that this statute applied to Mr. Warren, Congress amended the statute to exempt ministers and other professionals. This amendment was enacted in 1891. Although the change occurred before *Holy Trinity* reached the Supreme Court, the statute was not retroactive and thus did not apply to the case. Act of March 3, 1891, § 12, 26 Stat. 1084, 1086. Does this amendment lend support to the Court's holding? Or, is it irrelevant what a subsequent Congress concluded about the meaning of a previously enacted statute? (*See* Chapter 9.) Does it matter to you that in *United States v. Laws*, 163 U.S. 258, 265 (1896), the Court referred to the amendment when it held that a chemist was exempt from the act, even though the amendment was not in effect when the chemist came to the United States?

In the preceding case, Justice Brewer quickly dismissed the plain meaning of the statute in favor of an interpretation that furthered the statute's purpose. *Holy Trinity* was decided in 1892. With the reemergence of textualism, might a judge today feel more constrained by the statute's text? Read the more modern case below, and see if the judge finds it difficult to reject plain meaning in favor of purpose.

Ohio Div. of Wildlife v. Clifton
692 N.E.2d 253 (Ohio Mun. Ct. 1997)

JOHN R. ADKINS, JUDGE.

… The subject of [this] controversy is a certain grey squirrel, which was apparently dislodged from its nest shortly after birth. It was discovered by the defendant in this obviously imperiled state. The defendant exercised control over the squirrel, providing nutrition and hydration in such a way that notwithstanding the low potential for survival, the squirrel, in fact, was habilitated and survived. Nearly a year and a half passed, during which time the squirrel remained in the residence of Clifton and became habituated to that environment. Enthralled with the creature, Clifton carried it [dressed in a homemade costume] through the 1997 Pumpkin Show parade and won first prize in the most unusual pet category, thereby garnering the attention of Wildlife Officer Bebout. He and another officer drove to the residence of the alleged offender and attempted to take into custody this squirrel. Custody was refused by Clifton and she was cited into Circleville Municipal Court, the maximum possible penalty being $500 and sixty days in jail. The [state statute] section under which she was cited states as follows:

> Any person desiring ... to have game birds, quadrupeds, or fur-bearing animals in captivity, may apply in writing to the Division of Wildlife for a license to do so....
>
> Except as provided by law no person shall possess game birds, game quadrupeds, or fur-bearing animals....

In response to the issuance of the citation, on November 4, 1997, Clifton made an application for a ... permit, which was refused with an annotation at the bottom noting, "squirrel was taken from wild—no permit can be issued for this animal—must be released to the wild." ...

The Division has [no written rules setting out the criteria for the allowance or rejection of applications for licenses], but provided copies of [the administrative code entitled] "Hunting and trapping regulations for fur-bearing animals," the essence of which ... is that an animal listed may be hunted, trapped, taken, or possessed, if immediately thereafter it is put to death by any reasonable means.... It is clear ... that had Clifton captured this grey squirrel during the appropriate season and subsequently killed it, she would have committed no wrong.... The state's position, therefore, is clear: A person may take any such listed game animal during the appropriate season, having paid the appropriate licensing fee, and kill such animal. That is the only way a person may possess a listed animal, unless ... a license is issued. However, the state has no criteria by which a person may reasonably be adjudged worthy of or not worthy of possession of a wild animal having been acquired by other means....

The legislature of the state of Ohio expressly set forth that "[a]ny person" "may apply" for a license "to have game birds, game quadrupeds, or fur-bearing animals in captivity." R.C. 1533.71. That language is clear....

> In construing a statute, a court's paramount concern is the legislative intent in enacting the statute. Under Ohio law, it is a cardinal rule that a court must first look to the language of the statute itself to determine the legislative intent. In interpreting a statute, words and phrases shall be read in context and construed according to the rules of grammar and common usage. Courts do not have authority to ignore the plain and unambiguous language of a statute under the guise of statutory interpretation, but must give effect to the words used. In other words, courts may not delete words used or insert words not used....

[*State v. Conger*, 646 N.E.2d 238, 241 (Ohio 1994)].

In common law, "justice" was a title given to judicial officers of the King's Bench. It has come to be a term used in the United States to denote not only the individual empowered by the electorate to ensure appropriate checks and balances, but also the constant and perpetual disposition to place all men in equality. In the most expansive sense of the word, "justice" differs little from "virtue," which includes a gamut of Judeo-Christian values. Yet the common distinction between the terms "justice" and "virtue" is that virtue is wholly positive, while justice includes the imposition of punishment to ensure that people live within the law of their jurisdiction. "Justice" is not an abstract thought or concept, but sometimes the essence of justice, which is the common experience of man yielded from common sense, logic and decency, is lost in our society. Even though we charge jurors to apply the test of common sense that we use in our everyday lives, judges and lawyers often become lost in abstract thought and concepts, believing that they should apply statutes blindly. This court takes its obligation and its oath of office much more seriously.... No right of the victim is advanced, and no interest of the state served, by incarcerating the innocent. The Supreme Court of Ohio has stated, in a case that the state itself points to, that a trial before a judicial tribunal is primarily a truth-determining process, and if it in any sense loses its character as such, it becomes the veriest sort of a mockery. The ultimate aim of the criminal justice system, then, is not the balancing of rights, but the uncovering of truth.

The court finds that ... a citizen of the state of Ohio attempted to extend humanitarian aid to an otherwise helpless animal. The Wildlife Officer in this case would choose to reward her with a potential fine and incarceration and, obviously, death for the squirrel. Officer Lehman himself testified that the average life expectancy of a squirrel in the wild, due to Darwinian effects of predation and so forth, is eleven months. The court notes that the squirrel has so far survived seventeen. Officer Lehman further testified that the anticipated life expectancy of this squirrel in Clifton's residence is five to seven years. And yet, the state insists on regaining possession of this squirrel to return it to the wild, even though it knows that the animal would not survive. This makes no sense. Even a child could see that there is no justice or right in the position of the state.

Is there a rationale for the underlying statute? Of course! It must be learned from this case that citizens may not arbitrarily take animals from the wild to habituate, tame and otherwise domesticate them, for the obvious reason that the animals may be infected with various serious diseases, and they may pose a potential public safety risk to children and others. Therefore, the statute is logical and its general enforcement may be appropriate. As applied in this case, it is inappropriate....

When a person appears before the court having demonstrated only affection for an orphaned animal and an incredible regard for life, that person should be rewarded. But a narrow mind begets obstinacy and obviously it is very difficult to persuade arbitrary bureaucrats of concepts beyond the scope of their understanding....

The French philosopher Chamfort said, "Intelligent people make many blunders, because they never believe the world to be as stupid as it is." This court does not wish to be stupid and perpetuate the waste of time and resources of this court and the state of Ohio in pursuing this matter. At a time when the state is struggling to find resources to educate our children and to make them intelligent, compassionate people involved in honest, life-enhancing pursuits, it is more than ironic that the state ... would choose to allocate the resources of two uniformed officers to pursue a woman who demonstrates no moral culpability whatsoever. This court is not so foolhardy. Therefore, for all the reasons set forth above, the court finds the defendant's motion to be well taken and the case is dismissed forthwith. Further, this grey squirrel shall be permitted to be retained in and about the property of Mary Jane Clifton without further interference, although the court cautions Clifton that it does not expect to view this squirrel being bandied about in public in strange wearing apparel of any kind.

So ordered.

This opinion could have been reduced to a simple poem:

The court hereby announces a pearl,
It's sometimes OK to have a squirrel.
The legislature did a statute create,
The Wildlife Division obviously did not equate.
The necessity to be kind, thorough and specific,
The lack of these is legally terrific.
The result is this very short epistle,
The defendant/squirrel is granted a dismissal.

Notes and Questions

(1) *Was the Language of the Statute Clear?* Didn't the statute unambiguously prevent the defendant from owning the squirrel—"a fur-bearing animal"—without a license? If so, why did the squirrel get to return to the defendant's home?

(2) *Which Purpose Mattered?* What two purposes did the court identify? Which purpose mattered more in the court's final decision: the purpose behind the criminal justice system or the purpose of the specific statute?

(3) *A Court's Approach to Statutory Interpretation Matters.* Would a textualist judge have resolved this case in the same way? An intentionalist? What about a judge using Alaska's sliding scale approach, in which the willingness of the court to give weight to contrary extratextual sources decreases with the clarity of the text?

(4) *Absurdity.* Was the statute absurd on its face? If not, was it absurd as applied in this case? Should a judge use specific absurdity—*i.e.* absurd as applied in a case but not absurd generally—to avoid the plain meaning of the statute?

(5) *Other Cases.* In a number of older cases, the Supreme Court ignored the plain meaning when the Justices believed that the plain meaning defeated the statute's purpose. *See, e.g., United States v. Am. Trucking Ass'ns, Inc.*, 310 U.S. 534, 543–44 (1940) (there is no "rule of law" which forbids the use of extrinsic aids in construing the meaning of statutory language however clear the words may appear on "superficial examination"); *United States v. Ron Pair Enters., Inc.*, 489 U.S. 235, 242–43 (1989) ("The plain meaning of legislation should be conclusive, except in the 'rare cases [in which] the literal application of a statute will produce a result demonstrably at odds with the intentions of the drafters.'... In such cases, the intention of the drafters, rather than the strict language, controls.") (internal citation omitted); *Bob Jones Univ. v. United States*, 461 U.S. 574, 586 (1983) ("It is a well-established canon of statutory construction that a court should go beyond the literal language of a statute if reliance on that language would defeat the plain purpose of the statute.") Yet today, it is less common for the Justices to reject clear text for purpose.

Problem 10-2

Assume that you represent a person who was ticketed for driving a Segway™ (a motorized two-wheeled vehicle) on a sidewalk in violation of a statute prohibiting "vehicles" from being driven on a sidewalk. You are about to argue that a Segway™ is not a "vehicle." Assume that there is no definition of "vehicle" in the statute and that no other statue is relevant. Ignore the rule of lenity.

According to Dictionary.com your jurisdiction's preferred dictionary for determining ordinary meaning, a vehicle is:

1. A device or structure for transporting persons or things;

2. A self-propelled conveyance that runs on tires.

Thus, the plain meaning of the statute does not aid your client's case; a Segway™ is a "device or structure for transporting persons," is "self-propelled," and "runs on tires." As a good attorney, however, you do not stop with this conclusion. Instead, you learn that the legislative history includes a committee report that states: "this act is intended to apply to motorcycles, mopeds, and cars, which more properly belong on our roads and create unsafe conditions for pedestrians." How would you get a court to consider the report? How would the prosecutor respond?

Assume instead that the statute contained a purpose clause that stated: "It is the goal of this act to protect innocent citizens traversing the sidewalk by ensuring that all motorized vehicles capable of being driven on public throughways shall remain on the road at all times thereby making our sidewalks safe for those individuals and vehicles — such as pedestrians, strollers, and wheelchairs — that cannot travel on the public throughways." Does the clause aid your case? Can you convincingly argue that the statute is ambiguous? Absurd? Do you need to argue either to have the court consider the purpose clause? Does the answer to that question change depending on the judge's approach to statutory interpretation?

Chapter 11

The Relevance of Judicial Interpretations of an Identical or Similar Statute from Other Jurisdictions

This chapter analyzes the issues that can arise when a court interprets a statute using another jurisdiction's judicial interpretations of an identical or similar statute. We will look at three related, albeit different, situations: (1) when one state adopts a Model or Uniform Act; (2) when one state patterns a statute verbatim after another state's statute; and (3) when one state enacts its own statute, but other jurisdictions coincidentally have similar, though not identical, statutes.

The reasons to adopt another jurisdiction's judicial construction of the statute are different in each situation. As we will see, there is little controversy in some of these situations and more in others. For example, adopting interpretations by another state's courts where a Uniform Act is involved is relatively uncontroversial because one goal of adopting a Uniform Act is to achieve uniformity across state lines. Adopting another state's interpretation furthers uniformity and, thus, makes sense. In contrast, when a legislature patterns a statute after another state's existing statute, uniformity with the other state is not necessarily the goal. Perhaps most controversial of all is when a court interprets its own state's statute but looks to interpretations from another jurisdiction to do so — even though the language of the other jurisdiction's statute, though not its purpose, differs.

A. Other Jurisdictions' Interpretation of Model or Uniform Acts

It has become fairly common for organizations to draft and circulate model or uniform acts on particular subjects. These acts often deal with issues that are historically matters of state concern but which implicate multijurisdictional concerns. The number of model acts has grown exponentially over the years and today includes the Uniform Commercial Code, the Uniform Enforcement of Foreign Judgments Law, the Uniform Act for Out-of-State Parolee Supervision, and the Uniform Act to Secure the Attendance of Witnesses from Without a State in Criminal Proceedings, among countless others.

One goal of proponents of these acts is uniformity among states. Therefore, courts regularly look to the interpretation of a particular uniform act by another state and give deference to that state's interpretation:

> It is axiomatic that a purpose in enacting uniform laws is to achieve uniformity, not uniqueness. While opinions by courts of sister states construing a uniform act are not binding on this court, [I am] mindful that the objective of uniformity cannot be achieved by ignoring utterances of other jurisdictions. This court should strive to maintain the standardization of construction of uniform acts to carry out the legislative intent of uniformity. This does not mean that this court [should] blindly follow decisions of other states interpreting uniform acts, but this court [should] seriously consider the constructions given to comparable statutes in other jurisdictions and [should] espouse them to maintain conformity when they are in harmony with the spirit of the statute and do not antagonize public policy of this state.

> [B]y conforming [our] interpretation of [the U.C.C.] to that of our sister states, we are, in fact maintaining the standardization of construction of uniform acts and, in that way, carrying out the legislative intent of uniformity.

Pileri Indus., Inc. v. Consol. Indus., Inc., 740 So. 2d 1108, 1114 (Ala. Ct. App. 1999) (Crawley, J., dissenting).

Although uniformity may be a legislative goal, the courts are clear that other jurisdictions's interpretations carry great weight but are not controlling. As the North Dakota Supreme Court put it:

> The primary objective in interpreting a statute is to ascertain the intent of the Legislature. The courts attempt to construe uniform laws and model acts in the same manner as other jurisdictions to provide consistency and uniformity of the law. Consideration of similar statutes of other states and court decisions interpreting those statutes is appropriate and relevant. We consider the resolution of this issue by these other jurisdictions as highly persuasive authority.

Zuger v. N.D. Ins. Guar. Ass'n, 494 N.W.2d 135, 137–38 (N.D. 1992). *See Conn. Ins. Guar. Ass'n v. Fontaine*, 900 A.2d 18, 26 n.8 (Conn. 2006) (explaining that "Sister state decisions are helpful in construing and applying" model acts).

At times, legislatures make clear their desire for uniformity by adopting statutes that specifically direct courts to construe uniform statutes in uniformity with other states. *E.g.*, N.D. Cent. Code § 1-02-13 (2005) ("Any provision in this code which is a part of a uniform statute must be so construed as to effectuate its general purpose to make uniform the law of those states which enact it."); 1 Pa. Stat. Ann. § 1927 (West 2005) ("Statutes uniform with those of other states shall be interpreted and construed to effect their general purpose to make uniform the laws of those states which enact them."). Consider, however, whether it makes sense for a court to be careful to look at sister state interpretations when analyzing a model act, even when that court does not find any ambiguity in the text.

Construing uniform statutes in accordance with other state acts is non-controversial, but understanding that it is uniformity that drives statutory interpretation in this area will help your understanding and criticism of the next two areas we cover.

B. Adopting the Judicial Interpretations of a Borrowed Statute

Commonly, uniform acts are adopted in part to create uniformity across state lines. But it is also common for the legislature of one state to "borrow" a statute from another state by enacting an identical statute, without any apparent desire to achieve uniformity. Borrowing often occurs to simplify the drafting process; it is easier to copy than to create.

When borrowing occurs, how should a judge of the borrowing state interpret the borrowed statute? Should borrowing matter at all? Should a judge assume that when the legislature borrowed the statute the legislature also adopted any existing judicial interpretations from the patterning state? If so, what about subsequent decisions from the patterning state? Or, what if several states have identical statutes, but courts in each state have interpreted their own statute differently: Which interpretation should control? This section addresses these questions.

Generally, when a statute is adopted from another jurisdiction, a court will look to settled judicial construction in the patterning jurisdiction *as of the time the statute was adopted. Canfield v. Security-First Nat'l Bank of L.A.*, 87 P.2d 830, 836 (Cal. 1939) ("when a statute is adopted from a sister state that has been construed by the courts of that state, the judicial construction is likewise adopted"). This canon expands the presumption that a legislature knows of all prior interpretations of its own statutes; further, courts presume that the adopting legislature was aware of all the *other state's* judicial constructions of the statute and intended to adopt not only the statute, but these judicial constructions as well. *See State v. Schmidt,* 126 P.3d 507, 510 (Mont. 2005) ("We have long adhered to the rule that when Montana's Legislature adopts a statute from a sister state, Montana courts also adopt the construction of the statute as determined by the highest court of the sister state.") But how accurate do you think this presumption really is?

Even though the courts look to the decisions of the patterning states, courts in borrowing states disagree on whether the judicial interpretations of the patterning states are binding. Some states, like California and Montana, suggest that the legislature is deemed to adopt the judicial constructions, while other states suggest that the judicial constructions are persuasive, but not controlling. The principal case below (*Van Horn v. William Blanchard Co.*, 438 A.2d 552 (N.J. 1981)), illustrates the latter view; the majority noted that the patterning state's judicial constructions were merely significant — not controlling.

In contrast to the persuasive effect of interpretations from the patterning state that predated the borrowing, judicial interpretations of the borrowed statute in the patterning state issued *after* the borrowing state adopts its statute are, at most, only informative. What affects whether a court in interpreting a statute that has been adopted from another jurisdiction should accept the patterning jurisdiction's judicial interpretations? And how can a court be sure it adopts the right state's interpretation when multiple state statutes were considered during the drafting process? The following cases explore these and other questions.

Van Horn v. William Blanchard Co.
438 A.2d 552 (N.J. 1981)

CLIFFORD, J.

... On September 25, 1975 plaintiff, Lloyd K. Van Horn, was employed ... [and working] on a building site in Clinton, New Jersey. The general contractor was defendant ... Blanchard.... Defendant Epic ... was [a] subcontractor.... [P]laintiff sustained injuries giving rise to this suit when he slipped and fell on the job site while running into a building to avoid a rain storm. The cause of action was predicated on defendants' failure to have maintained the building entrance in a safe condition....

Having been instructed that the combined negligence, if there were any, should total one hundred percent, the jury apportioned the negligence as follows: plaintiff, fifty percent; Blanchard, thirty percent; and Epic, twenty percent. Because the plaintiff's negligence exceeded the individual negligence of either of the joint tortfeasors, the trial court entered judgment for defendants.

On appeal plaintiff argued that "[i]n multiple defendant cases, in order to avoid harsh and unfair results, the negligence of an individual plaintiff must be compared to the combined negligence of the several tortfeasors." According to plaintiff he was entitled to a judgment on liability inasmuch as his negligence (fifty percent) was not greater than the aggregated negligence (fifty percent) of the two tortfeasors....

Both the plain meaning of the statute and long-standing judicial interpretation thereof lead [us to affirm.]

The Comparative Negligence Act was the Legislature's response to the harshness of the complete bar to recovery imposed by the rule of contributory negligence....

Section 1 of the Act reads as follows:

> Contributory negligence shall not bar recovery in an action by any person or his legal representative to recover damages for negligence resulting in death or injury to person or property, if such negligence was not greater than the negligence of the person against whom recovery is sought, but any damages sustained shall be diminished by the percentage sustained of negligence attributable to the person recovering. N.J.S.A. 2A:15-5....

The Comparative Negligence Act was taken nearly verbatim from the Wisconsin comparative negligence statute. A legislative enactment patterned after a statute of another state is ordinarily adopted with the prior constructions placed on it by the highest court of the parent jurisdiction. Hence it is significant that at the time New Jersey adopted the Wisconsin "modified" form of comparative negligence, the individual approach rather than the aggregate system was a fixture in Wisconsin law. In cases decided after New Jersey had embraced comparative negligence Wisconsin continued to adhere to the principle that the comparison of negligence in multiple defendant cases must be between the plaintiff and each defendant individually. Whereas it is true that Wisconsin flirted with the notion of embracing the aggregate approach, the departure was but a momentary aberration, as disclosed by *Reiter v. Dyken*.

> To change from the present rule to one in which a plaintiff would be allowed to recover against a person less negligent than himself would have significant ramifications throughout the tort system of allocating losses as it now exists in this state. Specifically, such a change would raise important questions about the extent of a less negligent defendant's liability and the operation of the rules of joint

and several liability, contribution, set-off and release. Indeed, unless accompanying changes are made in these related areas of law, the change requested by plaintiff may very well create far more serious problems than it is intended to resolve. For this reason we think plaintiffs' request would be better addressed to the legislature....

[A]ny change of our law in this area should come from the legislative rather than the judicial process.

Affirmed.

HANDLER, J., dissenting.

The Court in this case has ruled that New Jersey's Comparative Negligence Act, prevents a plaintiff injured in an accident from recovering damages from defendants whose combined fault for the accident equaled or exceeded that of the plaintiff. It does so notwithstanding the statute's intent to permit recovery by a plaintiff whose own fault for accidental injury constitutes no more than half of the total fault. The Court apparently feels bound to this result ... because this particular interpretation was reached by the courts of another jurisdiction whose decisions are said to be binding upon us. In my view, th[is] reason[] ... do[es] not justify the inequitable result embodied in the majority's interpretation of the Comparative Negligence Act. I therefore dissent.

The majority's interpretation of the New Jersey Comparative Negligence Act is known as the "individual" approach because it calls for the individual comparison of plaintiff's fault with that of each joint tortfeasor in a multi-defendant case in order to determine the liability of each defendant. The individual approach bars a plaintiff's recovery even though the combined negligence of all defendants contributing to the accident exceeds that of the plaintiff. This may be contrasted with the "aggregate" approach, which enables a plaintiff to recover from joint tortfeasors whose combined negligence exceeds that of the plaintiff even though some defendants individually may have been less at fault than the plaintiff....

[One] reason for the Court's conclusion that the New Jersey comparative negligence scheme embraces the individual approach is its belief that determinative weight must be given to the construction placed on the comparative negligence statute of Wisconsin by the courts of that state. It is true that New Jersey's Comparative Negligence Act mirrors Wisconsin's. The majority opinion assumes that in adopting a comparative negligence statute similar to Wisconsin's, our Legislature intended to embrace that state's judicial interpretation of its statute as well.

As a general rule, courts give a legislative enactment patterned after the statute of another state the same construction placed upon it by the highest court of that jurisdiction. New Jersey follows this approach. This rule, of course, is merely a tool for ascertaining the true intention of the Legislature. The judicial decisions of another state are not conclusive evidence of legislative intent. Thus, where the legislature of one state chooses to adopt as part of its laws the statute of another state, the judiciary of the adopting state may, if appropriate, choose to interpret its statute differently from the judicial interpretations of the source state. If there is some doubt that the adopting legislature fully intended to embrace the particular interpretations or applications by the courts of the source state, the courts of the adopting jurisdiction do not have to give greater weight to the originating state's judicial decisions than their intrinsic persuasiveness demands; and this is especially so where the public policies of the adopting state elicit different concerns and invoke priorities that are important or unique to that jurisdiction.

The assumption that the New Jersey Legislature intended to embrace not only Wisconsin's statute but also its judicial interpretations of that statute is questionable. The majority seemingly takes the view that the New Jersey law does not merely follow but is actually cloned from the Wisconsin statute. While references to the Wisconsin statute are present in the legislative history, there is nothing in that history to indicate that the Legislature, in adopting this statute, considered the central issue presented by this case — whether to employ the aggregate or the individual approach.

In addition, the sponsors' statement accompanying the bill introduced in the Assembly did not refer exclusively to the Wisconsin approach. Rather, it read, in pertinent part: "This State will not be unique if it adopts the law of comparative negligence. Other jurisdictions such as Wisconsin, Arkansas, Georgia, Maine, Florida, Iowa, Mississippi, Nebraska, South Dakota, Puerto Rico, the Canal Zone, the Canadian provinces, etc., have a form of comparative negligence." Therefore, it seems clear that the sponsors of the bill considered not only the law of Wisconsin but also that of a variety of jurisdictions, some of which adhere to the aggregate approach.

One such state, specifically mentioned by the sponsors, is Arkansas.... [T]hat state adopted the aggregate approach through judicial construction as early as 1962....

In 1978, the Oklahoma Supreme Court held that the state's comparative negligence statute ... should be interpreted to apply an aggregate approach. The court reasoned that its statute was based on the statutory scheme of both Wisconsin and Arkansas and that Arkansas' "aggregate" approach was preferable.

In opting to follow exactly or literally the Wisconsin judicial interpretation of the Comparative Negligence Act, this Court has abandoned any genuine interpretation of the Act and has walled off its analysis from any considerations of public policy. Yet no compelling argument is made why the decisions of the Wisconsin Supreme Court should be clamped around this State's comparative negligence law like an iron girdle, yielding no breathing room for our own tort law jurisprudence and public policy. In light of a legislative history that does not dictate such a course, our deliberations should be aired fully with reflections of our own public policy and legal traditions....[4]

In sum, I find no forceful argument in favor of construing the Comparative Negligence Act, as has the majority, to require the comparison of the negligence of a plaintiff with those of defendants on an individual basis. The language of the Act itself does not demand this. The decisions of the Wisconsin Courts do not constitute persuasive evidence of the intent of the New Jersey Legislature on this facet of the Act. Those decisions betray serious misgivings as to the soundness and wisdom of the interpretation of that state's law and are entitled to neither dispositive nor great weight by us in interpreting our law. Most importantly, our own public policy considerations strongly impel the aggregate approach to our Comparative Negligence Act.

Accordingly, I dissent.

---

4. Recently the Wisconsin Supreme Court, without expressly changing its position, voiced dissatisfaction with the individual approach in *May v. Skelley Oil Co.*, viz.

The majority of the court has become convinced that comparing the negligence of the individual plaintiff to that of each individual tortfeasor — rather than comparing the negligence of the individual plaintiff to that of the combined negligence of the several tortfeasors who have collectively contributed to plaintiff's injuries — leads to harsh and unfair results....

Notes and Questions

(1) *Was the Majority or the Dissent Correct?* Did the majority believe that the other state's interpretations were controlling, persuasive, or irrelevant? The dissent? Are opinions from courts in other states generally controlling or persuasive authority? Does this canon change that general presumption?

(2) *Why Not Arkansas or Oklahoma?* If, as the dissent contended, Wisconsin was not the sole patterning state, why did the majority defer to that state rather than Arkansas or Oklahoma, which had similar statutes and were also mentioned in the legislative history?

(3) *Wisconsin's Doubt.* The dissent, in a footnote, indicated that the Wisconsin Supreme Court had doubted the wisdom of its approach but ultimately left it to the legislature to amend the statute. What relevance, if any, should this fact have to the New Jersey court?

(4) *Subsequent Legislative Action in New Jersey.* After this decision, the New Jersey legislature amended the statute. In a later court case, the New Jersey Supreme Court wrote:

> [T]he Comparative Negligence Act was amended about a year after the trial [in this case]. The legislature acted to overturn our decision in *Van Horn v. Blanchard*, which interpreted the original Act as taking the "individual" approach to comparative negligence: plaintiff could recover only from those defendants who were more negligent than plaintiff, even if in the aggregate his negligence was less than the total percentage of fault on the part of all the defendants. To remedy the perceived inequity in that result the legislature adopted the "aggregate" approach: plaintiff in a negligence action may recover damages in any case in which his negligence is less than or equal to the combined negligence of multiple defendants.

Buckley v. Estate of Pirolo, 500 A.2d 703, 710 (N.J. 1985). Does this legislative response suggest that the dissent in *Van Horn* was correct? Or, was the majority right to let the legislature act?

Hillesland v. Fed. Land Bank Ass'n of Grand Forks
407 N.W.2d 206 (N.D. 1987)

Erickstad, Chief Justice.

… Hillesland began working at the Association in 1956.…

Through his position with the Association Hillesland in early 1983 learned that Ray and Eva Westby, customers of the Association, were experiencing financial difficulties. He also learned that they had received an offer to purchase their farm from another Association customer. Hillesland contacted the Westbys to offer financial counseling. They responded by expressing their desire to sell the farm.… [I]t is undisputed that these discussions eventually led to an offer to purchase the Westby farm by Hillesland's sons, David and Don.

In accordance with standard Association procedure, Hillesland submitted details of the proposed transaction … for approval. After meeting in a closed session with the Westbys, the board approved the transaction. Hillesland then submitted the matter to the Bank's Review Committee in St. Paul. In its report, the Review Committee stated that it was "not in a position to disapprove" the transaction, but it did express concern over the appearance of a conflict of interest and prohibited any further direct involvement in the transaction by Hillesland. The sale of the land to Hillesland's sons was completed shortly thereafter.

The Bank subsequently launched an investigation into the matter. On June 15, 1983, two representatives of the Bank appeared at a meeting of the Association board of directors in Grand Forks and advised Hillesland that he was being discharged from his employment with the Association. The Bank's rationale for Hillesland's termination was that he had violated written standards of conduct, had damaged the image and reputation of the Association and the Bank, and had exercised poor business judgment.

Hillesland commenced this action against the Association and the Bank alleging violation of provisions of the Farm Credit Act, breach of contract, age discrimination, and tortious interference by the Bank with Hillesland's employment contract with the Association. The district court granted summary judgment dismissing Hillesland's action, and he appeals....

Hillesland contends that there is an implied covenant of good faith and fair dealing in all employment contracts and that the Bank and the Association breached that covenant when they terminated his employment....

A brief historical perspective of the employment-at-will doctrine is helpful at this point. Prior to the mid-nineteenth century the prevailing theory was the "English rule," which provided that an employment without a set term was presumed to be for one year. Toward the end of the century the at-will rule was gaining popularity, and by the beginning of the twentieth century the at-will doctrine prevailed in the United States. The classic statement of the at-will rule is that an employer may discharge an employee "for good cause, for no cause or even for cause morally wrong, without being thereby guilty of legal wrong." *Payne v. Western & Atlantic Railroad Co.*, 81 Tenn. 507, 519–520 (1884), *overruled on other grounds, Hutton v. Watters*, 132 Tenn. 527, 179 S.W. 134, 137–138 (1915).

Congress and the legislatures of many states have enacted statutory provisions intended to afford some measure of protection to employees. Judicially created exceptions to or modifications of the at-will rule have also emerged to ameliorate the sometimes harsh consequences of strict adherence to the at-will rule. The two most common modifications are the public policy exception ... and the imposition of an implied covenant of good faith and fair dealing into the employment contract.

As previously noted, the at-will rule is statutory in this state. Section 34-03-01, N.D.C.C., provides in pertinent part: "An employment having no specified term may be terminated at the will of either party on notice to the other." Our statute is derived from the virtually identical California statute. Hillesland urges this court to imply into North Dakota employment contracts a covenant of good faith and fair dealing, as the California courts have done pursuant to that state's employment-at-will statute. Although we would normally attach great significance to a sister state's construction of a statute which served as the model for our state's provision, we decline to do so in this case.

The seminal California case is *Cleary v. American Airlines, Inc.*, 111 Cal.App.3d 443, 168 Cal.Rptr. 722 (1980)....

The Court of Appeal held that there was an implied covenant of good faith and fair dealing in every employment contract under California law. The court relied heavily upon two factors—the length of Cleary's employment and the existence of express procedures regarding termination in the company regulations. Thus, the court held that "the longevity of the employee's service, together with the expressed policy of the employer, operate as a form of estoppel, precluding any discharge of such an employee by the employer without good cause." ...

In later cases, the California Court of Appeal has grappled with the appropriate application of *Cleary* in a variety of fact situations. For example, in *Khanna v. Microdata Corp.*, 170 Cal.App.3d 250, 262, 215 Cal.Rptr. 860, 867 (1985), the First District Court of Appeal held that the application of the implied covenant was not limited to those situations where the employment was long-term and the employer acted contrary to its own stated procedures for discharge:

> "We cannot agree with appellant that the factors relied on by the court in *Cleary* are the *sine qua non* to establishing a breach of the covenant of good faith and fair dealing implied in every employment contract. The cases subsequent to *Cleary* discussing the breach of the implied covenant in employment contracts have indicated that the theory of recovery articulated in *Cleary* is not dependent on the particular factors identified in that case.... To the contrary, a breach of the implied covenant of good faith and fair dealing in employment contracts is established whenever the employer engages in 'bad faith action extraneous to the contract, combined with the obligor's intent to frustrate the [employee's] enjoyment of contract rights.'... The facts in *Cleary* establish only one manner among many by which an employer might violate this covenant." [Citations omitted.]

A few months later, the Second District Court of Appeal expressly disagreed with the holding in *Khanna,* concluding that to prove a violation of the covenant the employee "must show longevity of service, and breach of an express employer policy regarding the adjudication of employee disputes." ...

In those other jurisdictions which have found an implied-in-law covenant of good faith and fair dealing in employment contracts the application of the rule has been far from uniform. The Arizona Supreme Court, although holding that an implied covenant of good faith and fair dealing did apply to employment contracts, disagreed with the California rule that the covenant created a duty to terminate only in good faith:

> "We find neither the logic of the California cases nor their factual circumstances compelling for recognition of so broad a rule in the case before us. Were we to adopt such a rule, we fear that we would tread perilously close to abolishing completely the at-will doctrine and establishing by judicial fiat the benefits which employees can and should get *only* through collective bargaining agreements or tenure provisions.... While we do not reject the propriety of such a rule, we are not persuaded that it should be the result of judicial decision." *Wagenseller v. Scottsdale Memorial Hospital*, 147 Ariz. 370, 710 P.2d 1025, 1040 (1985). [Citation omitted.]

The court intimated that in Arizona the covenant would be breached only by a termination which contravened public policy.

Similarly, in *Magnan v. Anaconda Industries, Inc.*, 193 Conn. 558, 479 A.2d 781 (1984), the Supreme Court of Connecticut recognized that the covenant applied to employment contracts, but held that it should not be applied to transform an at-will employment into one terminable only for cause. To do so, the court stated, would be to "render the court a bargaining agent for every employee not protected by statute or collective bargaining agreement." The court concluded that an at-will employee could challenge his dismissal only when the reason for discharge involved a violation of an important public policy

Other jurisdictions similarly limit the rule. Massachusetts apparently applies the rule only if the discharge results in loss of compensation that is clearly identifiable and related to the employee's past service, such as future commissions based upon past sales. Alaska purports to follow the rule as formulated in Massachusetts.

Given the somewhat erratic development of this doctrine in the courts, we decline to follow either the California formulation or any of the variant theories developed in other jurisdictions. We choose to align ourselves with the emerging majority of our sister states which have rejected the implication of a covenant of good faith and fair dealing in employment contracts. *See, e.g., Zick v. Verson Allsteel Press Co.,* 623 F.Supp. 927 (N.D.Ill.1985) (applying Illinois law); *Parker v. National Corporation for Housing Partnerships,* 619 F.Supp. 1061 (D.D.C.1985) (applying District of Columbia law); *Satterfield v. Lockheed Missiles and Space Co.,* 617 F.Supp. 1359 (D.S.C.1985) (applying South Carolina law); *Fletcher v. Wesley Medical Center,* 585 F.Supp. 1260 (D.Kan.1984) (applying Kansas law); *Parnar v. Americana Hotels, Inc.,* 65 Hawaii 370, 652 P.2d 625 (1982); *Hunt v. IBM Mid America Employees Federal Credit Union,* 384 N.W.2d 853, 858 (Minn.1986); *Neighbors v. Kirksville College of Osteopathic Medicine,* 694 S.W.2d 822 (Mo.Ct.App.1985); *Murphy v. American Home Products Corp.,* 58 N.Y.2d 293, 461 N.Y.S.2d 232, 448 N.E.2d 86 (1983); *Thompson v. St. Regis Paper Co.,* 102 Wash.2d 219, 685 P.2d 1081 (1984); *Brockmeyer v. Dun & Bradstreet,* 113 Wis.2d 561, 335 N.W.2d 834 (1983).

We agree entirely with the policies and reasoning enunciated by the Supreme Court of Washington, sitting en banc, in *Thompson v. St. Regis Paper Co., supra,* 685 P.2d at 1086–1087 ... :

> "A number of courts have utilized a contract theory as a means of ameliorating the harshness of the rule. One contract theory utilized by a limited number of these courts is the adoption of a 'bad faith' exception.... Generally, these courts hold that in every employment contract there is an implied covenant of good faith and fair dealing which limited the employer's discretion to terminate an at will employee. Appellant urges us to adopt this approach.

> "We do not adopt this exception. An employer's interest in running his business as he sees fit must be balanced against the interest of the employee in maintaining his employment and this exception does not strike the proper balance. We believe that to imply into each employment contract a duty to terminate in good faith would ... subject each discharge to judicial incursions into the amorphous concept of bad faith. Moreover, while an employer may agree to restrict or limit his right to discharge an employee, to imply such a restriction on that right from the existence of a contractual right, which, by its terms has no restrictions, is internally inconsistent. Such an intrusion into the employment relationship is merely a judicial substitute for collective bargaining which is more appropriately left to the legislative process." ...

The Legislature has clearly spoken in Section 34-03-01, N.D.C.C. Adoption of the exception urged by Hillesland would effectively abrogate the at-will rule as applied in this state. We refuse to recognize a cause of action for breach of an implied covenant of good faith and fair dealing where, as in this case, the claimant relies upon an employment contract which contains no express term specifying the duration of employment. Accordingly, we conclude that the district court did not err in granting summary judgment against Hillesland on this issue.

Notes and Questions

(1) *The North Dakota Legislature Had Clearly Spoken, but did the Court Hear It?* The court said, "The Legislature has clearly spoken in Section 34-03-01, N.D.C.C." Further, the court said that North Dakota had modeled its statute after the one in California. Moreover, normally, North Dakota would give such interpretations "great significance." Given that California's statute was the model for North Dakota's statute and that California courts had implied the covenant of good faith and fair dealing in employment contracts, did the North Dakota Supreme Court ignore its legislature's intent? Other jurisdictions

that had adopted the implied covenant rule had various articulations of this rule. Did this lack of uniformity coupled with the fact that so many other jurisdictions had rejected the implied covenant rule support the court's holding?

(2) *But is Lack of Uniformity a Reason to not Follow Other Courts' Interpretations.* If a court can rely upon the lack of uniformity in other jurisdictions to justify not following the interpretation given to the model statute by the patterning state, then one might ask whether weight should be given to a patterning state's interpretations in any situation? After all, the only reason a split interpretation of a borrowed statute can arise is if another jurisdiction disagrees about the statute's meaning. This point suggests that perhaps no deference should be given to patterning state's interpretations.

(3) *But No Weight Defeats Uniformity and Presumes No Intent in Adopting the Other State's Statute.* If a borrowing court gives no weight to the patterning state's interpretations, then any intent by the legislature to adopt the patterning state's interpretations, or even to engender uniformity, will be lost. What of those goals? Does uniformity have little or no value because the statute is merely "borrowed" and not a "uniform act"? But if this point is true, why did the North Dakota court begin its analysis with California's interpretation?

(4) *Controlling Weight or Merely a Factor?* In the text preceding these cases, we noted that courts disagree about how much weight to give to judicial interpretations in the patterning state that are made prior to the borrowing state adopting the statute: Some states give such interpretations controlling weight (such as in *Blanchard*), while some states appear to give such interpretations little to no weight (such as in *Hillsland*). Which approach do you believe makes the most sense? Does it fly in the face of legislative competence to assume a legislature did not know of the interpretations? Does it ignore reality to assume that a legislature did?

(5) *Politics or Interpretation?* Do you believe that the North Dakota Supreme Court simply made a political, or policy, decision to reject the implied covenant exception? Notice that the court's primary justifications for rejecting California's interpretation were policy based. Did the court interpret a statute or decide a matter of policy without regard to legislative intent?

Problem 11-1

You represent Ed Dee, owner of Chicago Auto Dealers, Inc. ("CAD"). Mr. Dee would like to sue Whittle's Auto Imports, Inc. ("WAI") for deceptive trade practices. According to Mr. Dee, WAI, a competitor of CAD, published false car prices in a brochure and sent the brochure to CAD's potential customers. The issue for you to address is whether CAD would have standing to sue as a "consumer" under Mercer's Consumer Fraud and Deceptive Business Practices Act given that CAD neither relied on the brochure, nor can prove that it has been actually damaged by the false advertising in the brochure. The advertising is false; however, and CAD and WAI compete.

Read the materials below. What arguments would you make on behalf of Mr. Dee that he, as a corporation, has a cause of action under the consumer fraud statute (Mercer Rev. Stat. § 121.5(c))? What response might WAI offer? Who would be successful and why?

Problem Materials

The purpose clause to Mercer's consumer fraud statute states that the act was intended "to protect consumers and borrowers and businessmen against fraud, unfair methods of competition and unfair or deceptive acts or practices in the conduct of any trade or commerce." Mercer Rev. Stat. § 121.5(a), preamble to the Consumer Fraud and Deceptive Business Practices Act.

The substantive provisions include these:

First, Mercer Rev. Stat. § 121.5(c) provides:

> Unfair methods of competition and unfair or deceptive acts or practices, including but not limited to the use or employment of any deception, fraud, false pretense, false promise, misrepresentation or the concealment, suppression or omission of any material fact, with intent that others rely upon the concealment, suppression, or omission of such material fact, or the use or employment of any practice in the conduct of any trade or commerce are hereby declared unlawful whether any person has in fact been misled, deceived, or damaged thereby.

Your research has revealed that the statute was added in 1987. "Person" is not defined in the statute.

Second, Mercer Rev. Stat. § 121.5(d) provides:

> Any person who suffers damage as a result of a violation of the Act may bring an action against such person, and the court may in its discretion award damages.

Your research also reveals that another existing Mercer statute, enacted in 1921, permits individuals to sue businesses for fraud when "an individual is, in fact, (1) misled or deceived, and (2) damaged by an unfair business practice." Mercer Rev. Stat. 12.2 "Individual," in that statute, is defined as "a consumer."

Mercer patterned § 121.5(d) after a 1982 Utah statute. In 1985, in *M & G Corp. v. Dynometer*, the Utah Supreme Court had held that a business owner had standing to sue another business owner under its consumer protection statute. Then, in 1991, the Utah Supreme Court reversed itself in *Heritage Inc. v. Bank of Circio*, where it held that a business owner could not sue another business owner because the purpose of the statute was to protect unsophisticated consumers from the unfair business practices of more sophisticated businesses, not to protect competition or competitors. After *Bank of Circio*, a business could not take advantage of the lower standards of proof in the statute, but instead had to rely on traditional, harder-to-prove, common law fraud actions.

C. Interpretations of Similar Statutes from Other States

In the prior sections, the statutes being interpreted were virtually identical to the statute adopted in the other state, and legislative history reflected that the similarity was intended. In this section, we turn to statutes that have been adopted without any apparent influence from other states. If two states coincidentally have similar statutes, should one state's interpretations of the similar statute matter at all to the other state's court? In the case below, the court looked to interpretations from other states even though the statutes were worded differently and similarity was never intended.

While such a practice is fairly common in common law decision-making (*i.e.*, it is not uncommon for a court deciding whether a term is "conspicuous" in a contract to rely on cases from various jurisdictions that have similar facts), does this practice make any sense when statutes are involved? As we saw above, when one state patterns its statute after another state's statute, there is a presumption that the legislature of the borrowing state intended to adopt the judicial interpretations of the patterning state. Yet, the foundation for that presumption is lacking when a legislature drafts a statute that just happens to have the same words as another state's statute. So, how can the other state's interpretation of its own statute have any relevance at all? Aren't the courts simply debating the meaning of two differently worded statutes, enacted by two different legislatures, for two different but, perhaps, related purposes?

State v. Germonto

73 P.3d 978 (Utah Ct. App. 2003)

Jackson, Presiding Judge.

Frederick Germonto appeals from a conviction for escape from official custody, a second degree felony, in violation of Utah Code Annotated Section 76-8-309 (1999) (escape statute). We reverse.

On February 5, 2000, Germonto, an inmate at the Utah State Prison, attended chapel with a group of other inmates. While walking from the prison chapel back to his housing unit, Germonto broke rank and scaled a ten-foot chain link fence that separated the inmate housing yard from the outer perimeter area of the prison. He then proceeded to scale the perimeter fence, which had razor wire at the top. Prison guards arrived and ordered Germonto off the fence. Germonto dropped from the fence back onto the prison grounds, ran parallel to the perimeter fence, then stopped and was taken back into custody.

On March 9, 2000, the State filed an Information charging Germonto with violating the escape statute. A preliminary hearing was held ... at which Germonto argued that he could not be bound over on the crime of escape because he had not left the confines of the prison and therefore had not actually completed an escape.

The district court judge ... rejected Germonto's arguments and bound Germonto over for trial on the charge of escape....

In interpreting statutes, we first look to the plain language of the statute. In considering the plain language of a statute, courts presume that the legislature used each word advisedly and give effect to each term according to its ordinary and accepted meaning....

The plain language of Utah's escape statute requires that an inmate leave the confines of the prison to be guilty of escape. The escape statute plainly states that "[a] prisoner is guilty of escape if he leaves official custody without authorization." Utah Code Ann. §76-8-309(1). Subsection (7)(b) defines "official custody" as "confinement in the state prison" for purposes of this case.[2] Subsection (7)(a) further defines "confinement" as "housed in a state prison." Id. §76-8-309(7)(a)(i). Thus, to be guilty of escape, an inmate must leave his confinement or housing in the prison.

---

2. Subsection (7)(b) reads in full:

   "Official custody" means arrest, whether with or without warrant, or *confinement in a state prison*, jail, institution for secure confinement of juvenile offenders, or any confinement pursuant to an order of the court or sentenced and committed and the sentence has not been terminated or voided or the prisoner is not on parole....

The term "housing" is not defined in Utah's escape statute. The State argues, and the trial court agreed, that we should construe the term to include only the authorized areas of the prison. According to this definition, Germonto completed an escape because he stepped out of the queue of inmates without authorization. Germonto argues that we should construe the term to include the "confines of the prison," or the perimeter fence and all areas of the prison within the fence. We are persuaded that Germonto's construction of the term "housing" better accords with the legislative intent of the statute.

Although decisions from other jurisdictions interpreting statutes with distinct language provide little guidance in interpreting the language of Utah's escape statute, the decision in *State v. Gaines*, 372 So. 2d 552 (La. 1979) is worth noting because the statute at issue in that case is similar to Utah's escape statute. The statute at issue in *Gaines* defined escape as "the intentional departure ... of a person imprisoned, committed, detained, or otherwise in the lawful custody of any law enforcement officer ... *from any place where such person is lawfully confined.*" *Id.* at 554 (quoting La. R.S. 14:110(A)) (emphasis added). The court concluded that "any place where [a person is] legally confined" must necessarily be a place with physical barriers where the person is actually confined. In reaching that determination, the court recognized that "[a]ny less definitive or more ambiguous definition of place of confinement would render the statute unconstitutionally vague." In addition, the court recognized that even if the language were ambiguous, any ambiguity must be resolved in favor of the defendant. Because Gaines departed from an okra patch on prison grounds where he was on work detail but did not otherwise leave the confinement or boundaries of the prison, the court held that he did not commit an escape when he ran from the line where he was working and continued running even after a guard told him to stop and fired warning shots....

[The majority next concludes that the statute would be unconstitutionally vague if it] interpreted the statute so that an escape occurs even though the inmate has not left the official custody or confinement of the prison, the statute would violate the first two of these prohibitions.... [A] person of ordinary intelligence would not have notice as to what conduct is prohibited. The statute itself defines "official custody" as confinement in the state prison, and defines "confinement" as "housed in the state prison." While the statute defines the term "confinement," that term also has an ordinary and commonly understood meaning that is consistent with the statutory definition. "Confinement" means imprisonment or being confined, *i.e.*, being held within a boundary or bounded region. Webster's New World College Dictionary 306 (4th ed.1999). A person of ordinary intelligence could not read the escape statute and be given notice that he would be guilty of a completed escape even if he did not leave the confines of the prison....

In order to save the statute from constitutional conflicts or infirmities, the trial court's interpretation must be rejected. Instead, we must uphold the plain language of the statute, which requires an inmate to leave the confinement of the prison in order to commit an escape.

Our decision is bolstered by the portion of the code that outlines the elements for attempt crimes. *See* Utah Code Ann. § 76-4-101 (1999). "[A] person is guilty of an attempt to commit a crime if, acting with the kind of culpability otherwise required for the commission of the offense, he engages in conduct constituting a substantial step toward the commission of the offense." *Id.* The attempt statute further requires that any conduct be "strongly corroborative of the actor's intent to commit the offense" to constitute a "substantial step." *Id.*

We would eviscerate the crime of attempted escape if we considered any conduct by an inmate who moves to an area on prison grounds that is restricted or in which he is not supposed to be a completed escape. Any time an inmate is out of his cell when he is not supposed to be, fails to awake and vacate his cell when he is supposed to do so, is in the cell of another inmate, disregards the order of a guard, or otherwise moves out of bounds, the state could charge the inmate with a completed escape. Such an approach would run contrary to the legislative intent that an inmate leave official custody by leaving the confinement of the prison in order to commit a completed escape, and would do away with the crime of attempted escape.

The trial court's interpretation also disregards the purposes and principles set forth in Utah Code Ann. § 76-1-104 (1999), which requires that the provisions of the code be interpreted so that the elements of a crime are clearly defined, the penalties are proportionate to the seriousness of the offense, and arbitrary or oppressive treatment is prevented. The trial court's interpretation would allow for a punishment that is disproportionate to the crime because an inmate who did not leave the confinement of the prison would receive the same second degree felony punishment as an inmate who did leave the prison.…

In this case, there was not probable cause to believe Germonto completed the crime of escape because there is no evidence that he left the confines of the prison. While the evidence demonstrated that Germonto climbed over the inner fence, there is no evidence that he made it over the outer boundary fence and left the prison. Although the State presented sufficient evidence to bind Germonto over on the charge of attempted escape, it failed to establish probable cause to bind Germonto over on the crime of escape. Accordingly, the trial court erred in refusing to quash the bindover on that charge. We now reverse and remand.…

THORNE, JUDGE (dissenting):

… The majority concludes that under the plain language of our escape statute, an escape is not accomplished absent a prisoner successfully leaving the prison. The majority relies upon *State v. Gaines*, 372 So.2d 552 (La. 1979), to support this position. However, because the Louisiana escape statute is materially different from our own, the majority's reliance on *Gaines* is misplaced. In *Gaines*, the Louisiana Supreme Court examined whether a prisoner who fled from his assigned area within the prison, with the intent to leave the prison, had violated Louisiana's escape statute. The court examined the plain language of the Louisiana statute and determined that the legislature had amended the escape statute to require specific proof of two distinct elements: (1) The prisoner must escape from official custody; and (2) the prisoner must escape from a place of legal confinement.[1] Having so interpreted the statute, the Louisiana Supreme Court reversed Gaines's conviction, because while he escaped from official custody, at no point did he actually leave prison grounds.

In contrast, our escape statute, section 76-8-309, states that "[a] prisoner is guilty of escape if he leaves official custody without authorization." Utah Code Ann. § 76-8-309(1). Thus, unlike the statute at issue in *Gaines*, in Utah, an escape is complete once a prisoner "leaves official custody (making no reference to geographic boundaries) without authorization." *Id.* § 76-8-309(1). Accordingly, it is clear that our legislature has not seen fit to require the state to prove two conjunctive elements to establish that the crime of es-

---

1. During the relevant period, Louisiana's escape statute read as follows:

    Simple escape is: … The intentional departure, under circumstances wherein human life is not endangered, of a person imprisoned, committed, detained, or otherwise in the lawful custody of any law enforcement officer or officer of the Department of Corrections, from any place where such person is legally confined.

cape has been committed.[2] I therefore cannot join in the majority view that the analysis offered in *Gaines* provides constructive assistance in the present case.

Instead, I believe ... *Huffman v. State*, 659 N.E.2d 214 (Ind. Ct. App.1995),[3] to be particularly instructive. In *Huffman*, the defendant was a prisoner who had left his dormitory without authorization and hid on prison grounds until he was later discovered. Subsequently, the defendant was convicted of escape. On appeal, the defendant argued that "he could not properly be convicted of Escape because he had not made it off" prison grounds. In denying his claim, the Indiana Court of Appeals noted

> that our sister states have almost universally upheld Escape convictions where the prisoner did not make it outside the prison or detention facility where the states' statutes involved proscribed "escape from 'custody,' 'confinement,' or the like" (as opposed to statutes which proscribed "escape from 'prison,' 'detention facility,' or the like") and the prisoner exhibited an intention to leave the confines of the prison or institution.

Similarly, in *Urbauer v. State*, 744 P.2d 1274 (Okla. Crim. App.1987), the defendant was convicted of escape after scaling two of three fences surrounding the prison where he was incarcerated. On appeal the defendant argued that the evidence was insufficient to prove escape because he had not succeeded in leaving the prison grounds. The court, in denying his claim, noted that "[w]e think that for purposes of escape from a penal institution, 'custody' may be restraint by either physical means or by a superior force acting as a moral restraint. But there must be actual or constructive custody in order to escape from that custody." *Id.* The court further stated that "[a]ny departure from such restraint or control, with or without force, whether from custody of an officer or from *any place* where one is lawfully confined may be adjudged an escape." *Id.*

Finally, in *State v. Sugden*, 143 Wis. 2d 7284 (1988), the defendant was convicted of escape after highjacking a prison vehicle and driving it through the inner wall only to be stopped before reaching the outer wall. At trial, and on appeal, the state argued that the defendant's escape was complete when he broke out of the housing facility within the prison and that the defendant's point of capture was immaterial. The Wisconsin Supreme Court agreed, stating that within the meaning of the Wisconsin escape statute, "custody of an institution may exist within the perimeters of an institution because of special treatment that is given to particular inmates." *Id.* at 627. Thus, the court concluded, "[t]here may be custody without the walls and custody of various kinds, without limitation, within the walls."[4]

Much like the statutes at issue in *Sugden* and *Urbauer*, Utah's escape statute criminalizes "leav[ing] official custody without authorization." Utah Code Ann. § 76-8-309(1).

---

2. Admittedly, Utah Code Annotated section 76-8-309 (1999) offers a number of definitions for the term "official custody." I believe, however, that the broad range provided supports, rather than undermines, my conclusion. The definitions offered range from simple arrest, which can occur on the street and which is technically complete once a person is informed of the fact, with or without handcuffs or other restraining devices, to "confinement in a state prison, jail" or other area of secure confinement. *Id.* § 76-8-309(7)(b). Thus, unlike the majority, I do not believe the definitions offered create additional elements that must be proved by the state. Rather, I believe the definitions merely highlight those individuals who are subject to prosecution under section 76-8-309 should they "leave[] official custody without authorization." *Id.* § 76-8-309(1).

3. The Indiana escape statute in effect at the time of Huffman's action defined escape as follows: "A person who intentionally flees from lawful detention commits escape...." *Huffman v. State*, 659 N.E.2d 214, 215 (Ind. Ct. App. 1995) (quoting Ind. Code § 35-44-3-5(a)).

4. The Wisconsin court also noted that "'escape from prison' means something different from 'escape from custody of such institution [or prison].'" *State v. Sugden*, 422 N.W.2d 624, 628 (1988) (alterations in original) (citations omitted).

Thus, because "[t]here may be custody without walls and custody of various kinds, without limitation, within the walls," *Sugden*, 422 N.W.2d at 627; *see also* Utah Code Ann. § 76-8-309(7)(b) (defining the broad meaning of "official custody" under the statute), I would conclude that Germonto left official custody when he left his authorized area of confinement. It is clear from the record that Germonto's authorized area of confinement at the time of his escape was comprised of the yard through which he was traveling, following a church service, to return to his cell, and that when he scaled the fence into the "no-man's-land" area between the fences he had left official custody without authorization.

Moreover, inserting the definitions for "official custody" and "confinement" supplied in section 76-8-309(7)(a), (b), does not require a different result in this case. The application of the provided definitions changes the statute to read that Germonto is guilty of escape if he leaves "confinement in a state prison," where he is housed, without authorization. Utah Code Ann. § 76-8-309(7)(a)-(b). At the time of his escape, Germonto was "confined" to an area within the prison, bounded by a substantial fence, through which the guards transported the prisoners to and from the chapel. It was from this area of confinement within the prison that Germonto left without authorization when he successfully scaled the inner fence, knowing that if left unchecked he would reach "freedom." Thus, even considering the definitions provided for within the statute, Germonto's actions violated section 76-8-309.

While it is possible to read into section 76-8-309 the implied requirement that to be convicted of the crime of escape a prisoner must successfully escape all boundaries of the prison in which he finds himself, I believe that had the legislature intended that effect it could have, and would have, clearly communicated that intent in the statutory language. Instead, the legislature chose to criminalize the act of leaving official custody without authorization, an act that is accomplished not by escaping from the geographic boundaries of an institution, but by escaping from the authorized presence and immediate control of the institution or an arresting officer. Because the act of escaping official custody carries with it an inherent danger to the prisoner, police and correctional officers, and the public at large, the legislature is well within the bounds of reason in criminalizing the behavior as early in the process as is feasible.

Finally, I am also unpersuaded by the majority's arguments concerning attempted escape. First and foremost, it is clear from the statutory language, and the cases interpreting similar statutory language, that a prisoner must enjoy some level of success, albeit incomplete success, to be liable for the crime of escape.[4] It is the success of leaving an area of authorized confinement that defines the crime of escape. Thus, had Germonto failed to scale the inner fence—the limits of his authorized confinement area at the time of his escape—his crime would have been attempted escape. But, in the face of his success in scaling the fence, Germonto escaped from official custody....

Accordingly, I dissent from the majority opinion and would instead affirm the trial court's decision to bind Germonto over on the escape charge.

Notes and Questions

(1) *Looking Elsewhere?* Given the preeminent importance of text, shouldn't courts be very reluctant to look at another state's interpretations of statutes, even when the text is

---

4. Escape is defined variously to mean: "an act or instance of escaping: as [a] flight from confinement[, or the] evasion of something undesirable." Merriam-Webster's Collegiate Dictionary 395 (10th ed.1999). Accordingly, escape refers not to a successful act, but rather to the "flight" or "evasion" involved. *Id.*

virtually identical? In that regard, the dissent chided the majority for relying on the *Gaines* case from Louisiana. Yet, the dissent relied on cases from three other states: Indiana, Oklahoma, and Wisconsin. Who was right? Were the statutes in these states more or less similar to Utah's than Louisiana's? Can you tell? More significantly, if there is no indication that the legislature relied on those other statutes when it drafted the statute at issue, what reason does the court have for looking at the interpretations of the similar statutes? To avoid this problem, some courts hold that interpretations of sister states of similar or even identically worded statutes may not be considered unless the statute is ambiguous. *See, e.g., Jordache Enterprises, Inc. v. Brobeck, Phleger & Harrison,* 1999 WL 33842865 (1999) ("before we look to sister-state authorities..., we must first look to the statute itself. If the language of a statute is clear, its plain meaning should be followed. When a statute is unambiguous, there is no need for construction, and courts should not indulge in it.")

(2) *Wasn't the Majority's Interpretation Absurd?* Under the majority's approach, the defendant had not "left official custody without authorization" even though he climbed over one fence, climbed around the prison perimeter, and climbed to the top of the second fence, when he should have been being escorted back from prison chapel. Why, given the statute's text, isn't the majority's interpretation absurd?

(3) *Other Rationales.* The majority also relied upon the vagueness doctrine, concluding that no one would understand that leaving "official custody without authorization" included climbing over the fences. Do you agree? Similarly, the majority concluded that the "attempt" statute would be rendered superfluous if it construed the statute to cover the defendant's actions here. Do you agree, or does the dissent's argument have more force?

(4) *Lawyering Strategy.* As you have hopefully discerned by now, it is difficult enough to interpret and apply statutes. Citing to interpretations of similar statutes from another state may not be a good idea, especially where the text or purposes of the other state's statute vary even slightly from your jurisdiction's statute. As we stated in the introduction to this section, doing so may turn the debate into an irrelevant war of words.

Problem 11-2

Your client was inside a building with his friends when he fired a gun into an adjacent room. Among other things, he has been charged with violating Mercer Rev. Crim. Stat. § 27.001, which is quoted below. In addition, statutes from two other states that address similar crimes are provided. Each statute was adopted in the same year as Mercer's to address the then-growing problem of "drive by shootings." Be prepared to advise your client whether he likely violated Mercer Rev. Crim. Stat. § 27.001, and be prepared to explain why one or more of the related statutes matter or not. Would your conclusion about whether he violated the Mercer statute be the same if either other statute applied?

Problem Materials

Mercer Rev. Crim. Stat. § 27.001: Discharge of a firearm into an occupied structure

 a. Offense defined. — A person commits an offense if he knowingly, intentionally, or recklessly discharges a firearm from any location into an occupied structure.

 (b) Grading. — An offense under this section shall be a felony of the third degree.

(c) Defense.—It is a defense to prosecution under this section that:

   (1) the person discharging the firearm was a law enforcement officer engaged in the performance of his official law enforcement duties; or

   (2) the person discharging the firearm was engaged in a lawful hunting activity; and

      (i) the discharge of the firearm took place from a location where the hunting activity is lawful; and

      (ii) the passage of the projectile from the firearm into the occupied structure was not intentional, knowing or reckless.

(d) Definitions.—As used in this section, the following words and phrases shall have the meanings given to them in this subsection:

"Firearm." Any weapon which is designed to or may readily be converted to expel any projectile by the action of an explosion or the frame or receiver of any such weapon.

"Occupied Structure." Any structure, vehicle, or place adapted for overnight accommodation of persons or for carrying on business therein, whether or not a person is actually present.

Two other states, California and Kansas, have similar statutes. Below is the text of their statutes together with judicial interpretation of the statutes.

Cal. Penal Code § 246: Discharge of a firearm into an occupied structure

Any person who shall maliciously and willfully discharge a firearm at an inhabited dwelling house, occupied building, occupied motor vehicle, inhabited house car, or inhabited camper is guilty of a felony. As used in this section, 'inhabited' means currently being used for dwelling purposes, whether occupied or not.

The California provision was interpreted in *State v. Milani*, 100 P.4d 112 (Cal. 2009) not to apply to the discharge of a firearm from within an inhabited structure into an adjoining room. The court emphasized that the plain language of the statute required that the shooter shoot "at" the inhabited house and that in ordinary meaning one did not shoot "at" a house one was then "in." Based on that construction, the California court affirmed the dismissal of the charges against the defendant.

K.S. Penal Code § 435.170: Malicious and willful shooting, cutting or poisoning; shooting or throwing missile into train, station, steamboat, motor vehicle or building

Any person who shall maliciously or willfully shoot at or into any building shall be guilty of a felony.

The Kansas Supreme Court, in *State v. Edwards*, 10 S.W.4th 113 (Kan. 2007), held that the statute did not apply to a defendant who was in a building when he fired a shot from one room in the building through a doorway and into an adjoining room. The court relied on the plain language of the statute, unanimously holding that the phrase "shoot at or into any building" obviously was limited to shooting from outside a building either at or into a building, but did not include shots fired from within a building into an adjoining room.

Chapter 12

The Relevance of Time: Effective Dates, Prospective Effect, and Retroactivity

When a statute takes effect can be critically important. This chapter explores issues related to timing: how to determine the effective date of the statute and how to know whether the statute has retroactive or only prospective effect. This latter subject has special relevance in the criminal context; we cover that unique issue in another chapter because *ex post facto* laws create constitutional issues separate and apart from the issues discussed here.

A. Effective Date Provisions

The effective date of a new law can be critical. Suppose, for example, a new statute severely limits punitive damages. The value of a case filed after the effective date of the statute would obviously be lessened. But, sometimes, the effective date of a statute is unclear. When this happens, litigation over the effective date and its impact can arise.

Generally, federal statutes become effective on the date the president signs the bill, unless the bill expressly provides otherwise. Thus, many bills, like the College Fire Prevention Act (*See* Appendix B), are silent on this issue. If Congress wants a statute to have an effective date other than the signing date, the statute must expressly say so. Congress will often include delayed effective dates to provide advance notice to the public of changes in the law.

States take different approaches regarding when legislation that has been approved by the governor becomes law. Many states, by statute or constitution, provide that their statutes become effective on a particular date (usually several months after the legislative session ends), unless the bill provides otherwise. In other states, statutes become effective 90 days after the governor signs it, unless the legislation provides for a different effective date.

The following case analyzes these typically straightforward clauses. As with other statutory interpretation issues, sometimes what appears in the abstract to be certain and clear becomes less clear in application.

Fowler v. State
70 P.3d 1106 (Alaska 2003)

Steward, Judge.

On May 8, 2001, the Alaska Legislature passed a bill that amended the definition of felony driving while intoxicated, AS 28.35.030(n). Previously, driving while intoxicated had been a felony if a defendant had two prior convictions within the preceding five years. The 2001 amendment increased the "look-back" period to ten years.

Under Alaska law, a bill takes effect on the 90th day after the governor signs it, unless the legislature specifies otherwise. Here, the legislature did specify otherwise: the bill provided that the amended version of AS 28.35.030(n) would take effect on July 1, 2001 (about eight weeks after the legislature passed the bill). However, the legislature delayed transmitting the bill to the governor until June 20, and the governor did not sign the bill until July 3 — i.e., after the legislature's specified effective date.

On the following day — July 4, 2001 — Eric Fowler committed the offense of driving while intoxicated. He had two prior convictions within the preceding ten years, but not within the preceding five years. Thus, Fowler's offense would be a felony if the amended law was in effect on July 4, but only a misdemeanor if the amended law had not yet taken effect.

Fowler argues that because the governor did not sign the bill until after the effective date specified by the legislature, the bill must be treated as if the legislature had never specified a special effective date. According to this argument, the new law must be deemed to have gone into effect on October 1 — the 90th day following the governor's signature.

Alternatively, Fowler argues that even if the new law would normally have gone into effect on the day after the governor signed it, there was an additional delay in this case because the following day was July 4, a state holiday. Fowler argues that a new law cannot take effect on a holiday.

For the reasons explained here, we reject both of Fowler's arguments. We conclude that the new version of AS 28.35.030(n) took effect at 12:01 a.m. on July 4, 2001 — and that Fowler was therefore properly charged with felony driving while intoxicated.

A brief description of Alaska law on this subject

Article II, Section 18 of the Alaska Constitution states: "Laws passed by the legislature [normally] become effective ninety days after enactment [, but the] legislature may, by concurrence of two-thirds of the membership of each house, provide for another effective date." To clarify and carry out the mandate of this constitutional provision, the legislature enacted AS 01.10.070.

Under subsection (b) of this statute, a bill that does not specify a particular effective date takes effect at 12:01 a.m., Alaska Standard Time, on the 90th calendar day following the governor's signature. Under subsection (c), if a bill specifies that it takes effect "immediately," the bill takes effect at 12:01 a.m., Alaska Standard Time, on the day after it is signed by the governor.

Subsection (d) of AS 01.10.070 deals with bills that specify a particular effective date. The current version of subsection (d) codifies a rule that resolves situations like the one presented in Fowler's case:

(d) An Act that specifies a definite effective date becomes effective at 12:01 a.m., Alaska Standard Time, on the date specified. However, if the specified ... effective date is on or before the day the governor signs the Act, ... the Act becomes effective at 12:01 a.m., Alaska Standard Time, on the day after the governor signs the Act....

The problem is that when the events in Fowler's case arose in 2001, subsection (d) did not contain the second sentence. Thus, the 2001 version of AS 01.10.070(d) did not answer the question posed by this case: When does a bill take effect if the governor fails to sign the bill until after the legislatively specified effective date?

Although the current version of AS 01.10.070(d) resolves this problem, the current version of the statute does not govern Fowler's case.[6] We must therefore ascertain the common law on this topic as it existed in 2001, before AS 01.10.070(d) was amended to resolve this situation....

Fowler first argues that because the 2001 version of AS 01.10.070 did not contain an explicit rule to govern the situation presented in this case, we must presume that the "default" rule applied—that, unless the legislature specifies a different date, a statute takes effect on the 90th day after the governor signs it....

The basic question is to ascertain what the legislature would wish to have happen under these circumstances.

There are two ways in which the legislature can specify that they do not wish the usual 90-day rule to apply. The legislature can either (1) name a definite date on which the new law will take effect, or (2) declare that the new law will take effect "immediately."

Obviously, if the legislature follows this second course, the new law will not take effect immediately. Rather, the law will take effect on the day after the governor signs it—an event that the legislature has little control over. Thus, when the legislature declares that a law is to take effect "immediately," it means that the law should take effect "as soon as possible," consistent with the governor's role in the enactment process.

Fowler argues that the situation is different when the legislature specifies a date for a new law to go into effect. He contends that, by setting a specific future date, the legislature must mean for the public to get a certain amount of forewarning before the law takes effect. Thus, Fowler asserts, when the governor does not sign the bill until the specified date has transpired, a court must protect this desired period of forewarning by delaying the effective date of the law for 90 days.

But when the legislature specifies a definite date for a new law to take effect, they normally foresee that the governor will sign the law with time to spare—and that the new law will take effect on the specified date, regardless of when the governor signs it. In other words, there is no particular guaranteed period of forewarning, no particular buffer period between the signing of the bill and the time it takes effect.

We believe that when the legislature goes out of its way to specify a particular effective date, this date does not represent an imprecise description of how much forewarning the public should receive. Rather, it represents the legislature's intention that the new law should take effect on that specified date. Thus, when that specified date has already transpired by the time the governor signs the law, we believe it is reasonable to assume that the legislature would want the law to take effect as soon as possible—that is, on the day after the governor signs it. For this reason, we conclude that Fowler's suggested 90-day waiting period would not achieve the legislature's purpose.

---

6. See AS 01.10.090: "No statute is retrospective unless expressly declared therein."

In reaching this conclusion, we do not rely on any inference that might be drawn from the fact that, when the legislature addressed this problem, they codified the same rule that we now adopt as a matter of common law. However, we note that our interpretation is consistent with the rule of construction that was followed by the revisor of statutes up until AS 01.10.070(d) was amended to expressly resolve this problem.

The record in this case reveals that both the current revisor* of statutes and her predecessor encountered the problem of an after-signed law on other occasions. Without exception, these revisors concluded that the statutes in question should be deemed to have taken effect on the day after the governor signed the law. The revisors adopted this practice because they believed that it achieved a result "as close as possible to the legislature's intended effective date[.]" For example, SLA 1995, ch. 103 specified a particular effective date — June 30, 1995 — for § 70 of that session law. However, the governor did not sign the bill until that very date. When the bill was officially enrolled, the revisor substituted an effective date of July 1, 1995 — i.e., the day after the governor signed the bill.

The legislature has apparently acquiesced each time the revisor of statutes adjusted the effective dates of statutes in accordance with this practice. From this acquiescence, we conclude that the revisor's practice reflects the legislature's desired resolution of this problem.

Applying this rule of construction, we conclude that the new felony DWI law took effect at 12:01 a.m., Alaska Standard Time, (that is, at 1:01 a.m. Alaska Daylight Time) on July 4, 2001 — the day after the governor signed the law....

Fowler argues in the alternative that even if the new felony DWI law would normally have taken effect on the day after the governor signed it, the effective date of this new law was delayed by one day because July 4 was (and is) a state holiday. Fowler relies on AS 01.10.080, which states:

> The time in which an act provided by law is required to be done is computed by excluding the first day and including the last, unless the last day is a holiday, and then [that day] is also excluded.

Fowler contends that, pursuant to this statute, if a new law would normally take effect on a holiday, the effective date must be delayed by one day.

But it is plain from the wording of AS 01.10.080 that this statute is a codification of the common-law rule governing the computation of time for the *doing* of an act required by law. The statute allows an additional day for the accomplishment of the required act if the normal time limit expires on a holiday — a day when the usual operations of business are suspended and the courts [are] closed....

The effective date of a statute is not an "act" that must be accomplished within a specified time period. Thus, AS 01.10.080 does not address the question of when a newly enacted statute takes effect.

We note that, in the past, the legislature has expressly declared its intent to have new laws take effect on holidays. One of the prime examples is Alaska's present criminal code —

---

* Authors' footnote: In Alaska, the revisor is responsible for "edit[ing] and revis[ing] the laws for consolidation without changing the meaning of any law in the following manner...." Alaska Stat. § 01-05-030 (Michie 2002).

SLA 1978, ch. 166, §§ 3 & 25 specified that the new code would take effect on January 1, 1980....

For the reasons explained here, we hold that the 2001 amendment to AS 28.35.030(n) took effect at 12:01 a.m., Alaska Standard Time, on July 4, 2001. Because Fowler committed his offense approximately seven hours later (at around 8:00 a.m., Alaska Daylight Time), the new law applied to him.

The judgment of the superior court is affirmed.

Notes and Questions

(1) *Arguments.* What were the defendant's arguments that the statute should not apply to him? Do you find either argument convincing? Why did the court reject them?

(2) *Rule of Lenity.* In part of the opinion we omitted, the court dismissed the defendant's argument that the rule of lenity—under which courts must give narrower construction to an ambiguous penal statute—applied. The court concluded that the rule of lenity did not apply because "AS 01.10.070 is not a penal law. It is a law of general application that governs the effective date of all statutes enacted by the legislature, whether those statutes be criminal or civil." The rule of lenity provides that people must have notice that their activities are illegal before they can be penalized. Given that notice was the statute's purpose and that notice is constitutionally required, did the court err?

(3) *Subsequent Legislative Action.* The court pointed out that the legislature amended AS 01.10.070(d) to specifically address the situation that occurred in Fowler's case. Should that amendment have had any weight on the court's decision? Do you think the action of a later legislature should be at all relevant to the meaning intended by an earlier legislature? Even if it is legally irrelevant, is it logically compelling?

(4) *Constitutional Issues Created by Effective-Date Provisions.* Effective-date provisions can create constitutional issues in a variety of ways. For example, after enacting a cap of $150,000 for noneconomic damages, the Wisconsin legislature reconsidered the cap after several children died in horrific circumstances and increased it to $500,000 for all cases filed after a certain date. The statute was held unconstitutional because it violated the due process rights of tortfeasors who committed the tort before the effective date but who were sued afterward. *Schultz v. Natwick*, 653 N.W.2d 266 (Wis. 2002). Can you explain why?

Problem 12-1

You work for a state legislator who is concerned that her state does not have a default statute for the effective date of statutes. Case law currently holds that a statute takes effect from the date of its passage unless another time is provided in the statute itself. The date of passage is the date of the completion of the last act necessary to fulfill the constitutional requirements and to give a bill the force of law—in this case, signature by the governor. Draft a bill that would alter this common-law rule such that laws would become effective 90 days after they have been signed by the governor. In doing so, consider what should happen if (1) the governor vetoes the bill, but the veto is overridden, (2) the 90th day falls on a holiday or weekend, (3) the bill is never signed but still becomes law (as in the case of a pocket veto), and (4) at what time of day the 90th day will start (i.e.: 12:01 AM or something later). Are there any other issues you should consider?

B. Prospective Effect and Retroactivity

1. General Rule: Statutes Have Only Prospective Effect

As a general principle, statutes are presumed to have only prospective effect. *Landsgraf v. USI Film Prods.*, 511 U.S. 244, 270 (1994). For example, the enactment of a statute creating a cause of action against those who discriminate on the basis of race will not permit a person who was discriminated against the day before the statute's effective date to file suit. Courts presume that statutes have only prospective effect, in part, because retrospective effectiveness could impose liability where none existed before. *See id.*; *see generally Lundeen v. Canadian Pac. R.R. Co.*, 532 F.3d 682 (2008) (addressing due process and other challenges to expressly retroactive statute). (The constitutional issues that can arise when a statute imposes *criminal* liability retroactively are discussed in a later chapter.)

This general presumption itself has significant limitations. For example, while a new cause of action cannot be adopted to arise retroactively, some states hold that a statute that "merely provides a new remedy, enlarges an existing remedy, or substitutes a remedy is not unconstitutionally retrospective." *McMickle v. Griffin*, 254 S.W.3d 729, 747 (Ark. 2008) (holding that an amendment to existing wrongful-death action, which modified the measure of damages but did not create wrongful-death claim, applied to pending cases). Likewise, some states do not apply the presumption against retroactivity to statutes that are procedural. *Id.*

If a statute is given retroactive effect, then constitutional concerns can arise: Due process, for example, may require that a party have notice that an act will result in civil liability, and so retroactively imposing liability on acts that were lawful at the time committed can violate due process. *United States v. Lopez-Solis*, 447 F.3d 1201 (9th Cir. 2006) (holding that clarification could not be given retroactive effect without constituting an *ex post facto* law). Another issue can arise when a statute extends a statute of limitation, thus "reviving" what were time-barred claims. *See, e.g., Nixon v. State*, 704 N.W.2d 643 (Iowa 2005) (construing statutes not to revive barred claims absent clear legislative intent to do so). In other words, giving a statute retroactive effect can have serious repercussions.

Even when it applies, the general presumption against retroactive effect is just that: a presumption. Because it is only a presumption, it may be overcome either by express statutory language or by implication. *Myers v. Philip Morris Co., Inc.*, 50 P.3d 751 (Cal. 2002). The following section explores one of the exceptions to this presumption: Statutes that merely clarify existing statutes may be given retroactive effect.

2. The Clarification Exception to Prospective-Only Effect

Sometimes, a legislature will adopt a statute that purports to merely clarify an existing statute. For example, the legislature may state that a new statute is "merely declarative of existing law." Because the new statute simply restates the existing law, the new statute would technically have retroactive affect: It would be effective from the time the existing statute took effect. But if the new statute does not simply clarify new law, then the new statute should not have retroactive effect. Perhaps not surprisingly, legislatures and courts do not always agree on whether the new statute merely clarifies existing law. This section analyzes how courts respond to such declarations.

If you put to the side the question of whether a later legislature can ever know whether it is stating what an earlier legislature intended, then how should courts address the retroactive effect of a statute that purports to merely "clarify" an already existing statute? If, in fact, the purported amendment does not change the meaning of the existing statute, then it would be sophistry to say that the amendment is "retroactive" because the amendment did not change the existing statute. But, if in fact the meaning of the existing statute was changed, then the legislature made a retroactive change. Hence, constitutional and other retroactivity problems may arise.

As you might expect, courts take different approaches when responding to these legislative declarations. First, some courts have stated that whether a clarification, rather than a change, has occurred turns on whether the existing statute was ambiguous or clear. When the existing statute was clear, any amendment to that statute was likely intended to change the law; hence, retroactivity would be inappropriate. In contrast, when the existing statute was ambiguous, an amendment may or may not have been intended to change the law. Therefore, retroactivity may be appropriate. *Williams v. Staples*, 804 N.E.2d 489, 498 (Ill. 2004) ("amendment of an unambiguous statute indicates a purpose to change the law, while no such purpose is indicated by the mere fact of an amendment of an ambiguous provision."). But does this approach make sense? Consider whether a legislature is changing the meaning of an ambiguous statute when the legislature chooses one of the possible meanings? By definition, isn't a "clarification" a change?

Second, some courts do not rely on ambiguity alone, but instead apply multi-factor tests to determine whether a change or a clarification has occurred:

> To determine whether the legislature enacted a statutory amendment with the intent to clarify existing legislation, we look to various factors, including, but not limited to (1) the amendatory language; (2) the declaration of intent, if any, contained in the public act; (3) the legislative history; and (4) the circumstances surrounding the enactment of the amendment, such as, whether it was "enacted in direct response to a judicial decision that the legislature deemed incorrect"; or "passed to resolve a controversy engendered by statutory ambiguity. In the cases wherein this court has held that a statutory amendment had been intended to be clarifying and, therefore, should be applied retroactively, the pertinent legislative history has provided uncontroverted support for the conclusion that the legislature considered the amendatory language to be a declaration of the legislature's original intent rather than a change in the existing statute.

Town of Middlebury v. Dep't of Envtl. Prot., 927 A.2d 793, 804 (Conn. 2007); *Martin v. Union Pac. R.R. Co.*, 186 P.3d 61, 66 (Colo. Ct. App. 2007) ("To distinguish between a change and a clarification, we look to (1) whether the provision was ambiguous before it was amended; (2) the plain language used in the amendment; and (3) the legislative history surrounding the amendment.").

The following three cases explore this issue, which raises many issues of statutory interpretation that are the subject of the first part of this book, including separation of powers and approaches to interpretation. Note the decreased importance of text in the following cases, notes, and questions. We begin with a fairly basic case and then move toward the more difficult issues created by "clarifications" of prior statutes.

McClung v. Employment Dev. Dep't
99 P.3d 1015 (Cal. 2004)

CHIN, J.

"It is, emphatically, the province and duty of the judicial department, to say what the law is. Those who apply the rule to particular cases, must of necessity expound and interpret that rule." (*Marbury v. Madison* (1803) 1 Cranch 137, 5 U.S. 137, 177.)

This basic principle is at issue in this case. In *Carrisales v. Department of Corrections* (1999) 988 P.2d 1083 (*Carrisales*), we interpreted Government Code section 12940 (hereafter section 12940), part of the California Fair Employment and Housing Act (FEHA). Later, the Legislature amended that section by adding language to impose personal liability on persons *Carrisales* had concluded had no personal liability. (§ 12940, subd. (j)(3).) Subdivision (j) also contains a statement that its provisions "are declaratory of existing law...." (§ 12940, subd. (j)(2).) Based on this statement, plaintiff argues that the amendment did not *change*, but merely *clarified*, existing law. Accordingly, she argues, the amendment applies to this case to impose personal liability for earlier actions despite our holding in *Carrisales* that no personal liability attached to those actions.

We disagree. Under fundamental principles of separation of powers, the legislative branch of government enacts laws. Subject to constitutional constraints, it may *change* the law. But *interpreting* the law is a judicial function. After the judiciary definitively and finally interprets a statute, as we did in *Carrisales*, the Legislature may amend the statute to say something different. But if it does so, it *changes* the law; it does not merely state what the law always was. Any statement to the contrary is beyond the Legislature's power. We also conclude this change in the law does not apply retroactively to impose liability for actions not subject to liability when performed.

I. FACTS AND PROCEDURAL BACKGROUND

In January 1998, plaintiff Lesli Ann McClung filed a complaint against the Employment Development Department and Manuel Lopez, alleging claims of hostile work environment and failure to remedy a hostile work environment under the FEHA.... The superior court granted summary judgment for defendants....

The Court of Appeal ... reversed it as to Lopez....

We granted Lopez's petition for review to decide whether section 12940, subdivision (j)(3), applies to this case....

The FEHA declares certain kinds of discrimination and harassment in the workplace to be "unlawful employment practice[s]." (§ 12940.) In *Carrisales*, we interpreted the FEHA as imposing "on the *employer* the duty to take all reasonable steps to prevent this harassment from occurring in the first place and to take immediate and appropriate action when it is or should be aware of the conduct," but as not imposing "personal liability for harassment on nonsupervisory coworkers." Later, effective January 1, 2001, the Legislature amended the subdivision of section 12940 that we interpreted in *Carrisales* (now subdivision (j)). (Stats.2000, ch. 1049, §§ 7.5, 11.) As amended, section 12940, subdivision (j)(3), provides in relevant part: "An employee of an entity subject to this subdivision is personally liable for any harassment prohibited by this section that is perpetrated by the employee...." It seems clear, and no one disputes, that this provision imposes on nonsupervisory coworkers the personal liability that *Carrisales* said the FEHA had not imposed. Subdivision (j) also states that its provisions "are declaratory of existing law...." (§ 12940, subd. (j)(2).)

We must decide whether the amendment to section 12940 applies to actions that occurred before its enactment. If the amendment merely clarified existing law, no question of retroactivity is presented. A statute that merely *clarifies*, rather than changes, existing law does not operate retrospectively even if applied to transactions predating its enactment because the true meaning of the statute remains the same. In that event, personal liability would have existed at the time of the actions, and the amendment would not have changed anything. But if the amendment changed the law and imposed personal liability for earlier actions, the question of retroactivity arises. A statute has retrospective effect when it substantially changes the legal consequences of past events. In this case, applying the amendment to impose liability that did not otherwise exist would be a retroactive application because it would "attach[] new legal consequences to events completed before its enactment." Specifically, it would "increase a party's liability for past conduct...."

Accordingly, two separate questions are presented here: (1) Did the amendment extending liability in subdivision (j)(3) change or merely clarify the law? (2) If the amendment did change the law, does the change apply retroactively? ...

The legislative power rests with the Legislature. (Cal. Const., art. IV, § 1.) Subject to constitutional constraints, the Legislature may enact legislation. But the judicial branch *interprets* that legislation. Ultimately, the interpretation of a statute is an exercise of the judicial power the Constitution assigns to the courts. Accordingly, it is the duty of this court, when ... a question of law is properly presented, to state the true meaning of the statute finally and conclusively.

In *Carrisales*, *supra*, we interpreted the FEHA finally and conclusively as not imposing personal liability on a nonsupervisory coworker. This interpretation was binding on lower state courts....

It is true that if the courts have not yet finally and conclusively interpreted a statute and are in the process of doing so, a declaration of a later Legislature as to what an earlier Legislature intended is entitled to consideration. But even then, a legislative declaration of an existing statute's meaning is but a factor for a court to consider and is neither binding nor conclusive in construing the statute. This is because the Legislature has no authority to interpret a statute. That is a judicial task. The Legislature may define the meaning of statutory language by a present legislative enactment which, subject to constitutional restraints, it may deem retroactive. But it has no legislative authority simply to say what it *did* mean. A declaration that a statutory amendment merely clarified the law cannot be given an obviously absurd effect, and the court cannot accept the Legislative statement that an unmistakable change in the statute is nothing more than a clarification and restatement of its original terms. Because this court had already finally and definitively interpreted section 12940, the Legislature had no power to decide that the later amendment merely declared existing law....

Plaintiff points out that *Carrisales* itself postdated the acts alleged in this case and argues that before that decision, nonsupervisory coworkers had been personally liable under the statute. However, a judicial construction of a statute is an authoritative statement of what the statute meant before as well as after the decision of the case giving rise to that construction. This is why a judicial decision generally applies retroactively....

Our conclusion that the amendment to section 12940, subdivision (j)(3), changed rather than clarified the law does not itself decide the question whether it applies to this case. It just means that applying the amended section to this case would be a retroactive application.... We turn now to the question whether the amendment applies retroactively....

Generally, statutes operate prospectively only. The presumption against retroactive legislation is deeply rooted in our jurisprudence, and embodies a legal doctrine centuries older than our Republic. Elementary considerations of fairness dictate that individuals should have an opportunity to know what the law is and to conform their conduct accordingly.... For that reason, the principle that the legal effect of conduct should ordinarily be assessed under the law that existed when the conduct took place has timeless and universal appeal. The presumption against statutory retroactivity has consistently been explained by reference to the unfairness of imposing new burdens on persons after the fact.

This is not to say that a statute may never apply retroactively. A statute's retroactivity is, in the first instance, a policy determination for the Legislature and one to which courts defer absent 'some constitutional objection" to retroactivity. But it has long been established that a statute that interferes with antecedent rights will not operate retroactively unless such retroactivity be the unequivocal and inflexible import of the terms, and the manifest intention of the legislature. A statute may be applied retroactively only if it contains express language of retroactively *or* if other sources provide a clear and unavoidable implication that the Legislature intended retroactive application.

We see nothing here to overcome the strong presumption against retroactivity. Plaintiff and Justice Moreno argue that the statement in section 12940, subdivision (j)(2), that the subdivision's provisions merely declared existing law, shows an intent to apply the amendment retroactively. They cite our statement that where a statute provides that it clarifies or declares existing law, it is obvious that such a provision is indicative of a legislative intent that the amendment apply to all existing causes of action from the date of its enactment. In accordance with the general rules of statutory construction, we must give effect to this intention unless there is some constitutional objection thereto....

Moreover, the language of section 12940, subdivision (j)(2), namely, that "The provisions of this subdivision are declaratory of existing law," long predates the Legislature's overruling of *Carrisales.* That language was added to the section in reference to a different, earlier, change to the statute. (Stats.1987, ch. 605, §1, p.1945.) Any inference the Legislature intended the 2000 amendment to apply retroactively is thus far weaker than if the Legislature had asserted, *in the 2000 amending act itself,* that the amendment's provisions declared existing law.

Plaintiff and the Court of Appeal also cite statements in the legislative history to the effect that the proposed amendment would only "clarify" the law's original meaning. But these references may have been intended only to demonstrate that clarification was necessary, not as positive assertions that the law always provided for coworker liability. We see no indication the Legislature even thought about giving, much less expressly intended to give, the amendment retroactive effect to the extent the amendment did change the law. Specifically, we see no clear and unavoidable intent to have the statute retroactively impose liability for actions not subject to liability when taken. Requiring clear intent assures that the legislative body itself has affirmatively considered the potential unfairness of retroactive application and determined that it is an acceptable price to pay for the countervailing benefits....

For all of these reasons, we conclude that section 12940, subdivision (j)(3), does not apply retroactively to conduct predating its enactment....

We reverse the judgment of the Court of Appeal and remand the matter for further proceedings....

Concurring and Dissenting Opinion by Moreno, J.

We held in *Carrisales* that the California Fair Employment and Housing Act (FEHA) does not impose on nonsupervisory coworkers personal liability for harassment. The Legislature later amended Government Code section 12940, subdivision (j), to impose such personal liability. The statute as amended states that its provisions "are declaratory of existing law." (Gov.Code, § 12940, subd. (j)(2).)

I agree with the majority that the Legislature could not, by amending the statute, clarify its meaning in a manner inconsistent with our decision in *Carrisales*. Thus, the amendment must be deemed to have changed, rather than merely clarified, the law. But unlike the majority, I conclude that by purporting to clarify its original intent, the Legislature clearly intended to apply this statutory change retroactively. We must honor this legislative intent, unless prevented from doing so by constitutional concerns....

The majority ..."see[s] nothing here to overcome the strong presumption against retroactivity." I disagree. The statute at issue, subdivision (j)(2) of section 12940, states that its provisions "are declaratory of existing law...." In [another case], we recognized the importance of such legislative language: "[E]ven if the court does not accept the Legislature's assurance that an unmistakable change in the law is merely a 'clarification,' the declaration of intent may still effectively reflect the Legislature's purpose to achieve a retrospective change.... Thus, where a statute provides that it clarifies or declares existing law, it is obvious that such a provision is indicative of a legislative intent that the amendment apply to all existing causes of action from the date of its enactment."...

In the present case, ... we cannot give effect to the Legislature's statement that the amendment to section 12940, subdivision (j) was declaratory of existing law, but we can give effect to the Legislature's clear expression of its intent that this amendment be given retroactive effect.

The majority notes that the statutory language stating that the provisions of subdivision (j) of section 12940 are declaratory of existing law was originally added to the statute in reference to a 1987 amendment. The majority concludes from this that "[a]ny inference the Legislature intended the 2000 amendment to apply retroactively is thus far weaker than if the Legislature had asserted, *in the 2000 amending act itself*, that the amendment's provisions declared existing law." Again, I do not agree.

A statute that is amended is "re-enacted as amended." (Cal. Const., art. IV, §9.) "The amendment of a statute ordinarily has the legal effect of reenacting (thus enacting) the statute as amended, including its unamended portions." As amended, section 12940, subdivision (j) clearly states that its provisions are declaratory of existing law. The circumstance that the same statement had been made in reference to an earlier amendment of the same statute does not lessen the plain meaning of this statutory language. In general, we take it that the Legislature means what it says. In the present case, it is difficult to imagine how the Legislature could have more clearly expressed its intention that the 2000 amendment to subdivision (j) of section 12940, like the earlier amendment, was declaratory of existing law.

Because the Legislature clearly indicated its intent that the amendment to the statute be applied retroactively, we must honor that intent....

Notes and Questions

(1) *Was the Presumption Against Retroactivity Overcome?* The dissent agreed with the majority that the statute had changed the law. Nonetheless, the dissent found that the

presumption against retroactivity had been overcome. Why does the dissent believe that the presumption was overcome even though the court cannot give effect to the legislature's statement that the amendment did not change the law? Is the dissent a textualist? What was the majority's reason for finding that the presumption had not been overcome? How would a textualist view that reason?

(2) *The Dissent's Approach.* The dissent argued that retroactive effect had to be given unless doing so violated the Constitution. Can you explain why the majority believed that giving retroactive effect to the statute violated the Constitution, even if the substantive impact on the litigants themselves was constitutional?

(3) *Retroactive Application of Judicial Interpretation.* Notice that the events in the case took place before *Carrisales* was decided. If, as the plaintiff argued, the *Carrisales* court gave the statute the wrong interpretation, why wasn't it more appropriate to apply the amended statute to the defendant's actions, since the legislature obviously believed that *Carrisales* was wrong? In contrast, *Carrisales* applied to the defendant's conduct even though the conduct predated the decision. Why are judicial interpretations of a statute given retroactive effect, but statutes are not given retroactive effect?

(4) *Why Can't a Legislature Tell a Court it was Wrong?* Is the majority's point that a legislature cannot tell a court that the court was wrong? So long as there is no constitutional violation with the application of retroactivity, why, according to the majority, can't a legislature tell a court it was wrong? Do you agree with their point, for which the majority relies upon *Marbury v. Madison*?

(5) *Why Not?* The majority wrote that a court cannot accept a legislature's statement that an amendment merely clarified and restated existing law where the amendment "unmistakably" did more than that. Why does a legislature's disagreement with a prior interpretation mean that the legislature changed the law? Doesn't the legislature's disagreement mean that the court was wrong, not that the legislature changed anything? In addition, how does a later legislature know what the enacting legislature intended? More importantly, are these questions irrelevant in light of *Marbury v. Madison* and the principle of separation of powers?

(6) *A Proposed Demarcation on Separation of Powers.* Should the fact that a court has not yet interpreted a statute matter to the question of retroactivity? Consider what one South Carolina judge wrote:

> Whether a statutory amendment applies retroactively is ordinarily a matter of statutory construction and interpretation, not of constitutional law. The General Assembly has the authority to amend statutes, and to determine whether the amended statute applies to matters occurring before its effective date. The general rule is that "statutory enactments are to be considered prospective rather than retroactive unless there is a specific provision in the enactment or clear legislative intent to the contrary...." The only constitutional limit on retroactivity in a civil context[4] derives from due process guarantees, and from S.C. Const. art. I, § 4, prohibiting the passage of a law that has the effect of impairing the obligation of contract or divesting vested rights of property.
>
> Through a series of cases..., we have created two different rules regarding statutory retroactivity: If the Court never interpreted the prior statute, then the general rule recited above applies. If, however, the Court has issued an opinion

---

4. There are, of course, ex post facto concerns with criminal statutes.

interpreting a statute, any legislative change to that statute is deemed prospective only, lest the legislature invade the province of the Court. In my opinion, this "[] rule," premised on the separation of powers doctrine, has in fact led to its violation.

> The separation of powers doctrine prevents one branch of government from usurping the power and authority of another. It is not the legislature's amendment of a statute in response to a judicial interpretation which offends the doctrine, but rather our limitation on the General Assembly's authority to decide whether that statutory change should be given retroactive effect.

JRS Builders, Inc. v. Neunsinger, 614 S.E.2d 629, 632–33 (S.C. 2005) (Pleicones, J., dissenting). Does it make sense to apply a different rule if the amendment is made after a prior judicial interpretation? Is South Carolina law consistent with California's? Are both right, wrong, or divided? Consider the following case, which adds additional wrinkles to the analysis.

Ga. Dep't of Revenue v. Owens Corning
660 S.E.2d 719 (Ga. 2008)

MELTON, JUSTICE.

We granted certiorari in this case to determine whether the Court of Appeals erred by holding that the 1997 version of O.C.G.A. § 48-8-3(34)(A) clearly and unambiguously creates an exemption from taxation for machinery repair parts. Based on the applicable standards of review, the legislative history of the statute, and the Legislature's expressed intent that machinery repair parts not be extended a sales tax exemption prior to 2000, we find that no clear, unambiguous exemption for machinery repair parts existed in 1997. Therefore, we must reverse ...

At its inception in 1951 as part of the Retailers' and Consumers' Sales and Use Tax Act and for more than 40 years thereafter, machinery repair parts have been explicitly subjected to sales tax. At the outset, therefore, we begin with a clear and unambiguous legislative intent that machinery repairs parts are not exempt from sales tax. This clear intent to tax machinery repair parts must necessarily inform our consideration of future changes in the statute.

In 1994, O.C.G.A. § 48-8-3(34)(A) provided a sales tax exemption for "[m]achinery ... used directly in the manufacture of tangible personal property when the machinery is bought to replace or upgrade machinery in a manufacturing plant presently existing in this state." There was no reference to machinery repair parts in this statute, and it is undisputed that no exemption existed under this language. Therefore, the historical taxation of machinery repair parts continued as of 1994.

Likewise, no exemption was created under the revision of O.C.G.A. § 48-8-3(34)(A) in 1997. The 1997 statute provides for a sales tax exemption for "[m]achinery, *including components thereof,* which is used directly in the manufacture of tangible personal property when the machinery is bought to replace or upgrade machinery in a manufacturing plant presently existing in this state." (Emphasis supplied.) Nothing in this language creates an explicit exemption from sales tax for machinery repair parts. At best, this language may create some ambiguity that "replacement components" could possibly include repair parts. However, in cases of ambiguity, the statute must be interpreted in favor of the tax, not the exemption. Moreover, in light of the Legislature's explicit past declarations that machinery repair parts should be subject to tax, it stands to reason that, if the

Legislature wished to reverse this historical trend in the 1997 amendment, it would have done so explicitly.

The Legislature did not take that action, however, until 2000. That year, O.C.G.A. §48-8-3 was revised once more. The phrase "including components thereof" was deleted from subsection (34)(A). In addition, a new subsection was added which, for the first time, explicitly provides a phased-in exemption applicable to machinery repair parts. Until this point in time, every explicit mention by the Legislature of repair parts was made to show that these items were not allowed an exemption. The 2000 amendment is the first time the Legislature altered this rule.

The Legislature's intent that the exemption for machinery repair parts not take effect until 2000 is made evident from the stated purpose for the 2000 statutory revision, namely "to amend Code Section 48-8-3 ..., relating to exemption from sales and use taxes, so as *to clarify* that the exemption regarding certain components of machinery used directly in the manufacture of tangible personal property extends only to machinery components purchased to upgrade such machinery." (Emphasis supplied.) The Legislature then goes on to create a prospective phased-in exemption for machinery repair parts. This language shows that the Legislature wished to eradicate any ambiguity caused by the 1997 statute and make it clear that the 1997 statute did not extend the sales tax exemption to machinery repair parts.

Rather than narrowly construing the 1997 amendment, the dissent construes the statute in order to expand the scope of the sales tax exemption to cover machinery repair parts, despite the facts that the statute makes no mention of repair parts and these parts had been explicitly excepted from the exemption for decades, evidence of clear legislative intent that the dissent goes so far as to call "irrelevant." ... [T]he more reasonable conclusion is that the 2000 amendment was necessary to clarify that the 1997 exemption applied to only those components which upgraded machinery, because the former version of the statute was ambiguous and unclear in scope. By its express terms, the Legislature was not limiting an already existing exemption. In finding otherwise, the dissent distorts the standard that "subsequent legislation declaring the intent of the legislature in enacting an earlier statute is entitled to great weight." *Fleming v. State*, 523 S.E.2d 315 (1999). Ultimately, the dissent converts language designed to clarify that no exemption previously existed into a legislative acknowledgment of an exemption that needed to be limited.

At best, the 1997 amendment created an ambiguity as to whether the sales tax exemption applied to machine repair parts, and the law demands that, in such a case, we find that no exemption existed in fact.

Judgment reversed.

CARLEY, JUSTICE, dissenting.

... I respectfully dissent because ... the applicable rules of statutory construction compel the conclusion that the reference to machinery "components" in the 1997 version of O.C.G.A. §48-8-3(34)(A) unambiguously encompassed repair parts....

[I]n determining whether the 1997 version of O.C.G.A. §48-8-3(34)(A) clearly and unambiguously exempted repair parts from taxation, it is necessary that

> [w]e begin our analysis with the "golden rule" of statutory construction, which requires us to follow the literal language of the statute "unless it produces contradiction, absurdity or such an inconvenience as to insure that the legislature meant something else."

I submit that the majority does not adhere to this "golden rule." ...

The "literal language" of former O.C.G.A. § 48-8-3(34)(A) extended the tax exemption to "components" and, "[i]n all interpretations of statutes, the ordinary signification shall be applied to all words, except words of art or words connected with a particular trade or subject matter...." O.C.G.A. § 1-3-1(b). "Component," as it appeared in the applicable 1997 version of the statute, was not used as a term of art, and the usual definition of that word is "[a] constituent element, as of a system" or "[a] part of a mechanical or electrical complex." The American Heritage Dictionary (Second College Edition), p. 302. As thus defined, a single machine part can constitute a "component," without regard to the role that it plays in the operation of the machinery itself. Therefore, the "literal language" of former O.C.G.A. § 48-8-3(34)(A) did not limit the scope of the authorized exclusion to only certain constituent elements or parts of a machine which were used for specified purposes. Instead, it provided for a broadly inclusive tax exemption for any and all constituent elements or parts "bought to replace or upgrade" other constituent elements or parts of exempted machinery. Accordingly, the applicable rules of statutory construction compel the Court of Appeals' holding that the exemption for machinery "components" unambiguously included parts that were bought to repair and replace parts comprising [plaintiff's] machines in its Georgia manufacturing plants.

The initial flaw in the majority's analysis is that, rather than properly focusing on the controlling "literal language" of former O.C.G.A. § 48-8-3(34)(A), it relies instead on pre-1997 law to demonstrate that an ambiguity exists as to the meaning of "components." However, "components" did not appear in the statute before 1997, so the pre-existing law has absolutely no bearing on the "ordinary signification" which, under O.C.G.A. § 1-3-1 (b), is to be given to that word. To the contrary, the addition of "components" to the exemption in that year, when that term had never before appeared in the statutory language, gives rise to a very different presumption than that of ambiguity as to its meaning.

> From the addition of words it may be presumed that the legislature intended some change in the existing law; but it is also presumed that the legislature did not intend to effect a greater change than is clearly apparent either by express declaration or by necessary implication.

Thus, the addition of the phrase "including components thereof" in the 1997 statute should be presumed to have made some change in the pre-existing substantive law, and the duty of the court is to construe the change so as not to render it meaningless. Since the ordinary signification of "components" does include repair parts, the majority's reliance on the absence of an exemption for those parts in the pre-1997 law renders the General Assembly's addition of "components" to former O.C.G.A. § 48-8-3(34)(A) essentially meaningless....

The majority does not set forth any viable rationale for construing "components" narrowly so as to exclude repair parts. Instead, its interpretation of the 1997 revision is ultimately premised on reading into "components" a limitation which the General Assembly did not include in the statute when it changed the pre-existing law. However,

> under our system of separation of powers this Court does not have the authority to rewrite statutes. "(T)he doctrine of separation of powers is an immutable constitutional principle which must be strictly enforced. Under that doctrine, statutory construction belongs to the courts, legislation to the legislature. We can not add a line to the law."

According to its "literal language," former O.C.G.A. § 48-8-3 (34)(A) extended the tax exemption to "components." It did not extend the exemption to "components, *except for repair parts.*" The engrafting of such a limitation on the scope of the broad exemption granted to "components" by the General Assembly in 1997 is not appropriate statutory construction.

The majority not only relies upon the pre-1997 law, it also cites the 2000 revision to the statute as support for its wholesale rewriting of former O.C.G.A. § 48-8-3(34)(A). The applicable rule is that,

> [i]f examination of a subsequent statute in pari materia reveals the meaning that the legislature attached to the words of a former statute, it will amount to a legislative declaration of its meaning and will govern the construction of the former statute; and subsequent legislation declaring the intent of the legislature in enacting an earlier statute is entitled to great weight.

Fleming v. State, 523 S.E.2d 315 (Ga. 1999). That rule of statutory construction does not apply here, because the 2000 statute did not expressly declare the legislative intent which underlay the 1997 version of O.C.G.A. § 48-8-3(34)(A). Instead, the stated purpose of the subsequent statute was

> [*t*]*o amend* Code Section 48-8-3..., relating to exemption from sales and use taxes, *so as to clarify* that the exemption regarding certain components of machinery used directly in the manufacture of tangible personal property extends only to machinery components purchased to upgrade such machinery.... (Emphasis supplied.)

Ga. L. 2000, p. 615.

> "Amendment of a statute implies its survival and not destruction. It repeals or changes some provision, or adds something thereto ... [.] A law is amended when it is in whole or in part permitted to remain, and something is added to or taken from it, or it is in some way changed or altered to make it more complete or perfect, or to fit it the better to accomplish the object or purpose for which it was made, or some other object or purpose."

Wheeler v. Bd. of Trustees of Fargo Consolidated School Dist., 200 Ga. 323, 330(2), 37 S.E.2d 322 (1946).

If, as the majority holds, the General Assembly had intended to express the legislative intent in 2000 that the word "components" as it appeared in the 1997 revision of O.C.G.A. § 48-8-3(34)(A) exclude repair parts, then the 2000 legislation presumably would have provided for a *renewal* of the limited exemption that had been granted by the 1997 revision only to "machinery components purchased to upgrade ... machinery." However, the General Assembly recognized that the 1997 exemption granted to "components" was unambiguously broad enough to include repair parts and, in 2000, it changed that by amending the statute to provide otherwise. Thus, the clear legislative intent of the 2000 statute was "to clarify" that the former broad exemption for "components" granted under the 1997 version would no longer apply after the effective date of the amendment to O.C.G.A. § 48-8-3(34)(A)....

If the majority were correct, then the General Assembly could always effect a retroactive substantive change in the law simply by enacting a subsequent amendment so as "to clarify" that a statute had an entirely different meaning than that which was conveyed by the unambiguous language of its previous provisions. However,

> [r]etroactive statutes are forbidden by the first principles of justice. Retrospective laws which divest previously acquired rights on principle occupy the same position with ex post facto laws. Upon principle, every statute which takes away

or impairs vested rights acquired under existing laws, or creates a new obligation, imposes a new duty, or attaches a new disability, in respect to transactions or considerations already past, must be deemed retrospective.

London Guarantee & Accident Co. v. Pittman, 25 S.E.2d 60 (Ga. 1943). It is apparent that the General Assembly understood this constitutional limitation to its authority to divest taxpayers of the exemption provided for machinery repair parts by the 1997 revision of the statute and, by amending the statute in 2000, clarified that that exemption would not be continued in the future. Contrary to the holding of the majority, this Court cannot achieve what was forbidden to the General Assembly, and, by giving the 2000 statute retroactive effect, unconstitutionally deprive a taxpayer of a previously acquired exemption for repair parts.

Notes and Questions

(1) *Ambiguity as a Starting Point?* Should ambiguity be a factor for determining whether a later statute changes or merely clarifies an existing one? Recall that ambiguity only exists when there are two or more reasonable interpretations of a statute, not when the statute is vague. If there are two reasonable interpretations and a later legislature indicates its agreement with one of the two, why doesn't that choice signify change, not clarification?

(2) *Was the Georgia Tax Statute Ambiguous?* The three dissenting justices chastised the majority for engaging in an "unwarranted assumption" of ambiguity. Do you believe the majority properly determined that the statute was ambiguous?

(3) *The Relevance of Legislative Statements of Intent to Clarify.* One factor that courts consider is whether the legislature stated that it was merely clarifying an existing statute. First, does such a statement violate separation of powers, as some of the judges in the principal cases might argue? Second, can one legislature speak authoritatively about the intent of an earlier legislature? What if the later statute is enacted shortly after the earlier statute? Shortly after a judicial interpretation of the statute? *See McKenzie Check Advance of Fla., LLC v. Betts,* 928 So. 2d 1204, 1210 (Fla. 2006) ("Sometimes it may be appropriate to consider a subsequent amendment to clarify original legislative intent of a statute if such amendment was enacted soon after a controversy regarding the statute's interpretation arose.") And, finally, how much weight should such statements be given? Should the statements be given no weight at all? Merely be a factor? Be given strong weight?

(4) *Textualists and Intentionalists Might Agree on this Issue.* Do you believe that an intentionalist would find the approach of the courts to this issue to be off the mark? Would an intentionalist ever find "clarification" is proper? Would a textualist? A purposivist might endorse the multi-factor approach. Do you see why?

3. Defining Retroactivity

State Ethics Comm'n v. Evans
855 A.2d 364 (Md. 2004)

WILNER, J.

Maryland Code, §§ 15-701(a) and 15-703(a) of the State Government Article (SG) (2003 Supp.) require a lobbyist to file with the State Ethics Commission a registration statement for each client that has employed the lobbyist. Failure to file a required registration statement subjects the lobbyist to criminal sanctions. SG § 15-903.

SG § 15-405(e) permits the Commission to revoke a registration if the Commission determines that, based on acts arising from lobbying activities, the lobbyist has been convicted of bribery, theft, or other crime involving moral turpitude. A complaint charging such a conviction must be initiated within two years after the date the conviction becomes final. Section 15-405(e) was enacted in 2001 and took effect November 1, 2001. Prior to then, there was no express authority in the law for the Commission to suspend or revoke a registration and no statement of grounds upon which a registration could properly be suspended or revoked.

On July 14, 2000, Gerard Evans, a registered lobbyist, was convicted ... on nine counts of wire and mail fraud arising out of his lobbying activities. On September 29, 2000, he was sentenced to ... imprisonment, fined, and required to pay restitution.... As no appeal was taken, the conviction became final that day, some 13 months before § 15-405 took effect.

On May 24, 2002, Evans, having served his prison sentence, registered with the Commission as a lobbyist on behalf of five clients. On ... October 8, 2002, the Commission, acting under SG § 15-405(e), revoked the registrations. On Evans's petition for judicial review, the Circuit Court ... reversed the Commission's decision on the ground that it constituted an impermissible retroactive application of § 15-405(e). The issue before us, in this appeal by the Commission, is whether the Circuit Court was correct. We shall hold that it was.

In 1979, the General Assembly enacted a fairly comprehensive Public Ethics Law for State and local government officials and employees....

With three exceptions added over the years ... the law governing lobbyists was essentially restricted to requiring them to register with the State Ethics Commission and to file semi-annual reports. Although lobbyists were, of course subject to the criminal laws against bribery, fraud, and extortion, there were ... no more specific ethical standards set forth in the Public Ethics Law governing what they could or could not do. Nor was there any provision authorizing the Commission to suspend or revoke a registration or to impose any meaningful administrative sanction if inappropriate conduct was discovered. If the Commission found a violation of the law, it could issue an order to cease and desist the violation and seek judicial enforcement of that order or it could issue a reprimand. A court, in an enforcement action, could fine the violator.

The lack of clear ethical standards and effective administrative enforcement came dramatically to public attention when two prominent lobbyists..., the second being appellee, were indicted for, and ultimately convicted ... of, mail fraud based on conduct ... associated with their lobbying.... The essence of the nine wire and mail fraud charges of which Evans was convicted was that he had induced a member of the House of Delegates to commence the process for introducing legislation that would be detrimental to the economic interests of certain paint manufacturers, that he then, with some embellishment, presented that prospect to those manufacturers, falsely informing them that the Mayor of Baltimore intended to support that legislation, and that, through those false representations, he induced those companies to employ him as a lobbyist for the purpose of defeating the legislation. The parties inform us that "[s]chemes of this sort, premised on phony or outright phantom legislation, are colloquially known as 'bell ringing.'"

Even before the Evans indictment in December, 1999, the Legislature, in its January–April, 1999 Session, created a Study Commission on Lobbyist Ethics and charged it ... with collecting information about lobbying practices, formulating a Code of Ethics for lobbyists, proposing legislation, and reporting its findings to the Governor and General Assembly....

In its [November 2000] Report, the Study Commission declined the invitation to formulate a Code of Ethics for lobbyists but recommended instead a number of statutory changes designed to prohibit certain specific practices and provide greater regulation of lobbying activities and more effective enforcement of the regulatory requirements....

A bill embodying those recommendations was introduced and enacted in the 2001 Session of the General Assembly. Among other things, the bill created a new SG § 15-713 that listed 14 prohibited acts, one of which was "commit[ting] a criminal offense arising from lobbying activity." In SG § 15-405, dealing with the enforcement powers of the State Ethics Commission, the bill added the new suspension and revocation of registration provisions noted above. Section 15-405(e)(1) provides [generally that the Ethics Commission can suspend the registration of an individual regulated lobbyist if the individual was convicted of a criminal offense arising from lobbying activity]....

Section 4 of Ch. 631 provided that the Act would take effect November 1, 2001. The Act said nothing, one way or the other, about whether any of the sanctions it included could be applied to or based on conduct that occurred before its effective date.

As noted, Evans's conviction became final on September 29, 2000. On May 24, 2002, following his release from prison ... he filed lobbying registration forms with the Ethics Commission [which denied him registration]....

The issue before us is not whether, as a matter of public policy, a person who has engaged in the conduct Evans was convicted of committing should be permitted to continue to act as a compensated lobbyist. Nor, in our view, is the issue whether the Legislature had the Constitutional authority to draft the statute in such a way that would have allowed the Commission to preclude Evans from continuing to act as a compensated lobbyist based on his September, 2000 convictions. Indeed, Evans no longer contests, if he ever did, that the Legislature could have achieved that result. The only question is whether the record reveals a sufficiently clear intent by the Legislature that the statute have that effect or that it be applied in that manner.

[The majority then analyzed whether the statute applied retroactively. The majority applied these four basic principles:

> (1) statutes are presumed to operate prospectively unless a contrary intent appears; (2) a statute governing procedure or remedy will be applied to cases pending in court when the statute becomes effective; (3) a statute will be given retroactive effect if that is the legislative intent; but (4) even if intended to apply retroactively, a statute will not be given that effect if it would impair vested rights, deny due process, or violate the prohibition against *ex post facto* laws.

Applying these principles, the majority rejected the Commission's argument that because the General Assembly was keenly aware of Evans' behavior, "if the General Assembly had intended to exempt or give 'grandfather' status to Evans' conviction, it would have said so expressly." The majority reasoned, "The problem with this assertion is that it reverses the long-standing presumption against retroactivity.... [A] statute will be found to operate retroactively *only when the Legislature clearly expresses an intent that the statute apply retroactively*."]

The dissent agrees that, on the record before us, there is no evidence, or at least insufficient evidence, that the Legislature intended for § 15-405(e) to be applied retroactively, and it thus rejects, as do we, the Commission's argument to the contrary. On that issue, the Court is unanimous, and, apart from whether a retroactive application would or would not impair any vested rights of Evans, that alone would preclude giving the statute a retroactive application.

The dissent skirts that problem, which we regard as the determinative factor, by expressing the belief that termination of Evans's registration based on a conviction that occurred prior to the effective date of the statute does not constitute a retroactive application of the law. It rests that belief solely on the view that the Commission's action did not impair any vested right of Evans or change "the legal significance of completed transactions."

There are two problems with that proposition. First, assuming that the dissent's view that a criminal conviction is the equivalent of a "completed transaction" is correct, we are hard-pressed to understand how § 15-405(e) which, for the first time, permitted the State Ethics Commission to revoke a lobbyist's registration solely on the ground that the lobbyist has been convicted of certain criminal offenses, does not change the legal significance of a conviction that occurred prior to the effective date of the statute. Would the dissent also hold, under that view, that the Commission could suspend a registration for conduct, not then unlawful, that occurred prior to November 1, 2001?

To the extent that the dissent would define retroactivity in terms of whether a statute impairs vested rights, it conflates the concept of retroactivity with Constitutionally impermissible retroactivity and, as a logical consequence, would effectively prohibit any retroactive legislation. Under that view, a statute is retroactive if it impairs vested rights, but to the extent it impairs vested rights, it cannot be given retroactive effect—a classic "Catch-22." A statute may have retroactive effect without impairing a vested right. In [another case], we defined a retroactive statute as one "which purports to determine the legal significance of acts or events that have occurred prior to the statute's effective date," and we made clear that there is "no absolute prohibition against retroactive application of a statute."

A statute may affect dealings, contracts, or statuses that existed prior to the effective date of the statute, and, to the extent that it does so, it will be regarded as retroactive. Under clear and well-established Maryland case law, there are but two brakes or caveats on permitting statutes to have that effect: first, because there is a presumption that statutes apply only prospectively, there must be clear evidence, legally sufficient to rebut that presumption, that the legislature intended for the statute to apply retroactively; and second, even if such intent is adequately established, a statute will not be permitted to so apply if such an application would impair a vested right. The second brake is a Constitutional impediment, not a definitional element. It does not make the statute retroactive—that is accomplished by rules of statutory construction in aid of establishing legislative intent—but rather precludes the statute from applying retroactively, even though that was the legislative intent. If there is sufficient evidence of the requisite legislative intent and a retroactive application would not impair vested rights, the statute may be given retroactive effect. The problem in this case is that there was insufficient evidence of legislative intent that § 15-405(e) apply with respect to convictions that occurred prior to its effective date, a deficiency recognized by the dissent.

Because we find in this record no clear expression of an intent by the General Assembly to permit the revocation of a registration based on conduct that occurred before the effective date of the statute, it is not necessary for us to address the other issues raised by Evans....

Dissenting Opinion by HARRELL, J., which CATHELL, J., joins.

Were it necessary in this case to resolve the arguments directed to retroactivity, I would agree with the Majority that, on this record, the Legislature failed to express sufficiently and clearly an intent for the statutory amendments in question to have retrospective effect.... In my view, however, [this issue] need [not] be resolved here inasmuch as the application to Evans' lobbyist registration of § 15-405(e) by the State Ethics Commission was not retroactive in effect. The Commission's action neither impaired vested rights nor changed the legal consequences of completed transactions, as those criteria are understood in the accepted analysis of what constitutes the retrospective application of an enactment. Thus, neither the common law presumption against the retrospective application of legislation nor the question of legislative intent regarding retrospectivity are material to deciding this case. The application to Evans' situation of § 15-405(e) was entirely prospective and lawful. Accordingly, I would reverse the judgment of the Circuit Court for Anne Arundel County and remand this case with direction to affirm the State Ethics Commission's decision to revoke Evans' lobbyist registration.

Our cases considering whether particular statutes lawfully may be applied retrospectively tend to focus on the search for clues whether the Legislature, having failed to include clear direction to that end in the enactment, nevertheless evinced an intent for the statute in question to be applicable retroactively. Our cases, for the most part, however, have not considered in any depth the definition of, or developed an analytical paradigm for determining in the first instance, what constitutes retroactive application of a statute. Accordingly, I look elsewhere.

The U.S. Supreme Court dealt fully with this question in *Landgraf v. USI Film Products*, 511 U.S. 244, 268–83 (1994). While the Court eschewed a rigidly mechanical standard, it generally defined as a retrospective application of a statute one that "would impair rights a party possessed when he acted, increase a party's liability for past conduct, or impose new duties with respect to transactions already completed." The Court emphasized that "a statute does not operate 'retrospectively' merely because it is applied in a case arising from conduct antedating the statute's enactment." Rather, a statute is deemed to have retroactive effect if it purports to change the legal consequences of events completed before its enactment, with the analysis to be guided by "fair notice, reasonable reliance, and settled expectations." The Court urged caution in this analysis, stating: "[e]ven uncontroversially prospective statutes may unsettle expectations and impose burdens on past conduct: a new property tax or zoning regulation may upset the reasonable expectations that prompted those affected to acquire property; a new law banning gambling harms the person who had begun to construct a casino before the law's enactment or spent his life learning to count cards."

Landgraf dealt with the asserted imposition of civil tort liability (in the form of compensatory and punitive damages under the Civil Rights Act of 1991) for allegedly discriminatory conduct occurring prior to the effective date of the statute. The plaintiff-employee's immediate supervisor failed to respond to her complaints of sexual harassment by a co-worker. The plaintiff-employee allegedly suffered mental anguish because the situation was not corrected in a timely manner. While the defendant-employer would not have been liable under the previous statutory scheme, the Court assumed ... that application of the new statute to the past discrimination would support a finding of liability against the defendant-employer, along with a possible award of compensatory and punitive damages. To hold the defendant-employer liable for past conduct under these circumstances would impair the employer's previously vested legal right not to be forced to pay compensatory and punitive damages for acts or omissions which were not illegal at the time they occurred.[7] The Court found that to hold the defendant liable would

---

7. A vested right may be defined as an interest which is proper for the state to recognize and protect, and of which the individual may not be deprived arbitrarily without injustice. As such, it in-

have increased the employer's liability for past conduct. It observed that an award of compensatory damages is "quintessentially backward looking," and that introduction of a "right to compensatory damages" would "have an impact on private parties" planning." In other words, had the cause of action existed at the time of the conduct, the employer might have acted to terminate the harassment as a means to avoid civil liability. As such, the Court found that the proposed liability imposed new duties with respect to completed transactions. To hold an employer civilly liable for conduct not actionable at the time that it occurred would attach a "new legal burden" to the original conduct, and would impose a "new disability" with respect to completed transactions....

[The] application of § 15-405(e) to Evans impairs no vested right. Evans had no vested right to registration to practice as a lobbyist in the State of Maryland. The practice of public professions, such as law, medicine, and, by analogy, lobbying, is not a right, but a privilege subject to conditional public licensure. Such professions may harm the public if practiced improperly. A state necessarily reserves the power to condition such privileges on conditions consistent with the nature and purpose of the privilege. Thus, such privileges are subject to the State's inherent police power.

Furthermore, Evans had no vested right in the maintenance of existing regulations governing public lobbying registration. While the Supreme Court in *Landgraf* recognized that the presumption against statutory retroactivity is strongest where retroactive application would undermine the stability and predictability of property and contractual rights, stability or predictability of public licensing requirements are not essential to the existence of effective licensing regimes. The State must remain able to alter its licensing/registration requirements in order to accommodate evolving public needs and concerns. Evans cannot argue persuasively that he did not have "fair notice" that he would be subject to the specific requirements of § 15-405(e) at the time that he engaged in his criminal conduct. He was on notice that his last previous registration inevitably would expire on its own terms, which it did. Evans also was on notice that the regulations governing any application for future registrations were subject to change, and that he could only register anew by re-applying under whatever regulations were in place at the time of each subsequent application.

Second, application of § 15-405(e) to Evans did not subject him to new duties or increased liability within the meaning of *Landgraf* or our cases. The contemplated tort liability in *Landgraf* ... implicated new, affirmative, and unconditional requirements that the employer make restitution in the form of damages or reinstatement, respectively. Section 15-405(e) placed no similar duties upon Evans. It did not require Evans to report back to prison or to pay any additional damages or fines. The State Ethics Commission, by revoking Evans' lobbying registration, followed the mandate of § 15-405 to protect the integrity of the regulated public profession committed to its supervision. The Commission was given the opportunity to do so because Evans applied for registration within two years of being convicted of a crime of moral turpitude arising out of lobbying activities.

Section 15-405(e) imposed no new burdens or duties on transactions completed by Evans before the effective date of the statute. Unlike the defendants in *Landgraf* ... Evans

---

cludes an immediate right of present enjoyment or a present fixed right of future enjoyment which, under particular circumstances, will be protected from legislative interference. Walter v. Gunter, 367 Md. 386, 415 (2002) (Harrell, J., Dissenting). In the context of *Landgraf*, the defendant-employer impliedly had a vested right not to be forced arbitrarily to pay monetary damages to another individual. The fact that the conduct in question was not illegal under the previous statutory scheme, and was completed before the law was changed, would have meant holding the defendant liable for damages based on past conduct for which the defendant could not have foreseen such liability.

effectively had a pre-existing legal duty not to commit crimes of moral turpitude arising out of lobbying activities: such activities already were unlawful under federal law at the time of his misconduct. Thus, § 15-405(e) imposed no new duty on Evans than previously existed under federal law.

Further unlike the cases discussed above, all of the events precipitating the application of § 15-405(e) to Evans were not completed before § 15-405(e) became effective. The Commission applied § 15-405(e) to revoke the registration Evans sought after its effective date. As noted earlier, his previous registration had expired of its own terms. In order for § 15-405(e) to apply to him, it was necessary that Evans apply for a new lobbying registration within two years of his conviction, which he obligingly did. Thus, the final precipitating event for the application of § 15-405(e) was not Evans' pre-enactment criminal conviction, but his application for the registration, after the effective date of the statutory change, and within two years of his conviction. Because this event was not completed until after the statutory effective date, it did not constitute a "transaction already completed" within the meaning of *Landgraf*....

The Majority opinion's conclusion in the present case that § 15-405(e) was applied retroactively to Evans improperly expands the definition of "retroactive application." Under the Majority's view, the presumption against retroactivity successfully may be invoked whenever a statute or licensing scheme operates on past events in any way, ignoring the qualified definition and caveat of caution in this regard found in Supreme Court, other state court, and our own cases. The Majority labels retroactive the Commission's application of the statute to Evans despite the fact that § 15-405(e) did not impair in this case any previously vested rights, was applied only to a post-effective-date registration application, and was not applied to a transaction completed before the statutory effective date.

For the foregoing reasons, I would reverse the judgment of the Circuit Court for Anne Arundel County and remand the matter to that Court with directions to affirm the action of the State Ethics Commission.

Notes and Questions

(1) *What is Retroactivity?* All of the judges agreed that the presumption against retroactive application had not been overcome. But they disagreed on whether applying the statute to Evans's conduct constituted retroactive application. Why? Who was right?

(2) *What if There is Another Amendment?* Suppose the legislature amends the statute to require that for a person to register as a lobbyist, he or she must have lived in Maryland for the preceding ten years, and Evans had only lived in Maryland for five years. The statute clearly states that it applies only prospectively. Can it be applied to Evans if he registers to be a lobbyist after its effective date?

(3) *Conflation or Not?* According to the majority, the dissent conflated the questions of whether a statute applied retroactively and whether the statute was constitutional. Was the majority right?

(4) *Constitutional Issues.* As the principal cases suggest, retroactive statutes can create constitutional issues. *See, e.g., In re ADC Telecomms., Inc. Sec. Litig.*, 409 F.3d 974 (8th Cir. 2005) (collecting cases holding that an amendment that extends an existing statute of limitation to revive barred claims increases liability and so implicates constitutional concerns); *see also Republic of Austria v. Altmann*, 541 U.S. 677 (2004) (addressing retroactivity issues concerning foreign sovereign immunity).

Problem 12-2

You have been appointed as a public defender for Michael Lee Smith, who has been charged with aggravated assault. Mr. Smith tells you that he stabbed a fellow resident at the drug and alcohol rehabilitation center where both men resided. The victim saw Smith coming toward him with a knife. Another witness apparently saw the stabbing.

Smith also tells you that he has had two prior convictions. Specifically, on September 22, 1980, he was convicted of aggravated assault in Pennsylvania, and on July 17, 1987, he was convicted in North Carolina of armed robbery.

You have conducted research and identified the statutes below. The statute concerning retroactivity was adopted in 1961, as was the statute stating the sentence for aggravated assault. The section governing mandatory sentences was adopted in 1998. The stabbing occurred this past March.

Given the statutes below, how will you advise Mr. Smith concerning the potential sentence he faces?

Problem Materials

Mercer Stat. § 24-36-24 (Retroactivity not Presumed)

> No statute shall be construed as retroactive unless clearly and manifestly so intended by the Legislature.

Mercer Stat. § 13-11-22 (Aggravated Assault)

> The sentence for aggravated assault shall be no less than 1 year and no more than 4 years.

Mercer Stat. § 13-13-24 (Mandatory Sentencing)

> (a) Where a person has at the time of the commission of the current offense previously been convicted of two or more such crimes of violence arising from separate criminal transactions, the person shall be sentenced to a minimum sentence of at least 25 years total confinement, notwithstanding any other provision of this title or other statute to the contrary. Upon conviction for a third or subsequent crime of violence the court may, if it determines that 25 years of total confinement is insufficient to protect the public safety, sentence the offender to life imprisonment without parole.

> (b) Definition.— As used in this section, the term "crime of violence" means murder of the third degree, voluntary manslaughter, aggravated assault, rape, involuntary deviate sexual intercourse, aggravated indecent assault, incest, sexual assault, arson, kidnapping, burglary, robbery, or criminal attempt, criminal conspiracy or criminal solicitation to commit murder, or any of the offenses listed above, or equivalent crime under the laws of Mercer, whether the crime is committed in Mercer or elsewhere.

Problem 12-3

Your clients, Rob Pemberton and Janet Bland, have been charged with unlawful acceptance of corporate political contributions and money laundering. They have asked you whether you likely can have the charges dismissed. The indictment charges that they knowingly accepted political contributions from corporations to a political committee called Mercerians For a Totalitarian Majority ("MTM"). More specifically, the indictment charges that each had received a check for more than $100,000 from corporations and provided the money to MTM. According to the indictment, Janet had received a cashier's check, but Rob received just an ordinary check. A cashier's check is guaranteed to be paid. An ordinary check, in contrast, is a "written message to the drawee to pay money in accordance with an order, and thus its primary function is to facilitate payment of an obligation." Fred H. Miller & Alvin C. Harrell, The Law of Modern Payment Systems and Notes § 1.01(4)(a) (2002).

The indictment includes several charges, one of which is money laundering. At the time of the events, the statute provided that a person commits money laundering if he or she "conducts, supervises, or facilitates a transaction involving the funds of criminal activity." Mercer Penal Code § 34.02(a)(2). "Funds" was, at the time of the events, defined as follows:

(a) coin or paper money of the United States or any other country that is designated as legal tender and that circulates and is customarily used and accepted as a medium of exchange in the country of issue;

(b) United States silver certificates, United States Treasury notes, Federal Reserve System notes; and

(c) official bank notes that are customarily used and accepted as a medium of exchange in a foreign country and foreign bank drafts.

Mercer General Code § 34.01(2). Shortly after Pemberton and Bland had been indicted, the legislature approved, and Mercer's governor signed into law, the "Money Laundering Clarification and Clean Up Act of 2009." This bill changed the definition of "funds" by adding a new subsection (d) to the statute, which reads as follows:

(d) currency or its equivalent, including an electronic fund, personal check, bank check, traveler's check, money order, bearer negotiable instrument, bearer investment security, or certificate of stock that allows title to pass on delivery.

The legislative history of the amendment shows that a version of the bill had been pending since the original money laundering statute had been adopted. No amendment was adopted, however, until the indictments against Bland and Pemberton were announced.

The legislative history further shows that with the first iteration of the bill, the sponsor had stated that "This bill is necessary to clarify that the definition of 'funds' in the money laundering statute includes all negotiable instruments." It also shows that when the version of the bill that was finally approved was being debated, the accompanying senate committee report stated that "This bill is intended only to clarify existing law, not to make a change."

The money laundering statute had not been interpreted by a court prior to enactment of the Money Laundering Clarification and Clean Up Act of 2009.

Chapter 13

Conflicting Statutes

This chapter addresses two related topics that arise from conflicts among statutes. While legislatures are presumed to know all existing statutes, sometimes it seems as if a legislature enacts a new statute without taking into account the existence or scope of an earlier statute. What does a court do, for example, when one statute prohibits something that another statute expressly permits? In this chapter we will explore issues related to conflicting statutes.

First, we examine how courts approach conflicting statutes. Sometimes two statutes both seem to apply to a particular circumstance, but they conflict with one another. How should a court resolve that conflict? Courts first strive to interpret the statutes so that a conflict does not exist, typically by using the textual canons or by relying on extrinsic or policy-based sources. However, when a conflict remains, courts must determine which statute controls. Generally, courts will first try to determine whether one statute is "more specific" than the other and whether one statute was enacted later than the other. A later-enacted and more specific statute will often "trump" an earlier, general statute. When that effort fails, courts examine whether the later-enacted statute impliedly repealed the earlier one; however, courts do not easily reach the conclusion that one statute impliedly repealed another statute.

Second, we will examine how courts construe statutes that conflict with settled and significant policies and, particularly, federalism and foreign relations. Courts look closely, for example, at federal statutes that intrude into matters historically of state concern and apply special rules to statutes that seem to conflict with state policies. This close scrutiny is a species of the general problem of conflicting statutes that arises when a federal statute appears to conflict with an important interest, such as sovereign immunity. (Preemption may also be implicated, which we later address in Chapter 14.)

A. Conflicting Statutes

1. The Last-Enacted Rule: Harmonize General and Specific Statutes

When two statutes facially conflict, the judicial approach is to attempt first to interpret the two to avoid finding a conflict by using the canons of construction or other available interpretive techniques. If a conflict is impossible to avoid, then, ordinarily, specific statutes control general ones and later-enacted statutes control earlier-enacted ones. These principles make sense: A statute that specifically addresses a topic should trump a more generalized statute, and an earlier-enacted statute should be read in light of, and be subject to, a later-enacted one. Rather than relying upon these judicial canons, some state legislatures have enacted legislative directives telling their courts to take this approach. For example, a New Mexico statute provides:

> If statutes appear to conflict, they must be construed, if possible, to give effect to each. If the conflict is irreconcilable, the later-enacted statute governs. However, an earlier-enacted specific, special or local statute prevails over a later-enacted general statute unless the context of the later-enacted statute indicates otherwise.

New Mexico Stat. § 12-2A-10 (1978). *See* Tex. Gov't Code § 311.025 (same principle).

Neither the general rule nor the statute above address what happens when there is an earlier-enacted, specific statute and a later-enacted, general statute that conflict. Which controls? Most states give effect to the earlier-enacted, specific statute unless the context of the later-enacted statute indicates otherwise.

The following case shows that further complexities can arise when more than one statute applies to the same issue before a court. In this case, a number of statutes had been enacted at various times. You might find the opinion difficult to follow because of this fact. We have actually edited the opinion significantly to make it easier for you to read. But complex cases are typical in statutory interpretation. See if you can figure out a way to keep the statutes clear in your mind as you read. We provide our strategy in the notes that follow.

Williams v. Commonwealth
829 S.W.2d 942 (Ky. Ct. App. 1992)

HOWERTON, JUDGE.

Robert Williams appeals from his conviction … for manslaughter, second degree, for which he received a five-year prison sentence.…

On March 30, 1990, Williams killed Albert Combs with a shotgun.…

Williams'.… argument is that the court erred by refusing to consider the alternative sentencing provisions of KRS 500.095. Subsection (1) of that statute, which was enacted in 1990, provides:

> *In every case in which a person* pleads guilty to or *is convicted of a crime punishable by imprisonment, the judge shall*
>
> *consider* whether the person should be sentenced to a term of *community service as an alternative to the prison term.…* (Emphasis added.)

The trial court declined to consider alternative sentencing, however, because of KRS 533.060(1), which was enacted in 1976. That statute reads:

> *When a person has been convicted of an offense* or has entered a plea of guilty to an offense classified as *a Class A, B, or C felony and the commission* of such offense *involved the use of a weapon from which a shot or projectile may be discharged that is readily capable of producing death* or other serious physical injury, *such person shall not be eligible for probation, shock probation or conditional discharge.* (Emphasis added.)

Williams argues that KRS 500.095 is more specific, and that it was enacted subsequent to KRS 533.060(1), and it is therefore controlling.

Several principles of statutory construction come in for consideration in resolving this problem. Where a conflict exists between two statutes, the later statute enacted is generally controlling. This principle standing alone would favor KRS 500.095, which was enacted in 1990. KRS 533.060(1) was enacted in 1976. We also note, however, that where there is conflict between statutes or sections thereof, it is the duty of the court to attempt to harmonize the interpretation so as to give effect to both sections or statutes, if possible. The court must not interpret a statute so as to bring about an absurd or unreasonable result. If we agreed with Williams and concluded that KRS 500.095 were controlling, we would make a nullity of KRS 533.060(1).

Another rule of statutory construction is that specific provisions of a statute take precedence over general provisions. The language in KRS 500.095(1) is very specific when it directs that in every case the judge shall consider alternatives to prison, but we also note that KRS 533.060(1) is very specific when it directs that anyone convicted of using a firearm in the commission of a Class A, B, or C felony must be sentenced to a term in prison....

[T]he General Assembly clearly intended to provide severe penalties for convicted and paroled felons who commit subsequent felonies. It is also clear that the General Assembly specifically intended to provide a prison sentence for anyone convicted of using a firearm in the commission of a serious crime.

On the other hand, it is just as clear that the legislature has recognized the need and value for giving the courts some options and alternatives to incarceration when imposing just sentences. The General Assembly's dilemma is now this Court's problem. Having to resolve the conflict, we determine that KRS 533.060(1) is controlling over KRS 500.095. If the legislature intends otherwise, it must rewrite several conflicting statutes. Using the principles we have discussed, we could have decided this case either way. However, while digging deeper to find the true legislative intent, we took note of [two] additional statutes not otherwise presented and argued in this appeal. They are ... KRS 533.010, and KRS 533.070....

KRS 533.010 was originally enacted in 1974. It authorized probation or conditional discharge in any case except where the death penalty was imposed. In 1976, KRS 533.060 toughened the law and required prison sentences in some instances [such as when a defendant uses a firearm]....

[In 1990, the legislature] added a new section (3) to KRS 533.010. It reads:

When the court deems it in the best interest of the defendant and the public, the court may order the person to work at community service related projects under the terms and conditions specified in *KRS 533.070*.... (Emphasis added.)

KRS 533.070(1) reads in pertinent part as follows: "In any case where imprisonment is an authorized penalty and *where imprisonment is not required* by the statute relating to the crime committed, a court may, as a form of conditional discharge, sentence the defendant to work at community service related projects...." (Emphasis added.) This enactment clearly indicates that the legislature was aware of some mandatory prison requirements which it did not wish to repeal.

Because KRS 533.070 was enacted in 1990, just as was KRS 500.095, we determine that the legislature intended to continue mandatory imprisonment in the specific situations set out in KRS 533.060(1). The trial court properly declined to consider alternatives to incarceration for Williams....

HUDDLESTON, JUDGE, concurring in part and dissenting in part.

I dissent from that portion of the Court's opinion which rejects Williams' argument that the trial court erred by refusing to consider the alternative sentencing provisions of KRS 500.095(1). That statute, enacted in 1990, provides that:

In *every case* in which a person pleads guilty to or is convicted of a crime punishable by imprisonment, *the judge shall consider* whether the person should be sentenced to a term of community service as an alternative to the prison term.... (Emphasis supplied.)

[In 1990,] KRS 533.010 was amended and reenacted. It now provides that

(1) *Any person* who has been convicted of a crime and who has not been sentenced to death may be sentenced to probation, probation with an alternative sentencing plan, or conditional discharge....

(2) Before imposition of a sentence of imprisonment, *the court shall consider the possibility of probation, probation with an alternative sentencing plan, or conditional discharge*.... (Emphasis supplied.)

The trial court's refusal to consider probation was based on the prohibitive language contained in KRS 533.060(1):

When a person has been convicted of an offense or has entered a plea of guilty to an offense classified as a Class A, B, or C felony and the commission of such offense involved the use of a weapon from which a shot or projectile may be discharged that is readily capable of producing death or other serious physical injury, such person shall not be eligible for probation, shock probation or conditional discharge.

The statutes clearly contain conflicting language. Where a conflict exists, the latter statute controls. The Legislature, in enacting KRS 500.095(1) and in reenacting KRS 533.010 in 1990, is presumed to have been aware of KRS 533.060(1), which has been in effect since 1976, and which was amended as recently as 1986.

As used in KRS 500.095(1) and KRS 533.010(2), the word "shall" is mandatory. And as used in KRS 533.010(1), the phrase "any person" means everyone (except, according to the statute, those sentenced to death). The trial court was thus obliged, when sentencing Williams to consider the possibility of probation, probation with an alternative sentencing plan, or conditional discharge, despite the language of the earlier statute, KRS 533.060(1), prohibiting such consideration.

I would set aside the sentencing in this case and remand ... with directions to consider the sentencing alternative set forth in KRS 533.010 and KRS 500.095(1).

Notes and Questions

(1) *Application of Specific v. General.* In this case, the majority concluded that both statutes were "specific." If the majority had held KRS § 500.095 to be "general," would that conclusion have lead to a different result? What if KRS § 533.060(1) were the general statute? Same result? If both statutes were specific, why didn't the later-enacted statute control?

(2) *Absurd Result?* The majority reasoned that it had to give effect to both statutes and "not interpret a statute so as to bring about an absurd result." The majority then concluded that if KRS § 500.095 (enacted in 1990; requiring probation in all cases) controlled, then KRS § 533.060(1) (enacted in 1976; prohibiting probation in cases involving a gun) would no longer be effective, *i.e.*, it was impliedly repealed. Was the majority correct? Or, could KRS § 553.060(1) simply be an exception to KRS § 500.095?

(3) *Bad Lawyering?* The majority noted that it was not persuaded by the parties' arguments. Rather, it found convincing the existence of the other statutes, which were not "otherwise presented and argued in this appeal." Did the parties' lawyers do a competent job?

(4) *What's "General" and What's "Specific"?* How should a judge determine whether a statute is "general" or "specific"? In another case, the Ohio Supreme Court stated: "the common meaning of 'general' is that which is 'universal, not particularized, as opposed to special.'" *State v. Conyers*, 719 N.E.2d 535, 539 (Ohio 1999) (quoting BLACK's LAW DICTIONARY 682 (6th Ed. 1990)). Putting to the side the easy cases (a statute regulating all fruit is general relative to one concerning bananas, for example), do you find this definition helpful? Would it have been helpful in the principal case?

(5) *Presumption of Legislative Awareness.* Both the majority and dissent found it reasonable to presume that a legislature is aware of existing law (including common law, statutes, and regulations) when it enacts new or amends existing statutes. Is this presumption realistic? Would an opposite presumption be disrespectful of the legislature?

(6) *In Pari Materia.* The majority did not find any canon helpful and relied on *in pari materia*. Do you find the arguments regarding KRS § 533.010 and KRS § 533.070 convincing? How did the dissent respond to them, if at all?

(7) *Lawyering Strategy.* As a lawyer, you will read many complicated cases involving multiple statutes. Once useful technique to help you keep track of the statutes is to create a timeline with each statute identified. For example, in the preceding case, your timeline might look something like this:

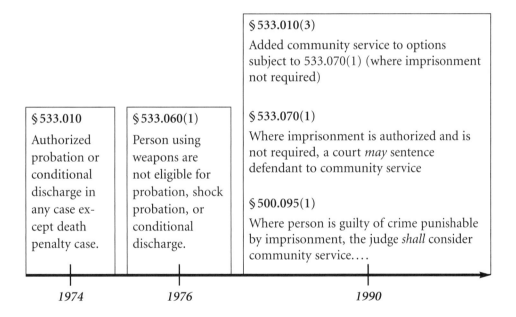

2. Implied Repeal

Courts disfavor repeal by implication because it is at odds with the presumption that the legislature knew about existing statutes and so would have expressed its intention to repeal one explicitly. Although one might question whether this presumption is realistic, given the statutorification of American law, the presumption persists. As a result, courts are very reluctant to hold that a later-enacted statute impliedly repeals an earlier-enacted one without first finding that the two statutes are in "irreconcilable conflict" or that the later-enacted statute "covers the whole subject of the earlier one and 'is clearly intended as a substitute.'" *Carcieri v. Salazar*, 129 S. Ct. 1058, 1068 (2009) (quoting *Branch v. Smith*, 538 U.S. 254, 273 (2003)).

What happens, then, when a legislature enacts a statute that conflicts with an existing one and the conflict cannot be reconciled? On the one hand, if the legislature knew of the conflict, then arguably it implicitly intended to repeal the earlier statute. On the other hand, there is a strong likelihood that the legislature never considered the issue raised by the conflict. Because of the presumption that legislatures are aware of all other statutes when they act, repeals by implication are not favored. This case explores these issues. Notice as you read it the role that the specific/general canon plays.

Morton v. Mancari
417 U.S. 535 (1974)

JUSTICE BLACKMAN delivered the opinion for a unanimous Court.

The Indian Reorganization Act of 1934 ... accords an employment preference for qualified Indians in the Bureau of Indian Affairs (BIA or Bureau). Appellees, non-Indian BIA employees, challenged this preference as contrary to the anti-discrimination provisions of the Equal Employment Opportunity Act of 1972. ...

Section 12 of the Indian Reorganization Act, provides:

> "The Secretary of the Interior is directed to establish standards of health, age, character, experience, knowledge, and ability for Indians who may be appointed, without regard to civil-service laws, to the various positions maintained, now or hereafter, by the Indian Office, in the administration of functions or services affecting any Indian tribe. Such qualified Indians shall hereafter have the preference to appointment to vacancies in any such positions."

In June 1972, pursuant to this provision, the Commissioner of Indian Affairs, with the approval of the Secretary of the Interior, issued a directive ... stating that the BIA's policy would be to grant a preference to qualified Indians ... in the situation where an Indian and a non-Indian, both already employed by the BIA, were competing for a promotion within the Bureau. The record indicates that this policy was implemented immediately. ... [Petitioners challenge this policy.]

[T]he District Court concluded that the Indian preference was implicitly repealed by § 11 of the Equal Employment Opportunity Act of 1972, proscribing discrimination in most federal employment on the basis of race.[6] ...

[T]he first issue in the present case [is]: whether the Indian preference was repealed by the Equal Employment Opportunity Act of 1972. Title VII of the Civil Rights Act of 1964, was the first major piece of federal legislation prohibiting discrimination in private employment on the basis of "race, color, religion, sex, or national origin." 42 U.S.C. s 2000e-2(a). Significantly, §§ 701(b) and 703(i) of that Act explicitly exempted from its coverage the preferential employment of Indians by Indian tribes or by industries located on or near Indian reservations. 42 U.S.C. §§ 2000e(b) and 2000e-2(i).[19] This exemption

---

6. Section 2000e-16(a) reads:
   "All personnel actions affecting employees or applicants for employment..., and in those units of the legislative and judicial branches of the Federal Government having positions in the competitive service, ... shall be made free from any discrimination based on race, color, religion, sex, or national origin."

19. Section 701(b) excludes "an Indian Tribe" from the Act's definition of "employer." Section 703(i) states: "Nothing contained in this subchapter shall apply to any business or enterprise on or near

reveals a clear congressional recognition, within the framework of Title VII, of the unique legal status of tribal and reservation-based activities....

The 1964 Act did not specifically outlaw employment discrimination by the Federal Government. Yet the mechanism for enforcing longstanding Executive Orders forbidding Government discrimination had proved ineffective for the most part. In order to remedy this, Congress, by the 1972 Act, amended the 1964 Act and proscribed discrimination in most areas of federal employment. In general, it may be said that the substantive anti-discrimination law embraced in Title VII was carried over and applied to the Federal Government.... Nowhere in the legislative history of the 1972 Act, however, is there any mention of Indian preference.

Appellees assert, and the District Court held, that since the 1972 Act proscribed racial discrimination in Government employment, the Act necessarily, albeit *sub silentio*, repealed the provision of the 1934 Act that called for the preference in the BIA of one racial group, Indians, over non-Indians....

We disagree. For several reasons we conclude that Congress did not intend to repeal the Indian preference and that the District Court erred in holding that it was repealed....

Appellees encounter head-on the "cardinal rule ... that repeals by implication are not favored." They and the District Court read the congressional silence as effectuating a repeal by implication. There is nothing in the legislative history, however, that indicates affirmatively any congressional intent to repeal the 1934 preference. Indeed, there is ample independent evidence that the legislative intent was to the contrary.

This is a prototypical case where an adjudication of repeal by implication is not appropriate. The preference is a longstanding, important component of the Government's Indian program. The anti-discrimination provision, aimed at alleviating minority discrimination in employment, obviously is designed to deal with an entirely different and, indeed, opposite problem. Any perceived conflict is thus more apparent than real.

In the absence of some affirmative showing of an intention to repeal, the only permissible justification for a repeal by implication is when the earlier and later statutes are irreconcilable. Clearly, this is not the case here. A provision aimed at furthering Indian self-government by according an employment preference within the BIA for qualified members of the governed group can readily co-exist with a general rule prohibiting employment discrimination on the basis of race. Any other conclusion can be reached only by formalistic reasoning that ignores both the history and purposes of the preference and the unique legal relationship between the Federal Government and tribal Indians.

Furthermore, the Indian preference statute is a specific provision applying to a very specific situation. The 1972 Act, on the other hand, is of general application. Where there is no clear intention otherwise, a specific statute will not be controlled or nullified by a general one, regardless of the priority of enactment.

The courts are not at liberty to pick and choose among congressional enactments, and when two statutes are capable of co-existence, it is the duty of the courts, absent a clearly expressed congressional intention to the contrary, to regard each as effective.

---

an Indian reservation with respect to any publicly announced employment practice of such business or enterprise under which a preferential treatment is given to any individual because he is an Indian living on or near a reservation."

When there are two acts upon the same subject, the rule is to give effect to both if possible.... The intention of the legislature to repeal must be clear and manifest. In light of the factors indicating no repeal, we simply cannot conclude that Congress consciously abandoned its policy of furthering Indian self-government when it passed the 1972 amendments....

Judgment ... reversed and case[] remanded.

Notes and Questions

(1) *Can a Statute that Prohibits all Hiring Decisions Based on Race Co-exist with a Statute Specifically Allowing Hiring Preferences Based on a Specific Race?* Is the Court's argument — that the two statutes are reconcilable — convincing? Or, even well reasoned? Doesn't the BIA statute become an exception to the Civil Rights Act under the Court's ruling? Did the Court simply dislike the result it should have reached?

(2) *Is the Result in* Morton *Consistent with* Williams v. Commonwealth*?* The *Morton* court says that a specific statute will always trump a general statute absent legislative intent to the contrary. Is this statement correct?

(3) *If Repeal by Implication is not Favored, How Explicit Must a Statute be Before Repeal will be Found?* Should it be sufficient if the statute has a general provision saying that "all acts or parts of acts inconsistent or in conflict herewith are repealed"? Isn't the legislature making the courts do its work by requiring courts to determine which statutes are inconsistent and, thus, repealed? Or, does this process ensure that if the legislature misses an act or two, the catchall provision will allow the court to correct the omission?

(4) *If a Later-Enacted Statute is Comprehensive, Should Courts Find Repeal More Readily?* What if only part of an existing statute is repugnant to a later-enacted one? Is only that part of the former statute repealed? Here is how the Idaho Supreme Court answered these questions:

> Since laws are presumed to be passed with deliberation, and with full knowledge of existing ones on the same subject, it is but reasonable to conclude that the legislature, in passing a statute, did not intend to interfere with or abrogate any former law relating to the same matter, unless the repugnancy between the two is irreconcilable. Except where an act covers the entire subject matter of earlier legislation, is complete in itself, and is evidently intended to supersede the prior legislation on the subject, a later act does not, by implication, repeal an earlier act unless there is such a clear, manifest, controlling, necessary, positive, unavoidable, and irreconcilable inconsistency and repugnancy, that the two acts can not, by a fair and reasonable construction, be reconciled, made to stand together, and be given effect or enforced concurrently. Moreover, a statute is only repealed by the repugnancy of matter in a subsequent statute to the extent of such repugnancy, and if any part of the earlier act can stand as not superseded or affected by the later act, it is not repealed. For one statute to repeal another by implication, they must both relate to the same object or purpose. The policy against implied repeals has peculiar and special force when conflicting provisions, which are thought to work a repeal, are contained in a special or specific act in a later or general or broad act. In such case, there is a presumption that the general or broad law was not designed to repeal the special or specific act.

Meade v. Freeman, 462 P.2d 54, 62–63 (Idaho 1969).

Tenn. Valley Auth. v. Hill

437 U.S. 153 (1978)

CHIEF JUSTICE BURGER delivered the opinion of the Court.

The questions presented in this case are (a) whether the Endangered Species Act of 1973 requires a court to enjoin the operation of a virtually completed federal dam — which had been authorized prior to 1973 — when … the Secretary of the Interior has determined that operation of the dam would eradicate an endangered species; and (b) whether continued congressional appropriations for the dam after 1973 constituted an implied repeal of the Endangered Species Act, at least as to the particular dam....

In [the] area of the Little Tennessee River the Tennessee Valley Authority, a wholly owned public corporation of the United States, began constructing the Tellico Dam and Reservoir Project in 1967, shortly after Congress appropriated initial funds for its development....

The Tellico Dam has never opened, however, despite the fact that construction has been virtually completed and the dam is essentially ready for operation. Although Congress has appropriated monies for Tellico every year since 1967, progress was delayed, and ultimately stopped, by a tangle of lawsuits and administrative proceedings....

[While litigation was pending], a discovery was made in the waters of the Little Tennessee which would profoundly affect the Tellico Project.... [A] University of Tennessee ichthyologist, Dr. David A. Etnier, found a previously unknown species of perch, the snail darter, or Percina (Imostoma) tanasi....

Until recently the finding of a new species of animal life would hardly generate a cause célèbre. This is particularly so in the case of darters, of which there are approximately 130 known species, 8 to 10 of these having been identified only in the last five years. The moving force behind the snail darter's sudden fame came some four months after its discovery, when the Congress passed the Endangered Species Act of 1973 (Act), 87 Stat. 884, 16 U.S.C. § 1531 et seq. (1976 ed.). This legislation, among other things, authorizes the Secretary of the Interior to declare species of animal life "endangered"[8] and to identify the "critical habitat" of these creatures. When a species or its habitat is so listed, the following portion of the Act — relevant here — becomes effective:

> "The Secretary [of the Interior] shall review other programs administered by him and utilize such programs in furtherance of the purposes of this chapter. All other Federal departments and agencies shall, in consultation with and with the assistance of the Secretary, utilize their authorities in furtherance of the purposes of this chapter by carrying out programs for the conservation of endangered species and threatened species listed pursuant to section 1533 of this title and *by taking such action necessary to insure that actions authorized, funded, or carried out by them do not jeopardize the continued existence of such endangered species and threatened species or result in the destruction or modification of habitat of such species* which is determined by the Secretary, after consultation as appropriate with the affected States, to be critical." 16 U.S.C. § 1536 (1976 ed.) (emphasis added)....

---

8. An "endangered species" is defined by the Act to mean "any species which is in danger of extinction throughout all or a significant portion of its range other than a species of the Class Insecta determined by the Secretary to constitute a pest whose protection under the provisions of this chapter would present an overwhelming and overriding risk to man." 16 U.S.C. § 1532(4) (1976 ed.)....

[T]he Secretary formally listed the snail darter as an endangered species on October 8, 1975 [and said]....

> "[T]he snail darter occurs only in the swifter portions of shoals over clean gravel substrate in cool, low-turbidity water. Food of the snail darter is almost exclusively snails which require a clean gravel substrate for their survival. *The proposed impoundment of water behind the proposed Tellico Dam would result in total destruction of the snail darter's habitat.*" (emphasis added).

Subsequent to this determination, the Secretary declared the area of the Little Tennessee which would be affected by the Tellico Dam to be the "critical habitat" of the snail darter. Using these determinations as a predicate, and notwithstanding the near completion of the dam, the Secretary declared that pursuant to § 7 of the Act, "all Federal agencies must take such action as is necessary to insure that actions authorized, funded, or carried out by them do not result in the destruction or modification of this critical habitat area." This notice, of course, was pointedly directed at TVA and clearly aimed at halting completion or operation of the dam....

Meanwhile, Congress had also become involved in the fate of the snail darter. Appearing before a Subcommittee of the House Committee on Appropriations in April 1975—some seven months before the snail darter was listed as endangered—TVA representatives described the discovery of the fish and the relevance of the Endangered Species Act to the Tellico Project. At that time TVA [argued] that the Act did not prohibit the completion of a project authorized, funded, and substantially constructed before the Act was passed.... Thereafter, the House Committee on Appropriations, in its June 20, 1975, Report, stated the following in the course of recommending that an additional $29 million be appropriated for Tellico:

> "The *Committee* directs that the project, for which an environmental impact statement has been completed and provided the Committee, should be completed as promptly as possible...." H.R.Rep.No.94-319, p. 76 (1975). (Emphasis added.)

Congress then approved the TVA general budget, which contained funds for continued construction of the Tellico Project....

In February 1976, ... respondents filed the case now under review, seeking to enjoin completion of the dam and impoundment of the reservoir on the ground that those actions would violate the Act by directly causing the extinction of the species Percina (Imostoma) tanasi.... Shortly thereafter the House and Senate held appropriations hearings which would include discussions of the Tellico budget....

The District Court found that closure of the dam and the consequent impoundment of the reservoir would "result in the adverse modification, if not complete destruction, of the snail darter's critical habitat," making it "highly probable" that "the continued existence of the snail darter" would be "jeopardize[d]." Despite these findings, the District Court declined to embrace the plaintiffs' position on the merits....

> "At some point in time a federal project becomes so near completion and so incapable of modification that a court of equity should not apply a statute enacted long after inception of the project to produce an unreasonable result...."

To accept the plaintiffs' position, the District Court argued, would inexorably lead to what it characterized as the absurd result of requiring "a court to halt impoundment of water behind a fully completed dam if an endangered species were discovered in the river on the day before such impoundment was scheduled to take place...."

Less than a month after the District Court decision, the Senate and House Appropriations Committees recommended the full budget request of $9 million for continued work on Tellico. In its Report accompanying the appropriations bill, the Senate Committee stated:

> "During subcommittee hearings, TVA was questioned about the relationship between the Tellico project's completion and the November 1975 listing of the snail darter (a small 3-inch fish which was discovered in 1973) as an endangered species under the Endangered Species Act. TVA informed the Committee that it was continuing its efforts to preserve the darter, while working towards the scheduled 1977 completion date. TVA repeated its view that the Endangered Species Act did not prevent the completion of the Tellico project, which has been under construction for nearly a decade. The subcommittee brought this matter, as well as the recent U. S. District Court's decision upholding TVA's decision to complete the project, to the attention of the full Committee. *The Committee does not view the Endangered Species Act as prohibiting the completion of the Tellico project at its advanced stage and directs that this project be completed as promptly as possible in the public interest.*" S.Rep.No.94-960, supra, at 96. (Emphasis added.)

On June 29, 1976, both Houses of Congress passed TVA's general budget, which included funds for Tellico....

Thereafter, [the Court of Appeals reversed the District Court Opinion].... The reviewing court ... rejected TVA's contention that the word "actions" in §7 of the Act was not intended by Congress to encompass the terminal phases of ongoing projects....

As far as the Court of Appeals was concerned, it made no difference that Congress had repeatedly approved appropriations for Tellico, referring to such legislative approval as an "advisory opinio[n]" concerning the proper application of an existing statute. In that court's view, the only relevant legislation was the Act itself, "[t]he meaning and spirit" of which was "clear on its face." ...

Following the issuance of the permanent injunction, members of TVA's Board of Directors appeared before Subcommittees of the House and Senate Appropriations Committees to testify in support of continued appropriations for Tellico. The Subcommittees were apprised of all aspects of Tellico's status, including the Court of Appeals' decision. TVA reported that the dam stood "ready for the gates to be closed and the reservoir filled," and requested funds for completion of certain ancillary parts of the project, such as public use areas, roads, and bridges....

Both Appropriations Committees subsequently recommended the full amount requested for completion of the Tellico Project. In its June 2, 1977, Report, the House Appropriations Committee stated:

> "It is *the Committee's view* that the Endangered Species Act was not intended to halt projects such as these in their advanced stage of completion, and [the Committee] strongly recommends that these projects not be stopped because of misuse of the Act." H.R.Rep.No.95-379, p. 104. (Emphasis added.)

As a solution to the problem, the House Committee advised that TVA should cooperate with the Department of the Interior to relocate the endangered species to another suitable habitat so as to permit the project to proceed as rapidly as possible. Toward this end, the Committee recommended a special appropriation of $2 million to facilitate relocation of the snail darter and other endangered species which threatened to delay or stop TVA projects. Much the same occurred on the Senate side, with its Appropriations

Committee recommending both the amount requested to complete Tellico and the special appropriation for transplantation of endangered species. Reporting to the Senate on these measures, the Appropriations Committee took a particularly strong stand on the snail darter issue:

> "This *committee has not viewed* the Endangered Species Act as preventing the completion and use of these projects which were well under way at the time the affected species were listed as endangered. If the act has such an effect which is contrary to *the Committee's understanding* of the intent of Congress in enacting the Endangered Species Act, funds should be appropriated to allow these projects to be completed and their benefits realized in the public interest, the Endangered Species Act notwithstanding." S.Rep.No.95-301, p. 99 (1977). (Emphasis added.)

TVA's budget, including funds for completion of Tellico and relocation of the snail darter, passed both Houses of Congress and was signed into law on August 7, 1977.

We granted certiorari to review the judgment of the Court of Appeals....

[The Court first concludes that the legislative history of the Endangered Species Act shows clearly that Congress did not intend there to be any exception to the act for projects near completion when the Act passed.]

Notwithstanding Congress' expression of intent in 1973, we are urged to find that the continuing appropriations for Tellico Dam constitute an implied repeal of the 1973 Act, at least insofar as it applies to the Tellico Project. In support of this view, TVA points to the statements found in various House and Senate Appropriations Committees' Reports; ... those Reports generally reflected the attitude of the Committees either that the Act did not apply to Tellico or that the dam should be completed regardless of the provisions of the Act. Since we are unwilling to assume that these latter Committee statements constituted advice to ignore the provisions of a duly enacted law, we assume that these Committees believed that the Act simply was not applicable in this situation. But even under this interpretation of the Committees' actions, we are unable to conclude that the Act has been in any respect amended or repealed.

There is nothing in the appropriations measures, as passed, which states that the Tellico Project was to be completed irrespective of the requirements of the Endangered Species Act. These appropriations, in fact, represented relatively minor components of the lump-sum amounts for the *entire* TVA budget. To find a repeal of the Endangered Species Act under these circumstances would surely do violence to the "'cardinal rule ... that repeals by implication are not favored.'" *Morton v. Mancari*, 417 U.S. 535, 549, (1974).... [T]he intention of the legislature to repeal must be clear and manifest. In practical terms, this "cardinal rule" means that "[i]n the absence of some affirmative showing of an intention to repeal, the only permissible justification for a repeal by implication is when the earlier and later statutes are irreconcilable." *Mancari, supra*, at 550.

The doctrine disfavoring repeals by implication applies with full vigor when ... the subsequent legislation is an appropriations measure. This is perhaps an understatement since it would be more accurate to say that the policy applies with even greater force when the claimed repeal rests solely on an Appropriations Act. We recognize that both substantive enactments and appropriations measures are "Acts of Congress," but the latter have the limited and specific purpose of providing funds for authorized programs. When voting on appropriations measures, legislators are entitled to operate under the assumption that the funds will be devoted to purposes which are lawful and not for any purpose forbidden. Without such an assurance, every appropriations measure would be pregnant with prospects of altering substantive legislation, repealing by implication any prior statute which might prohibit the expenditure. Not only would this lead to the absurd result of requiring Members to review exhaustively the background of every authorization before voting on an appropriation, but it would flout the very rules the Congress carefully adopted to avoid this need. House Rule XXI(2), for instance, specifically provides:

> "No appropriation shall be reported in any general appropriation bill, or be in order as an amendment thereto, for any expenditure not previously authorized by law, unless in continuation of appropriations for such public works as are already in progress. *Nor shall any provision in any such bill or amendment thereto changing existing law be in order.*" (Emphasis added.)

Thus, to sustain petitioner's position, we would be obliged to assume that Congress meant to repeal *pro tanto* §7 of the Act by means of a procedure expressly prohibited under the rules of Congress.

Perhaps mindful of the fact that it is "swimming upstream" against a strong current of well-established precedent, TVA argues for an exception to the rule against implied repealers in a circumstance where, as here, Appropriations Committees have expressly stated their "understanding" that the earlier legislation would not prohibit the proposed expenditure. We cannot accept such a proposition. Expressions of committees dealing with requests for appropriations cannot be equated with statutes enacted by Congress, particularly not in the circumstances presented by this case. First, the Appropriations Committees had no jurisdiction over the subject of endangered species, much less did they conduct the type of extensive hearings which preceded passage of the earlier Endangered Species Acts, especially the 1973 Act. We venture to suggest that the House Committee on Merchant Marine and Fisheries and the Senate Committee on Commerce would be somewhat surprised to learn that their careful work on the substantive legislation had been undone by the simple—and brief—insertion of some inconsistent language in Appropriations Committees' Reports.

Second, there is no indication that Congress as a whole was aware of TVA's position, although the Appropriations Committees apparently agreed with petitioner's views. Only recently ... we declined to presume general congressional acquiescence in a 34-year-old practice of the Securities and Exchange Commission, despite the fact that the Senate Committee *having jurisdiction over the Commission's activities* had long expressed approval of the practice. Mr. Justice Rehnquist, speaking for the Court, observed that we should be "extremely hesitant to presume general congressional awareness of the Commission's construction based only upon a few isolated statements in the thousands of pages of legislative documents." *A fortiori*, we should not assume that petitioner's views—and the Appropriations Committees' acceptance of them—were any better known, especially when the TVA is not the agency with primary responsibility for administering the Endangered Species Act.

Quite apart from the foregoing factors, we would still be unable to find that in this case "the earlier and later statutes are irreconcilable," *Mancari*, 417 U.S., at 550; here it is entirely possible "to regard each as effective." *Id.*, at 551. The starting point in this analysis must be the legislative proceedings leading to the 1977 appropriations since the earlier funding of the dam occurred prior to the listing of the snail darter as an endangered species. In all successive years, TVA confidently reported to the Appropriations Committees that efforts to transplant the snail darter appeared to be successful; this surely gave those Committees some basis for the impression that there was no direct conflict between the Tellico Project and the Endangered Species Act. Indeed, the special appropriation for 1978 of $2 million for transplantation of endangered species supports the view that the Committees saw such relocation as the means whereby collision between Tellico and the Endangered Species Act could be avoided. It should also be noted that the Reports issued by the Senate and House Appropriations Committees in 1976 came within a month of the District Court's decision in this case, which hardly could have given the Members cause for concern over the possible applicability of the Act. This leaves only the 1978 appropriations, the Reports for which issued after the Court of Appeals' decision now before us. At that point very little remained to be accomplished on the project; the Committees understandably advised TVA to cooperate with the Department of the Interior "to relocate the endangered species to another suitable habitat so as to permit the project to proceed as rapidly as possible." It is true that the Committees repeated their earlier expressed "view" that the Act did not prevent completion of the Tellico Project. Considering these statements in context, however, it is evident that they represent only the personal views of these legislators, and however explicit, they cannot serve to change the legislative intent of Congress expressed before the Act's passage....

Affirmed.

Justice Powell, with whom Justice Blackmun joins, dissenting.

The Court today holds that §7 of the Endangered Species Act requires a federal court, for the purpose of protecting an endangered species or its habitat, to enjoin permanently the operation of any federal project, whether completed or substantially completed....

In my view §7 cannot reasonably be interpreted as applying to a project that is completed or substantially completed[1] when its threat to an endangered species is discovered. Nor can I believe that Congress could have intended this Act to produce the "absurd result"—in the words of the District Court—of this case. If it were clear from the language of the Act and its legislative history that Congress intended to authorize this result, this Court would be compelled to enforce it. It is not our province to rectify policy or political judgments by the Legislative Branch, however egregiously they may disserve the public interest. But where the statutory language and legislative history, as in this case, need not be construed to reach such a result, I view it as the duty of this Court to adopt a permissible construction that accords with some modicum of common sense and the public weal....

In 1975, 1976, and 1977, Congress, with full knowledge of the Tellico Project's effect on the snail darter and the alleged violation of the Endangered Species Act, continued to appropriate money for the completion of the Project. In doing so, the Appropriations Committees expressly stated that the Act did not prohibit the Project's completion, a view that Congress presumably accepted in approving the appropriations each year. For example, in June 1976, the Senate Committee on Appropriations released a report noting the District Court decision and recommending approval of TVA's full budget request for the Tellico Project. The Committee observed further that it did "not view the Endangered Species Act as prohibiting the completion of the Tellico project at its advanced stage," and it directed "that this project be completed as promptly as possible in the public interest." The appropriations bill was passed by Congress and approved by the President....

In June 1977 [after the Court of Appeals reversed the District Court], and after being informed of the decision of the Court of Appeals, the Appropriations Committees in both

---

1. Attorney General [Griffin] Bell advised us at oral argument that the dam had been completed, that all that remains is to "[c]lose the gate," and to complete the construction of "some roads and bridges." The "dam itself is finished. All the landscaping has been done.... [I]t is completed."

Houses of Congress again recommended approval of TVA's full budget request for the Tellico Project. Both Committees again stated unequivocally that the Endangered Species Act was not intended to halt projects at an advanced stage of completion:

> "[The Senate] Committee has not viewed the Endangered Species Act as preventing the completion and use of these projects which were well under way at the time the affected species were listed as endangered. If the act has such an effect, which is contrary to the Committee's understanding of the intent of Congress in enacting the Endangered Species Act, funds should be appropriated to allow these projects to be completed and their benefits realized in the public interest, the Endangered Species Act notwithstanding."

> "It is the [House] Committee's view that the Endangered Species Act was not intended to halt projects such as these in their advanced stage of completion, and [the Committee] strongly recommends that these projects not be stopped because of misuse of the Act."

Once again, the appropriations bill was passed by both Houses and signed into law.

II

Today the Court ... adopts a reading of § 7 of the Act that gives it a retroactive effect and disregards 12 years of consistently expressed congressional intent to complete the Tellico Project. With all due respect, I view this result as an extreme example of a literalist construction, not required by the language of the Act and adopted without regard to its manifest purpose. Moreover, it ignores established canons of statutory construction.

A

The starting point in statutory construction is, of course, the language of § 7 itself. I agree that it can be viewed as a textbook example of fuzzy language, which can be read according to the "eye of the beholder."[11] The critical words direct all federal agencies to take "such action [as may be] necessary to insure that actions authorized, funded, or carried out by them do not jeopardize the continued existence of ... endangered species ... or result in the destruction or modification of [a critical] habitat of such species...." Respondents—as did the Sixth Circuit—read these words as sweepingly as possible to include all "actions" that any federal agency ever may take with respect to any federal project, whether completed or not.

The Court today embraces this sweeping construction. Under the Court's reasoning, the Act covers every existing federal installation, including great hydroelectric projects and reservoirs, every river and harbor project, and every national defense installation— however essential to the Nation's economic health and safety. The "actions" that an agency would be prohibited from "carrying out" would include the continued operation of such projects or any change necessary to preserve their continued usefulness. The only precondition, according to respondents, to thus destroying the usefulness of even the most important federal project in our country would be a finding by the Secretary of the Interior that a continuation of the project would threaten the survival or critical habitat of a newly discovered species of water spider or amoeba.

---

11. The purpose of this Act is admirable. Protection of endangered species long has been neglected. This unfortunate litigation—wasteful for taxpayers and likely in the end to be counterproductive in terms of respondents' purpose—may have been invited by careless draftsmanship of otherwise meritorious legislation.

"[F]requently words of general meaning are used in a statute, words broad enough to include an act in question, and yet a consideration of the whole legislation, or of the circumstances surrounding its enactment, or of the absurd results which follow from giving such broad meaning to the words, makes it unreasonable to believe that the legislator intended to include the particular act." *Church of the Holy Trinity v. United States*, 143 U.S. 457, 459 (1892). The result that will follow in this case by virtue of the Court's reading of §7 makes it unreasonable to believe that Congress intended that reading. Moreover, §7 may be construed in a way that avoids an "absurd result" without doing violence to its language.

The critical word in §7 is "actions" and its meaning is far from "plain." It is part of the phrase: "actions authorized, funded or carried out." In terms of planning and executing various activities, it seems evident that the "actions" referred to are not all actions that an agency can ever take, but rather actions that the agency is deciding whether to authorize, to fund, or to carry out. In short, these words reasonably may be read as applying only to prospective actions, i. e., actions with respect to which the agency has reasonable decisionmaking alternatives still available, actions not yet carried out. At the time respondents brought this lawsuit, the Tellico Project was 80% complete at a cost of more than $78 million. The Court concedes that as of this time and for the purpose of deciding this case, the Tellico Dam Project is "completed" or "virtually completed and the dam is essentially ready for operation." Thus, under a prospective reading of §7, the action already had been "carried out" in terms of any remaining reasonable decisionmaking power....

As indicated above, this view of legislative intent at the time of enactment is abundantly confirmed by the subsequent congressional actions and expressions. We have held, properly, that post-enactment statements by individual Members of Congress as to the meaning of a statute are entitled to little or no weight. The Court also has recognized that subsequent Appropriations Acts themselves are not necessarily entitled to significant weight in determining whether a prior statute has been superseded. But these precedents are inapposite. There was no effort here to "bootstrap" a post-enactment view of prior legislation by isolated statements of individual Congressmen. Nor is this a case where Congress, without explanation or comment upon the statute in question, merely has voted apparently inconsistent financial support in subsequent Appropriations Acts. Testimony on this precise issue was presented before congressional committees, and the Committee Reports for three consecutive years addressed the problem and affirmed their understanding of the original congressional intent. We cannot assume — as the Court suggests — that Congress, when it continued each year to approve the recommended appropriations, was unaware of the contents of the supporting Committee Reports. All this amounts to strong corroborative evidence that the interpretation of §7 as not applying to completed or substantially completed projects reflects the initial legislative intent.

I have little doubt that Congress will amend the Endangered Species Act to prevent the grave consequences made possible by today's decision. Few, if any, Members of that body will wish to defend an interpretation of the Act that requires the waste of at least $53 million, and denies the people of the Tennessee Valley area the benefits of the reservoir that Congress intended to confer....

Notes and Questions

(1) *Repeal by Implication.* Does anyone really suggest that the Endangered Species Act was repealed by implication? What, precisely, was the issue in this case? Are you convinced that the Endangered Species Act and the appropriation bills were reconcilable, as the majority concluded?

(2) *The Dissent's View*. Why was the dissent willing to ignore the longstanding rule that repeal by implication is disfavored? Did the dissent avoid the rule against implied repeals or conclude that the requirements for finding implied repeal were present?

(3) *Repeal by Implication and Appropriations Bills*. The majority said that repeal by implication, which is generally disfavored, is strongly disfavored when it comes to appropriations bills. Why should a court treat appropriation bills differently than other bills? Why did the dissent ignore House Rule XXI(2) stating, "Nor shall any provision in [any appropriation bill] changing existing law be in order"? Does it make sense to rely on a House rule, but ignore what the House members said about the statute? Or, is that not what happened here?

(4) *Absurdity*. According to the dissent, the majority's interpretation was absurd. Why? Did the dissent find the Endangered Species Act to be absurd generally, just in this case, or in all cases in which a project was substantially completed?

(5) *Legislative Response*. The dissent expected Congress to act immediately to "correct" the majority's erroneous decision. The dissent was not disappointed. After a protracted fight, in 1980 Congress added a rider to an appropriations bill that specifically excepted the Tellico Dam. Energy and Water Appropriation Act of 1980, Pub. L. No. 96-69, tit. IV, 93 Stat. 449 (1979) (stating that the Tennessee Valley Authority Corporation was "authorized and directed to complete construction, operate and maintain the Tellico Dam and Reservoir project ... notwithstanding the provisions of" the Endangered Species Act.) President Jimmy Carter signed the bill into law. Why did the 1980 appropriations rider partially repeal the Endangered Species Act, yet the earlier appropriations bills did not?

(6) *Implied Repeal as an Uncertain Doctrine*. Some have argued that the approach of the courts toward implied repeal allows courts to "exercise interpretive freedom while signaling interpretive restraint." Karen Petroski, *Retheorizing the Presumption Against Implied Repeals*, 92 Cal. L. Rev. 487, 495 (2004). Do you agree that the process of deciding whether two statutes conflicts is one that "necessarily involve[s] considerable interpretive and rhetorical creativity" and so allows for greater room for "activist" interpretations? *Id.* at 494.

Problem 13-1

You represent Mark Stelter. You previously represented Mark in his 2002 divorce from Tracy. Tracy and Mark had one child, Kim (a boy), prior to their divorce. Tracy was awarded sole custody, but every other weekend Mark had custody, and Kim would reside with Mark. They have "shared parental responsibility" in terms of Section 71.21, discussed below.

Mark has returned to you because Kim recently vandalized his school. The school has filed suit, naming both Tracy and Mark as defendants pursuant to Section 471.24 of the Mercer Statutes. Mark has asked you whether or not he is likely to be held liable under this statute.

Your research has revealed the following.

In 1956, Mercer adopted Mercer Rev. Stat. §471.24, which imposed liability on parents for certain damage caused by minors. The preamble to that statute explained that its purpose was to "aid in reducing juvenile delinquency by imposing liability upon parents who control minors." Further, a findings clause stated that "The legislature finds that it is in the public interest of this State that each and every parent of this State shall be re-

sponsible for the damages caused by minors that the parent controls." In full, that statute—
which has existed largely unchanged—provides:

> Mercer Rev. Stat. §471.24. Civil action against parents; willful destruction or
> theft of property by minor
>
> (1) Any municipal corporation, county, school district, or department of
> Mercer; any person, partnership, corporation, or association; or any religious
> organization, whether incorporated or unincorporated, shall be entitled to
> recover damages in an appropriate action at law, in a court of competent ju-
> risdiction, from the parents of any minor under the age of 18 years, living
> with the parents, who maliciously or willfully destroys or steals property, real,
> personal, or mixed, belonging to such municipal corporation, county, school
> district, department of the state, person, partnership, corporation, associa-
> tion, or religious organization.
>
> (2) The recovery shall be limited to the actual damages in addition to taxable
> court costs.

Later, in 1997, the Mercer legislature adopted a comprehensive statute to address child
custody. The provisions of that statute pertinent here follow:

> Mercer Rev. Stat. §71.21. Custody; financial responsibility; best interests of child
>
> (a) As used in this Section the following definitions apply:
>
> (1) "Custodial parent" or "primary residential parent" means the parent with
> whom the child maintains his or her primary residence.
>
> (2) "Shared parental responsibility" means a court-ordered relationship in
> which both parents retain full parental rights and responsibilities with respect
> to their child and in which both parents confer with each other so that major
> decisions affecting the welfare of the child will be determined jointly.
>
> (3) "Sole parental responsibility" means a court-ordered relationship in which
> one parent makes decisions regarding the minor child.
>
> (b) A court shall award custody in the best interest of the child. In awarding cus-
> tody of any minor child, and whether or not custody is awarded jointly or pri-
> marily to one parent, the court shall order that the parental responsibility for a
> minor child be shared by both parents unless the court finds that shared parental
> responsibility would be detrimental to the child. The court shall award the non-
> custodial parent reasonable visitation rights consistent with the best interest of
> the child.

B. The Clear Statement Rule

The "clear statement rule" is a canon of interpretation that applies only when a federal
statute can be read to conflict with certain important principles, such as sovereign immunity
or the balance of power between federal and state government. *See, e.g., Gregory v. Ashcroft*,
501 U.S. 452, 461 (1991) (federal interference with state law is at "the heart of representative government"); *Atascadero State Hosp. v. Scanlon*, 473 U.S. 234, 243, (1985) ("Congress must express its intention to abrogate the Eleventh Amendment [protection of
sovereign immunity] in unmistakable language in the statute itself.") In general, the clear

statement rule provides that a federal statute will be construed to interfere with or affect those principles only when the language of the statute unmistakably states that intent.

This section explores several aspects of the clear statement rule, including how "clear" the statement has to be. This section further catalogues the principal areas where courts have traditionally applied clear statement rules.

Oregon v. Ashcroft
368 F.3d 1118 (9th Cir. 2004)
aff'd Gonzales v. Oregon, 546 U.S. 243 (2006)

TALLMAN, CIRCUIT JUDGE.

A doctor, a pharmacist, several terminally ill patients, and the State of Oregon challenge an interpretive rule issued by Attorney General John Ashcroft which declares that physician assisted suicide violates the Controlled Substances Act of 1970 ("CSA"), 21 U.S.C. §§ 801–904. This so-called "Ashcroft Directive," published at 66 Fed.Reg. 56,607, criminalizes conduct specifically authorized by Oregon's Death With Dignity Act, Or.Rev.Stat. § 127.800-127.897. We hold that the Ashcroft Directive is unlawful and unenforceable....

The Ashcroft Directive purports to interpret and implement the CSA.... The stated purpose of the CSA is "to provide increased research into, and prevention of, drug abuse and drug dependence ... and to strengthen existing law enforcement authority in the field of drug abuse."

Under the CSA, it is unlawful to prescribe or dispense controlled substances without a federal registration. The CSA originally provided automatic federal registration for state-licensed health-care practitioners. The Attorney General could revoke a practitioner's federal registration only if the practitioner falsified his or her registration application, was convicted of a felony related to a controlled substance, or had his or her state license suspended or revoked.

In 1971, pursuant to his authority to issue rules regulating controlled substances under the CSA, then Attorney General John Mitchell promulgated the following regulation:

> A prescription for a controlled substance to be effective must be issued for a legitimate medical purpose by an individual practitioner acting in the usual course of his professional practice.... An order purporting to be a prescription issued not in the usual course of professional treatment ... is not a prescription within the meaning and intent of ... the Act and the person knowingly filling such a purported prescription, as well as the person issuing it, shall be subject to the penalties provided for violations of the provisions of law relating to controlled substances.

21 C.F.R. § 1306.04. This regulation exposed properly licensed and registered physicians to federal prosecution for distributing prescription drugs outside "the usual course of professional practice."

In 1984, Congress amended the CSA to give broader authority to the Attorney General. The Attorney General is now authorized to revoke a physician's prescription privileges upon his determination that the physician has "committed such acts as would render his registration ... inconsistent with the public interest[.]" 21 U.S.C. § 824(a)(4). When determining which acts are inconsistent with the public interest, the Attorney General must consider the following factors:

(1) The recommendation of the appropriate State licensing board or professional disciplinary authority;

(2) The applicant's expertise in dispensing ... controlled substances;

(3) The applicant's conviction record under Federal or State laws relating to the manufacture, distribution, or dispensing of controlled substances;

(4) Compliance with applicable State, Federal, or local laws relating to controlled substances;

(5) Such other conduct which may threaten the public health and safety.

21 U.S.C. § 823(f). Although this provision gives the Attorney General new discretion over the registration of health care practitioners, Congress explained that "the amendment would continue to give deference to the opinions of State licensing authorities, since their recommendations are the first of the factors to be considered[.]" S.Rep. No. 98-225, at 267 (1984).

Against this backdrop of federal regulation, in 1994, the State of Oregon enacted by ballot measure the country's first law authorizing physician assisted suicide. *See* Or.Rev.Stat. § 127.800-897. Oregon's Death With Dignity Act authorizes physicians to prescribe lethal doses of controlled substances to terminally ill Oregon residents according to procedures designed to protect vulnerable patients and ensure that their decisions are reasoned and voluntary. Oregon voters reaffirmed their support for the Death With Dignity Act on November 4, 1997, by defeating a ballot measure that sought to repeal the law.

Soon thereafter, several members of Congress, including then Senator John Ashcroft, urged then-Attorney General Janet Reno to declare that physician assisted suicide violated the CSA. She declined to do so. In a letter dated January 5, 1998, Attorney General Reno explained that the CSA was not "intended to displace the states as the primary regulators of the medical profession, or to override a state's determination as to what constitutes legitimate medical practice." She concluded that "the CSA does not authorize [the Drug Enforcement Administration ("DEA")] to prosecute, or to revoke DEA registration of, a physician who has assisted in a suicide in compliance with Oregon law."

With a change of administrations came a change of perspectives. On November 9, 2001, newly appointed Attorney General John Ashcroft reversed the position of his predecessor and issued the Directive at issue here. The Ashcroft Directive proclaims that physician assisted suicide serves no "legitimate medical purpose" under 21 C.F.R. § 1306.04 and that specific conduct authorized by Oregon's Death With Dignity Act "may 'render [a practitioner's] registration ... inconsistent with the public interest' and therefore subject to possible suspension or revocation." The Directive specifically targets health care practitioners in Oregon and instructs the DEA to enforce this determination "regardless of whether state law authorizes or permits such conduct by practitioners."

To be perfectly clear, we take no position on the merits or morality of physician assisted suicide. We express no opinion on whether the practice is inconsistent with the public interest or constitutes illegitimate medical care. This case is simply about who gets to decide. All parties agree that the question before us is whether Congress authorized the Attorney General to determine that physician assisted suicide violates the CSA. We hold that the Attorney General lacked Congress' requisite authorization. The Ashcroft Directive violates the "clear statement" rule, contradicts the plain language of the CSA, and contravenes the express intent of Congress.

We begin with instructions from the Supreme Court that the "earnest and profound debate about the morality, legality, and practicality of physician-assisted suicide" belongs among state lawmakers. . . .

The principle that state governments bear the primary responsibility for evaluating physician assisted suicide follows from our concept of federalism, which requires that state lawmakers, not the federal government, are the primary regulators of professional [medical] conduct. The Supreme Court has made the constitutional principle clear: "Obviously, direct control of medical practice in the states is beyond the power of the federal government." *Linder v. United States*, 268 U.S. 5, 18 (1925). The Attorney General "may not . . . regulate [the doctor-patient] relationship to advance federal policy." *Conant*, 309 F.3d at 647 (Kozinski, J., concurring).[6]

By criminalizing medical practices specifically authorized under Oregon law, the Ashcroft Directive interferes with Oregon's authority to regulate medical care within its borders and therefore alters the usual constitutional balance between the States and the Federal Government. Under these circumstances, it is incumbent on the federal courts to be certain of Congress' intent before finding that federal authority supersedes state law.

Unless Congress' authorization is "unmistakably clear," the Attorney General may not exercise control over an area of law traditionally reserved for state authority, such as regulation of medical care. This concern is heightened where an administrative interpretation alters the federal-state framework by permitting federal encroachment upon a traditional state power. Unless Congress conveys its purpose clearly, it will not be deemed to have significantly changed the federal-state balance. In divining congressional intent, it is a "cardinal principle" of statutory interpretation that "where an otherwise acceptable construction of a statute would raise serious constitutional problems, [federal courts shall] construe the statute to avoid such problems unless such construction is plainly contrary to the intent of Congress.

The Ashcroft Directive is invalid because Congress has provided no indication—much less an "unmistakably clear" indication—that it intended to authorize the Attorney General to regulate the practice of physician assisted suicide. By attempting to regulate physician assisted suicide, the Ashcroft Directive invokes the outer limits of Congress' power by encroaching on state authority to regulate medical practice. Because Congress has not clearly authorized such an intrusion, the Ashcroft Directive violates the clear statement rule. We need not, and therefore do not, decide whether the Ashcroft Directive actually exceeds Commerce Clause boundaries, but only that it invokes the outer limits of Congress' power without explicit authority from Congress. Absent an unmistakably clear expression of intent to alter the usual constitutional balance between the States and the Federal Government, we will interpret a statute to preserve rather than destroy the States' substantial sovereign powers. . . .

The injunction previously entered by the district court is ordered continued in full force and effect as the injunction of this court.

---

6. As noted in *Younger v. Harris*, 401 U.S. 37, 44–45 (1971):

The concept [of federalism] does not mean blind deference to "States' Rights" any more than it means centralization of control over every important issue in our National Government and its courts. The Framers rejected both these courses. What the concept does represent is a system in which there is sensitivity to the legitimate interests of both State and National Governments, and in which the National Government, anxious though it may be to vindicate and protect federal rights and federal interests, always endeavors to do so in ways that will not unduly interfere with the legitimate activities of the States.

WALLACE, SENIOR CIRCUIT JUDGE, dissenting.

... The majority asserts that the Attorney General lacks authority to decide whether physician-assisted suicide is consistent with "the public interest" and a "legitimate medical practice" under the Controlled Substances Act and its implementing regulations because Congress intended to preserve the states' traditional authority to make these determinations. This argument ignores the Controlled Substances Act's text and controlling Supreme Court decisions....

[T]he majority argues that the Ashcroft Directive exceeds the Attorney General's statutory authority because Congress has not clearly authorized the Attorney General to upset the delicate balance between federal regulation of controlled substances and state control of medical practices....

[The] clear statement rule is based upon understandable and significant federalism concerns, the importance of which I do not doubt. The question we must ask ourselves, however, is whether this canon of statutory interpretation applies to the case before us.

Not every colorable constitutional question triggers [the] clear statement rule. Our past decisions dictate that we must scrutinize constitutional objections to [the] agency interpretation skeptically. Only if the agency's proffered interpretation raises *serious* constitutional concerns may we refuse to defer.... As such, the proper approach here is to proceed directly to the merits of Petitioners' constitutional challenge, deciding whether the agency interpretation raises the sort of grave and doubtful constitutional questions that could lead us to invalidate the regulations in order to save the statute from unconstitutionality. Only if the Attorney General's proposed interpretation would likely render the statute unconstitutional do we apply [the] clear statement canon. Applying these principles, we should not require a clear statement in this case because controlling precedent compels the conclusion that the Attorney General's interpretation did not invoke "the outer limits" of Congress's Commerce Clause power....

The majority cannot have it otherwise. Their argument that "*direct* control of medical practice in the states is beyond the power of the federal government" misses the point. Unless and until the Supreme Court directs us differently, our opinions and other binding precedent compel the conclusion that Congress acts comfortably within its Commerce Clause power when it regulates the prescription and dispensation of controlled substances. General Ashcroft's interpretation of 21 C.F.R. § 1306.04(a) does not, therefore, invoke the outer limits of Congress' power, the clear statement rule does not apply, and we must evaluate the Ashcroft Directive according to ordinary standards of deference....

Therefore, I dissent.

Notes and Questions

(1) *The Purpose of the Clear Statement Rule.* The dissent narrowly defined what triggers application of the clear statement rule by suggesting that so long as the subject is within the scope of the Commerce Clause, the clear statement rule does not apply. In other words, the Commerce Clause established the dividing line between state and federal powers. Do you believe that view is too narrow?

(2) *Constitutional Question Avoidance Doctrine.* In a later chapter, you will learn that statutes will be construed, if possible, to avoid questions about their constitutionality. Here, the majority used this canon to support its argument that the clear statement rule

applied (*i.e.*, applying the clear statement rule avoided the necessity of reaching the constitutional question). The dissent reached the constitutional question first, found no concern, and then decided that the clear statement rule had no application. Has the dissent merged these two related—but different—doctrines?

(3) *Other Illustrations.* Throughout this text, there are other examples of the clear statement rule: For example, there is one in Chapter 14 in *Burch v. Secretary of Health & Human Services*, 2001 WL 180129 (Fed. Cl. 2001) (holding that in the absence of a clear statement that Congress meant to abdicate the general presumption of sovereign immunity, a remedial statute would be narrowly construed); another is in Chapter 7 in *Texas Natural Resource & Conservation Commission v. White*, 13 S.W.3d 819 (Tex. Ct. App. 2000) (refusing to find that sovereign immunity had been waived despite a conflicting statutory directive). Courts have applied the clear statement rule in a variety of other contexts as well: federal court jurisdiction (*see Bellsouth Telecomm., Inc. v. MCImetro Access Transmission Servs., Inc.*, 317 F.3d 1270 (11th Cir. 2003) (en banc)); foreign sovereign immunity (*see Spector v. Norwegian Cruise Line Ltd.*, 545 U.S. 119 (2005)); and, as in *Ashcroft*, matters historically of state concern (*see John v. United States*, 247 F.3d 1032 (9th Cir. 2001) (en banc) (addressing federal statute that purported to regulate fishing in state waterways)). Arguably, the presumption against implied repeals is a form of the clear statement rule. Can you explain why?

(4) *Where is the Line?* The designation of a statute as being subject to the clear statement rule means that the statute will be narrowly construed. For this reason, by designating a statute as subject to this rule, courts may further their own public policy choices. For example, by declaring the regulation of physicians to be historically a matter of state concern, a court can then interpret a regulation or statute narrowly to avoid "impinging" on state's rights and invalidating the statute. Is there a way to cabin the doctrine to prevent political decision-making? Did the dissent present the best way? Does the subjective nature of the inquiry make the clear statement rule questionable as an interpretive canon?

(5) *Affirmed on Appeal.* Justice Kennedy, writing for Justices Stevens, O'Connor, Souter, Ginsberg, and Breyer, affirmed, holding that the Controlled Substances Act did not delegate the power to "cede medical judgements to an Executive official who lacks medical expertise." *Id.* at 266. The clear statement rationale was dismissed: "It is unnecessary even to consider the application of clear statement requirements. . . ." *Id.* at 274.

Problem 13-2

Many states have "felon disenfranchisement" statutes. These statutes are common, and many have been in force since the mid- to early-1800s. Under these state statutes, a person who has been convicted of a felony generally loses the right to vote until that person has been pardoned, has served the maximum term in prison, or has been discharged from parole. *See, e.g.*, N.Y. ELECTION LAW § 5-106.

Congress adopted the Voting Rights Act ("VRA") in 1965. At the time it was adopted, Section 2 of the VRA, 42 U.S.C. § 1973, provided: "No voting qualification or prerequisite to voting, or standard, practice, or procedure shall be imposed or applied by any State or political subdivision to deny or abridge the right of any citizen of the United States to vote on account of race or color."

In 1980, the Supreme Court held that Section 2 of the VRA was violated only if a racially neutral state action was motivated by a discriminatory purpose; a statute, in other words, that had a racial impact, but which was not adopted for a discriminatory purpose, did not violate the VRA. *See City of Mobile v. Bolden*, 446 U.S. 55 (1980).

Congress, in 1982, responded to the Court's opinion by amending the VRA. Two provisions are pertinent here.

- First, Section 2(a) was amended to read: "No voting qualification or prerequisite to voting, or standard, practice or procedure shall be imposed or applied by any State or political subdivision in a manner which results in a denial or abridgment of the right of any citizen of the United States to vote on account of race or color."

- Second, new subsection (b) was added, which provides: "A violation of subsection (a) ... is established if, based on the totality of the circumstances, it is shown that ... members [of protected minority groups] have less opportunity than other members of the electorate to participate in the political process and to elect representatives of their choice."

Felons have filed suit, alleging that Mercer's felon disenfranchisement statute, which is identical to New York's, violates Section 2 of the VRA, as amended. They have alleged that racial discrimination in the criminal justice system causes members of protected minority groups to lose the right to vote on account of their race or color. They also allege that the statute was adopted with discriminatory intent and that it results in denial or abridgment of their right to vote on account of their race.

You are a clerk for a judge who must decide whether the clear statement rule applies to the VRA: absent a clear statement that Congress intended to upset the long-standing state practice of felon disenfranchisement, should the VRA be interpreted not to apply to felon disenfranchise statutes, even if the state statutes are adopted with a discriminatory intent or if they have a discriminatory impact. If the clear statement rule does apply, does the VRA make a clear statement? In formulating your answers, consider these excerpts from opinions from other circuits that have addressed this issue.

Problem Materials

Farrakhan v. Washington
338 F.3d 1009 (9th Cir. 2003)

PAEZ, CIRCUIT JUDGE (for a unanimous panel):

... As a preliminary matter, we agree with the district court that Plaintiffs' claim of vote denial is cognizable under Section 2 of the VRA. Felon disenfranchisement is a voting qualification, and Section 2 is clear that any voting qualification that denies citizens the right to vote in a discriminatory manner violates the VRA. 42 U.S.C. § 1973. Indeed, the Supreme Court has made clear that states cannot use felon disenfranchisement as a tool to discriminate on the basis of race, and Congress specifically amended the VRA to ensure that, "in the context of all the circumstances in the jurisdiction in question," any disparate racial impact of facially neutral voting requirements did not result from racial discrimination, Senate Report at 27.

Permitting a citizen, even a convicted felon, to challenge felon disenfranchisement laws that result in either the denial of the right to vote or vote dilution on account of race animates the right that every citizen has of protection against racially discriminatory voting practices. Although states may deprive felons of the right to vote without violating the Fourteenth Amendment, when felon disenfranchisement results in denial of the right to vote or vote dilution on account of race or color, Section 2 affords disenfranchised felons the means to seek redress....

Johnson v. Bush

405 F.3d 1214 (11th Cir. 2005) (en banc)

KRAVITCH, CIRCUIT JUDGE (for the majority).

[W]e believe that the plaintiffs' interpretation of the VRA raises grave constitutional concerns.[35] For the plaintiffs' interpretation to be correct, we must look for a clear statement from Congress that it intended such a constitutionally-questionable result. Instead of a clear statement from Congress indicating that the plaintiffs' interpretation is correct, the legislative history indicates just the opposite — that Congress never intended the Voting Rights Act to reach felon disenfranchisement provisions....

Congress most recently amended the Voting Rights Act in 1982 in response to the Supreme Court's decision in *City of Mobile v. Bolden*, 446 U.S. 55 (1980), in an attempt to clarify the standard for finding Section 2 violations. In revising the statute, Congress intended to depart from the intent-based standard of the Supreme Court's Equal Protection jurisprudence and establish an effects-based standard.... After the 1982 amendment, a state practice could survive Equal Protection Clause scrutiny but fail Section 2 Voting Rights Act scrutiny.

Neither the plain text nor the legislative history of the 1982 amendment declares Congress's intent to extend the Voting Rights Act to felon disenfranchisement provisions. The Senate Report, which details many discriminatory techniques used by certain jurisdictions, made no mention of felon disenfranchisement provisions.[39] Although it is conceivable that certain legislators may have wanted the Voting Rights Act to encompass felon disenfranchisement provisions, we should not assume that Congress intended to produce a statute contrary to the plain text of the Fourteenth Amendment without a clear statement. As the Second Circuit noted, "considering the prevalence of felon disenfranchisement [provisions] in every

---

35. We also note that application of the VRA to Florida's felon disenfranchisement provision could raise federalism concerns in that it significantly alters the constitutionally mandated balance of power between the States and the Federal Government. *See Gregory v. Ashcroft*, 501 U.S. 452, 457–61 (1991). Whenever Congress intrudes upon "a decision of the most fundamental sort for a [State], ...'it is incumbent upon the federal courts to be certain of Congress' intent before finding that federal law overrides' this balance." *Gregory v. Ashcroft*, 501 U.S. at 461. Congress's intent must be "unmistakably clear in the language of the statute." *Id.* at 460–61. In *Gregory*, Missouri state court judges challenged a provision of the Missouri Constitution that required certain judges to retire at the age of seventy as being in violation of the Age Discrimination in Employment Act of 1967 (ADEA). After concluding that "the authority of the people of the States to determine the qualifications of their most important government officials ... lies at the heart of representative government," the Court found that state judges were not covered by the ADEA because Congress did not make their inclusion unmistakably clear. *Id.* at 467. As in *Gregory*, the balance of power between the States and the Federal Government is at issue in this case. If defining the qualifications of important government officials lies at the heart of representative government, then surely defining who decides what those qualifications will be is equally important. Although the States' power in this regard must be exercised in accordance with the Fourteenth and Fifteenth Amendments, § 2 of the Fourteenth amendment establishes an explicit constitutional balance between the States and the Federal Government by giving the States authority to continue the prevalent practice of disenfranchising felons. If Congress wishes to alter the balance of power in this area, its intention must be unmistakably clear.

39. The one-sided legislative history is buttressed by subsequent Congressional acts. Since 1982, Congress has enacted laws making it easier for states to disenfranchise felons. For instance, in 1993, Congress enacted the National Voter Registration Act (NVRA), Pub. L. No. 103-31, 107 Stat. 77 (1993), which authorizes states to purge felons from voter rolls. The Act also instructs federal prosecutors to give written notice to state election officials of persons convicted of felonies. In this same Act, Congress sought to eliminate certain practices that dampen minority participation in the electoral process. Although not dispositive, this suggests that Congress did not intend to sweep felon disenfranchisement laws within the scope of the VRA.

region of the country since the Founding, it seems unfathomable that Congress would silently amend the Voting Rights Act in a way that would affect them." There is simply no discussion of felon disenfranchisement in the legislative history surrounding the 1982 amendments.

Thus, we believe that applying Section 2 of the Voting Rights Act to felon disenfranchisement provisions raises grave constitutional concerns.[40] Chiefly, the plaintiffs' interpretation calls for a reading of the statute which would prohibit a practice that the Fourteenth Amendment permits Florida to maintain. As a matter of statutory construction, we should avoid such an interpretation. The case for rejecting the plaintiffs' reading of the statute is particularly strong here, where Congress has expressed its intent to exclude felon disenfranchisement provisions from Voting Rights Act scrutiny. Accordingly, we affirm the district court's grant of summary judgment to the defendants on the Voting Rights Act claim.

BARKETT, CIRCUIT JUDGE, dissenting.

... Nor does the "plain statement" rule of *Gregory v. Ashcroft* prevent plaintiffs from proceeding under the VRA. The canon of construction at issue in *Gregory* holds that where Congress intends to alter the "usual constitutional balance between the states and federal government," it must make its intent to do so unmistakably clear in the statute.... [H]owever, the Fourteenth and Fifteenth Amendments altered the constitutional balance between the two sovereigns—not the Voting Rights Act, which merely enforces the guarantees of those amendments.

Moreover, the Supreme Court has explicitly held that the *Gregory* "plain statement" canon is wholly inapplicable where the statutory language unambiguously applies to a particular state function. *Pa. Dep't of Corr. v. Yeskey*, 524 U.S. 206, 209 (1998). In *Yeskey*, the petitioners contended that under *Gregory*, state prisons were not subject to the Americans with Disabilities Act based on the lack of a "plain statement" indicating congressional intent to alter the constitutional balance by regulating state prisons. The Court limited *Gregory's* plain statement rule, holding it inapplicable because the prison fell squarely within statutory language providing for coverage of "public entities." Similarly, Congress need not have included a "plain statement" on the VRA's application to criminal disenfranchisement statutes, as those statutes fall squarely within the VRA's textual prohibition on any "qualification or prerequisite to voting ... which results in a denial or abridgement of the right of any citizen of the United States to vote on account of race or color." 42 U.S.C. § 1973(a)....

I would remand for determination by the trier of fact whether, under the totality of the circumstances, plaintiffs' votes were denied "on account of race" in violation of the VRA.

Hayden v. Pataki

449 F.3d 305 (2d Cir. 2006) (en banc)

CARBRANES, CIRCUIT JUDGE (for the majority):

Our decision not to apply § 1973 to felon disenfranchisement provisions is confirmed and supported by the operation of the clear statement rule (also known as the "plain statement rule"), a canon of interpretation which requires Congress to make its intent "'unmistakably clear'" when enacting statutes that would alter the usual constitutional bal-

---

40. In addition to the constitutional concerns, there are prudential concerns as well. If we were to accept the plaintiffs' interpretation of the statute, states might lose their ability to exclude felons currently in prison from the franchise.

ance between the Federal Government and the States. *Gregory v. Ashcroft*, 501 U.S. 452, 460 (1991). Accordingly, to the extent that the Voting Rights Act would affect this balance if applied to felon disenfranchisement statutes, we must construe the statute not to encompass such provisions if it is even unclear whether Congress intended the Voting Rights Act to apply to such laws.

The clear statement rule provides that, "[i]f Congress intends to alter the 'usual constitutional balance between the States and the Federal Government,' it must make its intention to do so 'unmistakably clear in the language of the statute.'" *Gregory*, 501 U.S. at 460–61. According to the Supreme Court, "[i]n traditionally sensitive areas, such as legislation affecting the federal balance, the requirement of clear statement assures that the legislature has in fact faced, and intended to bring into issue, the critical matters involved in the judicial decision." *Id.* at 461. Thus, we have stated that federal courts will construe a statute to alter the federal balance only when Congress expresses an affirmative intention to do so.

For the clear statement rule to apply here in defendants' favor, we would therefore need to conclude (1) that applying § 1973 to prisoner disenfranchisement laws would alter the constitutional balance between the States and the Federal Government and (2) that Congress has not made its intention to alter that balance unmistakably clear.

The threshold question to be confronted is whether the clear statement rule applies here at all. Plaintiffs forcefully argue that the clear statement rule only guides our statutory construction when the statutory language is ambiguous, relying on *Gregory* and post-*Gregory* decisions by the Supreme Court, and insist that the broad language of the Voting Rights Act is not ambiguous. We are not persuaded by plaintiffs' arguments.

The *Gregory* Court stated, in describing the operation of the clear statement rule, that "we must be absolutely certain that Congress intended such an exercise [of legislative power]," *Gregory*, 501 U.S. at 464, and that "it must be plain to anyone reading the Act that it covers" the issue in question. *Id.* at 467. Subsequent to *Gregory*, the Supreme Court, in *BFP v. Resolution Trust Corp.*, formulated the analysis as follows: "[t]o displace traditional state regulation…, the federal statutory purpose must be 'clear and manifest.'" 511 U.S. 531, 544.

A few years later, the Supreme Court concluded that the clear statement rule did not apply in two cases. In 1997, in *Salinas v. United States*, the Court described *Gregory* as noting that "the principle it articulated did not apply when a statute was unambiguous." 522 U.S. 52, 60 (1997). The Court stated that "[t]he plain-statement requirement articulated in Gregory … does not warrant a departure from the statute's terms. The text of [the statute] is unambiguous on the point under consideration here…." *Id.* The next term, the Court *decided Pennsylvania Department of Corrections v. Yeskey*, in which it assumed *arguendo* that the clear statement rule applied and held that "the requirement of the rule is amply met" because the statute was unambiguous. 524 U.S. 206, 209 (1998).[21]

---

21. Plaintiffs argue that Yeskey governs this case, as the Court, in addressing whether the Americans with Disabilities Act ("ADA") covers inmates in state prisons, noted there that "the ADA plainly covers state institutions without any exception that could cast the coverage of prisons into doubt." *Yeskey*, 524 U.S. at 209. As such, the Court concluded that the general language of the ADA constituted a sufficiently clear statement of Congress's intent for the purposes of the clear statement rule.

We believe Yeskey is easily distinguishable from this case. There was no reason to believe that Congress, in enacting the ADA, had given any thought whatsoever to the coverage of prisons. In light of the broad language of the ADA, and the absence of any exception from its coverage of state institutions, there was no basis on which to conclude that Congress had meant to exempt prisons. The present situation is substantially different. Here, for the reasons stated at length above, there is a significant amount of evidence that Congress did not intend the VRA to encompass felon disenfranchisement laws, and, at the very least, was convinced it had not done so. Accordingly, the broad language of the VRA

The Court recently addressed the clear statement rule in a different context, but in terms that shed light on its operation here. *Spector v. Norwegian Cruise Line, Ltd.*, 545 U.S. 119 (2005). Discussing the "internal affairs" clear statement rule, which concerns "the presumption against applying general statutes to foreign vessels' internal affairs," the plurality opinion noted that "[i]mplied limitation rules avoid applications of otherwise unambiguous statutes that would intrude on sensitive domains in a way that Congress is unlikely to have intended had it considered the matter," *id.* at 2182 (plurality opinion of Kennedy, J.) and that "[t]hese clear statement rules ensure Congress does not, by broad or general language, legislate on a sensitive topic inadvertently or without due deliberation." *Id.*

For the reasons discussed above, we believe Congress's intent regarding the coverage of felon disenfranchisement provisions by the Voting Rights Act is, at the very least, uncertain, despite the "broad and general language" used in that statute. Given the "sensitive topic" at issue, we would expect Congress to have specified that felon disenfranchisement provisions are covered by the Voting Rights Act if that were its intent. Inasmuch as Congress did not do so—and the evidence of Congressional intent suggests that Congress did not in fact intend to cover such provisions—we believe that the statute is sufficiently ambiguous for the clear statement rule to be applied here.

In applying the clear statement rule, we must first decide whether bringing felon disenfranchisement laws within the scope of the Voting Rights Act—as plaintiffs ask us to do—would "alter the usual constitutional balance between the States and the Federal Government." *Gregory*, 501 U.S. at 460. As a preliminary matter, plaintiffs argue that the application of the Voting Rights Act to felon disenfranchisement provisions could not affect the "federal balance" because that balance was already changed by the passage of the Fourteenth and Fifteenth Amendments, and the sole task of the Voting Rights Act is to effectuate those constitutional provisions. Consequently, plaintiffs assert that bringing their claim within the scope of the VRA would not alter the federal balance.

We do not find this argument persuasive, for, while it undoubtedly rings true for the Voting Rights Act in general, Section 2 of the Fourteenth Amendment explicitly leaves the federal balance intact with regard to felon disenfranchisement laws specifically. *See* U.S. Const. amend. XIV, § 2 ("[W]hen the right to vote at any [federal] election ... is denied to any of the male inhabitants of [a] state ... or in any way abridged, except for participation in rebellion, or *other crime*, the basis of representation therein shall be reduced....") (emphasis added). Therefore, extending the coverage of the Voting Rights Act to these provisions would introduce a change in the federal balance not contemplated by the framers of the Fourteenth Amendment.

---

notwithstanding, it is not entirely clear that Congress meant to alter the federal balance by encompassing felon disenfranchisement laws within the coverage of the VRA, and the clear statement rule must therefore be applied.

These statements indicate that the clear statement rule does not require courts engaged in statutory interpretation to search for a construction of the statute that will not affect the federal balance, but rather, reveal the canon to be a default rule: when a particular construction of a statute would alter the federal balance, to the extent there is any doubt about whether Congress intended that construction, courts should assume that Congress did not mean to alter the federal balance. When the terms of a statute admit of no uncertainty, the statute, of course, serves as its own clear statement. In other words, a clear statement is only necessary when the statute does not itself constitute a clear statement on the relevant issue. Therefore, we will apply the clear statement rule when a statute admits of an interpretation that would alter the federal balance but there is reason to believe, either from the text of the statute, the context of its enactment, or its legislative history, that Congress may not have intended such an alteration of the federal balance.

We have little difficulty concluding that application of the Voting Rights Act to prisoner disenfranchisement provisions like that of New York would effect a change in the federal balance. These laws, applying as they do only to currently incarcerated felons and parolees, implicate no less than three important state interests: (1) the regulation of the franchise; (2) the State's authority to craft its criminal law; and (3) the regulation of correctional institutions. We address each of these interests in turn.

There is no question that regulation of the franchise is an important state interest and that interfering with a State's power to govern this area would disrupt the federal balance. "No function is more essential to the separate and independent existence of the States and their governments than the power to determine within the limits of the Constitution the qualifications of their own voters for state, county, and municipal offices and the nature of their own machinery for filling local public offices." *Oregon v. Mitchell*, 400 U.S. 112, 125 (1970) (opinion of Black, J.). In deciding that the Voting Rights Act did not apply to felon disenfranchisement provisions like that of Florida, the Eleventh Circuit drew an analogy to *Gregory v. Ashcroft*, which had addressed whether state judges could be subject to the provisions of the Americans with Disabilities Act and had concluded that "the authority of the people of the States to determine the qualifications of their most important government officials ... lies at the heart of representative government." 501 U.S. at 463. Judge Kravitch, writing for the Eleventh Circuit *en banc*, noted that "[i]f defining the qualifications of important government officials lies at the heart of representative government, then surely defining who decides what those qualifications will be is equally important." *Johnson*, 405 F.3d at 1232 n.35.... We agree with each of these formulations.

Second, the State of New York has made clear that its statute, § 5-106, constitutes an integral part of its criminal and penal systems. The New York statute, which formerly disenfranchised felons for life, was amended in 1971 to reach only currently incarcerated felons and parolees.... The Model Penal Code likewise considers prisoner disenfranchisement provisions an integral part of the criminal law. It is undisputed that "[u]nder our federal system, the States possess primary authority for defining and enforcing the criminal law." United *States v. Lopez*, 514 U.S. 549, 561 n. 3 (1995).... Accordingly, applying the Voting Rights Act to prisoner disenfranchisement provisions would intrude on New York's "sovereign power to punish offenders" and would thus alter the federal balance.

Third, as a related yet distinct matter, the State has a powerful interest in the administration of its prisons. Indeed, "[o]ne of the primary functions of government is the preservation of societal order through enforcement of the criminal law, and the maintenance of penal institutions is an essential part of that task." *Procunier v. Martinez*, 416 U.S. 396, 412 (1974). The Supreme Court has gone so far as to say that "'[i]t is difficult to imagine an activity in which a State has a stronger interest.'" *Yeskey*, 524 U.S. at 209. Inasmuch as New York's prisoner disenfranchisement provision is limited to those confined in penal institutions and on parole, applying the Voting Rights Act to the provision would surely affect the State's powers in this area as well.

In light of these three separate compelling state interests, we have little difficulty concluding that construing the VRA to encompass prisoner disenfranchisement provisions like that of New York would unquestionably alter the federal balance. Accordingly, we proceed to the second prong of the clear statement test, which requires us to determine whether Congress has clearly signaled its intent to alter the federal balance by subjecting state prisoner disenfranchisement laws to the provisions of the Voting Rights Act.

As discussed at greater length above, our review of the legislative history of both the 1965 enactment and 1982 revision of the Voting Rights Act as well as our examination of other proposed legislation on this issue demonstrate Congress's lack of intent to include felon disenfranchisement provisions in the coverage of the Voting Rights Act, and compel us to conclude that Congress unquestionably did not manifest an "unmistakably clear" intent to include felon disenfranchisement laws under the VRA. As a result, we hold that the requirements of the clear statement rule are not met, and we will accordingly not construe the Voting Rights Act to reach these laws.

We therefore hold that the Voting Rights Act must be construed to not encompass prisoner disenfranchisement provisions like that of New York because (a) Congress did not intend the Voting Rights Act to cover such provisions; and (b) Congress made no clear statement of an intent to modify the federal balance by applying the Voting Rights Act to these provisions. Accordingly, we conclude that plaintiffs' vote denial claim, which seeks to challenge New York's prisoner disenfranchisement statute under the Voting Rights Act, must be dismissed and the judgment of the District Court must be affirmed.

SACK, CIRCUIT JUDGE with whom JUDGE STRAUB joins with concurring in part and concurring in judgment.

I write separately principally to respond to a portion of the dissent of my colleague, Judge Calabresi, in which he concludes that Judge Straub and I, being "motivated in large part by skepticism that Congress could have intended the result that the plaintiffs urge," have confused the views of the current Congress with that of the Congress that enacted the Voting Rights Act and its 1982 amendments. Judge Calabresi may or may not be right on the merits of this case, but in this respect he is surely wrong. What the current Congress, or a Congress that will next consider voting rights, thinks or will think is Congress's business, not ours. The question here is what the statute means.

It is in response to that question that we ... conclude[] that Congress did not intend the Voting Rights Act to encompass the type of felon disenfranchisement law at issue in this case. By amending Section 2 of the Voting Rights Act in 1982, Congress apparently sought to make clear that Section 2 covered both vote denial and vote dilution, and to reinstate the "results test," which Congress found to be the rule developed in the voting rights case law before the Supreme Court's decision in *City of Mobile v. Bolden*, 446 U.S. 55 (1980)....[1] Whatever one's view of the uses and misuses of legislative history to enlighten, or even to contradict plain meaning, insofar as the 1982 amendment was aimed specifically at overruling *Bolden* and reinstating previous case law, it is not that difficult to discern what Congress meant to do when it said what it said....

RAGGI, CIRCUIT JUDGE, concurring.

I fully concur in the majority opinion's thoughtful analysis.... I write separately only to expand on its discussion of why we require a clear statement of congressional intent to allow plaintiffs to pursue a VRA challenge to § 5-106....

While acknowledging the presumptive validity of felon disenfranchisement laws, plaintiffs and supporting *amici* submit that New York's practice of prisoner disenfranchisement violates the VRA because there is a gross racial disparity in the state prison population. If permitted to pursue their claim, they seek to show that this disparity is a product of per-

---

1. As the Senate Report declared: "This Amendment is designed to make clear that proof of discriminatory intent is not required to establish a violation of section 2. It thereby restores the legal standards, based on the controlling supreme Court precedents, which applied in voting discrimination claims prior to the litigation involved in *Mobile v. Bolden*. The Amendment also adds a new subsection to Section 2 which delineates the legal standards under the results test by codifying the leading pre-*Bolden* vote-dilution case ..."

vasive racism infecting every part of the New York criminal justice system, from stop and frisk determinations by police officers on the street, to charging decisions by prosecutors, to detention and sentencing rulings by state court judges. In short, plaintiffs propose to use the VRA to indict the New York criminal justice system for racism.

So employed, the VRA would not only significantly intrude on, but also seriously disrupt, the orderly administration of criminal justice in New York, obviously a matter of legitimate state interest. Plaintiffs' suit would effectively impugn the constitutionality of countless state convictions without necessarily proving that any one prosecution or sentence was, in fact, discriminatory. Equally disturbing, the state's criminal justice system could be adjudged discriminatory without New York being required to release, retry, or resentence a single prisoner. New York would just have to give prisoners the vote. Such a result would undoubtedly undermine public confidence in all state criminal proceedings at the same time that it bred cynicism toward federal law for responding to such a serious problem with so ill-fitting a remedy.

Of course, Congress may enact laws that remedy aspects of particular problems— whether voter discrimination or invidious bias in the administration of criminal justice— without offering complete solutions. But when, as this case demonstrates, a VRA challenge to § 5-106 would so seriously undermine the legitimacy of the state's criminal justice system, it is appropriate to require a clear statement of congressional intent to have the VRA apply to felon disenfranchisement laws.

B.D. Parker, Jr. Circuit Judge, dissenting.

... [A] minority of this Court turns to the clear statement rule. This canon of interpretation requires Congress to make its intention "unmistakably clear" when enacting statutes that would alter the usual constitutional balance between the federal government and the states. The minority's concern is that application of the VRA to New York Election Law § 5-106 would intrude into three important state functions: (1) the regulation of the franchise; (2) the state's authority to craft its criminal law; and (3) the regulation of correctional institutions. The minority reasons that, to the extent the VRA would affect this balance if applied to felon disenfranchisement statutes, it must be construed not to encompass such provisions if it is unclear whether Congress intended the VRA to apply to such laws.

For several reasons, the clear statement rule does not apply. First, for it to apply, ambiguity must exist, and § 2(a) is unambiguous. *See, e.g., Penn. Dep't of Corr. v. Yeskey*, 524 U.S. 206, 212 (1998) ("in the context of an unambiguous statutory text," arguments concerning whether Congress has made its intention clear are "irrelevant"); *Salinas v. United States*, 522 U.S. 52, 60 (1997) ("*Gregory* itself ... noted [that] the principle it articulated did not apply when a statute was unambiguous.") *Hilton v. S.C. Pub. Rys. Comm'n*, 502 U.S. 197, 206 (1991) (citing Supreme Court cases that "describe the plain statement rule as a rule of statutory construction to be applied where statutory intent is ambiguous").

Second, even if VRA § 2(a) were ambiguous, the clear statement rule would still not apply because the provision is broadly worded, and the rule does not apply to broadly worded remedial statutes. As the Supreme Court has made clear, a broad statute satisfies the clear statement rule even though it does not enumerate all of its intended applications: "[T]he fact that a statute can be 'applied in situations not expressly anticipated by Congress does not demonstrate ambiguity. It demonstrates breadth.'" *Yeskey*, 524 U.S. at 212. Congress used language in § 2 that was deliberately broad and generic. It is well-settled that "[a] statute can be unambiguous without addressing every interpretive theory offered by a party. It need only be 'plain to anyone reading the Act' that the statute encompasses the conduct at issue." *Salinas*, 522 U.S. at 60 (quoting *Gregory*, 501 U.S. at 467). Congress could hardly have been expected to have enumerated every conceivable voting qualification, prerequisite, practice, or procedure to which the statute could apply in the text, or even the legislative history, of § 2(a). To do so would have left the states free to devise new means to discriminate that were not listed. To hold that Congress did not intend the VRA to cover felon disenfranchisement statutes is to hold that Congress actually intended to allow some forms of race-based voter disenfranchisement. Such a result I find improbable—indeed inconceivable.

Third, the clear statement rule cannot be justified by contending that unless it is applied, the VRA would improperly interfere with "sensitive domains" such as the core state function of regulating the franchise. This contention overlooks the quite obvious fact that the very purpose of the VRA was to impose Congressional regulation on the traditional state function of regulating voting. *See Lopez v. Monterey County*, 525 U.S. 266, 284–85 (1999) ("In short, the Voting Rights Act, by its nature, intrudes on state sovereignty. The Fifteenth Amendment permits this intrusion, however...."). Time and time again, the Supreme Court has held that state voting requirements are comfortably within Congress' reach under the VRA.... Felon disenfranchisement is no more a core state function than any of these examples.

Fourth, while it is correct that the states possess the primary authority for defining and enforcing the criminal law, the short—and conclusive—answer is that New York Election Law § 5-106 is not a criminal law. It is a voting law found in New York's Election code, not among its criminal laws. As Judge Friendly pointed out, "[d]epriving convicted felons of the franchise is not a punishment but rather is a 'nonpenal exercise of the power to regulate the franchise.'" *Green v. Bd. of Elections*, 380 F.2d 445, 450 (2d Cir.1967).

Fifth, the clear statement rule is particularly inappropriate in the context of the VRA, which was enacted and amended pursuant to Congress's powers under both the Fourteenth and Fifteenth Amendments. Contrary to the suggestion of some members of this Court, the seismic shift created by the Fourteenth and Fifteenth Amendments clearly altered the federal-state balance in an attempt to address a truly compelling national interest—namely, reducing racial discrimination perpetuated by the states. Indeed, these Amendments "were specifically designed as an expansion of federal power and an intrusion on state sovereignty." *Gregory*, 501 U.S. at 468.

Finally, were a clear statement required, VRA § 2(a) supplies it: "No voting qualification or prerequisite to voting or standard, practice, or procedure shall be imposed or applied by any State or political subdivision in a manner which results in a denial or abridgement of the right of any citizen of the United States to vote on account of race or color...." 42 U.S.C. § 1973(a). Since § 2(a) covers all voting qualifications, it indisputably covers felon disenfranchisement laws like New York Election Law § 5-106. If anything is clear from the legislative history of the VRA it is that Congress intended to eliminate all race-based disfranchisement, no matter the means by which it was achieved.

SOTOMAYOR, CIRCUIT JUDGE, dissenting.

I ... write this separate opinion only to emphasize one point. I fear that the many pages of the majority opinion and concurrences—and the many pages of the dissent that are necessary to explain why they are wrong—may give the impression that this case is in some way complex. It is not.

It is plain to anyone reading the Voting Rights Act that it applies to all "voting qualification[s]." And it is equally plain that § 5-106 disqualifies a group of people from voting. These two propositions should constitute the entirety of our analysis. Section 2 of the Act by its unambiguous terms subjects felony disenfranchisement and all other voting qualifications to its coverage.

The duty of a judge is to follow the law, not to question its plain terms. I do not believe that Congress wishes us to disregard the plain language of any statute or to invent exceptions to the statutes it has created. The majority's "wealth of persuasive evidence" that Congress intended felony disenfranchisement laws to be immune from scrutiny under §2 of the Act, includes not a single legislator actually saying so. But even if Congress had doubts about the wisdom of subjecting felony disenfranchisement laws to the results test of §2, I trust that Congress would prefer to make any needed changes itself, rather than have courts do so for it.

Chapter 14

Statutes and Legal Hierarchy

Statutes interact with other forms of substantive law. Illustratively, common law often affects the meaning of statutes. Thus, it is a canon of construction that, "'absent contrary indications,' Congress is presumed to have adopted 'the common law definition of statutory terms.'" *United States v. Chipps*, 410 F.3d 438, 449 (8th Cir. 2005), *quoting United States v. Shabani*, 513 U.S. 10, 13 (1994). This canon reflects the belief that legislatures know that judges, who are steeped in common law, interpret statutes. Judges likely apply that basic canon without even being aware that they are reading statutes in light of common law.

While the impact of common law on statutes is fairly obvious, statutes can also affect common law. A statute can, for example, repeal a common law cause of action or create one where none existed before. Or, a federal statute might conflict with a state statute or state common law. This chapter explores the hierarchy of federal statutes and state law. This chapter first explores two substantive canons of interpretation: One provides that statutes in derogation of the common law should be construed narrowly, and the other provides that remedial statutes should be construed liberally to further their purposes. We will see that, under some circumstances, these canons can be in tension with each other. At this chapter's conclusion, we will see that sometimes federal statutes preempt state statutes or state common law, effectively displacing state law with federal.

A. Statutes in Derogation of the Common Law

An oft-cited canon of statutory construction is that statutes in derogation of the common law must be strictly construed. *E.g.*, *Washington Metro. Area Transit Auth. v. Johnson*, 467 U.S. 925, 945–46 (1984) (stating it to be a "settled principle that a provision limiting common-law rights must be strictly construed, for no statute is to be construed as altering the common law, farther than its words import. It is not to be construed as making any innovation upon the common law which it does not fairly express."). This canon of construction was developed long ago, when there were generally fewer statutes and the common law was the most important source of rights and obligations. Additionally, some formulations of this canon arose at a time when the public's skepticism of the legislative and political processes was high. *See Bandfield v. Bandfield*, 75 N.W. 287, 288 (Mich. 1898) ("The legislature should speak in no uncertain manner when it seeks to abrogate the plain and long-established rules of the common law ... for statues are not presumed to make any alteration of the common law, further or otherwise than the act expressly declares.").

The derogation canon arguably served two different purposes. First, because there was an early reluctance by American courts to allow legislatures to restrict rights recognized by the common law, the canon was perceived as protecting common law rights. For example, the canon prevented the legislature from accidentally "repealing" a settled common law cause of action. Second, constitutional issues could unexpectedly arise if a legislature abrogated an individual's common law right; for example, the legislature might enact a statute that restricted an individual's interest in property, which would implicate the Due Process Clause. Sometimes one act implicated both of these twin purposes. For example, a statute that eliminated a common law cause of action both potentially allowed legislative intrusion into the judicial arena and deprived a plaintiff of an existing, constitutionally protected right. To limit these intrusions and deprivations, the judiciary crafted the canon that statutes that were in derogation of the common law should be narrowly construed so that legislatures had to be very clear about their objectives.

But not all statutes intruded into the judicial sphere or deprived litigants of rights. Some statutes expanded the available common law rights and remedies. In other words, a *remedial* statute might create rights or remedies that were unavailable at common law, instead of eliminating or restricting them. Depending on what "derogation" means (an issue we explore below), the policies identified in the last paragraph that support strict construction of statutes in derogation of the common law would not be implicated in cases where the statute was "remedial" in nature. Therefore, the courts broadly interpreted these statutes to further their remedial purposes. Hence, when a court characterized a statute as "remedial," strict construction was not appropriate. Whether a statute is strictly or broadly construed depends on a court's characterization of a statute as being remedial or in derogation.

While the canon fell out of favor for awhile, recent legislation in the area of tort reform has made this characterization important once again. For example, a recent New Mexico statute limited landowner liability for accidents arising out of off-road motor vehicles. *Martin v. Middle Rio Grande Conservancy Dist.*, 194 P.3d 766, 770 (N.M. Ct. App. 2008). The court reasoned that the statute was "in derogation of the common law because it strip[ed] from a class of plaintiffs ... the right to recover damages caused by negligence." *Id.* Thus, the court construed "the statute against a broad conferral of immunity...." *Id.*; *See Lostritto v. Cmty. Action Agency of New Haven, Inc.*, 848 A.2d 418, 434 (Conn. 2004) ("Both statutes ... were drafted as part of ... tort reform and are therefore in derogation of the common law.").

As you can see, characterization matters. Consider whether a court's decision to characterize a statute as in derogation of the common law can justify narrow interpretation, which may frustrate the legislative agenda. *See* Gregory C. Sisk, *Interpretation of the Statutory Modification of Joint and Several Liability: Resisting the Deconstruction of Tort Reform*, 16 U. Puget Sound L. Rev. 1, 18–19 (1992) (arguing that "the flame of tort reform must not be smothered beneath the blanket of that legal cliché which states that statutes in derogation of the common law should be given a narrow construction"). The following cases explore the application of the derogation canon and the problem of characterization. Among the issues that you should consider are these: (1) Does the canon further any substantive goal of interpretation, such as accuracy, efficiency, or separation of powers? (2) Is the characterization of a statute as "remedial" as meaningful or as clear as the courts suggest it is, given that any expansion of a right or remedy on behalf of a plaintiff necessarily curtails the rights and expands the liability of a defendant?

Compare the use of the derogation canon in each of the next two cases. Although the issue is identical—whether the state's wrongful death statute allows a plaintiff to recover punitive damages—the courts reach opposite conclusions. Be sure you can explain why.

Behrens v. Raleigh Hills Hosp., Inc.

675 P.2d 1179 (Utah 1983)

STEWART, JUSTICE.

The issue ... is whether punitive damages may be awarded in a wrongful death action....

I. THE FACTS

Plaintiff's decedent, Robert Alan Behrens, was admitted to the defendant Raleigh Hills Hospital to undergo treatment for alcohol abuse. On the third day of his stay, a hospital employee allowed decedent to use a razor to shave. Instead, decedent used the razor to slash his wrists; he died four days later.

Decedent's wife, individually and on behalf of their infant son, filed this action for wrongful death seeking compensatory damages only. The jury trial resulted in a judgment for plaintiff in the amount of $100,000. However, the trial court granted defendant's motion for [a new trial for reasons unrelated to this appeal].

After the motion for a new trial was granted, plaintiff moved to amend her complaint to include a claim for punitive damages....

III. PUNITIVE DAMAGES IN WRONGFUL DEATH ACTIONS

The key substantive issue in this case is whether the Utah wrongful death statute allows for recovery of punitive damages or only permits compensatory damages. The relevant portion of U.C.A., 1953, § 78-11-7 states: "In every action under this [section] ... such damages may be given as under all the circumstances of the case may be just." Whether this provision allows for recovery of punitive damages in a wrongful death action is a question of first impression in Utah.

The common law recognized no action for the wrongful death of a human being. Lord Campbell's Act, which was enacted in England in 1846 to override the common law, created a statutory action for wrongful death. That act provided for the recovery of damages which the jury found resulted from the death. Although English courts have restricted recovery under that act to pecuniary losses suffered by the survivors, American courts have not ruled consistently one way or the other....

Defendant contends that the Utah statute, being in derogation of the common law, must be strictly construed and that the claim for punitive damages must consequently be denied because the statute neither expressly nor impliedly allows for such damages.

The Utah wrongful death act was originally passed by the Territorial Legislature in 1874 to remedy the harsh effects of the common law rule which did not recognize wrongful death actions at all. At statehood, a cause of action for wrongful death was guaranteed by the Constitution which also prohibited any statutory limits on the amount recoverable. Article XVI, § 5 states:

> The right of action to recover damages for injuries resulting in death, shall never be abrogated, and the amount recoverable shall not be subject to any statutory limitation....

The Utah wrongful death statute, implementing the constitutional provision, although in derogation of the common law, traditionally has been liberally construed by the courts. Indeed, a liberal construction is supported by one of our earliest statutes, U.C.A., 1953, § 68-3-2:

> The rule of the common law that statutes in derogation thereof are to be strictly construed has no application to the statutes of this state. The statutes establish the laws of this state respecting the subjects to which they relate, and their provisions and all proceedings under them *are to be liberally construed* with a view to effect the objects of the statutes and to promote justice.

Thus, unlike those wrongful death statutes which disallow punitive damages because those statutes are construed strictly, the Utah wrongful death statute is not required to be strictly construed because it deviates from the common law.

The traditional, liberal construction of the Utah statute has been applied specifically to the damages clause of the act which provides for "such damages ... as under all the circumstances of the case may be just." U.C.A., 1953 §78-11-7. This Court, at an early date, construed the statute to allow recovery of damages for both pecuniary and nonpecuniary losses, even though damages for nonpecuniary losses are not expressly authorized by the statute. In [another case], we recently stated: "[T]he statute is broadly phrased, and this Court has construed it accordingly."

Most commentators agree that absent an express prohibition against recovery of punitive damages in wrongful death actions, the position most consistent with fairness and sound public policy is to allow punitive damages where the circumstances warrant. For example, in his comprehensive treatise, Speiser comments:

> Under existing systems, many jurisdictions do not allow recovery of punitive damages in wrongful death actions, unless the statutes are fairly explicit in sanctioning such recovery. This would make sense in states (and there are a few) that do not allow punitive damages at all. But it makes no sense for a state that allows punitive damages for a willful, wanton, malicious, reckless or grossly negligent tort that results in personal injury, emotional anguish, or property damage, to deny such punitive damages where the injury victim happens to die. Death is, after all, the final injury—the ultimate insult. Such a result defies logic and distorts symmetry in the law....

This state has traditionally permitted recovery of punitive damages in personal injury cases. Consistency with general tort law suggests that the Utah wrongful death statute should be construed to permit punitive damages. If the Legislature intended to prohibit the award of punitive damages, it could have done so expressly....

In sum, because of the broad language of the wrongful death statute which permits recovery for nonpecuniary losses, the liberal construction that has been placed on that language, and the desirability of having the rule of law in wrongful death cases consistent with general tort law, we hold that the wrongful death statute permits the recovery of punitive damages in appropriate cases.

Cohen v. Rubin

(Md. Ct. App. 1983)

GETTY, JUDGE.

This appeal arises out of an action for negligent operation of an automobile, negligent entrustment of the vehicle by the owner-father to his son and wrongful death. On February 2, 1982, a Baltimore County jury rendered the following verdicts.

1. $2,000.00 compensatory damages in favor of the Estate of Philip Scott Rubin against the defendants, Steven and Sidney Cohen.

2. $250,000.00 punitive damages in favor of the Estate of Philip Scott Rubin against the defendant, Steven Cohen....

On April 26, 1982, judgment absolute was entered for the above amount[] with the exception of the $250,000.00 punitive damage award against Steven Cohen....

The ... appellants contend that the court erred in [denying the] punitive damage claim in the Wrongful Death Action.

The statute involved provides:

(d) Damages if spouse or minor child dies. — For the death of a spouse, minor child or parent of a minor child, the damages awarded under subsection (c) are not limited or restricted by the "pecuniary loss" or "pecuniary benefit" rule but may include damages for mental anguish, emotional pain and suffering, loss of society, companionship, comfort, protection, marital care, parental care, filial care, attention, advice, counsel, training, guidance, or education where applicable.

At common law a right of action for wrongful death did not exist. The Maryland Legislature, in 1852, enacted the wrongful death act that, for the first time, gave a right of action under certain conditions to designated relative of a deceased person, as opposed to the personal representatives of the decedent, where death resulted from a wrongful act or negligence. The Act is nearly identical to England's Lord Campbell's Act enacted six years earlier....

In the present case we are faced with the precise question as to the recovery of exemplary damages under the wrongful death statute. Prior to the enactment of 3-904(d) in 1969, recovery in these cases was limited to pecuniary loss.

The preamble to section 3-904(d) states clearly the legislative intent embodied in the amendment.

WHEREAS, Strict application of this test (pecuniary loss) ... in the case of a minor's death ... results in a minus figure, since the value of his services lost by death in modern society is generally much less than the probable cost of raising the child; and

WHEREAS, It is desirable to substitute a valid test for determining damage for the fictional test of the 'pecuniary benefit' rule in which emotional facts frequently enter; now therefore....

Amelioration of the harsh "pecuniary rule"* was all the legislature intended by the 1969 amendment. We do not accept ... appellants' argument that punitive damages are recoverable because the statute does not expressly preclude or limit such recovery. The negligence causing death statute is in derogation of the common law and, therefore, should be strictly construed. We are of the opinion, therefore, that punitive damages are not recoverable in cases arising under the wrongful death statute unless and until the legislature so provides.

Notes and Questions

(1) *Why did the Courts Reach Different Results?* If you cannot come up with a reasoned basis for the different results, does that mean that characterization of a statute as being in "derogation of the common law" is an objective characteristic or a subjective conclusion?

---

* Authors' footnote: The pecuniary benefit rule allowed recovery only for loss that could be valued in money.

(2) *Defining Derogation.* Derogation is defined, at least in Black's Law Dictionary, as "[t]he partial repeal or abolishing of a law, as by a subsequent act which limits its scope or impairs its utility and force." BLACK'S LAW DICTIONARY 399 (5th ed. 1979). Are wrongful death statutes in derogation of the common law? The principal cases split on this issue, as do other cases. *Compare Corkill v. Knowles*, 955 P.2d 438, 442 (Wyo. 1998) ("Wrongful death acts do not take away any common law right; they were designed to mend the fabric of the common law, not to weaken it. Remedial acts are not strictly construed, although they do change a rule of the common law."), *with Cockrum v. Fox*, 199 S.W.3d 69, 73 (Ark. 2004) ("a wrongful-death action is an action in derogation of common law and, as a statutory construction, it must be strictly construed"). Doesn't the question of whether a wrongful death statute is in derogation of the common law depend on whether you're asking the plaintiff or the defendant in the wrongful death case? Although courts seldom address that question, in Illinois, "statutes in derogation of the common law are to be strictly construed in favor of persons sought to be subjected to their operation." *People v. Perry*, 864 N.E.2d 196, 209 (Ill. 2007). If Illinois's perspective is proper, are courts that characterize wrongful death acts as remedial (because they create a new claim) looking at the issue from the wrong perspective—the plaintiff's rather than the defendant's? Or, does "derogation of the common law" merely mean the same thing as "changing the common law," and so *any* change to the common law would be in derogation?

Interestingly, one common assumption—that wrongful death actions did not exist at common law—may be inaccurate, and if so, the reason for viewing wrongful death statutes as in derogation of the common law may be wrong. *Sanzi v. Shetty*, 2002 WL 1371044, at *4 n.2 (R.I. Super. Ct. 2002) ("It is not at all clear … that an action for wrongful death was not available at common law.").

(3) *What About Time?* Even assuming wrongful death statutes were in derogation of the common law, many legislatures adopted these statutes in the 1800s. Does it make sense to continue to characterize them this way now? To press the issue further, suppose that, today, a legislature simply re-enacted the exact same statutory language that had been on the books since 1852: Should a court still characterize the statute as being in derogation of the common law? Do you believe that a typical legislator would agree with the statement that wrongful death statutes should be strictly construed? If not, should that fact affect how a court interprets a wrongful death statute enacted long ago? Should it affect how a court interprets one that was reenacted word-for-word from an old statute? How would an intentionalist, purposivist, and textualist answer these questions?

(4) *Public Policy Paramount?* Does it make sense to deny punitive damages in wrongful death actions when punitive damages would be available if the decedent had survived? Put another way, does denying punitive damages in wrongful death actions lead to less precaution by potential defendants? If so, why doesn't that policy argument mean that courts should hold that punitive damages are available?

(5) *Continued Vitality.* What drives this canon? If you perceive the driver to be judicial hostility toward statutes, then arguably the historical basis for the canon's origins have diminished. As one judge wrote:

> Statutes then were not created from common law methodology. Indeed, 18th century judges felt then rather subject to tyrannical majorities and shifting whims. England had suffered through the civil wars of the Seventeenth Century and the abuses of unchecked majorities in Parliament. The beheading of Charles I was followed by the post-restoration instability leading to the Glorious Revolution in 1685. [Judges] viewed the common law as a source of social stability, cast from

the wisdom of the ages and forged in cases evolving over the long sweep of history. Statutes often emerged from ephemeral, narrow and parochial interests, but the common law was eternal and universal.

Blankfeld v. Richmond Health Care, Inc., 902 So. 2d 296, 305 (Fla. Dist. Ct. App. 2005) (Farmer, J., concurring). In this regard, what do you make of the fact that many state legislatures have, by statute, abolished this canon, either generally, *e.g.*, KY. REV. STAT. § 446.080(1) (2003) ("All statutes of this state shall be liberally construed with a view to promote their objects and carry out the intent of the legislature, and the rule that statutes in derogation of the common law are to be strictly construed shall not apply to the statutes of this state."), or with respect to particular statutes, such as wrongful death acts. *BellSouth Telecomms., Inc. v. Meeks*, 863 So.2d 287, 290 (Fla. 2003) (explaining that legislature had stated that the state's "public policy" was "to shift the losses resulting when wrongful death occurs ... to the wrongdoer" and so wrongful death statutes "are remedial and shall be liberally construed.").

Problem 14-1

You are on the Mercer Supreme Court and have just heard oral argument in the case of *Crystal v. Stevens*. Janis Crystal sued James Stevens, her neighbor, for the wrongful death of her teenage son, Thomas. Stevens wrongfully shot Thomas in the eye with a B.B. gun. Thomas was allegedly trespassing on Stevens's property "again." For purposes of this appeal only, the parties stipulate that the homicide had been committed in a willful and wanton manner. Using the problem materials below and the previous cases, decide whether you would overrule *Engle v. Finch* (excerpted below) and why you would reach your decision. Prepare an outline of your ruling.

Problem Materials

Mercer Crim. Code § 19-7-1. Parental power; recovery for homicide of child

> (c) (1) In every case of the homicide of a child, minor or *sui juris*, there shall be some party entitled to recover the full value of the life of the child, either as provided in this Code section or as provided in Chapter 4 of Title 51....

Mercer Crim. Code § 19-8-1. As used in this chapter, the term:

> (1) "Full value of the life of the decedent" means the full value of the life of the decedent without deducting for any of the necessary or personal expenses of the decedent had he lived.

> (2) "Homicide" includes all cases in which the death of a human being results from a crime, from criminal or other negligence, or from property which has been defectively manufactured, whether or not as the result of negligence.

Mercer Crim. Code § 51-12-5.1. Punitive damages (enacted in 1938)

> (a) As used in this Code section, the term "punitive damages" is synonymous with the terms "vindictive damages," "exemplary damages," and other descriptions of additional damages awarded because of aggravating circumstances in order to penalize, punish, or deter a defendant.

> (b) Punitive damages may be awarded only in such tort actions in which it is proven by clear and convincing evidence that the defendant's actions showed willful misconduct, malice, fraud, wantonness, oppression, or that entire

want of care which would raise the presumption of conscious indifference to consequences.

(c) Punitive damages shall be awarded not as compensation to a plaintiff but solely to punish, penalize, or deter a defendant.

In *Engle v. Finch*, the Mercer Supreme Court held that punitive damages were not recoverable in wrongful death actions. The court based its decision on the fact that Mercer's wrongful death statute was enacted in 1850, following Lord Campbell's Act (of England), which was enacted in 1847. Because the English courts had construed Lord Campbell's Act to not allow vindictive, exemplary, or punitive damages, the Mercer Supreme Court followed suit. Thereafter, however, the legislature enacted the general punitive damages statute in 1938. There have been no other cases in Mercer to address this question since *Engle v. Finch* was decided.

Engle v. Finch

165 Mercer 131 (1927)

HINES, JUDGE.

At the common law no recovery could be had for an injury resulting in death, because the right of action died with the person. So a widow or child could not recover for the homicide of the husband or parent, and the husband could not recover for the homicide of his wife. This was changed in England, by Lord Campbell's act, which was passed in 1846. The common-law rule was changed in this state by the act of 1850. That act provided that:

> "In all cases hereafter where death shall ensue from or under circumstances which would entitle the deceased, if death had not ensued, to an action against the perpetrator of the injury, the legal representative of such deceased shall be entitled to have and maintain an action at law against the person committing the act from which the death has resulted; one half of the recovery to be paid to the wife and children, or the husband of the deceased, if any, in case of his or her estate being insolvent."

Lord Campbell's act and our act of 1850 are substantially the same. Neither act provided any measure of recovery. In construing Lord Campbell's act the English courts held that that act was compensatory, and that vindictive, punitive, or exemplary damages could not be recovered thereunder. In construing our act of 1850 [in another case], this court construed it as the English courts had construed Lord Campbell's act; and ..., this court ... said:

> "It is admitted that in actions of this sort, the jury can not find vindictive, punitive, or exemplary damages; and that they are confined to injuries of which a pecuniary estimate can be made."

By the act of 1856 it was provided:

> "That if any one shall be killed by the carelessness, negligence or improper conduct of any of said railroad companies, their officers, agents or employees, by the running of the cars or engines of any of said companies, that the right of action to recover damages, shall vest in his widow, if any, if no widow, it shall vest in his children if any, and if no child or children, it shall vest in his legal representatives."

In construing the act of 1850, as amended by the act of 1856, this court laid down the measure of damages as the pecuniary damages to the wife from the homicide, to be ascertained by inquiring what would be a reasonable support, according to the circumstances in life of the husband, as they existed at his death, and as they may be reasonably expected to exist in view of his character, habits, occupation and prospects in life, and when the annual money value of that support has been found, to give, as damages, its present worth, according to the expectation of the life of the deceased, as ascertained by the mortuary tables of well-established reputation.... [I]t was said that:

> "It was intended only to give to the wife damages for her loss, or, if no wife, then to the children, for their loss. What, then, is the loss of the wife? Her legal loss? It is that which she was, by law, entitled to from her husband, a reasonable support, according to his condition in life."

... This is a legislative imposition of a penalty upon the person who causes the death of another by negligence, the penalty to go to the person injured. It is penal, in that the measure of the recovery is the full value of the life of the deceased, irrespective of its real value to the person in whom the cause of action is vested. In a case of aggravating circumstances, can the jury give additional damages, either to deter the wrongdoer from repeating the trespass, or as compensation for the wounded feelings of the plaintiff? "In every tort there may be aggravating circumstances, either in the act or the intention, and in that event the jury may give additional damages, either to deter the wrongdoer from repeating the trespass, or as compensation for the wounded feelings of the plaintiff." Civil Code 1910, § 4503. To hold that the jury can award additional exemplary damages under this section would have the effect of imposing upon the person committing the homicide a double penalty. While the Legislature could impose double damages, such intention is not to be imputed to it, except in cases which are clear and free from doubt. The right to sue at all depends upon this statute. The amount of recovery is fixed by it, and excludes exemplary or punitive damages. The measure of damages is the full value of the life of the deceased husband or parent. The statute giving the right of action and fixing the measure of damages, we cannot hold that it was the intention of the Legislature to permit the recovery of additional damages under section 4503 of the Code. So we are of the opinion that the question propounded by the Court of Appeals should be answered in the negative.

All the Justices concur.

B. Remedial Statutes

Sometimes statutes broaden common law rights or create new rights. Such statutes are called "remedial." "Remedial" means "intended as or providing a remedy," "concerned with the correction, removal, or abatement of an evil, defect, or disease," and "relating to, or being a law enacted for the purpose of providing a method of enforcing an already existing substantive right." www.dictionary.com (citing Merriam-Webster's Dictionary of Law).

Courts generally agree that remedial statutes should be interpreted broadly to advance the statute's purpose. *Dep't of Labor & Indus. v. Gongyin*, 109 P.3d 816, 821 (Wash. 2005); *Samish Indian Nation v. United States*, 419 F.3d 1355, 1367 (Fed. Cir. 2005) (collecting cases). Interpreting a statute broadly can create tension with two other canons. First, interpreting a statute broadly may be at odds with the plain meaning canon. As a result, some courts hold that the fact that a statute is remedial and should be construed broadly only matters when the text is ambiguous or would lead to unworkable results. *E.g., Vincent v.*

City of New Haven, 941 A.2d 932, 941 n.16 (Conn. 2008) ("the principle of statutory construction that instructs us to construe the act broadly to achieve its remedial purpose does not guide us in the present case because that principle is applicable only when the statutory language is susceptible of more than one reasonable interpretation or when the text of the statute, although plain and unambiguous, yields absurd or unworkable results."). Yet, this approach to broadly interpreting remedial statutes severely cabins its applicability because it allows for a broad interpretation only in instances of ambiguity.

Second, when a statute is characterized as "remedial," the "broad reading" canon can directly conflict with the canon that statutes in derogation of the common law should be construed narrowly. For example, characterizing a wrongful death statute as "remedial" results in liberal construction; characterizing it as "in derogation of the common law" results in a narrow construction. Viewed in this light, a court's categorization of a statute's purpose as "remedial" can be critical. Yet, that categorization may be largely subjective.

The Supreme Court struggled with this second point in *Babbitt v. Sweet Home Chapter of Communities for a Great Oregon,* 515 U.S. 687 (1995). The Endangered Species Act made it unlawful to "take" an endangered species. *Id.* at 690 (citing 16 U.S.C. § 1531 (1988 ed. and Supp. V). The statute defined "take" to include "harass, harm, pursue, hunt, shoot, wound, kill, trap, capture, or collect ..." *Id.* at 691 (citing 16 U.S.C. § 1532(19)). Pursuant to that statute, the Secretary of the Interior had promulgated a regulation that defined the word "harm" in the definition of the word "take" to include "an act which actually kills or injures wildlife." Such act may include significant habitat modification or degradation where it actually kills or injures wildlife by significantly impairing essential behavioral patterns, including breeding, feeding, or sheltering." *Id.* at 691 (citing 50 C.F.R. § 17.3 (1994)).

The defendants wanted to log certain wilderness areas where endangered species bred, fed, and obtained shelter. *Id.* at 692. Logging would degrade the habitat and, potentially at least, kill some endangered species. *Id.* As a result, the defendants sought a declaratory judgment that the regulation's definition of "harm" as including habitat modification and degradation was invalid. *Id.* They contended that the definition of "take" in the statute was limited to actions taken directly against an endangered animal or plant. *Id.* at 693. Hence, the agency had no authority to promulgate a regulation that prohibited indirect harm. *Id.*

The majority disagreed and upheld the broad regulation. *Id.* at 695. The majority emphasized the "broad purpose" of the act as a basis for its conclusion that the agency had authority for the more expansive regulation. *Id.* at 699–703. In contrast, Justice Scalia, in a dissent joined by Justice Thomas, refused to interpret "harm" to encompass indirect harm. *Id.* at 714–736 (Scalia, J., dissenting). Justice Scalia based his analysis on the plain language of the statute and on the textual canons. *Id.* Further, and pertinent here, he chided the majority for relying upon the act's "broad purpose" to justify an expansive grant of authority to the agency. *Id.* at 726. According to Justice Scalia: "'The Act must do everything necessary to achieve its broad purpose' is the slogan of the enthusiast, not the analytical tool of the arbiter." *Id.*

The following case and notes explore these issues further.

Burch v. Sec'y of Health & Human Serv.

2001 WL 180129 (Fed. Cl. 2001)

Hastings, Special Master.

... The following facts appear to be undisputed. Shon S. Burch and Jonathan Burch are the mother and father, respectively, of Sabian E. Burch.... While Shon Burch was pregnant with Sabian, she received an "MMR" (measles, mumps, rubella).... After Sabian was born, the infant was determined to be suffering from a serious neurologic abnormality known as Aicardi's Syndrome. Sabian has suffered from a seizure disorder, brain malformation, and significant developmental delay....

The instant petition ... alleged that Sabian's severe neurologic abnormality was a result of the MMR vaccination that her mother received ... while pregnant with Sabian.... [R]espondent [argued that] the evidence does not support a conclusion that Sabian's neurologic abnormality was caused by the MMR vaccination in question.... [T]he parties agreed that [the] crucial legal issue is whether Sabian, while *in utero*, "received" the MMR vaccine from the MMR vaccination administered to her mother ... as the term "received" is used at § 300aa-11(c)(1)(A)....

Under the Program, compensation is available ... to a person who has suffered an injury after having "received" a vaccine.... The relevant statutory provision reads, in pertinent part, as follows:

> A petition for compensation ... for a vaccine-related injury ... shall contain—
>
> (1) ... an affidavit, and supporting documentation, demonstrating that the person who suffered such injury ...—
>
> (A) received a vaccine....

§ 300aa-11(c)(1)(A). Thus, the person whose injury is the subject of the Program petition must have "received" a vaccine....

[R]espondent has argued that ... I am bound by the "sovereign immunity" principles of statutory construction, which would mean that I should "strictly" and "narrowly" construe the statute. On the other hand, there also exists a principle of statutory construction that states that a "remedial" statute is generally to be construed in a "liberal" fashion so as to give broad effect to the "remedial" purpose behind the statute. Accordingly, ... I will examine each of these principles....

The starting point of the doctrine of "sovereign immunity," a judge-made doctrine which dates from the early days of our country, is that the federal government, as this nation's "sovereign," may not be sued without its consent. From that initial principle, the federal courts have derived certain principles of *statutory construction* that have been applied in interpreting legislation which is said to have *waived* that immunity with respect to a particular type of suit against the United States. One principle is that a statutory waiver of sovereign immunity must be "definitely and unequivocally expressed." The second is that the statutory language setting forth such a waiver is to be "construed strictly" or "construed narrowly" in favor of the government.

In this case, ... the "Vaccine Act" unquestionably *does* waive the government's immunity from suit, in order to permit monetary awards to persons whose circumstances fall within that Act's requirements. The sovereign immunity principles of statutory construction set forth above, however, are still of great significance here, because in this case I am required to determine the meaning of *one particular provision* of the Vaccine Act. Respondent argues that because this particular provision is *part* of the Vaccine Act, which *as a whole* constitutes a waiver of sovereign immunity, in reaching an interpretation I must "narrowly and strictly" construe the statutory language....

[I]t is clear that the doctrine of sovereign immunity applies to the interpretation of this provision of the Vaccine Act....

Another principle of statutory construction, however, must also be considered...."[R]emedial" or "welfare" legislation should be given a "broad construction" or a "liberal interpretation" in order to further the "remedial," "beneficent," or "humanitar-ian" purposes behind the statute. Thus, the question arises whether the Vaccine Act should be viewed as legislation that is "remedial" in nature, and therefore should be "liberally" construed so as to give a wider application to the remedial purposes behind the statute.[3] The cases ... mentioning this "remedial legislation" rule do not provide any precise defi-nition of what legislation should be considered to be "remedial" in nature. However, the cases all seem to refer to statutes that are designed to benefit or protect classes of persons who have been harmed or disadvantaged in some fashion. In that light, it seems reason-able to conclude that the Vaccine Act, which is designed to benefit persons injured by vaccinations, does constitute a "remedial" statute. Does it follow, therefore, that the pro-visions of that Act are to be "liberally" or "broadly" interpreted? I conclude that it does not. Rather, my analysis of the case law is that with respect to statutes which are *both* "re-medial" in nature *and* also waive the federal government's immunity from suit, it is the sovereign immunity doctrine which "trumps" the competing principle of statutory con-struction, so that *strict and narrow construction* remains the controlling principle with respect to such statutes....

First, ... in all of the cases ... concerning "remedial legislation," as in all of the Supreme Court opinions and nearly all of the other federal cases that I have found that also describe the same rule of "liberal construction," the statute that was being interpreted pertained to relief against *private entities*, rather than against the federal government. So those cases provide no authority for the proposition that it is correct to use the "remedial legislation" principle to construe liberally a statute that authorizes relief against the *United States*. More importantly, the recent Supreme Court precedent seems to point strongly to the conclusion that the "remedial legislation" principle has *no* application to statutes afford-ing relief against the *government*. For example, in *Lane v. Pena*, that court was interpret-ing the Rehabilitation Act of 1973, an act protecting the handicapped which certainly does seem to be an example of "remedial legislation." Yet the Court applied the sovereign immunity "strict construction" rule, and mentioned nothing about the remedial nature of the statute being a reason to mitigate the application of that rule. Another example is *Library of Congress v. Shaw*, in which the Supreme Court was interpreting a provision of the Civil Rights Act of 1964, which allows victims of racial discrimination to obtain re-dress, and, thus, also seems to fit the description of "remedial legislation." Again, the Court applied the "strict construction" principle as part of the sovereign immunity doc-trine. Thus, the Supreme Court ... seems clearly to have taken the view that when a statute waives the federal government's immunity from suit, such a statute, *even when "reme-dial" in nature*, must be strictly construed in the government's favor.

To be sure, I have identified two appellate court decisions in which it is asserted that a "remedial" statute affording relief against the United States should be interpreted "lib-erally." In addition, the court in *McMahon v. United States*, 186 F.2d 227, 229 (3rd Cir.1950), *aff'd* 342 U.S. 25 (1951), suggested that in the case of a statute that is *both* "remedial" *and* constitutes a waiver of sovereign immunity, the two competing statutory construction principles would in effect cancel each other out, so that the court would construe the statutory language "without throwing any weights on either side of the scale." I conclude, however, that [this] appellate court decision[was] simply overruled by the recent Supreme Court decisions..., which establish a contrary rule....

---

3. The petitioners in this case have not cited these cases, nor have they cited this principle of lib-eral construction of remedial statutes. Nevertheless, I have found it appropriate to consider on my own this potentially-applicable theory of statutory construction.

This means that I must "constru[e] ambiguities in favor of immunity." It means that if there exist more than one "plausible" reading of the statutory provision at issue or two possible interpretations of "equal likelihood" then I must choose the interpretation that produces the more limited award....

The question of whether an unborn child *in utero* "receives" a vaccine that is administered to his mother, under the meaning of the word "received" as used in § 300aa-11(c)(1)(A), presents a difficult issue of statutory interpretation. Petitioners argue that Sabian "received" the MMR vaccine administered to her mother while Sabian was *in utero,* contending as a matter of fact that the vaccine injected into the mother's body would automatically pass into the unborn child's system, "just as that fetus receives the nutrients that the mother ingests." Petitioners argue that since the vaccine passes into the unborn child's system, that child has "received" the vaccine. Respondent argues, on the other hand, that the term "received" applies only to situations in which a person was *directly administered* the vaccine by the vaccine administrator — *i.e.,* was injected with a vaccine or ingested it (took it orally). Respondent argues that Sabian did not "receive" the vaccine within the statutory meaning; only her mother did....

I find this statutory interpretation question to be a difficult one, with reasonable arguments on both sides. However, I ultimately must conclude that the sovereign immunity doctrine dictates the outcome of this issue. I conclude that the statutory language of § 300aa-11(c)(1)(A) is ambiguous in its application to this situation, and that both competing interpretations are at least "plausible." Therefore, ... I must adopt respondent's interpretation, since that produces the more narrow waiver.

In reaching this conclusion, I acknowledge that I find much that is persuasive in petitioners' arguments.... First, I find considerable merit in the argument ... that an unborn child can be said to have "received" a vaccine under the ordinary meaning and usage of the term "received." That is, assuming that it is true as a factual matter that the MMR vaccine would have naturally flowed through the mother's system into Sabian's system at that stage of the pregnancy, then it does seem logical to conclude that Sabian "received" the vaccine. Although Sabian did not receive it *directly* from the vaccine administrator, it is reasonable to say that she did "receive" it through her mother's system.... [T]here seems to be no particular reason to restrict the word "received" in the statute to receipt by *injection* or *ingestion,* as respondent argues. Certainly, under the ordinary usage of the word "receive," a person can "receive" things by means other than injection or ingestion. I see no inherent reason why a person could not be said to "receive" a vaccine in this third fashion — that is, by transfer from a pregnant woman's system into the system of the unborn child.

Second, I agree ... that petitioners' interpretation of the term "received" would be more in keeping with the general spirit and the remedial nature of the Program, which was intended to "generously" assist injured persons whose injuries may have been vaccine-caused.

However, on the other hand, I can also see merit in respondent's argument. Although a person can "receive" other things by means other than injection or ingestion, it is true that when one thinks of "receiving" *a vaccine,* one would normally think of having the vaccine administered by injection or ingestion. So, there is some appeal to respondent's argument that when Congress used the phrase "received a vaccine" in § 300aa-11(c)(1)(A), Congress likely had in mind only receipt by injection or ingestion....[9]

---

9. I note that I have not found any legislative history that relates specifically to the statutory provision at issue here....

[Also,] I must respectfully disagree with the ultimate legal conclusion of [another court that addressed the same issue: *Rooks v. Secretary of HHS*, 2000 WL 816825 (Fed. Cl. Spec. Mstr. No. 93-689V, June 5, 2000)]. My view is that the *Rooks* decision failed to give full effect to the rigorous application of the sovereign immunity doctrine that has been directed by the [recent] Supreme Court [decisions] highlighted above. Specifically, I note the following discussion in the judge's opinion in *Rooks:*

> Within the context of the Act's purpose, the language of clause (c)(1)(A) does not itself clearly settle the issue. *The term "received" is ambiguous* because it could refer to receipt of the actual vaccine or receipt of the injection or pill to be swallowed. *Each is plausible....* Based on the underlying policy and object of the Act, the court believes that the term "received" should be given broader scope. The court finds that the potential to "receive" a vaccine while in utero exists because such an interpretation would fulfill the purpose behind the statute.

(35 Fed. Cl. at 6, emphasis added.)

Thus, in this passage, the judge in *Rooks* clearly acknowledges that the statutory provision in question is "ambiguous," and that each of two proposed interpretations thereof is "plausible." The judge further indicates that he chose the petitioner's "broader" interpretation over the respondent's interpretation, "[b]ased on the underlying policy and object of the [Vaccine] Act," as determined from the legislative history. But while this method of statutory interpretation would seem quite persuasive to me outside the context of the sovereign immunity doctrine, in my view it is contrary to the Supreme Court ... decisions ... discussed above. That is, the judge's reliance upon the legislative history and statutory purpose seems to be erroneous in light of the direction of those Supreme Court rulings that if the waiver is not unambiguously apparent in the statutory text itself, a court *must not utilize the legislative history* to interpret the text. Moreover, it seems to me to have been incorrect, under the recent Supreme Court decisions, for the *Rooks* court to find the statutory provision to be "ambiguous" and the respondent's narrower interpretation to be "plausible," but to nevertheless choose the petitioner's "broader" interpretation. Rather, the recent cases have specified that a court must "constru[e] ambiguities in favor of immunity." Those decisions have also mandated that if there exist more than one "plausible" reading of the statutory provision at issue or two possible interpretations of "equal likelihood" then a court must choose the interpretation that produces the *narrower* waiver of immunity.

In short, on this issue of statutory interpretation, I agree with ... *Rooks* that the statutory language is "ambiguous" as to its application here, and that both statutory interpretations advanced in this case are "plausible." Therefore, as dictated by the recent Supreme Court sovereign immunity decisions cited above, I am bound to choose the interpretation that produces the more narrow waiver of immunity. Here, that is the respondent's interpretation of the statute....

As a final point, I note that I reach my decision on this case even though I am well aware of the statement in the legislative history indicating that Vaccine Act awards are to be made with "generosity." H.R. Rept. No. 99-908, 99th Cong., 2d Sess. at 3. Also, as the judge pointed out in *Rooks*, it seems clear that the *general spirit* behind enactment of the Act was one of generosity to persons who have suffered very unfortunate injuries. Therefore, I candidly acknowledge that my own initial intuitive inclination was to resist the idea that the sovereign immunity doctrine should apply to questions of statutory interpretation in Vaccine Act cases, requiring use of the most narrow interpretation as to close questions. It seems counter-intuitive to apply this doctrine to a statute with such a generous, remedial purpose. Moreover, I personally find some of the dissenting opinions in the 1990s Supreme Court cases cited above to be persuasive in arguing against the recent trend to rigorously apply the sovereign immunity doctrine. However, those dissenting opinions are, of course, *dissents;* I am bound to follow, instead, the *majority* opinions in those cases, which mandate strict enforcement of the doctrine, even in cases where the statutory scheme involves a remedial program....

Sabian Burch clearly suffers from a tragic condition, and she and her parents are clearly deserving of great sympathy. However, I have concluded as a legal matter, for the reasons set forth above, that petitioners are barred under current law from receiving Program compensation for Sabian's neurologic condition, because Sabian did not "receive" the vaccine in question as that term is used at § 300aa-11(c)(1)(A)....

Notes and Questions

(1) *Rejecting the Plain Meaning.* The court found "considerable merit in the argument" that pursuant to the plain meaning of the statute, the child "received" the vaccine. Nonetheless, the court rejected that meaning. Why? Which canon mattered more to the court? Do you believe that it gave that canon too much weight in light of the plain meaning?

(2) *When Canons Conflict.* The court recognized that the general rule is that remedial statutes should be liberally construed; yet, the court strictly construed this statute. Why did the court not construe the statute liberally? Was it because the statute was in derogation of the common law or for some other reason?

(3) *Was the Court Correct?* The court also looked at the legislative history, plain meaning, and purpose of the statute. According to the court, each aid to construction supported the parents' position. Yet, the court relied exclusively on the canon of construction necessitated by the sovereign immunity doctrine. Given that all other aids pointed to a different interpretation, should the court have interpreted the statute differently?

(4) *Competent Lawyering?* The parents' attorney failed to mention the remedial canon to the court. In footnote 3, the court indicated that despite the attorney's failure, it would consider the canon anyway. How would you like this opinion if you were the attorney?

(5) *Statutory Approach.* Which interpretation, that of *Rook* or *Burch*, do you believe an intentionalist would adopt? A textualist? A purposivist?

(6) *Eye of the Beholder?* Consider this observation: "it is not at all apparent just what is and what is not remedial legislation; indeed all legislation might be thought remedial in some sense — even massive codifications. We suspect that the phrase typically has been used to give judicial approval to a particular set of policy viewpoints." *Ober United Travel Agency, Inc. v. U.S. Dep't of Labor*, 135 F.3d 822, 825 (D.C. Cir. 1998). Does it make sense to give such significantly different interpretations to a statute — narrow versus broad interpretation — depending on whether the purpose is remedial when that characterization seems subjective at best? Does the *Ober* court's statement echo what we noted above: that whether a statute is in derogation of the common law depends on whose ox is being gored?

(7) *Remedial Statutes in Derogation of the Common Law.* A common example of statutes that clearly have both remedial and derogation aspects are Workers' Compensation Acts: Employers may be held liable without proof of fault (in derogation of the common law), but the purpose of the acts is to provide remedies to injured workers (a remedial purpose). What happens when a statute is remedial but is also in derogation of the common law? *See Cabatbat v. County of Hawai'i Dep't of Water Supply*, 78 P.3d 756, 762 (Haw. 2003)

("Compensation acts being highly remedial in character, though in derogation of the common law, should generally be liberally and broadly construed to effectuate their beneficent purposes."); *see also Seahorse Marine Supplies, Inc. v. P.R. Sun Oil Co.*, 295 F.3d 68, 73–74 (1st Cir. 2002) (noting that the statute "is a remedial statute, and as such, merits a relatively expansive construction. We are mindful, however, that the statute is in derogation of common law rights, and therefore should not be interpreted to reach beyond its original language and purpose."); *Santa Fuel, Inc. v. Varga*, 823 A.2d 1249, 1255 (Conn. Ct. App. 2003) ("Although the mechanic's lien statute creates a statutory right in derogation of the common law … its provisions should be liberally construed in order to implement its remedial purpose of furnishing security for one who provides services or materials.") Are these statements consistent? Do they provide any real guidance for interpretation?

(8) *Should Remedial Statutes in Derogation of the Common Law be Considered "Exceptions" to the Rule of Strict Construction?* A dissenting judge in a case involving a wrongful death action made this argument:

> The majority argues our wrongful death statute is in derogation of the common law and therefore should be strictly construed. Initially, it should be noted that despite being in derogation of the common law, our wrongful death statute is a remedial statute. Furthermore, we have long recognized that "every remedial law must, of necessity, be in derogation of the common law." … As a result, "The rule that remedial statutes are construed liberally is one of the most common exceptions to the rule that statutes in derogation of the common law are to be construed strictly." … Accordingly, the majority's narrow approach would serve to defeat the purposes behind enacting the statute.

Crosby v. Glasscock Trucking Co., 532 S.E.2d 856, 863 (S.C. 2000) (Toal, J., dissenting). Does this argument resolve the tension created by these two canons or simply recast it?

Problem 14-2

Under the "American Rule," the prevailing party in a lawsuit is not entitled to its attorneys' fees from the loser, unless a statute or contract authorizes it. Thus, if a party sues another for breach of contract, the party may prevail, but the victory may be hollow because attorneys' fees can be substantial. This has been the common law rule in America since its founding and stands in stark contrast to the "British Rule," under which the losing party pays the prevailing party's fees.

You are a lawyer in a state where the legislature recently adopted a statute that permits an award of attorneys' fees to the prevailing party in contract actions. As part of the legislative history, you uncover testimony from the bill's sponsor that the statute was intended to be remedial and that it should not be construed strictly. During floor debates, another representative stated: "This narrow exception to the common law rule will allow those aggrieved by breach of a written contract to recover attorney fees." The statute simply provides: "In actions for breach of contract, and notwithstanding anything in the common law of this State to the contrary, the prevailing party in actions for breach of contract shall be entitled to recover its attorneys' fees."

After winning a verdict for your client in a case involving an *implied* contract, you are preparing for oral argument in which you will argue for an award of attorneys' fees. You need to be prepared to argue your client's position and to anticipate the losing party's arguments: that the statute should be construed narrowly as one that is in derogation of the common law.

C. Federal Preemption of State Law

The Supremacy Clause of the U.S. Constitution provides that federal law "shall be the supreme Law of the Land; and the Judges in every State shall be bound thereby, any Thing in the Constitution or Laws of any State to the Contrary notwithstanding." U.S. Const. art. VI, cl. 2. Under the Supremacy Clause, federal law—whether created by statute, Constitution, treaty, or federal regulation—prevails over state law. Thus, under our federal system of government, federal law is supreme. As a result, a state law—statute, common law, or other form—that conflicts with a federal law may be "preempted" by federal law: Federal law controls in the case of any conflict.

Sensitive issues arise in preemption analysis, however, because of the careful balance of state and federal interests. Perhaps as a consequence, in analyzing whether a federal statute preempts state law, courts often look beyond the text of the federal statute or regulation, turning immediately to examine the enacting Congress's intent or purpose. "Federal preemption can be express or implied, but in either case is primarily a question of Congressional intent." *Clearing House Ass'n, LLC v. Cuomo*, 510 F.3d 105, 113 (2d Cir. 2007). Thus, the preemption doctrine, in some ways, puts the current interpretation approach on its head, giving primacy to purpose and intent, rather than text.

There are three types of federal preemption, one express and two implied. Express preemption obviously turns on the existence of a statute expressly preempting state law. In addition to express preemption, preemption can be implied in two other situations: "[(1)] where Congress has legislated so comprehensively that federal law occupies an entire field of regulation and leaves no room for state law, or [(2)] where federal law conflicts with state law." *Id.*

Some extraordinarily difficult policy issues underlie preemption. We have edited the following cases to avoid many of the constitutionally related issues that arise with preemption, focusing instead on the statutory interpretation issues that preemption creates. Notice, however, that the importance of text fades rapidly as the preemption analysis deepens—a fact that has led to criticisms by some judges, including justices on the Supreme Court.

1. Express Preemption

If Congress chooses to include a preemption clause, then the first step of preemption analysis is to determine the scope and meaning of the clause. The "task of statutory construction must in the first instance focus on the plain wording of the clause, which necessarily contains the best evidence of Congress' pre-emptive intent." *CSX Transp., Inc. v. Easterwood*, 507 U.S. 658, 664 (1993). The following case examines the scope of an express preemption provision.

Medtronic, Inc. v. Lohr
518 U.S. 470 (1996)

Justice Stevens delivered the opinion of the Court.

Congress enacted the Medical Device Amendments of 1976.... The question presented is whether that statute pre-empts a state common-law negligence [and strict liability claims] against the manufacturer of an allegedly defective medical device....

I

Throughout our history the several States have exercised their police powers to protect the health and safety of their citizens. Because these are primarily, and historically, ... matter[s] of local concern, the States traditionally have had great latitude under their police powers to legislate as to the protection of the lives, limbs, health, comfort, and quiet of all persons.

Despite the prominence of the States in matters of public health and safety, in recent decades the Federal Government has played an increasingly significant role in the protection of the health of our people. Congress' first significant enactment in the field of public health was the Food and Drug Act of 1906, a broad prohibition against the manufacture or shipment in interstate commerce of any adulterated or misbranded food or drug. Partly in response to an ongoing concern about radio and newspaper advertising making false therapeutic claims for both "quack machines" and legitimate devices such as surgical instruments and orthopedic shoes, in 1938 Congress broadened the coverage of the 1906 Act to include misbranded or adulterated medical devices and cosmetics. See Federal Food, Drug, and Cosmetic Act of 1938 (FDCA).

While the FDCA provided for premarket approval of new drugs, it did not authorize any control over the introduction of new medical devices. As technologies advanced and medicine relied to an increasing degree on a vast array of medical equipment ... including kidney dialysis units, artificial heart valves, and heart pacemakers, policymakers and the public became concerned about the increasingly severe injuries that resulted from the failure of such devices....

In response ... [In 1976,] Congress enacted the statute at issue here: the Medical Device Amendments of 1976 (MDA or Act). The Act classifies medical devices in three categories based on the risk that they pose to the public. Devices that present no unreasonable risk of illness or injury are designated Class I and are subject only to minimal regulation by "general controls." 21 U.S.C. § 360c(a)(1)(A). Devices that are potentially more harmful are designated Class II.... § 360c(a)(1)(B). Finally, devices that either "presen[t] a potential unreasonable risk of illness or injury," or which are "purported or represented to be for a use in supporting or sustaining human life or for a use which is of substantial importance in preventing impairment of human health," are designated Class III. § 360c(a)(1)(C). Pacemakers [at issue here] are Class III devices.

Before a new Class III device may be introduced to the market, the manufacturer must provide the FDA with a "reasonable assurance" that the device is both safe and effective. Despite its relatively innocuous phrasing, the process of establishing this "reasonable assurance," which is known as the "premarket approval," or "PMA" process, is a rigorous one. Manufacturers must submit detailed information regarding the safety and efficacy of their devices, which the FDA then reviews, spending an average of 1,200 hours on each submission.

Not all, nor even most, Class III devices on the market today have received premarket approval because of two important exceptions to the PMA requirement. First, Congress realized that existing medical devices could not be withdrawn from the market while the FDA completed its PMA analysis for those devices. The statute therefore includes a "grandfathering" provision which allows pre-1976 devices to remain on the market without FDA approval until such time as the FDA initiates and completes the requisite PMA. Second, to prevent manufacturers of grandfathered devices from monopolizing the market while new devices clear the PMA hurdle, and to ensure that improvements to existing devices can be rapidly introduced into the market, the Act also permits devices that are "substantially equivalent" to pre-existing devices to avoid the PMA process.

Although "substantially equivalent" Class III devices may be marketed without the rigorous PMA review, such new devices ... are subject to the requirements of § 360(k). That section imposes a limited form of review on every manufacturer intending to market a new device by requiring it to submit a "premarket notification" to the FDA (the process is also known as a "§ 510(k) process," after the number of the section in the original Act). If the FDA concludes on the basis of the § 510(k) notification that the device is "substantially equivalent" to a pre-existing device, it can be marketed without further regulatory analysis.... The § 510(k) notification process is by no means comparable to the PMA process; in contrast to the 1,200 hours necessary to complete a PMA review, the § 510(k) review is completed in an average of only 20 hours. As one commentator noted: The attraction of substantial equivalence to manufacturers is clear. [Section] 510(k) notification requires little information, rarely elicits a negative response from the FDA, and gets processed very quickly.

Congress anticipated that the FDA would complete the PMA process for Class III devices relatively swiftly. But because of the substantial investment of time and energy necessary for the resolution of each PMA application, the ever-increasing numbers of medical devices, and internal administrative and resource difficulties, the FDA simply could not keep up with the rigorous PMA process. As a result, the § 510(k) premarket notification process became the means by which most new medical devices—including Class III devices—were approved for the market....

II

... Medtronic took advantage of § 510(k)'s expedited process in October 1982, when it notified the FDA that it intended to market its Model 4011 pacemaker lead as a device that was "substantially equivalent" to devices already on the market. (The lead is the portion of a pacemaker that transmits the heartbeat-steadying electrical signal from the "pulse generator" to the heart itself.) On November 30, 1982, the FDA found that the model was "substantially equivalent to devices introduced into interstate commerce" prior to the effective date of the Act, and advised Medtronic that it could therefore market its device.... The agency emphasized, however, that this determination should not be construed as an endorsement of the pacemaker lead's safety.

Cross-petitioner Lora Lohr is dependent on pacemaker technology for the proper functioning of her heart. In 1987 she was implanted with a Medtronic pacemaker equipped with one of the company's Model 4011 pacemaker leads. On December 30, 1990, the pacemaker failed, allegedly resulting in a "complete heart block" that required emergency surgery. According to her physician, a defect in the lead was the likely cause of the failure.

In 1993, Lohr and her husband filed this action.... Their complaint contained both a negligence count and a strict-liability count. The negligence count alleged a breach of Medtronic's "duty to use reasonable care ..." in several respects, including the use of defective materials in the lead and a failure to warn or properly instruct the plaintiff or her physicians of the tendency of the pacemaker to fail, despite knowledge of other earlier failures. The strict-liability count alleged that the device was in a defective condition and unreasonably dangerous to foreseeable users at the time of its sale.

Medtronic ... filed a motion for summary judgment arguing that both the negligence and strict-liability claims were pre-empted by 21 U.S.C. § 360k(a). That section, which is at the core of the dispute between the parties in this suit, provides:

"§ 360k. State and local requirements respecting devices

(a) General rule

Except as provided in subsection (b) of this section, no State or political sub-division of a State may establish or continue in effect with respect to a device intended for human use any requirement—

(1) which is different from, or in addition to, any requirement applicable under this chapter to the device, and

(2) which relates to the safety or effectiveness of the device or to any other matter included in a requirement applicable to the device under this chapter.

To carry out this grant of authority, the FDA has issued regulations under the statute which both construe the scope of § 360k(a) and address the instances in which the FDA will grant exemptions to its pre-emptive effect....

The District Court ... dismissed the Lohrs' entire complaint.

The Court of Appeals reversed in part and affirmed in part.

Medtronic filed a petition for certiorari seeking review of the Court of Appeals' decision insofar as it affirmed the District Court and the Lohrs filed a cross-petition seeking review of the judgment insofar as it upheld the pre-emption defense.... [W]e granted both petitions.

III

... [W]e are presented with the task of interpreting a statutory provision that expressly pre-empts state law. While the pre-emptive language of § 360k(a) means that we need not go beyond that language to determine whether Congress intended the MDA to pre-empt at least some state law, we must nonetheless identify the domain expressly pre-empted by that language. Although our analysis of the scope of the pre-emption statute must begin with its text, our interpretation of that language does not occur in a contextual vacuum. Rather, that interpretation is informed by two presumptions about the nature of pre-emption.

First, because the States are independent sovereigns in our federal system, we have long presumed that Congress does not cavalierly pre-empt state-law causes of action. In all pre-emption cases, and particularly in those in which Congress has legislated ... in a field which the States have traditionally occupied, we start with the assumption that the historic police powers of the States were not to be superseded by the Federal Act unless that was the clear and manifest purpose of Congress....

Second, our analysis of the scope of the statute's pre-emption is guided by our oft-re-peated comment that "[t]he purpose of Congress is the ultimate touchstone" in every pre-emption case. As a result, any understanding of the scope of a pre-emption statute must rest primarily on a fair understanding of *congressional purpose.* Congress' intent, of course, primarily is discerned from the language of the pre-emption statute and the statu-tory framework surrounding it. Also relevant, however, is the structure and purpose of the statute as a whole as revealed not only in the text, but through the reviewing court's reasoned understanding of the way in which Congress intended the statute and its sur-rounding regulatory scheme to affect business, consumers, and the law....

IV

... Medtronic argues ... the plain language of the statute pre-empts any and all com-mon-law claims brought by an injured plaintiff against a manufacturer of medical devices.

Medtronic's argument ... is implausible. Under Medtronic's view of the statute, Con-gress effectively precluded state courts from affording state consumers any protection from injuries resulting from a defective medical device. Moreover, because there is no explicit private cause of action against manufacturers contained in the MDA, and no suggestion that the Act created an implied private right of action, Congress would have barred most, if not all, relief for persons injured by defective medical devices. Medtronic's construction of § 360k would therefore have the perverse effect of granting complete immunity from design defect liability to an entire industry that, in the judgment of Congress, needed more stringent regulation in order "to provide for the safety and effectiveness of medical devices intended for human use," 90 Stat. 539 (preamble to Act)....

An examination of the basic purpose of the legislation as well as its history entirely supports our rejection of Medtronic's extreme position. The MDA was enacted "to provide for the safety and effectiveness of medical devices intended for human use." Medtronic asserts that the Act was also intended, however, to "protect innovations in device technology from being 'stifled by unnecessary restrictions,'" and that this interest extended to the pre-emption of common-law claims. While the Act certainly reflects some of these concerns, the legislative history indicates that any fears regarding regulatory burdens were related more to the risk of *additional* federal and state regulation rather than the danger of pre-existing duties under common law. *See, e.g.,*122 Cong. Rec. 5850 (1976) (statement of Rep. Collins) (opposing further "redundant and burdensome Federal requirements"); *id.,* at 5855 (discussing efforts taken in MDA to protect small businesses from the additional requirements of the Act). Indeed, nowhere in the materials relating to the Act's history have we discovered a reference to a fear that product liability actions would hamper the development of medical devices. To the extent that Congress was concerned about protecting the industry, that intent was manifested primarily through fewer substantive requirements under the Act, not the pre-emption provision; furthermore, any such concern was far outweighed by concerns about the primary issue motivating the MDA's enactment: the safety of those who use medical devices.

The legislative history also confirms our understanding that § 360(k) simply was not intended to pre-empt most, let alone all, general common-law duties enforced by damages actions. There is ... nothing in the ... debates suggesting that any proponent of the legislation intended a sweeping pre-emption of traditional common-law remedies against manufacturers and distributors of defective devices. If Congress intended such a result, its failure even to hint at it is spectacularly odd, particularly since Members of both Houses were acutely aware of ongoing product liability litigation.[13] ...

V

Medtronic asserts several specific reasons why, even if § 360k does not pre-empt all common-law claims, it at least pre-empts the Lohrs' claims in this suit. In contrast, the Lohrs argue that their entire complaint should survive a reasonable evaluation of the pre-emptive scope of § 360k(a).... First, the Lohrs claim that the Court of Appeals correctly held that their negligent design claims were not pre-empted because the § 510(k) pre-market notification process imposes no "requirement" on the design of Medtronic's pacemaker. Second, they suggest that even if the FDA's general rules regulating manufacturing practices and labeling are "requirements" that pre-empt *different* state requirements, § 360k(a) does not pre-empt state rules that merely duplicate some or all of those federal requirements. Finally, they argue that because the State's general rules imposing com-

---

13. Furthermore, if Congress had intended the MDA to work this dramatic change in the availability of state-law remedies, one would expect some reference to that change in the extensive contemporary reviews of the legislation. We have been able to find no such reference.

mon-law duties upon Medtronic do not impose a requirement "with respect to a device," they do not conflict with the FDA's general rules relating to manufacturing and labeling and are therefore not pre-empted.

Design Claim

The Court of Appeals concluded that the Lohrs' defective design claims were not pre-empted because the requirements with which the company had to comply were not sufficiently concrete to constitute a pre-empting federal requirement. Medtronic counters by pointing to the FDA's determination that Model 4011 is "substantially equivalent" to an earlier device as well as the agency's continuing authority to exclude the device from the market if its design is changed. These factors, Medtronic argues, amount to a specific, federally enforceable design requirement that cannot be affected by state-law pressures such as those imposed on manufacturers subject to product liability suits.

The company's defense exaggerates the importance of the §510(k) process and the FDA letter to the company regarding the pacemaker's substantial equivalence to a grandfathered device.... [T]he 510(k) process is focused on *equivalence,* not safety. As a result, substantial equivalence determinations provide little protection to the public. These determinations simply compare a post-1976 device to a pre-1976 device to ascertain whether the later device is no more dangerous and no less effective than the earlier device. If the earlier device poses a severe risk or is ineffective, then the later device may also be risky or ineffective. The design of the Model 4011, as with the design of pre-1976 and other "substantially equivalent" devices, has never been formally reviewed under the MDA for safety or efficacy.

The FDA stressed this basic conclusion in its letter to Medtronic finding the 4011 lead "substantially equivalent" to devices already on the market. That letter only required Medtronic to comply with "general standards" — the lowest level of protection "applicable to all medical devices," and including "listing of devices, good manufacturing practices, labeling, and the misbranding and adulteration provisions of the Act." It explicitly warned Medtronic that the letter did "not in any way denote official FDA approval of your device," and that "[a]ny representation that creates an impression of official approval of this device because of compliance with the premarket notification regulations is misleading and constitutes misbranding." FDA Substantial Equivalence Letter.

Thus, even though the FDA may well examine §510(k) applications for Class III devices ... with a concern for the safety and effectiveness of the device, it did not "require" Medtronics' pacemaker to take any particular form for any particular reason; the agency simply allowed the pacemaker, as a device substantially equivalent to one that existed before 1976, to be marketed without running the gauntlet of the PMA process.... In providing for this exemption to PMA review, Congress intended merely to give manufacturers the freedom to compete, to a limited degree, with and on the same terms as manufacturers of medical devices that existed prior to 1976. There is no suggestion in either the statutory scheme or the legislative history that the §510(k) exemption process was intended to do anything other than maintain the status quo with respect to the marketing of existing medical devices and their substantial equivalents. That status quo included the possibility that the manufacturer of the device would have to defend itself against state-law claims of negligent design. Given this background behind the "substantial equivalence" exemption, the fact that "[t]he purpose of Congress is the ultimate touchstone" in every pre-emption case, and the presumption against pre-emption, the Court of Appeals properly concluded that the "substantial equivalence" provision did not pre-empt the Lohrs' design claims.

Identity of Requirements Claims

The Lohrs next suggest that even if "requirements" exist with respect to the manufacturing and labeling of the pacemaker, and even if we can also consider state law to impose a "requirement" under the Act, the state requirement is not pre-empted unless it is "different from, or in addition to," the federal requirement. § 360k(a)(1).... [T]he Lohrs' allegations may include claims that Medtronic has ... violated FDA regulations. At least these claims, they suggest, can be maintained without being pre-empted by § 360k, and we agree.

Nothing in § 360k denies Florida the right to provide a traditional damages remedy for violations of common-law duties when those duties parallel federal requirements. Even if it may be necessary as a matter of Florida law to prove that those violations were the result of negligent conduct, or that they created an unreasonable hazard for users of the product, such additional elements of the state-law cause of action would make the state requirements narrower, not broader, than the federal requirement. While such a narrower requirement might be "different from" the federal rules in a literal sense, such a difference would surely provide a strange reason for finding pre-emption of a state rule insofar as it duplicates the federal rule. The presence of a damages remedy does not amount to the additional or different "requirement" that is necessary under the statute; rather, it merely provides another reason for manufacturers to comply with identical existing "requirements" under federal law....

Manufacturing and Labeling Claims

Finally, the Lohrs suggest that with respect to the manufacturing and labeling claims, the Court of Appeals should have rejected Medtronic's pre-emption defense in full.

[The FDA] labeling regulations ... require manufacturers of every medical device, with a few limited exceptions, to include with the device a label containing "information for use, ... and any relevant hazards, contraindications, side effects, and precautions." 21 CFR §§ 801.109(b) and (c) (1995). Similarly, manufacturers are required to comply with "Good Manufacturing Practices," or "GMP's," which are set forth in 32 sections and less than 10 pages in the Code of Federal Regulations....

While admitting that these requirements exist, the Lohrs suggest that their general nature simply does not pre-empt claims alleging that the manufacturer failed to comply with other duties under state common law....

The Lohrs' theory is supported by the FDA regulations, which provide that state requirements are pre-empted "only" when the FDA has established "specific counterpart regulations or ... other specific requirements applicable to a particular device." 21 CFR § 808.1(d) (1995).... The regulations even go so far as to state that § 360k(a) generally "does not preempt a state or local requirement prohibiting the manufacture of adulterated or misbranded devices" unless "such a prohibition has the effect of establishing a substantive requirement for a specific device." § 808.1(d)(6)(ii)....

Although we do not believe that this statutory and regulatory language necessarily precludes "general" federal requirements from ever pre-empting state requirements, or "general" state requirements from ever being pre-empted, it is impossible to ignore its overarching concern that pre-emption occur only where a particular state requirement threatens to interfere with a specific federal interest....

[T]he Lohrs' common-law claims are not pre-empted by the federal labeling and manufacturing requirements. The generality of those requirements make this quite unlike a case in which the Federal Government has weighed the competing interests relevant to the particular requirement in question, reached an unambiguous conclusion about how those competing considerations should be resolved in a particular case or set of cases, and implemented that conclusion via a specific mandate on manufacturers or producers. Rather, the federal requirements reflect important but entirely generic concerns about device regulation generally, not the sort of concerns regarding a specific device or field of device regulation that the statute or regulations were designed to protect from potentially contradictory state requirements.

Similarly, the general state common-law requirements in this suit were not specifically developed "with respect to" medical devices. Accordingly, they are not the kinds of requirements that Congress and the FDA feared would impede the ability of federal regulators to implement and enforce specific federal requirements. The legal duty that is the predicate for the Lohrs' negligent manufacturing claim is the general duty of every manufacturer to use due care to avoid foreseeable dangers in its products. Similarly, the predicate for the failure to warn claim is the general duty to inform users and purchasers of potentially dangerous items of the risks involved in their use. These general obligations are no more a threat to federal requirements than would be a state-law duty to comply with local fire prevention regulations and zoning codes, or to use due care in the training and supervision of a work force. These state requirements therefore escape pre-emption, not because the source of the duty is a judge-made common-law rule, but rather because their generality leaves them outside the category of requirements that § 360k envisioned to be "with respect to" specific devices such as pacemakers. As a result, none of the Lohrs' claims based on allegedly defective manufacturing or labeling are pre-empted by the MDA...

Accordingly, the judgment of the Court of Appeals is reversed insofar as it held that any of the claims were pre-empted and affirmed insofar as it rejected the pre-emption defense. The cases are remanded for further proceedings.

JUSTICE BREYER, concurring in part and concurring in the judgment.

This action raises two questions. First, do the Medical Device Amendments of 1976 (MDA) to the Federal Food, Drug, and Cosmetic Act ever pre-empt a state-law tort action? Second, if so, does the MDA pre-empt the particular state-law tort claims at issue here?

I

My answer to the first question is that the MDA will sometimes pre-empt a state-law tort suit. I basically agree with Justice O'CONNOR's discussion of this point and with her conclusion. The statute's language, read literally, supports that conclusion. It says:

> "[N]o State ... may establish ... with respect to a device ... any [state] *requirement* ... which is different from, or in addition to, any [federal] requirement...."

One can reasonably read the word "requirement" as including the legal requirements that grow out of the application, in particular circumstances, of a State's tort law....

Finally, a contrary holding would have anomalous consequences. Imagine that, in respect to a particular hearing aid component, a federal MDA regulation requires a 2-inch wire, but a state agency regulation requires a 1-inch wire. If the federal law, embodied in the "2-inch" MDA regulation, pre-empts the state "1-inch" agency regulation, why would it not similarly pre-empt a state-law tort action that premises liability upon the defendant manufacturer's failure to use a 1-inch wire (say, an award by a jury persuaded by expert testimony that use of a more than 1-inch wire is negligent)? The effects of the state agency regulation and the state tort suit are identical. To distinguish between them for pre-emption purposes would grant greater power (to set state standards "different from, or in addition to," federal standards) to a single state jury than to state officials acting through state administrative or legislative lawmaking processes. Where Congress likely did not focus specifically upon the matter, I would not take it to have intended this anomalous result.

Consequently, I believe that ordinarily, insofar as the MDA pre-empts a state require-ment embodied in a state statute, rule, regulation, or other administrative action, it would also pre-empt a similar requirement that takes the form of a standard of care or behav-ior imposed by a state-law tort action. It is possible that the plurality also agrees on this point, although it does not say so explicitly.

II

The answer to the second question turns on Congress' intent. Although Congress has not stated whether the MDA does, or does not, pre-empt the tort claims here at issue, several considerations lead me to conclude that it does not.

First, the MDA's pre-emption provision is highly ambiguous. That provision makes clear that federal requirements may pre-empt state requirements, but it says next to noth-ing about just when, where, or how they may do so. The words "any [state] requirement" and "any [federal] requirement," for example, do not tell us *which* requirements are at issue, for *every* state requirement that is not identical to even *one* federal requirement is "different from, or in addition to," that single federal requirement; yet, Congress could not have intended that the existence of one single federal rule, say, about a 2-inch hear-ing aid wire, would pre-empt *every* state law hearing aid rule, even a set of rules related only to the packaging or shipping of hearing aids. Thus, Congress must have intended that courts look elsewhere for help as to just which federal requirements pre-empt just which state requirements, as well as just how they might do so.

Justice O'Connor, with whom The Chief Justice [Rehnquist], Justice Scalia, and Justice Thomas join, concurring in part and dissenting in part.

... [B]ecause Congress has expressly provided a pre-emption provision, we need not go beyond that language to determine whether Congress intended the MDA to pre-empt state law. We agree, then, on the task before us: to interpret Congress' intent by reading the statute in accordance with its terms. This, however, the Court has failed to do.

The cases require us to determine whether the Lohrs' state common-law claims sur-vive pre-emption under § 360k. I conclude that state common-law damages actions do im-pose "requirements" and are therefore pre-empted where such requirements would differ from those imposed by the FDCA. The plurality acknowledges that a common-law action might impose a "requirement," but suggests that such a pre-emption would be "rare in-deed." To reach that determination, the opinion ... states that pre-emption occurs only "where a particular state requirement threatens to interfere with a specific federal inter-est," and ... concludes that common-law claims are almost never pre-empted, and that the Lohrs' claims here are not pre-empted. This decision is bewildering and seemingly without guiding principle.

The language of § 360k demonstrates congressional intent that the MDA pre-empt "any requirement" by a State that is "different from, or in addition to," that applicable to the device under the FDCA. The Lohrs have raised various state common-law claims in connection with Medtronic's pacemaker lead. Analysis, therefore, must begin with the question whether state common-law actions can constitute "requirements" within the meaning of § 360k(a)....

If the statute contains an express pre-emption clause, the task of statutory construction must in the first instance focus on the plain wording of the clause, which necessarily contains the best evidence of Congress' pre-emptive intent.... Title 21 U.S.C. § 360k(a)(1) directs the pre-emption of "any [state] requirement" "which is different from, or in addition to, any requirement applicable under [the FDCA] to the device." ... [T]he term "requirement" encompasses state common-law causes of action.... The statute makes no mention of a requirement of specificity, and there is no sound basis for determining that such a restriction on "any requirement" exists.

I conclude that a fair reading of § 360k indicates that state common-law claims are pre-empted, as the statute itself states, to the extent that their recognition would impose "any requirement" different from, or in addition to, FDCA requirements applicable to the device. From that premise, I proceed to the question whether FDCA requirements applicable to the device exist here to pre-empt the Lohrs' state-law claims.

I agree with the Court that the Lohrs' defective design claim is not pre-empted by the FDCA's § 510(k) "substantial equivalency" process. The § 510(k) process merely evaluates whether the Class III device at issue is substantially equivalent to a device that was on the market before 1976, the effective date of the MDA; if so, the later device may be also be marketed. Because the § 510(k) process seeks merely to establish whether a pre-1976 device and a post-1976 device are equivalent, and places no "requirements" on a device, the Lohrs' defective design claim is not pre-empted.

I also agree that the Lohrs' claims are not pre-empted by § 360k to the extent that they seek damages for Medtronic's alleged violation of federal requirements. Where a state cause of action seeks to enforce an FDCA requirement, that claim does not impose a requirement that is "different from, or in addition to," requirements under federal law. To be sure, the threat of a damages remedy will give manufacturers an additional cause to comply, but the requirements imposed on them under state and federal law do not differ. Section 360k does not preclude States from imposing different or additional *remedies,* but only different or additional *requirements.*

I disagree, however, with the Court's conclusion that the Lohrs' claims survive pre-emption insofar as they would compel Medtronic to comply with requirements different from those imposed by the FDCA.... Some, if not all, of the Lohrs' common-law claims regarding the manufacturing and labeling of Medtronic's device would compel Medtronic to comply with requirements different from, or in addition to, those required by the FDA. The FDA's Good Manufacturing Practice (GMP) regulations impose comprehensive requirements relating to every aspect of the device-manufacturing process, including a manufacturer's organization and personnel, buildings, equipment, component controls, production and process controls, packaging and labeling controls, holding, distribution, installation, device evaluation, and recordkeeping. The Lohrs' common-law claims regarding manufacture would, if successful, impose state requirements "different from, or in addition to," the GMP requirements, and are therefore pre-empted. In similar fashion, the Lohrs' failure to warn claim is pre-empted by the extensive labeling requirements imposed by the FDA. See, *e.g.,* 21 CFR § 801.109 (1995) (requiring labels to include such information as indications, effects, routes, methods, frequency and duration of administration, relevant hazards, contraindications, side effects, and precautions). These extensive federal manufacturing and labeling requirements are certainly applicable to the device manufactured by Medtronic. Section 360k(a) requires no more specificity than that for pre-emption of state common-law claims....

Notes and Questions

(1) *Express Preemption.* This case involved an express preemption provision. Why? Do you agree with the dissent that the term "requirements" is clear and indicates Congress's intent to preempt any state requirement that is more stringent than the federal requirements? Why did the plurality disagree with this point?

(2) *Clear Statement Rule.* Why, according to the plurality, must Congress be clear when it intends to preempt state law? Was Congress clear here? Should the Court require even greater clarity than was present here before finding preemption?

(3) *Dissent v. Plurality.* Where did the dissent and plurality part ways? The Lohrs raised three claims: defective design, failure to abide by federal requirements, and violations of state manufacturing and labeling laws. Which claims did both the plurality and dissent believe were not preempted? Which claims did the dissent believe were preempted and the plurality believed were not? Why the difference?

(4) *Approach.* Did approach matter at all? Or, did the two opinions differ in their understanding of the plain meaning of the word "requirements"? Assuming the latter, what different interpretations did the plurality and dissent have? Which do you think was correct?

(5) *Intent, Purpose, and More?* Although the Justices disagreed on the outcome, each of them relied to some extent on extratextual sources, such as agency regulations. The plurality, in fact, relied heavily on legislative history to determine intent. Is preemption, by its nature, an inquiry that must be extratextual, even in cases involving express preemption provisions?

(6) *The FDA's Preemption Regulation.* The FDA promulgated a regulation that provided:

> State ... requirements are preempted only when ... there are ... *specific* [federal] requirements applicable to a particular device ... thereby making any existing *divergent* State ... requirements applicable to the device different from, or in addition to, the *specific* [federal] requirements....

Medronic, Inc., 518 U.S. at 499 (citing 21 C.F.R. § 808.1(d)(1995)). Can a federal agency determine that Congress intended to preempt state law? Assuming not, then what—if any—is the relevance of this regulation?

In the previous section, we examined the contours of express preemption clauses and saw that Congress isn't always so clear. We turn now to implied preemption claims.

2. Implied Preemption

Two types of implied preemption have been identified: field preemption and conflict preemption. Field preemption arises when federal statutes are so comprehensive that they occupy an entire field. It is a very narrow doctrine, rarely invoked, and so we address it in the notes following the case below. In contrast, conflict preemption is more common. Conflict preemption arises when there is a conflict between federal and state law such that either (a) it is impossible for a party to comply with both laws or (b) state law "stands as an obstacle to the accomplishment" of federal objectives.

In the following case, the defendant raised implied preemption, but the Court found none. Many commentators view this case as indicating a sharp shift away from finding implied preemption and toward a more textualist approach to this issue. See if you agree.

Wyeth v. Levine

129 S. Ct. 1187 (2009)

JUSTICE STEVENS delivered the opinion of the Court.

Directly injecting the drug Phenergan into a patient's vein creates a significant risk of catastrophic consequences. A Vermont jury found that petitioner Wyeth, the manufacturer of the drug, had failed to provide an adequate warning of that risk and awarded damages to respondent Diana Levine to compensate her for the amputation of her arm. The warnings on Phenergan's label had been deemed sufficient by the Federal Food and Drug Administration (FDA) when it approved Wyeth's new drug application in 1955 and when it later approved changes in the drug's labeling. The question we must decide is whether the FDA's approvals provide Wyeth with a complete defense to Levine's tort claims. We conclude that they do not....

The injectable form of Phenergan can be administered intramuscularly or intravenously, and it can be administered intravenously through either the "IV-push" method, whereby the drug is injected directly into a patient's vein, or the "IV-drip" method, whereby the drug is introduced into a saline solution in a hanging intravenous bag and slowly descends through a catheter inserted in a patient's vein. The drug is corrosive and causes irreversible gangrene if it enters a patient's artery.

Levine's injury resulted from an IV-push injection of Phenergan. On April 7, 2000, ... she received ... Phenergan for her nausea.... [T]he physician assistant administered the drugs by the IV-push method, and Phenergan entered Levine's artery, either because the needle penetrated an artery directly or because the drug escaped from the vein into surrounding tissue (a phenomenon called "perivascular extravasation") where it came in contact with arterial blood. As a result, Levine developed gangrene, and doctors amputated first her right hand and then her entire forearm. In addition to her pain and suffering, Levine incurred substantial medical expenses and the loss of her livelihood as a professional musician....

Levine brought an action for damages against Wyeth, relying on common-law negligence and strict-liability theories. Although Phenergan's labeling warned of the danger of gangrene and amputation following inadvertent intra-arterial injection, Levine alleged that the labeling was defective because it failed to instruct clinicians to use the IV-drip method of intravenous administration instead of the higher risk IV-push method. More broadly, she alleged that Phenergan is not reasonably safe for intravenous administration because the foreseeable risks of gangrene and loss of limb are great in relation to the drug's therapeutic benefits....

The evidence presented during the 5-day jury trial showed that the risk of intra-arterial injection or perivascular extravasation can be almost entirely eliminated through the use of IV-drip, rather than IV-push, administration.... While Phenergan's labeling warned against intra-arterial injection and perivascular extravasation and advised that "[w]hen administering any irritant drug intravenously it is usually preferable to inject it through the tubing of an intravenous infusion set that is known to be functioning satisfactorily," the labeling did not contain a specific warning about the risks of IV-push administration ...

[T]he trial judge instructed the jury that it could consider evidence of Wyeth's compliance with FDA requirements but that such compliance did not establish that the warnings were adequate. He also instructed, without objection from Wyeth, that FDA regulations "permit a drug manufacturer to change a product label to add or strengthen a warning about its product without prior FDA approval so long as it later submits the revised warning for review and approval."

... [T]he jury found that Wyeth was negligent [and] that Phenergan was a defective product as a result of inadequate warnings and instructions.... It awarded total damages of $7,400,000 ...

The Vermont Supreme Court affirmed....

The question presented by the petition is whether the FDA's drug labeling judgments preempt state law product liability claims premised on the theory that different labeling judgments were necessary to make drugs reasonably safe for use....

Wyeth makes two separate pre-emption arguments: first, that it would have been impossible for it to comply with the state-law duty to modify Phenergan's labeling without violating federal law, and second, that recognition of Levine's state tort action creates an unacceptable obstacle to the accomplishment and execution of the full purposes and objectives of Congress, because it substitutes a lay jury's decision about drug labeling for the expert judgment of the FDA. As a preface to our evaluation of these arguments, we identify two factual propositions decided during the trial court proceedings, emphasize two legal principles that guide our analysis, and review the history of the controlling federal statute.

The trial court proceedings established that Levine's injury would not have occurred if Phenergan's label had included an adequate warning about the risks of the IV-push method of administering the drug.... In finding Wyeth negligent as well as strictly liable, the jury also determined that Levine's injury was foreseeable. That the inadequate label was both a but-for and proximate cause of Levine's injury is supported by the record and no longer challenged by Wyeth.

The trial court proceedings further established that the critical defect in Phenergan's label was the lack of an adequate warning about the risks of IV-push administration.... [T]he jury verdict established only that Phenergan's warning was insufficient. It did not mandate a particular replacement warning, nor did it require contraindicating IV-push administration: [As the Vermont Supreme Court explained,] "There may have been any number of ways for [Wyeth] to strengthen the Phenergan warning without completely eliminating IV-push administration." We therefore need not decide whether a state rule proscribing intravenous administration would be pre-empted. The narrower question presented is whether federal law pre-empts Levine's claim that Phenergan's label did not contain an adequate warning about using the IV-push method of administration.

Our answer to that question must be guided by two cornerstones of our pre-emption jurisprudence. First, "the purpose of Congress is the ultimate touchstone in every pre-emption case." *Medtronic, Inc. v. Lohr*, 518 U.S. 470, 485 (1996). Second, "[i]n all pre-emption cases, and particularly in those in which Congress has 'legislated ... in a field which the States have traditionally occupied,'... we 'start with the assumption that the historic police powers of the States were not to be superseded by the Federal Act unless that was the clear and manifest purpose of Congress.'" *Lohr*, 518 U.S., at 485.[3]

---

3. Wyeth argues that the presumption against pre-emption should not apply to this case because the Federal Government has regulated drug labeling for more than a century. That argument misunderstands the principle: We rely on the presumption because respect for the States as "independent sovereigns in our federal system" leads us to assume that "Congress does not cavalierly pre-empt state-law causes of action." *Medtronic, Inc. v. Lohr*, 518 U.S. 470, 485 (1996). The presumption thus accounts for the historic presence of state law but does not rely on the absence of federal regulation.

For its part, the dissent argues that the presumption against pre-emption should not apply to claims of implied conflict pre-emption at all, but this Court has long held to the contrary....

In order to identify the "purpose of Congress," it is appropriate to briefly review the history of federal regulation of drugs and drug labeling. In 1906, Congress enacted its first significant public health law, the Federal Food and Drugs Act, ch. 3915, 34 Stat. 768. The Act, which prohibited the manufacture or interstate shipment of adulterated or misbranded drugs, supplemented the protection for consumers already provided by state regulation and common-law liability. In the 1930s, Congress became increasingly concerned about unsafe drugs and fraudulent marketing, and it enacted the Federal Food, Drug, and Cosmetic Act (FDCA), ch. 675, 52 Stat. 1040, as amended, 21 U.S.C. § 301 *et seq.* The Act's most substantial innovation was its provision for premarket approval of new drugs. It required every manufacturer to submit a new drug application, including reports of investigations and specimens of proposed labeling, to the FDA for review. Until its application became effective, a manufacturer was prohibited from distributing a drug. The FDA could reject an application if it determined that the drug was not safe for use as labeled, though if the agency failed to act, an application became effective 60 days after the filing. FDCA, § 505(c), 52 Stat. 1052.

In 1962, Congress amended the FDCA and shifted the burden of proof from the FDA to the manufacturer. Before 1962, the agency had to prove harm to keep a drug out of the market, but the amendments required the manufacturer to demonstrate that its drug was "safe for use under the conditions prescribed, recommended, or suggested in the proposed labeling" before it could distribute the drug. In addition, the amendments required the manufacturer to prove the drug's effectiveness by introducing "substantial evidence that the drug will have the effect it purports or is represented to have under the conditions of use prescribed, recommended, or suggested in the proposed labeling." § 102(d), *id.*, at 781.

As it enlarged the FDA's powers to "protect the public health" and "assure the safety, effectiveness, and reliability of drugs," *id.*, at 780, Congress took care to preserve state law. The 1962 amendments added a saving clause, indicating that a provision of state law would only be invalidated upon a "direct and positive conflict" with the FDCA. § 202, *id.*, at 793. Consistent with that provision, state common-law suits continued unabated despite ... FDA regulation. And when Congress enacted an express pre-emption provision for medical devices in 1976 it declined to enact such a provision for prescription drugs.

In 2007, after Levine's injury and lawsuit, Congress again amended the FDCA. For the first time, it granted the FDA statutory authority to require a manufacturer to change its drug label based on safety information that becomes available after a drug's initial approval. In doing so, however, Congress did not enact a provision in the Senate bill that would have required the FDA to preapprove all changes to drug labels. Instead, it adopted a rule of construction to make it clear that manufacturers remain responsible for updating their labels....

Wyeth first argues that Levine's state-law claims are pre-empted because it is impossible for it to comply with both the state-law duties underlying those claims and its federal labeling duties. The FDA's premarket approval of a new drug application includes the approval of the exact text in the proposed label. Generally speaking, a manufacturer may only change a drug label after the FDA approves a supplemental application. There is, however, an FDA regulation that permits a manufacturer to make certain changes to its label before receiving the agency's approval. Among other things, this "changes being effected" (CBE) regulation provides that if a manufacturer is changing a label to "add or strengthen a contraindication, warning, precaution, or adverse reaction" or to "add or strengthen an instruction about dosage and administration that is intended to increase the safe use of the drug product," it may make the labeling change upon filing its supplemental application with the FDA; it need not wait for FDA approval.

Wyeth argues that the CBE regulation is not implicated in this case because a 2008 amendment provides that a manufacturer may only change its label "to reflect newly acquired information." 73 Fed. Reg. 49609. Resting on this language (which Wyeth argues simply reaffirmed the interpretation of the regulation in effect when this case was tried), Wyeth contends that it could have changed Phenergan's label only in response to new information that the FDA had not considered. And it maintains that Levine has not pointed to any such information concerning the risks of IV-push administration. Thus, Wyeth insists, it was impossible for it to discharge its state-law obligation to provide a stronger warning about IV-push administration without violating federal law. Wyeth's argument misapprehends both the federal drug regulatory scheme and its burden in establishing a pre-emption defense.

We need not decide whether the 2008 CBE regulation is consistent with the FDCA and the previous version of the regulation, as Wyeth and the United States urge, because Wyeth could have revised Phenergan's label even in accordance with the amended regulation. As the FDA explained..., "'newly acquired information'" is not limited to new data, but also encompasses "new analyses of previously submitted data." *Id.*, at 49604. The rule accounts for the fact that risk information accumulates over time and that the same data may take on a different meaning in light of subsequent developments: "[I]f the sponsor submits adverse event information to FDA, and then later conducts a new analysis of data showing risks of a different type or of greater severity or frequency than did reports previously submitted to FDA, the sponsor meets the requirement for 'newly acquired information.'" *Id.*, at 49607.

... Levine did ... present evidence of at least 20 incidents prior to her injury in which a Phenergan injection resulted in gangrene and an amputation. After the first such incident came to Wyeth's attention in 1967, it notified the FDA and worked with the agency to change Phenergan's label. In later years, as amputations continued to occur, Wyeth could have analyzed the accumulating data and added a stronger warning about IV-push administration of the drug.

Wyeth argues that if it had unilaterally added such a warning, it would have violated federal law governing unauthorized distribution and misbranding. Its argument that a change in Phenergan's labeling would have subjected it to liability for unauthorized distribution rests on the assumption that this labeling change would have rendered Phenergan a new drug lacking an effective application. But strengthening the warning about IV-push administration would not have made Phenergan a new drug. Nor would this warning have rendered Phenergan misbranded. The FDCA does not provide that a drug is misbranded simply because the manufacturer has altered an FDA-approved label; instead, the misbranding provision focuses on the substance of the label and, among other things, proscribes labels that fail to include "adequate warnings." Moreover, because the statute contemplates that federal juries will resolve most misbranding claims, the FDA's belief that a drug is misbranded is not conclusive. And the very idea that the FDA would bring an enforcement action against a manufacturer for strengthening a warning pursuant to the CBE regulation is difficult to accept—neither Wyeth nor the United States has identified a case in which the FDA has done so.

Wyeth's cramped reading of the CBE regulation and its broad reading of the FDCA's misbranding and unauthorized distribution provisions are premised on a more fundamental misunderstanding. Wyeth suggests that the FDA, rather than the manufacturer, bears primary responsibility for drug labeling. Yet through many amendments to the FDCA and to FDA regulations, it has remained a central premise of federal drug regulation that the manufacturer bears responsibility for the content of its label at all times. It is charged both with crafting an adequate label and with ensuring that its warnings remain adequate as long as the drug is on the market.

Indeed, prior to 2007, the FDA lacked the authority to order manufacturers to revise their labels. When Congress granted the FDA this authority, it reaffirmed the manufacturer's obligations and referred specifically to the CBE regulation, which both reflects the manufacturer's ultimate responsibility for its label and provides a mechanism for adding safety information to the label prior to FDA approval. Thus, when the risk of gangrene from IV-push injection of Phenergan became apparent, Wyeth had a duty to provide a warning that adequately described that risk, and the CBE regulation permitted it to provide such a warning before receiving the FDA's approval.

... [A]bsent clear evidence that the FDA would not have approved a change to Phenergan's label, we will not conclude that it was impossible for Wyeth to comply with both federal and state requirements....

Wyeth has offered no such evidence. It does not argue that it attempted to give the kind of warning required by the Vermont jury but was prohibited from doing so by the FDA. And while it does suggest that the FDA intended to prohibit it from strengthening the warning about IV-push administration because the agency deemed such a warning inappropriate in reviewing Phenergan's drug applications, both the trial court and the Vermont Supreme Court rejected this account as a matter of fact. In its decision on Wyeth's motion for judgment as a matter of law, the trial court found "no evidence in this record that either the FDA or the manufacturer gave more than passing attention to the issue of" IV-push versus IV-drip administration. App. 249. The Vermont Supreme Court likewise concluded that the FDA had not made an affirmative decision to preserve the IV-push method or intended to prohibit Wyeth from strengthening its warning about IV-push administration. Moreover, Wyeth does not argue that it supplied the FDA with an evaluation or analysis concerning the specific dangers posed by the IV-push method. We accordingly cannot credit Wyeth's contention that the FDA would have prevented it from adding a stronger warning about the IV-push method of intravenous administration. Impossibility pre-emption is a demanding defense. On the record before us, Wyeth has failed to demonstrate that it was impossible for it to comply with both federal and state requirements....

Wyeth also argues that requiring it to comply with a state-law duty to provide a stronger warning about IV-push administration would obstruct the purposes and objectives of federal drug labeling regulation. Levine's tort claims, it maintains, are pre-empted because they interfere with "Congress's purpose to entrust an expert agency to make drug labeling decisions that strike a balance between competing objectives." We find no merit in this argument, which relies on an untenable interpretation of congressional intent and an overbroad view of an agency's power to pre-empt state law.

Wyeth contends that the FDCA establishes both a floor and a ceiling for drug regulation: Once the FDA has approved a drug's label, a state-law verdict may not deem the label inadequate, regardless of whether there is any evidence that the FDA has considered the stronger warning at issue. The most glaring problem with this argument is that all evidence of Congress' purposes is to the contrary. Building on its 1906 Act, Congress enacted the FDCA to bolster consumer protection against harmful products. Congress did not provide a federal remedy for consumers harmed by unsafe or ineffective drugs in the 1938 statute or in any subsequent amendment. Evidently, it determined that widely available state rights of action provided appropriate relief for injured consumers.[7] It may

---

7. Although the first version of the bill that became the FDCA would have provided a federal cause of action for damages for injured consumers, witnesses testified that such a right of action was unnecessary because common-law claims were already available under state law. See Hearings on S.1944 before a Subcommittee of the Senate Committee on Commerce, 73d Cong., 2d Sess., 400 (1933)

also have recognized that state-law remedies further consumer protection by motivating manufacturers to produce safe and effective drugs and to give adequate warnings.

If Congress thought state-law suits posed an obstacle to its objectives, it surely would have enacted an express pre-emption provision at some point during the FDCA's 70-year history. But despite its 1976 enactment of an express pre-emption provision for medical devices, Congress has not enacted such a provision for prescription drugs.[8] Its silence on the issue, coupled with its certain awareness of the prevalence of state tort litigation, is powerful evidence that Congress did not intend FDA oversight to be the exclusive means of ensuring drug safety and effectiveness. The case for federal pre-emption is particularly weak where Congress has indicated its awareness of the operation of state law in a field of federal interest, and has nonetheless decided to stand by both concepts and to tolerate whatever tension there [is] between them." . . .

We conclude that it is not impossible for Wyeth to comply with its state and federal law obligations and that Levine's common-law claims do not stand as an obstacle to the accomplishment of Congress' purposes in the FDCA. Accordingly, the judgment of the Vermont Supreme Court is affirmed.

Justice Thomas, concurring in the judgment.

I agree with the Court that the fact that the Food and Drug Administration (FDA) approved the label for petitioner Wyeth's drug Phenergan does not pre-empt the state-law judgment before the Court. . . .

I write separately, however, because I cannot join the majority's implicit endorsement of far-reaching implied pre-emption doctrines. In particular, I have become increasingly skeptical of this Court's "purposes and objectives" pre-emption jurisprudence. Under this approach, the Court routinely invalidates state laws based on perceived conflicts with broad federal policy objectives, legislative history, or generalized notions of congressional purposes that are not embodied within the text of federal law. Because implied pre-emption doctrines that wander far from the statutory text are inconsistent with the Constitution, I concur only in the judgment. . . .

In order to ensure the protection of our fundamental liberties, the Constitution establishes a system of dual sovereignty between the States and the Federal Government. The Framers adopted this constitutionally mandated balance of power, to reduce the risk of tyranny and abuse from either front, because a federalist structure of joint sovereigns preserves to the people numerous advantages, such as a decentralized government that will be more sensitive to the diverse needs of a heterogeneous society and increase[d] opportunity for citizen involvement in democratic processes. Furthermore, as the Framers observed, the "compound republic of America" provides "a double security . . . to the rights of the people" because "the power surrendered by the people is first divided between two distinct governments, and then the portion allotted to each subdivided among distinct and separate departments." The Federalist No. 51, p. 266 (M. Beloff ed., 2d ed.1987).

Under this federalist system, the States possess sovereignty concurrent with that of the Federal Government, subject only to limitations imposed by the Supremacy Clause. In this

---

(statement of W.A. Hines); see *id.,* at 403 (statement of J.A. Ladds) ("This act should not attempt to modify or restate the common law with respect to personal injuries").

8. In 1997, Congress pre-empted certain state requirements concerning over-the-counter medications and cosmetics but expressly preserved product liability actions. See 21 U.S.C. §§ 379r(e), 379s(d) ("Nothing in this section shall be construed to modify or otherwise affect any action or the liability of any person under the product liability law of any State").

way, the Supremacy Clause gives the Federal Government a decided advantage in a delicate balance between federal and state sovereigns. As long as it is acting within the powers granted it under the Constitution, Congress may impose its will on the States....

Nonetheless, the States retain substantial sovereign authority. U.S. Const., Amdt. 10 ("The powers not delegated to the United States by the Constitution, nor prohibited by it to the States, are reserved to the States respectively, or to the people") In accordance with the text and structure of the Constitution, "[t]he powers delegated by the proposed constitution to the federal government, are few and defined" and "[t]hose which are to remain in the state governments, are numerous and indefinite."The Federalist No. 45, at 237–238. Indeed, in protecting our constitutional government, "the preservation of the States, and the maintenance of their governments, are as much within the design and care of the Constitution as the preservation of the Union and the maintenance of the National government." *Texas v. White,* 7 Wall. 700, 725 (1869).

As a result, in order to protect the delicate balance of power mandated by the Constitution, the Supremacy Clause must operate only in accordance with its terms. The clause provides:

> This Constitution, and the Laws of the United States which shall be made in Pursuance thereof; and all Treaties made, or which shall be made, under the Authority of the United States, shall be the supreme Law of the Land; and the Judges in every State shall be bound thereby, any Thing in the Constitution or Laws of any state to the Contrary notwithstanding. Art. VI, cl. 2.

With respect to federal laws, then, the Supremacy Clause gives "supreme" status only to those that are "made in Pursuance" of "[t]his Constitution." *Ibid.;* see 3 J. Story, Commentaries on the Constitution of the United States § 1831, p. 694 (1833) (hereinafter Story) ("It will be observed, that the supremacy of the laws is attached to those only, which are made in pursuance of the constitution").

Federal laws "made in Pursuance" of the Constitution must comply with two key structural limitations in the Constitution that ensure that the Federal Government does not amass too much power at the expense of the States. The first structural limitation ... is the Constitution's conferral upon Congress of not all governmental powers, but only discrete, enumerated ones.[1]

The second structural limitation is the complex set of procedures that Congress and the President must follow to enact Laws of the United States[: bicameralism and presentment]. The Supremacy Clause thus requires that pre-emptive effect be given only to federal standards and policies that are set forth in, or necessarily follow from, the statutory text that was produced through the constitutionally required bicameral and presentment procedures. See 3 J. Story § 1831, at 694 (Actions of the Federal Government "which are not pursuant to its constitutional powers, but which are invasions of the residuary authorities of the smaller societies," are not "the supreme law of the land. They will be merely acts of usurpation, and will deserve to be treated as such")....

In light of these constitutional principles, I have become increasingly reluctant to expand federal statutes beyond their terms through doctrines of implied pre-emption. My

---

1. This structural limitation may be implicated in a pre-emption case if the federal law at issue is beyond the scope of Congress' enumerated powers. Expansion of congressional power through an increasingly generous ... interpretation of the commerce power of Congress," for example, creates "a real risk that Congress will gradually erase the diffusion of power between State and Nation on which the Framers based their faith in the efficiency and vitality of our Republic.

review of this Court's broad implied pre-emption precedents, particularly its "purposes and objectives" pre-emption jurisprudence, has increased my concerns that implied pre-emption doctrines have not always been constitutionally applied. Under the vague and "potentially boundless" doctrine of "purposes and objectives" pre-emption, for example, the Court has pre-empted state law based on its interpretation of broad federal policy objectives, legislative history, or generalized notions of congressional purposes that are not contained within the text of federal law.

Congressional and agency musings ... do not satisfy the Art. I, § 7 requirements for enactment of federal law and, therefore, do not pre-empt state law under the Supremacy Clause. When analyzing the pre-emptive effect of federal statutes or regulations validly promulgated thereunder, evidence of pre-emptive purpose [must be] sought in the text and structure of the [provision] at issue to comply with the Constitution. Pre-emption analysis should not be a freewheeling judicial inquiry into whether a state statute is in tension with federal objectives, but an inquiry into whether the ordinary meanings of state and federal law conflict. Pre-emption must turn on whether state law conflicts with the text of the relevant federal statute or with the federal regulations authorized by that text.

This Court has determined that there are two categories of conflict pre-emption, both of which Wyeth contends are at issue in this case. First, the Court has found pre-emption where compliance with both federal and state regulations is a physical impossibility for one engaged in interstate commerce. Second, the Court has determined that federal law pre-empts state law when, under the circumstances of a particular case, state law stands as an obstacle to the accomplishment and execution of the full purposes and objectives of Congress.[2] ...

Wyeth first contends that it would have been impossible for it to comply with the state-law duty to modify Phenergan's labeling without violating federal law. But, as the majority explains, the text of the relevant federal statutory provisions and the corresponding regulations do not directly conflict with the state-law judgment before us....

Wyeth also contends that state and federal law conflict because recognition of [this] state tort action creates an unacceptable obstacle to the accomplishment and execution of the full purposes and objectives of Congress because it substitutes a lay jury's decision about drug labeling for the expert judgment of the FDA. This Court's entire body of "purposes and objectives" pre-emption jurisprudence is inherently flawed. The cases improperly rely on legislative history, broad atextual notions of congressional purpose, and even congressional inaction in order to pre-empt state law. I, therefore, cannot join the majority's analysis of this claim, or its reaffirmation of the Court's "purposes and objectives" jurisprudence....

The Court's "purposes and objectives" pre-emption jurisprudence is ... problematic because it encourages an overly expansive reading of statutory text. The Court's desire to divine the broader purposes of the statute before it inevitably leads it to assume that Congress wanted to pursue those policies "at all costs"—even when the text reflects a different balance. As this Court has repeatedly noted, it frustrates rather than effectuates legislative in-

---

2. The majority's pre-emption analysis relies in part on a presumption against pre-emption. Because it is evident from the text of the relevant federal statutes and regulations themselves that the state-law judgment below is not pre-empted, it is not necessary to decide whether, or to what extent, the presumption should apply in a case such as this one, where Congress has not enacted an express-pre-emption clause.

tent simplistically to assume that *whatever* furthers the statute's primary objective must be the law. Federal legislation is often the result of compromise between legislators and groups with marked but divergent interests. Thus, a statute's text might reflect a compromise between parties who wanted to pursue a particular goal to different extents. Therefore, there is no factual basis for the assumption underlying the Court's "purposes and objectives" pre-emption jurisprudence that every policy seemingly consistent with federal statutory text has necessarily been authorized by Congress and warrants pre-emptive effect. Instead, our federal system in general, and the Supremacy Clause in particular, accords pre-emptive effect to only those policies that are actually authorized by and effectuated through the statutory text. The majority, while reaching the right conclusion in this case, demonstrates once again how application of "purposes and objectives" pre-emption requires inquiry into matters beyond the scope of proper judicial review....

In this case, the majority has concluded from silence that Congress believed state lawsuits pose no obstacle to federal drug-approval objectives. That is the required conclusion, but only because it is compelled by the text of the relevant statutory and regulatory provisions, not judicial suppositions about Congress' unstated goals. The fact that the Court reaches the proper conclusion does not justify its speculation about the reasons for congressional inaction. In this case, the Court has relied on the perceived congressional policies underlying inaction to find that state law is *not* pre-empted. But once the Court shows a willingness to guess at the intent underlying congressional inaction, the Court could just as easily rely on its own perceptions regarding congressional inaction to give unduly broad pre-emptive effect to federal law....

The origins of this Court's "purposes and objectives" pre-emption jurisprudence ... illustrate that this brand of the Court's pre-emption jurisprudence facilitates freewheeling, extratextual, and broad evaluations of the "purposes and objectives" embodied within federal law. This, in turn, leads to decisions giving improperly broad pre-emptive effect to judicially manufactured policies, rather than to the statutory text enacted by Congress pursuant to the Constitution and the agency actions authorized thereby. Because such a sweeping approach to pre-emption leads to the illegitimate—and thus, unconstitutional—invalidation of state laws, I can no longer assent to a doctrine that pre-empts state laws merely because they "stan[d] as an obstacle to the accomplishment and execution of the full purposes and objectives" of federal law, as perceived by this Court. I therefore respectfully concur only in the judgment.

JUSTICE ALITO, with whom THE CHIEF JUSTICE [ROBERTS] and JUSTICE SCALIA join, dissenting.

This case illustrates that tragic facts make bad law. The Court holds that a state tort jury, rather than the Food and Drug Administration (FDA), is ultimately responsible for regulating warning labels for prescription drugs....

The Court frames the question presented as a "narro[w]" one—namely, whether Wyeth has a duty to provide "an adequate warning about using the IV-push method" to administer Phenergan. But that ignores the antecedent question of who—the FDA or a jury in Vermont—has the authority and responsibility for determining the "adequacy" of Phenergan's warnings....

More to the point, ... the real issue is whether a state tort jury can countermand the FDA's considered judgment that Phenergan's FDA-mandated warning label renders its intravenous (IV) use "safe." ...

To the extent that "[t]he purpose of Congress is the ultimate touchstone in every preemption case," *Medtronic, Inc. v. Lohr*, 518 U.S. 470, 485 (1996)), Congress made its "purpose" plain in authorizing the FDA—not state tort juries—to determine when and under what circumstances a drug is "safe." ...

Where the FDA determines, in accordance with its statutory mandate, that a drug is on balance "safe," our conflict pre-emption cases prohibit any State from countermanding that determination....

Thus, as the Court itself recognizes, it is irrelevant in conflict pre-emption cases whether Congress "enacted an express pre-emption provision at some point during the FDCA's 70-year history." Rather, the ordinary principles of conflict pre-emption turn solely on whether a State has upset the regulatory balance struck by the federal agency....

By their very nature, juries are ill-equipped to perform the FDA's cost-benefit-balancing function.... Indeed, patients like respondent are the only ones whom tort juries ever see, and for a patient like respondent—who has already suffered a tragic accident— Phenergan's risks are no longer a matter of probabilities and potentialities.

In contrast, the FDA has the benefit of the long view. Its drug-approval determinations consider the interests of all potential users of a drug, including "those who would suffer without new medical [products]" if juries in all 50 States were free to contradict the FDA's expert determinations. And the FDA conveys its warnings with one voice, rather than whipsawing the medical community with 50 (or more) potentially conflicting ones. After today's ruling, however, parochialism may prevail....

To be sure, state tort suits can peacefully coexist with the FDA's labeling regime, and they have done so for decades. But this case is far from peaceful coexistence. The FDA told Wyeth that Phenergan's label renders its use "safe." But the State of Vermont, through its tort law, said: "Not so."

The state-law rule at issue here is squarely pre-empted. Therefore, I would reverse the judgment of the Supreme Court of Vermont.

Notes and Questions

(1) *The Basis for Implied Preemption.* The majority addressed both arguments that the federal labeling law impliedly preempted state tort law: (1) that it would have been impossible for it to comply with the state-law duty without violating federal law and (2) that recognition of a state tort action creates an unacceptable obstacle to the accomplishment and execution of the full purposes and objectives of Congress. How did the majority respond to each argument? Do you find the responses convincing? Or, do you agree with the dissent that the "FDA told Wyeth that [the drug's] label renders its use 'safe.' But the State of Vermont, through its tort law, said: 'Not so.'"?

(2) *Is Implied Preemption That Distinct from Express Preemption?* In both preemption cases, most of the Justices readily looked beyond text. Who was the exception? What extra-textual sources were considered? Does the fact that both preemption doctrines turn on extratextual sources strike you as unusual compared to the typical approach to interpretation?

(3) *Justice Thomas's Dissent.* By definition, either form of implied preemption is not based on statutory text. Justice Thomas believes that this fact makes these forms of preemption unconstitutional. What do you make of his argument? Given that he finds implied preemption problematic, why did he agree with the majority in this case? Does the implied preemption analysis seem jarring to you in light of the otherwise heavy focus on text that pervades statutory interpretation today? Do you believe that intentionalism,

purposivism, or something else best explains the issues that the Court finds important in implied preemption analysis?

(4) *Field Preemption*. Field preemption, or complete preemption, is another form of implied preemption. It arises only when Congress adopts "a scheme of federal regulation" that is either (a) so pervasive that the only reasonable inference is "Congress left no room for the states to supplement it" or (b) where an Act of Congress "touche[s] a field in which the federal interest is so dominant that the federal system will be assumed to preclude the enforcement of state laws on the same subject." *English v. Gen. Elec. Co.*, 496 U.S. 72, 79 (1990). Field preemption is quite narrow. Indeed, the Supreme Court has questioned whether field preemption can arise without an express Congressional statement. *See Camps Newfound/Owatonna, Inc. v. Town of Harrison, Maine*, 520 U.S. 564, 614–15 (1997). The Supreme Court has found field preemption in only three areas: (a) claims alleging breach of a collective bargaining agreement that fall under section 301 of the Labor Management Relations Act; (2) claims for benefits or enforcement of rights under the Employee Retirement Income Security Act ("ERISA"); and (3) claims against a national bank chartered under the National Bank Act. *See Rogers v. Yonce*, 2008 WL 2853207, at 10 (N.D. Okla. July 21, 2008) (cataloging areas and collecting cases).

(5) *Is There Implied Preemption of State Law by State Statutes?* Preemption arises because of the supremacy of federal law over state law. Obviously, a state statute cannot "preempt" federal law, but can a state statute displace state common law or local regulation? In part, this issue implicates statutes in derogation of the common law and remedial statutes. We saw earlier that, as a general rule, statutes in derogation of the common law are strictly construed, while remedial statutes are broadly interpreted to effectuate their purposes. Another body of law exists, often independently of derogation cases, that addresses "preemption" of state law by state statutes. Often, state courts apply a federal preemption doctrine to determine if a state statute displaces state common law without analyzing whether the federal doctrine fits. *E.g., People v. Kasben*, 2006 WL 3077685, at 7 (Mich. Ct. App. Oct. 31, 2006) ("While the preemption doctrine is traditionally applied when a federal law takes precedence over a state law, preemption may also be applied when a state statute acts to preempt the common law."); *Summit Water Distr. Co. v. Mountain Reg'l Water Special Serv. Dist.*, 108 P.3d 119, 122 (Utah Ct. App. 2005) ("In addressing whether a state statute preempts a local government act or common law, Utah courts have looked at the preemption model of the United States Supreme Court for guidance."). Other state courts are more attuned to the purpose of federal preemption doctrine; thus, they recognize that the question of displacement of state common law by a state statute is not properly analyzed under that rubric. *See Kraft v. Detroit Entm't, LLC*, 683 N.W.2d 200, 206 n.5 (Mich. Ct. App. 2004) (explaining that "preemption" was a "misnomer" in this context). However, even courts that recognize that the preemption doctrine does not apply sometimes, nonetheless, use the term "preemption." *See id.; Colo. Mining Ass'n v. Bd. Of County Comm'rs of Summit County*, 199 P.3d 718 (Colo. 2009) (majority and minority disagreed on proper approach to analyze preemption, with dissent emphasizing that "conflicts between state and county laws are not subject to a constitutional analysis"). Can you explain why it may be important, particularly if a federal judge is analyzing the impact of a state statute on state common law, to be careful not to use the word "preemption" to describe this analysis?

(6) *What about Derogation?* We located only a few cases in which courts utilized the derogation canon while analyzing preemption. *See, e.g., Corvello v. New England Gas Co.*, 532 F. Supp. 2d 396, 401 (D. R.I. 2008) (reasoning that it was "especially true" that preemption can be found only where intent is "clear and unequivocal" if the statute operates

"in derogation of the common law"); *Welsh v. Century Prods., Inc.*, 745 F. Supp. 313, 316 (D. Md. 1990) (finding no express preemption and stating that the principle that any such expression must be clear was "bolstered … by the enduring maxim that statutes in derogation of the common law are to be narrowly construed."). Yet, it would seem that the derogation canon ought to apply in preemption analysis, particularly when state courts are analyzing whether a state statute displaces state common law. Can you explain the silence? Does the "presumption against preemption" implicate the derogation canon, at least at the federal level?

(7) *Only Express State Statutory Displacement?* Commentators have argued that courts that liberally interpret state statutes to displace state law may, contrary to legislative intent, repeal or otherwise limit settled common law torts. *See, e.g.,* Jarod S. Gonzalez, *State Antidiscrimination Statutes and Implied Preemption of Common Law Torts: Valuing the Common Law*, 59 S.C. L. Rev. 115 (2007). Do you believe that courts should interpret state statutes to displace common law torts only if the legislature clearly expresses that intent to protect against this concern? Some courts harmonize the derogation canon and the notion of preemption by taking that approach. *See Hardy v. State*, 482 A.2d 474, 478 (Md. Ct. App. 1984) (There "is a presumption against statutory interpretation of the common law. This presumption is easily dissipated if the statute expressly overrides a common-law principle."). While a bright line, does recognizing only express preemption go too far?

Problem 14-3

You represent three passengers who each want to sue Mercer Airlines and a fourth who is an airline employee. Analyze whether the claim each is preempted by federal law based upon the following materials.

Your first client, Brad, believes that the airlines have falsely advertised their fares. Specifically, when booking on-line, Mercer Airlines does not disclose that it charges a $10 per ticket "convenience fee." Your research shows that, absent preemption, he can bring a claim for fraud under Mercer law.

Your second client, Abby, was on a Mercer flight that, due to bad weather, was forced to stay on a runway for 8 hours. The toilets overflowed, and conditions were generally miserable. Your research shows that, absent preemption, she has a state law claim for false imprisonment.

Your third client, Christopher, alleges that he was discriminated against due to his handicap. He was not allowed to board a particular flight because of a handicap that meant the airline would have been forced to provide him two seats, not one. Your research confirms that, absent preemption, he could state a claim for intentional infliction of emotional distress under Mercer common law.

Your fourth client, David, is a homosexual employee of Mercer Airlines who believes the airline is discriminating by not providing him and his partner with equal benefits. A Mercer state statute requires that companies provide same sex couples with the same benefits as married, heterosexual couples. You have concluded that, absent preemption, he can state a claim for violation of the Mercer anti-discrimination statute.

Your legal research reveals the following.

In 1938, Congress created the Civil Aeronautics Board (a federal agency) and authorized it to regulate entry into the interstate airline industry, the routes that airlines could fly, and the fares that airlines could charge consumers. The 1938 Act included a "savings clause" which provided:

> Nothing contained in this chapter shall in any way abridge or alter the remedies now existing at common law or by statute, but the provisions of this chapter are in addition to such remedies.

49 U.S.C.A. § 1506 (West 1976). States could, under this savings clause, regulate price, fares, and all other matters relating to airlines.

In 1978, Congress enacted the Airline Deregulation Act of 1978 ("ADA") with the stated purpose "to encourage, develop, and attain an air transportation system which relies on competitive market forces to determine the quality, variety and price of air services." H.R.Rep. No. 95-1779, 95th Cong., 2d Sess., 53, reprinted in 1978 U.S.C.C.A.N. 3737.

To avoid the frustration of that goal by the substitution of state regulations for the recently removed federal regulations, Congress enacted § 1305(a) of the ADA. Although it has since been recodified, the language of the preemption provision now in effect is identical to the language as adopted in 1978:

    a.   Definition.—In this section, "State" means a State, the District of Columbia, and a territory or possession of the United States.

    (b)   Preemption.—

        (1)   Except as provided in this subsection, a State, political subdivision of a State, or political authority of at least 2 States may not enact or enforce a law, regulation, or other provision having the force and effect of law related to a price, route, or service of an air carrier that may provide air transportation under this subpart.

        (2)   This subsection does not limit a State, political subdivision of a State, or political authority of at least 2 States that owns or operates an airport served by an air carrier holding a certificate issued by the Secretary of Transportation from carrying out its proprietary powers and rights.

        (3)   Transportation by air carrier or carrier affiliated with a direct air carrier.—

            (A)   General rule.—Except as provided in subparagraph (B), a State, political subdivision of a State, or political authority of 2 or more States may not enact or enforce a law, regulation, or other provision having the force and effect of law related to a price, route, or service of an air carrier or carrier affiliated with a direct air carrier through common controlling ownership when such carrier is transporting property by aircraft or by motor vehicle (whether or not such property has had or will have a prior or subsequent air movement).

            (B)   Matters not covered.—Subparagraph (A)—

                (i)   shall not restrict the safety regulatory authority of a State with respect to motor vehicles, the authority of a State to impose highway route controls or limitations based on the size or weight of the motor vehicle or the hazardous nature of the cargo, or the authority of a State to regulate motor carriers with regard to minimum amounts of financial responsibility relating to insurance requirements and self-insurance authorization; and

(ii) does not apply to the transportation of household goods, as defined in section 13102 of this title.

(C) Applicability of paragraph (1).—This paragraph shall not limit the applicability of paragraph (1).

49 U.S.C.A. § 1305. Congress has also retained the savings clause, quoted above, that preserves common law and statutory remedies. 49 U.S.C.A. § 40120.

The legislative history shows that because Congress did not want states to undo federal deregulation by regulating airlines on their own, it included the preemption clause, above.

In promulgating regulations pursuant to the ADA, the Civil Aeronautics Board focused on the two underlying purposes of the Act—to prevent state economic regulation from frustrating the benefits of federal deregulation and to clarify the confusion under the prior law, which permitted some dual state and federal regulation of the rates and routes of the same carrier:

> One policy behind the preemption provision was to prevent State economic regulation from frustrating the benefits of decreased Federal regulation. In the section-by-section analysis of a precursor to the ADA, the House managers of the Bill stated:
>
> > [W]ith the passage of legislation ... loosening Federal regulation of airline service and fares, it is possible that some States will enact their own regulatory legislation, imposing utility type regulation on interstate airline service and fares. The [Act] includes a specific statutory provision precluding State interference with interstate service and fares.
>
> Section-by-section analysis of H.R. 8813 Cong. Rec., September 23, 1977, H. 10007-8.

According to the regulations, another policy was to avoid the confusion caused under existing law which permitted dual State and Federal regulation of the same carrier. 44 Fed. Reg. 9948-49 (1979). The Civil Aeronautics Board also stated:

> Section 105 forbids state regulation of a federally authorized carrier's routes, rates, or services. Clearly, states may not interfere with a federal carrier's decision on how much to charge or which markets to serve.... Similarly, a state may not interfere with the services that carriers offer in exchange for their rates and fares. For example, liquidated damages for bumping (denial of boarding), segregation of smoking passengers, minimum liability for loss, damages, and delayed baggage, and ancillary charges for headsets, alcoholic beverages, entertainment, and excess baggage would clearly be "service" regulation within the meaning of section 105.
>
> Additionally, we conclude that regulation of capital structure, minimum insurance requirements, bonding, etc. motivated by a desire to protect the quality of service is included with the preemption imposed in section 105.

Id. at 9951.

The Supreme Court has, in one case, discussed the scope of "related to." The Court stated:

> The ordinary meaning of these words is a broad one—"to stand in some relation; to have bearing or concern; to pertain; refer; to bring into association with

or connection with," Black's Law Dictionary 1158 (5th ed. 1979)—and the words thus express a broad pre-emptive purpose. We have repeatedly recognized that in addressing the similarly worded pre-emption provision of the Employee Retirement Income Security Act of 1974 (ERISA), 29 U.S.C. § 1144(a), which pre-empts all state laws "insofar as they ... relate to any employee benefit plan." We have said, for example, that the "breadth of [that provision's] pre-emptive reach is apparent from [its] language," ... that it has a "broad scope," ... and an "expansive sweep," ... and that it is "broadly worded," ..."deliberately expansive," ... and "conspicuous for its breadth,".... True to our word, we have held that a state law "relates to" an employee benefit plan, and is pre-empted by ERISA, "if it has a connection with or reference to such a plan." ... Since the relevant language of the ADA is identical, we think it appropriate to adopt the same standard here: State enforcement actions having a connection with or reference to airline "rates, routes, or services" are pre-empted under [the ADA].

Morales v. Trans World Airlines, 504 U.S. 374, 384 (1992).

Several tests for what constitutes a "service" have been put forth by the appellate courts. The Ninth Circuit has held that "services" encompasses "the prices, schedules, origins and destinations of the point-to-point transportation of passengers, cargo, or mail" but does not include "provision of in-flight beverages, personal assistance to passengers, the handling of luggage, and similar amenities." *Charas v. Trans World Airlines, Inc.*, 160 F.3d 1259, 1266 (9th Cir. 1998) (*en banc*) (interpreting "service" to refer only to the "provision of air transportation to and from various markets at various times"). *See Taj Mahal Travel, Inc. v. Delta Airlines, Inc.*, 164 F.3d 186, 193–94 (3d Cir. 1998) (similar interpretation). The Fifth Circuit has held that it includes the "contractual features of air transportation" including "ticketing, boarding procedures, provision of food and drink, and baggage handling." *Hodges v. Delta Airlines, Inc.*, 44 F.3d 334, 336 (5th Cir. 1998). The Second Circuit has held, for example, that "requiring airlines to provide food, water, electricity, and restrooms to passengers during lengthy ground delays does relate to the service of an air carrier" and stat[ed] that "services" included "the provision or anticipated provision of labor from the airlines to its passengers and encompasses matters such as boarding procedures, baggage handling, and food and drink...." *Air Transp. Ass'n of Am., Inc. v. Cuomo*, 520 F.3d 218, 223 (2d Cir. 2008).

Chapter 15

Implied Remedies and Causes of Action: Where Purpose and Intent Are Primary

We have repeatedly seen that today's judges more often emphasize the text of the statute over its purpose or any perceived legislative intent. Yet, in some key areas, intent and purpose are the focus of statutory interpretation. This chapter explores two areas where text is less significant: implied remedies and implied causes of action. We will see, however, the difficulties that emphasis on intent and purpose create, and we will also see judges express concern about the role of extra-textual sources. Yet, is there any other way to approach these issues?

A. Express Statutory Remedies: Exclusive or Not?

This section addresses questions related to implied remedies. Suppose, as is typical, a statute authorizes a cause of action and specifies that damages are recoverable to those who are harmed by someone violating that statute. Are damages the exclusive remedy, or should other remedies, such as injunctive relief, be available? A distinct, but related, issue is whether a statute that does not expressly permit a cause of action should be interpreted to allow one by implication. If so, a number of issues arise: What is the scope of liability? What damages are recoverable? What statute of limitations applies? The cases that analyze these questions also raise fundamental issues of statutory interpretation that we have addressed throughout the book.

If a statute authorizes a cause of action and provides for damages, should damages be exclusive or should equitable relief also be available? What if the converse is true—the statute authorizes equitable relief but not damages—should damages be available as well? Some courts apply a purposivist analysis to answer this question: They ask whether the specified relief alone will achieve the purpose of the statute. That approach is directly at odds with textualism. The following cases and notes explore these issues.

Orloff v. L.A. Turf Club, Inc.

180 P.2d 321 (Cal. 1947)

CARTER, JUSTICE

Plaintiff commenced this action for injunctive relief, alleging in his complaint that defendant Los Angeles Turf Club ... is engaged in operating a horse racing course ... and invites the public to attend. In January ... plaintiff, an adult, purchased a ticket for admission to the defendant's place of business and was admitted thereto. Thereafter plaintiff was ejected from the establishment by defendant and its employees. In February he was again admitted thereto and was again ejected. The ousting of plaintiff was without cause, he being of a good moral character and having conducted himself properly at all times. At the time of the ejections above mentioned "defendants and each of them unlawfully ordered plaintiff not to return to said race course thereafter, and unlawfully threatened to thereafter refuse to admit plaintiff thereto, or if admitted to forcibly remove and eject plaintiff therefrom." By reason of defendant's conduct, plaintiff was humiliated and embarrassed and sustained mental anguish.

Defendant's demurrer was sustained with leave to plaintiff to amend his complaint to claim only damages. Upon his refusal so to do, a judgment dismissing his action was entered and he appeals therefrom.

Plaintiff's action is based upon the so called civil rights statutes. Generally it is provided that all citizens are entitled to full and equal accommodations, advantages, facilities, and privileges of places of amusement and accommodations subject to conditions and limitations established by law applicable to all alike. Civil Code, sec. 51. And whoever denies the privileges accorded by the foregoing, except for reasons applicable alike to every race and color, or discriminates on the latter ground, is liable in damages for not less than $100, which may be recovered in an action at law. Civil Code, sec. 52. But in addition to those provisions ... there are specific statutory mandates which are here applicable. "It is unlawful for any corporation, person, or association, or the proprietor, lessee, or the agents of either, of any opera-house, theater, melodeon, museum, circus, caravan, race-course, fair or other place of public amusement or entertainment, to refuse admittance to any person over the age of twenty-one years, who presents a ticket of admission acquired by purchase, or who tenders the price thereof for such ticket, and who demands admission to such place...." Civil Code, sec. 53. The following section reads: "Any person who is refused admission to any place of amusement contrary to the provisions of the last preceding section, is entitled to recover from the proprietor, lessee, or their agents, or from any such person, corporation, or association, or the directors thereof, his actual damages, and one hundred dollars in addition thereto." Civil Code, sec. 54. And it is that section which is invoked by defendant as establishing the exclusive remedy for the violation of section 53. It is argued that ... the remedy provided by section 54 is exclusive. Thus preventative or specific relief such as injunction or mandamus is not available in the instant case inasmuch as $100 and compensatory damages are the only remedies available....

The statute in the instant case is in the Civil Code and it is provided therein: "The rule of the common law, that statutes in derogation thereof are to be strictly construed, has no application to this code. The code establishes the law of this state respecting the subjects to which it relates, and its provisions are to be liberally construed with a view to effect its objects and to promote justice." Civil Code, sec. 4.

A factor of importance in interpreting the statute and in applying the above-mentioned rule of statutory construction is the adequacy of the remedy provided by the statute. It has been intimated in regard to the rule of statutory interpretation here discussed, that it should not apply when the remedy provided by statute is inadequate. A recovery of compensatory damages and $100 is plainly inadequate relief in a case of this character. Compensable damages would be extremely difficult if not impossible to measure and prove. The sum of $100 is a relatively insignificant recovery when we consider that a positive and unequivocal right has been established and violated.... The right of admission to the places designated is clearly and positively stated (Civil Code, sec. 53) and the inadequacy of the remedy provided in section 54 is manifest in both cases. If the objects of the Civil Code are to be effectuated, and justice promoted as required by section 4 thereof, certainly specific relief should be available where the object is to prevent the exclusion of persons from certain places and there are no valid reasons why such relief should be denied.

Reliance is placed upon Woolcott v. Shubert, 169 App.Div. 194, and White v. Pasfield, 212 Ill.App. 73, holding that a similar statutory remedy provided for in civil rights statutes is exclusive. Those cases failed to take into consideration the factors herein discussed which we believe are of controlling significance and should therefore not be followed....

The judgment is reversed.

Notes and Questions

(1) *Judicial Legislation?* The statute seemed clear: Those who were tossed out received $100 plus compensatory damages. Yet, the court looked elsewhere to determine whether injunctive relief was available. What approach did the court take? Does it make sense to use textualism to answer the question of whether a remedy is adequate?

(2) *Test the Court's Approach.* Suppose the statute had imposed a $10,000 fine? $100,000? $1,000,000? In each instance, would it still be necessary to award injunctive relief? Doesn't the court simply disagree with the legislature's judgment that $100 plus compensatory damages was sufficient to effectuate the purpose of the statute? Put even more dramatically, doesn't the court simply replace the legislature's specific intent—requiring payment of $100 plus compensatory damages—with its own purpose of ending discrimination?

(3) *Equitable v. Legal.* Suppose § 54 had provided: "Any person who is refused admission to any place of amusement, contrary to the provisions of the last section, is entitled to enjoin the proprietor, lessee, or their agents, or any such person, corporation, association, their agents, or the directors thereof." Would money damages have been available?

(4) *Compare the Other Cases.* In the last paragraph of its opinion, the court rejected cases decided in 1915 and 1918 in other jurisdictions that held money damages to be the exclusive remedy for violations of somewhat similar statutes. The *Woolcott* case involved the exclusion from a theater of a *New York Times* reviewer; the *White* case involved minorities who had been excluded from a private park. More recent cases had also denied injunctive relief to minorities. *E.g., Fletcher v. Coney Island, Inc.,* 134 N.E.2d 371 (Ohio 1956). Should the same conclusion as to the adequacy and the exclusivity of the remedy be reached in those states today? In other words, does it matter whether damages would have been sufficient at the time these statutes were passed? Why?

Orloff was decided long ago, at a time when courts were, perhaps, more open to expansive judicial activity in statutory construction. In the following case, the dissent believes that the majority's decision to imply injunctive relief is out of line with modern statutory interpretation. Is it?

Dowdell v. Bloomquist

847 A.2d 827 (R.I. 2004)

FLAHERTY, JUSTICE.

> "Tree at my window, window tree, My sash is lowered when night comes on;
> But let there never be curtain drawn Between you and me."

Robert Frost

In the matter before us, four western arborvitae trees are at the plaintiff's window. Sadly, however, the curtains between the neighboring parties have long since been drawn, forever dividing what was once an amicable relationship between them. The fate of the offending trees now hangs in the balance.

The plaintiff, Cheryl Dowdell, brought this action in Superior Court alleging that the defendant, Peter Bloomquist, planted four western arborvitae trees on his Charlestown property solely to exact revenge against her, to retaliate by blocking her view, and in violation of the spite fence statute, G.L.1956 § 34-10-20.[1] She sought legal and equitable relief. After considering the testimony and evidence presented at a nonjury trial, the presiding Superior Court justice found that the trees planted to satisfy defendant's malicious intent, not his pretextual desire for privacy, and that defendant had violated § 34-10-20. The trial justice granted plaintiff injunctive relief. We affirm the judgment of the trial justice.

The facts pertinent to this appeal are as follows. The parties' homes are on adjoining lots in a subdivision of Charlestown, each approximately one acre in size. Dowdell's home sits at a higher elevation than Bloomquist's and has a distant view of the ocean over the Bloomquist property. In June 2000, defendant acquired the home from his mother, Lorraine Bloomquist. Prior to that time, the Dowdell family had an amicable relationship with defendant's mother. Change was in the wind in the fall of 2000, however, when defendant petitioned for a zoning variance from the Charlestown zoning board seeking permission to build a second-story addition to his home. The plaintiff expressed concern about the petition, anxious that the addition would compromise her view of the Atlantic Ocean. For six months the parties argued before the Charlestown Zoning Board of Review as to the merits of the addition. As a result, the relationship between the neighbors became less than friendly. In March 2001, defendant began clearing land and digging holes to plant the disputed trees in a row between their homes. In April, defendant's counsel sent a letter to plaintiff warning him against trespass onto the Bloomquist property. In May, one day after the zoning board closed its hearing on defendant's variance request, defendant began planting the four western arborvitae trees that now stand in a row bordering the property line. Although the forty-foot-high trees enabled little light to pass into Dowdell's second- and third-story picture windows, testimony at trial evidenced that the vegetation was not a bar to the unkind words between the neighbors.

After the trial justice heard four days of testimony and viewed the property, he made a finding that the row of trees were a fence, based on the language of § 34-10-1. He further

---

1. General Laws 1956 § 34-10-20 provides as follows:
   "**Spite fences.** — A fence or other structure in the nature of a fence which unnecessarily exceeds six feet (6') in height and is maliciously erected or maintained for the purpose of annoying the owners or occupants of adjoining property, shall be deemed a private nuisance, and any owner or occupant who is injured, either in the comfort or enjoyment of his or her estate thereby, may have an action to recover damages for the injury."

found that the objective of privacy claimed by defendant was "no more than a subterfuge for his clear intent to spite his neighbors by erecting a fence of totally out of proportion trees." Hence, the trial justice found that the trees constituted a spite fence in violation of §34-10-20. He noted testimony that plaintiff's real estate values had depreciated by as much as $100,000. Nonetheless, he found that money damages could not adequately compensate her and that equitable relief was more appropriate. Bloomquist was ordered "to cut the four Western Arborvitae to no more than 6' in height and keep them at that level or remove them entirely with no more Western Arborvitae to be planted." ...

[Among other things, on appeal] defendant alleges that the trial justice lacked the authority to award injunctive relief based ... the specific language of the spite fence statute, which states that one "may have an action to recover damages for the injury." ...

[D]efendant correctly asserts that the statute specifically allows for "an action to recover damages." Specifically, the statute states that one who is injured by a spite fence "*may* have an action to recover damages for the injury." Section 34-10-20. (Emphasis added.) However, contrary to defendant's assertion, we believe this language merely sanctions the additional remedy of damages, but does not exclude injunctive relief, which is a remedy logically rooted in the nature and purpose of the statute. To support this holding, we look to the remedial practice in other states that recognize the erection of a spite fence as actionable. Connecticut, Idaho, Indiana, Massachusetts, Montana, New Hampshire, and South Dakota all allow injunctive relief for violations of spite fence law. Especially illustrative is the law as it stands in Massachusetts, whose statute is strikingly similar to §34-10-20. The Massachusetts statute provides:

> "A fence or other structure in the nature of a fence which unnecessarily exceeds six feet in height and is maliciously erected or maintained for the purpose of annoying the owners or occupants of adjoining property shall be deemed a private nuisance. Any such owner or occupant injured ... may have an action of tort for damages...."

In interpreting this law, the Supreme Judicial Court of Massachusetts recognized that despite the lack of explicit language, the court had the authority to order a spite fence to be "abated," in addition to damages and costs. *Rice v. Moorehouse*, 150 Mass. 482, 23 N.E. 229 (1890) (trial justice properly ordered abatement of so much of a spite fence as exceeded six feet in height). The Court relied on the law of nuisance as the basis for its decision, just as we do today....

For the reasons set forth above, we affirm the judgment of the Superior Court. The record shall be remanded to the Superior Court.

FLANDERS, JUSTICE, concurring in part and dissenting in part.

... I would hold that the Superior Court did not have the power to issue an injunction in favor of the plaintiff for the defendant's violation of that statute because it provides only for "an action to recover damages." ... Accordingly, it is up to the General Assembly, not this Court, to provide a cause of action for equitable relief to parties entitled to recover damages under the spite-fence statute.

The spite-fence statute, §34-10-20, specifically states that a party seeking relief pursuant to its terms "may have *an action to recover damages* for the injury." (Emphasis added.) It does not say that any injured owner or occupant may have an action to obtain equitable or injunctive relief for any such injury. Citing this limited right to recover damages for a violation of the spite-fence statute, defendant argues that the trial justice erred in awarding injunctive relief to this plaintiff when the statute creating such a right provided plaintiff with no such cause of action or remedy. I agree with this conclusion.

It is well settled that when the language of a statute is clear and unambiguous, this Court must interpret the statute *literally* and must give the words of the statute their *plain and ordinary meanings.* As defendant correctly notes in his brief, the plain and obvious meaning of "an action to recover damages" does not include an equitable remedy such as an injunction. Although the trial justice conclusorily said that he believed a damages remedy "cannot compensate [plaintiff] for this spiteful act" and that "[e]quitable relief is far more appropriate," the evidence in this case showed that the spite fence in question caused a permanent and quantifiable diminution in the value of plaintiff's property, one that could be remedied via an award of damages....

In this case, the spite-fence statute creates a right not recognized at common law because it deems to be a private nuisance a fence or a fence-like structure that unnecessarily exceeds six feet in height and that "is maliciously erected or maintained for the purpose of annoying the owners or occupants of adjoining property." Section 34-10-20. As this Court observed in [in another case], under the common law

> "[a] landowner has no right to the light and air coming to him across his neighbor's land. True, if the light and air be shut off damage may well result to his property for residential purposes, as is alleged here, but it is *damnum absque injuria.* It is damage which the law does not recognize because there is no injury. Where there is no right, a deprivation works no injury."

Courts should not infer causes of actions and remedies that are not expressly provided for in a statute such as this one that creates a right and a remedy that was not available at common law. Indeed, as a general rule, when a statute does not plainly provide for a private cause of action ... such a right cannot be inferred." ...

By a parity of reasoning, in this case we should not infer a right to seek and obtain equitable relief for a violation of the spite-fence statute because, like the statutes at issue in [the other jurisdictions], the statute already expressly provides a remedy—albeit not one for the type of relief that plaintiff would prefer, but one "to recover damages for the injury." Section 34-10-20.

Moreover, the mere fact that the statute deems the creation of a spite fence to constitute a private nuisance does not imply that the General Assembly intended for an equitable remedy to be available for such a nuisance when the statute fails to provide for such relief. Deeming the erection of a spite fence to constitute a private nuisance only suffices to establish the perpetrator's civil *liability* for violating the statute. But it does not speak to what civil *remedy* is available for creating such a private nuisance, especially when an equitable remedy was not available to abate a spite fence at common law. Moreover, if the General Assembly's purpose had been to incorporate any and all remedies that might be available to remedy a private nuisance at common law, why would it have specified in the statute that an aggrieved party may have an action to recover damages for the injury? Is this not a classic instance of *expressio unius est exclusio alterius* ("to express or include one thing implies the exclusion of the other")? If the General Assembly had intended to provide for both equitable and legal relief, why would it not have said so expressly, instead of providing only for a damages action? When the General Assembly wants to empower courts to award equitable or injunctive relief, in addition to damages, for the violation of a statutorily created right, it certainly knows how to do so. *See, e.g.,* Deceptive Trade Practices Act, G.L.1956 §6-13.1-5.2(b) ("In any action brought under this section, the court may in its discretion order, in addition to damages, injunctive or other equitable relief."). As this Court observed many years ago..., "[t]he function of adjusting remedies to rights is a legislative rather than a judicial one, and up to the present time the legislature of this

[s]tate has omitted to provide a remedy" for the right in question. When, as here, a statute expressly provides [a] remed[y], courts must be extremely reluctant to expand its sweep by augmenting the list of prescribed anodynes. Instead, a court should ordinarily conclude that the legislature provided precisely the redress it considered appropriate, and should not expand the remedies available.

The majority relies on *Rice v. Moorehouse*, 150 Mass. 482, 23 N.E. 229, 229 (1890), for the proposition that both damages and injunctive relief are appropriate sanctions to impose on the violator of a spite-fence statute. But the language in the Massachusetts spite-fence statute that the court construed in *Rice*—namely, Mass. Gen. Laws ch. 348, §§ 1–2 (1887)—was markedly different from the language of § 34-10-20.[11] Chapter 348, § 2 of the Mass. Gen. Laws provided that one injured by a spite fence had "an action of tort for the damage sustained thereby, and *the provisions of chapter one hundred and eighty of the Public Statutes concerning actions for private nuisances shall be applicable thereto.*" (Emphasis added.) As the *Rice* court noted, chapter 180 specifically "authorize[d] the court ... to enter judgment that the nuisance be abated and removed." *Rice*, 23 N.E. at 229. Therefore, unlike the provisions of § 34-10-20, the text of the statute at issue in *Rice* specifically provided that a law authorizing the abatement and removal of a private nuisance "shall be applicable" to the statutorily created right of action for spite fences. *See* Mass. Gen. Laws ch. 348, § 2. Here, § 34-10-20 contains no such reference to a statute authorizing the enforcing court to abate or remove the nuisance....

Given that the General Assembly easily could have included a cause of action for equitable remedies in the spite-fence statute, we should deem this omission as evincing a legislative intent to limit a spite-fence claimant's remedy to "an action to recover damages." Section 34-10-20.

Also, the General Assembly has had more than fifty years to act since the 1950 *Musumeci* decision, in which this Court indicated that the common law provided no equitable relief for the erection of a spite fence, and noted that the spite-fence statute only provided for a damages remedy. Nevertheless, the General Assembly has declined to expand that statute to provide for equitable relief. But inaction upon the part of the legislature, however long continued, can not confer legislative functions upon the judiciary. Accordingly, a party seeking an injunction under the spite-fence statute should petition the Legislature, not this Court, for relief, because for this Court to create such a cause of action and remedy would be interpretation by amendment of the statute. In other words, the remedy is to be found in the state house not the courthouse....

Notes and Questions

(1) *Should a Presumption Against Additional Remedies Apply?* In *Orloff*, the court did not presume that the remedies were exclusive, but instead directly analyzed whether it believed that the listed remedies were sufficient to carry out the purpose of the statute. The Rhode Island Supreme Court, in contrast, based its holding on the notion that injunctive relief was "logically rooted in the nature and purpose of the statute." These tests are sim-

---

11. The majority quotes the text of Mass. Gen. Laws Ann. ch. 49, § 21 (West 1994) to buttress its conclusion that the language in the Massachusetts statute is "strikingly similar" to the language of G.L.1956 § 34-10-20. But the statute that the Rice court interpreted was not the 1994 law quoted by the majority but an earlier spite-fence statute—namely, Mass. Gen. Laws ch. 348, §§ 1–2 (1887)— one that expressly incorporated an abatement and removal statute for remedying a nuisance that is conspicuously absent from the provisions of § 34-10-20.

ilar but not identical. Which do you think reflects an intentionalist approach? Purposivist? Textualist? Returning to a question we asked earlier, does it make sense to apply a textualist approach to this issue? If not, does that mean that remedies should never be implied?

(2) *Exclusio Unius?* Why doesn't the fact that the statute includes one remedy mean that the legislature intended to exclude all others? At minimum, shouldn't there be a presumption that identified remedies are exclusive? Is *Orloff* close to that approach? If a presumption applied, what would overcome it?

In the next section, we'll explore when courts will imply a cause of action, or a claim, with remedies. As you read the rest of this chapter, ponder whether the approach courts take to determining whether to imply a cause of action also might be appropriate to determining whether to allow an implied remedy to an express cause of action.

B. Implied Causes of Action

A private cause of action is the right of an individual to sue either (1) to recover for an injury caused by another party's violation of a legal obligation or (2) to prevent injury from a threatened violation. Although a duty can arise from various sources, our focus is on the obligations arising from statutes. We have seen that many statutes expressly authorize aggrieved parties to sue. While those statutes present issues of interpretation, the existence of the right to sue is not, itself, in doubt.

In the first section of this chapter, we examined whether, for an express cause of action, courts should imply remedies beyond those remedies identified in the statute. Again, the existence of the claim was not in doubt: only whether non-expressed remedies were.

What may not be intuitive is that a statute can prohibit something and yet not authorize anyone to enforce that prohibition. For example, some statutes impose obligations and authorize a government agency to enjoin violators of the statute. Commonly, these statutes do not expressly provide private individuals with any way to enforce those obligations or to seek damages when violation of the statute injures them. In other words, the statutes make no mention of private-party suits of any kind. Some statutes do not authorize anyone, the government or a private party, to enforce the obligations. When a private party sues to enforce such statutes or to obtain damages for their violation, courts must confront the issue of whether a cause of action in favor of a private plaintiff should be implied. One commentator described a typical implied private cause of action scenario as follows:

> [T]he plaintiff institutes a civil action to prevent an injury or to recover damages, and he alleges that he is entitled to relief because of something contained in a legislative text. He says the defendant has acted or proposes to act in a manner contrary to the text. He relies upon the legislation even though the words of the text do not actually state that he has a right to bring an action of this kind, and here the defendant raises a defense. The defendant argues that the legislation does not support the plaintiff's claim because it does not state that the plaintiff is entitled to maintain an action upon it. The court must then decide the issue.

H. Miles Foy III, *Some Reflections on Legislation, Adjudication, and Implied Private Actions in the State and Federal Courts*, 71 CORNELL L. REV. 501, 503 (1986).

From both ends of the spectrum, implied rights present odd issues. On the one hand, the notion that a party can be damaged by the violation of a statute and yet have no ability either to recover damages or to stop the violation seems jarring. Every wrong has a right, or so the saying goes. On the other hand if a legislature has "chosen" not to create a claim, why should a court be free to imply one?

1. The Supreme Court's Development of this Doctrine

Despite these difficult issues, some statutes do allow private causes of action. Since at least the founding of this country, if not in English common law, the idea of an implied right of action has persisted. *See Wisniewski v. Rodale, Inc.*, 510 F.3d 294 (3rd Cir. 2007).* The Supreme Court was once much more willing to imply a cause of action than it is today. We'll examine the Supreme Court's approach to implied causes of action, and then we examine how state courts approach this issue. Early in its history, the Court viewed its decision to imply claims as part of its function to facilitate the legislative scheme or purpose. As will be seen, however, the Court has significantly curtailed what it perceives its function and role in this area to be.

In *J.I. Cace Company v. Borak*, 377 U.S. 426 (1964), the Court unanimously held that the Securities Exchange Act of 1934 impliedly authorized a private cause of action for rescission or damages to shareholders who alleged that they were injured by a consummated merger that was authorized with a false or misleading proxy statement in violation of § 14(a) of the Act. The Court stated that "it is the duty of the courts to be alert to provide such remedies as are necessary to make effective the congressional purpose." *Id.* at 433. The Court anchored its analysis in the purpose of the statute. Foremost, it relied on language in § 14(a) that explicitly granted the Securities and Exchange Commission ("SEC") the authority to make rules "in the public interest or for the protection of investors." The Court deemed "the protection of investors" to be among the section's primary purposes. *Id.* at 432. Because the SEC admitted that it did not have enough time or resources to examine every proxy statement for false and misleading statements, the Court stated that private enforcement was a "necessary supplement" to the SEC's efforts to protect investors. *Id.* at 433. Finally, the Court asserted that a federal right of action was necessary because state law might not be adequate to protect the federally created "rights" in the statute. *Id* at 434. Significantly, the *Borak* Court did not purport to discern Congress's intent to create a private right of action—instead, the Court focused on Congress's general purposes in enacting the statute. *Id.* at 431–32. The Court's approach is quite similar to the approaches taken in *Orloff* and *Dowdell* in determining whether to imply an additional remedy to an express cause of action.

Eleven years later, the Supreme Court replaced** *Borak's* purpose-driven approach in *Cort v. Ash*, 422 U.S. 66 (1975). In *Cort*, the Court adopted a four-factor test for determining whether an implied private right of action existed. Using its new test, the Court held that a criminal statute that prohibited corporations from making contributions to presidential campaigns did not provide an implied private right of action for shareholders to sue corporate directors who violated the statute. The Court described its test as follows:

> In determining whether a private remedy is implicit in a statute not expressly providing one, several factors are relevant. First, is the plaintiff "one of the class

---

* Authors' footnote: Much of the discussion of the cases in this section comes from this case.

** Authors' footnote: *Cort* did not expressly reject the *Borak* approach. In fact, it cited *Borak* several times to merely distinguish the statute in *Borak* from the one in *Cort*. *Cort*, 422 U.S. at 79–80 & n.11. Later cases recognize that *Cort* effectively overruled *Borak*. E.g., *Alexander v. Sandoval*, 532 U.S. 275, 287 (2001).

for whose especial benefit the statute was enacted"—that is, does the statute create a federal right in favor of the plaintiff? Second, is there any indication of legislative intent, explicit or implicit, either to create such a remedy or to deny one? Third, is it consistent with the underlying purposes of the legislative scheme to imply such a remedy for the plaintiff? And finally, is the cause of action one traditionally relegated to state law, in an area basically the concern of the States, so that it would be inappropriate to infer a cause of action based solely on federal law?

Id. at 78. The Court stated that, under the second factor, when federal law grants certain rights to a class of people (and thereby satisfies the first factor), "it is not necessary to show an intention to create a private cause of action, although an explicit purpose to deny such cause of action would be controlling." *Id.* at 82. Thus, the *Cort* test allowed courts to imply a private right of action even without any affirmative legislative intent to do so.

Although never formally overruled, "subsequent decisions have altered [*Cort*] virtually beyond recognition." *Wisniewski v. Rodale, Inc.*, 510 F.3d 294, 299 (3rd Cir. 2007). This is putting it mildly. The ink was not dry on *Cort* when the assault began.

First, in *Cannon v. University of Chicago*, 441 U.S. 677 (1979), the Court framed the implied right question as one of "statutory construction" in which a court must determine whether "Congress intended to make a remedy available." 441 U.S. at 688. The *Cannon* Court still relied on the four *Cort* factors as "indicative of such intent." *Id.* Thus, Congress's intent to create a private right of action—an issue virtually ignored in *Borak* and listed in *Cort* as just one of four factors—became *Cannon's* primary factor.*

In two cases later that same year, the Court emphasized that congressional intent was the exclusive factor, declaring that the inquiry was "limited solely to whether Congress intended to create the private right of action." *Touche Ross & Co. v. Redington*, 442 U.S. 560, 568 (1979) (instructing that the *Cort* factors should only be used to the extent they help to determine legislative intent); *Transamerica Mortg. Advisors, Inc. (TAMA) v. Lewis*, 444 U.S. 11, 15–16 (1979) ("what must ultimately be determined is whether Congress intended to create the private remedy asserted, as our recent decisions have made clear.").

2. The Supreme Court's Doctrine Today

The Court's decision in *Alexander v. Sandoval*, 532 U.S. 275 (2001), ended *Cort's* brief reign.** In *Sandoval*, the Court held that Title VI of the Civil Rights Act does not provide

---

* Authors' footnote: Only Justice Powell called for abandoning the *Cort* test. He argued in *Cannon* that *Cort* was actually unconstitutional because it permitted judicial lawmaking and so violated separation of powers. *Cannon*, 441 U.S. at 742–43 (Powell, J., dissenting). Justice Powell argued that courts should refuse to recognize implied private rights of action unless there was the "most compelling evidence that Congress in fact intended such an action to exist," and that courts should be "especially reluctant" to recognize them if the statute provided any alternative mechanism to enforce the rights it created. *Id.* at 749.

** Authors' footnote: The majority in *Sandoval* cited *Cort* only to point out that *Cort* marked the demise of the *Borak* approach. See *Sandoval*, 532 U.S. at 287. The *Sandoval* dissent, however, argued that *Cort* was viable. See *Sandoval*, 532 U.S. at 311 (Stevens, J., dissenting).

Some argue that Sandoval implicitly adopted Justice Powell's dissent in Cannon that the focus should be on congressional intent. *See, e.g.,* Matthew C. Stephenson, *Public Regulation of Private Enforcement: The Case for Expanding the Role of Administrative Agencies*, 91 VA. L. REV. 93, 105 (2005) ("The *Sandoval* Court thus seems to have adopted Justice Powell's view that the multifactor *Cort* analysis 'too easily may be used to deflect inquiry away from the intent of Congress, and to permit a court

an implied private right of action to enforce disparate-impact regulations promulgated under § 602 of the Act (42 U.S.C. § 2000d-1 (2000)). Although the Court did not expressly reject the *Cort* factors, it did not apply them to guide its inquiry. Instead, the Court set out the following new test to determine whether an implied private right of action exists:

> Like substantive federal law itself, private rights of action to enforce federal law must be created by Congress.... The judicial task is to interpret the statute Congress has passed to determine whether it displays an intent to create not just a private right but also a private remedy.... Statutory intent on this latter point is determinative.... Without it, a cause of action does not exist and courts may not create one, no matter how desirable that might be as a policy matter, or how compatible with the statute.

532 U.S. at 286–87 (citations omitted).

The Court concluded that the "text and structure" of § 602 did not show that Congress intended to create a private right, in light of the absence of "rights-creating language" that focuses on the protected individuals. 532 U.S. at 288–89. Next, the Court concluded that nothing in the text of § 602 demonstrated that Congress intended to create a private remedy and that the statute's provision of a remedial scheme suggests that Congress "intended to preclude" any other remedy. *Id.* at 290–91. The Court rejected the Government's position that Congress had "ratified" an implied private right of action under § 602 by failing to address this issue when it amended Title VI. Having applied what the Court called its "standard test for discerning private causes of action" and having found no congressional intent to create a personal right or private remedy in the statute's text or structure, the Court ended its inquiry. *Id.* at 293. *Cort* was no more. *See Correctional Servs. Corp. v. Malesko*, 534 U.S. 61, 67 n.3 (2001) (explaining that the Court had "retreated from [its] previous willingness to imply a cause of action where Congress has not provided one.").

Most recently, the Court has adopted a textualist approach to what admittedly should be entirely a non-textual issue, although whether textualism controls is still an open question. The first case below provides some additional details of this historic shift. Whether textualism's rise will continue this trend against implying private causes of action is an issue that the first case raises, along with more fundamental issues about the proper interpretive approach to this question. The second case examines some of the repercussions that result when courts imply a cause of action. The notes following each case explore these issues further.

Office Planning Group, Inc. v. Baraga-Houghton-Keweenaw Child Dev. Bd.
697 N.W.2d 871 (Mich. 2005)

YOUNG, J.

Plaintiff is a disappointed bidder that seeks disclosure from defendant of bid documents under ... a provision of the federal Head Start Act that requires Head Start agencies to provide for "reasonable public access" to information. Defendant Head Start agency contends that the act does not create a private cause of action to enforce

---

instead to substitute its own views as to the desirability of private enforcement.'" (quoting *Cannon,* 441 U.S. at 740 (Powell, J., dissenting)).

its provisions. We hold that the Head Start Act does not contemplate a private cause of action seeking disclosure of the contested bid documents.... Accordingly, we reverse....

Defendant, Baraga-Houghton-Keweenaw Child Development Board, Inc., is a private, nonprofit organization that is designated as a Head Start agency.... Defendant operates Head Start programs in Baraga, Houghton, and Keweenaw counties. In January 2001, defendant solicited bids for office supplies and furniture. Plaintiff, a private, for-profit corporation, submitted a bid. Defendant conducted an open meeting at which its building committee reviewed the bids and made a recommendation to its board of directors. Defendant accepted the lowest bid at the open meeting. Rodney Liimatainen, defendant's executive director, notified plaintiff's branch manager, Jack Hamm, that plaintiff's bid had exceeded the lowest bid by $10,000.

Hamm, suspicious that the lower bidders had offered lesser-quality merchandise, requested copies of all the bids submitted. Liimatainen informed Hamm that the details of the bids were unavailable for inspection by the public because the other bidders did not want the information disseminated....

[P]laintiff filed an action ... demanding a complete copy of each bid. Plaintiff later filed an amended complaint alleging that it was ... entitled to disclosure of the bid information under unspecified "federal legislation which requires disclosure of information by parties supplying service under the so-called Head Start Program." In subsequent motion papers, plaintiff indicated that the federal legislation on which it relied was 42 U.S.C. 9839(a), which provides, in relevant part:

> Each [Head Start] agency shall also provide for reasonable public access to information, including public hearings at the request of appropriate community groups and reasonable public access to books and records of the agency or other agencies engaged in program activities or operations involving the use of authority or funds for which it is responsible....

The trial court ... *sua sponte* granted summary disposition in favor of plaintiff ... on the ground that the requested information was subject to disclosure under § 9839(a)....

Because we conclude that § 9839(a) does not provide for a private cause of action, we reverse....

The Head Start Act was enacted for the purpose of "promot[ing] school readiness by enhancing the social and cognitive development of low-income children through the provision, to low-income children and their families, of health, educational, nutritional, social, and other services that are determined, based on family needs assessments, to be necessary." The secretary of the HHS is authorized under 42 U.S.C. 9836(a) to designate as a Head Start agency "any local public or private nonprofit or for-profit agency...."

Under 42 U.S.C. 9836a, the secretary is directed to establish by regulation standards applicable to Head Start agencies, including performance standards, administrative and financial management standards, and standards relating to the conditions and location of agency facilities. The secretary has promulgated regulations implementing these statutory directives. The secretary is directed under 42 U.S.C. 9836a(c) and (d) to monitor Head Start agencies for compliance with statutory and regulatory standards and to take corrective action if necessary. If an agency does not comply with such standards, the secretary may initiate proceedings to terminate the designation of the agency unless the agency corrects the deficiency.

At issue in this case is § 9839(a) of the act, which provides as follows:

Each Head Start agency shall observe standards of organization, management, and administration which will assure, so far as reasonably possible, that all program activities are conducted in a manner consistent with the purposes of this subchapter [42 U.S.C. 9831 *et seq.*] and the objective of providing assistance effectively, efficiently, and free of any taint of partisan political bias or personal or family favoritism. Each such agency shall establish or adopt rules to carry out this section, which shall include rules to assure full staff accountability in matters governed by law, regulations, or agency policy. *Each agency shall also provide for reasonable public access to information, including public hearings at the request of appropriate community groups and reasonable public access to books and records of the agency or other agencies engaged in program activities or operations involving the use of authority or funds for which it is responsible....* (Emphasis supplied.)

TC held it was implied COA

... The lower courts concluded that defendant was required under the "reasonable public access" provision of §9839(a) to disclose copies of all bids it received in connection with its January 2001 solicitation of bids for office supplies and furniture.... [W]e hold that §9839(a) does not provide for a private cause of action....

The fact that a federal statute has been violated and some person harmed does not automatically give rise to a private cause of action in favor of that person. Rather, like substantive federal law itself, private rights of action to enforce federal law must be created by Congress. Thus, in determining whether plaintiff may bring a private cause of action to enforce the public access requirement of §9839(a), we must determine whether Congress intended to create such a cause of action....

Although the United States Supreme Court in the last century embraced a short-lived willingness to create remedies to enforce private rights,[34] the Court "abandoned" that approach to statutory remedies in *Cort v. Ash* and "[has] not returned to it since." In *Cort*, the Court set forth a test for determining whether a private remedy is implicit in a statute that does not expressly provide such a remedy:

> First, is the plaintiff "one of the class for whose *especial* benefit the statute was enacted," ... that is, does the statute create a federal right in favor of the plaintiff? Second, is there any indication of legislative intent, explicit or implicit, either to create such a remedy or to deny one? ... Third, is it consistent with the underlying purposes of the legislative scheme to imply such a remedy for the plaintiff? ... And finally, is the cause of action one traditionally relegated to state law, in an area basically the concern of the States, so that it would be inappropriate to infer a cause of action based solely on federal law?

Post-*Cort*, the Court has become increasingly reluctant to imply a private cause of action, preferring to focus exclusively on the second *Cort* element, which requires indicia of congressional intent to create a cause of action. For example, as early as *Cannon v. Univ. of Chicago*[441 U.S. 677, 688 (1979)], although the Court applied each of the *Cort* factors, it characterized the determination whether a private remedy existed to enforce a statutory right as a matter of "statutory construction." In *Touche Ross & Co.*, 442 U.S. 560, the Court declined to even address the remaining *Cort* factors ... :

> It is true that in *Cort v. Ash*, the Court set forth four factors that it considered "relevant" in determining whether a private remedy is implicit in a statute not

---

34. *See, e.g., J I Case Co. v. Borak*, 377 U.S. 426, 433 (1964) (holding that "it is the duty of the courts to be alert to provide such remedies as are necessary to make effective the congressional purpose" of a federal statute).

expressly providing one. But the Court did not decide that each of these factors is entitled to equal weight. The central inquiry remains whether Congress intended to create, either expressly or by implication, a private cause of action. Indeed, the first three factors discussed in *Cort*—the language and focus of the statute, its legislative history, and its purpose, are ones traditionally relied upon in determining legislative intent. Here, the statute by its terms grants no private rights to any identifiable class and proscribes no conduct as unlawful. And the parties as well as the Court of Appeals agree that the legislative history of the 1934 Act simply does not speak to the issue of private remedies under § 17(a). At least in such a case as this, the inquiry ends there: The question whether Congress, either expressly or by implication, intended to create a private right of action, has been definitely answered in the negative....

In *Alexander*, the Court appears to have abandoned the *Cort* inquiry altogether in favor of a completely textual analysis in determining whether a private remedy exists under a particular statute. Rather than applying the *Cort* factors, the *Alexander* Court concluded, solely on the basis of the text of [the statute at issue], that private individuals could not sue to enforce disparate-impact regulations promulgated under Title VI of the Civil Rights Act of 1964. The Court rejected the plaintiff's argument that dispositive weight could be accorded to context shorn of text, holding that "legal context matters only to the extent it clarifies text." The *Alexander* majority additionally rejected the dissent's claim that the position adopted "blind[ed] itself to important evidence of congressional intent," noting that the methodology employed in the majority opinion was well established in earlier decisions that explained "that the interpretive inquiry begins with the text and structure of the statute ... and ends once it has become clear that Congress did not provide a cause of action."[46] ...

With the aforementioned principles in mind, we examine the text of the Head Start Act to determine whether it provides for a private cause of action to enforce § 9839(a)....

The act, of course, does not expressly provide for a private cause of action to enforce the disclosure requirement of § 9839(a). Thus, the question becomes whether the text of the act demonstrates an *implicit* intent to provide for a private cause of action.

analysis

Again, the stated purpose of the act is to promote school readiness by providing services to low-income children and their families. The act does not contemplate any benefit to private corporations such as plaintiff; nor does it indicate any intent that such a private corporation may sue to enforce its provisions. Where the intended beneficiaries are specifically identified, we are loath to create a private means of seeking redress under the act for nonbeneficiaries.

---

46. Our dissenting colleagues assert that we have incorrectly characterized Touche Ross & Co. and Alexander as representing a departure from the four-factor Cort test. Whether the United States Supreme Court will, in the future, continue to apply the four-part Cort test is, however, simply irrelevant where it is clear from the text of the statute at issue that Congress did not intend to create a private enforcement action. Indeed, this case is directly analogous to *Touche Ross & Co.* and *Alexander*. As the dissent points out, the provisions at issue in *Touche Ross & Co.* and *Alexander* neither conferred rights on individuals nor proscribed conduct as unlawful. The same can certainly be said of 42 U.S.C. 9839(a). Similarly, the dissent notes that the *Alexander* Court found it quite telling that the statute at issue expressly empowered governmental agencies to enforce regulations. The Head Start Act does precisely that, by directing the secretary to establish regulations governing Head Start agencies and to enforce those regulations, and, in 42 U.S.C. 9839(a), by requiring Head Start agencies to conduct program activities in conformity with the Head Start Act and to establish or adopt rules to carry out that duty....

More important, the act contains a comprehensive mechanism for ensuring agency compliance with its provisions.... [F]ar from demonstrating an intent to allow for a private cause of action, the act indicates that the *sole* remedy for a violation of § 9839(a) is an enforcement proceeding by the secretary of the HHS and the possible termination of Head Start agency status.

In light of this clear indication of congressional intent, we are precluded from venturing beyond the bounds of the statutory text to divine support for the creation of a private claim to enforce § 9839(a). To do so would be to substitute our own judgment for that of Congress and thus to usurp legislative authority, something that we of course decline to do....

Because the Head Start Act does not provide for a private cause of action to enforce the disclosure requirement of § 9839(a), plaintiff has failed to state a cognizable claim. Accordingly, we reverse....

WEAVER, J. (concurring in part and dissenting in part).

... I dissent from the majority holding that 42 U.S.C. 9839(a) of the federal Head Start Act does not permit plaintiff to seek disclosure of information relevant to the defendant's decision on competing bids for a contract....

For the reasons stated in Justice Kelly's dissent, I would hold that this statutory language does provide plaintiff a right to seek "reasonable" disclosure of records pertaining to contract bids submitted to a Head Start agency....

Though the majority may prefer that *Cort's* factors be abandoned and a "completely textual" approach be adopted, neither logic nor federal precedent supports its preference. First, it is absurd to advocate a "completely textual approach" where the need to examine whether a cause of action may be inferred from a statute is engendered by the *lack* of an expressly stated cause of action in the text of the statute. Further, the majority makes no attempt to explain how its "completely textual" approach differs from the *Cort* factors....

In this case we must necessarily look beyond the text of the statute at issue to discern whether Congress intended that a private person be able to seek disclosure of documents from a Head Start agency. The text of the statute at issue in this case, 42 U.S.C. 9839(a), does not expressly create a private cause of action to enforce its provision regarding public access to information. Thus, it is necessary to look beyond the text to determine whether Congress intended to create a private cause of action....

MARYLYN J. KELLY, J. (dissenting).

... I disagree with [the majority's] conclusion that the act ... does not provide a private cause of action. The statutory language, the focus of the legislation, its history, and its purpose imply a congressional intent to allow private actions. Therefore, I would find such a right and affirm....

Congress can create a private right of action in two ways. It can expressly provide for the right or it can imply it. Frequently, legislation does not clearly express whether a private right was intended. The growing volume of litigation and the complexity of federal legislation increase the need for careful scrutiny to ensure what Congress wanted.

To assist us ... the ... Court articulated a four-part test ... in *Cort*.... The key to this inquiry is determining the legislative intent in enacting the statute.

In *Touche Ross & Co.* the Court opined that the first three factors of *Cort* should be given greater weight than the fourth. The opinion states:

Indeed, the first three factors discussed in *Cort*—the language and focus of the statute, its legislative history, and its purpose are ones traditionally relied upon in determining legislative intent....

Contrary to the majority's conclusion, a full reading of *Alexander* indicates that the Court did not abandon *Cort*. Instead, *Alexander* stated that the analysis in that case need not extend beyond the first two *Cort* factors because the statute indicated that Congress did not intend a private cause of action. The *Cort* factors remain a valid and important means of discerning legislative intent. The *Alexander* decision provides no basis to conclude the contrary....

Despite espousing a textualist approach, the majority never deals with the actual language of 42 U.S.C. 9839(a). Instead, it focuses on ... the overall purpose of the Head Start Act.

Let us review the actual language in question....

This language indicates the intent of Congress to maintain open accountability in the use of Head Start funds. It explicitly provides a right of public access. After stating that "[e]ach agency shall also provide for reasonable public access to information," it spells out particulars on how to meet this requirement, including holding public meetings.

The statute specifically confers an individual right on members of the public to conduct inspections of books and records. The opposite situation existed in both *Touche Ross* and *Alexander*, where the statutes lacked language creating such a right. They offered neither the general public nor any private individual access to anything. The oversight they called for was by governmental agencies. The majority simply misses this important distinction.[6] ...

The majority also bases its decision on the general purpose of the Head Start Act. It assumes that the only purpose worth considering is the act's overarching goal of providing services to low-income children and their families. It ignores the congressional intent specifically written into 42 U.S.C. 9839(a).

42 U.S.C. 9839(a) specifies Congress's goal of maintaining open accountability in the use of public funds and effectuates it by providing a right of public access to books and records. By ignoring these specific provisions, the majority has effectively substituted its judgment for that of Congress. In reducing public oversight, it frustrates the paramount goals of the Head Start Act by facilitating the misuse of federal funds.

Application of the *Cort* factors to 42 U.S.C. 9839(a)

Given that the language of the statute does not contradict the existence of a private cause of action, it is appropriate to apply all the *Cort* factors. The first question is whether plaintiff is in the class for whose benefit Congress enacted 42 U.S.C. 9839(a). The statute indicates that Congress intended to grant access to the public at large. Plaintiff is a member of the public. Therefore, plaintiff is within the appropriate class.

---

6. The majority states that it "wholly disagree[s]" with the conclusion that 42 U.S.C. 9839(a) confers an individual right on a member of the public. It contends that 42 U.S.C. 9839(a) merely creates a disclosure requirement. Again, the majority fails to analyze the actual language of the statute. 42 U.S.C. 9839(a) mandates public access, such as public hearings, at the request of "appropriate community groups...." Only by allowing enforcement of this public inspection and access requirement can we effectuate Congress's specific goal of maintaining open accountability in the use of public funds. The majority simply ignores this clear congressional intent.

The second question, whether there is any indication that Congress intended to create or to deny a private right of action, has already been discussed. The language of 42 U.S.C. 9839(a) indicates a specific intent to create such an action. There is no legislative history or other material contradicting this intent.

The third question is whether it is consistent with the underlying legislative scheme to infer a private right of action. As the majority states, the overall purpose of the Head Start Act is to promote school readiness. As part of its plan to reach this goal, Congress expressed an intent to maintain open accountability in the use of public funds in 42 U.S.C. 9839(a). In the same section, to effectuate this intent, Congress provided the public with a right of access to books and records. Inferring a right of action to implement this right enforces that intent. [The dissent then analyzes each of the *Cort* factors.] Therefore, inferring a right of action is consistent with the legislative scheme.

Finally, there is no indication that this is a cause of action traditionally relegated to state law. And defendant makes no such argument. To the contrary, an action pursuant to 42 U.S.C. 9839(a) is the only means by which plaintiff could obtain the information it seeks. Therefore, the analysis [of the] *Cort* factors, points to the need to recognize a private right of action under 42 U.S.C. 9839(a).

Where a Legal Right Exists, so Does a Legal Remedy

"The very essence of civil liberty certainly consists in the right of every individual to claim the protection of the laws...." *Marbury v. Madison*, 163 U.S. (1 Cranch) 137, 163 (1803). One of the fundamental tenets of the American legal system is that, where there is a legal right, there is also a legal remedy. After it is determined that Congress intended a right of action, courts presume the availability of all appropriate remedies unless Congress has expressly indicated otherwise....

I would affirm....

Notes and Questions

(1) *Text Alone?* Is it absurd to determine whether an implied cause of action exists by looking only at the text? The notion that an "implied" right can be found in the text alone sounds like sophistry. Is it? If it is, then why was the dissent able to construct a reasonable argument that the text evidences such an intent?

(2) *The Purpose.* The judges disagreed on how purpose should be viewed. What was that disagreement, and who do you believe took the proper view? Can you construct an argument that, even with the majority's view of the statute's purpose, a cause of action should be implied?

(3) *Is* Cort *Consistent with the Court's Current Approach to Statutory Interpretation?* The judges disagreed about the vitality of the *Cort* factors, and as we noted, that issue is still open for debate, although the broad approach to implied rights represented by *Cort* is no longer dominant. If you believe that the move toward textualism and a more limited approach to implied causes of action is proper, what do you think of the fact that Congress often does not disturb courts' findings of implied causes of action (as the next case shows)?

(4) *Legal Context Revisited.* As we have seen, the willingness of the Court to find implied causes of action has waxed and waned over the years. It is fairly clear that the Supreme Court was, several decades ago, more willing to interpret statutes to provide an implied

cause of action. Should statutes that were enacted during that time be more liberally construed because the enacting legislature would have anticipated such legal treatment? *See Alexander v. Sandoval*, 532 U.S. 275, 288 (2001) (in refusing to find an implied cause of action, the Court noted that it had become less willing to find such rights and stated that "legal context matters only to the extent it clarifies text"). Do you think that the plain meaning of a statute ought to be determined by looking at legal context? If not, why not? *See* Bradford C. Mank, *Legal Context: Reading Statutes in Light of Prevailing Legal Precedent*, 34 Ariz. St. L.J. 815 (2002) (characterizing the approach of courts to this question as inconsistent and arbitrary).

(5) *Context Changes over Time?* In light of *Alexander*, litigants are now arguing that, even though courts previously found implied causes of action, the courts should reconsider their holdings if the implied right was found under *Cort* or its progeny. *E.g.*, *Jacobs v. Bremner*, 378 F. Supp. 2d 861 (N.D. Ill. 2005). In other words, the argument is being made that recent Supreme Court cases have adopted a narrower view of implied causes of action and that *Cort* was an improperly expansive view. *See, e.g., Olmsted v. Pruco Life Ins. Co. of N.J.*, 283 F.3d 429, 434 (2d Cir. 2002) (noting that earlier cases finding an implied right had been decided when "courts had more latitude to weigh statutory policy and other considerations than they do now."). From an interpretive standpoint, if *Alexander* and recent cases in fact overruled *Cort*, should they be applied only prospectively, so that any statute enacted between the time of *Cort* and the time of *Alexander* should still be interpreted in light of *Cort*? Why or why not? Would the different approaches—textualism, purposivism, or intentionalism—reach different answers to that question?

(6) *Stare Decisis and Statutory Interpretation Methodology.* The foregoing note raises issues of *stare decisis*. A legislature that enacts a statute at a time when implied causes of action would be easily found presumably relies upon the fact that courts take that approach. Should that assumption lead courts to more rigorously apply *stare decisis* to decisions concerning the proper methodology to statutory interpretation? *See generally*, Sydney Foster, *Should Courts Give Stare Decisis Effect to Statutory Interpretation Methodology?*, 96 Geo. L. J. 1863, 1863 (2008) (arguing that courts should give statutory interpretation doctrines "stronger stare decisis effect than their substantive law counterparts").

(7) *Should State Courts Follow the Supreme Court's Lead?* In the introduction, we noted that the Supreme Court has become more reluctant to find implied causes of action. Even after *Alexander*, state courts often apply the *Cort* factors to the question of whether a state statute creates implied rights. *E.g.*, *Ernst v. Burdick*, 687 N.W.2d 473 (N.D. 2004) (applying first three *Cort* factors). Other states adopt a different and ostensibly broader approach. For example, the Connecticut Supreme Court applies the following factors:

> First, is the plaintiff one of the class for whose ... benefit the statute was enacted ... ? Second, is there any indication of legislative intent, explicit or implicit, either to create a remedy or to deny one ... ? Third, is it consistent with the underlying purposes of the legislative scheme to imply such a remedy for the plaintiff?

Napoletano v. CIGNA Healthcare of Conn., Inc., 680 A.2d 127, 145 (1996). What benefits do you believe accrue from applying these broader tests? What detriments?

Problem 15-1

You work for a member of the U.S. House of Representatives. Congress is considering adopting the Junk Mail Recipient's Revenge Act. He has asked you whether the bill contains an express right of action, or if not, whether a court would likely imply one. Advise him. The operative text of the bill in its current form provides:

(a) Except for (1) free samples clearly and conspicuously marked as such, and (2) merchandise mailed by a charitable organization soliciting contributions, the mailing of unordered merchandise or of communications prohibited by subsection (c) of this section constitutes an unfair method of competition and are prohibited.

(b) Any merchandise mailed in violation of subsection (a) of this section, or within the exceptions contained therein, may be treated as a gift by the recipient, who shall have the right to retain, use, discard, or dispose of it in any manner he sees fit without any obligation whatsoever to the sender. All such merchandise shall have attached to it a clear and conspicuous statement informing the recipient that he may treat the merchandise as a gift to him and has the right to retain, use, discard, or dispose of it in any manner he sees fit without any obligation whatsoever to the sender.

(c) No mailer of any merchandise mailed in violation of subsection (a) of this section, or within the exceptions contained therein, shall mail to any recipient of such merchandise a bill for such merchandise or any dunning communications.

(d) For the purposes of this section, "unordered merchandise" means merchandise mailed without the prior expressed request or consent of the recipient.

C. The Contours of Implied Actions

The following case was decided just after *Office Planning Group*. The Justices disagreed regarding their need to address whether an implied cause of action should be found because, at least in one sense, that issue had been decided. In *Cannon v. University of Chicago*, 441 U.S. 677 (1979), the Supreme Court had already found an implied a cause of action under Title IX. In addition to debating this issue again, the Justices had to confront a key consequence of having found an implied cause of action: Its contours are left to the judiciary to define. Thus, the issue in the case, for our purposes, is less about whether there is an implied cause of action and more about whether this particular plaintiff is within the class of plaintiffs entitled to sue.

Jackson v. Birmingham Bd. of Educ.
544 U.S. 167 (2005)

JUSTICE O'CONNOR delivered the opinion of the Court.

Roderick Jackson, a teacher in the Birmingham, Alabama, public schools, brought suit against the Birmingham Board of Education (Board) alleging that the Board retaliated against him because he had complained about sex discrimination in the high school's athletic program. Jackson claimed that the Board's retaliation violated Title IX of the Education Amendments of 1972 ... 20 U.S.C. § 1681 *et seq.* The District Court dismissed Jackson's complaint on the ground that Title IX does not prohibit retaliation, and the Court of Appeals for the Eleventh Circuit affirmed. We consider here whether the private right of action implied by Title IX encompasses claims of retaliation....

According to the complaint, Jackson has been an employee of the Birmingham school district for over 10 years. In 1993, the Board hired Jackson to serve as a physical education teacher and girls' basketball coach. Jackson was transferred to Ensley High School in August 1999. At Ensley, he discovered that the girls' team was not receiving equal funding and equal access to athletic equipment and facilities. The lack of adequate funding, equipment, and facilities made it difficult for Jackson to do his job as the team's coach.

In December 2000, Jackson began complaining to his supervisors about the unequal treatment of the girls' basketball team, but to no avail. Jackson's complaints went unanswered, and the school failed to remedy the situation. Instead, Jackson began to receive negative work evaluations and ultimately was removed as the girls' coach in May 2001....

After the Board terminated Jackson's coaching duties, he filed suit.... He alleged ... that the Board violated Title IX by retaliating against him for protesting the discrimination against the girls' basketball team. The Board moved to dismiss on the ground that Title IX's private cause of action does not include claims of retaliation. The District Court granted the motion to dismiss.

The Court of Appeals for the Eleventh Circuit affirmed....

Title IX prohibits sex discrimination by recipients of federal education funding. The statute provides that "[n]o person in the United States shall, on the basis of sex, be excluded from participation in, be denied the benefits of, or be subjected to discrimination under any education program or activity receiving Federal financial assistance." 20 U.S.C. § 1681(a). More than 25 years ago, we held that Title IX implies a private right of action to enforce its prohibition on intentional sex discrimination. In subsequent cases, we have defined the contours of that right of action. [We also] held that it authorizes private parties to seek monetary damages for intentional violations of Title IX. We have also held that the private right of action encompasses intentional sex discrimination in the form of a recipient's deliberate indifference to a teacher's sexual harassment of a student, or to sexual harassment of a student by another student.

In all of these cases, we relied on the text of Title IX, which ... broadly prohibits a funding recipient from subjecting any person to "discrimination" "on the basis of sex." 20 U.S.C. § 1681. Retaliation against a person because that person has complained of sex discrimination is another form of intentional sex discrimination encompassed by Title IX's private cause of action. Retaliation is, by definition, an intentional act. It is a form of "discrimination" because the complainant is being subjected to differential treatment. Moreover, retaliation is discrimination "on the basis of sex" because it is an intentional response to the nature of the complaint: an allegation of sex discrimination. We conclude that when a funding recipient retaliates against a person *because* he complains of sex discrimination, this constitutes intentional "discrimination" "on the basis of sex," in violation of Title IX....

Congress certainly could have mentioned retaliation in Title IX expressly, as it did in §704 of Title VII of the Civil Rights Act of 1964, 42 U.S.C. §2000e-3(a) (providing that it is an "unlawful employment practice" for an employer to retaliate against an employee because he has "opposed any practice made an unlawful employment practice by [Title VII], or because he has made a charge, testified, assisted, or participated in any manner in an investigation, proceeding, or hearing under [Title VII]")…. Title VII, however, is a vastly different statute from Title IX. Title IX's cause of action is implied, while Title VII's is express. Title IX is a broadly written general prohibition on discrimination, followed by specific, narrow exceptions to that broad prohibition. See 20 U.S.C. § 1681. By contrast, Title VII spells out in greater detail the conduct that constitutes discrimination in violation of that statute. Because Congress did not list *any* specific discriminatory practices when it wrote Title IX, its failure to mention one such practice does not tell us anything about whether it intended that practice to be covered.

Title IX was enacted in 1972, three years after our decision in *Sullivan v. Little Hunting Park, Inc.*, 396 U.S. 229 (1969). In *Sullivan*, we held that 42 U.S.C. § 1982, which provides that "[a]ll citizens of the United States shall have the same right ... as is enjoyed by white citizens ... to inherit, purchase, lease, sell, hold, and convey real and personal property," protected a white man who spoke out against discrimination toward one of his tenants and who suffered retaliation as a result. Sullivan had rented a house to a black man and assigned him a membership share and use rights in a private park. The corporation that owned the park would not approve the assignment to the black lessee. Sullivan protested, and the corporation retaliated against him by expelling him and taking his shares. Sullivan sued the corporation, and we upheld Sullivan's cause of action under 42 U.S.C. § 1982 for "[retaliation] for the advocacy of [the black person's] cause." Thus, in *Sullivan* we interpreted a general prohibition on racial discrimination to cover retaliation against those who advocate the rights of groups protected by that prohibition.

Congress enacted Title IX just three years after *Sullivan* was decided, and accordingly that decision provides a valuable context for understanding the statute. As we recognized in *Cannon*, "it is not only appropriate but also realistic to presume that Congress was thoroughly familiar with *[Sullivan]* and that it expected its enactment [of Title IX] to be interpreted in conformity with [it]." Retaliation for Jackson's advocacy of the rights of the girls' basketball team in this case is "discrimination" "on the basis of sex," just as retaliation for advocacy on behalf of a black lessee in *Sullivan* was discrimination on the basis of race....

Nor are we convinced by the Board's argument that, even if Title IX's private right of action encompasses discrimination, Jackson is not entitled to invoke it because he is an "indirect victi[m]" of sex discrimination. The statute is broadly worded; it does not require that the victim of the retaliation must also be the victim of the discrimination that is the subject of the original complaint. If the statute provided instead that "no person shall be subjected to discrimination on the basis of *such individual's* sex," then we would agree with the Board. Cf. 42 U.S.C. § 2000e-2(a)(1) ("It shall be an unlawful employment practice for an employer ... to discriminate against any individual ... because of *such individual's* race, color, religion, sex, or national origin" (emphasis added)). However, Title IX contains no such limitation. Where the retaliation occurs because the complainant speaks out about sex discrimination, the "on the basis of sex" requirement is satisfied. The complainant is himself a victim of discriminatory retaliation, regardless of whether he was the subject of the original complaint.[3] As we explain above, this is consistent with *Sullivan*, which formed an important part of the backdrop against which Congress enacted Title IX. *Sullivan* made clear that retaliation claims extend to those who oppose discrimination against others.

---

3. Justice Thomas contends that "extending the implied cause of action under Title IX to claims of retaliation expands the class of people the statute protects beyond the specific beneficiaries." But Title IX's beneficiaries plainly include all those who are subjected to "discrimination" "on the basis of sex." 20 U.S.C. § 1681(a). Because, as we explain above, retaliation in response to a complaint about sex discrimination is "discrimination" "on the basis of sex," the statute clearly protects those who suffer such retaliation. The following hypothetical, offered by petitioner at oral argument, illustrates this point: If the male captain of the boys' basketball team and the female captain of the girls' basketball team together approach the school principal to complain about discrimination against the girls' team, and the principal retaliates by expelling them both from the honor society, then both the female and the male captains have been "discriminated" against "on the basis of sex."

Congress enacted Title IX not only to prevent the use of federal dollars to support discriminatory practices, but also to provide individual citizens effective protection against those practices. We agree with the United States that this objective would be difficult, if not impossible, to achieve if persons who complain about sex discrimination did not have effective protection against retaliation. If recipients were permitted to retaliate freely, individuals who witness discrimination would be loathe to report it, and all manner of Title IX violations might go unremedied as a result. See *Sullivan, supra*, at 237 (noting that without protection against retaliation, the underlying discrimination is perpetuated).

Reporting incidents of discrimination is integral to Title IX enforcement and would be discouraged if retaliation against those who report went unpunished. Indeed, if retaliation were not prohibited, Title IX's enforcement scheme would unravel. Recall that Congress intended Title IX's private right of action to encompass claims of a recipient's deliberate indifference to sexual harassment. Accordingly, if a principal sexually harasses a student, and a teacher complains to the school board but the school board is indifferent, the board would likely be liable for a Title IX violation. But if Title IX's private right of action does not encompass retaliation claims, the teacher would have no recourse if he were subsequently fired for speaking out. Without protection from retaliation, individuals who witness discrimination would likely not report it, indifference claims would be short-circuited, and the underlying discrimination would go unremedied....

Moreover, teachers and coaches such as Jackson are often in the best position to vindicate the rights of their students because they are better able to identify discrimination and bring it to the attention of administrators. Indeed, sometimes adult employees are the only effective adversaries of discrimination in schools....

To prevail on the merits, Jackson will have to prove that the Board retaliated against him *because* he complained of sex discrimination. The amended complaint alleges that the Board retaliated against Jackson for complaining to his supervisor, Ms. Evelyn Baugh, about sex discrimination at Ensley High School.... Accordingly, the judgment of the ... Eleventh Circuit is reversed, and the case is remanded....

JUSTICE THOMAS, with whom THE CHIEF JUSTICE [REHNQUIST], JUSTICE SCALIA, and JUSTICE KENNEDY, join, dissenting.

The Court holds that the private right of action under Title IX of the Education Amendments of 1972, for sex discrimination that it implied in *Cannon v. Univ. of Chicago*, extends to claims of retaliation. Its holding is contrary to the plain terms of Title IX, because retaliatory conduct is not discrimination on the basis of sex.... And, in cases in which a party asserts that a cause of action should be implied, we require that the statute itself evince a plain intent to provide such a cause of action. Section 901 of Title IX meets none of these requirements. I therefore respectfully dissent.

Title IX provides education funding to States, subject to § 901's condition that "[n]o person in the United States shall, on the basis of sex, be excluded from participation in, be denied the benefits of, or be subjected to discrimination under any education program or activity receiving Federal financial assistance." 20 U.S.C. § 1681(a). Section 901 does not refer to retaliation. Consequently, the statute prohibits such conduct only if it falls within § 901's prohibition against discrimination "on the basis of sex." It does not.

A claim of retaliation is not a claim of discrimination on the basis of sex. In the context of § 901, the natural meaning of the phrase "on the basis of sex" is on the basis of the plaintiff's sex, not the sex of some other person. For example, suppose a sexist air traffic controller withheld landing permission for a plane because the pilot was a woman. While the sex discrimination against the female pilot no doubt adversely impacted male passengers aboard that plane, one would never say that they were discriminated against "on the basis of sex" by the controller's action....

Jackson's assertion that the Birmingham Board of Education (Board) retaliated against him fails to allege sex discrimination in this sense. Jackson does not claim that his own sex played any role, let alone a decisive or predominant one, in the decision to relieve him of his position. Instead, he avers that he complained to his supervisor about sex discrimination against the girls' basketball team and that, sometime subsequent to his complaints, he lost his coaching position. At best, then, he alleges discrimination "on the basis of sex" founded on the attenuated connection between the supposed adverse treatment and the sex of others. Because Jackson's claim for retaliation is not a claim that his sex played a role in his adverse treatment, the statute's plain terms do not encompass it.

Jackson's lawsuit therefore differs fundamentally from other examples of sex discrimination, like sexual harassment. A victim of sexual harassment suffers discrimination because of her own sex, not someone else's.... Again, Jackson makes no such claim.

Moreover, Jackson's retaliation claim lacks the connection to actual sex discrimination that the statute requires. Jackson claims that he suffered reprisal because he *complained about* sex discrimination, not that the sex discrimination underlying his complaint occurred. This feature of Jackson's complaint is not surprising, since a retaliation claimant need not prove that the complained-of sex discrimination happened. Although this Court has never addressed the question, no Court of Appeals requires a complainant to show more than that he had a reasonable, good-faith belief that discrimination occurred to prevail on a retaliation claim. Retaliation therefore cannot be said to be discrimination on the basis of anyone's sex, because a retaliation claim may succeed where no sex discrimination ever took place.

The majority ignores these fundamental characteristics of retaliation claims. Its sole justification for holding that Jackson has suffered sex discrimination is its statement that "retaliation is discrimination 'on the basis of sex' because it is an intentional response to the nature of the complaint: an allegation of sex discrimination." But the sex-based topic of the complaint cannot overcome the fact that the retaliation is not based on anyone's sex, much less the complainer's sex. For example, if a coach complains to school officials about the dismantling of the men's swimming team, which he honestly and reasonably, but incorrectly, believes is occurring because of the sex of the team, and he is fired, he may prevail. Yet, he would not have been discriminated against on the basis of his sex, for his own sex played no role, and the men's swimming team over which he expressed concern also suffered no discrimination on the basis of sex. In short, no discrimination on the basis of sex has occurred.

At bottom, and petitioner as much as concedes, retaliation is a claim that aids in enforcing another separate and distinct right. In other contexts, this Court has recognized that protection from retaliation is separate from direct protection of the primary right and serves as a prophylactic measure to guard the primary right. As we explained with regard to Title VII's retaliation prohibition, a primary purpose of antiretaliation provisions is maintaining unfettered access to statutory remedial mechanisms. To describe retaliation as discrimination on the basis of sex is to conflate the enforcement mechanism with the right itself, something for which the statute's text provides no warrant....

Whether a statute supplies a cause of action is a matter of statutory interpretation. We must examine whether the statute creates a right. That right must be phrased in terms of the person benefited. And our inquiry is not merely whether the statute benefits some class of people, but whether that class includes the plaintiff in the case before us. Our role, then, is not "to provide such remedies as are necessary to make effective the congressional purpose expressed by a statute," but to examine the text of what Congress enacted into law. *Alexander v. Sandoval*, 532 U.S. 275, 287 (2001). If the statute evinces no intent to create a right for the plaintiff in the case before us, we should not imply a cause of action.

This Court has held that these principles apply equally when the Court has previously found that the statute in question provides an implied right of action and a party attempts to expand the class of persons or the conduct to which the recognized action applies. More specifically, this Court has rejected the creation of implied causes of action for ancillary claims like retaliation....

[I]mposing retaliation liability expands the statute beyond discrimination "on the basis of sex" to instances in which no discrimination on the basis of sex has occurred. Again, § 901 protects individuals only from discrimination on the basis of their own sex. Thus, extending the implied cause of action under Title IX to claims of retaliation expands the class of people the statute protects beyond the specified beneficiaries.... I find it instructive that § 901 does not expressly prohibit retaliation, while other discrimination statutes do so explicitly....

The Court establishes a prophylactic enforcement mechanism designed to encourage whistleblowing about sex discrimination. The language of Title IX does not support this holding. The majority also offers nothing to demonstrate that its prophylactic rule is necessary to effectuate the statutory scheme. Nothing prevents students—or their parents—from complaining about inequality in facilities or treatment. Under the majority's reasoning, courts may expand liability as they, rather than Congress, see fit. This is no idle worry. The next step is to say that someone closely associated with the complainer, who claims he suffered retaliation for those complaints, likewise has a retaliation claim under Title IX.

By crafting its own additional enforcement mechanism, the majority returns this Court to the days in which it created remedies out of whole cloth to effectuate its vision of congressional purpose. In doing so, the majority substitutes its policy judgments for the bargains struck by Congress, as reflected in the statute's text. The question before us is only whether Title IX prohibits retaliation, not whether prohibiting it is good policy. For the reasons addressed above, I would hold that § 901 does not encompass private actions for retaliation. I respectfully dissent.

Notes and Questions

(1) *Was this Case about Creating a New Implied Cause of Action or Defining the Contours of An Existing One?* The majority never addressed *Cort* or *Alexander* because the Court, in *Cannon*, had implied a cause of action under Title IX many years earlier. Was that a mistake? Wasn't the issue whether a victim of indirect discrimination should have an implied cause of action, and, therefore, whether *Cort* or *Alexander* was the appropriate case to apply? The dissent, in contrast, viewed this as the issue, but relied on the textualist approach we saw in *Office Planning Group* rather than *Cort* or *Alexander*. What is the difference between recognizing an implied claim and deciding that a particular person is among the class that has standing to bring one?

(2) *Text or Effectiveness?* The majority relied heavily on the fact that the purpose of Title IX would not be fulfilled if there was no private cause of action here. In contrast, the dissent contended that the Court's role was not to provide remedies necessary to make the statute effective, but simply to examine the statutory text to see if Congress intended such a remedy. Did the majority's approach differ from the dissent's?

(3) *Battling Analogies.* Both the dissent and majority suggested analogies to support their conclusions: The majority relied upon the expulsion of boys and girls from the honor club for complaining about inadequate funding of the girl's teams, and the dissent relied upon the men's coach complaining about unequal funding of the men's swim team. What language in the text are these analogies focused upon? Which analogy is more compelling?

(4) *Legal Context.* The majority relied heavily on the fact that Title IX was adopted just after *Sullivan* and so reasoned that *Sullivan* "provides a valuable context for understanding the statute." Again we ask: Do you believe that legal context is a reasonable interpretive tool? If we assume legislatures are aware of prior interpretations when they enact law, should we also rely on that presumption in this context? Why or why not?

(5) *What Remedy?* In a preceding section, we examined whether remedies for express causes of action should be exclusive. Where a court implies a cause of action, what remedy ought to be available? By definition, no statute authorizes a remedy, and so where should a court turn? General tort or contract law? An analogous, express statutory claim?

(6) *Which Statute of Limitations Applies to Implied Claims?* Remember that the court is interpreting a statute that does not expressly recognize an implied cause of action. By definition then, the statute does not contain a statute of limitations. What should a court do when claims are brought years after the fact—simply let them proceed since no statute of limitations applies? The usual approach is to adopt the time limitation for the claim that is most analogous to the case at hand. *E.g., Lampf, Pleva, Lipkind, Prupis & Petigrow v. Gilbertson*, 501 U.S. 350 (1991). As you can imagine, which statute of limitations is "most analogous" is often subject to disagreement. *See id.* (Justices disagreed on various issues underlying which statute of limitations applied to implied rights of action under Section 10(b)(5) of the federal securities laws). Incidentally, Congress responded to *Lampf* by adopting a specific statute of limitations for § 10(b)5. *See Nat'l Fire Ins. Co. v. Califinvest*, 1992 WL 35017, at *5 (S.D.N.Y. Feb. 14, 1992).

(7) *Another Case, Another Split.* 42 U.S.C. § 1981(a) provides that all "persons within the jurisdiction of the United states shall have the same right in every State and Territory to make and enforce contracts ... as is enjoyed by white citizens." Beginning in at least the 1970s, the Court had interpreted this statute to permit private causes of action. In 2008, the Court, in *CBOCS West, Inc. v. Humphries*, 128 S.Ct. 1951 (2008), held that the statute permitted a cause of action in favor of a person who was retaliated against because he reported to his employer that another employee's rights under the statute had been violated. Justices Thomas and Scalia dissented, arguing that neither the text nor *stare decisis* supported the majority's holding. *Id.* at 1961 (Thomas, J., dissenting).

Problem 15-2

You are a law clerk working for a state district court judge. A case is pending in which your judge must decide whether to imply a cause of action for a state statute. After doing some research, you determine that the statute was adopted after *Cort*, but before *Alexander* and the other recent cases limiting the implied rights analysis. However, the text of the statute had been taken from a federal statute that, in cases decided prior to *Cort*, had repeatedly been interpreted as authorizing an implied right of action. Today, of course, *Alexander* and the cases discussed above have been decided.

The judge believes that the three judges on the appellate court panel each has his or her own approach to statutory interpretation: one favors textualism; one purposivism; and one intentionalism. There is no legislative history or purpose clause to shed light on the issue—only the text of the statute itself. She does not want to be overruled, and so she has asked you to identify (1) what arguments each judge might find persuasive in arguing for or against an implied cause of action and (2) whether those arguments will negatively impact the opinions of the other judges.

While you are performing this task, consider what implications your analysis has for intentionalism, purposivism, and textualism.

Chapter 16

Constitutional Implications

This chapter explores the impact of constitutional doctrines on statutory interpretation. Throughout the book, we've seen that separation of powers and other constitutional principles can affect statutory interpretation. This chapter addresses how constitutional law affects statutory interpretation more directly.

We begin with a topic that flows from our chapter on ambiguity, absurdity, and scrivener's error: the constitutional avoidance doctrine. Like those other doctrines, courts can avoid the plain meaning of the text when that plain meaning raises constitutional issues that another, fair, interpretation would avoid. We then turn to two specific constitutional requirements that can directly affect the interpretive process: the requirements that (1) statutes satisfy due process by providing notice and (2) they not constitute prohibited *ex post facto* laws. Finally, we end with a discussion of legislative efforts to direct interpretation.

A. Avoiding Conflicts between Statutes and Constitutions

An important canon of statutory construction is that every state or federal statute should, if possible, be construed so that it does not violate the U.S. Constitution. Similarly, state statutes should be interpreted, if possible, not to violate the enacting state's constitution. Thus, "where a statute is susceptible of two constructions, by one of which grave and doubtful constitutional questions arise and by the other of which such questions are avoided, our duty is to adopt the latter." *U.S. ex rel. Attorney General v. Del. & Hudson Co.*, 213 U.S. 366, 408 (1909).

This canon stems from *Marbury v. Madison*, 5 U.S. (1 Cranch) 137 (1803), and respects the authority allocated in the Constitution between the judicial and the legislative branches for interpreting and making law. Thus, the primary rationale for this canon is that it promotes separation of powers: It requires courts to acknowledge legislative supremacy. "The Court presumes that the legislature acts in accordance with the Constitution, and the Court has no power even to consider the possibility that the legislature has not, unless a case or controversy forces it to...." William K. Kelley, *Avoiding Constitutional Questions as a Three-Branch Problem*, 86 Cornell L. Rev. 831, 837 (2001) (arguing that courts should abandon the canon because it conflicts "with both the power of the President to execute the law and the power of Congress to make the law"). By relying on this canon, a court "seeks to respect Congress's primacy in the sphere of lawmaking." *Id.* at 843.

By its terms, this canon only applies when there are at least two competing interpretations that are "fair" constructions of the statute. "Experience has shown, however, that the Court's conclusions about the interpretations that count as 'fair' constructions of statutes can be highly dubious." *Id.* at 855. At times, judges seem to strain to find an interpretation that avoids the constitutional question. See if you agree with the dissent in *Marshall* that the majority did just that. Another question you should ask yourself while you read this section is how explicit must a legislature be that it intended an interpretation that raises constitutional questions before a court should accept that interpretation? The note case, *NLRB v. Catholic Bishop*, tackles this question.

United States v. Marshall

908 F.2d 1312 (7th Cir. 1990) (en banc)
aff'd sub nom, Chapman v. United States, 500 U.S. 453 (1991)

EASTERBROOK, CIRCUIT JUDGE.

Stanley J. Marshall was convicted ... and sentenced to 20 years' imprisonment for ... distributing more than ten grams of LSD, enough for 11,751 doses. [The issue for the court is whether 21 U.S.C. §841(b)(1)(A)(v) and (B)(v), which set mandatory minimum terms of imprisonment—five years for selling more than one gram of a "mixture or substance containing a detectable amount" of LSD, ten years for more than ten grams—include the weight of a carrier medium.]

According to the Sentencing Commission, the LSD in an average dose weighs 0.05 milligrams.... But 0.05 mg is almost invisible, so LSD is distributed to retail customers in a carrier. Pure LSD is dissolved in a solvent such as alcohol and sprayed on paper or gelatin; alternatively the paper may be dipped in the solution. After the solvent evaporates, the paper or gel is cut into one-dose squares and sold by the square. Users swallow the squares or may drop them into a beverage, releasing the drug. Although the gelatin and paper are light, they weigh much more than the drug. Marshall's 11,751 doses weighed 113.32 grams; the LSD accounted for only 670.72 mg of this, not enough to activate the five-year mandatory minimum sentence, let alone the ten-year minimum....

If the carrier counts in the weight of the "mixture or substance containing a detectable amount" of LSD, some odd things may happen. Weight in the hands of distributors may exceed that of manufacturers and wholesalers. Big fish then could receive paltry sentences or small fish draconian ones. Someone who sold 19,999 doses of pure LSD (at 0.05 mg per dose) would escape the five-year mandatory minimum of §841(b)(1)(B)(v) and be covered by §841(b)(1)(C), which lacks a minimum term and has a maximum of "only" 20 years. Someone who sold a single hit of LSD dissolved in a tumbler of orange juice could be exposed to a ten-year mandatory minimum.... One way to eliminate the possibility of such consequences is to say that the carrier is not a "mixture or substance containing a detectable amount" of the drug. Defendants ask us to do this....

[W]e turn to the statute.

It is not possible to construe the words of §841 to make the penalty turn on the net weight of the drug rather than the gross weight of carrier and drug. The statute speaks of "mixture or substance containing a detectable amount" of a drug. "Detectable amount" is the opposite of "pure"; the point of the statute is that the "mixture" is not to be converted to an equivalent amount of pure drug....

Although the "mixture or substance" language shows that the statute cannot be limited to pure LSD, it does not necessarily follow that blotter paper is a "mixture or substance containing" LSD. . . . How much mingling of the drug with something else is essential to form a "mixture or substance"? The legislative history is silent, but ordinary usage is indicative. . . .

LSD is applied to paper in a solvent; after the solvent evaporates, a tiny quantity of LSD remains. Because the fibers absorb the alcohol, the LSD solidifies inside the paper rather than on it. You cannot pick a grain of LSD off the surface of the paper. Ordinary parlance calls the paper containing tiny crystals of LSD a mixture. . . .

[One] reason[has] been advanced to support a contrary conclusion: that statutes should be construed to avoid constitutional problems. . . .

A preference for giving statutes a constitutional meaning is a reason to construe, not to rewrite or "improve". Canons are doubt-resolvers, useful when the language is ambiguous and "a construction of the statute is fairly possible by which the question may be avoided." "[S]ubstance or mixture containing a detectable quantity" is not ambiguous, avoidance not "fairly possible". . . .

The canon about avoiding constitutional decisions, in particular, must be used with care, for it is a closer cousin to invalidation than to interpretation. It is a way to enforce the constitutional penumbra, and therefore an aspect of constitutional law proper. Constitutional decisions breed penumbras, which multiply questions. Treating each as justification to construe laws out of existence too greatly enlarges the judicial power. And heroic "construction" is unnecessary . . . [because] Congress possesses the constitutional power to set penalties on the basis of gross weight. . . .

A constitutional question remains, given our construction of the statute and guidelines. . . . [The court then turned to defendant's argument that the statute violated the Due Process and Equal Protection Clauses. The court rejected both arguments.]

That Congress could have written better laws does not mean that it had to. Amendments to the criminal code may be in order, but they are not ours to make under the banner of constitutional adjudication. . . .

[T]he judgment[] under review [is] affirmed.

CUMMINGS, CIRCUIT JUDGE, with whom BAUER, CHIEF JUDGE, and WOOD, JR., CUDAHY, and POSNER, CIRCUIT JUDGES, join, dissenting:

Two assumptions lie at the heart of the majority opinion. The first is that the words "mixture or substance" are not ambiguous and are not therefore susceptible of interpretation by the courts. The second is that the due process clause of the Fifth Amendment guarantees process but not substance. Both of these assumptions are unwarranted. . . .

The words "mixture or substance" are ambiguous, and a construction of those words that can avoid invalidation on constitutional grounds is therefore appropriate. . . . [The majority's interpretation of the statute violates] the defendants' Fifth Amendment right to due process of law. The Fifth Amendment prohibits the government from engaging in discrimination that is so unjustified that it violates due process of law. . . . [T]he statute and the Guidelines require two defendants convicted of selling the same number of doses of LSD for the same amount of money to be sentenced differently if they have chosen different inert carrier media to distribute the LSD. . . .

[A] difference in sentences based solely on the difference in the weight of an inert ingredient is not rationally related to the government's legitimate goal of eliminating the serious drug problem in this country. . . .

The majority has decided that ambiguous language is clear and that rational basis review is toothless. I therefore respectfully dissent.

POSNER, C. J., joined by BAUER, C. J., and CUMMINGS, WOOD, JR., and CUDAHY, CIRCUIT JUDGES, dissenting.

In [this] case[]..., the district court sentenced [a] seller[] of LSD in accordance with an interpretation of 21 U.S.C. § 841 that is plausible but that makes the punishment scheme for LSD irrational. It has been assumed that an irrational federal sentencing scheme denies the equal protection of the laws and therefore violates the due process clause of the Fifth Amendment. The assumption is proper, and in order to avoid having to strike down the statute we are entitled to adopt a reasonable interpretation that cures the constitutional infirmity, even if that interpretation might not be our first choice were there no such infirmity.

The statute fixes the minimum and maximum punishments with respect to each illegal drug on the basis of the weight of the "mixture or substance containing a detectable amount of" the drug.... The quoted words are critical. Drugs are usually consumed, and therefore often sold, in a diluted form, and the adoption by Congress of the "mixture or substance" method of grading punishment reflected a conscious decision to mete out heavy punishment to large retail dealers, who are likely to possess "substantial street quantities," which is to say quantities of the diluted drug ready for sale. That decision is well within Congress's constitutional authority even though it may sometimes result in less severe punishment for possessing a purer, and therefore a lighter, form of the illegal drug than a heavier but much less potent form....

Based as it is on weight, the system I have described works well for drugs that are sold by weight; ... it is as natural to punish its purveyors according to the weight of the product as it is to punish moonshiners by the weight or volume of the moonshine they sell rather than by the weight of the alcohol contained in it....

LSD, however, is sold to the consumer by the dose; it is not cut, diluted, or mixed with something else. Moreover, it is incredibly light. An average dose of LSD weighs .05 milligrams, which is less than two millionths of an ounce. To ingest something that small requires swallowing something much larger. Pure LSD in granular form is first diluted by being dissolved, usually in alcohol, and then a quantity of the solution containing one dose of LSD is sprayed or eyedropped on a sugar cube, or on a cube of gelatin, or, as in the cases before us, on an inch-square section of "blotter" paper.... After the solution is applied to the carrier medium, the alcohol or other solvent evaporates, leaving an invisible (and undiluted) spot of pure LSD on the cube or blotter paper. The consumer drops the cube or the piece of paper into a glass of water, or orange juice, or some other beverage, causing the LSD to dissolve in the beverage, which is then drunk. This is not dilution. It is still one dose that is being imbibed.... [A] quart of orange juice containing one dose of LSD is not more, in any relevant sense, than a pint of juice containing the same one dose, and it would be loony to punish the purveyor of the quart more heavily than the purveyor of the pint. It would be like basing the punishment for selling cocaine on the combined weight of the cocaine and of the vehicle (plane, boat, automobile, or whatever) used to transport it or the syringe used to inject it or the pipe used to smoke it. The blotter paper, sugar cubes, etc. are the vehicles for conveying LSD to the consumer.

The weight of the carrier is vastly greater than that of the LSD, as well as irrelevant to its potency. There is no comparable disparity between the pure and the mixed form (if that is how we should regard LSD on blotter paper or other carrier medium) with respect to the other drugs in section 841, with the illuminating exception of PCP. There Congress specified alternative weights, for the drug itself and for the substance or mixture containing the drug. For example, the five-year minimum sentence for a seller of

PCP requires the sale of either ten grams of the drug itself or one hundred grams of a substance or mixture containing the drug....

A person who sells LSD on blotter paper is not a worse criminal than one who sells the same number of doses on gelatin cubes, but he is subject to a heavier punishment. A person who sells five doses of LSD on sugar cubes is not a worse person than a manufacturer of LSD who is caught with 19,999 doses in pure form, but the former is subject to a ten-year mandatory minimum no-parole sentence while the latter is not even subject to the five-year minimum. If [the] defendant ... had sold the same number of doses in pure form, his Guidelines sentence would have been ... four years rather than twenty.... In none of these computations, by the way, does the weight of the LSD itself make a difference — so slight is its weight relative to that of the carrier — except of course when it is sold in pure form. Congress might as well have said: if there is a carrier, weigh the carrier and forget the LSD.

This is a quilt the pattern whereof no one has been able to discern. The legislative history is silent, and since even the Justice Department cannot explain the why of the punishment scheme that it is defending, the most plausible inference is that Congress simply did not realize how LSD is sold....

Well, what if anything can we judges do about this mess? The answer lies in the shadow of a jurisprudential disagreement that is not less important by virtue of being unavowed by most judges. It is the disagreement between the severely positivistic view that the content of law is exhausted in clear, explicit, and definite enactments by or under express delegation from legislatures, and the natural lawyer's or legal pragmatist's view that the practice of interpretation and the general terms of the Constitution (such as "equal protection of the laws") authorize judges to enrich positive law with the moral values and practical concerns of civilized society. Judges who in other respects have seemed quite similar, such as Holmes and Cardozo, have taken opposite sides of this issue. Neither approach is entirely satisfactory. The first buys political neutrality and a type of objectivity at the price of substantive injustice, while the second buys justice in the individual case at the price of considerable uncertainty and, not infrequently, judicial willfulness. It is no wonder that our legal system oscillates between the approaches. The positivist view, applied unflinchingly to this case, commands the affirmance of prison sentences that are exceptionally harsh by the standards of the modern Western world, dictated by an accidental, unintended scheme of punishment nevertheless implied by the words (taken one by one) of the relevant enactments. The natural law or pragmatist view leads to a freer interpretation, one influenced by norms of equal treatment; and let us explore the interpretive possibilities here. One is to interpret "mixture or substance containing a detectable amount of [LSD]" to exclude the carrier medium — the blotter paper, sugar or gelatin cubes, and orange juice or other beverage....

Interpreted to exclude the carrier, the punishment schedule for LSD would make perfectly good sense; it would not warp the statutory design.... This interpretation leaves "substance or mixture containing" without a referent, so far as LSD is concerned. But we must remember that Congress used the identical term in each subsection that specifies the quantity of a drug that subjects the seller to the designated minimum and maximum punishments. In thus automatically including the same term in each subsection, Congress did not necessarily affirm that, for each and every drug covered by the statute, a substance or mixture containing the drug must be found.

The flexible interpretation that I am proposing is decisively strengthened by the constitutional objection to basing punishment of LSD offenders on the weight of the carrier medium rather than on the weight of the LSD. Courts often do interpretive handsprings to avoid having even to decide a constitutional question. In doing so they expand, very questionably in my view, the effective scope of the Constitution, creating a constitutional penumbra in which statutes wither, shrink, are deformed. A better case for flexible interpretation is presented when the alternative is to nullify Congress's action: when in other words there is not merely a constitutional question about, but a constitutional barrier to, the statute when interpreted literally. This is such a case....

Our choice is between ruling that the provisions of section 841 regarding LSD are irrational, hence unconstitutional, and therefore there is no punishment for dealing in LSD—Congress must go back to the drawing boards, and all LSD cases in the pipeline must be dismissed—and ruling that, to preserve so much of the statute as can constitutionally be preserved, the statutory expression "substance or mixture containing a detectable amount of [LSD]" excludes the carrier medium. Given this choice, we can be reasonably certain that Congress would have preferred the second course; and this consideration carries the argument for a flexible interpretation over the top....

The literal interpretation adopted by the majority is not inevitable. All interpretation is contextual. The words of the statute—interpreted against a background that includes a constitutional norm of equal treatment, a (closely related) constitutional commitment to rationality, an evident failure by both Congress and the Sentencing Commission to consider how LSD is actually produced, distributed, and sold, and an equally evident failure by the same two bodies to consider the interaction between heavy mandatory minimum sentences and the Sentencing Guidelines—will bear an interpretation that distinguishes between the carrier vehicle of the illegal drug and the substance or mixture containing a detectable amount of the drug. The punishment of the crack dealer is not determined by the weight of the glass tube in which he sells the crack; we should not lightly attribute to Congress a purpose of punishing the dealer in LSD according to the weight of the LSD carrier. We should not make Congress's handiwork an embarrassment to the members of Congress and to us.

Notes and Questions

(1) *Finding Ambiguity.* Do you understand the two steps taken by the majority to reach its holding that the plain meaning of "mixture" included the blotter paper? The dissenters did not find the term clear. Thus, the judges on the Seventh Circuit had mixed views about the meaning of the term "mixture." Which arguments were most convincing?

(2) *The Likely Effect of Reaching the Constitutional Question.* Judge Easterbrook wrote that the canon about avoiding constitutional decisions "is a closer cousin to invalidation than to interpretation." What did he mean? Do you agree?

(3) *Avoiding, Not Deciding.* Be sure you understand that the dissent would have avoided holding that one interpretation was unconstitutional. Instead, the dissent recognized that one interpretation would create a constitutional issue. So, the dissent chose an interpretation that would avoid the constitutional question altogether:

> This cardinal principle, which has for so long been applied by the Court that it is beyond debate, requires merely a determination of serious constitutional doubt, and not a determination of unconstitutionality. That must be so, of course, for otherwise the rule would mean that our duty is to first decide that a statute is unconstitutional and then proceed to hold that such ruling was unnecessary because the statute is susceptible of a meaning which causes it not to be repugnant to the Constitution.

Almendarez-Torres v. United States, 523 U.S. 224, 250 (1998). Thus, if a court applies the canon and interprets a statute to avoid a constitutional question, that holding would not prevent the legislature from rejecting the court's interpretation by amending the statute and forcing the constitutional issue.

(4) *On Appeal.* The Supreme Court affirmed *Marshall* in *Chapman v. United States*, 500 U.S. 453 (1991). The Justices were also divided about what "mixture" meant. The majority opinion by Chief Justice Rehnquist relied on a dictionary definition of "mixture" to mean "two substances blended together so that the particles of one are diffused among the particles of the other" to interpret "mixture" to include the weight of the blotter paper. Given the context of the use of the word, should the Court have looked to the definition in a pharmacological dictionary? Why or why not?

(5) *Subsequent Agency Action.* In November 1993, the Sentencing Commission, the agency responsible for interpreting the statute in *Marshall*, revised the Sentencing Guidelines. Abandoning its former approach of including the weight of the blotter paper, the Commission amended the Guidelines directing that each dose of LSD on a carrier had a presumed weight of 0.4 mg. U.S. Sentencing Comm'n, U.S. Sentencing Guidelines Manual § 2D1.1I, n.* (H). Does the amendment necessarily mean that the courts were wrong to have interpreted the statute otherwise?

(6) *How Clear Must the Problem Be?* In *NLRB v. Catholic Bishop*, 440 U.S. 490 (1979), the Court held that the National Labor Relations Act did not cover lay teachers employed by church-operated schools. In so holding, the majority reasoned:

> [I]n the absence of a *clear expression* of Congress' intent to bring teachers in church-operated schools within the jurisdiction of the Board, we decline to construe the Act in a manner that could in turn call upon the Court to resolve difficult and sensitive questions arising out of the guarantees of the First Amendment Religion Clauses.

Id. at 508–11 (emphasis added). Thus, the majority would not construe a statute to violate the Constitution "if any other possible construction remain[ed] available." *Id.* at 500. Is this the appropriate standard? Or, was the majority "do[ing] interpretive handsprings to avoid having even to decide a constitutional question"? *Marshall*, 908 F.2d at 1335 (Posner, J., dissenting).

What if the construction that ostensibly was intended by the legislature violates the Constitution and all other interpretations violate legislative intent? In other words, doesn't the alternate construction have to be one the legislature intended?

The dissent in *Catholic Bishop* chastised the majority for adding an element to this canon:

> The general principle of construing statutes to avoid unnecessary constitutional decisions is a well-settled and salutary one. The governing canon, however, is *not* that expressed by the Court today. The Court requires that there be a "clear expression of an affirmative intention of Congress" before it will bring within the coverage of a broadly worded regulatory statute certain persons whose coverage might raise constitutional questions. But those familiar with the legislative process know that explicit expressions of congressional intent in such broadly inclusive statutes are not commonplace. Thus, by strictly or loosely applying its requirement, the Court can virtually remake congressional enactments. This flouts Mr. Chief Justice Taft's admonition "that amendment may not be substituted for construction, and that a court may not exercise legislative functions to save (a) law from conflict with constitutional limitation."

The settled canon for construing statutes wherein constitutional questions may lurk was stated in *Machinists v. Street*:

> When the validity of an act of the Congress is drawn in question, and even if a serious doubt of constitutionality is raised, it is a cardinal principle that this Court will first ascertain whether a construction of the statute is *fairly possible* by which the question may be avoided.

> This limitation to constructions that are "fairly possible," and "reasonable," acts as a brake against wholesale judicial dismemberment of congressional enactments. It confines the judiciary to its proper role in construing statutes, which is to interpret them so as to give effect to congressional intention. The Court's new "affirmative expression" rule releases that brake.

Catholic Bishop, 440 U.S. at 508–11 (Brennan, J., dissenting). Thus, the dissent suggested that if the traditional sources of statutory interpretation showed that the legislature intended the interpretation that raises the constitutional concerns, then the Court should address those concerns. Which position makes more sense?

(7) *Positivism and Pragmatics.* Judge Posner explained that there is a:

> disagreement between the severely positivistic view that the content of law is exhausted in clear, explicit, and definite enactments by or under express delegation from legislatures, and the natural lawyer's or legal pragmatist's view that the practice of interpretation and the general terms of the Constitution (such as "equal protection of the laws") authorize judges to enrich positive law with the moral values and practical concerns of civilized society.

Marshall, 908 F.2d at 1335 (Posner, J., dissenting). What did he mean? Was he "pragmatic" or "positivistic"? How about the majority?

(8) *What Should Courts Do When Faced with Archaic Statutes?* What if long ago a legislature adopted a statute that was democratically popular at that time, but since then has lost favor and would likely not be re-enacted by a contemporary legislature? State laws prohibiting birth control or sodomy are good examples. The current state legislature is not going to take the time and effort to repeal such a statute, especially if it is not being enforced and, even more so, if the statute is one that might be highly controversial. (What legislator wants to be accused of being "in favor of sodomy"?) But, if the statute were enforced or if someone sued for a declaratory judgment to have the statute ruled unconstitutional, what should a court do? If the court declares the statute to be unconstitutional, then the court has, in a sense, trumped the legislature because the legislature can no longer repeal or amend the statute. But, if the court refuses to reach the constitutional question by giving the statute a very narrow construction and, thereby, construes it to mean something the legislature really had not intended, is the court interpreting the statute or legislating? If the latter, does "legislating" in this way serve a significant purpose such that it would be justified in this limited context? Or, does "legislating" from the bench always violate separation of powers? *See* GUIDO CALABRESI, A COMMON LAW FOR THE AGE OF STATUTES 21–26 (1982).

Problem 16-1

You represent James Beemer, who tells you the following: While acting as an officer for a labor union during 2000 and 2001, Mr. Beemer illegally accepted cash payments from a real estate company whose employees belonged to the union. On October 4, 2003, federal agents visited Mr. Beemer at his home. The agents identified themselves and explained that they were seeking his cooperation in an investigation of the real estate company and various individuals. They told Beemer that if he wished to cooperate, he should have an attorney contact the United States Attorney's Office and that if he could not afford an attorney, one would be appointed for him.

The agents then asked him if he would answer some questions, and he agreed. He was asked if he had received any cash or gifts from the real estate company when he was a union officer. He said "no." At that point, the agents disclosed that a search of the real estate company headquarters had produced company records showing otherwise. They also told him that lying to federal agents in the course of an investigation was a crime. Beemer refused to answer any more questions, and the interview soon ended.

Beemer has been indicted for accepting unlawful cash payments from an employer and making a false statement to a federal officer with the jurisdiction of a federal agency. He plans to plead guilty on the first charge, but wants to contest the second. Advise him whether he is likely to be convicted on the second charge for telling the federal officers "no" when asked whether he had received illegal payments.

Problem Materials

18 U.S.C.A. § 1001: Fraud and False Statements

Statements or entries generally

(a) Except as otherwise provided in this section, whoever, in any matter within the jurisdiction of the executive, legislative, or judicial branch of the Government of the United States, knowingly and willfully—

(1) falsifies, conceals, or covers up by any trick, scheme, or device a material fact;

(2) makes any materially false, fictitious, or fraudulent statement or representation; ...

shall be fined under this title or imprisoned not more than 5 years, or both.

U.S. Constitution, Amendment V

No person shall be ... compelled in any criminal case to be a witness against himself, nor be deprived of life, liberty, or property, without due process of law....

The following cases explain the exculpatory "no" and provide the arguments for you to make on your client's behalf.

United States v. Taylor
907 F.2d 801 (8th Cir. 1990)

John R. Gibson, Circuit Judge.

[The defendant was charged with forging his wife's name on bankruptcy pleadings. When the bankruptcy judge questioned the defendant, he denied knowing anything about the filings. He was charged with violating 18 U.S.C. § 1001(a). The defendant moved to dismiss the charge on the basis that it violated his Fifth Amendment privilege against self-incrimination. The court agreed.]

We begin by examining the language of the statute itself.... It is evident, as the government contends, that the plain language of the statute does not contain an "exculpatory no" exception.

Section 1001 originated from a statute passed in response to a spate of frauds upon the Government. Through amendments to the statute, which was enacted in 1863, Congress has expanded its scope beyond false statements causing pecuniary loss to the government to cover a wider range of fraudulent practices. Congress intentionally drafted section 1001 in an expansive fashion in order that it be accorded the broadest possible interpretation regarding the situations in which it would come into play....

Despite this expansive construction, the circuits which have squarely addressed the applicability of the "exculpatory no" doctrine have concluded that, under certain circumstances, the government may not prosecute an individual for false or fraudulent statements which were made in response to questioning initiated by the government where a truthful statement would have incriminated the defendant. An examination of these cases persuades us as well that we should apply the "exculpatory no" doctrine to this case.

The doctrine was initially articulated in *United States v. Stark*, where the court distinguished between affirmative representations and mere exculpatory denials, and held that the latter were not "statements" within the meaning of section 1001. The court declared that the statute's purpose was to protect the government from the affirmative or aggressive and voluntary actions of persons who take the initiative, or, in other words, to protect the government from being the victim of some positive statement, whether written or oral, which has the tendency and effect of perverting its normal proper activities.

In the leading case of *Paternostro v. United States*, the Fifth Circuit held that a defendant who gave allegedly false answers to questions asked by an IRS agent during an investigation did not violate section 1001. The court concluded that the defendant did not aggressively and deliberately initiate any positive or affirmative statement calculated to pervert the legitimate functions of Government. In *United States v. Bush*, the Fifth Circuit stated that there is a valid distinction between negative exculpatory denial of a suspected misdeed and an affirmative representation of facts peculiarly within the knowledge of the suspect not otherwise obtainable by the investigator....

The Fourth Circuit adopted the "exculpatory no" doctrine ... and held that a defendant's allegedly false statements to a Secret Service agent did not violate section 1001 because they were not volunteered with the intent to induce government action, but were instead exculpatory responses to questioning initiated by government agents. The court declared that the doctrine balance[d] the need for protecting the basic functions of government agencies with the concern that a criminal suspect not be forced to incriminate himself in order to avoid punishment under section 1001. The court identified the reason for the exception as follows: "False statements that pervert an agency's routine administrative functions are the specific target Congress intended the statute to reach, while the exception was created to protect negative responses to interrogation by a criminal investigator. The court then summed up its reasoning for adopting the doctrine:

> The sanction of section 1001 plays an important role in protecting the effectiveness of government agencies whose functions require them to rely on the accuracy of the information they receive. The statute, however, was not intended to compel persons suspected of crimes to assist criminal investigators in establishing their guilt....

The Sixth Circuit is the most recent circuit to adopt the "exculpatory no" exception. The court, in *United States v. Steele*, held the doctrine applicable to a defendant's statements to an IRS agent. The court noted that the doctrine, "which appears to be receiving widespread acceptance by federal courts of appeals, is anchored, *inter alia*, upon the

Fifth Amendment's protection against self incrimination through the use of compelled statements."

Our study of these decisions and the well-reasoned opinion of the district court causes us to conclude that section 1001 was not intended to proscribe mere exculpatory denials of guilt. We are persuaded ... that the 'exculpatory no' doctrine is a narrow yet salutory limitation on a criminal statute which, because of its breadth, is subject to potential abuse. Accordingly, we hold that the "exculpatory no" doctrine should be applied to this case....

We are satisfied that [the defendant's] exculpatory denials of guilt, made in a judicial proceeding in which he reasonably believed that affirmative responses would have been incriminatory, were not the type of false statements which section 1001 was intended to proscribe. Accordingly, we affirm the order of the district court dismissing the section 1001 charges against [him].

United States v. Rodriguez-Rios
14 F.3d 1040 (5th Cir. 1994)

JERRY E. SMITH, CIRCUIT JUDGE.

[The defendant had entered the country and told customs officials that he was carrying only "[a]bout a thousand dollars." Ultimately, a suitcase with $598,000 in cash was found in his car. The defendant was charged with violating a statute that required individuals to report the transport of more than $10,000. He was also charged with making a false, fictitious, or fraudulent statement or representation in violation of 18 U.S.C. § 1001. The court addressed the question of whether the "exculpatory no" exception to 18 U.S.C. § 1001 should be adopted. Rejecting it, the court said:]

The "exculpatory no" exception cannot be found in the plain language of § 1001.... [T]he relevant language of § 1001 is this: "Whoever, in any matter within the jurisdiction of any department or agency of the United States knowingly and willfully ... makes any false, fictitious or fraudulent statements or representations...."

A literal interpretation of the statute does not countenance the "exculpatory no" exception. Some courts have found the word "statements" to be a ready textual hook upon which to place concerns about legislative intent. Although that word may connote affirmative, aggressive, or overt declarations, we consider that as a matter of common sense and plain meaning, the word "no" is indeed a statement.

We are authorized to deviate from the literal language of a statute only if the plain language would lead to absurd results, or if such an interpretation would defeat the intent of Congress. Most recently, the Supreme Court has admonished that "[w]hen we find the terms of a statute unambiguous, judicial inquiry is complete except in rare and exceptional circumstances." Thus, we are told to follow a statute's plain meaning unless "[w]e can[ ] say that [it] is so bizarre that Congress 'could not have intended' it." Finding no such reason to deviate from the plain language of § 1001, we now discard the "exculpatory no" doctrine in this circuit.

It is said that the purpose of § 1001 is to protect the government from practices that would pervert its legitimate functions. The principal purpose of the "exculpatory no" exception, on the other hand, is to exclude from coverage those statements that do not so threaten. We conclude, however, that § 1001 should not be limited to those statements that pervert governmental functions but should be determined by the text and not by a judicial reconstruction of its purpose....

The Fifth Amendment right against self-incrimination is not applicable as an independent justification for the "exculpatory no" exception. Although the Fifth Amendment protects a person's right to remain silent in response to an incriminating question, an outright lie is not protected.... Thus, while the self-incrimination aspect of the "exculpatory no" exception may somehow be relevant to congressional intent, it is not an independent justification for that exception.

There is a concern that § 1001 forces persons who had committed a crime to choose between lying and incriminating themselves. This concern is not entirely correct. In such a situation, such individuals have the third option of remaining silent—a choice protected by the Fifth Amendment.

B. The Rule of Lenity

While ignorance of the law is no excuse, Due Process requires that criminal statutes give fair warning of the scope of criminal law. Consequently, a person cannot be punished for engaging in conduct that a reasonable person could not know was illegal. The rule of lenity thus reflects the principle that "individuals should not languish in prison unless the legislature has clearly articulated precisely what conduct constitutes a crime." *United States v. Gonzalez*, 407 F.3d 118, 125 (2d Cir. 2005). We will explore this canon more fully below.

There are two important conditions precedent to applying this rule. First, it applies only when the statute has a penal component to it. Thus, it applies to criminal statutes. It can also apply when a civil statute has a penal aspect to it. *United States v. Thompson/Center Arms Co.*, 504 U.S. 505, 517–18 & n.10 (1992) (applying the rule of lenity to interpret a tax statute in a civil setting because the statute had criminal implications). Thus, the characterization of a statute as penal is a threshold requirement for its application.

Second, the rule "is not a catch-all maxim that resolves all disputes in the defendant's favor—a sort of juristical 'tie goes to the runner.'" *Gonzalez*, 407 F.3d at 124. Instead, many courts hold that the rule applies, not if the statutory text is ambiguous, but only if the ambiguity remains after the court has examined other sources of statutory interpretation, including legislative history. *Reno v. Koray*, 515 U.S. 50, 65 (1995). The rule is reserved "for those situations in which a reasonable doubt persists about a statute's intended scope even *after* resort to the language and structure, legislative history, and motivating policies of the statute." *Moskal v. United States*, 498 U.S. 103, 108; *but see State v. Courchesne*, 816 A.2d 562, 618 n.24 (Zarella, J., dissenting) ("I would leave for another day the question of whether, because of the constitutional underpinnings embodied in its fair warning rationale, the rule of lenity should be employed immediately upon determining that the text of a criminal statute is ambiguous, or whether it should, along with other substantive presumptions, be employed only as a last resort after all of the relevant tools of construction have been employed.").

Despite these statements, you will note throughout this chapter that courts make reference to the rule of lenity without consulting the legislative history of the statute: Many courts apply the rule somewhat loosely, holding that, in general, they should interpret criminal statutes narrowly. *E.g.*, *Commonwealth v. O'Keefe*, 723 N.E.2d 1000 (Mass. Ct. App. 2000). Generally, however, courts require that the ambiguity exist after examining other sources of interpretation.

If the two conditions are satisfied, then the rule applies. Under the rule, where two reasonable interpretations of a penal statute exist—one inculpating and the other exculpating, or one imposing a harsher or longer punishment and the other imposing a milder or shorter punishment—a court must adopt the interpretation that favors the defendant. But how reasonable must the interpretations be?

> The rule ... is inapplicable unless two reasonable interpretations of the same provision stand in relative equipoise.... Thus, although true ambiguities are resolved in a defendant's favor, an appellate court should not strain to interpret a penal statute in defendant's favor if it can fairly discern a contrary legislative intent.

People v. Avery, 38 P.3d 1, 6 (Cal. 2002).

The case below addresses these issues. As you read this case, keep in mind that it involves an agency—the Bureau of Alcohol, Tobacco and Firearms—interpreting a statute. We have omitted most of the opinion that addresses the deference courts should give agency interpretations. We will address this issue in Chapter 17.

Modern Muzzleloading, Inc. v. Magaw
18 F. Supp. 2d 29 (D.D.C. 1998)

FLANNERY, DISTRICT JUDGE.

This case involves a challenge to the Bureau of Alcohol, Tobacco and Firearm's ("ATF") decision to classify the Knight Disc Rifle as a firearm for purposes of the Gun Control Act of 1968 ("GCA"), as amended, 18 U.S.C. §§ 921–930. The statute excludes "antique firearms" from the class subject to regulation. Modern Muzzleloading, Inc., the manufacturer of the Knight Disc Rifle, contends that the rifle is an antique firearm that should not be subject to regulation under the GCA. Acting on that view, for the fifteen-month period ending in December 1997, Modern Muzzleloading manufactured and distributed 30,000 Knight Disc Rifles without a license. In this action, Modern Muzzleloading has sued the Director of the ATF, seeking both (1) a declaration that the Knight Disc Rifle is not a firearm for purposes of the GCA and (2) an order enjoining ATF from enforcing its classification of the rifle....

The GCA defines the term "firearm" as "any weapon ... which will or is designed to ... expel a projectile by the action of an explosive." 18 U.S.C. § 921(a)(3). However, "[s]uch term does not include an antique firearm." The GCA defines the term "antique firearm" as follows:

(A) any firearm (including any firearm with a matchlock, flintlock, percussion cap, or similar type of ignition system) manufactured in or before 1898; and

(B) any replica of any firearm described in subparagraph (A) if such replica—

(i) is not designed or redesigned for using rimfire or conventional centerfire fixed ammunition, or

(ii) uses rimfire or conventional centerfire fixed ammunition which is no longer manufactured in the United States and which is not readily available in the ordinary channels of commercial trade.

18 U.S.C. § 921(a)(16). This case turns on whether the Knight Disc Rifle is a replica within the meaning of subparagraph (B). Since it is a currently-manufactured weapon, the rifle cannot qualify directly under subparagraph (A). It is also undisputed that the rifle does

not accept either rimfire or conventional centerfire ammunition and that, therefore, sub-paragraphs (B)(i) and (B)(ii) do not apply. Both parties agree that the term replica should or may be understood by referring to the parenthetical language found in subparagraph (A). Nevertheless, the parties disagree about the scope of this parenthetical and its affect on the determination of what constitutes a replica under subparagraph (B)....

[T]he key characteristic of the Knight Disc Rifle is its use of either a percussion cap or a shotgun primer as an ignition system. The rifle is designed so that each of those systems is held in place by a plastic disc with a hole in its center, into which the user inserts the ignition system. Modern Muzzleloading sells two discs for use in the rifle. One, a red disc that actually comes with the rifle, is designed to accept a percussion cap. The other, an orange disc that Modern Muzzleloading sells as an accessory, is designed to accept a shot-gun primer. The only difference in the discs is that the hole in the center of the orange disc is slightly larger, because the shotgun primer used in the rifle is slightly larger than a percussion cap. The use of the primer is viewed by the ATF as a defining characteristic in determining whether the Knight Disc Rifle is properly classified as an "antique." ...

In October 1997, ATF ... concluded that "(the Knight Disc Rifle) is designed to use shot-gun primers for an ignition system. It is not an antique firearm as defined in 18 U.S.C. § 921(a)(16) and it is a firearm as defined in 18 U.S.C. § 921(a)(3)." ...

The ATF explained that the Knight Disc Rifle is not an antique firearm because it is de-signed to use a modern centerfire shotgun primer as an ignition system. The ATF also explained why modern centerfire shotgun primers are not similar to the matchlock, flint-lock, and percussion cap ignition systems specified in the definition of an antique firearm found in 18 U.S.C. § 921(a)(16)(A)....

Plaintiff asserts that because the statute is criminal in nature, the rule of lenity applies, and the defendant's decision is not sustainable. In the Court's view, this is incorrect. Al-though the statute is criminal in nature, the rule of lenity does not apply and the ATF's decision is entitled to deference by the Court.

As defendant's counsel ably pointed out,

> The rule of lenity is premised on the idea that 'fair warning should be given to the world in language that the common world will understand, of what the law intends to do if a certain line is passed.' *Babbitt v. Sweet Home Chapter of Comms. for a Great Or.*, 515 U.S. 687 (1995). As the Supreme Court recently noted in interpreting the GCA, however, 'this Court has never held that the rule of lenity automatically permits [the person invoking the rule] to win.'

The fact that the statute is criminal in nature is simply not enough to invoke the rule of lenity. Rather, a Court must also find that there is a grievous ambiguity or uncertainty in the statute. That maxim of construction is reserved for cases where, after seizing every-thing from which aid can be derived, the Court is left with an ambiguous statute.

Defendant readily admits that the statute at issue is criminal in nature. Yet, plaintiff has failed to convince this Court that the statute contains a grievous ambiguity. In light of the structure and language of the statute, this Court finds that although the statute may be am-biguous to some degree, this ambiguity is slight, not grievous, and deference to the agency's interpretation of the statute is still warranted. Contrary to plaintiff's assertions, judicial deference to an agency's interpretation of a statute is not foreclosed simply because the statute contains criminal penalties. The statute at issue contains a section defining an an-tique firearm. The section is not devoid of guidance in terms of Congressional intent. The statute is somewhat ambiguous because it defines an antique firearm as including weapons with certain types of ignition systems as well as those using similar types of ignition systems. Nevertheless, the statute, when read as a whole, provides guidance as to an antique firearm's key criteria. Under these circumstances, it is inappropriate to apply the rule of lenity. ...

The plaintiff also cites *Crandon v. United States*, 494 U.S. 152 (1990), arguing that it strongly supports plaintiff's view that the rule of lenity applies to this suit and plaintiff should win. In *Crandon*, the Supreme Court was faced with the question of whether severance payments by a private corporation to former employees entering government service violated a provision of the Criminal Code that prohibits private parties from paying, and Government employees from receiving, substantial compensation for the employee's Government service. The corporation made these lump sum payments to mitigate the substantial financial loss each employee expected to suffer by reason of his change in employment. The Court faced an issue of statutory interpretation in deciding whether 18 U.S.C. § 209(a) required a recipient of funds to be employed by the government at the time of payment. The Court of Appeals had found that Congressional changes in 1962 concerning the wording of the applicable statute as well as public policy considerations counseled in favor of a broad interpretation. The Supreme Court disagreed, finding that the wording of the applicable statute, although awkward, indicated that employment status was an element of the offense. It is in this context that the Court found the rule of lenity an additional source of support for its conclusion that the statute required employment by the government at the time of payment.

This Court does not consider *Crandon* to have the far reaching effect that plaintiff asserts, namely resolving all issues in this case in favor of the plaintiff. Rather, after looking at the specific factual circumstances of *Crandon*, this Court is convinced that *Crandon's* significance is more narrow. In *Crandon*, the majority only used the rule of lenity to resolve any temporal issues about the statute that remained after the Court had exhaustively analyzed the language and history of the statute. Moreover, in that case, the Court found that the language and history of the statute weighed in favor of a narrow reading of the statute, thus complementing any application of the rule of lenity. In contrast, in the present case, applying the rule of lenity would conflict with the intent expressed in the language of the GCA. As this Court has previously explained, the applicable section of the GCA is somewhat ambiguous, but the Court need not apply the rule of lenity, since the ambiguity is not grievous and the overall structure of the statute counsels against plaintiff's interpretation. To apply the rule of lenity in the manner suggested by plaintiff would be contrary to the Congressional intent expressed in the statute. This rationale also illustrates the difference between this case and *United States v. Thompson/Center Arms Co.*, 504 U.S. 505, 517–18 (1992) (citing *Crandon* and applying the rule of lenity to a criminal statute at issue in a civil suit because the statute remained ambiguous even after applying traditional tools of statutory interpretation). ...

Instead of applying the rule of lenity, the Court believes that the appropriate standard of review is ... that "a reviewing court shall hold unlawful and set aside agency action, findings, and conclusions found to be arbitrary and capricious, an abuse of discretion, or otherwise not in accordance with law." Under this deferential standard of review, the Court is not to substitute its judgment for that of the ATF. A court need only examine whether the agency's decision was "based on a consideration of the relevant factors and whether there has been a clear error of judgment." ...

[The Court then upholds the ATF's interpretation of the GCA as consistent with the statute because "it seems like an entirely reasonable method of determining ... whether a weapon should be classified as an antique."]

For the reasons given above, the Court will grant the defendant's motion for summary judgment and deny the plaintiff's motion for summary judgment.

Notes and Questions

(1) *Finding Ambiguity.* Is a statute ambiguous only when the language itself lends itself to multiple interpretations, or must the language remain ambiguous after the court reviews the statute's legislative history, purpose, and context? How does the principal case resolve this question?

(2) *Using the Rule of Lenity as Added Support for the Other Statutory Aids.* How does the court distinguish the *Crandon* case? According to this court, does it matter whether the interpretation urged by the rule of lenity supports or contradicts the plain meaning and legislative history of the statute? In other words, should a court more readily turn to the rule of lenity if the interpretation that results simply confirms the ordinary meaning rather than contradicts it?

(3) *Babbitt v. Sweet Home Chapter.* In the so-called spotted owl case, which this case cites, the Supreme Court rejected the argument that because the Endangered Species Act allowed the agency to impose criminal penalties, the rule of lenity prohibited the Court from deferring to the Secretary of the Interior's interpretation of the Act. The Court wrote:

> The rule of lenity is premised on two ideas: First, a fair warning should be given to the world in language that the common world will understand, of what the law intends to do if a certain line is passed; second, legislatures and not courts should define criminal activity.

Babbitt v. Sweet Home Chapter of Comms. for a Great Or., 515 U.S. 687, 703 n.18 (1995). The Court reasoned that the rule did not answer the question of whether to defer to the agency's interpretation:

> We have never suggested that the rule of lenity should provide the standard for reviewing facial challenges to administrative regulations whenever the governing statute authorizes criminal enforcement. Even if there exist regulations whose interpretations of statutory criminal penalties provide such inadequate notice of potential liability as to offend the rule of lenity, the [regulation at issue here], which has existed for two decades and gives a fair warning of its consequences, cannot be one of them.

Id. at 704. Did the plaintiff in *Modern Muzzleloading* have inadequate notice of potential liability?

(4) *Criminal v. Civil.* As noted above, the rule applies to criminal statutes and to civil statutes with penal aspects. Is losing your driver's license a criminal or civil sanction? *Compare Harter v. N.D. Dep't of Transp.*, 694 N.W.2d 677, 681 (N.D. 2005) (holding that suspension of a driver's license is not criminal in nature; hence, the rule of lenity did not apply), *with Nunnally v. State Dep't of Pub. Safety & Corrections*, 663 So. 2d 254, 256 (La. Ct. App. 1995) (holding that statute revoking driving privileges is penal, so rule of lenity did apply). What about being civilly committed as a sexually violent person? *Compare In re Tiney-Bey*, 707 N.E.2d 751 (Ill. Ct. App. 1999) (holding that civil commitment act was civil, and thus rule of lenity did not apply), *with Townes v. Commonwealth*, 609 S.E.2d 1 (Va. 2005) (holding that civil commitment act was criminal, and so the rule of lenity did apply). Note that the rule does not apply to matters of criminal procedure—just to the

definitions of crime and the imposition of punishment. *See Commonwealth v. Shedlock*, 790 N.E.2d 722, 732 n.9 (Mass. Ct. App. 2003).

(5) *Does the Class of Defendant Matter?* In a case interpreting the federal mail fraud statute, Justice Stevens contended that it was appropriate to identify the class of litigants that would benefit from the Court's application of the rule of lenity to determine whether it should apply:

> When considering how much weight to accord to the doctrine of lenity, it is appropriate to identify the class of litigants that will benefit from the Court's ruling today. They are not uneducated, or even average, citizens. They are the most sophisticated practitioners of the art of government among us. There is an element of fiction in the presumption that every citizen is charged with a responsibility to know what the law is. But the array of government executives, judges, and legislators who have been accused, and convicted, of mail fraud under the well-settled construction of the statute that the Court renounces today are people who unquestionably knew that their conduct was unlawful.

McNally v. United States, 483 U.S. 350, 375 n.9 (1987) (Stevens, J., dissenting). Do you agree? Are educated defendants more likely to understand the meaning of a criminal statute? Should judges vary their decision to apply the rule of lenity based on who the defendant is?

(6) *Statutory Directives Abrogating the Rule of Lenity.* In specific instances, Congress has attempted to abrogate the rule of lenity. For example, the federal "RICO" statute— the Racketeer Influenced and Corrupt Organization Act—provides that its "provisions ... shall be liberally construed to effectuate [the bill's] remedial purposes...." Pub. L. No. 91-452, §904(a).* This directive has itself created issues of interpretation. The "applicability of the liberal construction standard has been questioned in criminal RICO cases in view of the general canon of interpretation that ambiguities in criminal statutes are to be construed in favor of leniency...." *Keystone Ins. Co. v. Houghton*, 863 F.2d 1125, 1128 n.3 (3d Cir. 1988). To resolve this conflict, the courts have continued to apply the rule of lenity to the criminal portions of the statute and have interpreted the civil penalties more liberally.

Some state legislatures have also tried to abrogate this rule by statute. *E.g.*, Cal. Penal Code §4 (2004) ("The rule of the common law, that penal statutes are to be strictly construed, has no application to this Code. All its provisions are to be construed according to the fair import of their terms, with a view to effect its objects and to promote justice."); N.Y. Penal Law §5.00 (McKinney 2004). However, because of the underlying due process concerns, state courts also narrowly interpret these "anti-lenity statutes." *E.g., People v. Ditta*, 422 N.E.2d 515, 517 (N.Y. 1981) ("Although [Penal Law §5.00] obviously does not justify the imposition of criminal sanctions for conduct that falls beyond the scope of the Penal Law, it does authorize a court to dispense with hypertechnical or strained interpretations...."); *People ex rel. Lungren v. Superior Court*, 926 P.2d 1042, 1053–54 (Cal. 1996) ("while ... the rule of the common law ... has been abrogated ... it is also true that the defendant is entitled to the benefit of every reasonable doubt, whether it arise out of a question of fact, or as to the true interpretation of words or the construction of language used in a statute."). Do you understand why legislative attempts to limit the rule of lenity have been largely unsuccessful?

---

* Authors' footnotes: RICO is a comprehensive federal anti-racketeering statute designed to eliminate corrupt influences on businesses.

Problem 16-2

You represent Chris Valentino. On July 26, 1986, he pled guilty to the felony offense of possession of heroin. The trial court sentenced him to five years imprisonment, suspended the imposition of the sentence, and then placed him on community supervision for five years. On September 1, 1991, the trial court, after finding that appellant satisfactorily fulfilled the conditions of community supervision, entered the following order:

> It is the order of the Court that the judgment of conviction entered in said cause be and is hereby set aside and the indictment against said defendant be and the same is hereby dismissed.

On November 6, 2004, Chris was a passenger in a car that was pulled over for a routine traffic violation. Chris and his friend were on their way hunting. The officer asked the driver and Chris whether they possessed any weapons. Chris informed the officer that he had a hunting rifle behind the seat. The officer then processed his license to check for prior criminal history and outstanding warrants, and learned of the 1986 conviction. Chris was subsequently arrested and indicted for the offense of unlawful possession of a firearm by a felon under Mercer Penal Code § 2-46-04.

What arguments would you make on Chris' behalf that the indictment should be dismissed? How would the prosecutor respond? How is a trial court likely to rule and why?

Problem Materials

Mercer Penal Code § 2-46-04:

(a) A person who has been convicted of a felony commits an offense if he possesses a firearm:

    (1) after conviction and before the fifth anniversary of the person's release from confinement following conviction of the felony or the person's release from supervision under community supervision, parole, or mandatory supervision, whichever date is later; or

    (2) after the period described by Subdivision (1), at any location other than the premises at which the person lives.

(b) **Findings and Purpose:**

    The legislature finds that the State of Mercer has an interest in protecting its citizens from convicted felons. But persons whose convictions are set aside pursuant to § 42-12-20(a) do not implicate these concerns for public safety. The underlying purpose of community supervision is to provide criminal defendants with a chance to "mend their ways." If a defendant accepts the challenge and successfully completes the terms and conditions of community supervision, he should not be stigmatized for the rest of his life. Such persons have demonstrated that they are ready to rejoin the community as law-abiding citizens.

Legislative History of § 2-46-05

Statements by Representative Longan, the sponsor of the bill:

    The prohibition against a felon possessing firearms has been part of our jurisprudence, in one form or another, since 1949. The legislature has changed the substance of this offense several times with the addition or deletion of just a few words. At times, the offense has only applied to people after their release from the penitentiary, but not to those who never went to prison. At times, the statute has applied specifically only to people who have committed crimes of violence. And at times, the statute has prohibited weapon possession only for certain kinds of guns or only if possessed away from home.

With this amendment, the statute will take on the broadest possible meaning it has ever had in order to best protect the citizens of Mercer from violent felons. For the first time, the prohibition against possessing a weapon will apply to all felons, regardless of whether the underlying offense involved an act of violence. And for the first time, a felon will be prohibited from possessing a gun, even at home, for five years after supervision ended.

This amendment makes the statute broader than all its previous versions. It applies regardless of the nature of the prior offense. And, it applies to a person whether or not he ever spent time in prison.

Mercer Code Crim. Procedure § 42-12-20(a):

At any time, after the defendant has satisfactorily completed one-third of the original community supervision period or two years of community supervision, whichever is less, the period of community supervision may be reduced or terminated by the judge. Upon the satisfactory fulfillment of the conditions of community supervision, and the expiration of the period of community supervision, the judge, by order duly entered, shall amend or modify the original sentence imposed, if necessary, to conform to the community supervision period and shall discharge the defendant. If the judge discharges the defendant under this section, the judge may set aside the verdict or permit the defendant to withdraw his plea, and shall dismiss the accusation, complaint, information or indictment against the defendant, who shall thereafter be released from all penalties and disabilities resulting from the offense or crime of which he has been convicted or to which he has pleaded guilty, except that:

(1) proof of the conviction or plea of guilty shall be made known to the judge should the defendant again be convicted of any criminal offense; and

(2) if the defendant is an applicant for a license or is a licensee under Chapter 42, Human Resources Code [for a child care facility], the Mercer Department of Human Services may consider the fact that the defendant previously has received community supervision under this article in issuing, renewing, denying, or revoking a license under that chapter.

OXFORD ENGLISH DICTIONARY 548, 737, 2117 (Compact Ed. 1971):

Convicted: "[p]roved or found guilty; condemned."

Penalty: "a loss, disability, or disadvantage of some kind."

Disability: "a restriction framed to prevent any person or class of persons from sharing in duties or privileges which would otherwise be open to them."

C. *Ex Post Facto* Laws

Closely related to the prior subjects in this chapter is the prohibition against *ex post facto* laws. *See* U.S. Const. art. I, § 9, cl. 3 ("No ... ex post facto Law shall be passed" by Congress); *see generally Smith v. Doe*, 538 U.S. 84 (2003). At its core, the clause prohibits: (1) statutes that criminalize an action that was completed before the law became effective; (2) statutes that inflict greater punishment for a crime than was possible when the crime was committed; and (3) statutes that deprive a criminal defendant of a defense that was available when the offense was allegedly committed. *Collins v. Youngblood*, 497 U.S. 37, 42 (1990).

The clause only applies in those narrow circumstances. Thus, a change of procedure, even if the change operates to disadvantage a defendant, is not prohibited so long as the change does not increase the punishment for a crime or make criminal conduct that was previously lawful. *United States v. Woods*, 399 F.3d 1144 (9th Cir. 2005) (change in time limits for new trial motions was not subject to clause). Likewise, a statute that makes it a crime for someone who has previously been convicted of a crime to carry a gun is not *ex post facto* because the conduct—carrying the gun—occured after enactment. *See State v. Schluter*, 653 N.W.2d 787 (Minn. Ct. App. 1987). The "focus of the *ex post facto* inquiry is not whether a legislative change produces some ambiguous sort of 'disadvantage'... but on whether any such change alters the definition of criminal conduct or increases the penalty by which a crime is punishable." *Cal. Dep't of Corrs. v. Morales*, 514 U.S. 499, 506 n.3 (1995).

While some of those principles may be counter-intuitive, there are difficult statutory interpretation issues that courts must face. Foremost, what if a statute is civil on its face, but it is also punitive in effect? Can a civil statute be "criminal" for purposes of *ex post facto* analysis?

The next two cases explore these issues: The first case explores whether the law is criminal; the second case explores whether the change was retroactive. Pay particular attention to how the judges decide whether the statute is criminal and whether it is retroactive. In other words, note how statutory interpretation is implicated.

People v. Leroy
828 N.E.2d 769 (Ill. Ct. App. 2005)

JUSTICE WELCH delivered the opinion of the court:

The defendant, Patrick Leroy, was charged in the circuit court of St. Clair County with unlawful failure to renew his address registration as a child sex offender. On February 5, 2002, the defendant pled guilty to the charge and was sentenced to one year's probation. On August 27, 2002, a petition to revoke the probation was filed, charging that the defendant lived within 500 feet of an elementary school. In an order issued December 27, 2002, the court found that the defendant admitted the charge, and the court ordered the defendant to move within 30 days.... At a hearing on April 11, 2003, the defendant stipulated that he lived within 500 feet of a school and that he was not the owner of the home but had lived there his whole life. The defendant was 36 years old at the time of the hearing. The defendant's mother owned the home in question, which is located in East St. Louis. In an order issued April 17, 2003, the court found that the defendant was in violation of his probation. On May 2, 2003, the court terminated the defendant's probation and prohibited him from residing at the home. The defendant now appeals, contending that the statute he violated is unconstitutional in that the statute ... is an *ex post facto* law.... For the reasons that follow, we affirm....

The statute in question, section 11-9.4(b-5) of the Criminal Code of 1961 (hereinafter subsection (b-5)), reads in pertinent part as follows:

"It is unlawful for a child sex offender to knowingly reside within 500 feet of a playground or a facility providing programs or services exclusively directed toward persons under 18 years of age. Nothing in this subsection (b-5) prohibits a child sex offender from residing within 500 feet of a playground or a facility providing programs or services exclusively directed toward persons under 18 years of age if the property is owned by the child sex offender and was purchased before the effective date of this amendatory Act of the 91st General Assembly."

We begin our analysis of subsection (b-5) with the Illinois Supreme Court's pronouncement that a statute is presumed constitutional, and the party challenging the statute bears the burden of demonstrating its invalidity. A reviewing court has a duty to construe a statute in a manner that upholds its validity and constitutionality if it can be reasonably done....

The defendant's ... argument on appeal is that subsection (b-5) is a prohibited *ex post facto* law because it "applies to sex offenders convicted before the statute's enactment." See U.S. Const., art. I, §§ 9, 10; Ill. Const.1970, art. I, § 16. These constitutional provisions restrain Congress and the state legislatures from enacting arbitrary or vindictive legislation and ensure that statutes give fair warning of their effect. A law is *ex post facto* if it is both retroactive and disadvantageous to the defendant. A law is disadvantageous to a defendant when that law criminalizes an act that was innocent when done, increases the punishment for a previously committed offense, or alters the rules of evidence by making a conviction easier. Although not coherently developed in the defendant's brief, presumably the defendant's argument in this case is that subsection (b-5) violates the prohibition against increasing the punishment for a previously committed offense. To determine if that is the case, we must first consider whether the restriction established by subsection (b-5) constitutes "punishment" and thus whether subsection (b-5) establishes criminal proceedings.

When faced with the question of whether a given statute imposes a punishment, a reviewing court must first ascertain whether the legislature meant the statute to establish "civil" proceedings. If the legislature intended to impose a punishment, the inquiry is complete. If, however, the intention of the legislature was to enact a regulatory scheme that is civil and nonpunitive, the reviewing court must further examine whether the statutory scheme is so punitive in either purpose or effect that it negates the state's intention to deem it civil. In making this determination, the reviewing court should ordinarily defer to the legislature's stated intent, and only the clearest proof will suffice to override legislative intent and transform what has been denominated a civil remedy into a criminal penalty.

As discussed above, we believe that the prohibitive subsections of section 11-9.4 of the Criminal Code of 1961 are intended to protect children from known child sex offenders. Where a legislative restriction is an incident of the state's power to protect the health and safety of its citizens, the restriction will be considered to evidence an intent to exercise that regulatory power, and not a purpose to add to a punishment. Accordingly, we conclude that the intent of the Illinois General Assembly in passing subsection (b-5) was to create a civil, nonpunitive statutory scheme to protect the public rather than to impose a punishment.

Having concluded that the intent behind the subsection was civil and not punitive, we next must consider whether the effect of the law is so punitive that it negates the state's attempt to craft civil restrictions. Whether a punitive effect results despite a statute's nonpunitive purpose is generally evaluated by employing the [following five]-factor test ... :

(1) whether the restriction has historically been regarded as a punishment, (2) whether the restriction imposes an affirmative disability or restraint, (3) whether the restriction promotes the traditional aims of punishment, namely retribution and deterrence, (4) whether the restriction has a rational connection to a nonpunitive purpose, and (5) whether the restriction is excessive with respect to this purpose. Although these factors are neither exhaustive nor dispositive, they are useful guideposts, and we shall employ them in our analysis of subsection (b-5).

With regard to the first factor—whether the restriction has historically been regarded as a punishment—the defendant contends that "[t]he effect of permanently preventing [the defendant] from living in the only home he has had for thirty-six years is banishment," which, in turn, has historically been regarded as a punishment. We do not agree that the defendant in this case has been banished. In colonial times, the most serious offenders within a community were banished, after which they could neither return to their original community nor, reputations tarnished, be admitted easily into new communities. The record in this case is completely devoid of evidence that the defendant cannot return to his original community of East St. Louis or that he cannot be admitted easily into a new community. Indeed, as discussed above, the record indicates that as of May 2, 2003, the date the circuit court entered its order in this case, the probation department had verified that the defendant was no longer living with his mother but was living instead in nearby Belleville. There is absolutely no evidence that the defendant has been unable to assimilate himself into this new community or that, did he so desire, he would be unable to procure appropriate housing in his hometown of East St. Louis.... Furthermore, although the defendant is prohibited from "residing" at the home his mother owns in East St. Louis because that home is located within 500 feet of a school, he is not precluded from visiting his mother at that home on a daily basis and thereby enjoying her support. Put simply, the restrictions placed on the defendant by subsection (b-5) in no way resemble the historical punishment of banishment, and only a tortured reading of the term banishment could lead us to conclude otherwise. On the record before us, we cannot conclude that the restrictions of subsection (b-5) are a historic form of punishment.

We turn now to the second factor—whether the restriction imposes an affirmative disability or restraint. To determine this, a reviewing court must consider how the effects of the statute in question are felt by those subject to it. If the disability or restraint is minor and indirect, its effects are unlikely to be punitive. Although subsection (b-5) does specifically restrict persons subject to it from living in certain areas, it does not otherwise restrict the movement and activities of such persons. Likewise, we are mindful that restricting the freedom of those deemed dangerous is a legitimate nonpunitive governmental objective and has been historically so regarded. Accordingly, although we would not characterize the disability or restraint imposed by subsection (b-5) as minor or indirect, we are not convinced that the presence of this factor alone is sufficient to create a punitive effect from subsection (b-5)'s nonpunitive purpose.

With regard to the third factor—whether the restriction promotes the traditional aims of punishment, namely, retribution and deterrence—we begin our analysis with the retribution factor. As discussed above, the purpose of the prohibitive subsections of section 11-9.4 is to protect children from known child sex offenders. Also as discussed above, subsection (b-5) bears a reasonable relationship to the purpose of protecting children from known child sex offenders and sets forth a reasonable method of furthering that purpose. There is no evidence that the subsection is designed as a form of retribution, nor does the defendant argue that it is. We reject the idea that subsection (b-5) promotes the traditional retribution aim of punishment. As to the deterrence factor, we noted above that it is reasonable to believe that a law that prohibits child sex offenders from living within 500 feet of a school will reduce the amount of incidental contact child sex offenders have with the children attending that school and that consequently the opportunity for the child sex offenders to commit new sex offenses against those children will be reduced as well. Accordingly, it is possible that the subsection might deter future crimes. However, even an obvious deterrent purpose does not necessarily make a law punitive. In fact, any number of governmental programs might deter crime without imposing punishment. We agree with the United States Supreme Court that to hold that the mere presence of a deterrent purpose renders a statute criminal would severely undermine the government's ability to engage in effective regulation. We reject the idea that subsection (b-5) promotes the traditional deterrence aim of punishment. We conclude that the subsection's purpose is the protection of the public and that it does not significantly promote either retribution or deterrence.

As to the fourth factor—whether the restriction has a rational connection to a nonpunitive purpose—we have repeatedly noted that the purpose of subsection (b-5) is to protect children from known child sex offenders. Given this purpose, it is reasonable to conclude that restricting child sex offenders from residing within 500 feet of a playground or a facility providing programs or services exclusively directed toward persons under 18 years of age might also protect society.

As to the fifth and final factor—whether the restriction is excessive with respect to its purpose—we conclude that it is not.... [A]mong the 13 states that have enacted some form of residency restriction applicable to sex offenders, the 500-foot restriction of subsection (b-5) is the least restrictive in geographical terms.... [A]lthough the law restricts residency to some extent, it does not otherwise restrict the movement and activities of child sex offenders. As the United States Supreme Court has noted, the excessiveness inquiry of *ex post facto* jurisprudence is not an exercise in determining whether the legislature has made the best choice possible to address the problem it seeks to remedy. The question is whether the regulatory means chosen are reasonable in light of the nonpunitive objective. Having concluded that prohibiting child sex offenders from living within 500 feet of a playground or a facility providing programs or services exclusively directed toward persons under 18 years of age bears a reasonable relationship to the purpose of protecting children from known child sex offenders and sets forth a reasonable method of furthering that purpose, we decline to now find subsection (b-5) excessive with respect to that purpose.

Our review of the effect of subsection (b-5) under the [five] factors convinces us that subsection (b-5) is not so punitive that it negates the state's attempt to craft civil restrictions. Accordingly, subsection (b-5) does not constitute an *ex post facto* law, and the defendant's fourth argument on appeal fails....

For the foregoing reasons, we affirm....

JUSTICE KUEHN, dissenting:

Patrick Leroy became a child sex offender in 1987, when the State of Illinois convicted him of criminal sexual assault. We are not told of the circumstances surrounding that offense, and the challenged law at issue here does not really care about any of the details that underlie a given child sex offender's crime. We only know that Leroy had to spend more than six years of his life confined with other state prisoners in order to satisfy the punishment imposed for having committed his crime.

As things have turned out, serving a term of imprisonment fell short of expiating Patrick Leroy's misconduct. Leroy must now suffer another restraint upon his personal liberty, an added consequence attendant to his aged criminal conviction. On July 7, 2000, 13 years after Leroy broke the law, the Illinois legislature enacted Public Act 91-91, a law that imposed a 500-foot residency restriction around playgrounds, schools, daycare centers, and the like and applied that ban retroactively to any child sex offender living at a residence in which he or she had no ownership interest. Thus, the family home where Patrick Leroy had been raised from birth, a home titled in his mother's name alone, suddenly became forbidden ground, a place where Leroy could no longer live without committing a felony offense.

The State of Illinois expelled Patrick Leroy from his home of 36 years. Since the expulsion is without time limitation, the ouster potentially constitutes a lifetime ban from the Leroy family home. As long as children attend the Miles Davis Elementary School, or as long as the playground that adjoins the school exists, no one who has ever been convicted of any offense that carries the mark of sexually offending against a child can live where Patrick Leroy once lived.

It took some time for the authorities to order Leroy out of his house. When they finally got around to seeking compliance with Public Act 91-911, almost 18 years had passed since Leroy had engaged in the criminal conduct that branded him a child sex offender. In May of 2003, Leroy bid farewell to his mother, and to the Leroy family home that he and she had shared for 36 years.

Leroy now lives by himself in a home located in Belleville, Illinois.

My colleagues do not believe that what has happened to Patrick Leroy offends any of the fundamental freedoms guaranteed as this nation's birthright. I believe that this law offends the constitutional prohibition against the enactment of *ex post facto* laws.... For the reasons that follow, I respectfully dissent.

The legislative intent behind Public Act 91-911 is beyond question. Legislators wanted to find a way to better protect children from people capable of taking sexual advantage of them. This desire resulted in Public Act 91-911, which removed *some known* child sex offenders from their homes, if they were located too close to playgrounds, schools, daycare centers, and any other facilities devoted exclusively to providing services to children or teenagers. For reasons unrelated to their legislative design, legislators permitted known child sex offenders who were purchasing their homes to continue living in close proximity to places where children gather.

In addition, our lawmakers passed Public Act 91-911 in order to create a barrier that would prohibit all future child sex offenders from living too close to these kinds of places.

Thus, it constitutes a felony offense for future child sex offenders, and for any past child sex offender not home-buying at the time Public Act 91-911 went into effect, to live anywhere within 500 feet of numerous places where children commonly assemble.

Public Act 91-911 was not passed for the purpose of further punishing convicted child sex offenders. However, a punitive effect unquestionably flows from this enactment. The retroactive application of the Act's residency restriction to people like Patrick Leroy, who have no ownership interest in their homes, violates our constitutional guarantee against the imposition of *ex post facto* punishment.

The first factor in weighing the potential punitive effect of an otherwise regulatory act is whether it resembles a historical form, or traditional means, of punishment. My colleagues scoff at the notion that Public Act 91-911 creates a restriction comparable to banishment, a punishment inflicted in colonial times. I believe that a banishment clearly resembles an expulsion of someone from his lifelong residence....

It is correct that the defendant has not been banished. Public Act 91-911 does not call for the banishment of child sex offenders. If it did, our inquiry would already be over. The Act would clearly impose added punishment in violation of the constitutional ban against *ex post facto* penalties.

Public Act 91-911 only created a retroactive residency restriction that, in its application to certain known child sex offenders, resembles banishment. The majority's conclusion to the contrary stems, at least in part, from a misunderstanding of what constitutes that traditional means of punishment.

A person is banished when he or she is expelled from a community and forbidden to return. Banishment has nothing to do with tarnishing reputations or making it difficult for someone to assimilate into new communities, as the majority opinion suggests....

When we understand what constitutes banishment and we consider the essence of its punitive aim, we find at its core the permanent expulsion of a criminal offender from his or her home. When a colonial offender was banished, he was ordered to leave his desired living space and was barred for life from ever returning to it. The underlying penal effect was the permanent loss of companionship and home of choice.

We do not have to torture the English language in order to conclude that what happened to Patrick Leroy resembles how people used to be punished in colonial times. Our inquiry into whether the retroactive residency restriction imposed by this law violates constitutional *ex post facto* constraints should progress from a finding that the restriction imposed resembles a historical form, and a traditional means, of punishment. We should find that criminalizing Patrick Leroy's long-standing home of choice, and imposing an indeterminate ban upon his ever living there again, constitutes an eviction very much akin to a banishment imposed in earlier times. To indefinitely expel a man from his family home, and separate him from family members with whom he has lived his entire life, seems decidedly similar to a method of punishment employed in colonial times. The only significant difference between a colonial banishment of some unwanted offender and the Act's retroactive expulsion of Patrick Leroy from where he wanted to live is how this reinvented form of permanent exclusion from home and family violates the constitutional protection against *ex post facto* punishment. As far as I know, our colonial ancestors would not have contemplated the banishment of people from their midst almost 18 years after they offended some colonial law....

My colleagues observe the obvious—that Public Act 91-911 imposes an affirmative disability and restraint of more-than-minor consequence. However, they give this factor only passing attention, dismissing it with the comment, "[A]lthough we would not characterize the disability or restraint imposed by subsection (b-5) as minor or indirect, we are not convinced that the presence of this factor alone is sufficient to create a punitive effect from subsection (b-5)'s nonpunitive purpose."

I am completely at odds with the majority about this factor. I would reach an exactly opposite conclusion. I believe that this *one factor alone* creates the kind of punitive effect that should bar the retroactive application of the residency restriction imposed by Public Act 91-911.

The majority's cursory deflection of the disability imposed by the retroactive application of the residency restriction contained in Public Act 91-911 unduly minimizes how significant and offensive its restraint really is to non-home-buying past offenders. Prohibiting someone from living where he has lived his entire life imposes a substantial disability.

Our legislature recognized as much, allowing known child molesters who were in the process of purchasing their homes to remain in them, regardless of how close the home was to a school, playground, or daycare center and regardless of how recent or reprehensible the home-buying child molester's conduct was....

While my colleagues readily observe how the Act's residency restriction might deter future crimes, they recast the inquiry from a discussion of whether the restriction at issue promotes deterrence, a traditional aim of punishment, to a discussion of how all regulatory schemes can carry a deterrent effect and how those regulations are not necessarily punitive in nature because of that fact. By focusing upon the assertion that all regulatory schemes that impose restrictions could be said to carry a deterrent effect, my colleagues skirt the issue, discounting the residency restriction's ability to promote deterrence, a traditional aim of punishment, just like they dismissed the question of whether this Act's restriction imposes the kind of disability and restraint that carries a punitive effect. In truth, this restriction provides deterrence every bit as effectively as other forms of punishment, a circumstance that no one even questions. The restriction clearly promotes a traditional aim of punishment.

The second common aim of punishment is retribution. We are told, "There is no evidence that [the residency restriction contained in Public Act 91-911] is designed as a form of retribution...." Again, the majority avoids any analysis of the real question posed, by misdirection. Our inquiry should not ask whether the legislature *designed* the residency restriction to exact retribution but should rather question whether the residency restriction's *application* tends to promote or advance retribution, a common aim of punishment.

While I am quite certain that legislators did not design the residency restriction contained in Public Act 91-911 to exact retribution, and thereby correct for wrongdoing, in which case the enactment would be *designed to punish* and therefore clearly violate the constitutional ban against *ex post facto* punishments, I believe that the restriction's application tends to promote retribution, a traditional aim of punishment.

Public Act 91-911 imposes a blanket residency restriction based upon only one criterion-conviction of the kind of criminal offense that marks the offender a "child sex offender." It does not discriminate based upon whether or not a particular individual actually presents some danger to children. The age of the conviction, the age of the offender, the nature of the crime, and the choice of the victim do not matter.

While there are numerous examples of how this Act's residency restriction advances a retributive purpose that commonly underlies the imposition of punishment, we need only look to Patrick Leroy's circumstance in order to understand how the Act's restriction tends to advance retribution, a traditional aim of punishment. The restriction casts Leroy out of his house because of an 18-year-old conviction, the details of which are unimportant to the expulsion's imposition. Without a better understanding of the nature of his offense, particularly his choice of victim, we cannot assess Leroy's likelihood for recidivism. Since we neither know nor care whether Leroy's removal from his home advances the safety of children attending Miles Davis Elementary School, we need to acknowledge that the automatic eviction, at least to a degree, promotes retribution for wrongdoing.

We might well ask ourselves two questions. What reason exists, in the absence of retribution, to expel Leroy from living in the Leroy family home when, as the majority points out, the prohibition does not preclude his daily unconstrained visitations there? Absent a tendency to promote retribution, what legitimate purpose would legislators have in removing Patrick Leroy from his home, given the fact that he has lived there for 10 years without reoffending, despite his close proximity to the hundreds upon hundreds of children who have matriculated to Miles Davis Elementary School during the same time span?

A restriction imposed without consideration for the likelihood of a particular offender to reoffend has to be grounded, at least in part, in furtherance of retribution. Here, the restriction is imposed without regard to the particulars of the offense, including the offender's choice of victim. The nature of the crime and the choice of the victim constitute important considerations in predicting what a prior offender's proximity to a given child-laden facility could mean in terms of reoffending. For example, a man branded a child sex offender for having had consensual sex with a 17-year-old girl could safely reside in close proximity to toddlers gathered at a daycare center but present a problem living across the street from a high school. On the other hand, a pedophile grandfather, branded a child sex offender for fondling his young grandchildren and their friends, presents a potential problem living across the street from a daycare center but could safely reside in close proximity to a high school. Since this Act treats all offenders alike, without consideration of whether a particular offender is likely to reoffend, its retroactive residency restriction promotes and furthers retribution, a traditional aim of punishment.

Finally, the residency restriction attaches without time limitation, expelling Patrick Leroy from his home and excluding his return forever, without regard for the likelihood of public danger. The retroactive application of the Act's residency restriction exceeds that which is necessary to protect children and enters the realm of retribution....

Public Act 91-911, viewed in light of the factors, exceeds its legislative intent to craft a civil regulatory scheme for the protection of children and is, in all truth, punitive in nature. It cannot be applied to Patrick Leroy, whose conviction predates the imposition of its disability and restraint by 13 years, without violating the constitutional guarantee against *ex post facto* punishment....

For these reasons, I respectfully dissent.

Notes and Questions

(1) *Purpose as the Key.* Notice that when determining whether an ostensibly non-criminal statute is, in fact, criminal, a court must in effect discern the statute's "purpose." Why is that step necessary? In making this determination, would a textualist look to extratextual sources? Imagine, for example, that the legislative history of the statute was replete with statements emphasizing the need for retribution and the desire to banish sex offenders to homes along freeways in isolated areas of the state. Would a textualist nonetheless reject this clear indication of the statute's purpose when determining whether the "civil" statute was "criminal" for purposes of analyzing it as an *ex post facto* law?

(2) *The Disagreement.* In some ways, the majority opinion can be read as simply holding that the defendant failed to prove the necessary facts. The majority repeatedly noted that the record lacked specific facts, and the majority took great comfort from the fact that the defendant had relocated to Belleville. No doubt that relocation formed part of the reason for the difference in opinions. Yet, the dissent believed that the majority set the bar too high — that the majority essentially would ignore all civil statutes with punitive effects. Who was right?

(3) *Legislative Intent.* One of the factors is whether the legislature intended a civil or punitive measure. The Supreme Court has stated that it "ordinarily defer[s] to the legislature's stated intent," and so "only the clearest proof will suffice to override legislative intent and transform what has been denominated a civil remedy into a criminal penalty." *Smith v. Doe*, 538 U.S. 84, 92 (2004). Does this statement reflect an interpretative approach or further separation of powers?

(4) *Distinguish Judicial "Law-Making."* Any time a court announces a new interpretation of a statute, isn't the court retroactively creating law? Suppose, for instance, that a court interprets a criminal statute for the first time and holds that intent is not required. Why shouldn't that interpretation be applicable only prospectively? In a sense, isn't all judicial interpretation retroactive?

In the prior case, the question was *whether the change in the law was criminal.* In the following case, the question is *whether there was a change* in the criminal law.

People v. Schaefer
703 N.W.2d 774 (Mich. 2005)

Young, J.

... In July 2003 ... defendant struck and killed an eleven-year-old girl who was riding her bicycle in the late afternoon.... Despite swerving in an attempt to avoid hitting the girl, the two collided. At the time of the accident, defendant had a 0.10 blood-alcohol level.

Defendant was charged with ... OUIL [driving while under the influence] causing death.... At defendant's preliminary examination, the prosecution called a sheriff's deputy who testified as an expert witness in accident reconstruction. The deputy testified that the accident was unavoidable, opining that the collision still would have occurred had defendant been sober and driving the speed limit. According to the deputy, a sober driver would have required at least 1 1/2 seconds to notice the girl and attempt to avoid hitting her. On the basis of his investigation, the deputy concluded that the girl emerged onto the road, and the impact occurred, all within less than one second.

The district court bound defendant over on all counts except OUIL causing death. On appeal to the circuit court, the court refused to reinstate the charge of OUIL causing death. The prosecution then appealed to the Court of Appeals, which affirmed the circuit court. Relying on [*People v. Lardie*, 551 N.W.2d 656 (Mich. 1996)], the Court of Appeals held that the prosecution failed to present sufficient evidence to justify a finding that defendant's intoxicated driving was a substantial cause of the victim's death.... In refusing to entertain the prosecutor's argument that *Lardie* was wrongly decided, the Court of Appeals stated that "[a] decision of the Supreme Court is binding upon this Court until the Supreme Court overrules itself. Therefore, we may not revisit the holding of *Lardie*." We granted the prosecutor's application for leave to appeal....

III. ANALYSIS

A. MCL 257.625(4)

Our Legislature first enacted the "OUIL causing death" statute as part of 1991 PA 98 in an attempt to increase the criminal penalties associated with driving while intoxicated. The Legislature evidently believed that sentences resulting from involuntary manslaughter and negligent homicide convictions inadequately deterred intoxicated drivers from getting behind the wheel. Thus, to address this concern, the Legislature enacted the OUIL causing death statute, which provides more severe penalties, with the apparent expectation that these heightened penalties would deter intoxicated individuals from driving.

Our OUIL causing death statute, MCL 257.625(4), provides:

A person, whether licensed or not, who operates a motor vehicle in violation of subsection (1) [under the influence of alcoholic liquor, a controlled substance, or a combination of alcoholic liquor and a controlled substance, or having an un-lawful body alcohol content], (3) [visibly impaired by the consumption of al-coholic liquor, a controlled substance, or a combination of alcoholic liquor and a controlled substance], or (8) [any body content of a schedule 1 controlled sub-stance] *and by the operation of that motor vehicle causes the death of another per-son* is guilty of a crime as follows:

(a) ... [A] felony punishable by imprisonment for not more than 15 years or a fine of not less than $2,500.00 or more than $10,000.00, or both.

B. PEOPLE V LARDIE

In *People v. Lardie*, this Court was presented with a due process challenge to the OUIL causing death statute.... In rejecting the defendants' due process arguments, this Court held that OUIL causing death is a general intent crime and that "the culpable act that the Legislature wishes to prevent is the one in which a person becomes intox-icated and then decides to drive." We further held that "there is no requirement [under §625(4)] that the people prove gross negligence or negligence" because "the Legisla-ture essentially has presumed that driving while intoxicated is gross negligence as a matter of law."

This Court then proceeded to examine the causation element of the OUIL causing death offense, stating:

> The Legislature passed [§625(4)] in order to reduce the number of alcohol-related traffic fatalities. The Legislature sought to deter drivers who are "will-ing to risk current penalties" from drinking and driving. In seeking to reduce fatalities by deterring drunken driving, the statute must have been designed to punish drivers when their *drunken* driving caused another's death. Other-wise, the statute would impose a penalty on a driver even when his wrongful decision to drive while intoxicated had no bearing on the death that resulted. Such an interpretation of the statute would produce an absurd result by di-vorcing the defendant's fault from the resulting injury. We seek to avoid such an interpretation.

Thus, relying on policy justifications and its belief that a contrary construction would lead to an "absurd result," the Lardie Court held that "in proving causation, the people must establish that the particular defendant's decision to drive while intoxicated pro-duced a change in that driver's operation of the vehicle that caused the death of the vic-tim." According to the Lardie Court, "[i]t is the change that such intoxication produces, and whether it caused the death, which is the focus of [the causation] element of the crime."

The *Lardie* Court summarized the three distinct elements the prosecution must prove in securing a conviction for OUIL causing death:

(1) [That] the defendant was operating his motor vehicle while he was intoxicated,
(2) that he voluntarily decided to drive knowing that he had consumed alcohol and might be intoxicated, and *(3) that the defendant's intoxicated driving was a sub-stantial cause of the victim's death.*

C. PRINCIPLES OF STATUTORY INTERPRETATION

When interpreting a statute, it is the court's duty to give effect to the intent of the Leg-islature as expressed in the actual language used in the statute. It is the role of the judiciary to interpret, not write, the law. If the statutory language is clear and unambiguous, the statute is enforced as written. Judicial construction is neither necessary nor permitted because it is presumed that the Legislature intended the clear meaning it expressed.

D. THE CAUSATION ELEMENT OF §625(4)

The plain text of §625(4) requires no causal link between the defendant's intoxication and the victim's death. Section 625(4) provides, "A person, whether licensed or not, who operates a motor vehicle [while intoxicated] and *by the operation* of that motor vehicle *causes* the death of another person is guilty of a crime...." Accordingly, it is the defendant's *operation* of the motor vehicle that must cause the victim's death, not the defendant's "intoxication." While a defendant's status as "intoxicated" is certainly an element of the offense of OUIL causing death, it is not a component of the *causation* element of the offense. Justice Weaver succinctly stated this point in her concurrence in *Lardie:*

> The plain language of the statute clearly indicates that the Legislature intended causation to turn on the fact that the defendant *operated* the vehicle while intoxicated, rather than the *changed manner in which*, or *how*, the defendant operated the vehicle while intoxicated.

The *Lardie* Court's reliance on policy considerations in construing §625(4) was misplaced. It is true that the cardinal rule of statutory interpretation is to give effect to the intent of the Legislature. However, the Legislature's intent must be ascertained from the actual text of the statute, not from extra-textual judicial divinations of "what the Legislature really meant." ... [R]ather than engaging in legislative mind-reading to discern [legislative intent], we believe that the best measure of the Legislature's intent is simply the words that it has chosen to enact into law.

The *Lardie* Court also erred in assuming that judicial adherence to and application of the actual text of §625(4) "would produce an absurd result." The result that the Court in *Lardie* viewed as "absurd"—imposing criminal liability under §625(4) when a victim's death is caused by a defendant's *operation* of the vehicle rather than the defendant's *intoxicated* operation—reflects a policy choice adopted by a majority of the Legislature. A court is not free to cast aside a specific policy choice adopted on behalf of the people of the state by their elected representatives in the Legislature simply because the court would prefer a different policy choice. To do so would be to empower the least politically accountable branch of government with unbridled policymaking power. Such a model of government was not envisioned by the people of Michigan in ratifying our Constitution, and modifying our structure of government by judicial fiat will not be endorsed by this Court.

Instead, we must construe the causation element of §625(4) according to the actual text of the statute. Section 625(4) plainly requires that the victim's death be caused by the defendant's *operation* of the vehicle, not the defendant's *intoxicated* operation. Thus, the manner in which the defendant's intoxication affected his or her operation of the vehicle is unrelated to the causation element of the crime. The defendant's status as "intoxicated" is a separate element of the offense used to identify the class of persons subject to liability under §625(4).

Accordingly, we overrule *Lardie* only to the extent it held that the prosecution must prove "that the defendant's *intoxicated* driving was a *substantial cause* of the victim's death." We hold that the prosecution, in proving OUIL causing death, must establish beyond a reasonable doubt that (1) the defendant was operating his or her motor vehicle in violation of MCL 257.625(1), (3), or (8); (2) the defendant voluntarily decided to drive, knowing that he or she had consumed an intoxicating agent and might be intoxicated; and (3) the defendant's operation of the motor vehicle caused the victim's death....

MICHAEL F. CAVANAGH, J. (concurring in part and dissenting in part).

... I dissent ... from the majority's decision to remand ... for further proceedings under the rule set forth in today's opinion because I believe that applying the new rule ... violates due process and infringes on the protections inherent in the Ex Post Facto Clauses of the United States and Michigan constitutions. US Const 1963, art I, § 10; Const, art 1, § 10....

In *Lardie*, this Court examined MCL 257.625(4) in great detail in an attempt to clarify its meaning. We engaged in extensive endeavors of statutory construction to determine things that were not evident on the statute's face. In particular, we examined whether the statute was meant to impose strict liability; if it was not, whether it created a general or specific intent crime; whether the Legislature intended that the prosecution prove some type of fault; and what the parameters of the statute's causation requirement were.

The resulting judicial interpretation of the statute had, of course, the force of law, and sufficiently explained to the citizenry what type of conduct on their part would lead to criminal culpability. Through that decision, the people of this state were given "fair warning" of a prohibited type of conduct.... There can be no doubt that a deprivation of the right of fair warning can result not only from vague statutory language but also from an unforeseeable and retroactive judicial expansion of narrow and precise statutory language.

Our decision in *Lardie*, which had the support of six justices, was the settled state of the law at the relevant time of these defendants' conduct. Due process precludes retroactive application of a judicial construction of a criminal statute that is unexpected and indefensible by reference to the law which had been expressed prior to the conduct in issue.... There was nothing in *Lardie* that suggested that the law was in some state of flux or that this Court's construction of the statute was less than clear or complete. No fair reading of *Lardie* would alert a person that *Lardie* would later be revisited or revised. Thus, at the time of these defendants' conduct, any construction different than that set forth in *Lardie* was both unexpected and indefensible.

The majority's assertion that "it is not 'indefensible or unexpected' that a court would, as we do today, overrule a case that failed to abide by the express terms of a statute,"* completely eliminates the protections against ex post facto punishments and due process violations. Under the majority's reasoning, no new court opinion would ever be "indefensible or unexpected," because the new opinion would always be "correct." But this ignores the fact that *every* court believes an opinion it issues is correct, just as the *Lardie* Court believed in 1996, or it would not issue the opinion.

Further, the majority's reasoning imposes on our citizenry the untenable burden of guessing and predicting when one court might overturn a prior court's settled interpretation of a statute. I find such a result in grave conflict with the notions of due process and, thus, fatally flawed.

As such, I disagree that [the defendant] must again undergo the criminal process under our new interpretation of what was, at the relevant time, settled law. Such a ruling vio-

---

* Authors' footnote: Apparently, the majority deleted this passage from its opinion after the dissent had written its opinion, but before the final decision was published.

lates the fundamental principles of due process and subjects defendants to ex post facto punishment. While the prosecution had a more difficult burden under *Lardie*, today's decision lessens that burden, making our new interpretation an unforeseeable judicial expansion of a criminal statute. Subjecting defendants to a new rule that increases the chance of culpability, when their conduct was committed when the old rule was settled law, is a clear violation of defendants' constitutional rights.

Accordingly, I would affirm the district court's dismissal of [the] defendant['s] case because the district court found that, under *Lardie*, probable cause that defendant committed a crime was nonexistent. The district court did not abuse its discretion in finding so....

Notes and Questions

(1) *Was There a Change in the Criminal Law?* Be sure you can articulate why the majority found that the prohibition against *ex post facto* laws was not an issue, but the concurring judge found it was. Can you argue that there was no change? That there was a change? Your analysis should lead you into the next question.

(2) *Is Reliance or Notice a Requirement?* The principle underlying the prohibition against *ex post facto* laws is that people should have notice that their conduct is unlawful *before* they engage in it. The facts of the defendant's case arguably press against that notion, or do they? Can you argue that the defendant "had notice" beforehand? That he did not have notice?

(3) *Was the* Lardie *Interpretation Correct?* No one contended that the *Lardie* interpretation was correct. Can you argue that the plain text supports the original interpretation in *Lardie*? Does the new interpretation render "and by the operation of that motor vehicle causes the death of another person" surplusage? Does the new interpretation ignore the clause's plain meaning?

(4) *Acquiescence?* Does it matter that, although *Lardie* had been decided in 1996, the legislature had not acted to change the wording of the statute in response? Does that fact suggest that the legislature had acquiesced in the *Lardie* interpretation? (*See* Chapter 9.) Did the defendant's lawyer miss a powerful argument?

Problem 16-3

You have been retained by Terry Draper. Draper advises you that a long time ago, in April 1992, he was charged with multiple traffic offenses, including driving while under the influence of alcohol. He pled guilty and was sentenced to one year of court supervision. The terms of his supervision required him to pay $500 in costs and to attend alcohol education classes. In May, 1993, he successfully completed the supervision, and the court discharged and dismissed the supervision.

Draper wants you to help him expunge the DUI from his arrest record. You conduct some research and conclude that, in April 1992, Mercer Rev. Stat. § 36-12-6(f) provided that a person could have a DUI arrest record expunged once five years had passed from the date dismissal occurred. However, effective in January 1997, the Mercer Legislature repealed that statute. In the same bill that repealed that statute, the legislature amended the civil statutes pertaining to drivers' licenses. Specifically, as part of the Drivers' License Improvement Act of 1997 ("DLIA"), the legislature enacted a new statute, § 23-2-9(a), which provided: "A person placed on supervision for [DUI] shall not have his or her record of arrest expunged." The preamble to the DLIA states: "The purpose of this statute is to facilitate safer driving on the streets of Mercer."

How will you argue that § 9(a) of the DLIA violates the *ex post facto* clause? What arguments do you expect the prosecution to raise in opposition? Ignore the rule of lenity.

D. Legislative Efforts to Direct *an Approach* to Interpretation

In the rest of this chapter, we turn to legislative efforts to direct interpretation. First, we examine the constitutionality of statutes in which the legislature tells courts how to interpret statutes. Second, we examine problems that can occur when the directives themselves create ambiguity.

1. Types of Legislative Directives

Statutory directives are statutes that tell the judiciary how to interpret a statute or statutes. There are many different kinds of directives. Directives vary from each other in the following ways. First, directives have different purposes. For example, some are definitional; they simply define terms that are used in other statutes. Other directives have a more theoretical impact: Some directives tell courts to interpret a statute broadly (or narrowly), while others tell the judiciary to take a specific approach to interpretation (such as purposivism, intentionalism, or textualism). Second, some directives by their terms only apply to specific statutes, while others apply to all statutes or to a particular type of statute. For example, a generally applicable directive might state that "unless context directs otherwise, the masculine includes the feminine for all statutes in this code." *See, e.g.*, 1 U.S.C.A. § 2 (West 2005). Third, statutory directives are either mandatory or permissive. A legislature may, for example, adopt a statute telling a court that it *must* construe a statute broadly to effectuate its remedial purposes or telling a court that it *may* do so.

Thus, directives come in various forms. Some directives raise constitutional issues, which we will explore in this chapter.

a. *Legislative Directives and Constitutional Concerns*

Some general directives are relatively benign and common. The federal statute below is an example. It directs courts to interpret specific words in all federal statutes in a specific manner:

> In determining the meaning of any Act of Congress, unless the context indicates otherwise—
>
> • words importing the singular include and apply to several persons, parties, or things;
>
> • words importing the plural include the singular;

- words importing the masculine gender include the feminine as well;
- words used in the present tense include the future as well as the present; ...
- the words "person" and "whoever" include corporations, companies, associations, firms, partnerships, societies, and joint stock companies, as well as individuals....

See 1 U.S.C. §1 (2005). There is very little controversy about the propriety of this kind of directive. Similarly, a general directive by which the legislature says "masculine" pronouns include the "masculine or feminine" does not seem problematic.

Where, however, the legislature goes beyond these simple, definitional directives, separation of powers can be implicated. Consider whether a legislative directive to a court to adopt a certain approach to interpretation violates separation of powers. *Marbury v. Madison,* 5 U.S. (1 Cranch) 137, 177 (1803) (holding that judges, in fulfilling their constitutionally delegated obligation to decide cases, "must of necessity expound and interpret" statutes).

Justice Scalia once commented, "I thought we had adopted a regular method for interpreting the meaning of a statute: first, find the ordinary meaning of the language in its textual context; and second, using established canons of construction, ask whether there is any clear indication that some permissible meaning other than the ordinary one applies." *Chisom v. Roemer,* 501 U.S. 380, 404 (1991) (Scalia, J., dissenting). As his sarcastic comment suggests, the Supreme Court has grappled throughout history with the appropriate approach to statutory interpretation, but has never settled on one. Congress has not enacted a statute that directs courts to use a particular theoretical approach. Some academics suggest it should, while others suggest that doing so would violate the Constitution. *Compare* Nicholas Quinn Rosenkranz, *Federal Rules of Statutory Interpretation,* 115 Harv. L. Rev. 2085 (2002) (arguing that Congress should provide federal rules of statutory interpretation), *with* Larry Alexander & Saikrishna Prakash, *Mother May I? Imposing Mandatory Prospective Rules of Statutory Interpretation,* 20 Const. Comment. 97 (2003) (rejecting Professor Rosenkranz's proposal and arguing that neither the courts nor Congress can limit the interpretation of statutes through rules of interpretation without violating entrenchment principles).

There is very little case law on this issue. *But see Evans v. State,* 872 A.2d 539, 552 (Del. 2005) (holding a state statute directing courts to "strictly interpret or construe legislative intent" and to "use the utmost restraint when interpreting ... the laws" violated separation of powers). However, the excerpt below directly addresses this question.

"Which Is to Be Master," The Judiciary or the Legislature?
When Statutory Directives Violate Separation of Powers
56 U.C.L.A. L. Rev. 837 (2009)[*]
Linda D. Jellum

Simply stated, ... [s]eparation of powers analysis examines the roles the legislature, the judiciary, and the executive should respectively have in creating, interpreting, and implementing law.... Ultimately, this analysis involves categorizing governmental power, allocating authority for that power to one of three institutions, and identifying which personnel should exercise that power in a way that best protects individual liberties and prevents tyranny.

---

[*] Copyright Linda D. Jellum and University of California at Los Angeles Law Review. Used by Permission.

Legal scholars have divided the Supreme Court's separation of powers doctrine into two approaches. The formalist approach emphasizes the need to maintain three distinct branches of government based on function. The functionalist approach emphasizes the need to maintain pragmatic flexibility to respond to modern government[al needs]....

Definitional directives, which define terms for one or more statutes, do not violate formal or functional separation of powers.... When the legislature enacts a definitional directive, the legislature is "affecting legal rights." Therefore, definitional directives are legislative in nature. To understand why they are legislative, assume that a legislature defined "buildings" in an arson statute to include vehicles. Assume further that the legislature defined "vehicles" to include bulldozers. Then, for purposes of this statute, a bulldozer would be a building (strange, but true). In this situation, the legislature has altered legal rights: Whereas normally bulldozers are not considered buildings and the arson statute would not protect their owners, the legislature has changed the norm by including bulldozers within the protected class. Simply put, the legislature has changed the bulldozer owner's legal status....

Because the legislature is performing a legislative act by defining terms, definitional directives do not violate formalist separation of powers.... Further, definitional directives do not violate functionalist separation of powers because these directives neither encroach impermissibly on a core judicial function nor aggrandize the legislative role. Practically speaking, "[l]egislative definitions or redefinitions of statutory terms are commonplace and generally quite desirable, as they render the legislature's intent more precise and easily discoverable." ...

[In contrast, theoretical directives are likely unconstitutional.] "Can Congress limit the Court's sources of knowledge?" This is precisely the question that theoretical directives raise. Theoretical directives, which identify what evidence a court may consider when interpreting statutes, seem to violate both the formalist and functionalist approaches to separation of powers notwithstanding pragmatic reasons supporting their use....

Theoretical directives violate formalist separation of powers quite simply because the legislature is performing a judicial act. Unlike definitional directives, theoretical directives do not affect legal rights. Indeed, affecting legal rights is not the purpose of theoretical directives. Instead, the purpose of theoretical directives is to tell the judiciary what evidence to consider when interpreting statutes.

Interpreting statutes is the quintessential judicial act. Determining what evidence to consider when deciding what a statute means is essential to the interpretive process because the court is determining how it will perform its function. When a legislature crafts a theoretical directive..., the legislature is not legislating; the legislature is not trying to alter legal rights. Rather, the legislature is trying to control the judicial function: interpreting statutes. "If officials in either of the [executive or legislative] branches were given final say over statutory interpretation ... or legislators could determine the meaning of their own statutes—this would sabotage both the constitutionally prescribed lawmaking procedures and the constitutional separation of powers." Saying what the law means is the judiciary's job. Hence, when the legislature enacts a theoretical directive, it is performing a judicial act, which is unconstitutional under formalist separation of powers.

[Additionally,] theoretical directives raise concerns under functionalism because they impermissibly allow Congress to intrude into a core judicial function and aggrandize its role while simultaneously contracting the roles of the judiciary and the executive....

First, theoretical directives impermissibly intrude on the judiciary's core function to interpret the law or "say what the law means." Saying what the law means is not just one core function of the judiciary; it is the most central constitutionally assigned function of the judiciary, as found in the vesting clause. As such, the Court should guard it jealously....

If the judiciary cannot tell the legislature or the executive how to do their respective jobs, and if the legislature cannot tell the executive how to do its job, and if the executive cannot tell the judiciary or legislature how to do their respective jobs, why then can the legislature tell the judiciary how to do its job? Why is it permissible for the legislature to tell the judiciary to look only at certain information when deciding what words mean?

Congress's role in lawmaking is to be as clear as it can be, given political and linguistic limitations. The judicial role is to take those words and give them the meaning Congress tried to convey within a particular factual setting. Certainly, the legislature can have a voice in interpretation and, indeed, already does. Congress may inform itself of how legislation is being implemented through the ordinary means of legislative investigation and oversight. If the legislature disagrees with the result in any particular case, it can legislatively overrule the decision. In this way, statutory interpretation becomes an ongoing dialogue between the judiciary and the legislature.

Allowing Congress a greater role at the front end of the judicial interpretation process, a role in controlling how statutes are interpreted, would allow Congress to become master of the interpretive process. Courts should be able to choose the method that, in their view, best accomplishes the job of interpreting statutes, just as the legislature chooses the best method for drafting statutes. Hence, theoretical directives allow the legislature to unduly encroach into the judicial sphere.

Notes and Questions

(1) *Master of the House.* Constitutions delegate to the legislature the power to make the laws and delegate to the courts the power to interpret them. When the legislature tells the judiciary how to interpret statutes, it arguably usurps the judicial power. *See Bd. of County Comm'rs v. Vail Assocs., Inc.,* 19 P.3d 1263, 1273 (Colo. 2001) (explaining that the court would construe a legislative directive as to what a statute meant to be "advisory, not binding" in order to avoid constitutional issues); *but see* Jonathan R. Siegel, *The Use of Legislative History in a System of Separated Powers,* 53 VAND. L. REV. 1457, 1501 (2000) (arguing that these directives do not violate separation of powers). Do you believe that statutory directives violate separation of powers by interfering with the delegation to the judiciary to decide cases and, in doing so, to interpret statutes?

(2) *Interpretive Directives.* We excised the portion of the article above which evaluates the constitutionality of interpretive directives, those directives that tell the judiciary how to interpret a statute or statutes. Consider, for example, whether it would violate separation of powers for a legislature to include an interpretive directive in a statute indicating that the statute should be interpreted liberally. *E.g.,* KAN. STAT. ANN. §60-1713 (2004) ("This act is remedial in nature and its purpose is to settle and provide relief from uncertainty and insecurity with respect to disputed rights, status and other legal relations and should be liberally construed and administered to achieve that purpose."). If you think such a statute would not violate separation of powers, consider whether a directive requiring courts to construe all statutes liberally would do so.

Some argue that *specific* interpretive directives—those directives that tell the judiciary how to interpret a specific statute—do not violate separation of powers, while general interpretive directives—those directives that tell the judiciary how to interpret many statutes—do violate separation of powers:

> General interpretive directives are unconstitutional because they interfere with the process of interpretation, much like theoretical directives, allowing for legislative aggrandizement. In contrast, specific interpretive directives seem less troubling because they are designed to promote specific policy choices arrived at via the constitutionally prescribed legislative process.

Jellum, *supra*, at 890. Do you agree or is the distinction too formalistic?

(3) *Other Constitutional Concerns Regarding Directives.* Consider whether a legislature could constitutionally direct courts to ignore the rule of lenity—which says that if a criminal statute is ambiguous it must be construed narrowly—in criminal cases? *E.g.*, Cal. Penal Code §4 (West 2004) ("The rule of the common law, that penal statutes are to be strictly construed, has no application to this Code."); N.Y. Penal Law §5.00 (McKinney 2004) ("The general rule that a penal statute is to be strictly construed does not apply..., but the provisions herein must be construed according to the fair import of their terms to promote justice and effect the objects of the law.") If such directives seem troubling, why is that so? Is it because of separation of powers or because of due process concerns? Note that the constitutional concerns raised by these directives are not limited to separation of powers.

There are no settled answers to these issues. There is, however, clearly tension between the constitutional obligation of courts to interpret statutes and legislative efforts to direct that task.

2. State Legislative Directives

In contrast to the federal legislature, several state legislatures have enacted theoretical directives mandating the interpretative approach that state judges must follow. Despite the argument that textualism reduces judicial activism, not every state legislature that has adopted a theoretical directive has chosen textualism or even eliminated consideration of extratextual sources. We provide some examples below.

a. Textualist Statutory Directives

The majority of states that have enacted general-approach directives have enacted directives that tell courts to focus on plain meaning. As we saw earlier, Connecticut's legislature specifically rejected the purposivist approach adopted by its judiciary in *Courchesne* and instead invoked textualism:

> The meaning of a statute shall, in the first instance, be ascertained from the text of the statute itself and its relationship to other statutes. If, after examining such text and considering such relationship, the meaning of such text is plain and unambiguous and does not yield absurd or unworkable results, extratextual evidence of the meaning of the statute shall not be considered.

Conn. Gen. Stat. Ann. §1-2z (West 2005); *accord*, 1 Pa. Cons. Stat. §1921(b) (2004); *see also* 2003 Pa. Cons. Stat. §1939 (2004) ("The comments or report of the commission, committee, association or other entity which drafted a statute may be consulted in the construction or application of the original provisions of the statute if such comments or report were published or otherwise generally available prior to the consideration of the statute by the General Assembly, but the text of the statute shall control in the event of conflict between its text and such comments or report.")

Iowa also codified a textualist approach, directing judicial consideration of intent only if a statute is ambiguous:

> *If a statute is ambiguous*, the court, in determining the intention of the legislature, may consider among other matters:
>
> (1) The object sought to be attained.
>
> (2) The circumstances under which the statute was enacted.
>
> (3) The legislative history.
>
> (4) The common law or former statutory provisions, including laws upon the same or similar subjects.
>
> (5) The consequences of a particular construction.
>
> (6) The administrative construction of the statute.
>
> (7) The preamble or statement of policy.

IOWA CODE ANN. § 4.6 (West 2005) (emphasis added); *accord* COLO. REV. STAT. § 2-4-203 (2005); HAW. REV. STAT. ANN. § 1-15 (LexisNexis 2004); OHIO REV. CODE ANN. § 1.49 (West 2005); N.D. CENT. CODE § 1-02-39 (2003). What should an Iowa court do if a statute is absurd? The statute doesn't say.

b. *Intentionalist and Purposivist Statutory Directives*

Not all state legislatures have adopted a textualist approach, however. New York, for example, seems firmly in the intentionalist camp:

> a. Generally
>
> The primary consideration of the courts in the construction of statutes is to ascertain and give effect to the intention of the Legislature.
>
> b. Ascertainment of intention
>
> The intention of the Legislature is first to be sought from a literal reading of the act itself, but if the meaning is still not clear the intent may be ascertained from such facts and through such rules as may, in connection with the language, legitimately reveal it.

N.Y. STATUTES LAW §§ 92(a) & (b) (McKinney 2005). The comments to this statute state:

> Since the intention of the Legislature, embodied in a statute, is the law, in the construction of statutes the basic rule of procedure and the primary consideration of the courts is to ascertain and give effect to the intention of the Legislature. Hence the legislative intent is said to be the "fundamental rule," "the great principle which is to control," "the cardinal rule" and "the grand central light in which all statutes must be read." So it is the duty of courts to adopt a construction of a statute that will bring it into harmony with the Constitution and with legislative intent, and no narrow construction of a statute may thwart the legislative design.
>
> The intent of the Legislature is controlling and must be given force and effect, regardless of the circumstance that inconvenience, hardship, or injustice may result. Indeed the Legislature's intent must be ascertained and effectuated whatever may be the opinion of the judiciary as to the wisdom, expediency, or pol-

icy of the statute, and whatever excesses or omissions may be found in the statute. The courts do not sit in review of the discretion of the Legislature and may not substitute their judgment for that of the lawmaking body.

Id. cmt. a.

Texas has a unique statute:

In construing a statute, *whether or not the statute is considered ambiguous on its face,* a court may consider among other matters the:

(1) object sought to be attained;

(2) circumstances under which the statute was enacted;

(3) legislative history;

(4) common law or former statutory provisions, including laws on the same or similar subjects;

(5) consequences of a particular construction;

(6) administrative construction of the statute; and

(7) title (caption), preamble, and emergency provision.

Tex. Gov't Code § 311.023 (West 2005) (emphasis added); *but see State v. Muller,* 829 S.W.2d 805, 811 n.7 (Tex. Crim. App. 1992) (applying this statute, the court noted that it was "important to restate again that under our established rules for statutory construction we look to a statute's legislative history *only* if the plain meaning of the literal text of that statute is ambiguous or leads to highly improbable results").

Georgia specifically directs courts to take an approach that mixes textualism, intentionalism, and purposivism:

(a) In all interpretations of statutes, the courts shall look diligently for the intention of the General Assembly, keeping in view at all times the old law, the evil, and the remedy....

(b) In all interpretations of statutes, the ordinary signification shall be applied to all words, except words of art or words connected with a particular trade or subject matter, which shall have the signification attached to them by experts in such trade or with reference to such subject matter.

Ga. Code Ann. §§ 1-3-1(a) & (b) (West 2005).

Notes and Questions

(1) *Are Texas Legislators Too Nice?* Some suggest that textualism is more deferential to a legislature than intentionalism or purposivism. If so, then why did the Texas legislature enact a statute that directs courts to consider the purpose of the statute, its legislative history, and essentially all other facts and circumstances? Was the legislature giving up power to the courts, reining them in, or neither?

(2) *Georgia.* Look again at the Georgia statute. Though acknowledging the statute, Georgia courts claim to follow the plain meaning approach. *Busch v. State,* 523 S.E.2d 21, 23 (Ga. 1999) ("If the words of a statute, however, are plain and capable of having but one meaning, and do not produce any absurd, impractical, or contradictory results, then this Court is bound to follow the meaning of those words."). The courts have tried to reconcile their approach with the statute:

> In construing a statute, our goal is to determine its legislative purpose. In this regard, a court must first focus on the statute's text. In order to discern the meaning of the words of a statute, the reader must look at the context in which the statute was written, remembering at all times that "the meaning of a sentence may be more than that of the separate words, as a melody is more than the notes." *If the words of a statute, however, are plain and capable of having but one meaning, and do not produce any absurd, impractical, or contradictory results, then this Court is bound to follow the meaning of those words.* If, on the other hand, the words of the statute are ambiguous, then this Court must construe the statute, keeping in mind the purpose of the statute and "the old law, the evil, and the remedy." O.C.G.A. 1-3-1(a).

State v. Brown, 551 S.E.2d 773, 775 (Ga. Ct. App. 2001) (emphasis added). Do you believe the Georgia courts are following the statute?

3. Interpreting Statutory Directives

In the last section, we examined the constitutionality of legislative directives. We turn now to a different issue: What happens when the directive itself creates ambiguity? Most commonly, this problem occurs when a directive is specific to one statute. For example, the federal "RICO" statute—the Racketeer Influenced and Corrupt Organization Act—directs that its "provisions ... shall be liberally construed to effectuate [the bill's] remedial purposes...." Organized Crime Control Act of 1970, Pub. L. No. 91-452, § 904(a), 84 Stat. 941, 947 (reproduced following 18 U.S.C. § 1961 (2005)).* Ironically enough, this statute-specific directive in RICO has required interpretation: the "applicability of the liberal construction standard has been questioned in *criminal* RICO cases in view of the general canon of interpretation that ambiguities in criminal statutes are to be construed in favor of leniency...." *Keystone Ins. Co. v. Houghton*, 863 F.2d 1125, 1128 n.3 (3d Cir. 1988), *overruled on other grounds*, *Klehr v. A. O. Smith, Corp.*, 521 U.S. 179 (1997). While the conflict between the statutory directive in the RICO statute and the rule of lenity has not been completely resolved, one court suggested that at a "minimum the liberal construction language requires that we resist the temptation to restrict *civil* RICO." *Keystone Ins. Co.*, 863 F.2d at 1128 (emphasis added).

Thus, directives can create, rather than resolve, ambiguity. The following case required a state court to interpret a specific directive. Notice how the court struggles with how to apply the legislature's direction.

Tex. Nat. Res. & Conserv. Comm'n v. White
13 S.W.3d 819 (Tex. Ct. App. 2000)

TERRIE LIVINGSTON, JUSTICE.

... White owned ... a business adjacent to ... Smith's land.... At some point, gasoline storage tanks located beneath Smith's property began to leak, and as a result gas fumes migrated onto White's property. After White complained to authorities about the fumes, TNRCC [Texas Natural Resources Conservation Commission] came onto appellee's land

---

* Authors' footnote: RICO is a comprehensive federal anti-racketeering statute designed to eliminate corrupt influences on businesses.

and, in an effort to remedy the situation, dug a trench and installed a motor-driven pump system to remove and dissipate the vapors. Two weeks later, however, TNRCC disengaged and removed the pump system. Six days later, the fumes migrated onto White's property, pooled in the corner of her store, ignited, and caused a fire that destroyed the building.....

[The doctrine of sovereign immunity protects the State of Texas, its agencies and its officials, from lawsuits for damages absent the State's consent to be sued. Hence, as a state agency, TNRCC is generally immune from suit. However, the Texas Tort Claims Act ("TTCA") waived immunity for property damage caused by a state agency's "operation or use of" motor-driven equipment.]

In 1976, the Texas Supreme Court held that "the statute [the TTCA] calls for liberal construction to effectuate its purposes." Indeed, the original version of the TTCA contained a provision calling for the liberal construction of its provisions to achieve the purposes of the act. [This act was repealed in 1985]. Unfortunately, without clear legislative explanation of the purposes of the act, such a call is inherently ambiguous. It is unclear whether the legislature intended the waiver provisions to be liberally construed, or whether governmental immunity should be liberally construed through narrow interpretation of the waiver provisions.[2] ...

Hence, we will interpret the TTCA waiver provisions broadly, but within reason and while keeping in mind that the legislature did not intend a general waiver of governmental immunity.....

[The court then evaluated the pleadings to determine whether White pleaded a cause of action.] We agree with TNRCC's first point that governmental immunity may properly be asserted in a plea to the jurisdiction. However, at this preliminary stage, before discovery has concluded, and under the appropriate standards for reviewing a trial court's denial of the State's assertion of immunity in a plea to the jurisdiction, we cannot say that White's pleadings are insufficient to state a cause of action or to raise the issue of waiver under the TTCA. We ... affirm.....

Notes and Questions

(1) *The Meaning of "Liberal Interpretation."* Why is the directive to give the statute a "liberal interpretation" subject to uncertainty here?

(2) *The Second Statutory Directive.* In footnote 2, the majority noted that the legislature had added a provision to the Texas Government Code directing that *all* statutes be liberally construed. According to the majority, this general interpretive directive did not resolve the conflict regarding how the immunity act should be interpreted. Why not?

(3) *On Appeal.* On appeal, the Texas Supreme Court reversed, holding that although TNRCC's motor-driven pump was "motor-driven equipment," plaintiff failed to assert that its "use," rather than "lack of use," caused her injury. Thus, she failed to demonstrate that the trial court had jurisdiction to hear her case. *Tex. Nat. Res. Conserv. Comm'n v. White*, 46 S.W.3d 864 (Tex. 2001). The statute at issue specifically covered "operation or use of" such equipment. In refusing to interpret the waiver to include non-use, the court stated: "We have refused to broaden section 101.021's waiver provision to include both use and non-use because doing so would be tantamount to abolishing governmental immu-

---

2. We note that although the government code now contains general provisions calling for the liberal construction of statutes, that provision is no less vulnerable to these ambiguities. *See* Tex. Gov't Code Ann. § 312.006(a) (Vernon 1998).

nity, contrary to the limited waiver the Legislature clearly intended." Did the Texas Supreme Court give a liberal or narrow interpretation to the statute? Unlike the appellate court, it did not find it necessary to determine whether the statute should be narrowly or broadly interpreted. Why not?

Problem 16-4

Assume you are a Texas legislator. You have a legislative aid working for you whom you believe to be an outstanding attorney. Your aid graduated from an unaccredited law school in another state, then took and passed that state's bar examination. Under the rules currently in place in Texas, your aid cannot sit for the bar because she has not graduated from an accredited law school. Nor will she ever be able to waive the bar examination requirement unless she attends an accredited law school. You believe that the rule should be changed to allow anyone who has passed a bar exam in any other state to be able to waive into Texas' bar without the need for an examination.

Ignoring any possible separation of powers concern, draft a statute to accomplish your goal. Assume that the Texas theoretical directive above applies. Assume also that the Texas Bar will be very opposed to this bill. Many Texas attorneys view the bar exam as a rite of passage and as an effective constraint on the number of attorneys able to practice in Texas. Additionally, the State Board of Bar Examiners will also be vehemently opposed to such a change. Therefore, you anticipate strong opposition during the debates. But you do know that many legislators do not support the current practice of requiring all licensed out-of-state attorneys to take another bar exam simply to practice in Texas.

Here are some questions you should consider while drafting: (1) Will you include a purpose or findings clause? (2) Will you add language directing the bill be narrowly or broadly interpreted? (3) Will you include a definitions section? (4) Will you permit graduates of accredited Wisconsin schools—who are admitted to Wisconsin's bar without taking a bar exam (otherwise known as the diploma privilege)—to waive in also? (5) Who or what will enforce your bill?

If instead you lived in the state of Connecticut, would you draft your bill any differently? If you lived in Alaska? New York?

Chapter 17

The Role of Agencies

A. Giving Deference to Agency Interpretations

For most of this text, we have watched as Congress has enacted a statute and then left resolution of any dispute about the statute's meaning to the courts. But often, Congress delegates power to federal agencies to act. Federal agencies have no authority to act until Congress grants, or *delegates*, power to them. Congress delegates power by enacting statutes—called enabling statutes—directing agencies to accomplish specific objectives, such as keeping the food supply safe. To accomplish these specific objectives, agencies often must interpret the enabling statute—and, potentially, other statutes related to that objective. For example, if Congress directed an agency to "regulate unsafe drugs," then the agency would have to interpret all three words. Hence, federal agencies play an important role in statutory interpretation. Similarly, state agencies, which must interpret statutes enacted by state legislatures, play an important role in interpreting state statutes.

Why would Congress delegate power to agencies? One answer is that Congress might wish to take advantage of an agency's expertise in the agency's area of authority. Consider the Environmental Protection Agency ("EPA") and the environment. Additionally, agencies may be better able than Congress to adjust policy expeditiously to address changing circumstances (such as a salmonella scare) and political opinion (such as a change in the executive). Moreover, agencies' personnel are more politically accountable than judges, who have life-time tenure. Finally, judges have limited powers: They can only resolve disputes. They do not have investigative powers, and they cannot prospectively regulate. Agencies can do all three: adjudicate, regulate, and investigate. When doing so, an agency will likely interpret a statute.

Courts review agency interpretations of statutes. What should courts do when confronted with an agency's interpretation? Should an agency's expertise, responsiveness, and political accountability affect a court's willingness to defer to the agency's interpretation of a statute? In other words, when an agency interprets a statute, should courts be required to accept the agency's interpretation; be required to review the interpretation without giving any deference to the agency's view; or be required to give some—and, if so, how much—deference to the agency's interpretation?

The answer to the question of how much deference courts give to agency interpretations has both practical and constitutional dimensions. First, the practical dimension: Today, all aspects of our society—business, social, and legal—are, to a greater degree than ever before, subject to agency regulation. As we pointed out earlier, modern society has seen tremendous growth in the number and complexity of administrative agencies. Because agency interpretations are so common, you should know when a court must adopt or may reject an agency's interpretation of a statute.

Second, the constitutional dimension: To the extent courts defer to agency interpretations, power may shift from the judicial and legislative branches to the executive branch. The Constitution requires cooperation from members of Congress and the executive for legislation to pass. Agencies do not play a role in a bill's passage, yet their subsequent interpretations may profoundly alter the bargains struck during this process. Suppose, for example, that Congress and the President enact a bill that delegates to the EPA the power to define and protect endangered species and their habitat. Suppose further that environmentally friendly Democrats control Congress by a one-vote majority. But the Republican president is more concerned with furthering business interests. Agencies operate within the executive branch, subject to the president's control. In our example, the EPA presumably would adopt policies that further the president's agenda of protecting business interests rather than the Democratic agenda of protecting the environment. This example is not entirely hypothetical. *See, e.g., Northern Spotted Owl v. Hodel*, 716 F. Supp 479 (W.D. Wash. 1988) (addressing the EPA's refusal to list the Northern Spotted Owl as an endangered species). This example shows that delegating power to agencies can alter the bargain struck during the legislative process.

Arguably, delegation may also provide the president with lawmaking power above that contemplated by the Constitution, for agencies, not courts, interpret ambiguous statutes when Congress delegates. And, as we said, the president controls agencies. Congress does retain some oversight over agencies, for it can hold hearings and amend enabling legislation. But ultimately, these control methods are slow and not always effective, especially when Congress does not have a veto-proof majority.

For these reasons, Congress attempted, in the 1970s, to assert more control over agencies with the legislative veto. The legislative veto was, at one time, Congress's favored method of trying to control the "'Imperial Presidency,' resulting from [an] over-aggrandizement of presidential power." Bernard Schwartz, *Curiouser and Curiouser: The Supreme Court's Separation of Powers Wonderland*, 65 Notre Dame L. Rev. 587, 598 (1990) (quoting Arthur M. Schlessinger, Jr., The Imperial Presidency (1973)). Legislative veto provisions in statutes provided a procedure whereby Congress delegated authority to an agency, but reserved for itself the power to oversee and veto the agency's use of that delegated authority. The Court held the legislative veto unconstitutional in *INS v. Chadha*, 462 U.S. 919, 959 (1983), because the constitutionally prescribed procedures for lawmaking—bicameral passage and presentment—were not followed. Hence, Congress lost one method for ensuring agency accountability. As you read this chapter, consider whether this power shift factored into the Court's analysis of the appropriate level of deference to give to agency interpretations of ambiguous statutory language.

Until 1984, the Supreme Court had not clearly delineated the appropriate level of deference that a court should give an agency's interpretation of a statute. Before 1984, whether courts would defer to agency interpretations turned on "the thoroughness evident in [the agency's] consideration, the validity of its reasoning, its consistency with earlier and later pronouncements, and all those factors which give it power to persuade, if lacking power to control." *Skidmore v. Swift & Co.*, 323 U.S. 134, 140 (1944). This minimal level of deference is known today as *Skidmore* deference. Also, at that time, some courts looked to see if the agency opinion had "'warrant in the record' and a reasonable basis in law." *NLRB v. Hearst Publ'ns, Inc.*, 322 U.S. 111, 131 (1944). Thus, while deference was accorded, the amount varied depending on the circumstances. In effect, agencies faced a balancing test: The more consistent, thorough, and considered their interpretations were, the more likely a court would defer to their interpretation.

In 1984, the Supreme Court decided the most cited administrative law case of all time, *Chevron U.S.A., Inc. v. Natural Resources Defense Council, Inc.*, 467 U.S. 837 (1984). The Court held that judges must defer to an agency's interpretation of an *ambiguous* statute — so long as the interpretation was reasonable — when that interpretation was made pursuant to an agency's rulemaking process.

1. Chevron's *Two-Step Test*

In *Chevron*, the Court identified a two-step process for affording deference. Be sure that you can identify both steps and the three reasons why the Court determined that deference was required.

Chevron U.S.A., Inc. v. Natural Res. Def. Council, Inc.
467 U.S. 837 (1984)

JUSTICE STEVENS delivered the opinion of the Court.

In the Clean Air Act Amendments of 1977, Congress enacted certain requirements applicable to States that had not achieved the national air quality standards established by the Environmental Protection Agency (EPA) pursuant to earlier legislation. The amended Clean Air Act required these "nonattainment" States to establish a permit program regulating "new or modified major stationary sources" of air pollution. Generally, a permit may not be issued for a new or modified major stationary source unless several stringent conditions are met.[1] The EPA regulation promulgated to implement this permit requirement allows a State to adopt a plantwide definition of the term "stationary source."[2] Under this definition, an existing plant that contains several pollution-emitting devices may install or modify one piece of equipment without meeting the permit conditions if the alteration will not increase the total emissions from the plant. The question presented by these cases is whether EPA's decision to allow States to treat all of the pollution-emitting devices within the same industrial grouping as though they were encased within a single "bubble" is based on a reasonable construction of the statutory term "stationary source." ...

[The lower Court] set aside the regulations embodying the bubble concept as contrary to law. ... We now reverse. ...

When a court reviews an agency's construction of the statute which it administers, it is confronted with two questions. First, always, is the question whether Congress has directly spoken to the precise question at issue. If the intent of Congress is clear, that is the end of the matter; for the court, as well as the agency, must give effect to the unambigu-

---

1. Section 172(b)(6), 42 U.S.C. §7502(b)(6), provides:
   "The plan provisions required by subsection (a) shall ... (6) require permits for the construction and operation of new or modified major *stationary sources* in accordance with section 173 (relating to permit requirements)" (emphasis added).

2. "(i) 'Stationary source' means any building, structure, facility, or installation which emits or may emit any air pollutant subject to regulation under the Act. (ii) 'Building, structure, facility, or installation' means all of the pollutant-emitting activities which belong to the same industrial grouping, are located on one or more contiguous or adjacent properties, and are under the control of the same person (or persons under common control) except the activities of any vessel." 40 C.F.R. §§51.18(j)(1)(i) and (ii) (1983).

ously expressed intent of Congress.[9] If, however, the court determines Congress has not directly addressed the precise question at issue, the court does not simply impose its own construction on the statute, as would be necessary in the absence of an administrative interpretation. Rather, if the statute is silent or ambiguous with respect to the specific issue, the question for the court is whether the agency's answer is based on a permissible construction of the statute.

The power of an administrative agency to administer a congressionally created ... program necessarily requires the formulation of policy and the making of rules to fill any gap left, implicitly or explicitly, by Congress. If Congress has explicitly left a gap for the agency to fill, there is an express delegation of authority to the agency to elucidate a specific provision of the statute by regulation. Such legislative regulations are given controlling weight unless they are arbitrary, capricious, or manifestly contrary to the statute. Sometimes the legislative delegation to an agency on a particular question is implicit rather than explicit. In such a case, a court may not substitute its own construction of a statutory provision for a reasonable interpretation made by the administrator of an agency.

We have long recognized that considerable weight should be accorded to an executive department's construction of a statutory scheme it is entrusted to administer, and the principle of deference to administrative interpretations has been consistently followed by this Court whenever decision as to the meaning or reach of a statute has involved reconciling conflicting policies, and a full understanding of the force of the statutory policy in the given situation has depended upon more than ordinary knowledge respecting the matters subjected to agency regulations.

> ... If this choice represents a reasonable accommodation of conflicting policies that were committed to the agency's care by the statute, we should not disturb it unless it appears from the statute or its legislative history that the accommodation is not one that Congress would have sanctioned.

In light of these well-settled principles it is clear that the Court of Appeals misconceived the nature of its role in reviewing the regulations at issue. Once it determined, after its own examination of the legislation, that Congress did not actually have an intent regarding the applicability of the bubble concept to the permit program, the question before it was not whether in its view the concept is "inappropriate" in the general context of a program designed to improve air quality, but whether the Administrator's view that it is appropriate in the context of this particular program is a reasonable one. Based on the examination of the legislation and its history ... we agree with the Court of Appeals that Congress did not have a specific intention on the applicability of the bubble concept in these cases, and conclude that the EPA's use of that concept here is a reasonable policy choice for the agency to make.

In these cases the Administrator's interpretation represents a reasonable accommodation of manifestly competing interests and is entitled to deference: the regulatory scheme is technical and complex, the agency considered the matter in a detailed and reasoned fashion, and the decision involves reconciling conflicting policies. Congress intended to accommodate both interests, but did not do so itself on the level of specificity presented by these cases. Perhaps that body consciously desired the Administrator to strike the balance at this level, thinking that those with great expertise and charged with responsibil-

---

9. The judiciary is the final authority on issues of statutory construction and must reject administrative constructions which are contrary to clear congressional intent. If a court, employing traditional tools of statutory construction, ascertains that Congress had an intention on the precise question at issue, that intention is the law and must be given effect.

ity for administering the provision would be in a better position to do so; perhaps it simply did not consider the question at this level; and perhaps Congress was unable to forge a coalition on either side of the question, and those on each side decided to take their chances with the scheme devised by the agency. For judicial purposes, it matters not which of these things occurred.

Judges are not experts in the field, and are not part of either political branch of the Government. Courts must, in some cases, reconcile competing political interests, but not on the basis of the judges' personal policy preferences. In contrast, an agency to which Congress has delegated policy-making responsibilities may, within the limits of that delegation, properly rely upon the incumbent administration's views of wise policy to inform its judgments. While agencies are not directly accountable to the people, the Chief Executive is, and it is entirely appropriate for this political branch of the Government to make such policy choices—resolving the competing interests which Congress itself either inadvertently did not resolve, or intentionally left to be resolved by the agency charged with the administration of the statute in light of everyday realities.

When a challenge to an agency construction of a statutory provision, fairly conceptualized, really centers on the wisdom of the agency's policy, rather than whether it is a reasonable choice within a gap left open by Congress, the challenge must fail. In such a case, federal judges—who have no constituency—have a duty to respect legitimate policy choices made by those who do. The responsibilities for assessing the wisdom of such policy choices and resolving the struggle between competing views of the public interest are not judicial ones: our Constitution vests such responsibilities in the political branches.

We hold that the EPA's definition of the term "source" is a permissible construction of the statute which seeks to accommodate progress in reducing air pollution with economic growth. The Regulations which the Administrator has adopted provide what the agency could allowably view as ... an effective reconciliation of these twofold ends....

The judgment of the Court of Appeals is reversed....

Notes and Questions

(1) *Step One.* *Chevron* created a two-step process. In the first step, a court must determine *de novo* whether Congress has unambiguously decided the issue. Whether Congress has unambiguously decided the issue or left ambiguity is a matter for the court to decide without regard to the agency's view. This first step focuses on Congress's role in drafting the statute. As the Court noted in footnote 9, "If a court, employing traditional tools of statutory construction, ascertains that Congress had an intention on the precise question at issue, that intention is the law and must be given effect." As we'll see below, despite this direction, some judges and commentators identify this first step as a search solely for textual clarity. Question whether "ambiguity" should mean precisely the same thing in this context as it does in statutory interpretation generally. Note that if the statute is not ambiguous, however determined, then no deference is due.

(2) *Step Two.* In the second step, which can be reached only if the court finds the statute is ambiguous, a court must examine how the agency resolved the ambiguity. Judicial review at this step is highly deferential, not *de novo*. At this step, the issue is not whether the court agrees with the interpretation, but whether the interpretation was reasonable. Consequently, to reject an agency's interpretation, a court must hold that either (1) Congress unambiguously decided the issue in a way that differs from the agency's resolution

or (2) Congress wrote an ambiguous statute and that the agency interpreted the statute in an unreasonable way.

(3) *Ignoring the Traditional Standard of Review.* In litigation, questions of fact are reviewed under a deferential standard of review. Deference is given to a lower court's fact findings, not just because the trial court heard the evidence first hand but also because of the functional distinction between the fact-finding process and review of that process. In contrast, appellate courts review questions of law, including statutory interpretation questions, *de novo.* No deference is given, in part, because appellate judges have greater resources to determine the law, but also because an error in the law will affect other litigants — not just those party to the dispute.

In administrative review, courts generally defer to findings of fact made by an agency. Such deference is appropriate for the same reasons that deference is appropriate for factual determinations of trial courts. Unlike review of trial courts' statutory interpretation holdings, courts also defer to an agency's interpretation of a statute, provided that the court first found that the legislature had not unambiguously addressed the issue. Why did the Supreme Court choose to defer to agencies on questions of law?

(4) *What Sources Are Relevant?* To determine whether the agency's interpretation is reasonable, what should a court look at — the text, the canons, the purpose, the legislative history, or all these things? Should any source matter more than the others? If *Chevron* requires a court to look at the identical sources under both steps, how do the steps differ? Note that challenges to agency interpretations tend to be successful, if at all, at step one. Does this suggest that there is a difference between the two steps, or might challenges be more successful at step one only because that step comes first?

(5) *Deference to Agency Interpretation of Regulations.* Agencies interpret not only statutes but their own regulations as well. An agency's interpretation of its own regulation will be rejected only when it is plainly wrong. *Bowles v. Seminole Rock & Sand Co.,* 325 U.S. 410, 414 (1945) (holding that agency interpretations of regulations are entitled to deference unless "plainly erroneous or inconsistent with the regulation"). This high level of deference is generally called either *Seminole Rock* or *Auer* deference; *Seminole Rock* preceded *Chevron,* while *Auer v. Robbins,* 519 U.S. 452 (1997), followed it. Why this more deferential standard?

Problem 17-1[*]

Susan Jones cracked her tooth while eating lunch in downtown Fort Landers, Mercer, which caused her immediate pain. Remembering that a dentist office was nearby, she dropped in and asked whether she could be seen on an emergency basis. The receptionist responded that this was a private, appointments-only dental office and asked whether Ms. Jones would like to be considered as a new patient. Ms. Jones said, "Yes please, my mouth is killing me. I have dental insurance." After checking the appointments schedule, the receptionist said that he could probably work her into the schedule in about a half-hour. He handed her a form, which contained a series of questions about her dental history and overall health. In answer to a specific inquiry on the form, she revealed that she had tested "positive" for HIV (the AIDS virus). The receptionist then told her that neither dentist would treat HIV-positive individuals and urged her to go to another facility that had a dental emergency clinic open

---

[*] This problem is based on an old exam question originally drafted by Professor Philip Frickey. Used by permission.

to the public on a walk-in basis. Ms. Jones did so and received treatment there. Ms. Jones subsequently filed a complaint with the Mercer Department of Health and Human Services (HHS), the state agency in charge of investigating discrimination claims.

The dentists contend that the discrimination statute (below) does not apply in this case. Their office is located on land owned by the business. The office is not a walk-in clinic, but rather requires patients to have an appointment. The dentists have refused to accept new or continuing patients over the years for a variety of reasons including lack of dental insurance, personality clashes, and failure to pay bills. Outside the office, over the sidewalk, a simple sign hangs. It reads "Dentists"—in large letters—next to a drawing of a tooth with a smile on it. Below the word "Dentists," in much smaller letters, the sign says: "By Appointment Only." There is a sign at the reception desk that says: "We have appointments available for new patients. Application forms for our services are available from the receptionist."

You are an investigator for HHS. Under the Mercer Human Rights Statute at issue here, HHS has the sole responsibility for enforcing the statute. Private persons, such as Ms. Jones, may not sue under the statute, but instead may only file a complaint with HHS. If HHS finds probable cause that a violation has occurred, HHS then brings suit on behalf of the aggrieved person, for whom compensatory damages may be recovered. Assume you have investigated Ms. Jones's complaint, found the facts to be as identified above, and read the relevant law below. Will you file a civil proceeding against the dentists, alleging that their refusal to treat Ms. Jones violated the Mercer Human Rights Statute? Why or why not? Assuming you file a complaint, how would a trial judge evaluate the agency's interpretation of the term "public accommodation"?

Problem Materials

Mercer Rev. Stat. § 129.211(c).

> It shall be an unlawful discriminatory practice for any person, being the owner, lessee, proprietor, manager, superintendent, agent, or employee of any place of public accommodation, to refuse, withhold from, or deny to any person any of the accommodations, advantages, facilities, or privileges thereof because of the race, creed, color, national origin, sex, disability, or marital status of such person.
>
> Clubs, businesses, and religious organizations, which are primarily private in nature, shall be exempt from the provisions of this statute.

(This statute was originally adopted in the 1940s as a race-discrimination statute, but has been amended at various times over the years to include prohibitions on other forms of discrimination, including, most recently, disability. There is no dispute that someone who is "HIV-positive" is "disabled" for purposes of this statute.)

Excerpt from Senate Report issued during the last amendment:

> Public-accommodations laws in some states were adopted as long ago as the era immediately following the Civil War. They were originally justified as being rooted in the common-law notion that certain callings—those that hold themselves out to, and are relied upon by, the public at large—have a "quasi-public character" that should include the obligation to serve the general public. The early statutes were usually limited to innkeepers, common carriers, theaters, and other places of public amusement. Over the years, the coverage of most of these statutes has grown bit by bit, by legislative amendment, to ensure that all people are treated fairly and equally by anyone serving the public generally.

One major exception to this trend is California, where, a couple of decades ago, this piecemeal approach was jettisoned in favor of a statute that simply states that all persons are entitled to the "full and equal accommodations, advantages, facilities, privileges, or services of all business establishments of every kind whatsoever." Finding California's approach too broad, the committee does not adopt it, but instead recommends [the language in Mercer Stat. § 129.211(c)]. This bill will protect both the rights of citizens who use places of public accommodation and the rights of private entities to be free from federal regulation.

Rule 1t-322.121, M.A.C. [Mercer Admin. Code].

The term "place of public accommodation" includes, inns; taverns; hotels; motels; restaurants; saloons; bars; or any facility where alcohol or food is sold; wholesale and retail stores and establishments dealing with goods or services of any kind; swimming pools; laundries; barber shops; beauty parlors; theaters; motion picture houses; music halls; skating rinks; amusement and recreation parks; bowling alleys; golf and mini-golf courses; billiard and pool parlors; clinics; hospitals; pharmacies; parking garages; all public conveyances operated on land or water or in the air, as well as the stations and terminals thereof; and all similar places open to the public.

"Place of public accommodation" shall not include any business, institution, or profession, which is wholly private in nature, but does include all businesses that serve the public, even if only in limited fashion.

The dictionary definition for "accommodation" is:

1) The act of accommodating or the state of being accommodated.

2) Something that meets a need; a convenience.

3) Accommodations

a) Room and board; lodgings.

b) A seat, compartment, or room on a public vehicle.

The dictionary definition for "public" is:

1) Of, concerning, or affecting the community or the people: *the public good.*

2) Maintained for or used by the people or community: *a public park....*

4) Participated in or attended by the people or community: "Opinions are formed in a process of open discussion and public debate."

B. The Relevance of the Type of Agency Action

The federal Administrative Procedure Act ("APA") governs the way federal administrative agencies can act. Most states have similar statutes governing the actions of state agencies. The text of the APA is at Title 5 of the United States Code, beginning at Section 500.

Under the APA, agencies "fill the gaps" in statutes by interpreting them in many ways. Three of them matter here: adjudication, legislative rulemaking, and non-legislative rulemaking. An agency might interpret a statute during any of these three processes. The way an agency acts affects the level of deference courts give to the interpretation. Thus, we next explore each way in more detail.

1. Adjudication

When an agency adjudicates, it may hold a formal, judicial-type hearing or act less formally. Formal administrative hearings resemble a civil trial with many of the same procedural accoutrements; the main differences between civil trials and formal administrative hearings are that (1) administrative hearings take place before an administrative law judge rather than a trial judge and (2) the rules of evidence do not apply in administrative hearings. While the APA identifies a number of required procedures for formal adjudication, other statutes may add procedural requirements. Although we oversimplify, for our purposes, you may consider formal administrative hearings to be the equivalent of civil trials.

While *formal* adjudication resembles civil adjudication, *informal* adjudication is altogether different. Very few procedures are required. The APA requires only two things when an agency acts pursuant to informal adjudication. First, the agency must decide the issue promptly and, second, the agency must notify the affected party of its decision and provide a brief statement of the reasons for the denial. 5 U.S.C. §§ 552(e) & 553(e) (2001). Informal adjudication is that simple.

Hence, an informal adjudication can be as straightforward as an agency administrator approving an individual's application for a hunting permit. While the APA requires only minimal procedures for informal adjudication, other statutes or the U.S. Constitution may require additional procedures. Even then, however, informal adjudication procedures are generally minimal compared to formal adjudication. However, during either formal or informal adjudication an agency may interpret a statute. The level of deference courts give to agency interpretations reached through these two different processes varies.

2. Legislative Rulemaking

Agencies also interpret statutes when they promulgate, or enact, regulations. Here again, agencies may act either formally or informally. Formal rulemaking resembles formal agency adjudication, meaning there is an administrative hearing with trial-like procedures. Oddly, the same procedural rules apply to both formal rulemaking and formal adjudication. The difference between the two is that at the end of the rulemaking process, the agency promulgates a regulation that applies broadly rather than an administrative opinion that binds only the parties to the proceeding. Formal rulemaking is less common at the federal level than formal adjudication and informal rulemaking. Yet, formal rulemaking is commonly used in the states.

Because Congress does not regularly require agencies to use the formal rulemaking process, informal rulemaking (or notice-and-comment rulemaking, as it is also known) is the norm. Notice-and-comment rulemaking requires an agency first to publish notice of a proposed regulation in the Federal Register, in which the agency solicits comments from the public about the proposed regulation. The agency then collects and responds to comments by publishing both in the Federal Register, explaining why it accepted or rejected the proposed changes to the regulation. At the end of this notice-and-comment process (which often takes years), the agency usually promulgates a regulation.

Notice-and-comment rulemaking is informal rulemaking in name only. The APA requires the agency to follow prescribed, time-consuming, and detailed procedures to adopt a regulation. But the APA is not the only source of procedural rules; many executive orders and statutes add procedural requirements beyond those required by the APA. The number and variety of additional procedures has led commentators to lament the slowing-down, or ossification, of the rulemaking process. Whether ossification is actually occurring is currently being debated. *See, e.g.,* Stephen M. Johnson, *Ossification's Demise? An Empirical Analysis of EPA Rulemaking from 2001–2005,* 38 ENVTL. L.J. 767 (2008) (noting that the rulemaking process *after publication* of a proposed rule has not been ossified, while acknowledging that it was possible that the process prior to the publication of a proposed rule may have been ossified).

3. Non-Legislative Rulemaking

Agencies also act in other less formal ways; for example, an agency may respond to a regulated entity's question about the meaning of a regulation or statute. Under the APA, the agency's written response is a non-legislative, interpretative rule, not a regulation or adjudication. Hence, the agency need not follow either formal or notice-and-comment rule-making processes. Indeed, the only required procedure under the APA for a non-legislative rule is that the agency publish the rule in the Federal Register or otherwise make it available to the public.

In addition, an agency may issue enforcement guidelines or publish procedural and policy manuals. The APA exempts from the notice-and-comment requirements three kinds of non-legislative rules: interpretative rules, general statements of policy, and rules of agency procedure and organization. 5 U.S.C. § 553(b)(3)(A). Because agencies need not follow a procedurally prescribed process when they enact non-legislative and procedural rules, those rules are easily modified and are not binding on the agency. The agency can change its mind about an interpretation or policy issued in a non-legislative rule immediately and easily. Because the process to enact these non-legislative rules is so much simpler, agencies increasingly opt for this process even when notice-and-comment procedures are statutorily mandated. Because notice-and-comment rulemaking requires agencies to jump through numerous hoops, many agencies avoid it altogether and use non-legislative rulemaking. Sometimes the agency's choice is proper under the APA, and sometimes it is not.

You likely won't fully appreciate the differences in these processes at this point. What should be clear, however, is that an agency can act with varying degrees of procedural formality. As you will see below, judicial deference to an agency interpretation seems to increase as the formality of the decision-making process under review increases.

Chevron addressed the degree of deference to be given to notice-and-comment rulemaking. (Remember that even though notice-and-comment rulemaking is called "informal rulemaking," the process involves defined procedures.) After *Chevron,* the Court initially applied its two-step framework to all agency interpretations. Later, however, the Court resurrected *Skidmore*'s less deferential "power-to-persuade" standard for review for non-legislative rulemaking. *See Christensen v. Harris County,* 529 U.S. 576, 587 (2000). The question for the Court in *Christensen* was whether a court should give *Chevron* deference to an interpretation the U.S. Department of Labor reached in an opinion letter (*i.e.,* a non-legislative, interpretative rule). A majority of the Court held that the agency's interpretation was not entitled to *Chevron* deference. In reaching this decision, the majority divided the agency-interpretation world into two categories: interpretations that carry the "force of law" and those that do not. Only those interpretations that carry the "force of law" should receive *Chevron* deference. An agency action has "force of law" when "Congress has delegated legislative power to the agency and [ ] the agency intended to exercise that power [when acting]." *Am. Mining Cong. v. Mine Safety & Health Admin.*, 995 F.2d 1106, 1109 (D.C. Cir. 1993). According to the *Christensen* majority, interpretations with the force of law include more formal actions such as formal adjudication, formal rulemaking, and notice-and-comment rulemaking. In contrast, "opinion letters ... policy statements, agency manuals, and enforcement guidelines" all lack the force of law and receive *Skidmore* deference, at most. *Christensen*, 529 U.S. at 587.

Thus, *Christensen* seemed to create a bright-line test: When the agency acted "formally" *Chevron* applied; when the agency acted less formally, *Chevron* did not. Yet, the Court's bright-line test did not last long. In the next term, the Court decided the following case; how did it change *Christensen*'s clear guidance?

United States v. Mead Corp.

533 U.S. 218 (2001)

Justice Souter delivered the opinion of the Court.

The question is whether a tariff classification ruling by the United States Customs Service deserves judicial deference.... We [hold] that a tariff classification has no claim to judicial deference under *Chevron*, there being no indication that Congress intended such a ruling to carry the force of law, but we hold that under *Skidmore v. Swift & Co.*, 323 U.S. 134 (1944), the ruling is eligible to claim respect according to its persuasiveness....

Respondent, the Mead Corporation, imports "day planners," three-ring binders with pages having room for notes of daily schedules and phone numbers and addresses, together with a calendar and suchlike. [Although the agency had classified the planners as duty-free "day planners" for several years, the agency changed its interpretation and issued a ruling letter classifying them as "bound diaries" subject to tariff.] That letter was short on explanation, but after Mead's protest, Customs Headquarters issued a new letter, carefully reasoned but never published, reaching the same conclusion....

Mead filed suit.... The Federal Circuit ... held that Customs classification rulings should not get *Chevron* deference [because r]ulings are not preceded by notice and comment (and thus) "do not carry the force of law and are not, like regulations, intended to clarify the rights and obligations of importers beyond the specific case under review." ...

We granted *certiorari* ... to consider the limits of *Chevron* deference owed to administrative practice in applying a statute. We hold that administrative implementation of a particular statutory provision qualifies for *Chevron* deference when it appears that Congress delegated authority to the agency generally to make rules carrying the force of law, and that the agency interpretation claiming deference was promulgated in the exercise of that authority. Delegation of such authority may be shown in a variety of ways, as by an agency's power to engage in adjudication or notice-and-comment rulemaking, or by some other indication of a comparable congressional intent. The Customs ruling at issue here fails to qualify, although the possibility that it deserves some deference under *Skidmore* leads us to vacate and remand....

We have recognized a very good indicator of delegation meriting *Chevron* treatment in express congressional authorizations to engage in the process of rulemaking or adjudication that produces regulations or rulings for which deference is claimed. It is fair to assume generally that Congress contemplates administrative action with the effect of law when it provides for a relatively formal administrative procedure tending to foster the fairness and deliberation that should underlie a pronouncement of such force. Thus, the overwhelming number of our cases applying *Chevron* deference have reviewed the fruits of notice-and-comment rulemaking or formal adjudication. That said, and as significant as notice-and-comment is in pointing to *Chevron* authority, the want of that procedure here does not decide the case, for we have sometimes found reasons for *Chevron* deference even when no such administrative formality was required and none was afforded. The fact that the tariff classification here was not a product of such formal process does not alone, therefore, bar the application of *Chevron*.

There are, nonetheless, ample reasons to deny *Chevron* deference here. The authorization for classification rulings, and Customs's practice in making them, present a case far removed not only from notice-and-comment process, but from any other circumstances reasonably suggesting that Congress ever thought of classification rulings as deserving the deference claimed for them here.

No matter which angle we choose for viewing the Customs ruling letter in this case, it fails to qualify under *Chevron*. On the face of the statute, to begin with, the terms of the congressional delegation give no indication that Congress meant to delegate authority to Customs to issue classification rulings with the force of law. . . .

Indeed, to claim that classifications have legal force is to ignore the reality that 46 different Customs offices issue 10,000 to 15,000 of them each year. Any suggestion that rulings intended to have the force of law are being churned out at a rate of 10,000 a year at an agency's 46 scattered offices is simply self-refuting. . . .

In sum, classification rulings are best treated like "interpretations contained in policy statements, agency manuals, and enforcement guidelines." *Christensen*, 529 U.S. at 587. They are beyond the *Chevron* pale. . . .

Underlying the position we take here, like the position expressed by Justice Scalia in dissent, is a choice about the best way to deal with an inescapable feature of the body of congressional legislation authorizing administrative action. That feature is the great variety of ways in which the laws invest the Government's administrative arms with discretion, and with procedures for exercising it, in giving meaning to Acts of Congress. . . .

Although we all accept the position that the Judiciary should defer to at least some of this multifarious administrative action, we have to decide how to take account of the great range of its variety. If the primary objective is to simplify the judicial process of giving or withholding deference, then the diversity of statutes authorizing discretionary administrative action must be declared irrelevant or minimized. If, on the other hand, it is simply implausible that Congress intended such a broad range of statutory authority to produce only two varieties of administrative action, demanding either *Chevron* deference or none at all, then the breadth of the spectrum of possible agency action must be taken into account. Justice Scalia's first priority over the years has been to limit and simplify. The Court's choice has been to tailor deference to variety. This acceptance of the range of statutory variation has led the Court to recognize more than one variety of judicial deference, just as the Court has recognized a variety of indicators that Congress would expect *Chevron* deference.[18]

Our respective choices are repeated today. Justice Scalia would pose the question of deference as an either-or choice. On his view that *Chevron* rendered *Skidmore* anachro-

---

18. It is, of course, true that the limit of *Chevron* deference is not marked by a hard-edged rule. But *Chevron* itself is a good example showing when *Chevron* deference is warranted, while this is a good case showing when it is not. Judges in other, perhaps harder, cases will make reasoned choices between the two examples, the way courts have always done.

nistic, when courts owe any deference it is *Chevron* deference that they owe. Whether courts do owe deference in a given case turns, for him, on whether the agency action (if reasonable) is "authoritative." The character of the authoritative derives, in turn, not from breadth of delegation or the agency's procedure in implementing it, but is defined as the "official" position of an agency and may ultimately be a function of administrative persistence alone.

The Court, on the other hand, said nothing in *Chevron* to eliminate *Skidmore's* recognition of various justifications for deference depending on statutory circumstances and agency action; *Chevron* was simply a case recognizing that even without express authority to fill a specific statutory gap, circumstances pointing to implicit congressional delegation present a particularly insistent call for deference. Indeed, in holding here that *Chevron* left *Skidmore* intact and applicable where statutory circumstances indicate no intent to delegate general authority to make rules with force of law, or where such authority was not invoked, we hold nothing more than we said last Term in response to the particular statutory circumstances in *Christensen*, to which Justice Scalia then took exception just as he does again today.

We think, in sum, that Justice Scalia's efforts to simplify ultimately run afoul of Congress's indications that different statutes present different reasons for considering respect for the exercise of administrative authority or deference to it. Without being at odds with congressional intent much of the time, we believe that judicial responses to administrative action must continue to differentiate between *Chevron* and *Skidmore*. ...

[W]e ... vacate the judgment and remand the case for further proceedings consistent with this opinion.

Justice Scalia, dissenting.

Today's opinion makes an avulsive change in judicial review of federal administrative action. Whereas previously a reasonable agency application of an ambiguous statutory provision had to be sustained so long as it represented the agency's authoritative interpretation, henceforth such an application can be set aside unless "it appears that Congress delegated authority to the agency generally to make rules carrying the force of law," as by giving an agency "power to engage in adjudication or notice-and-comment rulemaking, or ... some other [procedure] indicati[ng] comparable congressional intent," and "the agency interpretation claiming deference was promulgated in the exercise of that authority." What was previously a general presumption of authority in agencies to resolve ambiguity in the statutes they have been authorized to enforce has been changed to a presumption of no such authority, which must be overcome by affirmative legislative intent to the contrary. And whereas previously, when agency authority to resolve ambiguity did not exist the court was free to give the statute what it considered the best interpretation, henceforth the court must supposedly give the agency view some indeterminate amount of so-called *Skidmore* deference. We will be sorting out the consequences of the *Mead* doctrine, which has today replaced the *Chevron* doctrine, for years to come....

Only five years ago, the Court [decided]: "We accord deference to agencies under *Chevron* ... because of a presumption that Congress, when it left ambiguity in a statute meant for implementation by an agency, understood that the ambiguity would be resolved, first and foremost, by the agency, and desired the agency (rather than the courts) to possess whatever degree of discretion the ambiguity allows." Today the Court collapses this doctrine, announcing instead a presumption that agency discretion does not exist unless the statute, expressly or impliedly, says so.... [T]he Court now resurrects, in full force, the pre-*Chevron* doctrine of *Skidmore* deference.... The Court has largely replaced

Chevron, in other words, with that test most beloved by a court unwilling to be held to rules (and most feared by litigants who want to know what to expect): th'ol' "totality of the circumstances" test.

The Court's new doctrine is neither sound in principle nor sustainable in practice.

As to principle: The doctrine of *Chevron*—that all *authoritative* agency interpretations of statutes they are charged with administering deserve deference—was rooted in a legal presumption of congressional intent, important to the division of powers between the Second and Third Branches. When, *Chevron* said, Congress leaves an ambiguity in a statute that is to be administered by an executive agency, it is presumed that Congress meant to give the agency discretion, within the limits of reasonable interpretation, as to how the ambiguity is to be resolved. By committing enforcement of the statute to an agency rather than the courts, Congress committed its initial and primary interpretation to that branch as well....

The basis in principle for today's new doctrine can be described as follows: The background rule is that ambiguity in legislative instructions to agencies is to be resolved not by the agencies but by the judges. Specific congressional intent to depart from this rule must be found—and while there is no single touchstone for such intent it can generally be found when Congress has authorized the agency to act through (what the Court says is) relatively formal procedures such as informal rulemaking and formal (and informal?) adjudication, and when the agency in fact employs such procedures.... But ... [t]here is no necessary connection between the formality of procedure and the power of the entity administering the procedure to resolve authoritatively questions of law. The most formal of the procedures the Court refers to—formal adjudication—is modeled after the process used in trial courts, which of course are not generally accorded deference on questions of law. The purpose of such a procedure is to produce a closed record for determination and review of the facts—which implies nothing about the power of the agency subjected to the procedure to resolve authoritatively questions of law.

As for informal rulemaking: While formal adjudication procedures are *prescribed* (either by statute or by the Constitution), informal rulemaking is more typically *authorized* but not required. Agencies with such authority are free to give guidance through rulemaking, but they may proceed to administer their statute case-by-case, "making law" as they implement their program (not necessarily through formal adjudication). Is it likely—or indeed even plausible—that Congress meant, when such an agency chooses rulemaking, to accord the administrators of that agency, *and their successors,* the flexibility of interpreting the ambiguous statute now one way, and later another; but, when such an agency chooses [informal adjudication], to eliminate all future agency discretion by having that same ambiguity resolved authoritatively (and forever) by the courts? Surely that makes no sense. It is also the case that [non-legislative rules] ... are exempt from the requirements of informal rulemaking. Under the Court's novel theory, when an agency takes advantage of that exemption its rules will be deprived of *Chevron* deference, *i.e.,* authoritative effect. Was this either the plausible intent of the APA rulemaking exemption, or the plausible intent of the Congress that established the [exemption]? ...

As for the practical effects of the new rule:

The principal effect will be protracted confusion. As noted above, the one test for *Chevron* deference that the Court enunciates is wonderfully imprecise: whether "Congress delegated authority to the agency generally to make rules carrying the force of law, ... as by ... adjudication[,] notice-and-comment rulemaking, or ... some other [procedure] indicate[ng] comparable congressional intent." ... It is hard to know what the lower courts are to make of today's guidance.

Another practical effect of today's opinion will be an artificially induced increase in informal rulemaking.... Since informal rulemaking and formal adjudication are the only more-or-less safe harbors from the storm that the Court has unleashed; and since formal adjudication is not an option but must be mandated by statute or constitutional command; informal rulemaking—which the Court was once careful to make voluntary unless required by statute—will now become a virtual necessity....

Worst of all, the majority's approach will lead to the ossification of large portions of our statutory law.... As *Chevron* itself held, the Environmental Protection Agency can interpret "stationary source" to mean a single smokestack, can later replace that interpretation with the "bubble concept" embracing an entire plant, and if that proves undesirable can return again to the original interpretation. For the indeterminately large number of statutes taken out of *Chevron* by today's decision, however, ambiguity (and hence flexibility) will cease with the first judicial resolution.... [Under *Skidmore*, o]nce the court has spoken, it becomes *unlawful* for the agency to take a contradictory position; the statute now *says* what the court has prescribed....

There is, in short, no way to avoid the ossification of federal law that today's opinion sets in motion. What a court says is the law after according *Skidmore* deference will be the law forever, beyond the power of the agency to change even through rulemaking.

And finally, the majority's approach compounds the confusion it creates by breathing new life into the anachronism of *Skidmore* which sets forth a sliding scale of deference.... *Skidmore* deference is a recipe for uncertainty, unpredictability, and endless litigation. To condemn a vast body of agency action to that regime ... is irresponsible....

To decide the present case, I would adhere to the original formulation of *Chevron*.... Ambiguity means Congress intended agency discretion. Any resolution of the ambiguity by the administering agency that is authoritative—that represents the official position of the agency—must be accepted by the courts if it is reasonable....

The *authoritativeness* of the agency ruling may not be a bright-line standard—but it is infinitely brighter than the line the Court asks us to draw today.... And, most important of all, it is a line that focuses attention on the right question: not whether Congress "affirmatively intended" to delegate interpretive authority (if it entrusted administration of the statute to an agency, it did, because that is how our system works); but whether it is truly the agency's considered view, or just the opinions of some underlings, that are at issue....

For the reasons stated, I respectfully dissent.... I dissent even more vigorously from the reasoning that produces the Court's judgment, and that makes today's decision one of the most significant opinions ever rendered by the Court dealing with the judicial review of administrative action. Its consequences will be enormous, and almost uniformly bad.

Notes and Questions

(1) *Christensen's Relevance?* Did the *Mead* majority reject *Christensen's* bright-line test, and if so, why?

(2) *What Test?* What test would the majority apply to future agency interpretations? What test would the dissent apply? What are the advantages and disadvantages of each?

(3) *Skidmore's Resurrection.* The dissent chided the majority for "resurrecting" *Skidmore*. Was it ever dead? Did *Chevron* hold that all *authoritative* agency decisions are entitled to deference?

(4) *Some Other Indication of Comparable Congressional Intent.* According to the majority, when does an agency interpretation carry the force of law? What does "some other indication of a comparable congressional intent" mean?

(5) *Justice Scalia's Warning.* Justice Scalia lamented that the majority's decision would "lead to ossification of large parts of our statutory law...." He was concerned that agencies would be unable to alter their interpretation of a statute after a court had determined what that statute meant. We will reexamine whether he was correct after you read *National Cable & Telecommunications Association v. Brand X Internet Services,* excerpted below.

Justice Scalia's prediction that *Mead* would cause lower court confusion proved correct. Shortly after *Mead,* the Court again addressed the level of deference to be afforded an agency interpretation in the following case. Notice how the Court explains when an agency interpretation arrived at by a procedure other than formal adjudication, formal rule-making, or notice-and-comment rulemaking is entitled to *Chevron,* rather than *Skidmore,* deference. Is this articulation any more helpful than the one in *Mead*?

Barnhart v. Walton
535 U.S. 212 (2002)

Justice Breyer delivered the opinion of the Court.

The Social Security Act authorizes payment of disability insurance benefits and Supplemental Security Income to individuals with disabilities. For both types of benefits the Act defines the key term "disability" as an

> "*inability* to engage in any substantial gainful activity *by reason of* any medically determinable physical or mental *impairment* which can be expected to result in death or *which has lasted or can be expected to last for a continuous period of not less than 12 months.*" § 423(d)(1)(A) (1994 ed.) (Title II) (emphasis added).

This case presents two questions about the Social Security Administration's interpretation of this definition.

First, the Social Security Administration (which we shall call the Agency) reads the term "inability" as including a "12 month" requirement. In its view, the "inability" (to engage in any substantial gainful activity) must last, or must be expected to last, for *at least 12 months.* Second, the Agency reads the term "expected to last" as applicable only when the "inability" has *not yet* lasted 12 months. In the case of a later Agency determination— where the "inability" *did not* last 12 months—the Agency will automatically assume that the claimant failed to meet the duration requirement. It will not look back to decide hypothetically whether, despite the claimant's actual return to work before 12 months expired, the "inability" nonetheless *might have been* expected to last that long....

In 1996 Cleveland Walton, the respondent, applied for both Title II disability insurance benefits and Title XVI Supplemental Security Income. The Agency found that (1) by October 31, 1994, Walton had developed a serious mental illness involving both schizophrenia and associated depression; (2) the illness caused him then to lose his job as a full-time teacher; (3) by mid-1995 he began to work again part time as a cashier; and (4) by December 1995 he was working as a cashier full time.

The Agency concluded that Walton's mental illness had prevented him from engaging in any significant work, *i.e.*, from "engag[ing] in any substantial gainful activity," for 11 months—from October 31, 1994 (when he lost his teaching job) until the end of September 1995 (when he earned income sufficient to rise to the level of "substantial gainful activity"). And because the statute demanded an "inability to engage in any substantial gainful activity" lasting 12, not 11, months, Walton was not entitled to benefits.

Walton sought court review. The District Court affirmed the Agency's decision, but the Court of Appeals for the Fourth Circuit reversed.... The Government sought certiorari.... We now reverse.

The statutory definition of "disability" has two parts. First, it requires a certain kind of "inability," namely, an "inability to engage in any substantial gainful activity." Second it requires an "impairment," namely, a "physical or mental impairment," which provides "reason" for the "inability." The statute adds that the "impairment" must be one that "has lasted or can be expected to last ... not less than 12 months." But what about the "inability"? Must it also last (or be expected to last) for the same amount of time?

The Agency has answered this question in the affirmative. Acting pursuant to statutory rulemaking authority, it has promulgated formal regulations that state that a claimant is not disabled "regardless of [his] medical condition," if he is doing "substantial gainful activity." 20 CFR § 404.1520(b) (2001). And the Agency has interpreted this regulation to mean that the claimant is not disabled if "within 12 months after the onset of an impairment ... the impairment no longer prevents substantial gainful activity." 65 Fed. Reg. 42774 (2000). Courts grant an agency's interpretation of its own regulations considerable legal leeway. Auer v. Robbins, 519 U.S. 452, 461 (1997). And no one here denies that the Agency has properly interpreted its own regulation.

Consequently, the legal question before us is whether the Agency's interpretation of the statute is lawful. This Court has previously said that, if the statute speaks clearly "to the precise question at issue," we "must give effect to the unambiguously expressed intent of Congress." Chevron, 467 U.S. at 842–843. If, however, the statute "is silent or ambiguous with respect to the specific issue," we must sustain the Agency's interpretation if it is "based on a permissible construction" of the Act. Hence we must decide (1) whether the statute unambiguously forbids the Agency's interpretation, and, if not, (2) whether the interpretation, for other reasons, exceeds the bounds of the permissible.

First, the statute does not unambiguously forbid the regulation.... At the very least the statute is ambiguous in that respect....

Second, the Agency's construction is "permissible." The interpretation makes considerable sense in terms of the statute's basic objectives.... The Agency's interpretation supplies a duration requirement, which the statute demands, while doing so in a way that consistently reconciles the statutory "impairment" and "inability" language.

In addition, the Agency's regulations reflect the Agency's own longstanding interpretation. And this Court will normally accord particular deference to an agency interpretation of "longstanding" duration....

Walton also asks us to disregard the Agency's interpretation of its formal regulations on the ground that the Agency only recently enacted those regulations, perhaps in response to this litigation. We have previously rejected similar arguments.

Regardless, the Agency's interpretation is one of long standing. And the fact that the Agency previously reached its interpretation through means less formal than "notice and comment" rulemaking does not automatically deprive that interpretation of the judicial deference otherwise its due. If this Court's opinion in Christensen v. Harris County, 529 U.S. 576 (2000), suggested an absolute rule to the contrary, our later opinion in United States v. Mead Corp., 533 U.S. 218 (2001), denied the suggestion. Indeed, Mead ... indicated that whether a court should give such deference depends in significant part upon the interpretive method used and the nature of the question at issue. And it discussed at length why *Chevron* did not require deference in the circumstances there present—a discussion that would have been superfluous had the presence or absence of notice-and-comment rulemaking been dispositive....

In this case, the interstitial nature of the legal question, the related expertise of the Agency, the importance of the question to administration of the statute, the complexity of that administration, and the careful consideration the Agency has given the question over a long period of time all indicate that *Chevron* provides the appropriate legal lens through which to view the legality of the Agency interpretation here at issue....

The judgment of the Fourth Circuit is *Reversed.*

Justice Scalia, concurring in part and concurring in the judgment.

... I agree that deference is owed to regulations of the Social Security Administration (SSA) interpreting the definition of "disability." As the Court acknowledges, the recency of these regulations is irrelevant. I would therefore not go on, as the Court does, to address the SSA's prior interpretation of the definition of "disability" in [non-legislative rulemaking].

I do not believe, to begin with, that "particular deference" is owed "to an agency interpretation of 'longstanding' duration." That notion is an anachronism—a relic of the pre-*Chevron* days, when there was thought to be only one "correct" interpretation of a statutory text. A "longstanding" agency interpretation, particularly one that dated back to the very origins of the statute, was more likely to reflect the single correct meaning. But once it is accepted, as it was in *Chevron*, that there is a range of permissible interpretations, and that the agency is free to move from one to another, so long as the most recent interpretation is reasonable its antiquity should make no difference.

If, however, the Court does wish to credit the SSA's earlier interpretations—both for the purpose of giving the agency's position "particular deference" and for the purpose of relying upon congressional reenactment with presumed knowledge of the agency position, then I think the Court should state why those interpretations were authoritative enough (or whatever-else-enough *Mead* requires) to qualify for deference. I of course agree that more than notice-and-comment rulemaking qualifies, but that concession alone does not validate the [non-legislative rulemaking involved here]....

The SSA's recently enacted regulations emerged from notice-and-comment rulemaking and merit deference. No more need be said.

Notes and Questions

(1) *What Type of Agency Action Was Challenged?* Did the agency arrive at its interpretation of the statute through notice-and-comment rulemaking or non-legislative rulemaking? Was the process the agency used the basis for the majority's decision? Did the dissent believe that the process the agency used was central to the amount of deference to be given to the interpretation?

(2) *"Some Other Indication of a Comparable Congressional Intent."* According to the majority, when is an agency interpretation, which did not go through either formal agency action or notice-and-comment action, entitled to *Chevron* deference? Does this test make sense to you?

(3) *Pending Litigation.* Why did the *Walton* majority not care that the regulation was promulgated in response to the pending litigation? Did the dissent disagree? In *Mead*,

the Court stated that an interpretation advanced for the first time in a litigation brief would not be entitled to deference. 533 U.S. at 228. What, if anything, was different in *Walton*?

Problem 17-2

Chris Featherstone was convicted of violating a National Park Service ("Service") regulation regulating surfboarding at a national seashore park (the "park"). The Service's enabling statute provides that the Service may take "such measures as it deems necessary to provide for the enjoyment" of federal parks through either rulemaking or adjudication. The Service promulgated a regulation that allows the local park director to prohibit surfing when she determines that conditions are unsafe. By a non-legislative interpretative rule, the park director authorized the "on duty" park ranger to determine when conditions are unsafe and to then prohibit surfing. Chris was found surfing on a day when "no surfing" signs had been posted and was fined. He appealed the fine; the secretary of the Service upheld the fine. Chris appealed to the appropriate federal district court for review. He admits that he ignored the sign but contends that the agency's interpretation deserves no deference.

Assume that you are the trial judge reviewing the agency's decision to uphold the fine. What would be the appropriate standard of review? What additional information might you need to resolve that issue?

C. Critically Examining *Chevron*'s Step One

In *Chevron*'s first step, a court must determine whether Congress has unambiguously decided the issue. This step ignores the agency's interpretation and focuses solely on the statute. As you know well by now, there are different ways to decide whether a statute is ambiguous. Must the court find the text itself ambiguous or may a court look to other sources, such as the context, purpose, and legislative history? The article exerpt below explores this question and the change in the Court's approach to this issue over time.

Chevron's Demise: A Survey of *Chevron* from Infancy to Senescence
59 Admin. L. Rev. 725 (2007)[*]
Linda Jellum

In *Chevron* the Supreme Court decided what may well become the most cited case in legal history. Interestingly, neither the bench nor the bar considered the case revolutionary at the time. Indeed, what *Chevron* has become so well-known for—the appropriate standard of review courts apply to agency interpretations of statutes—was not even addressed in the court below. At the time the case was argued before the Supreme Court, the parties and the

Court focused attention on the political issue—the "bubble concept." But while the importance of the political issue has faded, the importance of the procedural issue has gained currency.

In *Chevron*, the Court resolved the question of how much deference courts must give to an agency's interpretation of a statute. At the time it was decided, many scholars believed that *Chevron* had clearly and simply delineated the appropriate framework for agency deference: first, determine whether Congress had decided the issue, and if not, then defer to any reasonable agency interpretation. But *Chevron* has proved to be less clear, predictable, and simple than originally envisioned. Its guidance is unclear; its application has been, at best, uncertain....

At step one, a court must determine whether Congress has spoken to the precise question at issue. But how should a court determine "whether Congress has directly spoken to the precise question at issue"? Should a court look broadly for congressional intent or more narrowly for textual clarity? ...

Chevron itself was relatively clear about which approach to take. Step one was supposed to be a search for the "intentions" of the legislature; legislative history, purpose, and even social context would all be relevant to this search. But concurrently with the rise of new textualism and the fall of intentionalism, a majority of the Supreme Court justices rejected intentionalism as the appropriate approach for *Chevron*'s first step. Today, many of the justices routinely equate step one of *Chevron* with a simple search for statutory clarity: the Court proceeds to step two whenever the text of a statute is [textually] ambiguous....

While the textualist-intentionalist divide, if you will, exists in all statutory interpretation cases, not just *Chevron* cases, it has unique application in *Chevron* cases because of the way this divide affects interpretative power. Assume, by way of example, that Congress writes a statute, which the legislature believes is clear. It is not; ambiguity becomes apparent only when that statute is applied to a particular set of facts. Who resolves this ambiguity: Congress or the judiciary? In a non-*Chevron* case, the judiciary must resolve ambiguity for there is no other branch to do so. It "is emphatically the province and duty of the judicial department to say what the law is." In these traditional statutory interpretation cases, the textualist-intentionalist divide addresses the distribution of power between only the judiciary and the legislature.

But if an agency is charged with implementing a statute, a third player has joined the power struggle: the executive. *Chevron*'s first step is about this power struggle: which branch should resolve administrative statutory ambiguity, the judiciary or the executive? Theoretically, the smaller role the judiciary has at step one, the more interpretative power the executive will have at step two. Conversely, the greater role the judiciary has at step one, the less interpretative power the executive will have at step two. Thus, in *Chevron* cases there is an interpretative power struggle between the judiciary and the executive—regardless of whether interpretative power flows to the judiciary or the executive—[that] does not exist in the simple statutory interpretation case.

For now, the Supreme Court has resolved the nature of the inquiry at step one: it is no longer a search for congressional intent; rather it is simply a search for statutory clarity....

By changing the nature of the inquiry from "what did Congress intend" to "are the words clear," the Court affected the power distribution among the various branches. With an intentionalist approach, law-making power would, theoretically, remain with the legislature while interpretative power would vest in the executive. This power distribution is consistent with *Chevron*'s implicit delegation doctrine: if Congress was silent or unclear, it implicitly delegated its law-making authority to the agency.

By turning *Chevron*'s first step textualist and limiting its application, the Court appears to have reclaimed the interpretative power it ceded when *Chevron* was decided. Under a textualist approach, what Congress intended is no longer relevant unless Congress clearly expresses that intention in the text itself: Congress's law-making power is curtailed. Intuitively, under this approach, agency interpretative power should increase. Language is inherently ambiguous. It is impossible for Congress to draft perfectly. If the justices dogmatically defer to the agency whenever a statute is ambiguous, agency deference should be the rule rather than the exception. Sure enough, "the Court's transition from intentionalism to textualism initially increased *Chevron* deference. However, as that transition has moved into subsequent phases, it is now having the opposite effect." As *Chevron*'s first step became more text based, the Court began to limit *Chevron*'s application. Today, *Chevron* applies in fewer cases than in the past [for several reasons]. In the end, the Court's reformulation of *Chevron*'s first step likely hastened *Chevron*'s demise.

Notes and Questions

(1) Chevron*'s Demise?* Do you agree that *Chevron* has become less relevant? Reread *Chevron* above, especially footnote 9. Was *Chevron*'s first step originally envisioned as an intentionalist step and later changed to a textualist step?

(2) *Power Shift.* According to the excerpt, how did the change to a textualist first step— if it occurred—affect the power distribution among the branches? Do you think that the Court returned to *Skidmore* for less formal interpretations, in part, because a textualist first step shifts too much power to agencies?

(3) *Does the Step Matter?* An empirical study found that agencies won 42 percent of the time at step one and 89 percent of the time at step two. Orin S. Kerr, *Shedding Light on* Chevron*: An Empirical Study of the* Chevron *Doctrine in the U.S. Courts of Appeals*, 15 YALE J. ON REG. 1, 31 (1998). Courts are more willing to find an enabling statute to be clear at step one than to find an agency's interpretation unreasonable under step two. *See* Thomas W. Merrill, *Judicial Deference to Executive Precedent*, 101 YALE L.J. 969, 980 (1992); *see also, e.g., AT&T Corp. v. Iowa Utilities Bd.*, 525 U.S. 366, 392 (1999) (finding unreasonable an FCC regulation under step two); *see generally* WILLIAM F. FUNK ET AL., ADMINISTRATIVE PROCEDURE AND PRACTICE: PROBLEMS AND CASES 151 (2d ed. 2001). If you represent the litigants, where should you focus your arguments? The agency?

In the case that follows, see if any of the opinions remained faithful to *Chevron*'s two-step formulation. Does this case support the author's assertion above that step one of *Chevron* has been transformed into a textualist step?

Zuni Pub. Sch. Dist. v. Dep't of Educ.

550 U.S. 81 (2007)

JUSTICE BREYER delivered the opinion of the Court.

[The federal Impact Aid Act provides financial assistance to certain local school districts. States are generally prohibited from offsetting the federal money by reducing state aid to those districts. An exception exists, however, for states that equalize expenditures for students across districts. The Act] sets forth a method that the Secretary of Education is to use when determining whether a State's public school funding program "equalizes expenditures" throughout the State. The statute instructs the Secretary to calculate the disparity in per-pupil expenditures among local school districts in the State. But, when doing so, the Secretary is to "disregard" school districts *with per-pupil expenditures ... above the 95th percentile or below the 5th percentile of such expenditures ... in the State."*

The question before us is whether the emphasized statutory language permits the Secretary to identify the school districts that should be "disregard[ed]" by looking to the *number of the district's pupils,* as well as to the size of the district's expenditures per pupil. We conclude that it does....

Zuni's strongest argument rests upon the literal language of the statute. Zuni concedes, as it must, that if the language of the statute is open or ambiguous—that is, if Congress left a "gap" for the agency to fill—then we must uphold the Secretary's interpretation as long as it is reasonable. See *Chevron....* For purposes of exposition, we depart from a normal order of discussion, namely an order that first considers Zuni's statutory language argument. Instead, because of the technical nature of the language in question, we shall first examine the provision's background and basic purposes. That discussion will illuminate our subsequent analysis.... It will also reveal why Zuni concentrates its argument upon language alone.

Considerations other than language provide us with unusually strong indications that Congress intended to leave the Secretary free to use the calculation method before us and that the Secretary's chosen method is a reasonable one. For one thing, the matter at issue—*i.e.,* the calculation method for determining whether a state aid program "equalizes expenditures"—is the kind of highly technical, specialized interstitial matter that Congress often does not decide itself, but delegates to specialized agencies to decide.

For another thing, the history of the [statute's enactment] strongly supports the Secretary.... The present statutory language originated in draft legislation that the Secretary himself sent to Congress in 1994.... Congress adopted that language without comment or clarification. No one at the time—no Member of Congress, no Department of Education official, no school district or State—expressed the view that this statutory language (which, after all, was supplied by the Secretary) was intended to require, or did require, the Secretary to change the Department's system of calculation, a system that the Department and school districts across the Nation had followed for nearly 20 years, without (as far as we are told) any adverse effect.

Finally, viewed in terms of the purpose [to exclude statistical outliers], the Secretary's calculation method is reasonable, while the reasonableness of a method based upon the number of districts alone (Zuni's proposed method) is more doubtful....

Thus, the history and purpose of [the statute] indicate that the Secretary's calculation formula is a reasonable method that carries out Congress' likely intent in enacting the statutory provision before us.

But what of the provision's literal language? The matter is important, for normally neither the legislative history nor the reasonableness of the Secretary's method would be determinative if the plain language of the statute unambiguously indicated that Congress sought to foreclose the Secretary's interpretation. And Zuni argues that the Secretary's formula could not possibly effectuate Congress' intent since the statute's language literally forbids the Secretary to use such a method. Under this Court's precedents, if the intent of Congress is clear and unambiguously expressed by the statutory language at issue, that would be the end of our analysis. A customs statute that imposes a tariff on "clothing" does not impose a tariff on automobiles, no matter how strong the policy arguments for treating the two kinds of goods alike. But we disagree with Zuni's conclusion, for we believe that the Secretary's method falls within the scope of the statute's plain language....

We [] find support for our view of the language in the more general circumstance that statutory "[a]mbiguity is a creature not [just] of definitional possibilities but [also] of statutory context." See also *FDA v. Brown & Williamson Tobacco Corp.*, 529 U.S. 120, 132–133 (2000) ("[m]eaning—*or ambiguity*—of certain words or phrases may only become evident when placed in context"). That may be so even if statutory language is highly technical. After all, the scope of what seems a precise technical chess instruction, such as "you must place the queen next to the king," varies with context, depending, for example, upon whether the instructor is telling a beginner how to set up the board or telling an advanced player how to checkmate an opponent....

Finally, we draw reassurance from the fact that no group of statisticians, nor any individual statistician, has told us directly in briefs, or indirectly through citation, that the language before us cannot be read as we have read it. This circumstance is significant, for the statutory language is technical, and we are not statisticians. And the views of experts (or their absence) might help us understand (though not control our determination of) what Congress had in mind.

The upshot is that the language of the statute is broad enough to permit the Secretary's reading. That fact requires us to look beyond the language to determine whether the Secretary's interpretation is a reasonable, hence permissible, implementation of the statute. For the reasons set forth..., we conclude that the Secretary's reading is a reasonable reading. We consequently find the Secretary's method of calculation lawful.

JUSTICE STEVENS, concurring.

... [I]n *Griffin v. Oceanic Contractors, Inc.*, 458 U.S. 564, 571 (1982), then-Justice Rehnquist wisely acknowledged that "in rare cases the literal application of a statute will produce a result demonstrably at odds with the intentions of its drafters, and those intentions must be controlling." And ..."[i]n such cases, the intention of the drafters, rather than the strict language, controls."

Today [Justice Scalia] correctly observes that a judicial decision that departs from statutory text may represent "policy-driven interpretation." As long as that driving policy is faithful to the intent of Congress (or, as in this case, aims only to give effect to such intent)—which it must be if it is to override a strict interpretation of the text—the decision is also a correct performance of the judicial function. Justice Scalia's argument today rests on the incorrect premise that every policy-driven interpretation implements a judge's personal view of sound policy, rather than a faithful attempt to carry out the will of the legislature. Quite the contrary is true of the work of the judges with whom I have worked for many years. If we presume that our judges are intellectually honest—as I do—there is no reason to fear "policy-driven interpretation[s]" of Acts of Congress.

In *Chevron*, we acknowledged that when "the intent of Congress is clear [from the statutory text], that is the end of the matter." But we also made quite clear that "administrative constructions which are contrary to clear congressional intent" must be rejected. In that unanimous opinion, we explained:

> "If a court, employing traditional tools of statutory construction, ascertains that Congress had an intention on the precise question at issue, that intention is the law and must be given effect."

Analysis of legislative history is, of course, a traditional tool of statutory construction. There is no reason why we must confine ourselves to, or begin our analysis with, the statutory text if other tools of statutory construction provide better evidence of congressional intent with respect to the precise point at issue.

As the Court's opinion demonstrates, this is a quintessential example of a case in which the statutory text was obviously enacted to adopt the rule that the Secretary administered both before and after the enactment of the rather confusing language found in [the statute]. That text is sufficiently ambiguous to justify the Court's exegesis, but my own vote is the product of a more direct route to the Court's patently correct conclusion. This happens to be a case in which the legislative history is pellucidly clear and the statutory text is difficult to fathom. Moreover, it is a case in which I cannot imagine anyone accusing any Member of the Court of voting one way or the other because of that Justice's own policy preferences.

Given the clarity of the evidence of Congress' "intention on the precise question at issue," I would affirm the judgment of the Court of Appeals even if I thought that petitioners' literal reading of the statutory text was correct.[3] The only "policy" by which I have been driven is that which this Court has endorsed on repeated occasions regarding the importance of remaining faithful to Congress' intent.

JUSTICE KENNEDY, with whom JUSTICE ALITO joins, concurring,

The district courts and courts of appeals, as well as this Court, should follow the framework set forth in *Chevron*, even when departure from that framework might serve purposes of exposition. When considering an administrative agency's interpretation of a statute, a court first determines "whether Congress has directly spoken to the precise question at issue." If so, "that is the end of the matter." Only if "Congress has not directly addressed the precise question at issue" should a court consider "whether the agency's answer is based on a permissible construction of the statute."

In this case, the Court is correct to find that the plain language of the statute is ambiguous. It is proper, therefore, to invoke *Chevron*'s rule of deference. The opinion of the Court, however, inverts *Chevron*'s logical progression. Were the inversion to become systemic, it would create the impression that agency policy concerns, rather than the traditional tools of statutory construction, are shaping the judicial interpretation of statutes. It is our obligation to set a good example; and so, in my view, it would have been preferable, and more faithful to *Chevron* to arrange the opinion differently. Still, we must give deference to the author of an opinion in matters of exposition; and because the point does not affect the outcome, I join the Court's opinion.

JUSTICE SCALIA, with whom THE CHIEF JUSTICE [ROBERTS] and JUSTICE THOMAS join, and with whom JUSTICE SOUTER joins as to Part I, dissenting.

In *Church of the Holy Trinity v. United States*, 143 U.S. 457 (1892), this Court conceded that a church's act of contracting with a prospective rector fell within the plain meaning of a federal labor statute, but nevertheless did not apply the statute to the church: "It is a familiar rule," the Court pronounced, "that a thing may be within the letter of the statute and yet not within the statute, because not within its spirit, nor within the intention of its makers." That is a judge-empowering proposition if there ever was one, and in the century since, the Court has wisely retreated from it, in words if not always in actions. But today *Church of the Holy Trinity* arises, Phoenix-like, from the ashes. The Court's contrary assertions aside, today's decision is nothing other than the elevation of judge-supposed legislative intent over clear statutory text. The plain language of the federal Impact Aid statute clearly and unambiguously forecloses the Secretary of Education's

---

3. See *Church of Holy Trinity v. United States*, 143 U.S. 457, 459 (1892) ("It is a familiar rule, that a thing may be within the letter of the statute and yet not within the statute, because not within its spirit, nor within the intention of its makers").

preferred methodology for determining whether a State's school-funding system is equalized. Her selection of that methodology is therefore entitled to zero deference under *Chevron*.

I. The very structure of the Court's opinion provides an obvious clue as to what is afoot. The opinion purports to place a premium on the plain text of the Impact Aid statute, but it first takes us instead on a roundabout tour of "[c]onsiderations *other* than language"—page after page of unenacted congressional intent and judicially perceived statutory purpose. Only after we are shown "why Zuni concentrates its argument upon language alone" (impliedly a shameful practice, or at least indication of a feeble case) are we informed how the statute's plain text does not unambiguously *preclude* the interpretation the Court thinks best. This is a most suspicious order of proceeding, since our case law is full of statements such as "We begin, as always, with the language of the statute," and replete with the affirmation that, when "[g]iven [a] straightforward statutory command, there is no reason to resort to legislative history." Nor is this cart-before-the-horse approach justified by the Court's excuse that the statute before us is, after all, a technical one.... As almost a majority of today's majority worries, "[w]ere the inversion [of inquiry] to become systemic, it would create the impression that agency policy concerns, rather than the traditional tools of statutory construction, are shaping the judicial interpretation of statutes." True enough—except I see no reason to wait for the distortion to become systemic before concluding that that is precisely what is happening in the present case. For some, policy-driven interpretation is apparently just fine. But for everyone else, let us return to Statutory Interpretation 101.

We must begin, as we always do, with the text.... [Justice Scalia concludes that the text is clear.]

II. How then, if the text is so clear, are respondents managing to win this case? The answer can only be the return of that miraculous redeemer of lost causes, *Church of the Holy Trinity*. In order to contort the statute's language beyond recognition, the Court must believe Congress's intent so crystalline, the spirit of its legislation so glowingly bright, that the statutory text should simply not be read to say what it says. Justice Stevens is quite candid on the point: He is willing to contradict the text. But Justice Stevens' candor should not make his philosophy seem unassuming. He maintains that it is "a correct performance of the judicial function" to "override a strict interpretation of the text" so long as policy-driven interpretation "is faithful to the intent of Congress." But once one departs from "strict interpretation of the text" (by which Justice Stevens means the actual meaning of the text) fidelity to the intent of Congress is a chancy thing. The only thing we know for certain both Houses of Congress (and the President, if he signed the legislation) agreed upon is the text. Legislative history can never produce a "pellucidly clear" picture of what a law was "intended" to mean, for the simple reason that it is never voted upon—or ordinarily even seen or heard—by the "intending" lawgiving entity, which consists of both Houses of Congress and the President (if he did not veto the bill). Thus, what judges believe Congress "meant" (apart from the text) has a disturbing but entirely unsurprising tendency to be whatever judges think Congress *must* have meant, *i.e.*, *should* have meant. In *Church of the Holy Trinity*, every Justice on this Court disregarded the plain language of a statute that forbade the hiring of a clergyman from abroad because, after all (they thought), "this is a Christian nation," so Congress could not have meant what it said. Is there any reason to believe that those Justices were lacking that "intellectua[l] honest[y]" that Justice Stevens "presume[s]" all our judges possess? Intellectual honesty does not exclude a blinding intellectual bias. And even if it did, the system of judicial amendatory veto over texts duly adopted by Congress bears no resemblance to the system of lawmaking set forth in our Constitution.

Justice Stevens takes comfort in the fact that this is a case in which he "cannot imagine anyone accusing any Member of the Court of voting one way or the other because of that Justice's own policy preferences." I can readily imagine it, given that the Court's opinion begins with a lengthy description of why the system its judgment approves is the *better* one. But even assuming that, in this rare case, the Justices' departure from the enacted law has nothing to do with their policy view that it is a bad law, nothing in Justice Stevens' separate opinion limits his approach to such rarities. Why should we suppose that in matters more likely to arouse the judicial libido — voting rights, antidiscrimination laws, or environmental protection, to name only a few — a judge in the School of Textual Subversion would not find it convenient (yea, *righteous!*) to assume that Congress *must* have meant, not what it said, but what he knows to be best? ...

Contrary to the Court and Justice Stevens, I do not believe that what we are sure the Legislature *meant* to say can trump what it *did* say. Citizens arrange their affairs not on the basis of their legislators' unexpressed intent, but on the basis of the law as it is written and promulgated. I think it terribly unfair to expect that the two rural school districts who are petitioners here should have pored over some 30 years of regulatory history to divine Congress's "real" objective (and with it the "real" intent that a majority of Justices would find honest and true). To be governed by legislated text rather than legislators' intentions is what it means to be "a Government of laws, not of men." And in the last analysis the opposite approach is no more beneficial to the governors than it is to the governed. By "depriving legislators of the assurance that ordinary terms, used in an ordinary context, will be given a predictable meaning," we deprive Congress of "a sure means by which it may work the people's will."

I do not purport to know what Congress thought it was doing when it amended the Impact Aid program in 1994. But even indulging Justice Stevens' erroneous premise that there exists a "legislative intent" separate and apart from the statutory text, I do not see how the Court can possibly say, with any measure of confidence, that Congress wished one thing rather than another....

The only sure indication of what Congress intended is what Congress enacted; and even if there is a difference between the two, the rule of law demands that the latter prevail. This case will live with *Church of the Holy Trinity* as an exemplar of judicial disregard of crystal-clear text. We must interpret the law as Congress has written it, not as we would wish it to be. I would reverse the judgment of the Court of Appeals.

JUSTICE SOUTER, dissenting.

I agree with the Court that Congress probably intended, or at least understood, that the Secretary would continue to follow the methodology devised prior to passage of the current statute in 1994. But for reasons set out in Justice Scalia's dissent, I find the statutory language unambiguous and inapt to authorize that methodology, and I therefore join Part I of his dissenting opinion.

Notes and Questions

(1) *Chevron's Two-Step.* Did the majority follow *Chevron's* two steps? If not, why not? Consider the point in Chevron's *Demise* that, because *Chevron's* first step has changed to a text-based inquiry, *Chevron's* relevance is fading. Doesn't the majority's decision to flip the analysis support that conclusion?

(2) *Writing Separately.* What are the points of Justice Souter's dissent and Justice Kennedy's concurrence?

(3) *Somewhat Clear Text Versus Crystal Clear Legislative History.* Do you agree with Justice Stevens that courts should reject the natural meaning of statutory text when legislative history is very clear that the natural meaning was not what Congress intended? Which approach do you think Justice Stevens follows?

(4) *"Above the 95th Percentile or Below the 5th Percentile."* Justice Scalia finds this text clear. Do you? If the text is as clear as Justice Scalia suggests, would the Court reach the second step of *Chevron* or has Congress conclusively decided the issue? According to Justice Scalia:

> In my experience, there is a fairly close correlation between the degree to which a person is … a "strict constructionist" … and the degree to which that person favors *Chevron* and is willing to give it broad scope. The reason is obvious. One who finds more often (as I do) that the meaning of a statute is apparent from its text and from its relationship with other laws, thereby finds less often that the triggering requirement for *Chevron* deference exists. It is thus relatively rare that *Chevron* will require me to accept an interpretation which, though reasonable, *I would not personally adopt*. Contrariwise, one who abhors a "plain meaning" rule, and is willing to permit the apparent meaning of a statute to be impeached by the legislative history, will more frequently find agency-liberating ambiguity, and will discern a much broader range of "reasonable" interpretation that the agency may adopt and to which the courts must pay deference. The frequency with which *Chevron* will require that judge to accept an interpretation he thinks wrong is infinitely greater.

Antonin Scalia, *Judicial Deference to Administrative Interpretations of Law*, 1989 Duke L.J. 511, 521 (1989) (emphasis added). Does Justice Scalia's view undermine *Chevron* deference? Do you think that a strict textualist should temper his views when the context is agency interpretation? Why or why not?

D. Agency Deference to Judicial Interpretation

Sometimes, courts must interpret statutes before an agency does. What should happen when an agency charged with implementing a statute disagrees with a court's interpretation? While agency interpretations are given deference (assuming the agency interpretation meets *Chevron*'s two-step analysis), should they be given the same deference when a court has already interpreted the same statutory language? The following case and problem explore the intersection of the *Chevron* doctrine and *stare decisis*.

Nat'l Cable & Telecomms. Assn. v. Brand X Internet Servs.
545 U.S. 967 (2005)

Justice Thomas delivered the opinion of the Court.

Title II of the Communications Act of 1934, as amended, subjects all providers of "telecommunications servic[e]" to mandatory common-carrier regulation. In the order under review, the Federal Communications Commission concluded that cable companies that sell broadband Internet service do not provide "telecommunications servic[e]" as the Communications Act defines that term, and hence are exempt from mandatory common-carrier regulation under Title II. We must decide whether that conclusion is a lawful construction of the Communications Act under *Chevron* and the Administrative Procedure Act. We hold that it is.

The traditional means by which consumers in the United States access the network of interconnected computers that make up the Internet is through "dial-up" connections provided over local telephone facilities.... "Broadband" Internet service, by contrast, transmits data at much higher speeds. There are two principal kinds of broadband Internet service: cable modem service and Digital Subscriber Line (DSL) service. Cable modem service transmits data between the Internet and users' computers via the network of television cable lines owned by cable companies. DSL service provides high-speed access using the local telephone wires owned by local telephone companies....

At issue in these cases is the proper regulatory classification under the Communications Act of broadband cable Internet service. The Act ... defines two categories of regulated entities relevant to these cases: telecommunications carriers and information-service providers. The Act regulates telecommunications carriers, but not information-service providers, as common carriers....

These two statutory classifications originated in the late 1970s, as the Commission ... distinguished between "basic" service (like telephone service) and "enhanced" service (computer-processing service offered over telephone lines).... The definitions of the terms "telecommunications service" and "information service" established by the 1996 Act are similar to the [former] basic- and enhanced-service classifications. "Telecommunications service" — the analog to basic service — is "the offering of telecommunications for a fee directly to the public ... regardless of the facilities used." 47 U.S.C. § 153(46). "Telecommunications" is "the transmission, between or among points specified by the user, of information of the user's choosing, without change in the form or content of the information as sent and received." § 153(43).... And "information service" — the analog to enhanced service — is "the offering of a capability for generating, acquiring, storing, transforming, processing, retrieving, utilizing, or making available information via telecommunications...." § 153(20).

In September 2000, the Commission initiated a rulemaking proceeding ... that ... culminated in the Declaratory Ruling under review in these cases. In the Declaratory Ruling, the Commission concluded that broadband Internet service provided by cable companies is an "information service" but not a "telecommunications service" under the Act, and therefore not subject to mandatory Title II common-carrier regulation.... Its logic was that ... cable companies do not "offe[r] telecommunications service to the end user, but rather ... merely us[e] telecommunications to provide end users with cable modem service." ...

The Court of Appeals ... held that the Commission could not permissibly construe the Communications Act to exempt cable companies providing Internet service from Title II regulation. Rather than analyzing the permissibility of that construction under the deferential framework of *Chevron*, however, the Court of Appeals grounded its holding in the *stare decisis* effect of *AT&T Corp. v. Portland*, 216 F.3d 871 (CA9 2000). *Portland* held that cable modem service was a "telecommunications service," though the court in that case was not reviewing an administrative proceeding and the Commission was not a party to the case. Nevertheless, *Portland*'s holding, the Court of Appeals reasoned, overrode the contrary interpretation reached by the Commission....

In *Chevron*, this Court held that ambiguities in statutes within an agency's jurisdiction to administer are delegations of authority to the agency to fill the statutory gap in reasonable fashion....

The *Chevron* framework governs our review of the Commission's construction. Congress has delegated to the Commission the authority to promulgate binding legal rules; the Commission issued the order under review in the exercise of that authority; and no one questions that the order is within the Commission's jurisdiction. Hence, as we have in the past, we apply the *Chevron* framework to the Commission's interpretation of the Communications Act....

The Court of Appeals declined to apply *Chevron* because it thought the Commission's interpretation of the Communications Act foreclosed by the conflicting construction of the Act it had adopted in *Portland, supra.* It based that holding on the assumption that *Portland's* construction overrode the Commission's, regardless of whether *Portland* had held the statute to be unambiguous. That reasoning was incorrect.

A court's prior judicial construction of a statute trumps an agency construction otherwise entitled to *Chevron* deference only if the prior court decision holds that its construction follows from the unambiguous terms of the statute and thus leaves no room for agency discretion. This principle follows from *Chevron* itself. *Chevron* established a "presumption that Congress, when it left ambiguity in a statute meant for implementation by an agency, understood that the ambiguity would be resolved, first and foremost, by the agency, and desired the agency (rather than the courts) to possess whatever degree of discretion the ambiguity allows." Yet allowing a judicial precedent to foreclose an agency from interpreting an ambiguous statute, as the Court of Appeals assumed it could, would allow a court's interpretation to override an agency's. *Chevron's* premise is that it is for agencies, not courts, to fill statutory gaps. The better rule is to hold judicial interpretations contained in precedents to the same demanding *Chevron* step one standard that applies if the court is reviewing the agency's construction on a blank slate: Only a judicial precedent holding that the statute unambiguously forecloses the agency's interpretation, and therefore contains no gap for the agency to fill, displaces a conflicting agency construction.

A contrary rule would produce anomalous results. It would mean that whether an agency's interpretation of an ambiguous statute is entitled to *Chevron* deference would turn on the order in which the interpretations issue: If the court's construction came first, its construction would prevail, whereas if the agency's came first, the agency's construction would command *Chevron* deference. Yet whether Congress has delegated to an agency the authority to interpret a statute does not depend on the order in which the judicial and administrative constructions occur. The Court of Appeals' rule, moreover, would "lead to the ossification of large portions of our statutory law," [*United States v. Mead Corp.*, 533 U.S. 218 (2001)] (Scalia, J., dissenting), by precluding agencies from revising unwise judicial constructions of ambiguous statutes. Neither *Chevron* nor the doctrine of *stare decisis* requires these haphazard results.

The dissent answers that allowing an agency to override what a court believes to be the best interpretation of a statute makes "judicial decisions subject to reversal by Executive officers." It does not. Since *Chevron* teaches that a court's opinion as to the best reading of an ambiguous statute an agency is charged with administering is not authoritative, the agency's decision to construe that statute differently from a court does not say that the court's holding was legally wrong.... The precedent has not been "reversed" by the agency, any more than a federal court's interpretation of a State's law can be said to have been "reversed" by a state court that adopts a conflicting (yet authoritative) interpretation of state law....

Against this background, the Court of Appeals erred in refusing to apply *Chevron* to the Commission's interpretation of the definition of "telecommunications service." Its prior decision in *Portland* held only that the *best* reading of § 153(46) was that cable modem service was a "telecommunications service," not that it was the *only permissible* reading of the statute. Nothing in *Portland* held that the Communications Act unambiguously required treating cable Internet providers as telecommunications carriers....

[The Court concluded that Congress had not spoken directly to the question at issue, and that the Commission's interpretation was reasonable.]

The Commission is in a far better position to address these questions than we are. Nothing in the Communications Act or the Administrative Procedure Act makes unlawful the Commission's use of its expert policy judgment to resolve these difficult questions. The judgment of the Court of Appeals is reversed, and the cases are remanded for further proceedings consistent with this opinion.

JUSTICE STEVENS, concurring.

While I join the Court's opinion in full, I add this caveat concerning [that part of the majority's opinion] which correctly explains why a court of appeals' interpretation of an ambiguous provision in a regulatory statute does not foreclose a contrary reading by the agency. That explanation would not necessarily be applicable to a decision by this Court that would presumably remove any pre-existing ambiguity.

JUSTICE BREYER, concurring.

I join the Court's opinion because I believe that the Federal Communications Commission's decision falls within the scope of its statutorily delegated authority—though perhaps just barely. I write separately because I believe it important to point out that Justice Scalia, in my view, has wrongly characterized the Court's opinion in *United States v. Mead Corp.*, 533 U.S. 218 (2001). He states that the Court held in *Mead* that "some unspecified degree of formal process" before the agency "was required" for courts to accord the agency's decision deference under *Chevron*.... [T]he existence of a formal rulemaking proceeding is neither a necessary nor a sufficient condition for according *Chevron* deference to an agency's interpretation of a statute. It is not a necessary condition because an agency might arrive at an authoritative interpretation of a congressional enactment in other ways, including ways that Justice Scalia mentions. It is not a sufficient condition because Congress may have intended *not* to leave the matter of a particular interpretation up to the agency, irrespective of the procedure the agency uses to arrive at that interpretation, say, where an unusually basic legal question is at issue....

JUSTICE SCALIA, with whom JUSTICE SOUTER and JUSTICE GINSBURG join as to Part I, dissenting.

... I. The first sentence of the FCC ruling under review reads as follows: "Cable modem service provides high-speed access to the Internet, *as well as* many applications or functions that can be used with that access, over cable system facilities." Does this mean that cable companies "offer" high-speed access to the Internet? Surprisingly not, if the Commission and the Court are to be believed.

It happens that cable-modem service is popular precisely because of the high-speed access it provides, and that, once connected with the Internet, cable-modem subscribers often use Internet applications and functions from providers other than the cable company. Nevertheless, for purposes of classifying what the cable company does, the Commission (with the Court's approval) puts all the emphasis on the rest of the package (the additional "applications or functions"). It does so by claiming that the cable company does not "offe[r]" its customers high-speed Internet access because it offers that access only in conjunction with particular applications and functions, rather than "separate[ly]," as a "stand-alone offering." ...

The Court concludes that the word "offer" is ambiguous in the sense that it has "'alternative dictionary definitions'" that might be relevant. It seems to me, however, that the analytic problem pertains not really to the meaning of "offer," but to the identity of what is offered. The relevant question is whether the individual components in a package being offered still possess sufficient identity to be described as separate objects of the offer, or whether they have been so changed by their combination with the other components that it is no longer reasonable to describe them in that way....

If, for example, I call up a pizzeria and ask whether they offer delivery, both common sense and common "usage" would prevent them from answering: "No, we do not offer delivery—but if you order a pizza from us, we'll bake it for you and then bring it to your house." The logical response to this would be something on the order of, "so, you *do* offer delivery." But our pizza-man may continue to deny the obvious and explain, paraphrasing the FCC and the Court: "No, even though we bring the pizza to your house, we are not actually 'offering' you delivery, because the delivery that we provide to our end users is 'part and parcel' of our pizzeria-pizza-at-home service and is 'integral to its other capabilities.'" Any reasonable customer would conclude at that point that his interlocutor was either crazy or following some too-clever-by-half legal advice.

In short, for the inputs of a finished service to qualify as the objects of an "offer" (as that term is reasonably understood), it is perhaps a sufficient, *but surely not a necessary*, condition that the seller offer separately "each discrete input that is necessary to providing ... a finished service." The pet store may have a policy of selling puppies only with leashes, but any customer will say that it *does* offer puppies—because a leashed puppy is still a puppy, even though it is not offered on a "stand-alone" basis....

After all is said and done, after all the regulatory cant has been translated, and the smoke of agency expertise blown away, it remains perfectly clear that someone who sells cable-modem service is "offering" telecommunications. For that simple reason set forth in the statute, I would affirm the Court of Appeals.

[T]he Court continues the administrative-law improvisation project it began four years ago in *Mead Corp.* To the extent it set forth a comprehensible rule, *Mead* drastically limited the categories of agency action that would qualify for deference under *Chevron.* For example, the position taken by an agency before the Supreme Court, with full approval of the agency head, would not qualify. Rather, some unspecified degree of formal process was required—or was at least the only safe harbor.

As I pointed out in dissent, this in turn meant (under the law as it was understood until today)[11] that many statutory ambiguities that might be resolved in varying fashions by successive agency administrations, would be resolved finally, conclusively, and forever, by federal judges—producing an "ossification of large portions of our statutory law." The Court today moves to solve this problem of its own creation by inventing yet another breathtaking novelty: judicial decisions subject to reversal by Executive officers.

---

11. The Court's unanimous holding in *Neal v. United States*, 516 U.S. 284 (1996), plainly rejected the notion that any form of deference could cause the Court to revisit a prior statutory-construction holding: "Once we have determined a statute's meaning, we adhere to our ruling under the doctrine of *stare decisis*, and we assess an agency's later interpretation of the statute against that settled law." The Court attempts to reinterpret this plain language by dissecting the cases *Neal* cited, noting that they referred to previous determinations of "'a statute's clear meaning.'" But those cases reveal that today's focus on the term "clear" is revisionist ...

Imagine the following sequence of events: FCC action is challenged as *ultra vires* under the governing statute; the litigation reaches all the way to the Supreme Court of the United States. The Solicitor General sets forth the FCC's official position (approved by the Commission) regarding interpretation of the statute. Applying *Mead*, however, the Court denies the agency position *Chevron* deference, finds that the *best* interpretation of the statute contradicts the agency's position, and holds the challenged agency action unlawful. The agency promptly conducts a rulemaking, and adopts a rule that comports with its earlier position — in effect disagreeing with the Supreme Court concerning the best interpretation of the statute. According to today's opinion, the agency is thereupon free to take the action that the Supreme Court found unlawful. . . .

It is indeed a wonderful new world that the Court creates, one full of promise for administrative-law professors in need of tenure articles and, of course, for litigators. I would adhere to what has been the rule in the past: When a court interprets a statute without *Chevron* deference to agency views, its interpretation (whether or not asserted to rest upon an unambiguous text) is the law. . . .

I respectfully dissent.

Notes and Questions

(1) *When an Agency Interpretation Trumps a Judicial Interpretation.* According to the majority opinion in *Brand X*, when would an agency interpretation be afforded *Chevron* deference even though that same language had already been interpreted to mean something different by a judge? When would the judicial interpretation triumph? Does this distinction make sense to you?

(2) *All or Nothing? Brand X* held that a judicial precedent would preclude *Chevron* deference only when the earlier court had held that "its construction follow[ed] from the unambiguous terms of the statute." Yet, the Court did not explain how to identify those holdings. Precedents following *Brand X* will likely make identification easy. However, some precedents likely predate *Chevron*, and so will not speak in *Chevron's* terms. And those precedents that post-date *Chevron* but predate *Brand X* may be unclear about whether the interpretation was the *only* reasonable one. Should the Court have established a test that is easier to apply?

(3) *Mead's Legacy.* Justice Scalia suggested that the majority opinion was nothing short of breathtaking because it allows judicial opinions to be reversed by executive officers. Is he correct? Does the majority respond to this criticism? What is the relevance of *Mead* to this discussion?

(4) *Scalia's Warning.* In *Mead*, excerpted earlier, Justice Scalia suggested that agencies would be unable to alter their interpretation of a statute once a court had determined what that statute meant. Was he correct? Does *Brand X* answer this question definitely or does it answer the question only for agency interpretations that are subject to *Chevron* deference? What if a judge determined the meaning of a statute and the agency then interpreted that same language to mean something different via a non-legislative interpretative rule? What, if any, level of deference would the agency's interpretation receive? *Chevron*, *Skidmore*, or no deference?

Problem 17-3

You represent a group of present and former employees of Cryodynamics Corporation aged 40 to 49. Last year, the company and its Union executed a collective bargaining agreement that eliminated the company's obligation to provide health benefits to retired employees, except as to employees at least 50 years old at the time the agreement was signed. Your clients objected to the agreement. They petitioned the Equal Employment Opportunity Commission (a federal agency) and claimed that the agreement violated the Age Discrimination in Employment Act of 1967. The EEOC agreed based on its interpretation of the statute as expressed in its regulation 29 C.F.R. § 1625.2(a). The employer disagreed with the agency's interpretation and has refused to settle with the employees. Your clients would like to bring suit against the company. Assuming *Chevron* applies, advise them on whether they would prevail on such a "reverse age discrimination" claim. What arguments would the employer make in response?

Problem Materials

Relevant provisions from the Age Discrimination in Employment Act (ADEA):

29 U.S.C. § 621(a)-(b) (2003): Congressional statement of findings and purpose

(a) The Congress hereby finds and declares that

> (1) in the face of rising productivity and affluence, older workers find themselves disadvantaged in their efforts to retain employment, and especially to regain employment when displaced from jobs....

> (b) It is therefore the purpose of this chapter to promote employment of older persons based on their ability rather than age; to prohibit arbitrary age discrimination in employment; to help employers and workers find ways of meeting problems arising from the impact of age on employment.

29 U.S.C. § 623(a): Prohibition of age discrimination

(a) Employer practices: It shall be unlawful for an employer—

> (1) to fail or refuse to hire or to discharge any individual or otherwise discriminate against any individual with respect to his compensation, terms, conditions, or privileges of employment, because of such individual's age....

29 U.S.C. § 631 (2003): Age limits

(a) Individuals at least 40 years of age

> The prohibitions in this chapter shall be limited to individuals who are at least 40 years of age.

29 C.F.R. § 1625.2(a) (assume that this federal regulation was enacted after *Hamilton v. Caterpillar, Inc.*, excerpted below, was decided):

> It is unlawful in situations where this Act applies, for an employer to discriminate in hiring or in any other way by giving preference because of age between individuals 40 and over. Thus, if two people apply for the same position, and one is 42 and the other 52, the employer may not lawfully turn down either one on the basis of age, but must make such decision on the basis of some other factor.

Select Legislative History on the ADEA:

Senate Hearings:

> – Statement of Sen. Harrison A. Williams: "Unfavorable beliefs and generalizations about older persons have grown up and have been translated into re-

strictive policies and practices in hiring new employees which bar older job-seekers from employment principally because of age."

- Statement of Sen. George Murphy: "[A]n older worker often faces an attitude on the part of some employers that prevents him from receiving serious consideration or even an interview in his search for employment."

House Hearings:

- Statement of Rep. Joshua Eilberg: "At age 40, a worker may find that age restrictions become common.... By age 45, his employment opportunities are likely to contract sharply; they shrink more severely at age 55 and virtually vanish by age 65."

- Statement of Rep. Claude Pepper: "We must provide meaningful opportunities for employment to the thousands of workers 45 and over who are well qualified but nevertheless denied jobs which they may desperately need because someone has arbitrarily decided that they are too old."

Hamilton v. Caterpillar, Inc.
966 F.2d 1226 (7th Cir. 1992)

CUDAHY, Circuit Judge.

In January 1986, Caterpillar announced that it was thinking about closing its plants in Davenport and Bettendorf, Iowa. Soon thereafter, Caterpillar began negotiations with Local 215 of the United Automobile, Aerospace and Agricultural Implement Workers of America, which represented Caterpillar's employees at the Iowa plants. As a result of the negotiations, in July 1986 Caterpillar agreed to establish a Special Early Retirement Program when and if the plants closed. Caterpillar's existing pension plan provided early retirement benefits to workers 60 years or older with 10 years of service and to workers 55 years or older with terms of service, that, when added to their age, totaled 85. The supplemental plan extends those early retirement benefits to workers 50 or older with 10 years of service.

The Davenport and Bettendorf plants were indeed shut down and all of Caterpillar's employees were laid off by June 1988. In 1990, Michael Hamilton brought a class action against Caterpillar, alleging that the Special Early Retirement Program violates the Age Discrimination in Employment Act (ADEA). The substance of the claim is more than a little bizarre: Hamilton and the other members of his class are between the ages of 40 and 50; they had ten years of service when the plants closed; and they are suing Caterpillar because they were too *young* to qualify for early retirement benefits....

This is the first time a reverse age discrimination case has reached this court.... [T]here is some arguable support for this position in the statute itself. Phrases like "because of such individual's age," "on the basis of such individual's age," or "because of his age" lend themselves to an interpretation that prohibits use of age as a factor, period. Finally, Hamilton points to a phrase in the Act's statement of purpose: "to prohibit arbitrary age discrimination in employment." 29 U.S.C. § 621(b)....

The findings that precede the congressional statement of purpose in section 621 refer specifically to the problems faced by "older workers" and "older persons." 29 U.S.C. §§ 621(a)(1), (a)(2) & (a)(3). In context, we believe that the phrase "arbitrary age discrimination" refers to Congress's understanding that discriminating against *older people* on the basis of their age is arbitrary. There is no evidence in the legislative history that

Congress had any concern for the plight of workers arbitrarily denied opportunities and benefits because they are too *young.* Age discrimination is thus somewhat like handicap discrimination: Congress was concerned that older people were being cast aside on the basis of inaccurate stereotypes about their abilities. The young, like the non-handicapped, cannot argue that they are similarly victimized.

The prohibitions in section 623 may be somewhat over inclusive, but the language Congress used is also more economical than the more precise alternatives. Perhaps Congress should have written "because such individual is older" or "on the basis of such individual's advancing age," but we are unwilling to open the floodgates to attacks on every retirement plan because Congress chose more graceful language.

The ADEA does not provide a remedy for reverse age discrimination. Accordingly, the judgment of the district court is *affirmed.*

Garrett v. Runyon
U.S. Equal Employment Opportunity Commission
Appeal Number 01960422
(September 5, 1997)

... Appellant had alleged [in a complaint filed with the EEOC] that officials at the Rome, Georgia Post Office discriminated against her on the basis of her age when, on October 1, 1994, her seniority standing was changed which resulted in her auxiliary route being awarded to another employee....

At the time this matter arose, appellant was employed by the agency at the Rome, Georgia Post Office as a Rural Carrier Associate. The evidence establishes that both appellant and another Rural Carrier Associate (hereinafter referred to as Comparison A) were hired by the agency effective August 1, 1987. Because both employees were hired on the same date, agency management deemed them to have equal seniority. At the time, there was no "tie-breaker" provision in the agency's collective bargaining agreement to establish the relative seniority standing for Rural Carrier Associates. However, it appears that the Postmaster borrowed the tie-breaker provision which did exist for another classification of carrier and deemed appellant to have the greater seniority because she had scored higher on the Rural Carrier Examination.

In 1988, the agency's collective bargaining agreement was amended to include tie breaker provisions for Rural Carrier Associates. Relevant to this case was a provision that "earliest date of birth" should be used to establish seniority between two employees with the same length of service.... [A]ppellant's seniority standing was adjusted, pursuant to the tie-breaker provisions of the collective bargaining agreement, to reflect that Comparative A, as the older employee, had the greater seniority. As a result, Comparative A, based on her greater seniority, was given the auxiliary route which had been worked by appellant prior to that date.

The record reveals that appellant filed a formal EEO complaint with the agency on November 21, 1994, alleging that the agency had discriminated against her on the basis of her age as referenced above. The agency accepted the complaint and conducted an investigation. At the conclusion of the investigation, appellant requested an administrative hearing.... In a final decision dated September 22, 1995, the agency ... entered a finding of no discrimination. It is from this decision that appellant now appeals....

The Commission's interpretive regulation, at 29 C.F.R. § 1625.2(a), specifically states:

(a) It is unlawful in situations where this Act applies, for an employer to discriminate in hiring or in any other way by giving preference because of age between individuals 40 and over. Thus, if two people apply for the same position, and one is 42 and the other 52, the employer may not lawfully turn down either one on the basis of age, but must make such decision on the basis of some other factor.

The plain language of this regulation appears to apply squarely to the instant matter, and works to prohibit the use of age as a seniority tie-breaker in this case. While the tie-breaker provision in question benefits the older employee, the Commission's regulation provides protection from age discrimination to both the older and younger individual who fall within the ambit of the ADEA. [We] recognize that at least one Circuit court has differed with our regulation. *See Hamilton v. Caterpillar Inc.* However, because the EEOC is the primary agency charged with the implementation of the ADEA, its interpretation of that statute is entitled to great deference. *See generally, Chevron, U.S.A., Inc. v. Natural Resources Defense Council.*

Accordingly, it is the decision of the Equal Employment Opportunity Commission to reverse the agency's final decision.

Notes and Questions

(1) Chevron *Step One.* Was the *Hamilton* opinion clear that, in *Brand X's* terms, "its construction follow[ed] from the unambiguous terms of the statute"? If so, does the agency's regulation receive deference? How much? If the opinion is unclear, does the agency's regulation receive deference? How much?

(2) *The* Mead *Mess.* If the agency had issued its interpretation through a non-legislative rule rather than through regulation, would the analysis be different?

(3) *Similarity to* Weber. Note the similarities between the issue raised by these cases and *Weber*. In *Weber*, the Court decided that a statute designed to protect minorities did not protect non-minorities from reverse discrimination, despite the plain language of the statute. Here, the issue was whether a statute designed to protect older workers from discrimination also protected younger workers from reverse discrimination. The Court has grown more conservative since *Weber* and has, more frequently, resorted to the plain meaning of the text to decide statutory issues. Despite this shift in philosophy, the Supreme Court held that the ADEA does not protect workers from reverse age discrimination in the case this problem was based on. *See General Dynamics Land Sys., Inc. v. Cline*, 540 U.S. 581 (2004). Because *General Dynamics* was decided in 2004, before *Brand X*, *General Dynamics* did not address the *Brand X* issue. Do you think the Court would have resolved the issue in Problem 17-3 and in the case differently if it had followed *Brand X*?

(4) *Expertise.* Does the EEOC have any particular expertise that would justify deferring to its decision that the ADEA forbids "reverse age discrimination"? If not, might deference nonetheless be appropriate?

Chapter 18

Severability and Inseverability Provisions

There are unique provisions in some statutes that create interesting issues for courts because of the interpretive challenges they create: severability and inseverability provisions. Both provisions are designed to show legislative intent as to how a court should proceed if the court holds that one part of a statute is unconstitutional: A severability provision indicates legislative intent that the remainder of the statute should remain in effect, while an inseverability provision indicates legislative intent that if one part of a statute is unconstitutional, the entire statute should be held invalid. These provisions are included in statutes fairly regularly. While they appear simple on their face, judicial reaction to them is curious. This chapter explores the problems that each of these provisions can create and the judicial resistance to treat them at face value.

A. Severability Provisions

Severability provisions serve essentially the same purpose in statutes as they do in contracts: to indicate the drafter's intent that if one provision is held invalid, then the remainder of the statute should remain in effect. Regardless of whether a statute includes such a provision, courts regularly consider whether a statute is severable. Thus, when a court finds a provision of a statute unconstitutional, that court will consider whether the remainder of the statute should remain valid. In other words, a court that strikes down a provision in a statute will not automatically strike down the entire statute. Instead, courts often leave the remaining provisions of the statute "fully operative as a law" unless "it is evident that the Legislature would not have enacted "the constitutional provisions independently of the unconstitutional aspects." *Alaska Airlines, Inc. v. Brock*, 480 U.S. 678, 684 (1987). Courts believe that by leaving as much of the statute as possible intact, they best implement legislative intent. *IMS Health Corp. v. Rowe*, 532 F. Supp.2d 183 (D. Me. 2008) ("Rules of statutory ... construction ... designed to effect legislative intent, do recognize that partial unconstitutionality of a statute ... does not necessarily result in tainting the whole legislation, even in the absence of a severability clause."). Hence, congressional "silence is just that—silence—and does not raise a presumption against severability." *Alaska Air*, 480 U.S. at 684.

Despite judicial willingness to sever even in the absence of such a provision, nonetheless many bills contain severability provisions. Additionally, some legislatures have enacted global severability provisions that direct courts to analyze whether an unconstitutional provision in a statute can be severed from the remainder in every case. This example is from a Washington state statute:

> If any chapter, section, subdivision of a section, paragraph, sentence, clause or word of this title for any reason shall be adjudged invalid, such judgment shall not affect, impair or invalidate the remainder of this title but shall be confined in its operation to the chapter, section, subdivision of a section, paragraph, sentence, clause or word of the title directly involved in the controversy in which such judgment shall have been rendered.... It is hereby expressly declared that had any chapter, section, subdivision of a section, paragraph, sentence, clause, word or any person, corporation, association or class of persons, corporations or associations as to which this title is declared invalid been eliminated from the title at the time the same was considered the title would have nevertheless been enacted with such portions eliminated.

Wash. Rev. Code Ann. § 82.98.030 (West 2004). Notice the final sentence, suggesting that the legislature would have had a specific intent in each situation. Consider whether this suggestion is accurate and whether such a directive would violate the constitutional enactment process.

While these clauses may appear to be boiler-plate, legislators often fight hard over whether to include a severability provision in a bill. *See generally*, Michael D. Shumsky, *Severability, Inseverability, and the Rule of Law*, 41 Harv. J. on Legis. 227 (2004) (discussing the McCain-Feingold campaign finance reform bill). Despite this fact, courts do not always give effect to severability provisions. Instead, as the Supreme Court recently stated, the inclusion of a severability provision merely "creates a presumption that Congress did not intend the validity of the statute in question to depend on the validity of the constitutionally offensive provision." *Alaska Air*, 480 U.S. at 686. However, that presumption may be overcome by "strong evidence that Congress intended otherwise." *Id.* This presumption seems odd: An unambiguous, express severability provision, part of the enacted text, is merely presumptively correct and can be overcome by other evidence showing that Congress intended inseverability. Surprisingly then, "the ultimate determination of severability will rarely turn on the presence or absence of ... a [severability] clause." *United States v. Jackson*, 390 U.S. 570, 585 n.27 (1968). Despite the fact that severability clauses may not be given their expressed effect, many statutes contain them. Inseverability clauses, which we will study in a moment, are less common.

In the following case, the two defendants argued that the unconstitutional provision in a statute required reversal of their convictions. The court, however, found a way to avoid that result. Notice the relevance of the severability provision.

Elliott v. Commonwealth

593 S.E.2d 263 (Va. 2004)

Lemons, Justice.

On the night of May 2, 1998, Richard J. Elliott, ("Elliott") and Jonathan S. O'Mara ("O'Mara") erected a cross in the yard of ... Elliott's next-door neighbor, and attempted to ignite it. According to the record, Elliott conceived of the cross burning as revenge against [the neighbor] because [the neighbor] had complained to Elliott's mother about gunfire in Elliott's backyard. Elliott convinced two friends, O'Mara and David Targee, to aid him in the burning.

The Commonwealth prosecuted Elliott and O'Mara for attempted cross burning and conspiracy to commit cross burning.... O'Mara pled guilty to attempted cross burning and conspiracy to commit cross burning but conditioned his plea upon the reservation of his right to challenge the constitutionality of [the statute] on appeal. Elliott chose to be tried by a jury.... A jury found Elliott guilty of attempted cross burning but acquitted him of conspiracy to commit cross burning....

[W]e held that [the statute] was facially invalid as selective regulation of speech based upon content ... because it singled out a particular form of intimidating symbolic speech for punishment while leaving other forms unregulated. Additionally, we held that the language of the prima facie evidence provision of the statute was overbroad because of its chilling effect upon the exercise of free speech under the First Amendment.

The Commonwealth appealed our decision to the United States Supreme Court. In a plurality opinion authored by Justice O'Connor, the Supreme Court held that the Commonwealth may engage in content discrimination when the basis for the content discrimination consists entirely of the very reason the entire class of speech at issue is proscribable. Thus, the Commonwealth may prohibit cross burning with intent to intimidate, even though it fails to prohibit the burning of other objects, because cross burning is significantly more likely to intimidate.

Although it concluded that the core provisions of [the statute] were constitutional, the Supreme Court held that the prima facie evidence provision of the statute was unconstitutional.... [T]he Supreme Court held that the provision as interpreted by the model jury instruction was unconstitutionally overbroad.

The Supreme Court ... remanded the *Elliott* and *O'Mara* cases to this Court to determine ... whether the prima facie evidence provision could be severed from the statute if a constitutional interpretation could not be found....

> [The statute], in effect at the time defendants committed the offenses, provided:
>
> It shall be unlawful for any person or persons, with the intent of intimidating any person or group of persons, to burn or cause to be burned, a cross on the property of another, a highway or other public place....
>
> Any such burning of a cross shall be prima facie evidence of an intent to intimidate a person or group of persons....

Elliott and O'Mara have argued that the unconstitutional prima facie evidence provision cannot be severed from the remainder of the statute.... We reject [the argument]....

Code § 1-17.1, first enacted in 1986, provides that "[t]he provisions of all statutes are severable unless (i) the statute specifically provides that its provisions are not severable; or (ii) it is apparent that two or more statutes or provisions must operate in accord with one another." Prior to the enactment of this statute, "[a]bsent a severability provision, a legislative act [was] presumed to be non-severable." Code § 1-17.1 changed that rule and provided a rule of construction for the courts to apply to interpret even statutes passed prior to 1986. If the General Assembly intended for § 1-17.1 to apply only to statutes passed after 1986, it could have included such language in the section. Instead, the statute refers broadly to "[t]he provisions of statutes in this Code," without reference to dates of enactment.

Code § 18.2-423 does not fall within either of the exceptions to the rule of severability established in § 1-17.1. The cross burning statute does not contain language stating that its parts are not severable, nor is the prima facie evidence provision necessary to the operation of the remainder of the statute. The fact that the provision is not inextricably intertwined with the rest of the statute is illustrated by the fact that the cross burning statute, now codified at § 18.2-423, existed for 16 years, from 1952 to 1968, without the prima facie evidence provision. *See* Code § 18.1-365 (Supp.1968). The statute was and can be effective now in punishing intimidation without the prima facie evidence provision....

For the reasons discussed above, we hold that ... the statute is severable and that the core provisions of the statute that remain do not violate the First Amendment or Article I, § 12 of the Constitution of Virginia. There is no need to order retrials; consequently, the convictions of Richard J. Elliott and Jonathan S. O'Mara will be affirmed.

Notes and Questions

(1) *Note the Argument.* The criminal defense lawyer used the unconstitutional *prima facie* provision to try to reverse his clients' convictions. How? Be sure you can explain why the fact that the Supreme Court found the *prima facie* portion of the statute unconstitutional could result in reversal of his clients' conviction—even if no jury instruction about *prima facie* intent to intimidate had been given at the defendants' trial.

(2) *Retroactive Effect.* Notice that in Virginia, the presumption before 1986 was that absent a severability provision, a statute was presumed non-severable. Then the legislature enacted § 1-17.1, which reversed this presumption. The *prima facie* statute, though, was enacted in 1968, long before the severability provision became effective. Why does this court hold § 1-17.1 applies to a provision added to a statute before § 1-17.1 had been enacted?

(3) *At Odds with Textualism?* Is the approach of the courts to severability clauses— that they merely create a presumption of severability—consistent with textualism? Some commentators say that they are merely boilerplate that express nothing about legislative intent. *E.g.*, Max Radin, *A Short Way with Statutes*, 56 Harv. L. Rev. 388, 419 (1942) ("Are we really to imagine that the legislature had, as it says it had, weighted each paragraph literally and come to the conclusion that it would have enacted that paragraph if all the rest of the statute were invalid?"). Can you identify a policy reason why the plain text of a severability clause should not be enforced as written? In responding, consider the fact that textualists believe that they cannot know what motivated particular legislators to vote for particular bills. Is enforcing severability provisions as written at least in tension with that view? Finally, if a particular statute *lacks* a severability provision and if, as many say, they are "boilerplate," ought the rule be that where there is no severability provision, the statute should stand or fall as a whole?

(4) *Taking Textualism Too Far?* In *Louisville/Jefferson County Metro Gov't v. Metro Louisville Hosp. Coalition, Inc.,* ___ S.W.3d ___, 2009 WL 350694 (Ct. App. Ky. Feb. 13, 2009), the Louisville City Council adopted an ordinance that banned smoking, except at Churchill Downs, home of the Kentucky Derby. The exception was found to violate the Equal Protection Clause of the Kentucky Constitution. Although the ordinance contained a severability clause, the district court invalidated the entire ordinance. In reaching its conclusion that the City Council would not have adopted the ordinance without the exception for Churchill Downs, the district court relied on the fact that an ordinance without the exception had been rejected by the City Council. The appellate court reversed. It held that reliance on legislative history was improper: "[I]f the Ordinance at hand is not ambiguous, it would violate basic rules of statutory construction to consider the debates on amendments to determine legislative intent." Does the appellate court's approach go too far? Or, does it make sense, but only if the statute contains a severability provision? In answering those questions, recall that the Supreme Court in *Alaska Airlines, Inc. v. Brock*, 480 U.S. 678, 686 (1987) stated that a severability clause merely creates a presumption of severability that may be overcome by "strong evidence that Congress intended otherwise." How likely is it that text alone will be evidence to overcome the presumption?

(5) *Section by Section.* In *Sloan v. Wilkins*, 608 S.E.2d 579 (S.C. 2005), the statute at issue contained a severability provision that provided:

> If any section, subsection, paragraph, subparagraph, sentence, clause, phrase, or word of this act is for any reason held to be unconstitutional or invalid, such holding shall not affect the constitutionality or validity of the remaining portions of this act, the General Assembly hereby declaring that it would have passed this act, and each and every section, subsection, paragraph, subparagraph, sentence, clause, phrase, and word thereof, irrespective of the fact that any one or more other sections, subsections, paragraphs, subparagraphs, sentences, clauses, phrases, or words hereof may be declared to be unconstitutional, invalid, or otherwise ineffective.

Id. at 584. The court concluded that a bill that had, among other things, created a culinary institute at a community college and authorized a feasibility study for a state law school, violated the "one subject rule." The court held that in light of the severability provision, however, it would enforce those provisions of the bill that were within "one subject" and hold unconstitutional those provisions that related to another subject. It then found the "subject" of the act to have been "to foster economic growth in this state through development of the life sciences industry." *Id.* The court severed and upheld provisions that, among other things, promoted venture capital for life sciences and allowed for depreciation of machinery used in biotechnology fields. It found provisions that gave raises and better insurance benefits to graduate students to violate the one subject rule. Isn't the determination of whether a legislature would have enacted some of provisions but not others speculative? *See also Alaskans for a Common Language, Inc. v. Kritz,* 170 P.3d 183 (Alaska 2007) (court split on whether voters would have approved referendum without the unconstitutional section).

(6) *Statutory Directives.* Some legislatures have adopted statutes that provide specific direction to courts as to how to determine when a statute should be held invalid when one provision is struck down. Pennsylvania, for example, has a statute of general application that provides that provisions of *every* statute are severable, unless one of two exceptions applies:

> The provisions of every statute shall be severable. If any provision of any statute or the application thereof to any person or circumstance is held invalid, the remainder of the statute, and the application of such provision to other persons or circumstances, shall not be affected thereby, unless the court finds that the valid provisions of the statute are so essentially and inseparably connected with, and so depend upon, the void provision or application, that it cannot be presumed the General Assembly would have enacted the remaining valid provisions without the void one; or unless the court finds that the remaining valid provisions, standing alone, are incomplete and are incapable of being executed in accordance with the legislative intent.

1 Pa. C.S. § 1925. How should a court in such a jurisdiction determine whether an exception applies?

B. Inseverability Provisions

In contrast to a severability provision, which indicates legislative intent that the provisions of a statute should not stand or fall together, *inseverability* clauses indicate legislative intent that the legislature would *not* have enacted the statute without every provision; hence, all provisions should stand or fall together. Used this way, inseverability provisions serve "a key function of preserving legislative compromise;" they "bind[] the benefits and concessions that constitute the deal into an interdependent whole." Israel E. Friedman, *Comment, Inseverability Clauses in Statutes*, 64 U. Chi. L. Rev. 903, 914 (1997).

Perhaps surprisingly, given their purpose at ensuring that a legislative compromise is maintained in the courts, inseverability clauses are less common than severability provisions. *See* Shumsky, *supra*, at 243. Although less common, inseverability clauses raise fundamental issues of statutory interpretation, as the following case shows.

Louk v. Cormier
622 S.E.2d 788 (W. Va. 2005)

Davis, Justice.

Rita Mae Louk, appellant/plaintiff below (hereinafter referred to as "Ms. Louk"), appeals from an order of the Circuit Court of Randolph County denying her motion for a new trial. A jury returned a non-unanimous verdict against Ms. Louk in her medical malpractice action against Dr. Serge Cormier, appellee/defendant below (hereinafter referred to as "Dr. Cormier"). Here, Ms. Louk contends that the circuit court erred by ruling that the non-unanimous verdict provision of W. Va.Code § 55-7B-6d (2001) (Supp.2004) was constitutional. After reviewing the briefs, listening to the arguments of the parties and considering the relevant authority, we reverse....

The sparse record in this case indicates that ... Dr. Cormier performed a hysterectomy and salpingo-oophorectomy on Ms. Louk.... Several days after Ms. Louk was released from the hospital, she became gravely ill. Consequently ... Ms. Louk returned to the hospital complaining of a fever ... and a tender abdomen. On the day that Ms. Louk returned to the hospital, exploratory surgery was performed. The exploratory surgery revealed that Ms. Louk had suffered a perforation of her cecum....

Ms. Louk filed a medical malpractice action against Dr. Cormier. The central allegation ... was that Dr. Cormier perforated Ms. Louk's cecum when he performed the hysterectomy.... Dr. Cormier defended ... on a theory that the cecum spontaneously ruptured.

The case proceeded to trial ... before a twelve person jury.... Among the instructions given was an instruction that informed the jury that it was not necessary to reach a unanimous verdict. The jury returned a verdict in which ten jurors found in favor of Dr. Cormier. Two jurors found in favor of Ms. Louk.

Thereafter, Ms. Louk filed a post-trial motion seeking a new trial arguing that the non-unanimous verdict instruction authorized by W. Va.Code § 55-7B-6d was unconstitutional. On December 19, 2003, the circuit court entered an order denying the motion for a new trial. Ms. Louk filed this appeal from that ruling ...

[After considerable analysis the court held] that the provisions contained in W. Va.Code § 55-7B-6d (2001) (Supp.2004) were enacted in violation of the Separation of Powers Clause, Article V, § 1 of the West Virginia Constitution, insofar as the statute addresses procedural litigation matters that are regulated exclusively by this Court pursuant to the Rule-Making Clause, Article VIII, § 3 of the West Virginia Constitution. Consequently, W. Va.Code § 55-7B-6d, in its entirety, is unconstitutional and unenforceable....

Because of an amendment to the MPLA's Severability statute in 2001,[17] our determination that the non-unanimous verdict provision in W. Va.Code § 55-7B-6d is invalid impacts other provisions of the MPLA, as well as another statute. The MPLA's Severability statute, W. Va.Code § 55-7B-11 (2001) (Supp.2004), reads as follows:

> (a) If any provision of this article ... or the application thereof to any person or circumstance is held invalid, such invalidity shall not affect other provisions or applications of this article, and to this end, the provisions of this article are declared to be severable.

> (b) *If any provision of the amendments to section five of this article, any provision of new section six-d of this article or any provision of the amendments to section eleven, article six, chapter fifty-six of this code as provided in House Bill 601 ... is held invalid, or the application thereof to any person is held invalid, then, notwithstanding any other provision of law, every other provision of said House Bill 601 shall be deemed invalid and of no further force and effect.*

> (c) If any provision of the amendments to sections six or ten of this article or any provision of new sections six-a, six-b or six-c of this article as provided in House Bill 60l ... is held invalid, such invalidity shall not affect other provisions or applications of this article, and to this end, such provisions are deemed severable.

(Emphasis added).

A fair reading of the Severability statute indicates that it is a hybrid, *i.e.*, it contains both *severability* provisions and a *non-severability* provision. It is the non-severability provision, W. Va.Code § 55-7B-11(b), that is relevant to our decision in this case. Under the non-severability provision, the Legislature has determined that, if this Court invalidates a provision to the 2001 amendments to W. Va.Code § 55-7B-5, W. Va.Code § 56-6-11, or the newly created W. Va.Code § 55-7B-6d, then all of said provisions are invalid. In other words, the non-severability provision has presumptively invalidated the remaining twelve juror provision in W. Va.Code § 55-7B-6d, and the 2001 amendments to W. Va.Code § 55-7B-5 and W. Va.Code § 56-6-11, as a result of our determination that the non-unanimous verdict provision in W. Va.Code § 55-7B-6d is unconstitutional. The issue of the deference to be accorded a non-severability provision appears to be one of first impression for this Court.

It has been observed that a non-severability clause is almost unheard of and constitutes a legislative finding that every section is so important to the single subject that no part of the act can be removed without destruction of the legislative purpose.[18] Our research

---

17. . "It has come to be common legislative drafting practice to include in each bill a separability clause (sometimes called a severability clause or saving clause) to the effect that if any part of the act be found invalid, the remainder of the act shall nevertheless be upheld. Such clauses must be considered by the courts in deciding the separability of an enactment. The separability clause is a comparatively modern legislative device, the courts having developed the principle and practice of holding statutes separable long before the innovation of separability clauses." Norman J. Singer, *Statutes and Statutory Construction* § 44:8, at 585 (2001).

18. "[C]ontroversial legislation sometimes includes [a non-]severability clause, a clause declaring that, if any one provision of the statute is held invalid, the remainder of the statute shall not have effect." Mark L. Movsesian, *Severability in Statutes and Contracts*, 30 Ga. L.Rev. 41, 77 (1995). Further, it has been suggested that legislatures include a non-severability provision in a statute "in an effort to prevent the courts from sustaining a piece of controversial legislation in the event that they invalidate one central provision." Lars Noah, *The Executive Line Item Veto and the Judicial Power to Sever: What's The Difference?*, 56 Wash. & Lee L.Rev. 235, 237–38 (1999). *See also* Michael D. Shumsky, *Severability, Inseverability, and the Rule of Law*, 41 Harv. J. on Legis. 227, 267–68 (2004) ("When [a legislature] includes [a non-] severability clause in constitutionally questionable legislation, it does so in order to insulate a key legislative deal from judicial interference. Such clauses are iron-clad guaran-

indicates that only a few courts have addressed the issue of non-severability provisions. A majority of those courts have enforced non-severability provisions without comment.

A few courts, however, have commented on the degree of deference to be accorded to non-severability provisions. These courts have held that a non-severability clause cannot ultimately bind a court, it establishes (only) a presumption of non-severability. That is, despite the unambiguous command of … (non)severability clauses, … they create only a rebuttable presumption that guides-but does not control-a reviewing court's severability determination.

We have discerned from courts and commentators that statutory construction principles that apply to "severability" provisions are equally applicable to "non-severability" provisions. Consequently, we now hold that a non-severability provision contained in a legislative enactment is construed as merely a presumption that the Legislature intended the entire enactment to be invalid if one of the statutes in the legislation is found unconstitutional. When a non-severability provision is appended to a legislative enactment and this Court invalidates a statute contained in the enactment, we will apply severability principles of statutory construction to determine whether the non-severability provision will be given full force and effect.

1. Severability principles of statutory construction. Under this Court's severability principles of statutory construction we do not defer, as a matter of course, to severability provisions contained in statutes. Instead, we engage in an independent analysis to determine legislative intent and the effect of the severability section of the statute….

This Court has adopted the following statutory construction principle that is applied in determining the issue of severability:

> A statute may contain constitutional and unconstitutional provisions which may be perfectly distinct and separable so that some may stand and the others will fall; and if, when the unconstitutional portion of the statute is rejected, the remaining portion reflects the legislative will, is complete in itself, is capable of being executed independently of the rejected portion, and in all other respects is valid, such remaining portion will be upheld and sustained.

The most critical aspect of severability analysis involves the degree of dependency of statutes. Thus, where the valid and the invalid provisions of a statute are so connected and interdependent in subject matter, meaning, or purpose as to preclude the belief, presumption or conclusion that the Legislature would have passed the one without the other, the whole statute will be declared invalid.

The foregoing severability statutory construction principles will be applied to determine whether the remaining twelve juror provision in W.Va.Code § 55-7B-6d and the 2001 amendments to W. Va.Code § 56-6-11 and W. Va.Code § 55-7B-5 must be invalidated as inseverable from W. Va.Code § 55-7B-6d.

2. The twelve juror provision of W. Va.Code § 55-7B-6d. The remaining provision in W. Va.Code § 55-7B-6d directs that "the jury in any trial of an action for medical professional liability shall consist of twelve members." As will be shown, this provision is invalid because it is in conflict with a specific rule promulgated by this Court

---

tees-clear statements by [the legislature] that it would not have enacted one part of a statute without the others. Legislation containing [a non-]severability clause can thus be conceived of as a contract among competing political interests containing a structural enforcement mechanism designed to alleviate the concerns of those legislators who were willing to vote for … a particular statutory scheme only if credibly assured that certain limiting provisions would be secure in the enacted legislation.").

and because it is not severable from the unconstitutional non-unanimous jury verdict provision.

The issue of the number of jurors in a civil action is addressed in Rule 47(b) of the West Virginia Rules of Civil Procedure. Rule 47(b) states, in relevant part, that "[u]nless the court directs that a jury shall consist of a greater number, a jury shall consist of six persons." Under W. Va.Code § 55-7B-6d, it is mandatory that a trial court seat twelve jurors in a medical malpractice action. However, under Rule 47(b), a jury is limited to six members unless, in the exercise of the trial court's discretion, a greater number is imposed....

Additionally, the twelve juror requirement is dependent upon and intertwined with the unconstitutional non-unanimous jury verdict provision of W. Va.Code § 55-7B-6d. In order for the non-unanimous jury verdict provision to take effect, twelve jurors must be chosen so that a minimum of nine jurors may render a verdict. Consequently, the twelve juror provision is invalid because it is not severable from the unconstitutional non-unanimous jury verdict provision of W. Va.Code § 55-7B-6d.

3. Six Member Jury Exemption in Amendment to W. Va.Code § 56-6-11. The 2001 amendment to W. Va.Code § 56-6-11 added subsection (c), which provides:

> The provisions of this section providing for a six member jury trial do not apply to any proceeding had pursuant to article seven-b, chapter fifty-five of this code, the provisions of which apply to all cases involving a medical professional liability action.

Clearly, W. Va.Code § 56-6-11(c)'s exemption of a six person jury in medical malpractice cases is dependent upon the twelve person provision in W. Va.Code § 55-7B-6d, which we have invalidated. Consequently, we find the 2001 amendment to W. Va.Code § 56-6-11(c) is inseverable from W. Va.Code § 55-7B-6d and is therefore invalid.

4. Proscription of Bad Faith Claims Against Medical Malpractice Insurers in Amendment to W. Va.Code § 55-7B-5. The 2001 amendment to W. Va.Code § 55-7B-5 added subsections (b) and (c) ...

The issues addressed in W. Va.Code §§ 55-7B-5(b) and (c) pertain to the ability of a bad faith claim to be asserted against an insurer of a health care provider. Whether a litigant may or may not be able to file a bad faith claim against a health care insurer is not dependent in any way upon whether a verdict may be non-unanimous. That is, W. Va.Code §§ 55-7B-5(b) and (c) are independent of W. Va.Code § 55-7B-6d....

Consequently, W. Va.Code §§ 55-7B-5(b) and (c) are severable from W. Va.Code § 55-7B-6d and are, therefore, not invalidated by our decision to strike down the non-unanimous jury verdict provision of W. Va.Code § 55-7B-6d....

Reversed and Remanded.

ALBRIGHT, CHIEF JUSTICE, concurring

I concur with the result in this case but pause to offer some words of caution. The authority relied upon by the majority regarding the non-severability clause is quite tenuous. I fear the reasoning employed by the majority creates serious potential for mischief. On the other hand, the use by the Legislature of a so-called "non-severability" clause—especially on a regular basis—has equal or even greater potential for mischief.

In this case, I would have preferred that the Court postpone the issuance of the mandate in order to give the Legislature the time needed to reconsider whether it truly desired to have its entire enactment on medical malpractice fail because it had inadvertently strayed into an area of constitutional responsibility reserved to this Court. For this reason I concur with reservation.

Benjamin, Justice, concurring, in part, and dissenting, in part

I dissent from ... the majority's analysis of the non-severability clause contained in W. Va.Code § 55-7B-11(b). Instead of invalidating the clause in question as unconstitutional, the majority utilizes a statutory interpretation approach to the clause. The result is that the majority premises its invalidity finding on the statutory interpretation of a clause which is clear and unambiguous. Principles of statutory interpretation should only be invoked where the statutory language is ambiguous. The language contained within W. Va.Code § 55-7B-11(b) is not ambiguous and is as clear as any that this Court has been called upon to consider. By its terms, the clause is either a valid exercise of power or it is an invalid attempt to appropriate power. The middle ground of invoking statutory interpretation principles to determine validity is simply not a option, in my opinion, for deciding the validity of W. Va.Code § 55-7B-11.

I conclude that a legislative body may not, years after it has dissolved and been replaced by a new legislative body, reach out from the grave to invalidate an otherwise valid law of this state in the manner intended by this clause. The insertion of a "poison pill" clause into otherwise valid legislation constitutes a usurpation of this Court's role in determining the validity of lawfully enacted statutes. Our system of governance does not envision legislative "dares" to this Court to not invalidate unconstitutional legislative enactments. A non-severability clause, such as here, improperly seeks to protect an unconstitutional enactment from legitimate scrutiny by the judicial branch by linking it to viability of valid law (law which has been followed and properly relied upon in this State for years). By such "poison pills", the message to this Court is clear—either we permit unconstitutional legislation to stand, or otherwise valid statutes which have been relied upon and used for years by citizens of West Virginia become collateral damage. The Judiciary must resist such an injection of politics into this Court's decisions. This Court's duty to determine the constitutionality of legislation must not be impeded, constrained, threatened or cajoled. Separation of Powers, a foundation of our constitutional system of governance, proscribes any such legislative posturing which would cause us indirectly to do that which we would not do directly.

The non-severability provision of W. Va.Code § 55-7B-11(b) violates the Separation of Powers Clause of our Constitution. It constitutes an improper attempt by the Legislature to usurp this Court's independent consideration of the constitutionality of individual statutes. Any attempt to improperly influence this Court's duty of constitutional scrutiny by hinging the validity of otherwise constitutional legislation upon the requirement that this Court uphold otherwise unconstitutional legislation is intolerable and, therefore, invalid. The 2001 Legislature cannot now act to repeal otherwise valid legislation in 2005. Should the current Legislature seek to do so, it may.

Maynard, Justice, dissenting:

A court should exercise the greatest caution and restraint when deciding its own power. I wish the majority had done so here. By ruling that this Court, simply by its own judge-made rules, can strike down a statute passed by the entire legislature is sobering indeed! This ruling not only invalidates important provisions of the medical malpractice reform package but also serves as a warning that this Court has the absolute power to declare null and void any part or the entire reform package. The mechanism for grinding a statute out of existence is for the Court simply to declare that the statute conflicts with an existing rule of this Court or to make a new rule which conflicts with the statute. In either case, the statute becomes unconstitutional....

I note that the majority also strikes a non-severability provision. The reader should understand that the Legislature passed, as part of its reform package, what I call a "poison pill" non-severability provision. Simply put, it says that if this Court strikes down any part of specified articles in House Bill 601, which makes up part of the Medical Professional Liability Act, then every other provision of House Bill 601 shall be deemed invalid and of no further force and effect. The majority now says the Legislature cannot do that. This I find astonishing. The majority actually says the Legislature cannot reverse a statute *it* passed. It seems to me if the Legislature has the power to enact a law, it certainly has the power to repeal the same law. At any rate, I do not need to reach that provision in this dissent. Since there is no conflict between the statute and this Court's rule, I would find the statute to be valid and constitutional. Thus, the non-severability clause would not be implicated.

Accordingly, for the reasons stated above, I dissent to the majority opinion.

Notes and Questions

(1) *Who was Right?* The majority viewed its job as interpreting the inseverability provision and applying it as an interpretive guide. One dissenter believed that the inseverability provision should be enforced as written and that any other result would be "astonishing." The first dissenter viewed the inseverability provision as a usurpation of judicial and legislative power. Who was right?

(2) *Repealing Valid Legislation?* One dissent believed that the prior legislature was "reaching out" and repealing valid legislation by including an inseverability provision. Is that a correct view? Or, is the court re-writing the statute the legislature enacted by choosing to enforce only part of the statute?

(3) *Ignoring the Compromise?* Given the nature of compromise inherent in the legislative process, do you believe the presumption should be toward inseverability when a severability clause is lacking? If an inseverability clause indicates that the legislation was a compromise that would not have been passed except *in toto*, does a court ignore legislative intent if it fails to give the provision full effect? What policies would suggest that a court should not give full and immediate effect to inseverability provisions? Which of these should carry the most weight? Or, does your answer suggest that an all-or-nothing view is inappropriate?

(4) *Varying Judicial Approaches.* In a few states, courts presume statutes to be inseverable unless the legislature specifies otherwise. The greater number of states reason that statutes are presumed severable but that presumption is overcome by the inclusion of an inseverability provision. Given that it is within the court's province to determine the constitutionality of a statute, does an inseverability clause violate separation of powers? If inseverability clauses are constitutional, does the resulting statute that is enforced by the court somehow violate the bicameral and presentment clauses of the constitution because the "remaining" statute is one that was never passed by a legislature and presented to the executive?

(5) *Pernicious Motive and Unconstitutional Effect?* One commentator has argued that inseverability clauses can be inspired by ill motives and have negative impact. Consider these observations:

> Typically, an inseverability clause is used because the legislature is justifiably concerned that a reviewing court, in invalidating only part of a statute, might leave standing an unworkable law, or one that the legislature would not have enacted in the form that it took after the unconstitutional part was removed. Most courts will sever the unconstitutional provisions of a statute only if they believe the contrary: that the valid provisions of a statute are functionally capable of stand-

ing alone, and that the legislature would have enacted the valid provisions of the statute without the invalid ones. But this is guesswork by definition, and it is understandable for legislators to fear that the courts might guess wrong....

The two other uses of inseverability clauses are tactical, and questionable. In the first of these ... the inseverability clause serves an in terrorem function, as the legislature attempts to guard against judicial review altogether by making the price of invalidation too great.... [A]n inseverability clause might provide that in case the courts invalidated any part of a wide-ranging, indispensable law (such as a budget bill), the entire law, and perhaps other, previously enacted laws, would cease to exist. The other questionable use of inseverability, a sort of poison-pill device..., involves an attempt to sabotage a statute. The legislators might assume that the statute contains some unconstitutional provision already (probably a safe assumption in such constitutionally tortuous areas as campaign finance), or they might insert both an inseverability clause and a new provision whose unconstitutionality was fairly plain (such as a provision to outlaw flag burning). Such a clause can serve a dual purpose: it can ensure invalidation of the law, and at the same time legislators who oppose the bill in principle, but whose constituents favor it, can feel comfortable voting for the bill and gaining political advantage without concern that the bill might survive judicial scrutiny.

On the surface, in terrorem clauses seem especially troubling, because they represent an attempt by the legislature to prevent the judiciary from exercising a power that rightly belongs to it (whereas poison-pill clauses invite the judiciary to exercise that power). These clauses, in other words, amount to coercive threats, and the principle that people should not be subject to such threats, or should be free of the consequences of their acts if the acts are coerced, is about as basic as legal principles get.

Fred Kameny, *Are Severability Clauses Constitutional*, 28 STATUTE L. REV. 131, 135–36 (2007). Assuming these observations are true, how should a court respond? Should a court consider evidence in the legislative history as to why the inseverability provision was adopted? If a court finds an improper legislative motive, should that finding matter to the ultimate question of severability or inseverability?

Problem 18-1

The judiciary in the state had not been given a salary increase by the state legislature in five years. Despite judicial requests and public support for the idea, the current legislature also seemed cold to the idea. However, on the last day of the session, the legislature approved a bill that sought to accomplish two major objectives. First, it provided for a 4% increase in judicial salaries, effective immediately. Second, it provided that a criminal defendant could be convicted by a majority vote of a jury comprised of at least six jurors. During floor debates on what was called "the four for four" bill, several legislators commented that the state supreme court had repeatedly held that a conviction could be constitutional only if the jury were comprised of six members, if the verdict were unanimous, and if there were twelve jurors, nine of whom voted to convict. Thus, the law seemed patently unconstitutional. After those statements were made, the bill was amended to include the judicial raise and an inseverability provision.

You are representing a defendant who has been convicted by a vote of four out of six jurors. It is absolutely clear that the conviction is unconstitutional. How would you argue to the judge that the impact of its unconstitutionality on the salary increase should be handled? If you represent the prosecution, how would you respond? Ignore the one subject rule.

Appendix A

Canons of Construction

Excerpted from Karl N. Llewellyn,
*Remarks on the Theory of Appellate Decision and the Rules
of Cannon about How Statutes are to be Construed*
3 Vand. L Rev. 395 (1949)*

THRUST	BUT	PARRY
1. A statute cannot go beyond its text.		1. To effect its purpose a statute may be implemented beyond its text.
2. Statutes in derogation of the common law will not be extended by construction		2. Such acts will be liberally construed if their nature is remedial.
3. Statutes are to be read in the light of the common law and a statute affirming a common law rule is to be construed in accordance with the common law.		3. The common law gives way to a statute which is in consistent with it and when a statute is designed as a revision of a whole body of law applicable to a given subject it supersedes the common law.
4. Where a foreign statute which has received construction has been adopted, previous construction is adopted too.		4. It may be rejected where there is conflict with the obvious meaning of the statute or where the foreign decisions are unsatisfactory in reasoning or where the foreign interpretation is not in harmony with the spirit or policy of the laws of the adopting state.
5. Where various states have already adopted the statute, the parent state is followed.		5. Where interpretations of other states are inharmonious, there is no such restraint.
6. Statutes *in pari materia* must be construed together.		6. A statute is not *in pare materia* if its scope and aim are distinct or where a legislative design to depart from the general purpose or policy of previous enactments may be apparent.
7. A statute imposing a new penalty or forfeiture, or a new liability or disability, or creating a new right of action will not		7. Remedial statutes are to be liberally construed and if a retroactive interpretation will promote the ends of

---

* Copyright Vanderbilt Law Review. Used by permission.

be construed as having a retroactive effect.

justice, they should receive such construction.

8. Where design has been distinctly started no place is left for construction.

8. Courts have the power to inquire into real as distinct from ostensible purpose.

9. Definitions and rules of construction contained in an interpretation clause are part of the law and binding.

9. Definitions and rules of construction in a statute will not be extended beyond their necessary import nor allowed to defeat intention otherwise manifested.

10. A statutory provision requiring liberal construction does not mean disregard of unequivocal requirements of the statute.

10. Where a rule of construction is provided within the statute itself the rule should be applied.

11. Titles do not control meaning; preambles do not expand scope; section headings do not change language.

11. The title may be consulted as a guide when there is doubt or obscurity in the body; preambles may be consulted to determine rationale, and thus the true construction of terms; section headings may be looked upon as part of the statute itself.

12. If language is plain and unambiguous it must be given effect.

12. Not when literal interpretation would lead to absurd or mischievous consequences or thwart manifest purpose.

13. Words and phrases which have received judicial construction before enactment are to be understood according to that construction.

13. Not if the statute clearly requires them to have a different meaning.

14. After enactment, judicial decision upon interpretation of particular terms and phrases controls.

14. Practical construction by executive officers is strong evidence of true meaning.

15. Words are to be taken in their ordinary meaning unless they are technical terms or words of art.

15. Popular words may bear a technical meaning and technical words may have a popular signification and they should be so construed as to agree with evident intention or to make the statute operative.

16. Every word and clause must be given effect.

16. If inadvertently inserted or if repugnant to the rest of the statute, they may be rejected as surplusage.

17. The same language used repeatedly in the same connection is presumed to bear the same meaning throughout the statute.

17. This presumption will be disregarded where it is necessary to assign different meanings to make the statute consistent.

18. Words are to be interpreted according to the proper grammatical effect of their arrangement within the statute.

18. Rules of grammar will be disregarded where strict adherence would defeat purpose.

19. Exceptions not made cannot be read.

19. The letter is only the "bark." Whatever is within the reason of the law is within the law itself.

20. Expression of one thing excludes another.

20. The language may fairly comprehend many different cases where some only are expressly mentioned by way of example.

21. General terms are to receive a general construction.

21. They may be limited by specific terms with which they are associated or by the scope and purpose of the statute.

22. It is a general rule of construction that where general words follow an enumeration they are to be held as applying only to persons and things of the same general kind or class specifically mentioned (*ejusdem generis*).

22. General words must operate on something. Further, *ejusdem generis* is only an aid in getting the meaning and does not warrant confining the operations of a statute within narrower limits than were intended.

23. Qualifying or limiting words or clauses are to be referred to the next preceding antecedent.

23. Not when evident sense and meaning require a different construction.

24. Punctuation will govern when a statute is open to two constructions.

24. Punctuation marks will not control the plain and evident meaning of language.

25. It must be assumed that language has been chosen with due regard to grammatical propriety and is not interchangeable on mere conjecture.

25. "And" and "or" may be read interchangeably whenever the change is necessary to give the statute sense and effect.

26. There is a distinction between words of permission and mandatory words.

26. Words imparting permission may be read as mandatory and words imparting command may be read as permissive when such construction is made necessary by evident intention or by the rights of the public.

27. A proviso qualifies the provision immediately preceding.

27. It may clearly be intended to have a wider scope.

28. When the enacting clause is general, a proviso is construed strictly.

28. Not when it is necessary to extend the proviso to persons or cases which come within its equity.

Appendix B

The College Fire Prevention Act

108th CONGRESS

1st Session

S. 620
(H. R. 1613)

To establish a demonstration incentive program within the Department of Education to promote installation of fire sprinkler systems, or other fire suppression or prevention technologies, in qualified student housing and dormitories, and for other purposes.

IN THE HOUSE OF REPRESENTATIVES

April 3, 2003

Mrs. JONES of Ohio introduced the following bill; which was referred to the Committee on Education and the Workforce

———

A BILL

To establish a demonstration incentive program within the Department of Education to promote installation of fire sprinkler systems, or other fire suppression or prevention technologies, in qualified student housing and dormitories, and for other purposes.

Be it enacted by the Senate and House of Representatives of the United States of America in Congress assembled,

SECTION 1. SHORT TITLE; FINDINGS.

(a) SHORT TITLE—This Act may be cited as the 'College Fire Prevention Act'.

(b) FINDINGS—The Congress finds the following:

(1) On Wednesday, January 19, 2000, a fire occurred at a Seton Hall University dormitory. Three male freshmen, all 18 years of age, died. Fifty-four students, 2 South Orange firefighters, and 2 South Orange police officers were injured. The dormitory was a 6-story, 350-room structure built in 1952, that housed approximately 600 students. It was equipped with smoke alarms but no fire sprinkler system.

(2) On Mother's Day 1996 in Chapel Hill, North Carolina, a fire in the Phi Gamma Delta Fraternity House killed 5 college juniors and injured 3. The 3-story plus basement fraternity house was 70 years old. The National Fire Pro-

561

tection Association identified several factors that contributed to the tragic fire, including the lack of fire sprinkler protection.

(3) It is estimated that between 1980 and 1998, an average of 1,800 fires at dormitories, fraternities, and sororities, involving 1 death, 70 injuries, and $8,000,000 in property damage were reported to public fire departments.

(4) Within dormitories, fraternities, and sororities the leading cause of fires is arson or suspected arson. The second leading cause of college building fires is cooking. The third leading cause is smoking.

(5) New dormitories are generally required to have advanced safety systems such as fire sprinklers. But such requirements are rarely imposed retroactively on existing buildings.

(6) In 1998, 93 percent of the campus building fires reported to fire departments occurred in buildings where there were smoke alarms present. However, only 34 percent had fire sprinklers present.

SEC. 2. ESTABLISHMENT OF FIRE SUPPRESSION DEMONSTRATION INCENTIVE PROGRAM.

(a) GRANTS—The Secretary of Education (in this Act referred to as the 'Secretary'), in consultation with the United States Fire Administration, shall establish a demonstration program to award grants on a competitive basis to eligible entities for the purpose of installing fire sprinkler systems, or other fire suppression or prevention technologies, in student housing and dormitories owned or controlled by such entities.

(b) ELIGIBLE ENTITY—For purposes of this Act, the term 'eligible entity' means any of the following:

(1) An accredited public or private institution of higher education (as that term is defined in section 101 of the Higher Education Act of 1965 (20 U.S.C. 1001)).

(2) An accredited historically Black college or university (as that term is used in section 322 of the Higher Education Act of 1965 (20 U.S.C. 1061)).

(3) An accredited Hispanic-serving institution (as that term is defined in section 502 of the Higher Education Act of 1965 (20 U.S.C. 1101a)).

(4) An accredited Tribally Controlled College or University (as that term is defined in section 2 of the Tribally Controlled College or University Assistance Act of 1978 (25 U.S.C. 1801)).

(5) A social fraternity or sorority exempt from taxation under section 501(a) of the Internal Revenue Code of 1986 (26 U.S.C. 501(a)), the active membership of which consists primarily of students in attendance at an accredited institution of higher education.

(c) SELECTION PRIORITY—In making grants under subsection (a), the Secretary shall give priority to eligible entities that demonstrate the greatest financial need.

(d) RESERVATIONS—Of the amount made available to the Secretary for grants under this section for each fiscal year, the Secretary shall award—

(1) not less than 10 percent to eligible entities that are historically Black colleges and universities, Hispanic-serving institutions, and Tribally Controlled Colleges and Universities; and

(2) not less than 10 percent to eligible entities that are social fraternities and sororities.

(e) APPLICATION—To seek a grant under this section, an eligible entity shall submit an application to the Secretary at such time, in such manner, and accompanied by such information as the Secretary may require.

(f) MATCHING REQUIREMENT—As a condition on receipt of a grant under subsection

(a), the applicant shall provide (directly or through donations from public or private entities) non-Federal matching funds in an amount equal to not less than 50 percent of the cost of the activities for which assistance is sought.

(g) LIMITATION ON ADMINISTRATIVE EXPENSES—Not more than 10 percent of a grant made under subsection (a) may be expended for administrative expenses with respect to the grant.

(h) REPORTS—Not later than 12 months after the date of the first award of a grant under this section and annually thereafter until completion of the program, the Secretary shall provide to the Congress a report that includes the following:

(1) The number and types of eligible entities receiving assistance under this section.

(2) The amounts of such assistance, the amounts and sources of non-Federal funding leveraged for activities under grants under this section, and any other relevant financial information.

(3) The number and types of student housing fitted with fire suppression or prevention technologies with assistance under this section, and the number of students protected by such technologies.

(4) The types of fire suppression or prevention technologies installed with assistance under this section, and the costs of such technologies.

(5) Identification of Federal and State policies that present impediments to the development and installation of fire suppression or prevention technologies.

(6) Any other information determined by the Secretary to be useful to evaluating the overall effectiveness of the program established under this section in improving the fire safety of student housing.

(i) AUTHORIZATION OF APPROPRIATIONS—There is authorized to be appropriated to carry out this Act $100,000,000 for each of the fiscal years 2004 through 2008. At the end of fiscal year 2008, all unobligated appropriations authorized under this subsection shall revert to the general fund of the Treasury.

SEC. 3. ADMISSIBILITY AS EVIDENCE.

(a) PROHIBITION—Notwithstanding any other provision of law and subject to subsection (b), any application for assistance under this Act, any negative determination on the part of the Secretary with respect to such application, or any statement of reasons for the determination, shall not be admissible as evidence in any proceeding of any court, agency, board, or other entity.

(b) EXCEPTION—This section does not apply to the admission of an application, determination, or statement described in subsection (a) as evidence in a proceeding to enforce an agreement entered into between the Secretary of Education and an eligible entity under section 2.

Index